The
Tahoe Sierra

A Natural History Guide
to 112 Hikes in the Northern Sierra

Jeffrey P. Schaffer

WILDERNESS PRESS

BERKELEY

FIRST EDITION 1975
Second printing 1977
Third printing 1978
Revised fourth printing 1979
Second Edition 1984
THIRD EDITION 1987
Second printing January 1989
Third printing November 1990
Fourth printing October 1992
Fifth printing May 1994
Sixth printing October 1996
FOURTH EDITION June 1998
Second printing September 1999
Third printing March 2001
Fourth printing October 2002

Photographs by the author
U. S. Geological Survey topographic maps revised and updated by the author in the field.
Principal map drafting by the author, aided by his daughter, Mary Anne Schaffer.
Book design by Margaret Copeland—Terragraphics
Cover design by Larry Van Dyke
Front cover photo: Sand Point at Lake Tahoe. Copyright © 1998 by Ed Cooper
Back cover photo: Middle Loch Leven Lake. Copyright © 1998 by Jeffrey P. Schaffer

Library of Congress Card Catalog Number 98-12308
International Standard Book Number 0-89997-220-9

Manufactured in the United States of America

Published by **Wilderness Press**
                1200 5th Street
                Berkeley, CA 94710
                (800) 443-7227; FAX (510) 558-1696
                mail@wildernesspress.com
                Contact us for a free catalog
                Visit our web site at **www. wildernesspress.com**

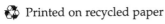 Printed on recycled paper

Library of Congress Cataloging-in-Publication Data

Schaffer, Jeffrey P.
     The Tahoe Sierra : a natural history guide to 112 hikes in the northern Sierra /
Jeffrey P. Schaffer. -- 4th ed.
        p. cm.
     Includes bibliographical references (p.) and index.
     ISBN 0-89997-220-9
     1. Hiking--Sierra Nevada (Calif. and Nev.)--Guidebooks. 2. Rock climbing--Sierra
Nevada (Calif. and Nev.)--Guidebooks. 3. Natural history--Sierra Nevada (Calif. and Nev.)
4. Sierra Nevada (Calif. and Nev.)--Guidebooks.   I. Title
GV199.42.S55S3 1998   98-12308
                                                                              CIP

Contents

Acknowledgements

In the first edition and its three subsequent printings, I acknowledged four professors at my alma mater, the University of California, Berkeley. Garniss Curtis (Geology Department gave me a better understanding of the area's history. Mitchell Reynolds (also of the Geology Department, but later with the U.S. Geological Survey) was unrelenting in pushing me to my limits of field-mapping ability—hence my obsession with producing accurate maps. Theodore Oberlander (Geography Department) also helped my field mapping by sharpening my interpretation of topographic maps. Finally, Robert Stebbins (Zoology Department) verified my conclusions about certain reptiles.

For the second edition one or more of the manuscript's chapters were sent to various government employees for review—a procedure which proved to be necessary. Those people reviewing a substantial part of the manuscript were: Keith Thurlkill and Glenn Hampton (USFS Lake Tahoe Basin Management Unit), Robert K. Henley (Eldorado N.F.) and Doug Hatch and Ann Westling (Tahoe N.F.). Checking smaller portions of the manuscript were: Karl Stein and Harlow Scott (Eldorado N.F.), Edwin Gregg, Andrea Holland, and Robert G. Lancaster (Tahoe N.F.), R.W. Jessen (Plumas N.F.), Dale R. Gerry (Toiyabe N.F.), Woody Banks and Dave Harris (B.L.M., Folsom District Office), Brenda Boswell (Calif. Dept. Parks & Rec.), Mike Callen (Malakoff Diggins S.H.P.), K.R. Fetherston (Sugar Pine Point S.P.). The fish chapter was reviewed by James H. Ryan (Calif. Dept. Fish & Game), and the geology chapter by Scott A. Mathieson (U.S. Geological Survey). Since this book first appeared in 1975, tremendous progress has been made in interpreting the area's geologic history, and this chapter was completely rewritten in the third edition, then again in this present edition. For this last edition I thank David Jones (U.S. Geological Survey and U.C., Berkeley) for comments on my unabridged manuscript, which then was shortened and simplified for this book. From the third edition onward, I have included wildflower plates, and I was very fortunate to have the Tahoe area's foremost botanist, Gladys L. Smith, check my plant identifications on these plates as well as review the chapter.

George Cardinet, Jr., a past president of the California State Horsemen's Association, was one of the driving forces for the construction of the Tahoe Rim Trail, and in the 1980s he reviewed my material on that trail. Others who supplied information on it were "Mac" Magary (USFS Lake Tahoe Basin Management Unit), Vicki Raucci (Tahoe Rim Trail's former Executive Director), and Lynda McDowell (Tahoe Rim Trail's present Executive Director).

Finally, working in the mountains can be a lonely task, so it is good when you can get someone to share your hiking and camping activities, plus shuttle you around the terrain. For eleven of my twelve guidebooks, including this one, Ken Ng has helped me in the field work. For the second edition, my wife, Bonnie Myhre, accompanied me on two trips, and in later editions provided support.

—Jeffrey P. Schaffer
Napa, California
January 1998

Part One   Introductory Chapters

Lake Tahoe, viewed from the Rubicon Trail in D.L. Bliss State Park

Waterfall at union of Umpa Lake and Twin Lakes creeks

Chapter 1
Introduction

The Tahoe Sierra

Due to its unique mode of origin Lake Tahoe greatly surpasses all other Sierra Nevada lakes in area and depth. Indeed, the lake ranks as one of the world's great lakes; few mountain lakes are larger, and few lakes at any elevation are deeper. Each summer, multitudes of bathers and boaters flock to its shores, while thousands of hikers explore its rim of snow-capped mountains.

This book is mainly about the trails in and around the Lake Tahoe Basin. However, the area defined by me as the Tahoe Sierra is considerably larger. The northern limit is fairly easy to define: Plumas-Eureka State Park. Beyond this park you enter prime Feather River country, and both the quantity and quality of natural lakes decrease dramatically. In that country the best recreation lakes are man-made: Little Grass Valley Reservoir, Bucks Lake, and Lake Almanor.

The south boundary of the Tahoe Sierra is harder to define. Carson Pass is only a mile south of the Lake Tahoe Basin rim, so it had to be included. After all, the shortest way into the basin's southern lakes is on trails from the Carson Pass environs. But the best trails from the Carson Pass area lead south, away from the basin, climbing up to lakes below the ruins of an old volcano, Round Top peak. These lakes, which are within the northern part of Mokelumne Wilderness, are too alluring to be omitted. Here, near an east-west ridge dominated by Round Top, the Tahoe Sierra's southern boundary was drawn. Mokelumne Wilderness, like the Tahoe Sierra's Desolation Wilderness, is blessed with lakes, though except for the northern ones, most are quite small, typically one to several acres in size. An exception is 16-acre Fourth of July Lake, which is about a mile southwest of Round Top, and it is included in this book. Several miles southeast of Round Top lies the Blue Lakes area, which is popular among campers, who have come mostly to fish. Hikers and equestrians are certainly in the minority.

The Tahoe Sierra's east boundary lies along the Sierra Nevada's east edge, where its mountain vegetation gives way to Great Basin vegetation. In the Lake Tahoe area proper, this edge is along the east base of the Carson Range, which is a subsidiary range of the Sierra Nevada. If it stood isolated, the Carson Range would be fairly impressive, for in stature it equals southern California's highest range, the San Bernardino Mountains.

The western boundary is poorly defined. I would like to have covered all the trail down through the lower montane forest to its western edge, which lies at roughly 1000-2000 feet elevation. Unfortunately, few good trails exist in this land of tall pines and firs. The land has been extensively utilized, first by miners, then by loggers, and presently by Californians enlarging their settlements. This latest commercial episode presents grave danger to the forest and its associated plants and animals. At present only one sizable park exists—Malakoff Diggins. Much more sanctuary is needed if we are to preserve the native plants and animals. Deer in particular are hampered as their migratory routes get blocked by development. They are preyed upon by mountain lions, which increasingly are sighted by the growing numbers of residents.

Scope and Purpose of this Book

This guidebook has four purposes. First, it is primarily a guide to virtually all the trails in the Tahoe Sierra that are, in my opinion, worth hiking. Most of the area's trails below 6000 feet are not worth hiking, while most above it are. In these higher lands, new trails have been constructed in the last quarter of the 20th century. The first half of this quarter has seen the construction of many miles of the Pacific Crest Trail, the second half, many miles of the Tahoe Rim Trail. When the latter is completed, roughly at the start of the third millennium, it will undoubtedly be one of California's most scenic and most used trails. Much shorter trails also have been built, my favorite being the very popular Mt. Judah Loop Trail. While this guidebook is aimed primarily at hikers, who will compose the great majority of its users, it is also intended for equestrians. I have not addressed mountain bikers, who have become quite numerous in the 1990s, and in places, the dominant trail users. Guides for them exist, stating which trails are open to them and which are not. Unfortunately, a significant number of mountain bikers ride closed trails, much to the consternation of hikers, including me (and I own a mountain bike).

Second, this book is a natural history of the Tahoe Sierra. As a matter of opinion, I consider the book more of a natural-history guide than a trail guide. If the natural history were omitted, the book would be only half as heavy as it now is (which, for some hikers, is not a bad idea). The geology chapter is extensive so that you can appreciate all the major changes in the Tahoe landscape over its entire existence. The botany chapter introduces you to the area's major plant communities, to all its conifers, and to over 70 of its common wildflowers. The zoology chapter completes the natural-history triad. Hopefully, each will be thought-provoking. In addition to these chapters I've mentioned the common rocks and vegetation seen along virtually every hike. In many hikes I've elaborated on the local natural history, particularly on summits from which you see much of the landscape. Up high the assemblage of plants is quite different from that of mid-elevation lands, so I've

included additional wildflower plates. In all, over 150 species are illustrated. Julie Stauffer Carville, in her *Lingering in Tahoe's Wild Gardens,* has produced an equally heavy trail guide that is almost entirely enchanting discourses on native plants.

Third, this is a fishing guide. In Chapter 4 virtually all the named lakes that you can reach by trail, plus ones near the trailheads, have been included in a chart, which shows the kind of trout you can expect to catch at each lake. However, because this book is more of a trail guide than a fishing guide, it does omit the lower-elevation lakes which are frequented by campers. The following Table of Activities indicates the hikes along which you can do some fishing.

Last, this book is a climbing guide. Since the late 1960s the vertical walls of Yosemite Valley have been overpopulated with climbers. Looking for new, less crowded routes, climbers have often turned to the high country of the central Sierra, but not until the early 1970s did they actively pursue cliffs near and around the Tahoe Basin. (Lovers Leap, above Highway 50 near Strawberry, was an exception. Today, climbers also flock to the Donner Pass area, along old Highway 40.) For climbers in search of isolated cliffs in the northern Sierra, this guide identifies almost all that can be reached by trail. Those reached by roads or by short walks from them are described in *Climber's Guide to Tahoe Rocks,* by Mike Carville (son of Julie, mentioned just above). Both books are listed in "Recommended Reading and Source Materials," at the back of this guidebook. My Table of Activities identifies the appropriate hikes with climbing possibilities.

Selecting your Hike

If you are familiar with the Tahoe region, you may already know which of this book's 100+ hikes will interest you. If not, then you can make an acquaintance with the region by reading each hiking chapter's introduction, which tells you what you can expect in that particular area. Alternatively, you can get a brief idea of what to expect by referring to the two following tables, which list some general characteristics of every hike in the book. Once you select a hike, read its description and see if it still sounds appealing.

The first table lists each hike's classification plus activities you can do while on it. The classification ranges from an easy 1A to a hard 5E. The numbers refer to each hike's mileage, and the letters refer to the net elevation gain:

1 = 0.0–4.9 miles	A = 0–499 feet
2 = 5.0–9.9 miles	B = 500–999 feet
3 = 10.0–14.9 miles	C = 1000–1999 feet
4 = 15.0–19.9 miles	D = 2000–2999 feet
5 = 20.0+ miles	E = 3000+ feet

Net elevation gain *usually* is the difference between the hike's highest and lowest elevations. An example of a conspicuous exception is Hike 8. On it you start at a high trailhead and end at a low trailhead. In the hike's described direction you have a net gain of 720 feet, a "B." But if you were to hike it in reverse—from the low trailhead to the high trailhead—you would have a net gain of 1170 feet, a "C." In reality, you may do a lot more gaining than the net elevation gain implies, particularly on the longer routes, which may climb and descend a number of ridges. Nevertheless, it does give you a rough estimate of the climbing involved. The distance given for each hike is for the farthest destination people are likely to visit, which is usually, though not always, the farthest point. The distance, in most cases, is the total distance to and from the main destination, not just a one-way hike. (One-way distances to each major destination are listed at the start of each hike.) Take, for example, Hike 71, which goes to Lake Sylvia, Lyons Lake, and Pyramid Peak. It is rated a 3C because it is a 10.0-mile round trip to and from Lyons Lake. If people rarely visited this lake, then this hike would become a 2C, a 9.8-mile round trip to and from Lake Sylvia. On the other hand, if most people ascended Pyramid Peak, it would become a 3E, a 12.6-mile round trip to and from the summit—one involving about 3300 feet of net elevation gain. For each hike the distance does *not* include distances along lateral trails which you may pass along the main route. For example, in Hike 20, the trailhead-to-trailhead distance is 14.4 miles, but if you take all the lateral trails, the distance becomes 17.2 miles.

In the first table a plus (+) indicates that a certain activity can be found along a hike; a minus (–), its absence. Four straight minuses don't mean a hike is completely unrewarding. Hike 29, for example, has four straight minuses, yet it stands out because it is the *only* hike that goes to giant sequoias. If a hike were indeed unrewarding, it wouldn't be in this book.

Where there is water there are usually, but not always, fishing and swimming opportunities. In like manner the presence of a lake doesn't always mean these two activities are available. No one, for instance, would knowingly swim in leech-infested Bloodsucker Lake (Hike 70), nor can you swim in some shallow lakes and creeks. If you're more interested in fishing than in swimming, you'll want to consult Chapter 4, which is devoted to this subject.

Most hikes give you views, some give you good views. Summit views, as used in the table, are those obtained from a notable summit—views which alone make the hike worth the effort.

Rock climbing can be done in many places in the Tahoe Sierra, but much of it wouldn't be worth your effort. In this table rock climbing is limited to hikes that pass cliffs worth climbing, and these hikes specifically identify them.

The second table lists sights, which should help photographers and nature lovers plan their hikes. "Lake" is taken to mean any large body of water, natural or man-made. A hike with only ponds along it would be classified as minus (–) for lakes.

Rocks are divided into three groups: granitic, metamorphic, and volcanic. Granitic rocks are the most common rock type. Volcanic rocks are the least common of the three, but where they occur, they are usually very conspicuous and are often the dominant rock type. Along the hikes, volcanic rocks are more prevalent than metamorphic rocks, which lie mostly in the trail-poor western half of our area. Sedimentary rocks, which are rare in the entire Sierra Nevada, are not included. The largest exposures of these rocks are found in Hike 5, which explores the Malakoff Diggins.

Table of Activities

Hike	Classification	Fishing	Swimming	Summit views	Rock climbing	Hike	Classification	Fishing	Swimming	Summit views	Rock climbing
1	1A	+	+	−	−	57	1A	+	+	−	−
2	2C	+	+	−	−	58	1A	+	+	−	−
3	2B	+	+	−	−	59	5B	+	+	−	−
4	1C	+	+	−	−	60	3C	+	+	+	−
5	1A	−	−	−	−	61	4C	+	+	−	−
6	1A	+	+	−	−	62	2A	+	+	−	−
7	2A	−	−	−	−	63	3C	+	+	−	−
8	2B	+	+	−	−	64	4C	+	+	−	+
9	1A	+	−	−	−	65	5C	+	+	−	+
10	3D	+	−	−	−	66	5D	+	+	−	+
11	1A	+	−	−	−	67	2C	+	+	−	−
12	3E	−	−	+	−	68	2C	+	+	−	−
13	2E	−	−	+	−	69	2C	+	+	−	−
14	2C	+	+	−	−	70	1B	−	−	−	−
15	2D	+	+	+	−	71	3C	+	+	+	+
16	2C	−	−	+	−	72	2E	+	+	+	+
17	2B	+	+	−	−	73	2D	−	−	+	−
18	2C	+	+	−	−	74	3D	+	+	+	−
19	1B	+	+	−	−	75	4C	+	+	−	−
20	3A	+	+	−	−	76	4D	+	+	−	+
21	1A	+	+	−	−	77	2C	+	+	−	+
22	1A	+	+	−	+	78	2C	+	+	−	−
23	2B	+	+	−	+	79	2E	+	+	+	−
24	3C	+	+	+	+	80	2B	+	+	−	−
25	1A	+	+	−	−	81	3E	+	+	+	−
26	1A	+	+	−	−	82	3C	+	+	−	−
27	3D	+	+	+	+	83	3C	+	+	−	−
28	1A	−	−	−	−	84	2D	+	+	+	−
29	1A	−	−	−	−	85	3C	+	+	+	+
30	1A	+	−	−	−	86	3C	+	+	+	+
31	1A	+	+	−	−	87	3C	+	+	−	+
32	2A	+	+	−	−	88	3C	−	−	−	−
33	2B	+	+	+	+	89	4C	+	+	−	−
34	2C	+	+	−	+	90	1B	−	−	−	−
35	3C	+	+	+	−	91	2C	+	+	−	+
36	4C	+	+	+	−	92	2B	+	+	−	+
37	3D	−	−	+	−	93	3A	+	+	−	−
38	4B	+	+	−	−	94	2B	+	+	+	−
39	3B	−	−	+	−	95	1A	+	+	−	+
40	2A	−	−	−	−	96	2B	+	+	−	−
41	2A	−	−	−	+	97	2D	+	+	+	−
42	3C	+	+	−	+	98	3C	+	+	−	−
43	3C	−	−	+	+	99	3B	+	+	−	−
44	4D	−	−	+	+	100	3C	−	−	−	+
45	4D	+	+	+	+	101	3C	+	+	+	+
46	1C	+	+	−	−	102	4C	+	+	−	−
47	2C	+	+	−	+	103	3C	−	−	+	−
48	4C	+	+	−	+	104	3C	−	−	+	−
49	4C	+	+	−	+	105	3D	−	−	+	−
50	3D	+	+	+	−	106	5D	−	−	+	−
51	3D	−	−	+	+	107	5B	−	+	+	−
52	4C	+	+	−	−	108	3C	−	−	+	−
53	2A	+	+	−	+	109	5C	−	−	+	−
54	1A	+	+	−	−	110	2C	−	−	+	−
55	1A	−	−	−	−	111	3B	+	+	−	−
56	1A	−	−	−	−	112	5C	+	+	−	−

Table of Sights

Hike	Lakes	Granitic	Metamorphic	Volcanic	Lower Montane	Upper Montane	Subalpine	History
		Rocks			**Vegetation**			
1	−	+	+	−	+	−	−	−
2	−	−	+	−	+	−	−	−
3	−	−	+	−	+	−	−	−
4	−	−	+	−	+	−	−	−
5	−	−	+	−	+	−	−	+
6	+	−	+	−	+	−	−	+
7	−	−	+	+	+	−	−	−
8	−	−	+	−	+	−	−	−
9	−	−	+	−	+	+	−	−
10	−	+	+	−	+	+	−	−
11	−	−	+	−	+	−	−	−
12	−	−	+	−	+	+	+	−
13	−	−	+	−	+	+	+	+
14	+	−	+	−	−	+	−	+
15	+	−	+	−	−	+	+	−
16	−	−	+	−	−	+	+	−
17	+	−	+	−	−	+	−	−
18	+	−	+	−	−	+	−	−
19	+	−	+	−	−	+	−	−
20	+	−	+	−	−	+	−	−
21	+	−	+	−	−	+	−	−
22	+	−	+	−	−	+	−	−
23	+	−	+	−	−	+	−	−
24	+	−	+	−	−	+	−	−
25	+	−	+	−	+	+	−	−
26	+	−	+	−	+	+	−	−
27	+	−	+	+	+	+	−	−
28	−	−	+	−	−	+	−	−
29	−	−	+	−	+	+	−	−
30	−	+	+	+	+	−	−	+
31	+	+	+	+	−	+	−	−
32	+	+	+	−	−	+	−	−
33	+	+	+	+	−	+	−	−
34	+	+	−	−	−	+	−	−
35	+	+	−	+	−	+	−	−
36	+	+	−	+	−	+	+	−
37	−	+	−	+	−	+	+	−
38	+	+	+	+	−	+	−	−
39	−	+	+	+	−	+	−	−
40	−	+	+	+	−	+	−	−
41	+	+	−	−	−	+	−	−
42	+	+	+	+	−	+	−	−
43	−	+	+	+	−	+	+	−
44	−	+	+	+	−	+	+	−
45	+	+	−	+	−	+	+	−
46	+	+	−	+	−	+	−	−
47	−	+	+	+	+	+	−	−
48	−	+	+	+	+	+	−	−
49	−	+	+	+	+	+	+	−
50	+	+	+	+	−	+	+	−
51	−	+	−	+	−	+	+	−
52	+	+	−	−	+	+	−	−
53	+	+	−	−	+	+	−	−
54	+	+	−	−	+	+	−	+
55	−	+	−	−	−	+	−	+
56	+	+	−	−	+	+	−	+
57	+	+	−	−	−	+	−	−
58	+	+	−	−	−	+	−	−
59	+	+	−	+	−	+	−	−
60	+	+	−	+	−	+	+	−
61	+	+	−	−	−	+	−	−
62	+	+	−	−	−	+	−	−
63	+	+	−	−	−	+	−	−
64	+	+	+	−	−	+	−	−
65	+	+	+	−	−	+	−	−
66	+	+	+	−	−	+	+	−
67	+	+	−	−	−	+	−	−
68	+	+	−	−	−	+	−	−
69	+	+	−	−	−	+	−	−
70	+	+	−	−	−	+	−	−
71	+	+	−	−	−	+	+	−
72	+	+	−	−	−	+	+	−
73	−	+	−	−	−	+	+	−
74	+	+	−	−	−	+	+	−
75	+	+	−	+	−	+	−	−
76	+	+	−	−	−	+	−	−
77	+	+	−	−	−	+	−	−
78	+	+	−	−	−	+	−	−
79	+	+	+	−	−	+	+	−
80	+	+	+	−	−	+	−	+
81	+	+	+	−	−	+	−	−
82	+	+	+	−	−	+	−	−
83	+	+	+	−	−	+	−	−
84	+	+	+	−	−	+	+	−
85	+	+	−	−	−	+	+	−
86	+	+	−	−	−	+	−	−
87	+	+	−	−	−	+	−	−
88	−	+	−	−	−	+	−	−
89	+	+	−	+	−	+	+	−
90	−	+	−	−	−	+	−	+
91	+	+	−	+	−	+	−	−
92	+	+	−	+	−	+	−	−
93	+	+	−	+	−	+	+	−
94	+	+	−	+	−	+	+	−
95	+	+	−	−	−	+	−	−
96	+	+	−	+	−	+	−	−
97	+	+	−	+	−	+	+	−
98	+	+	−	+	−	+	+	−
99	+	+	−	+	−	+	+	−
100	−	+	−	+	−	+	+	−
101	+	+	−	−	−	+	+	−
102	+	+	−	−	−	+	+	+
103	+	+	+	−	−	+	+	−
104	+	+	+	−	−	+	+	−
105	+	+	−	+	−	+	+	−
106	−	+	−	+	−	+	+	−
107	+	+	−	+	−	+	−	−
108	−	+	−	+	−	+	+	−
109	+	+	−	+	−	+	+	−
110	−	−	−	+	−	+	−	−
111	+	−	−	+	−	+	−	−
112	+	−	−	+	−	+	−	−

Vegetation, too, is divided into three groups: lower montane, upper montane, and subalpine. The first is a low-elevation forest whose dominant species include ponderosa pine, white fir, sugar pine, incense-cedar, Douglas-fir, and black oak. The second is a mid-elevation forest that includes Jeffrey pine, red fir, western white pine, and western juniper. The third is a high-elevation *sparse* forest that includes whitebark pine, mountain hemlock, and lots of hardy herbs.

Finally, historical places are mentioned for the sake of history buffs. Each hike with a plus (+) is one that contains an elaboration of the history of that hike's nearby area and/or related areas, or that visits historic structures, such as the Vikingsholm (Hike 54).

Interpreting Each Hike's Basic Data

Certain data are given at the beginning of each hike. The first two are distance(s) and low/high elevations, which are quite obvious.

Season is the period of the year when you should be able to drive to a trailhead and then hike an essentially snow-free trail. Weather varies considerably from year to year, so the hiking season may be shorter or longer, depending largely on whether the winter-spring precipitation (most of it as snow) has been above or below normal. Tahoe Sierra summer days are usually ideal at higher elevations, warming to the 70s during the day and cooling to the 40s by sunrise. Major summer storms are rare, but near the crest, thunderstorms can douse a local area. They may occur daily for a whole week or more, or more likely, may not occur for weeks at a time. Generally, the summer morning is cloudless, but clouds build up in the afternoon, only to dissipate around dusk. At lower elevations, such as at Malakoff Diggins, daytime temperatures soar into the 90s, and such an area is best visited during spring or fall, unless you specifically intend to go sunbathing and/or swimming.

Those who like to go swimming will generally find lakes warmer than nearby streams. Most lakes warm up to the mid- or high 60s—cool Lake Tahoe is a conspicuous exception—and a few of the lower lakes even top 70°F. Almost all are at their maximum in late July

through mid-August, although Lake Tahoe tops out later, in late August or early September, reaching the low to mid-60s. Rivers and streams, continuously being fed by cold ground water, rarely get above the 50s, except lower down, where one can expect the South Yuba River (Hikes 2 and 8) to warm into the 70s by mid afternoon, then cool through the night.

The fourth category, *classification*, is a bit subjective. Hikes range from "very easy" to "very strenuous," though most of them fit in the "moderate" range. Four parameters were used in determining the classification rating: length, elevation gain, steepness of trail, and altitude of trail (at high elevations, you tire more easily).

Studying the map at the Pacific Crest/Tahoe-Yosemite trail junction (Hikes 98-99)

The *map* refers to the appropriate topographic map (or maps) that show the hike. Where several maps are required, they are listed in the order you will need them. On this chapter's four-page general map of the Tahoe Sierra, all of the topographic maps are shown as well as what page each appears on. Most maps are aligned so that the north edge is along the top of the page. Where a map is turned sideways, a north-arrow is given (even though the orientation of letters and numbers tells you which side is up, north). All of the maps *except* Map 11 are at the same scale, about 1:42,100, which is about 1½ inches equals 1 mile, and a mileage scale bar is provided below. It, however, is not that necessary, since township-and-range *sections* appear on the maps, and in their north-south directions (and *usually* in their east-west directions) the distance across each section is about 1 mile. Also, for all these topographic maps, the following legend applies.

The *trailhead* mentions directions to the start of each hike and usually mentions the amount of parking spaces available. In most cases this space is adequate, but for some routes, such as Hike 77, demand far exceeds available sites. Finally, the *introduction* tells you what you can expect. It is useful in your decision of what hike to take.

Legend

Heavy-duty paved road	
Medium-duty paved road	
Light-duty paved road	
Gravel road	
Described trail	
Other trail or jeep road	
Permanent stream	
Seasonal stream	
Lake	

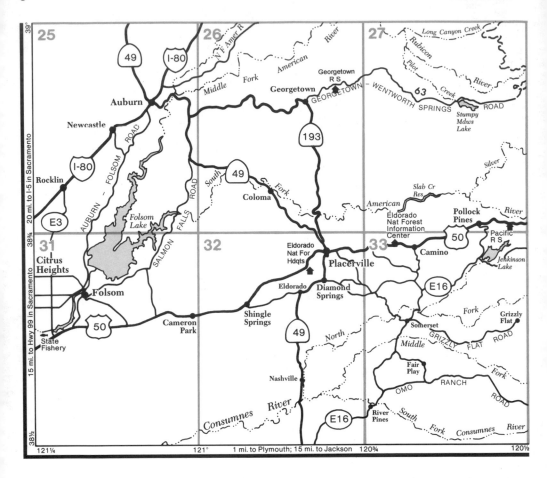

A General Map of the TAHOE SIERRA

Index to *Tahoe Sierra* Topographic Maps

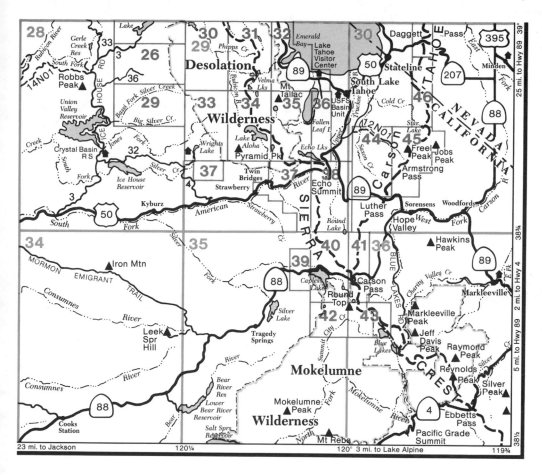

and Vicinity

U.S. Geological Survey 15′ Topographic Maps
(Numbers 1–36 of the light grid)

1	Bucks Lake	19	Grass Valley
2	Quincy	20	Colfax
3	Blairsden	21	Duncan Peak
4	Portola	22	Granite Chief
5	Chilcoot	23	Tahoe
6	Dogskin Mountain	24	Carson City
7	Mooreville Ridge	25	Auburn
8	Downieville	26	Georgetown
9	Sierra City	27	Saddle Mountain
10	Sierraville	28	Robbs Peak
11	Loyalton	29	Fallen Leaf Lake
12	Reno	30	Freel Peak
13	Nevada City	31	Folsom
14	Alleghany	32	Placerville
15	Emigrant Gap	33	Camino
16	Donner Pass	34	Leek Spring Hill
17	Truckee	35	Silver Lake
18	Mt. Rose	36	Markleeville

Legend

U.S. Geological Survey
15-minute topographic
map

> 34

Tahoe Sierra topographic map.
Index to these maps
on the opposite page.

> 43

Highways
Interstate Route   I-80
U.S. Route   50
State Route   49

Roads
County Road   E16
Other All-Weather Road
Gravel Road

U.S.F.S. Office or Ranger Station   ♠

N

0   5   10 mi

Declination averages 16½°e

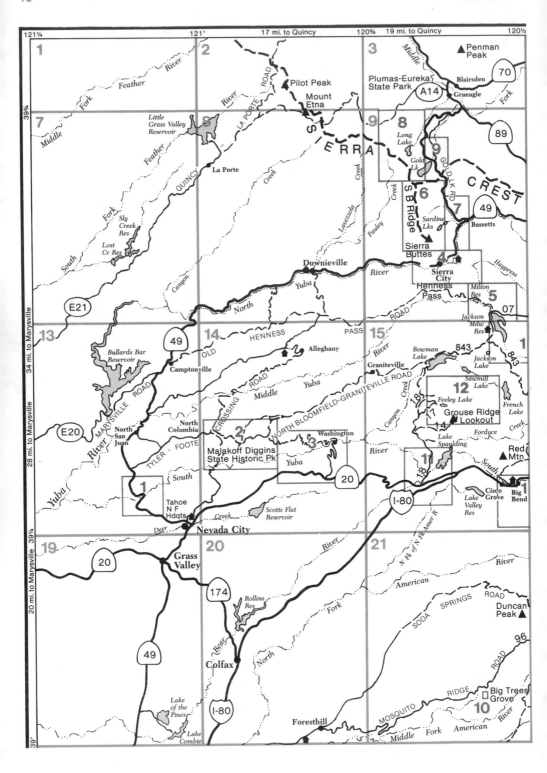

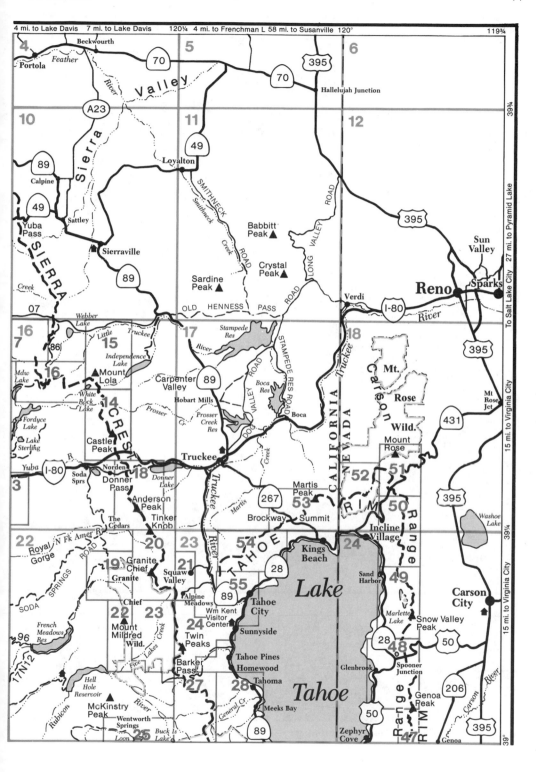

Upper and Lower Sardine Lakes, Sierra Buttes

Chapter 2
Towns, Resorts, Lodges, and Campgrounds

Introduction

For camping and lodging, the Tahoe Sierra can be divided into two areas: lands within the Lake Tahoe Basin and lands outside it. Outside the basin the milieu is generally relaxed and tranquil. Within the basin the setting still is quite pleasant in campgrounds and lodges along the lake's west shore, although one generally has to put up with the fairly heavy traffic along its Highway 89. Along the lake's north and south shores, the setting is urban and traffic jams occur far too often—there simply are too many vehicles in the basin. The lake's east shore is the least developed, deficient in both camping and lodging. The Toiyabe National Forest and Lake Tahoe Nevada State Park claim almost half of the lake's east shore and the great bulk of the lands above it, yet neither entity has even a single campground. This is unfortunate, since at least during the summer, the Forest Service and State Park campgrounds along the lake's south shore are filled to capacity. However, most of the basin's campgrounds, like its hotels, motels, resorts, and lodges, do take reservations, and you can eliminate a lot of frustration by making them. Outside the basin only the larger, popular campgrounds take reservations.

Towns

The Tahoe Sierra's towns can be grouped according to the services they provide the visitor. The first category is the full-service town, which has everything—car dealerships, hospitals, government administrative offices, shopping centers—plus a broad choice of gas stations, restaurants, and lodging. Auburn, Grass Valley-Nevada City, Placerville, and South Lake Tahoe-Stateline certainly fit into this category. Lake Tahoe's swath of north-shore settlements, which extends from Tahoe City east to Incline Village, has considerable gas stations, restaurants, and lodging, but lacks most of the other urban characteristics. With somewhat less offerings, but nevertheless having nearly every necessity a visitor might need, is the Donner Lake-Truckee area.

The second category is towns with one to several of each of the following: gas station, restaurant or coffee shop, motel or lodge, and general store or food market. Only the towns convenient for this book's users are considered. These are Downieville, Sierra City, and Graeagle, all in the Chapter 9 area, plus most of Lake Tahoe's west-shore towns.

Finally, there are smaller settlements which offer gas or food or lodging, but not always all three. Along Highway 49 there are North San Juan, which is not far past Nevada City, and Sierraville, which lies in a beautiful east-side agricultural valley. Neither is particularly tourist-oriented. Along Interstate 80 and Highway 50 there are a number of settlements, generally one every few miles. Most have only a gas station and attendant cafe or ministore.

Resorts and Lodges

These can run $200+ per night per room or cottage, so I recommend that you first visit any resort or lodge that may sound interesting. What I prefer and think is worth the money may not appeal to you, for different people like different amenities.

The Highway 49 country offers some picturesque resorts and lodges close to the Sierra crest. Other lodging exists around Downieville, but these aren't considered, since this book deals only with Highway 49 trails that are above Sierra City. Above that Gold Rush town, which also has food and lodging, all the resorts occur in one area: along side roads branching west from the Gold Lake road. Driving north on this broad, well-graded highway, you pass roads to Sardine Lake Resort (Map 7), Packer Lake Lodge and Salmon Lake Resort (both Map 6), and Gold Lake, Elwell, and Gray Eagle lodges (all Map 8). The first three lie along lakeshores, while the last three lie closer to the Gold Lake Road but are nevertheless within a short walking distance of two or more lakes. When the snowpack begins to break up in June, the resorts usually open for business, and they generally stay open at least through the start of deer-hunting season, which is the last weekend in September.

Along Interstate 80 and its feeder roads there are few resorts which would cater to hikers. However, one worth mentioning is Rainbow Lodge (Map 13), located a mere 0.3 mile east of the Loch Leven Lakes trailhead (Hike 34). Highway 50 is equally deficient in acceptable resorts, having only two candidates. The first is Camp Sacramento (Map 37), which is primarily for Sacramento's residents, although, if space is available, it does take nonresidents. The second is off the highway at the gateway to Desolation Wilderness: Echo Lake Resort (Map 36). Although each has its good points, neither can offer the solitude found at the Gold Lake Road resorts.

The Tahoe Sierra, as defined in this book, extends south to the Highway 88 region. In this area you'll find popular, fisherman-oriented Caples Lake Resort (Map 40), which lies just across from a Forest Service campground. Silver Lake is just west of and outside the book's area, but it offers additional lodging and camping. In the opposite direction from Caples is Sorensen's Resort, which lies just 0.9 mile east of the Highways 88/89 junction. Just 0.5 mile east of this resort is Hope Valley Resort, operated under the same management as is Sorensen's.

Then there are three resorts in the southwest part of the Lake Tahoe Basin that deserve mention. From south to north these are Angora Lakes Resort (Map 35), Camp Richardson (Map 32 inset) and Meeks Bay Resort (Map 28). Angora Lakes Resort is tiny and isolated, and perhaps because of its pleasant ambiance it is always booked. For this summer-only resort you may have to make reservations a year in advance—if you can get any at all. The other two, along Highway 89, are readily accessible and have a longer season. Both Meeks Bay Resort and Camp Richardson lie along Lake Tahoe. Each has a small marina, and each is strongly oriented toward water sports. In addition, Camp Richardson has horse stables, with miles of horse trails awaiting the equestrian. There are also stables adjacent to Meeks Bay Resort.

Campgrounds

Most of this book's users will stay at campgrounds rather than at lodges, resorts, or motels. Consequently, I have attempted to list all the appropriate Tahoe Sierra campgrounds. Out-of-the-way campgrounds, such as those in the lower parts of the Eldorado and Tahoe national forests, are omitted. In the following list of campgrounds, some appear on the book's topographic maps, and the map for each of them is indicated. Also, campground seasons are listed, but these are approximate, since they vary, with the weather, from year to year. Some of the larger, more popular Forest Service campgrounds are maintained by private corporations, and the result is that their camp fees are higher. Fallen Leaf Campground is one of the more expensive ones, because like all Tahoe Basin sites that produce sewage, its sewage is pumped out of the basin, which is quite expensive to do. Expect to pay about $12-16 for the more popular Forest Service campgrounds, about double that for private campgrounds. Some of the more primitive Forest Service campgrounds are free.

Given the popularity of Sierran campgrounds during the summer, you should consider making reservations, preferably 2 to 4 months in advance. For Forest Service campground reservations, phone 800-280-2267 (280-CAMP); for State Park campground reservations, phone 800-444-7275 (444-PARK). *All* of the *group* sites in national-forest campgrounds are reserved. *Note:* campgrounds with reservable sites are identified with an asterisk (*).

ELDORADO NATIONAL FOREST

Caples Lake C.G. 35 sites. 7840'. On Hwy. 88 at Caples Lake. Open June through mid-Oct. Map 40.

Fashoda C.G. 30 walk-in tent sites. 4850'. On Union Valley Reservoir's peninsula. Open June through mid-Oct.

*Gerle Creek C.G. 50 sites. 6300'. Entrance road is 2¾ mi. n. of jct. where For. Rte. 30 leaves For. Rte. 3 (Loon Lake Rd.). Open June through mid-Oct.

*Ice House C.G. 38 sites. 5450'. Drive 10½ miles up For. Rte. 3 to For. Rte. 32, and 1.2 mi. e. up it. At Ice House Reservoir. Open June through mid-Oct.

Kirkwood Lake C.G. 12 sites. 7680'. Narrow entrance road begins from Hwy. 88 just 0.6 mi. west of Kirkwood Ski Resort, which lies between Silver and Caples lakes. Open mid-June through mid-Oct. Map 39.

*Loon Lake C.G. 62 sites plus 3 group camps and 2 equestrian camps. 6430'. At Loon Lake. Open mid-June through mid-Sept. Map 25.

*Loon Lake Chalet 6430'. Along west shore of Loon Lake. Open year-round. Not a campground, but rather a cabin with a kitchen, with space for up to 20 people. Map 25.

Lovers Leap C.G. 21 sites. 5800'. At the base of Lovers Leap, an imposing cliff, just east of Hwy. 50's Strawberry. Take Strawberry Lane, which begins immediately northeast of Strawberry Lodge. The lane quickly bridges the South Fork American River, and you branch left. The campground is heavily used by rock climbers. Open mid-May through Oct.

Northshore C.G. 15 sites. 6430'. Along northwest shore of Loon Lake. For R.V.s (no piped water). Open mid-June through mid-Sept. Map 25.

Northwind C.G. 9 sites. 5450'. Drive 10½ miles up For. Rte. 3 to For. Rte. 32, and 2.3 mi. e. up it. At Ice House Reservoir. Open mid-May through Oct.

*Red Fir Group C.G. 1 group site. 6430'. Along northwest shore of Loon Lake. Open mid-June through mid-Sept. Map 25.

Schneider Camping Area Primitive c.g. with several sites. 8300'. About 1¼ mi. n.w. of Caples Lake Maintenance Station, via rough rd. Open mid-July through mid-Oct. Map 40.

Silver Creek C.G. 12 sites. 5200'. Narrow, rough entrance road begins about 9 mi. up For. Rte. 3 and 0.2 mi. before Ice House Resort. Open June through mid-Oct.

*Silver Lake C.G. 62 sites. 7270'. Along Hwy. 88 near lake's n. shore. Open July through mid-Oct.

South Fork C.G. 17 sites. 5160'. North of Union Valley Reservoir. From a jct. 0.2 mi. n. of the For. Rtes. 1/3 jct., drive 1.2 mi. n.w. on 13N28. Open June through mid-Oct.

Strawberry Point C.G. 10 sites. 5450'. Drive 10½ miles up For. Rte. 3 to For. Rte. 32, and 2.8 mi. e. up it. At Ice House Reservoir. Open mid-May through late Oct.

*Sunset C.G. 131 sites. 4850'. On Union Valley Reservoir's peninsula. Open June through mid-Oct.

Wench Creek C.G. 100 sites plus 2 group camps. 4900'. Above Union Valley Reservoir's east shore. Open June through mid-Oct. Its two group sites require reservations.

Woods Lake C.G. 14 sites. 8240'. Near Hwy. 88's Carson Pass. Open July through early Oct. Map 40.

*Wrights Lake C.G. 83 sites. 6940'. At Wrights Lake. Open mid-June through mid-Oct.

*Yellowjacket C.G. 40 sites. 4900'. Above Union Valley Reservoir's northeast shore. Open June through mid-Oct.

LAKE TAHOE BASIN MANAGEMENT UNIT (USFS)

Bayview C.G. 16 sites. 6850'. On Hwy. 89, above Emerald Bay. Open late May through mid-Oct. 48-hr. limit; no drinking water. Map 32.

*Fallen Leaf C.G. 205 sites. 6340'. Between Hwy. 89 and n. shore of Fallen Leaf Lake. Open mid-May through mid-Oct. Map 32.

Luther Pass Overflow Camping Area (formerly Big Meadow Camping Area, mentioned in trailhead 92) Undeveloped sites along old road (former Highway 89) starting near the Big Meadow trailhead (Hike 92), which has restrooms. 7000-7300'. Open June through Oct. Map 38.

*Meeks Bay C.G. 40 sites. 6230'. At Meeks Bay. Open mid-June through mid-Sept. Map 28.

*Nevada Beach C.G. 63 sites. 6240'. Along s.e. Lake Tahoe. Leave Hwy. 50 about 2 mi. n. of the Calif.-Nev. border. Open late May through late Sept.

*William Kent C.G. 95 sites. 6250'. Along Hwy. 89, 2¼ mi. s. of Tahoe City. Open May through Sept. Map 55.

PLUMAS NATIONAL FOREST

Gold Lake Camping Area Primitive c.g. with about 10 sites. 6420' Along Gold Lake, just off Gold Lake Rd. Poor rd. to c.g. Open July through mid-Oct. Map 10.

Lakes Basin C.G. 24 sites plus 1 group site. 6300'. About midway along Gold Lake Rd. Narrow rd. through c.g. Open late June through Sept. Map 8.

TAHOE NATIONAL FOREST

Ahart C.G. 12 sites. 5340'. Along For. Rte. 96 above n.e. corner of French Mdws. Res. and 1 mi. beyond Middle Fork American River bridge. Open June through mid-Oct.

*Aspen Group C.G. 3 sites. 6100'. Jackson Mdw. Res., n. shore. Open June through Oct. Map 5.

Berger Creek C.G. Primitive c.g. with about 10 sites. 5940'. Along Packer Lake Road (County Route S621), 2¼ mi. above the Gold Lake Rd. jct. Open late June through mid-Oct. Map 6.

Big Bend C.G. 15 sites. 5730'. Along I-80, behind Big Bend Visitor Information Center (use Big Bend exit). Open late May through early Sept. Map 13.

*Black Bear Group C.G. 1 site. 5300'. Along rd. above n.e. shore of French Mdws. Res. Open June through Oct.

Carr Lake C.G. 4 sites. 6700'. Primitive c.g. near end of For. Rte. 17-4. Open July through mid-Oct. Map 12.

Chapman Creek C.G. 27 sites. 5840'. Along Hwy. 49, 3.1 mi. above the Gold Lake Rd. jct. Open June through mid-Oct.

*Coyote Group C.G. 3 sites. 5300'. Along For. Rte. 96 above n.e. corner of French Mdws. Res. and 0.2 mi. beyond Middle Fork American River bridge. Open June through Oct.

Diablo C.G. Primitive C.G. with about 10 sites. 5900'. Along Packer Lake Road (County Route S621), 1.9 mi. above the Gold Lake Rd. jct. Open late June through mid-Oct. Map 6.

*East Meadow C.G. 46 sites. 6100'. Jackson Mdw. Res., n.e. shore. Open June through Oct. Map 5.

*Faucherie Group C.G. 1 site. 6100'. At Faucherie Lake, Grouse Ridge Recreation Area. Open June through mid-Oct. Map 12. Rough road; not recommended.

*Findley C.G. 14 sites. 6240'. Jackson Mdw. Res., w. shore. Open June through Oct. Map 17.

*Fir Top C.G. 12 sites. 6100'. Jackson Mdw. Res., w. shore. Open June through Oct. Map 17.

*French Meadows C.G. 75 sites. 5300'. Along For. Rte. 96 above s.e. shore of French Mdws. Res. Open June through mid-Oct.

*Gates Group C.G. 3 sites. 5330'. Above east end of French Mdws. Res. Take For. Rte. 68 briefly up to c.g. entrance rd. Open mid-June through mid-Oct.

*Goose Meadows C.G. 24 sites. 5980'. Along Hwy. 89, about 4½ mi. s. of I-80 (west Truckee exit). Open May through mid-Sept.

*Granite Flat C.G. 75 sites. 5880'. Along Hwy. 89, about 1½ mi. s. of I-80 (west Truckee exit). Open May through mid-Sept.

Grouse Ridge C.G. 9 sites. 7440'. Primitive c.g. near end of rough For. Rte. 14. Open mid-July through mid-Oct. Map 12.

*Hampshire Rocks C.G. 31 sites. 5890'. Along I-80 at the Rainbow Rd. exit and located 1 mi. e. of Big Bend Visitor Information Center. Open June through early Sept. Map 13.

Indian Springs C.G. 35 sites. 5500'. About 2 mi. n.w. of I-80's Cisco Grove. Open late May through mid-Oct.

Lakeside C.G. Primitive c.g. with about 30 sites. 5760'. Along Prosser Res. Leave Hwy. 89 about 3⅔ mi. n. of I-80. Open late Apr. through late Oct.

Lasier Mdw. Horse Camp 6 sites. 6500'. Along For. Rte. 70 (Pass Cr. Loop Rd.), 1¼ mi. s.e. past the entrance to Jackson Mdw. Reservoir's East Meadow C.G. Open June through Oct. Map 17.

*Lewis C.G. 40 sites. 5350'. Along rd. above n.e. shore of French Mdws. Res. Open late May through late Oct.

Lindsey Lake C.G. 10 sites. 6250'. Primitive c.g. near end of For. Rte. 17. Last 0.6 mile is a narrow, rough road. Open July through mid-Oct. Map 12.

Loganville C.G. 19 sites. On Hwy. 49 about 1½ mi. w. of Sierra City. Open May through Oct.

*Lower Little Truckee C.G. 15 sites. 6120'. Along Hwy. 89, 11¼ mi. n. of I-80. Open late May through early Nov.

Packsaddle C.G. 14 sites plus 2 equestrian sites. 6140'. Along Packer Lake Road (County Route S21), 2.7 mi. above the Gold Lake Rd. jct. Open late June through mid-Oct. Map 6.

*Pass Creek C.G. 30 sites. 6100'. Jackson Mdw. Res., n. shore. Open June through Oct. Map 5.

Prosser C.G. 29 sites and 1 group site. 5770'. Near Prosser Res. Leave Hwy. 89 about 3⅔ mi. n. of I-80. Open late May through mid-Oct.

Salmon Creek C.G. 32 sites. 5700'. Along s. part of Gold Lake Rd., 0.2 mi. n. of the Packer Lake Rd. jct. Open mid-June through mid-Oct. Map 7.

Sardine Lake C.G. 27 sites. 5740'. Near s. part of Gold Lake Rd. Open mid-June through mid-Oct. Map 7.

Sierra C.G. 16 sites. 5670'. Along Hwy. 49, 1.2 mi. above the Gold Lake Rd. jct. Open June through Oct.

*Silver Creek C.G. 27 sites. 6060'. Along Hwy. 89, 1⅓ mi. n. of the Squaw Valley jct. and 7 mi. s. of I-80 (west Truckee exit). Open mid-May through mid-Oct.

Silvertip Group C.G. 1 site. 6070'. Jackson Mdw. Res. Open June through Oct. Map 17.

Snag Lake C.G. Primitive c.g. with about 16 sites. 6670'. Along Gold Lake Rd., 1½ mi. s.e. of Gold Lake. Open July through mid-Oct. Map 10.

Talbot C.G. Primitive c.g. with 5 sites. 5600'. Near the Hike 42 trailhead. Open mid-June through mid-Oct. Map 19.

Union Flat C.G. 11 sites. 3380'. Along Hwy. 49, about 6½ mi. below Sierra City. Open May through Oct.

*Upper Little Truckee C.G. 26 sites. 6170'. Along Hwy. 89, 11¾ mi. n. of I-80. Open late May through early Nov.

Wild Plum C.G. 42 sites. 4400'. E. of sierra City, at end of Wild Plum Rd. Open May through Oct. Map 4.

*Woodcamp C.G. 20 sites. 6100'. Jackson Mdw. Res., w. shore. Open June through Oct. Map 17.

Woodchuck Flat C.G. Primitive c.g. with about 8 sites. 6260'. 2¾ mi. up Forest Route 85., which begins ⅓ mi. n.w. of Cisco Grove. Open late June through early Sept.

*Yuba Pass C.G. 20 sites. 6710'. Along Hwy. 49 at Yuba Pass. Open July through mid-Oct.

TOIYABE NATIONAL FOREST

*Hope Valley C.G. 26 sites. 7140'. 1.7 mi. s. on Blue Lakes Rd., whose jct. with Hwy. 88 is 6.3 mi. n.e. of Carson Pass and 2.4 mi. s.w. of the Hwys. 88/89 jct. Open late May through mid-Oct.

Kit Carson C.G. 12 sites. 6880'. Along Hwy. 88, 1½ mi. e. of Hwy. 89 jct. Open late May through mid-Oct.

Mt. Rose C.G. 24 sites. 8920'. Near Mt. Rose Summit, at top of Nev. Hwy. 431. Open late June through mid-Sept.

Snowshoe Springs C.G. 13 sites. 6670'. Along Hwy. 88, about 2 mi. e. of Hwy. 89 jct. Open late May through mid-Oct.

BUREAU OF LAND MANAGEMENT

South Yuba C.G. 15 sites. 2500'. Just off the North Bloomfield-Graniteville Rd., opposite the Hike 2 trailhead. Open all year except when snowbound. Map 2.

STATE PARKS AND RECREATION AREAS

*D.L. Bliss S.P. 168 sites in 5 camping areas. 6230'-6650'. W. shore of Lake Tahoe. Open mid-June through early Sept. Map 32.

*Donner Memorial S.P. 154 sites. 5950'. E. shore of Donner Lake. Open late May through late Sept.

*Emerald Bay S.P. 100 sites in 2 camping areas. 6300'-6600'. W. shore of Lake Tahoe. Open mid-June through early Sept. Map 32.

*Malakoff Diggins S.H.P. 30 sites plus 1 group site plus 2 cabins. 3650'. N.e. of Nevada City. See Hike 3 trailhead. Open all year except when snowbound. Map 2.

Plumas-Eureka S.P. 70 sites. 5250'. West of Graeagle, via Co. Rd. A14. Open late May through mid-Oct. Map 8.

*Sugar Pine Point S.P. (General Creek C.G.) 175 sites. 6340'. Along Hwy. 89 between Tahoma and Meeks Bay. Open all year.

*Tahoe S.R.A. 38 sites. 6240'. At n.e. edge of Tahoe City. Open all year. Map 55.

CITY PARKS

Lake Forest C.G. 19 sites. 6240'. Just n.e. of Tahoe City. From Hwy. 28 in Lake Forest, take Lakeforest Rd. Open mid-May through early Sept.

*South Lake Tahoe-Eldorado Recreation Area (Campground by the Lake) 153 sites. 6230'. In n.e. S. Lake Tahoe city. Open Apr. through Oct. Reservations: 530-542-6096.

PACIFIC GAS AND ELECTRIC COMPANY

Lake Spaulding C.G. 10 sites. 5000'. From I-80, take Hwy. 20 exit and go about 2 mi. w. on it, then ½ mi. up rd. toward lake. Open June through Sept.

Lodgepole C.G. 18 sites. 5750'. From I-80, take Yuba Gap exit and follow signs 1.9 mi. s.e. to c.g., below Lake Valley Reservoir's dam.

Silver Lake West C.G. 35 sites. 7240'. Along Hwy. 88 near lake's n. shore. Open July through mid-Oct.

The following campgrounds are along the Blue Lakes Rd., whose jct. with Hwy. 88 is 6.3 mi. n.e. of Carson Pass and 2.4 mi. s.w. of the Hwys. 88/89 jct. Blue Lakes Rd. goes 10.7 mi. s. to a jct. with Indian Valley rd., then 1.2. mi. s.w. to a jct. with Twin Lakes rd., where it turns north. The following mileages are from this last jct. All c.g.s are open from about mid-July through mid-Sept.

Lower Blue Lake C.G. 15 sites. 8080'. Immediately past last jct.

Middle Creek C.G. 8 sites. 8120'. 1.4 mi. past last jct.

Upper Blue Lake Damsite C.G. 10 sites. 8180'. 1.8 mi. past last jct. Map 43.

Upper Blue Lake C.G. 32 sites. 8200'. 3.0 mi. past last jct. Map 43.

PRIVATE

Feather River KOA 55 sites. 4700'. Along Hwy. 70, about 5 mi. e. of Blairsden. Open Apr. 1 through Nov. 1. Res.: 530-836-2688.

Hope Valley Resort C.G. 24 sites. 6840'. Along Hwy. 88 about 1.4 mi. east of the Hwy. 89 jct. Open early June through mid-Sept. Operated by Sorensen's Resort.

Lake Tahoe KOA 68 sites. 6370'. Along Hwy. 50, immediately s.w. of Upper Truckee Rd. jct., about 5½ mi. s. of S. Lake Tahoe Y. Open all year, with limited winter facilities. Res.: 530-577-3693.

Little Bear C.G. and R.V. Park 57 sites. 4300'. Along Hwy. 70/89, about 1 mi. n.w. of Blairsden. Open May 1 through Nov. 1. Res.: 530-836-2774.

Meeks Bay Resort 28 sites. 6240'. Along Hwy. 89 at Meeks Bay. Open mid-June through mid-Sept. Res.: 530-525-7242. Map 28.

Movin' West Trailer Ranch 36 sites. 4360'. Near Graeagle, 0.3 mi. w. on Co. Rd. A14. Open all year. Res.: 530-836-2614.

Richardson's Resort (Camp Richardson) C.G. 335 sites. 6240'. Along Hwy. 89 about 2½ mi. n.w. of S. Lake Tahoe Y. Open early May through mid-Oct. Reservations: 530-541-1801; 800-544-1801. Map 32 inset.

River Rest Resort 100 sites. 2620'. In Washington, along South Yuba River. See Hike 8 trailhead. Open all year. Res.: 530-265-4306. Map 3.

Sandy Beach C.G. 34 sites. 6240'. N. shore of Lake Tahoe, in Tahoe Vista, 1.2 mi. east of Hwy. 267 jct. Open May 1 through mid-Oct. Res.: 530-546-7682.

Sierra Skies R.V. Park 30 sites. 4170'. In Sierra City. Open mid-Apr. through Oct. Res.: 530-862-1166. Map 4.

Sierra Springs Trailer Resort 30 sites. 4900'. Along Hwy. 70, about 3½ mi. e. of Blairsden. Open all year. Res.: 530-836-2747.

Tahoe Pines C.G. 60 sites. 6320'. Along Hwy. 50, immediately n.e. of Upper Truckee Rd., about 5¼ mi. s. of S. Lake Tahoe Y. Memorial weekend through Labor Day weekend. Res.: 530-577-1653.

Tahoe Valley C.G. 300 sites. 6280'. Just e. of Hwy. 50, about 0.4 mi. s. of S. Lake Tahoe **Y**. Open all year. Res.: 530-541-2222.

Zephyr Cove Resort C.G. 180 sites. 6240'. Along s.e. Lake Tahoe. Along Hwy. 50 about 4 mi. n. of the Calif.-Nev. border. Open mid-Apr. through Nov. 1. Res.: 702-588-6644.

Hikers approaching Mt. Tallac's summit

Chapter 3
Exploring the Tahoe Sierra on Foot, Horseback, or Skis

Introduction

Most of this book is devoted to trails—where they go, what they are like, what lakes, peaks, or views you'll see, and what significant plants, animals, or geologic formations you're likely to encounter along the trails. Although this book is aimed mainly at hikers, it should be equally useful for equestrians. Cross-country skiers certainly will find it less useful, since during their sport's season the trails are under snow. Still, I hope they will find some merit in the text and its accompanying maps. This chapter covers the rules and beneficial practices that apply to all outdoor users, regardless of their mode of travel or time of year. The first thing you must know is that if you enter Desolation Wilderness (Hikes 59-62, 64-69, 71-87), you will need a wilderness permit. If you enter Mokelumne Wilderness (Hikes 96-99), you will need a wilderness permit if you stay in it *overnight* anytime from April 1 through November 30. At present, you do not need a wilderness permit to enter Granite Chief Wilderness or Mt. Rose Wilderness.

Wilderness Permits

Introduction During the decade from 1960 to 1969, backpacking, with its new, lightweight technology, came of age, and hikers proliferated through the Sierra Nevada. By the time Desolation Wilderness was officially created in late 1969, it was already crowded, and a guidebook printed a few months later added to its popularity. It looked like this infant wilderness was about to be trampled to death. Concerned, the Forest Service began a permit system in 1971, in part to determine just how many people were flooding the wilderness, what spots they visited, and how long they stayed. In 1975, the year that the first edition of *The Tahoe Sierra* appeared, about 3400 visitors could be found in the wilderness on a typical summer day, and about 90% of the wilderness' recreational activity took place in about 10% of its area. The Forest Service judged this human impact to be too great and, after a detailed study, determined the wilderness' optimum capacity to be about 2100 persons at one time. Since this number was less than the number of persons actually using the wilderness, the Forest

Service began limiting, in 1978, the number of persons entering the wilderness. *Today, anyone contacted by a ranger within the wilderness without a permit will be issued a violation notice.*

When In Desolation Wilderness, permits are required year-round, even in the dead of winter. The period from November through May may be the best time to visit for those *experienced in mountain ways,* for then it is truly wild, traces of man being buried beneath the snow and solitude reigning supreme.

How Many As of the late 1990s the Forest Service was issuing permits for up to 700 people per day to backpackers and equestrians entering Desolation Wilderness. At present they don't limit the number of day users, but this could change in the future. Day users can self-register at the popular trailheads, although on busy weekends, permits sometimes run out. Regardless of whether you spend just an hour or the legal maximum of two weeks in the wilderness, your party, which currently is limited to 15 persons, will need a permit. (The Forest Service hopes the size of your party will be much smaller.) At present there is no stock limit. Before the Fourth of July and after Labor Day, backpackers usually can get a permit easily; however, during the height of the hiking season, particularly on weekends, they may find wilderness permits extremely scarce. Of the permits issued daily to overnighters, up to half can be reserved, and knowledgeable wilderness visitors do just that.

Where   To *reserve* a permit for Desolation Wilderness, contact the Eldorado National Forest Information Center within 90 days of the start of your proposed excursion. This center is open seven days a week, year-round, except for certain holidays. It is located alongside Highway 50 about 5 miles east of Placerville. Reach them at:

Eldorado National Forest
Information Center
3070 Camino Heights Drive
Camino, CA 95709
(530) 644-6048.

You can get a permit in person, or phone or fax the center, which takes credit cards (there is a fee if you *reserve* a permit). Be sure to mention your trip dates, size of party, number of stock (if any), and proposed itinerary (for example: 8/11, Wrights Lake trailhead to Lake Schmidell; 8/12, Lake Schmidell to Middle Velma Lake; 8/13, Middle Velma Lake to Lake Aloha; 8/14, Lake Aloha to Lake Doris; 8/15, Lake Doris to Wrights Lake trailhead).

You cannot reserve a permit anywhere else, although you can pick one up, *in the off season,* at:

Lake Tahoe Basin Management Unit
870 Emerald Bay Road (a.k.a. Highway 89)
South Lake Tahoe, CA 96150
(530) 573-2694.

They are located in the Plaza 89 center about 0.3 mile northwest of the city's Highways 50/89 split. The staff requests that you pick up a permit at the *Lake Tahoe Visitor Center* when it is open, which is about from early June through late September. It is located along Highway 89 about 3.2 miles northwest of the Highways 50/89 split in South

Lake Tahoe, and just 150 yards beyond the junction with the southbound Fallen Leaf Road. Additionally, if you are heading south on Highway 89 from Tahoe City, you can pick up a permit at the *William Kent Visitor Center,* which dispenses permits from about the Fourth of July weekend through the Labor Day weekend. This center, at the entrance to the William Kent Campground, is located 2¼ miles south of the major junction by Lake Tahoe's outlet at Tahoe City.

For the hikes in Mokelumne Wilderness that are covered in this guide, overnight users can self-register at the Carson Pass Information Center, which is at the south end of a long turnout at Carson Pass. This center is operated during the summer. For the rest of the year, overnight users, driving east up Highway 88, should get a permit at:

Amador Ranger District
26820 Silver Drive
Pioneer, CA, 95666
(209) 295-4251.

This office is about 18 miles east of Jackson. The staff prefers that you pick up your permit in person. They are open Monday through Friday 8 A.M. to 4:30 P.M. off season, and also on Saturdays from the Memorial Day weekend through the Labor Day weekend.

Backpacking and Day Hiking

General   Most of the hikes in this book can be done as day hikes rather than as overnight hikes—although you may want to take more than one day to do many of them. Generally, you have to do very little planning and preparation for each. Backpacking novices can learn the art by reading Winnett and Findling's *Backpacking Basics*—aimed directly at them.

Accurate, up-to-date topographic maps are included in this guide, which allow you to visualize the difficulty of the terrain any hike traverses as well as allow you to gauge your hiking progress. Each hike lists the distances to major goals, mostly lakes. In addition, shorter distances are often mentioned in a hike's description. There are numerous instances where vertical distance in feet and horizontal distance in yards are given. The first is given to tell you how much you will have to climb, thereby informing those who like easy hikes what they're in for. The second has a more practical reason: some trail junctions are easily missed, particularly in early season when snow lingers on. Therefore, potentially hard-to-find junctions are identified by their distance from the nearest identifiable feature—often a creek crossing. Yards are given because they approximately equal long strides—when in doubt the hiker can pace off the distance.

Your progress along a trail is often measured with respect to a prominent feature in the landscape, such as a mountain or hill above you. On this guide's topographic maps, many unnamed high points are identified by an **X**, which marks the point, and a number, which gives its elevation. This guide usually refers to these high points as summits or peaks—for example, peak 9224.

Some trails in this guide are potentially hard to follow in a few spots. Others may have early-season snow patches hiding them. For both, you can usually find your way by watching for blazes or ducks that mark the trail. A *blaze* is a conspicuous scar on a tree trunk, created where someone has carved away a patch or two of bark. A *duck* is one or more rocks, usually stacked one upon another in an obviously unnatural (e.g., man-made) manner.

Minimal-impact hiking If thousands of hikers walk through a mountain landscape, especially across fragile areas such as boggy meadows or sandy soils, they are almost bound to degrade it. The following suggestions are offered in the hope they will reduce human impact on the landscape, thus keeping it attractive for those who follow.

First, if you are healthy enough to make an outdoor trip in the mountains, you are in good enough condition to do so on foot. Leave horses or other pack animals behind. One horse can do more damage than a dozen backpackers. It will contribute at least as much excrement as all of them, but moreover, it will do so indiscriminately, sometimes in creeks or at lake shores. Another problem with horses is that they can trample meadow trails into a string of muddy ruts, particularly in early season. Finally, grazing can adversely impact the native vegetation. For example, only 30 years after Yosemite Valley was set aside as a park, its luxuriant native grasses and wildflowers were reduced to about one-fourth their original number, largely replaced by hardier, less showy alien species. However, cattle more than horses keep many of Tahoe's mountain meadows in a flower-poor state. If you do bring stock animals into Desolation Wilderness, you are required to provide them with supplemental feed, and you are not allowed to tie or picket them in any meadow or within 200 feet of water. Just as hikers can engage in certain practices and behaviors to reduce their impact on the environment, so can equestrians, and there are a number of books with advice for them. Some of these are listed in the "General" section under "Recommended Reading and Source Materials."

If at all possible, those on foot should day hike rather than overnight-hike. You can, for example, make easy-to-moderate day hikes to over half of the Desolation Wilderness lakes, and the same applies to the lakes outside the wilderness. Actually, if you're *really* in shape, there's no reason you can't day hike to *any* lake under 8½ miles away and *enjoy* it. Such a lengthy hike should take only 6 hours or less, round trip, if you're truly in shape. Of course anglers will object, since the best time for fishing is early morning. And who wants to get up at three in the morning to fish a lake at dawn? For them, backpacking is a must. Still, trout-stocked mountain lakes are an unnatural phenomenon, and some people question continuance of the stocking program. In our area, some lakes are no longer planted.

Why do day hikers have less impact on the environment? Fore one thing, they usually use toilets near trailheads rather than soil near lakes. Seven-hundred backpackers in Desolation Wilderness contribute about a ton of human waste per week, and the bulk of this is within 100 yards of a lake, stream, or trail. Around a popular lake excrement can lead to deterioration of its water quality. Always defecate *at least 50 yards away* from any lake or stream, and the Forest Service recommends you bury feces 6-8 inches deep. Apparently, the spread of *Giardia*, which is discussed at the end of this chapter, has become a real problem in many Sierra lakes and streams largely because of human feces contaminated with this intestinal parasite.

If, in order to have a satisfactory wilderness experience, you decide to backpack, you might consider the following advice, which is specifically aimed at those visiting Desolation Wilderness, but is applicable to all backpackers (and equestrians).

1. Pack out toilet paper. Popular lakes can receive over a thousand visitors during summer, and there's a limit to how much paper can be buried. You could burn the toilet paper, but this requires a campfire, which is illegal in our area's wildernesses.

2. If you are camping outside a wilderness, don't build a campfire unless you absolutely have to do so, as in an emergency. Downed wood is already too scarce, and cutting or defacing standing vegetation, whether living or dead, is strictly prohibited. *Use a stove instead.* Stoves cook meals faster, leave pots and pans cleaner, and save downed wood for the soil's organisms, which are necessary food for larger animals. Campfires can leave an unsightly mess and, as winter's snowpack melts, campfire ashes can be carried into lakes, reducing their water quality. If you intend to build a fire, you will need a *campfire permit*. These can be obtained at ranger stations, at Forest Service headquarters, or at the Eldorado National Forest Information Center, mentioned earlier. A campfire permit requires a group to carry a shovel. If you don't build any fires but use only a gas stove, then you can leave the shovel behind, but you'll still need the campfire permit (unless you have a wilderness permit).

3. Don't pollute lakes and streams by washing clothes or dishes in them. And don't lather up in them, even with biodegradable soap. *All* soaps pollute. Do your washing and pot scrubbing well away from lakes and streams, and bury fish entrails rather than throw them back into the water.

4. Set up camp at least 100 feet from trails, streams, and lakeshores. At some lakes this may be practically impossible, and then you must be extremely careful not to degrade the environment. Always camp on mineral soil (or perhaps even on bedrock, if you've brought sufficient sleep padding), but never in meadows or other soft, vegetated areas. It's best to use a site already in use rather than to brush out a new campsite. That would result in one more human mark upon the landscape.

5. Leave your campsite clean. Don't leave scraps of food behind, for they only attract mice, bears, and other camp marauders. If you can carry it in, you can carry it out. After all, your pack is lighter on the way out and the trail is probably mostly downhill.

6. Don't build structures. Rock walls, large fireplaces, and bough beds were fine through the 1950s, before throngs flocked to the mountains, but they are not appropriate today. There are just too many humans on this planet, and one goes into the wilderness for a bit of solitude away from them. The wilderness user shouldn't have to be confronted with continual reminders of human presence. Leave the wilderness at least as pure as you found it.

7. Noise and loud conversations are inappropriate. Have some consideration for other campers in the vicinity. Always camp far enough away from others to assure privacy to both them and you.

Regardless of whether you are day hiking or overnighting, you should observe the following advice.

1. The smaller your party, the better. In an official wilderness, parties currently are limited to 15 individuals, though at the more popular trailheads the size is as small as six. If your party is more than six, you should avoid the more popular trails in any wilderness. This is also good advice to follow outside the wilderness. You can lessen your group's impact on others by avoiding the main hiking season, which lasts from about late July through the Labor Day weekend, when lakes are fairly warm and mosquitoes are minimal.

2. If you're 16 or older, you'll need a California fishing license if you plan to fish (see next chapter). You'll also need a license to hunt. Observe all fishing and hunting regulations.

3. Destruction, injury, defacement, removal, or disturbance in any manner of any natural feature or public property is prohibited. This includes molesting any animal; picking flowers or other plants; cutting, blazing, marking, driving nails in, or otherwise damaging growing trees or standing snags; writing, carving, or painting of name or other inscription anywhere; destruction, defacement, or moving of signs.

4. Smoking is not allowed while traveling through vegetated areas. You may stop and smoke in a safe place.

5. Pack and saddle animals have the right of way on trails. Hikers should get completely off the trail, on the downhill side if possible, and remain quiet until the stock has passed. Mountain bikers should yield to both hikers and equestrians.

6. When traveling on a trail, stay on the trail. Don't cut switchbacks, since this destroys trails. When going cross-country, don't mark your route in any way. Let the next person route-find just as you did. Use a compass and map.

7. Be prepared for sudden, adverse weather. It's good to carry a poncho even on a sunny day hike. It can double as a ground cloth or emergency tent. A space blanket (2 oz. light) is also useful. Some day hikes accidentally turn into overnight trips, due to injury, getting lost, bad weather, or slower-than-anticipated hiking. Early-season and late-season hikers may encounter snow flurries and, rarely, full-fledged storms; and if they plan to camp out overnight, they should have a tent or at least some covering. Before you drive off to your trailhead, find out what the weather is supposed to be like, but be prepared— Sierra weather has been known to go from clear blue sky to all-out thunderstorm in only an hour. Never climb to a summit if clouds are building above it, particularly if you hear thunder or see lightning in the area.

8. The farther you are from your trailhead, the greater is the problem if you are injured. Rock climbers and mountaineers, who are in a higher-risk category, should bear this in mind. You shouldn't hike alone, since then you may have no one but yourself to rescue you in an emergency. In particular, crossing large streams in early season can be dangerous. However, in the area covered by this book, most of the trails are popular and you are likely to meet other people, should you need help.

Giardiasis

Our clear mountain lakes and streams unfortunately sometimes contain disease-producing organisms. One hidden hazard you should particularly know about is a disease called *giardiasis* (jee-ar-dye-a-sis). It can cause severe intestinal discomfort. The disease is caused by a microscopic organism, *Giardia lamblia*. The cystic form of giardia can occur in mountain streams and lakes. These natural waters may be clear, cold, and free-running; they may look, smell, and taste fine; still giardia may be present.

Although giardiasis can be incapacitating, it is not usually life-threatening. After ingestion by humans, giardia organisms normally attach themselves to the small intestine. Disease symptoms usually include diarrhea, gas, abdominal cramps, and bloating. Weight loss may occur from nausea and loss of appetite. These discomforts may last up to six weeks. Most people are unaware that they have been infected, and may return home from the mountains before the onset of symptoms. If not treated, the symptoms may disappear on their own, only to recur intermittently over a period of many months. Other diseases can have similar symptoms, but if you drank untreated water, you should suspect giardiasis and so inform your doctor. If the disease is properly diagnosed, it is curable with medication prescribed by a physician.

There are several ways for you to treat raw water to make it relatively safe to drink. The treatment most certain to destroy giardia is to boil the water, preferably for 3-5 minutes.

Chemical disinfectants, such as iodine or chlorine, are not as reliable as boiling unless you wait for a long time, such as an hour, before drinking the treated water. This, obviously, is a long time to wait for a drink, so carry two water bottles. While you're drinking from one, the second can be sitting in your pack, with the disinfectant working in it. The recommended dosages, per quart, for these substances are: 5 tablets of chlorine or 4 drops of household bleach, or 2 tablets of iodine or ten drops of 2% tincture of iodine. To avoid the nuisance of boiling or the bad taste of chemicals, you can instead carry a water filter. These are fairly expensive, bulky, and sometimes a nuisance to use, but you can pump a quart of cool, refreshing, good-tasting water in only about two minutes. Finally, you can avoid drinking untreated water altogether by day hiking and carrying you own safe supply of water.

Llamas, for better or for worse, have become increasingly popular pack animals

Chapter 4
Lakes and Fish of the Tahoe Sierra

Introduction

No guide to the Tahoe Sierra could be complete without a chapter on the area's trout and trout lakes. In general, the larger lakes produce the larger fish. Lake Tahoe has produced some whoppers—to over 30 pounds—for lake trout. The lake's average fish, however, is considerably less, only a couple of pounds. Still, this is a lot larger than most Desolation Wilderness trout, which are typically less than a pound. This wilderness has been touted as an angler's paradise, for virtually every lake is stocked. Even so, less than 10% of the wilderness visitors are serious anglers, although many visitors do carry a rod "just in case." Most of the serious anglers in the Tahoe Sierra visit its rivers and major streams plus its larger lakes, which include Loon, Fallen Leaf, Donner, Spaulding, and Bowman lakes and Union Valley, Hell Hole, French Meadows, Prosser Creek, Boca, Stampede, and Jackson Meadow reservoirs. In the table that follows, most of the larger lakes, which typically lie below 6000 feet, are omitted. Only the lakes that are shown on this book's topographic maps (or just off them) are included.

General Fishing Regulations

Everyone 16 years or older needs a fishing license. These are short-term or annual, resident or nonresident. The license plus detailed regulations are available at most sporting-goods stores and at mountain resorts. Also, you can contact the Department of Fish and Game (1701 Nimbus Road, Rancho Cordova, CA 95670; 916-358-2900). Most of the Tahoe Sierra lies within the Sierra Fishing District. In this district the late April through mid-November daily limit is typically five fish. Lake Tahoe lies partly in Nevada, and anywhere on this lake either a California or a Nevada fishing license will do.

Principal Trout and Salmon

There are only two trout species native to the Tahoe Sierra, rainbow and cutthroat. All other species have been introduced. Originally, rainbow trout occurred in western Sierra streams, usually below the lakes, since they much prefer to spawn on stream beds rather than on lake bottoms. Consequently, to maintain their populations in mountain lakes, the Department of Fish and Game must continually plant rainbows, annually in many lakes. There are about a half dozen subspecies of rainbow trout in California, and they all can be cross-bred (even with cutthroat trout). One such hybrid is a cross of the Shasta rainbow with the British Columbian Kamloops rainbow. This hybrid of two nonnative subspecies has been popular in the Tahoe area since 1978. The Lahontan cutthroat trout is native to the Truckee, Carson, and Walker river drainages. It occurred in Lake Tahoe until the 1940s, when it apparently disappeared. The introduction of the aggressive lake trout (mackinaw), from Michigan, is cited as the prime cause for its demise. The brown trout, of European descent, is another introduction, and is found in a few lakes. The arctic grayling, a more recent introduction, has not caught on.

The most successful introduction, from the northeastern United States, is the brook trout, or "brookie." Unlike the rainbow, it spawns in mountain lakes and therefore can maintain its population. Many mountain anglers consider it the tastiest of the Sierra's trout. Another successful introduction, from the southern end of the High Sierra, is the golden trout. It prefers high mountain lakes, and in the Tahoe Sierra that is where it has been planted. These lakes typically are also the most remote, so to catch a golden trout is a rewarding experience.

The only common salmon in our area is the kokanee, which is a landlocked version of the oceangoing sockeye salmon. Most trout its size eat insects or small fish, but the kokanee prefers to eat plankton. It does well only in the cool, larger lakes, such as Donner and Tahoe. Tahoe has one more native species that is closely related to trout—the mountain whitefish. This edible fish does not occur in any other Tahoe Sierra lake.

Lakes and Fish of the Tahoe Sierra

Lake's name	Mentioned in hike(s)	Shown on map(s)	Elevation (feet)	Size (acres)	Depth (in feet, if known)	Trout or salmon
Aloha, Lake	66, 72, 83, 87	34	8116	610	30	BK
Alta Morris Lake	82	34	8150	4 ½	18	BK, GT
American Lake	72	34	8100	11	40	BK
Angora Lake, Lower	58	35	7390	8	32	CT
Angora Lake, Upper	58	35	7460	14	48	CT
Audrain, Lake	89	38	7140	11	10	BK, RT
Avalanche Lake	72	35, 37	7490	2	10	BK, RT
Azure Lake	55	31, 32	7700	30	103	BK, RT
Barrett Lake	63	33	7635	6	30	BT, RT
Bear Lake	75	27	7530	6	—	BK
Bear Lake, Big	21, 22	8	6485	24	69	RT
Bear Lake, Little	21, 22	8	6489	4	15	RT
Berts Lake	—	25	6730	1 ½	10	BK, RT
Beyers Lake	33	12	6856	18	30	CT
Beyers Lake, upper	33	12	6860	6	8	BK
Blue Lake	—	11	5964	47	160	RT
Blue Lake, Upper	—	43	8136	298	177	CT, RT
Boomerang Lake	68	33	8060	1	10	BK
Bowman Lake	—	n. of 12	5558	825	160	RT
Buck Island Lake	59	25, 27	6430	45	40	BK, BN, RT
Cagwin Lake	85	35	7750	2	12	RT
Caples Lake	96	39, 40	7798	623	70	BN, LK, RT
Carr Lake	31	12	6664	15	22	BK, RT
Cathedral Lake	79	35	7630	2	25	BK, GT
Channel Lake	72	34	8090	4	16	BK, RT
Cliff Lake	76	31	8390	4	<20	BK
Clyde Lake	66	34	8060	21	35	BK, GT
Crag Lake	76	31	7470	22	—	BK, BN
Cub Lake	21, 22	8	6580	2	10	BK
Culbertson Lake	32	12	6442	71	50+?	RT
Cup Lake	73	37	8500	2 ½	30+?	BK, GT
Dardanelles Lake	91, 92	38	7750	16	23	BK
Dark Lake	61	33	6900	14	11	BN, RT
Deer Lake	17-19	6	7100	28	40	RT
Desolation Lake	72	34	7980	3 ½	13	BK
Devils Oven Lake	36	14	7874	4	fi	BK, GT
Dicks Lake	66, 77, 78	34	8425	61	65	BK, RT
Dipper Pond	76	31	7475	1 ½	—	BK, RT
Donner Lake	—	18	5933	840	220	KOK, LT, RT
Doris, Lake	64-66	33	8350	2 ½	12	GT
Downey Lake	33	12	6870	12	40	RT
Eagle Lake	77	32	6990	20	25	BK, RT
Echo Lake, Lower	85-87	35, 36	7414	250	180	BK, KOK, RT
Echo Lake, Upper	85-87	35	7414	80	—	BK, KOK, RT
Elbert Lake	—	38	7550	4	10	BK, RT
Emigrant Lake	96	42	8590	21	80	BK
Eureka Lake	27 Trhd.	n. of 8	6180	33	30	BK, RT
Fallen Leaf Lake	56	32, 35, 36	6377	1410	365	BN, KOK, LT, RT
Faucherie Lake	33	12	6132	140	120	BN, RT
Fawn Lake	—	25, 27	6350	6	12	RT
Feeley Lake	31, 32	12	6728	51	64	BN, RT
Fisher Lake	Ch. 10 Intro.	13	7035	3	50	BK
Five Lakes (Granite Chief)	46	20, 21	7510-7540	1-5	5-20	BK, RT in s.&w. lakes
Five Lakes (Grouse Ridge)	33	12	6990-7220	2-6	—	RT in 3 largest lakes
Floating Island Lake	79	35	7220	2	15	BK
Fontanillis Lake	66, 77, 78	31	8300	25	76	BK
Forni Lake	60	26	7930	6	>27	BK, GT
4-Q Lake, lower	65	30	7470	2 ½	16	BK
4-Q Lake, middle	65	30	7475	3	19	BK
4-Q Lake, upper	65	30	7480	6	21	BK
Fourth of July Lake	98	42	8164	16	60	BT, RT
Fox Lake	59	30	6550	4	15	BK

Fish: AG: arctic grayling BK: brook trout BN: brown trout CT: cutthroat trout GT: golden trout KOK: kokanee salmon LT: lake trout (mackinaw) RT: rainbow trout (mostly hybrids)

Lake's name	Mentioned in hike(s)	Shown on map(s)	Elevation (feet)	Size (acres)	Depth (in feet, if known)	Trout or salmon
Frata Lake	72	35	8065	2	9	BK
Frog Lake	98, 99	41	8850	7	27	CT, RT
Fuller Lake	—	11	5343	64	31	BN, RT
Gefo Lake	72	34	7870	3 ½	9	BK
Genevieve, Lake	76	31	7420	7	12	BK
Gertrude Lake	67	33	7995	2 ½	11	BK, GT
Gilmore Lake	81	35	8310	78	250	BK, LT, RT
Glacier Lake	33	12	7540	3	30+?	GT
Gold Lake	20	8, 9	6407	480	80	BN, RT
Gold Lake, Little	20 Trhd.	6, 8	6435	6	13	BK
Granite Lake	78	32	7660	8	30+?	BK
Grass Lake (Desol. Wild.)	80	35	7235	18	25	BK, RT
Grass Lake (Luther Pass)	100	44	7690	10	5	BK
Grouse Lake	69	33	8140	4	15	RT
Grouse Lake, Lower	76	31	8030	1	—	BK
Grouse Lake, Upper	76	31	8195	2	—	BK
Half Moon Lake	82	34	8140	23	19	BK, GT
Heather Lake	66, 83	34	7900	34	>50	BK, BN
Hemlock Lake	69	33	8390	1	14	BK
Hidden Lake	76	31	7575	5	—	BT, RT
Highland Lake	65	30	7810	13	88	RT
Horseshoe Lake	65	30	7540	8	10	BK
Island Lake (Grouse Ridge)	31, 32	12	6830	35	80	BT, LT, RT
Island Lake (Desol. Wild.)	68	33, 34	8140	20	30+?	BK, GT
Jabu Lake	—	35	8460	1 ½	>20	GT
Jackson Lake	—	n. of 12	6585	50	60	RT
Jackson Meadow Reservoir	39, 40	5, 17	6036	960	125	RT
Jamison Lake	27	8	6275	23	28	BK, RT
Kalmia Lake	—	34	8590	4	15	GT
Kirkwood Lake	—	39	7670	18	30	RT
Lake of the Woods	72, 74, 87	35	8050	69	70	BK, RT
Lawrence Lake	63	33	7820	8	>35	BK, RT
LeConte, Lake	87	34	8180	6	35	BK, RT
Leland Lake, Lower	65	30	8125	5	32	GT
Leland Lake, Upper	65	30	8190	4	13	GT
Lily Lake	25	8	5918	3	21	BK
Lindsey Lake, lower	32	12	6236	25	44	BN, RT
Lindsey Lake, middle	32	12	6436	20	40	CT
Loch Leven Lake, High	34	13	6870	6	9	BK, RT
Loch Leven Lake, Middle	34	13	6780	11	25	BK, RT
Loch Leven Lake, Upper	34	13	6790	5	26	RT
Lois, Lake	64-66	30, 33	8290	23	73	BK
Long Lake (Lakes Basin)	22-24, 27	8	6555	147	191	RT
Long Lake (Grouse Ridge)	31, 32	12	6870	4	17	RT
Loon Lake	59	25	6378	1450	40+?	RT
Lost Lake (by Duck Lake)	52	28	7700	10	—	RT
Lost Lake (by Barrett Lake)	63	33	7790	3	15	DK
Lost Lake (by Triangle Lake)	85	35	8110	2	—	BK, GT
Lost Lake, lower	—	43	8630	13	25	BK
Lost Lake, upper	—	43	8670	17	37	BK
Lucille, Lake	87	35	8170	8	20	BK
Lyons Lake	71	34	8380	7	50	BK, RT
Margaret Lake	95	39	7530	5 ½	20	BK
Margery, Lake	87	35	8225	4	10	BK
Marlette Lake	104	48	7823	350	52	CT (no fishing)
Maude Lake	64-66	33	7660	7	20	RT
McConnell Lake	65	30	7830	5	8	GT
Meiss Lake	92-94	40	8314	10	6	BK
Mildred Lake, middle	42	22	7950	2	—	GT
Milk Lake	31	12	6997	13	—	RT
Miller Lake	75 Trhds.	27	7115	25	8	BK
Milton Reservoir	10	5	5690	26	8	BN, CT, RT
Needle Lake	45	20	8510	1 ½	—	LT
Needle Lake, Little	45	20	8070	2	—	BK
Number 3, Lake	63	30	8230	7	25	GT
Number 5, Lake	63	33	7940	3 ½	8	BK
Packer Lake	15	6	6224	11	27	RT
Paradise Lake	35, 38	14	7728	19	30+?	BT, RT
Pearl Lake	62	33	7350	4	34	RT
Penner Lake	32	12	6895	20	—	BK, RT
Phipps Lake	75, 76	31	8550	10	—	BK
Pyramid Lake	72	34	8030	9	>20	BK

Fish: AG: arctic grayling BK: brook trout BN: brown trout CT: cutthroat trout GT: golden trout
KOK: kokanee salmon LT: lake trout (mackinaw) RT: rainbow trout (mostly hybrids)

Lake's name	Mentioned in hike(s)	Shown on map(s)	Elevation (feet)	Size (acres)	Depth (in feet, if known)	Trout or salmon
Ralston Lake	85	35	7790	12	35	BK, RT
Red Lake	—	41	7860	85	30	BK
Richardson Lake	75	27	7395	11	31	BK, RT
Rock Lake (Jamison Creek)	27	8	6315	15	—	BK
Rock Lake (Grouse Ridge)	32	12	6710	20	—	BK
Rock Lake, Lower	32	12	6622	9	—	BK
Rockbound Lake	59	27, 30	6529	114	95	RT
Ropi Lake	72, 74	34	7625	18	50	BK
Round Lake (Lakes Basin)	21	8	6716	14	40	BK, CT
Round Lake (Grouse Ridge)	31, 32	12	6900	5	—	RT
Round Lake (Upper Truckee)	91, 92	38, 40	8037	14	40	BK, CT
Round Top Lake	96-98	40	9340	9	40	GT
Rubicon Lake	76	31	8305	8	30	BK
Rubicon Reservoir	59	30	6548	80	30	RT
Rucker Lake	—	11	5462	54	—	RT
Salmon Lake	34	13	6700	3	15	BT, RT
Salmon Lake, Lower	—	6	6380	25	11	BK
Salmon Lake, Upper	19	6	6501	37	46	BK, RT
Sand Ridge Lake	35	14	7798	4	10	BK
Sanford Lake	33	12	7058	6	22	RT
Sardine Lakee, Lower	14	6, 7	5762	35	81	BK, RT
Sardine Lake, Upper	14	6	5995	54	159	RT
Saucer Lake	—	35, 37	8590	1	20	GT
Sawmill Lake	32	n. of 12	5863	120	20	RT
Saxonia Lake	15	6	6496	10	40	RT
Schmidell, Lake	64-66	30	7870	36	>100	BK
Secret Lake	69	33	8300	1	10	BK
Shadow Lake (near Loon Lake)	60	26	7260	6	15	BK
Shadow Lake (near Meeks Bay)	76	31	7660	5	—	RT
Shotgun Lake	32	12	6520	22	—	RT
Showers Lake	89, 93, 94	40	8647	6	20	BK
Silver Lake	21	8	6670	10	16	BK
Smith Lake (Lakes Basin)	26, 27	8	6079	21	—	BK
Smith Lake (Desol. Wild.)	69	33, 34	8700	9	60	BK
Snag Lake	—	9	6670	20	9	BK
Snake Lake	20	8	6730	6	—	RT
Snow Lake	55	32, 35	7390	14	20	BK
Spider Lake	59	25	6710	42	45	RT
Spooner Lake	104	48	6980	84	10	BK, RT (catch & release only)
Squaw Lake	—	9	6670	5	25	BK
Star Lake	101, 102	45, 46	9110	20	30+?	BK
Stony Ridge Lake	76	31	7820	53	84	BK, LT
Summit Lake	36	14	7398	7	15	BK
Susie Lake	66, 83	34	7795	37	68	BK, RT
Sylvia Lake	71	34	8060	3	20	GT
Tahoe, Lake	53, 54	32	6229	122,000	1645	BN, KOK, LT, RT
Tallac Lake	—	35	7900	1	—	GT
Tamarack Lake	85	35	7830	23	31	BK
Tamarack Lake, Lower	15	6	6715	2 ½	9	BK
Tamarack Lake, Upper	15	6	6754	3	14	RT
Toem Lake	72	34	7635	9	—	RT
Top Lake	63	33	8260	5	20	GT
Triangle Lake	84, 85	35	8010	1	20	RT
Twin Lake, Lower	68	33	7980	9	—	RT
Twin Lake, Upper	68	33	7982	13	—	RT
Tyler Lake	67	33	8220	2	20	BK
Velma Lake, Lower	77	31	7700	34	61	BK, RT
Velma Lake, Middle	66, 75-78	31	7890	43	44	RT
Velma Lake, Upper	77, 78	31	7950	14	29	BK, RT
Waca Lake	72	34	8190	5	>38	BK
Wades Lake	20, 27	8	6549	10	36	BK
Warren Lake	35, 36	14	7210	31	—	CT
Watson Lake	111, 112	54	7770	5	—	CT
West Lake, lower	35, 36, 41	14	7180	3	5	BK
West Lake, upper	35, 36, 41	14	7240	2 ½	15	BK
White Rock Lake	38	16	7818	89	—	RT
Winnemucca Lake	97, 98	41	8980	52	100	RT
Woods Lake	97	40	8220	13	51	AG, RT
Wrights Lake	62-70	33	6941	65	7	BK, RT
Young America Lake	15	6	7250	6	48	GT
Zitella, Lake	65	30	7660	8	15	BK

Fish: AG: arctic grayling BK: brook trout BN: brown trout CT: cutthroat trout GT: golden trout
KOK: kokanee salmon LT: lake trout (mackinaw) RT: rainbow trout (mostly hybrids)

Chapter 5
Geology

Introduction

Until the 1990s, the story of the origin of the Sierra Nevada landscape went like this. In the last few million years, the range experienced major uplift, which steepened the gradients of its rivers, causing them to flow faster and erode more effectively, creating major canyons. Large glaciers then flowed down these canyons, greatly deepening and widening them. In short, the range underwent radical transformation, mostly in the last 10 million years, from a low, gentle landscape to a high, rugged one. This version is not true, although because it originated back in the mid-1800s, geologists have forgotten how it arose. Like others, I believed this view, but in the 1990s had the opportunity to study it. The results are presented in my comprehensive *Geomorphic Evolution of the Yosemite Valley and Sierra Nevada Landscapes: Solving the Riddles in the Rocks*. The book documents the history of geological research in the range as well as uplift evidence and glacial evidence. Since the book is readily available—see "Recommended Reading and Source Materials"— I will present only a general account of how the uplift misconception arose.

The misconception had its roots with Louis Agassiz, who in 1837 presented evidence of a widespread former glaciation in Europe, and he logically assumed that the ice originated at the North Pole and spread southward. But as glacial evidence mounted, geologists came to realize that European glaciers flowed north from the Alps, not south from the North Pole. Since the glaciation had been geologically recent, geologists assumed that the Alps were almost as recent. So by about 1860 the misconception had arisen: the Alps and other glaciated ranges experienced major uplift, followed by tremendous, rapid erosion, first by rivers, and then by glaciers. The earliest geologists, exploring the Sierra Nevada in the 1860s, carried this misconception with them. By the late 1890s, the geology of the range had been mapped in sufficient detail to absolutely disprove the misconception, virtually all of the crucial evidence lying in the Tahoe Sierra or in the lower lands west of it. Nevertheless, the misconception had become entrenched, and no one would question it until I (and then several others) did so *a full century later*, in the 1990s.

The Present as a Key to the Past

As the early European geologists recognized, geologic processes occurring today occurred in the past. However, we now know what the early geologists did not. First, until about 33 million years ago, most of the earth's lands experienced wet, warm climates, ones that create higher rates of weathering and erosion than found in the Sierra Nevada today. Second, starting about 2½ million years ago, the Sierra Nevada experienced alternating cycles of glaciation and interglaciation. (Since about 10,000 years ago, the world has been in

the latest interglaciation, a span during which glaciation has been minimal and sea-level elevation has been maximal.) Third, early geologists did not know about plate tectonics (continental drift) and the complex faulting associated with it.

With the present as a key to the past, we can examine what is occurring today and apply it to the past. Along most of California, the San Andreas fault is the approximate boundary between the Pacific plate, on the west, and the North American plate, on the east. This primary fault is one of a series of nearly parallel major faults of the San Andreas fault *system*. Movement on these major faults is right-lateral—the block of crust on the west side of each fault moves north with respect to the block of crust on the east side. The San Andreas fault currently has the most movement, but in the past other faults were more active, and in the future other faults probably will become more active.

About 5 million years ago, the direction of the Pacific plate's motion began to change, so that instead of its east edge sliding smoothly north past the west edge of the North American plate, the east edge increasingly was compressed against it. The continental crust riding on the two plates, being of relatively low density, could not sink out of the way, so the compressive forces caused uplift, and the Coast Ranges were born. Because the major faults aren't perfectly parallel, irregularities have arisen. Where parallel faults tend to converge, as along central California, a block of submerged continental crust was raised thousands of feet above sea level to create the Santa Lucia Range, among others. But to the north, where parallel faults tend to diverge, a lowland developed, the San Francisco Bay.

If the change in the direction of the Pacific plate continues, the Coast Ranges will continue to grow, rivaling the Sierra Nevada in only a few million years. Eventually the angle between the two plates may increase to the point that the Coast Ranges will be thrust across the Central Valley, obliterating it. If so, they will be compressed against the western Sierra Nevada, and this compression will cause an *orogeny*, or mountain-building episode.

During it, the Coast Ranges will become attached, or *accreted* to the range, which then will have become a bit wider. This accreted belt of continental crust will be similar to previously accreted belts, each called a *terrane*—a usually complex, fault-bounded geologic unit (as opposed to terrain—a geographical area). In the Tahoe Sierra, the Northern Sierra terrane is easily the largest, but in lands west of it there are several others, all somewhat linear and roughly north-south in orientation.

While the continental crust can't sink, the denser oceanic crust as well as the dense, upper-mantle rock underlying both crusts can, and so an oceanic plate will dive under a continental plate. With increasing pressure and depth, the diving plate will begin to undergo partial melting, and the melt, or *magma*, being of relatively low density, will ascend through the continental crust. If the magma solidifies before reaching the earth's surface, it becomes *granitic* rock, and a body of granitic rock is called a *pluton*. If it reaches the surface as eruptions of ash or lava, it becomes *volcanic* rock. Voluminous eruptions can create a mountain range, such as the Cascade Range of Washington, Oregon, and northern California. That range is largely the result of an oceanic plate diving eastward beneath the Pacific Northwest.

Magma that solidifies beneath the surface forms *plutonic* rock, and in the Sierra Nevada most of this rock, where exposed, is light-gray *granitic* rock. Together, volcanic and plutonic rocks are classified under *igneous* rocks, which are any that solidify from a molten mass. The common types of igneous rocks are listed in the accompanying table.

IGNEOUS ROCKS

generally increasing oxides of silicon, sodium, and potassium ↑	Volcanic Rocks		Plutonic Rocks	*generally increasing oxides of magnesium, iron and calcium; also, increasing melting point and increasing density* ↓
	rhyolite	*approximately equals*	granite	
	rhyodacite	*approximately equals*	quartz monzonite	
	dacite	*approximately equals*	granodiorite	
	andesite	*approximately equals*	diorite	
	basalt	*approximately equals*	gabbro	

The Paleozoic Tahoe Sierra
(570-245 million years ago)

Ancient volcanic islands Until roughly 365 million years ago, the western shoreline of North America lay in what is now central Nevada, and the Tahoe Sierra lay submerged in the adjacent ocean. In our area, evidence of this ancient time occurs as now-metamorphosed sediments and ocean crust that collectively make up the Shoo Fly Complex, which is the oldest—and easily the largest—of three units of the Northern Sierra terrane. Its eastern part includes the Sierra Buttes-Lakes Basin area, the Grouse Ridge Recreation Area, and Union Valley Reservoir. Although the oldest marine sediments are "only" about 450 million years old, some incorporated grains of quartzite (metamorphosed sandstone), found near Culbertson Lake (Hike 31), range up to 2.7 billion years old. The Shoo Fly's western part includes the east half of Malakoff Diggins State Historic Park and lands south to Placerville. Isolated remnants of this complex also occur in Granite Chief Wilderness.

In the Tahoe Sierra, volcanism began about 420 million years ago, and it has continued on and off until geologically recent time. Before the creation of the Sierra Nevada range proper, there were several periods of arc volcanism, eruptions produced by a curved line of volcanoes, such as the Ryukyu Islands between Japan and Taiwan. Just as a *back-arc basin*—the shallow South China Sea—separates the chain of volcanic islands from the coast of China, a similar basin separated a chain of volcanic islands in the vicinity of the Sierra Nevada from the coast of North America, located in today's Nevada.

After initial sputtering, volcanoes began to erupt in earnest around 400 million years ago and did so until about 365 million years ago. Some magma fed the erupting volcanoes, but also some solidified in the crust beneath them to form granitic rock. Only a linear remnant of this granitic rock, the Bowman Lake batholith, still exists, and it extends from about Highway 49 midway between Downieville and Sierra City south to the impressive South Yuba River gorge just north of Interstate 80's Emigrant Gap. The best remains of this volcanic arc occur in the vicinity of the Sierra Buttes. While the Sierra Buttes may appear to be the eroded ruins of an old volcano, this sawtooth ridge is not; it is merely the eroded remains of metamorphosed volcanic rocks and deposits.

Antler and Sonoma orogenies The Sierra Buttes volcanism ended during the Antler orogeny, which occurred about 365 to 350 million years ago. In the Tahoe Sierra, the Shoo Fly Complex was compressed and broken up, and its sedimentary and volcanic rocks were metamorphosed by heat and pressure into

Horizontally layered volcanic strata stand above Caples Lake

metasediments and metavolcanics. Sierran arc volcanism continued through the Antler orogeny, and the record is partly preserved in rocks extending from Plumas-Eureka State Park south to the North Yuba River/Haypress Creek confluence. After the Antler orogeny the Tahoe Sierra's lands underwent extension, causing the volcanic realm to sink and become buried under accumulating marine sediments. After tens of millions of years the sea retreated and the upper marine sediments were eroded away, leaving about a 50-million-year gap in the geologic record.

In the Tahoe Sierra, land formed once again with a second round of arc volcanism, which began about 260 million years ago and lasted at least until the Sonoma orogeny, which occurred from about 250 to 240 million years ago. The rocks with evidence of arc volcanism are scattered, but include those around Frazier Falls (Hike 28). It was during the Sonoma orogeny that the Northern Sierra terrane was accreted to the western edge of North America.

The Mesozoic Tahoe Sierra (245-65 million years ago)

Triassic-Jurassic volcanism During the Triassic period (245-208 million years ago), a line of volcanoes extended from the north end of the Carson Range south to the southern Sierra Nevada. As earlier, these did not form a towering volcanic range, but rather developed close to sea level, and some of their flows reached the sea. Desolation Wilderness remained a very shallow part of that sea, lying under perhaps less than 50 feet of water until volcanism waned about 220 million years ago. By then the coastline had retreated at least 50 miles east of the vicinity of Lake Tahoe. About the same time, the limestone comprising the shallow sea floor of Desolation Wilderness was part of a crustal mass that began to sink between faults, transforming it into a deep-sea basin. That basin collected sediments from about 204 to 163 million years ago, during the Jurassic period (208-140 million years ago). A remnant preserved in the Mt. Tallac vicinity is composed of a 5000-foot-thick assemblage of tilted, metamorphosed sediments lying on granitic bedrock. Where peaks, ridges, cliffs, and slopes have developed in this metamorphic rock, it is very prominent, painting the east-central part of Desolation Wilderness in earth tones. It is equally prominent north of Interstate 80, composing monolithic English Mountain.

Some magma that produced basaltic lava also solidified beneath the surface to form gabbro, and other magma that produced

English Mountain, a resistant mass of metamorphosed volcanic rocks

andesitic lava also solidified beneath the surface to form diorite. Quite a lot of these two dark, intrusive rocks occur in Desolation Wilderness from Maude Lake and most of the way up to Rockbound Pass, and then from Lake Lois to Lake Schmidell (Hike 64).

Nevadan orogeny No sooner had the volcanic sediments accumulated than the volcanic arc producing them was tilted during extensional faulting. This, in turn, was quickly followed by compressional faulting accompanied by voluminous, rising magma, and several plutons developed. There were two large ones, the Haypress Creek and Emigrant Gap plutons, each about 10 miles across, and each forming between 168 to 164 million years ago. In southwestern Desolation Wilderness are four smaller plutons of similar age. All of these plutons were deformed during the Nevadan orogeny proper.

The Sierra Nevada finally became a mountain range during a compressional "event" that may have peaked about 155 million years ago. This used to be called the Nevadan orogeny, but the term has fallen out of favor. Compression has been quite protracted, lasting from about 163 to at least 143 million years ago before waning over the next few million years. During this time, a series of linear terranes were accreted. The compressive forces uplifted the newly assembled range, and when the forces ceased, the Tahoe Sierra may have stood at about three-fourths of its modern elevations. As in previous orogenies, this one compressed the existing rocks, metamorphosing them through heat and pressure, and they were folded and faulted.

Development of a Granitic Landscape Compression can thicken continental crust only to a certain extent before it becomes too heavy to be supported by the underlying plastic, slowly deforming rock. As the underlying rock began to flow, the newly formed Sierra Nevada began to stretch apart through extensional faulting, and its crust thinned, in part fracturing the existing plutons. This rifting greatly facilitated the upward flow of magma, and the range entered a period of voluminous volcanism and plutonism. Large volcanoes developed on the surface, while large bodies of magma just below them solidified to form plutons. The oldest plutons are about 143 to 140 million years old, and on Highway 50 east you drive past their exposed granitic rocks first near the west part of Placerville and then later from about Riverton onward for several miles. Many of the Tahoe Sierra's granitic rocks found along the Sierra crest and in the Carson Range are considerably younger. There, a second group of plutons developed late in the Cretaceous period (140-65 million years ago), and they are about 100 to 80 million years old. Unlike previous ones, these have not been deformed. They too once had volcanoes and lava flows above them, but not being metamorphosed, the volcanic rocks were readily eroded and deposited as sediments in the Central Valley.

The extension that caused voluminous late-Cretaceous volcanism and plutonism also rifted the crust along faults, and some formerly subsurface plutons became rapidly exposed. The crust immediately east of the Sierra crest was down-faulted, creating the Truckee-Lake Tahoe basin and other depressions. Note that at this time the Sierra crest came into existence—it is a very old feature. Rivers that previously flowed west across the newly formed Sierra crest were decapitated as their upper drainages east of the crest sank. Along today's crest are three preserved canyons of Cretaceous rivers, these at Paradise Lake north of Donner Pass, at Donner Pass, and at Echo Summit. Volcanism and plutonism ceased by about 80 to 75 million years ago, and about then the Sierra Nevada began its last pulse of uplift. By 65 million years ago, the time when dinosaurs went extinct, the range had reached its present height.

The Cenozoic Tahoe Sierra (65 million years ago to present)

Past climates The climate during the days of the dinosaurs was tropical, and after their demise it generally remained moist and warm until about 33 million years ago, when it began to change toward California's modern summer-dry climates. Under moist and warm climates the sedimentary and volcanic rocks weathered and eroded quite rapidly, and the tops of granitic plutons were exposed in as little as several million years. By 65 million years ago, if not sooner, the Sierra Nevada had become a largely granitic landscape. By 33 million years ago this landscape had evolved to one extremely similar to today's granitic landscape. Indeed, you could have identified all the major features by using today's topographic maps, for since that time most of the resistant granitic and metamorphic ridges, benches, and summits have been lowered by only 10 to 100 feet.

Volcanism, burial, and faulting The last pulse of Cretaceous uplift rejuvenated erosion, and coarse sediments derived largely from upper Sierra lands were deposited in the lower parts of some drainages. The most important locale is the South Yuba River drainage in the vicinity of Malakoff Diggins State Historic Park, north of Nevada City. Minor remnants of these prevolcanic auriferous (gold-rich) gravels let us reconstruct the topography that they buried some 50+ million years ago. What they show is that the South Yuba River canyon back then was essentially as deep as it is today.

The 33-million-year date, besides marking climate change, marked the beginning of renewed volcanism in the north half of the range. At first there were infrequent, if violent, eruptions of rhyolite. With time, however, there were sufficient eruptions to bury Tahoe's lands under as much as 1000 feet of rhyolite. As with the prevolcanic gravels, volcanic remnants let us reconstruct the topography they buried. Just west of Donner Pass is a sequence of volcanic deposits. The lowest and oldest is 33-million-year-old rhyolite, and it lies on the granitic floor of upper Summit Valley, showing that back then the valley already was broad and flat-floored. Past glaciers here were up to 1000 feet thick, yet they barely eroded through the granitic bedrock.

Former geologists have concluded that the Sierra crest had not yet come into existence, since if the volcanoes lay in a depression east of today's crest, then the rhyolite deposits could not have gotten over the crest and into western lands. However, we know that a Long Valley volcano, a few miles east of the Sierra crest near Mammoth Lakes, cataclysmically erupted about 760,000 years ago and buried the headwaters of the San Joaquin River, west of the crest, under about 1000 feet of rhyolite. In massive eruptions, a major crest is only a minor obstacle. The rhyolitic eruptions likely were facilitated by extensional faulting, and so the existing east-side depressions would have sank some more.

The rhyolite outbursts lasted until about 20 million years ago, when floods of volcanic lavas, volcanic mudflows, and volcanic sediments, chiefly andesite in composition, had already begun to inundate the lands. Once called the Mehrten Formation, these volcanic products later were subdivided into various units, and combined, they eventually buried our area under as much as 3000 feet of deposits. Still, the volcanic landscape was usually quiet, for eruptions probably were no more common than those in today's Cascade Range.

In the western part of the Great Basin—more specifically, east and north of the Carson Range—volcanism was in high-gear by 15 million years ago, and the faulting that accompanied the volcanism resulted in about 3000 feet of subsidence in the ensuing 2 million years. The zone of volcanism moved westward with time, the Sierra crest becoming inundated by flows and deposits from crest or near-crest volcanoes starting mostly around 13 million years ago. Desolation Wilderness largely escaped burial by both rhyolitic and andesitic volcanism, standing high as an island of granitic and metamorphic rock. Between 9 and 5 million years ago the largely andesitic volcanism waned, causing erosion to outpace deposition, and the old river canyons were exhumed. By about 3 million years ago, Sierra-crest volcanism had virtually ceased, but important volcanism was about to begin just to the east, in the Truckee-Lake Tahoe depression.

Creation of Lake Tahoe As was mentioned earlier, the basin that now holds Lake Tahoe began to form late in the days of the dinosaurs, and by 33 million years ago, the southern half (Lake Tahoe part) of the basin had topography that closely resembled today's. The lake began to form only about 2¼ million years ago, when lava erupted in the northern half of the basin, creating a volcanic dam and effectively impounding water south of it. Between 2¼ and 1¼ million years ago there were at least seven major lava flows, which at times dammed the lake as much as 800 feet above its current 6229-foot level. However, the lake's outlet, the Truckee River, continued to erode through successive flows.

Concluding our look into the origin of Lake Tahoe, we might note that the processes which brought about its creation—early faulting and late volcanism—also denied it national park status. That is because some of the volcanic rocks laid down just east of the Lake Tahoe Basin were faulted, the most famous one being the Comstock fault. Along it, silver, gold, and mercury were injected, creating the Comstock Lode. When it was discovered in 1859, a tide of miners flooded the mining area (see Hike 90 for a bit of mining history). The Tahoe forests were raped for mine timbers, buildings, and firewood, while the mountain meadows were desecrated with livestock that helped feed the hungry hordes. Desolation Wilderness, in contrast, was largely spared, except for the livestock. There were no minerals to mine, and because glaciers had removed soils, the trees that grew there were too sparse to be lumbered.

Glaciation In the Tahoe area, small glaciers may have appeared sporadically as early as 15 million years ago. Major glaciation, however, did not begin until about 2½ million years ago. Since then the landscape has been appreciably glaciated perhaps four dozen times. During each major glaciation, glaciers advanced over deposits of previous glaciations, eradicating evidence of their existence. The best glacial records lie not in mountain ranges but rather in ocean sediments, which record alternating periods of glaciation and interglaciation (like the one we are in now). In our area there remains evidence from only two glaciations, the Tahoe and the Tioga. The Tahoe existed from about 200,000 to 130,000 years ago, the slightly smaller Tioga from about 35,000 to 13,000 years ago. Between the

two there were up to three periods that produced relatively small glaciers.

Because the Carson Range lay in the rainshadow of the Sierra Nevada crest, it received less snow, and glaciers were few and small. In contrast, glaciers were numerous and large on the Sierra's west slopes, where snowfall was greatest (see glacier map). The South Yuba River glacier was over 25 miles long, and the Rubicon River glacier was over 30—comparable in length and thickness to the Merced River glacier through Yosemite Valley. On east slopes, glaciers were of intermediate length, but nevertheless were sufficiently long to reach Lake Tahoe, spewing icebergs into the frigid water.

Glaciers not only discharged into Lake Tahoe; a few large ones managed to dam it. These glaciers descended east to the north-flowing Truckee River—Lake Tahoe's outlet stream—and blocked its flow. The glacier dams were immense, high enough to raise the lake's level by 600 feet during an early glaciation. But when water pressure became too great, the ice dams broke, sending inconceivably large walls of water down the Truckee River canyon. During the Tahoe glaciation, one or more glacier dams raised the lake by 90 feet. Consequently, the lake was larger, and it expanded south over the South Lake Tahoe plain and into the lower part of the Upper Truckee River canyon. Lake-bed sediments were deposited in both areas. During the Tioga glaciation, the glaciers were a bit shorter, and apparently no ice dam formed in the Truckee River canyon.

When the Tioga glaciers finally retreated into oblivion about 13,000 years ago, they left behind moraines, which are accumulations of material—mostly rockfall—that the glaciers had transported. In our area, the Tahoe and Tioga moraines are most conspicuous about Fallen Leaf Lake, Cascade Lake, and Emerald Bay. The Tahoe Sierra's most photographed set of lateral moraines is the pair that border this bay. Here, *lateral* moraines formed as boulders carried atop the glaciers fell from their sides, accumulating as a veneer on bedrock ridges. By viewing these moraines, which would have been slightly lower than the surfaces of the glaciers responsible for

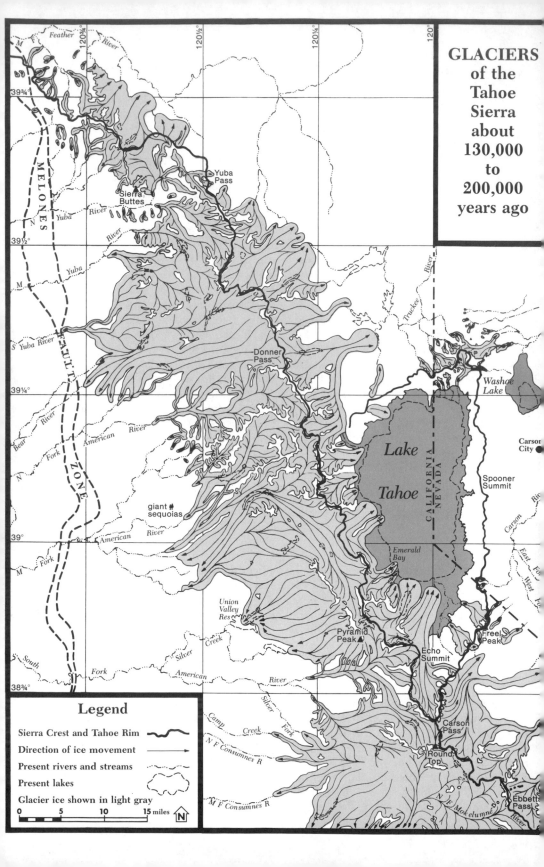

GLACIERS
of the
Tahoe
Sierra
about
130,000
to
200,000
years ago

Feather River

Yuba Pass

Sierra Buttes

Yuba River

Yuba River

S. Yuba River

MELONES

FAULT ZONE

Bear River

American River

Fork

giant sequoias

American River

Donner Pass

Truckee River

Washoe Lake

Lake Tahoe

CALIFORNIA NEVADA

Emerald Bay

Carson City

Spooner Summit

Carson Ri

East Fork

West F

Union Valley Res

Pyramid Peak

Echo Summit

Freel Peak

American River

Silver Creek

Fork

South Fork

American River

Silver Fork River

Camp. Creek

N F Consumnes R

M F Consumnes R

N F Mokelumne River

Carson Pass

Round Top

Ebbetts Pass

Legend

Sierra Crest and Tahoe Rim

Direction of ice movement

Present rivers and streams

Present lakes

Glacier ice shown in light gray

0   5   10   15 miles

N

them, one can visualize the length and thickness of these former glaciers. Another kind of moraine is a *terminal* moraine, which extends from the lateral moraines around the snout of the glacier. Behind the terminal moraine there usually lie several *recessional* moraines, each left where the retreating glacier stagnated, leaving enough debris to form a sizable ridge, such as the ones damming Fallen Leaf Lake and Wrights Lake.

Overall, Sierra glaciers did not radically transform their lands. Glaciers probably were effective at removing volcanic silts, sands, gravels, and thin lava flows, as were the preglacial rivers. Before glaciation, granitic bedrock locally had undergone considerable weathering, particularly on flat-floored canyon bottoms, where the weathering front penetrated along fractured bedrock. Glaciers removed this weathered bedrock, excavating hollows that then became today's lakes. In addition to excavating lake basins, glaciers have modified the landscape by accelerating two processes of mass wasting. First, they have caused accelerated rockfall due to pressure release. Large, thick glaciers exist for thousands of years, and their mass applies considerable pressure to the bedrock. When they melt away, which happens rather suddenly, the bedrock becomes depressurized. Slopes and cliffs then undergo accelerated mass wasting, spalling rock slabs that break and accumulate below as talus (which future glaciers will remove and then deposit some of it to form moraines). Second, because glaciers produce extremely cold local climates, freeze-and-thaw prying of rocks is also accelerated. This is particularly true at the heads of glaciers, that is, in the bowl-shaped canyon heads, the *cirques*.

Parts of our area remain almost as pristine and desolate as the day the glaciers left them, for in areas of soil-free bedrock, the granite has weathered only a fraction of an inch in the last 13,000 years. In some places, no discernible weathering has occurred, and the polish and striations imparted to the bedrock through glacial action still remain. Without faulting and volcanism, changes in a mountain landscape are exceedingly slow.

Glacial evidence: erratic boulder, polish, striations, chatter marks

Chapter 6
Botany

Introduction

Reconnaissance satellites monitor the earth's vegetation today, and it is unfortunate they weren't around 65 million years ago, when the last of the dinosaurs became extinct. If we had a continuous video record from that time onward—in other words, for all of the Cenozoic era—what a show it would be. Back then, 65 million years ago, the earth had attained 98½% of its present age, yet in the ensuing 1½% of its aging, its surface would experience great changes in landscapes, plants, and animals. In the Tahoe Sierra the changes in plants were quite dramatic.

History of the Tahoe Sierra Flora

By the start of the Cenozoic era the Sierra Nevada had already achieved modern heights, and it had a warm, wet, nearly tropical climate. Unfortunately, due to lack of fossils we don't know what the vegetation was near the high crest lands, but we do know that at mid- and low elevations there were trees similar to today's laurel, maple, beech, fig, magnolia, walnut, and oak. The climate stayed warm and wet until about 33 million years ago, when the earth as a whole cooled, due to a reorganization of ocean currents in response to ongoing plate tectonics ("continental drift"). During this time, the usually wet landscape would have had a forest rich in species, not unlike today's tropical rain forests. And intense chemical weathering coupled with vigorous stream erosion transformed the land from a mostly metamorphic one to a mostly granitic one, the latter producing relatively nutrient-deficient soils for plants. While these soils are ideal for conifers, which dominate the range today, the wet climate was not.

When the climate changed, populations of conifers (and their associated shrubs and herbs) from the drier interior were able to migrate west into the range. The timing of the change was most fortunate, for lands between the Rocky Mountains and the Sierra Nevada began to collapse, the process starting in the east and advancing westward. Over millions of years a rugged, mountainous highland province slowly evolved into today's lower Basin and Range province. The lands just east of the Tahoe Sierra sank to about their present elevations by about 12 million years ago.

As those lands sank, their climates became progressively warmer and drier, and water-loving species such as giant sequoias disappeared, replaced with drought-resistant species such as juniper and sagebrush. A serious summer-dry climate originated in California about 15 million years ago, giving pines and firs an additional advantage over their broad-leaved competitors. Then the drought intensified as the inland sea occupying California's Central Valley gradually dried up and as the Coast Ranges began to

---

Some common shrubs of the Tahoe Sierra. All have white flowers except as noted in parentheses. **Top row, left to right:** *bush chinquapin (flowers inconspicuous), pinemat manzanita (pale pink), Labrador tea, bog kalmia (rose).* **Row 2:** *red mountain heather (rose), white mountain heather, American (or creek) dogwood, snow bush.* **Row 3:** *tobacco brush, mountain spiraea (rose), bitter cherry, thimbleberry. Bottom row: serviceberry, mountain ash, red elderberry, mountain snowberry (pink).*

rise, these events occurring over the last several million years. Less moisture reached the range, and even less reached its eastern slopes.

The start of climate change 33 million years ago was also accompanied in the northern half of the Sierra Nevada with the start of volcanic eruptions. Over millions of years, the deep, generally granitic Sierra canyons became buried under volcanic sediments and lava flows, which certainly made the landscape less dramatic. However, they were a double bonus for many plants. First, volcanic soils hold more water and nutrients than do granitic ones. Second, the volcanic topography overall was less rugged, allowing plant populations to migrate across buried, formerly obstructing canyons. As the Sierra climate became progressively drier, such migration likely occurred, water-loving plants gradually shifting their distributions northward into the southern Cascade Range.

But as water-loving plants were migrating out, or being reduced in numbers, or going extinct, drought-tolerant plants were moving in. These came from southern California, invading the Sierra's foothills, cloaking them with live oaks and chaparral (drought-tolerant, fire-adapted shrubs).

The onset of major glaciation, roughly 2½ million years ago, brought even more stress to the Tahoe flora. During times of maximum glaciation, most of the area covered by this book—that is, the land above 6000 feet—lay under glacier ice. The higher peaks and ridges, however, did protrude above the sea of ice, and cold environments, which are very restricted today, were more extensive. This is especially true of the relatively unglaciated lands of the Carson Range and those above the north shore of Lake Tahoe. Alpine and subalpine plants expanded their range at the expense of less frost-tolerant plants.

During the last 2½ million years, there have been several dozen major glacial episodes, and with each one, the plants would descend to lower elevations to escape the colder climates. When the glaciers retreated, they left a bedrock landscape devoid of its former soils. Lower down, the glaciers left locally abundant deposits—mostly transported,

ground-up rockfall—and on them rather sterile soils developed that nevertheless supported dense stands of conifers, especially lodgepole pines and red firs. Before glaciation commenced, giant sequoias in the Tahoe Sierra's higher lands may have coexisted with red firs, as they did in western Nevada millions of years earlier, according to the fossil record. Whereas the red firs have been able to recolonize glaciated lands, the sequoias have not, for the thick, water-rich yet well-drained preglacial soils are gone. The sequoias barely hang on in one small area, the enigmatic Placer County Big Trees Grove, discussed in Hike 29.

Higher up, the glaciers generally scoured the bedrock landscape, leaving precious few deposits—and sparser vegetation. Also higher up, the glaciers scoured out hollows on relatively flat lands, which quickly filled to form lakes and ponds. These provided new Tahoe-area habitats to exploit—though with each glacier readvance, the lakes and ponds were obliterated, only to resurrect phoenix-like in the next interglaciation, like the one we currently are in. During this time, various Indian groups entered the range, and they set fires. Natural fires had been part of the Sierra scene for millions of years, but now the fires probably became more frequent, and plants better adapted to fire would have expanded their distribution at the expense of less-adapted plants.

The final trauma to Tahoe Sierra flora began with the Gold Rush. Forests were razed to supply firewood and timber to mining settlements. Alien plants were brought in, some unintentionally and some on purpose, and their aggressive competition proved to be detrimental to some native plants, especially lower down. Higher up in mountain meadows, native plants were impacted by overgrazing from sheep and cattle. Today, ponderosa pine, and to a lesser extent other conifers, face a newer problem—air pollution. As California's Central Valley becomes increasingly urbanized, air pollution may increase, weakening these trees and making them highly susceptible to death by bark-beetle infestation. Additionally, the range's lower lands are becoming increasingly populated, and native plants are being replaced with nonnative ones. As the native-plant populations are being reduced and fragmented, they are becoming increasingly vulnerable to extinction.

Identifying Tahoe Sierra Plants

In the Tahoe Sierra proper, which is defined as that region mostly above 6000 feet and extending from the Carson Pass environs north to Plumas-Eureka State Park, there are about 1000 species of vascular plants. Vascular plants include trees, shrubs, and herbs. Herbs include, in addition to "wildflowers," such groups as grasses, sedges, and rushes. However, for the aspiring botanist, and particularly for the average hiker, such herbs usually are ignored. So too are the other vascular plants: ferns, fern allies, horsetails, club-mosses, spike-mosses, and related kin.

The average hiker can't fail to notice the trees, though he or she may be more impressed with their size or shape than with what species they are. The vast majority of trees one sees in the Tahoe Sierra are conifers, and most are quite easy to identify. Since only 17 species are found along this area's trails, all are included in the next section. Other kinds of trees, such as oaks and aspens, may be locally abundant, but certainly above 6000 feet elevation they make up a small percentage of the overall forest canopy. If you are interested in all of the area's trees but not in the shrubs and herbs, then consider carrying Watts' 2-ounce wonder, the *Pacific Coast Tree Finder* (for this book and others, see "Recommended Reading and Source Materials," at the back of this guidebook).

The authoritative reference to Lake Tahoe's vascular plants is Smith's monograph and its later supplement. Unfortunately, neither is readily available to the general public, though serious botanists will want to acquire both. They list the species and where each has been collected, but neither has a plant key. For that you'll need Hickman or Weeden. Professional botanists may carry Hickman's fairly expensive, 5-pound *Jepson Manual,* but most will prefer Weeden's economical, 13-ounce *Sierra Nevada Flora.* Plant keys usually intimidate nonprofessionals, but Weeden's are as user-friendly as one could expect. Not only does Weeden give species distribution, he also gives, where available, species edibility. However, his book has relatively few drawings, so to compensate for this, I've included over 150 species of wildflowers on 17 plates. (For scientific names, see the appendix at the back of the book.) Flowers that are found along many of this guidebook's trails are grouped together in this chapter's eight plates. Those with a more restricted, though often locally abundant, distribution are on the remaining nine plates, which are found in the hiking chapters (all plates are indexed in the "Contents"). If you are interested only in wildflowers and abhor keys, then Niehaus and Ripper's *Field Guide to Pacific States Wildflowers* is your best bet. Be aware that many plant species have more than one common name. For the 17 plates I have listed *my* preferred common name, but have listed others in parentheses. Take, for example, plant 6 in Plate 1: elk (leafy) thistle. Hickman, Weeden, and Niehaus and Ripper call it elk thistle, but Smith calls it leafy thistle.

The Conifers: Cone-bearing Trees

All of the conifers in the Tahoe Sierra have evergreen leaves, which are either needlelike or scalelike. In the key below, the conifers are listed by leaf and cone characteristics. In the descriptions that follow, the conifers in each group are listed in the order you would encounter them as you ascended east up the Sierra's western slopes.

1. **Pines:** except for one species, pines have needles in bundles of 2-5; cones hanging (1.a. 1 needle, 1.b. 2 needles, 1.c. 3 needles, 1.d. 5 needles).
2. **True firs:** needles in rows along branches; cones upright atop only upper branches.
3. **False fir and hemlock:** needles not in rows; cones hanging.
4. **Other conifers:** leaves small, scalelike, about ⅛-¼" long.

1.a. Pine with 1 needle.
Pinyon pine Needles drab, sharp-pointed, 1-1½" long. Found only along the east flank of the

Carson Range, generally below its crest. Not likely to be seen.

1.b. Pine with 2 needles.
Lodgepole pine   Bark thin, scaly, sappy—don't touch it. Very common in Tahoe Sierra, especially between 6000 and 9000'.

1.c. Pines with 3 needles.
Gray (foothill, Digger) pine   Needles gray-green, 7-12" long. Cones 6-10" long, on short stalks. Below 4000' (Hikes 1-8, especially Hikes 2 and 8).
Knobcone pine   Needles green, 3-7" long. Cones 3-6" long, stalkless. Below 4000' (Hikes 1-8, especially Hikes 2 and 8).
Ponderosa pine   Needles yellow-green, 5-10" long. Cones 3-5" long, with out-turned prickles (they stick you). Bark yellow and platy in mature trees. Tree 150-220' tall. Common from about 1500 to 6500', occasional to 7500'.
Jeffrey pine   Needles blue-green, 5-10" long. Cones 5-10" long, with in-turned prickles. Bark reddish brown, with butterscotch odor detected in bark furrows of mature trees. Tree 50-180' tall. Common from about 5000 to 8500'. Hybridizes with ponderosa pine, making identification difficult where the two species overlap.
Washoe pine   Needles gray-green, 4-6" long. Cones usually less than 5" long. Closely resembles the Jeffrey pine. Tree occurs in significant numbers only in the Mt. Rose area (Hike 108), from about 6000 to 8500'.

1.d. Pines with 5 needles.
Sugar pine   Needles 3-4" long. Cones long and narrow, 10-16" long, growing at ends of long, graceful branches. Tree 150-240' tall. Common from about 3000 to 6500' west of the Sierra crest; uncommon in the Tahoe basin.
Western white pine   Needles 3-4" long. Cones narrow, 4-8" long. Checkerboard pattern on bark of mature trees. Tree 50-150' tall. Occurs from about 6000 to 9500', but common only from 7000 to 9000'.
Whitebark pine   Needles stiff, 1½-3" long. Cones 1½-3" long. Bark thin and scaly, like that of lodgepole pine. Tree up to 50' tall, but a prostrate shrub at highest elevations. Common from about 8500 to 10,800'.

2. True firs.
White fir   Needles 1-2½" long, in two rows. Each needle with a half twist at base. Cones 3-5" long.

Bark of mature tree grayish brown, deeply furrowed. Tree 150-230' tall. Common from about 3000 to 6500', but occasional up to 7500'.
Red fir   Needles ¾-1½" long, stout, curving up and densely covering branches. Cones 5-8" long. Bark of mature tree reddish brown, deeply furrowed. Tree 120-200' tall. Common from about 6500 to 9000', but occasional down to 5500'.

3. False fir and hemlock.
Douglas-fir   Needles about 1" long, soft, and growing all around the branches. Cones 2-4" long, lightweight, with toothed bracts projecting from scales. Bark dull-brown, deeply furrowed. Tree 150-230' tall (but to 330' tall in Pacific Northwest). Locally common, especially on north-facing slopes, from about 1000 to 6000'. Occasional to 6500', but rare in Tahoe basin.
Mountain hemlock   Needles about 1" long, soft, and growing all around the branches. Cones 1-3" long, lightweight, without bracts. Bark purplish brown to reddish brown. Tree 25-100' tall. Grows in areas of deep snowpack from about 7000 to 10,000'.

4. Other conifers.
Incense-cedar   Leaves yellow-green, in flat, horizontal sprays. Cones about 1" long, with only two fertile scales (two seeds each). Bark cinnamon-brown, fibrous. Tree 80-150' tall. Fairly common, it associates with white firs and ponderosa pines, growing from about 1000 to 6500', rarely higher.
Western juniper   Leaves gray-green, clasping the branchlets. Cones berrylike, blue-black when mature, though covered with a whitish powder. Bark cinnamon-brown, shreddy. Trunk short and broad. Locally common in dry, rocky areas, particularly in Desolation Wilderness, from about 5000 to 9500'.
Giant sequoia   Found only in one small grove (Hike 29). When this Placer County grove was discovered, only six trees existed there, but more have been planted around them.

Plant Distribution
Given the area covered by this guidebook, I have divided the vegetation into four major vegetation zones. Increasing in elevation, these are: lower montane vegetation, upper montane vegetation, subalpine vegetation, and alpine vegetation. (For the first three types many botanists say "forest" instead of

"vegetation," but each of these zones has locally large areas of nonforest vegetation such as brush and grass.) Although many species grow in only one vegetation zone, many others grow in two zones, less in three zones, and perhaps a few in all four zones. An example of the last category is the woolly sunflower, which extends, as one variety or another, from sea level up to the highest Tahoe Sierra elevations. Obviously then, the following classification is not a perfect one.

LOWER MONTANE VEGETATION ZONE

This zone extends from about 2000 to 6000 feet in elevation, broadly speaking. To the west lies the foothills vegetation zone, which barely gets a toehold in the Tahoe Sierra. The only hikes described in this guidebook which traverse through this lower zone are those along the South Yuba Trail, Hikes 2 and 8. Here, this vegetation is on dry, south-facing slopes, at elevations up to 3000 feet. But on the shady, relatively moist north-facing slopes of the South Yuba River canyon, the lower montane vegetation extends west down to 1000 feet. On the Independence Trail, Hike 1, you're traversing through a lush, verdant Douglas-fir forest.

The primary conifers of this zone are ponderosa pine and white fir, with lesser numbers of Douglas-fir, incense-cedar, sugar pine and giant sequoia, this last species growing only in the Placer County grove (Hike 29). Within this zone, as in all four zones, temperature and precipitation vary considerably. Ponderosa pine prefers the warm, dry sites, white fir and Douglas-fir prefer the cool, moist sites, and the other conifers fall in between. The occurrence of frequent fires favors ponderosa pine, black oak, and their shrubby associates, such as mountain misery, deer brush, and whiteleaf and Indian manzanitas. In any given spot in the Sierra Nevada, lightning fires tend to occur about once every 7-15 years. When fires are prevented, white fir and incense-cedar take over. This is what happened in Yosemite Valley, much to everyone's consternation, since the original pine-and-oak woodland provided superior views of the cliffs and waterfalls.

Near the lower end of this zone, precipitation is about 35 inches per year, with about 5% of it as snow, and the growing season is about 7 months. Near the upper end of this zone, the precipitation can double that, with about half of it as snow, and the growing season is only about 5 months. That is quite some difference. To appreciate the difference, visit Malakoff Diggins State Historic Park (Hikes 3-7), then drive up to Sierra City and explore its environs (Hikes 9-11).

UPPER MONTANE VEGETATION ZONE

At about 6000 feet the lower-montane conifers give way to their look-alikes. Ponderosa pine yields to Jeffrey pine, white fir to red fir, sugar pine to western white pine, and incense-cedar to western juniper. Shrubs do likewise, the lower manzanitas yielding to greenleaf and pinemat manzanitas, and deer brush to tobacco brush and snow bush. The oaks are no longer trees, but rather shrubs: the bush chinquapin and the huckleberry oak. As with the previous zone, the boundary can be quite irregular. White fir may grow on sunny south-facing slopes up to 7500 feet, while red fir may grow on snowy north-facing slopes down to 5500 feet. The upper boundary also is hard to define, but it is roughly at 9000 feet.

The upper montane vegetation zone spreads across a landscape that has been repeatedly glaciated, and this has increased the number of habitats for plants to exploit. These new habitats, listed in an order of increasing wetness, are bedrock slabs and cliffs, lateral moraines, ground moraines, meadows, and lakes. Desolation Wilderness has many bedrock outcrops, and these are particularly exploited by western junipers and, to a lesser extent, by Jeffrey pines. These pines prefer instead the dry, gravelly soils of slopes, and compete for them with huckleberry oak, greenleaf manzanita, tobacco brush, snow bush, bush chinquapin, and bitter cherry. The flats with deep soils support magnificent forests of red fir, but where the ground water table is high, the lodgepole pine takes over. If ground water is too pervasive, no tree can survive, and meadows result. Shrubs such as willows, alders, and huckleberries can thrive in meadows, but typically

Wildflower Plate 1. White or pinkish white flower of the parsley (carrot) family (photos 1-5) and the sunflower family (6-9). Note: the scientific names of all the wildflowers on Plates 1-17 are listed on page 393. Flower colors and alternate names of some wildflowers are shown in parentheses.
1 Parish's yampah, 2 Gray's lovage, 3 Brewer's angelica, 4 cow parsnip, 5 ranger's buttons (swamp white heads),
6 elk (leafy) thistle, 7 rosy everlasting, 8 white-flowered hawkweed, 9 dusty maidens (hoary chaenactis).

Wildflower Plate 2. Whitish flowers of other plant families.
1 Nude buckwheat (naked eriogonum), 2 western bistort (snakeweed), 3 alpine knotweed, 4 Nevada lewisia, 5 spreading phlox (white, pale pink, or pale blue), 6 white-veined wintergreen, 7 death camas, 8 California corn lily, 9 Sierra rein (crane) orchid (white-flowered bog orchid).

Wildflower Plate 3. Off-yellow or partly yellow flowers.
1 Pearly everlasting (white with yellow center), 2 (common) yarrow (white with yellow center), 3 wandering daisy (violet with yellow center), 4 Fendler's meadow rue (yellow-green), 5 marsh marigold (white with yellow center), 6 mountain jewel flower (white-yellow to red-purple), 7 dwarf (pine-woods) lousewort (dull yellow flowers *beneath* leaves), 8 Leichtlin's Mariposa tulip (lily), 9 Davis' knotweed (white-yellow to purple-green).

Wildflower Plate 4. Yellow flowers of the sunflower family.
1 Seep-spring arnica, 2 soft (cordilleran) arnica, 3 arrow-leaved balsamroot, 4 Brewer's aster, 5 woolly sunflower (yarrow), 6 nodding microseris (scorzonella), 7 single-stemmed senecio (tower butterweed, groundsel), 8 arrow-leaved senecio (arrowhead butterweed, groundsel), 9 mountain mule ears.

Wildflower Plate 5. Yellow flowers of other plant families.
1 Sierra stonecrop, 2 pretty face, 3 sticky cinquefoil, 4 sulfur flower, 5 common (woolly) mullein, 6 common monkey flower, 7 Baker's violet, 8 mountain violet, 9 Sierra wallflower.

Wildflower Plate 6. Orange, scarlet, or red flowers.
1 California fuchsia (scarlet), 2 wavy-leaved (Applegate's) paintbrush (scarlet), 3 mountain pride (red), 4 alpine (Sierra tiger) lily (red-orange), 5 crimson columbine (red with yellow center), 6 scarlet gilia (desert trumpet), 7 Anderson's thistle (reddish flowers and stem), 8 pinedrops (orange-to-rust plant), 9 snow plant (red plant).

Wildflower Plate 7. Pink, pinkish violet, or rose flowers.
1 Swamp onion, 2 Sierra onion, 3 nettle-leaved horsemint, 4 alpine shooting star, 5 Richardson's geranium, 6 baby (little) elephant heads, 7 glaucous (waxy) sidalcea (checker), 8 pussy paws, 9 (red) fireweed.

Wildflower Plate 8. Blue, blue-violet, violet, or purple flowers.
1 crest (spur) lupine (violet to blue), 2 ballhead (waterleaf) phacelia (dull-purple to blue to brown), 3 coyote mint (mountain monardella) (violet), 4 Nuttall's larkspur (bilobed delphinium) (purple), 5 tall larkspur (tower delphinium) (purple), 6 monk's hood (purple), 7 velvety stickseed (blue with white center), 8 Sierra penstemon (purple), 9 meadow penstemon (rose-purple).

most meadow vegetation is herbs. Here, plant diversity is at its peak, which is in stark contrast to the somber, shady red-fir forest, whose floor is largely barren. If you want to see a hundred plant species in one day, you certainly should visit at least one meadow, for it will put you well on your way toward your goal. The final new habitat, lakes, most novice botanists pass up. A number of species do grow on lake bottoms, but they are generally out of sight and reach unless you're willing to dive after them.

The upper montane vegetation zone not only spreads across severely glaciated lands, but also enters progressively drier lands the farther east one goes from the Sierra crest. In a space of about 20 miles, from the Sierra crest east across Lake Tahoe to the Carson Range crest, the precipitation can be cut in half. In the *central* Carson Range, this lesser precipitation

Top left: *cones of ponderosa pine (top), Douglas-fir (right), and sugar pine (bottom).* Top right: *cones of western white pine (left) and red fir (right).* **Bottom:** *white-fir branches (left) versus red-fir branches (right).*

was insufficient to develop glaciers. Hence, the soils there are older and are relatively uniform, the meadows are few, and the land is lakeless except for man-made reservoirs. While the western-land shrubs and herbs can sleep through winter under a protective blanket of snow, the Carson Range plants must battle winter's icy chill head-on. With less water and more severe winters, the vegetation takes on a remarkably different character. The forest is more open, western white pines dominating over red firs. Some of the common shrubs are gone, replaced by Great Basin shrubs, such as sagebrush, antelope bush (bitterbrush), and mountain mahogany.

Plants can also adapt to a specific kind of bedrock. In the upper montane vegetation zone there are exposures of granitic, metamorphic, and volcanic bedrock, and mule ears grow in soils derived from each. However, where volcanic soils are rich, mule ears can grow in huge colonies, forming dry meadows that are tens of acres in extent. In Granite Chief Wilderness (42-50), these aromatic, large-leaved sunflowers locally put on a show.

SUBALPINE VEGETATION ZONE

The gradation from the upper montane vegetation zone to the subalpine vegetation zone is irregular. Near the Sierra crest, red fir and Jeffrey pine of the lower zone stay mostly below 8000 feet, although in the Carson Range they can be found up to about 9000 feet. Lodgepole and western white pines can occur in both areas in abundance at 9000 feet and even reach 9500 feet. The latter is about 500 feet above the base of Tahoe's subalpine zone (though at the Sierra Buttes, to the north, this base is at about 8200 feet). Locally these pines can outnumber the subalpine zone's primary indicator, the whitebark pine. The zone's other prominent tree, the mountain hemlock, is a poor indicator, for though it can thrive at 10,000 feet, it can also thrive at 7000 feet. The problem of defining the subalpine zone isn't so much one of what trees exist, but rather of how they exist. In the subalpine realm, the trees no longer exist as continuous forest, but rather as open woods or in small, compact clusters.

The subalpine zone is a realm of severe climate. Almost all the precipitation is in the form of snow, and there usually is a lot of it. Among hemlocks, which grow in snowy sites and actually help to preserve the snow by their extremely dense, shady clustering, the snow can cover the ground for up to 10 months of the year. In more exposed sites gusty winds can blow the snow away, leaving the ground barren and exposed to months of subfreezing temperatures. In this harsh environment the growing season is only about two months long. During that brief period, shrubs and herbs must sprout new vegetation, produce flowers and seeds, and stock up on carbohydrate reserves for the oncoming winter.

As you climb up through the subalpine realm, you'll notice that the trees decrease in stature. By 10,000 feet the whitebark pine is the only species of tree, if you call the stunted specimens trees. They may be 20 feet high in favorable spots, but more likely they will be only a few feet high. And as you climb toward a high summit, particularly Freel Peak, Jobs Peak, or Jobs Sister, the trees become reduced to a dense mat of knee-high vegetation.

Shrubs and herbs also decrease in stature with increasing vegetation. The pine's and shrubs's adaptations are to the harsh winter climate, for keeping low allows them to stay within a blanket of protective snow. Any parts of the plants that protrude above it are pruned back by the icy, subfreezing winter winds. The herbs, on the other hand, are adapted to the summer climate. They are typically matted or prostrate, usually less than 4 inches high. By keeping low, they are protected from buffeting winds, which are rarely effective within the first few inches from the ground.

But pollination of these flowers by the wind is ineffective. The plants are too few and far between to rely on the wind for this vital process. This is true for wildflowers *everywhere* in the Tahoe Sierra, not just above 9000 feet. However, conifers, grasses, and sedges rely on wind for pollination. This mode of pollination is perhaps a clue to why the dwarfed whitebark pines grow in such dense clusters. If they were evenly spaced across the terrain, the ovules in the female cones would be far less likely to be pollinated, resulting in very few seeds. Compactness, however, assures pollination. The seeds, being heavy, are not readily distributed, but animals tend to that. The Clark's nutcracker is particularly effective at this task, burying caches of seeds to last it through the year. The bird will eat most of the seeds, but some will survive to create another cluster of whitebark pines.

ALPINE VEGETATION ZONE

Perhaps the alpine vegetation zone does not truly exist in the Tahoe Sierra, for whitebark pines approach or reach the highest summits. In our area there are only three serious contenders for this designation: Round Top (Hike 97), Freel Peak-Jobs Sister (Hikes 102-103), and Mt. Rose (Hike 108). I consider myself in the alpine realm when I sight the sky pilot, which I have never seen below treeline. In Yosemite, one sees this blue-flowered member

of the phlox family at 12,000-13,000 feet. It does not grow north of the park.

Still, there are Tahoe shrubs and herbs that do prefer to grow on land above the trees. All of the nine wildflowers that appear on Plate 17 (Mt. Rose, Hike 108) fall into this category. Other wildflowers include silky raillardella and skunk-leaved polemonium (Plate 11, Hike 16), alpine sorrel (Plate 13, Hike 71), and shaggy hawkweed (Plate 14, Hike 81). Finally, a variety of showy penstemon (Plate 15, Hike 97) also fits into this category. At high elevations this variety can form dense mats with showy clusters of brilliant blue flowers.

During glacial times, a true alpine realm existed, for Tahoe's high peaks had temperatures like those found today on the Sierra's highest peaks. The relict populations of quasi-alpine plants are enduring the current interglacial "heat wave," waiting for the time when they can once again expand their domain.

Chapter 7
Zoology

Introduction

We humans are unique animals. We may be the only life form in our galaxy that can comprehend nature from its least scale—the subatomic quarks and leptons—up to its grandest scale—the entire universe. We have the potential to give rise, directly or indirectly, to advanced life forms that could, theoretically, colonize our galaxy in considerably less than a million years, which is a mere tick of the universal time clock. Yet, despite our accomplishments and our potential (if we don't destroy ourselves in the near future), we are superfluous animals. But it's not only we who are superfluous; the same applies to all the vertebrates, be they fishes, amphibians, reptiles, birds, or mammals. The only necessary animals are the invertebrates, those lowly animals we seldom think about unless they're pestering us, our homes, or our gardens. Without pollinating insects, many flowering plants would face extinction. Humans, in contrast, hold the record for causing extinctions, having eliminated an untold number of plant and animal species over the last 10,000+ years, including in this century the former monarch of the Sierra, the California grizzly bear.

Top: *three common insects. Fir sawyer (beetle), sphinx moth at Davidson's penstemons, ceanothus sphinx moth cocoon attached to manzanita branch.* **Bottom:** *three forest arthropods. Millipede (a scavenger), tick engorged with blood, crab spider on balsamroot flower.*

Invertebrates

In a mountain meadow there can be thousands of invertebrates in every square yard. In meadow-splotched Desolation Wilderness, their numbers are in the countless billions. As in other land environments, insects make up the bulk of the species, spiders placing a poor second. California has about 30,000 species of insects and perhaps a sixth of them can be found in the Tahoe Sierra. That amounts to about five species for every species of vascular plant. Many are pollinators, including species of moths, butterflies, beetles, bees, flies, and mosquitoes. Yes, mosquitoes, which, as much as we may despise them, are important pollinators. Honey bees fare poorly in the mountains, but bumblebees, which can regulate their body temperature, can thrive even in Tahoe's alpine flower gardens. Up there above 10,000 feet, they sometimes get competition from sphinx moths, which are among the Sierra's largest pollinators, being close to a hummingbird in size.

But moths lead most of their lives as larvae, which are well known for their leaf-eating habits. One equally large cousin of the sphinx moth is the ceanothus silk moth, which is found up to about 7500 feet in the Tahoe Sierra. It devours not only ceanothus leaves, but also those of other shrubs such as manzanitas and willows. Then, too, there are bark beetles, which in effect devour forests. They supposedly kill more trees than all other agents combined—fire, fungi, and other insects.

Birds keep insects and other invertebrates in check, consuming impressive quantities of them, but in all likelihood insects and spiders consume ever larger quantities of their brethren. For example, woodwasp larvae parasitize the larvae of bark beetles, fir sawyers, and other wood borers. Crab spiders climb into flowers that match their coloration, then snatch unsuspecting creatures, such as mosquitoes. Spiders, in turn, are sought after by mud daubers, which are wasps. But even some wasps are subject to attack, ironically by their relatives, the ichneumonid wasps. In short, invertebrates by themselves do a commendable job of regulating their own numbers while keeping the forests and meadows healthy.

Fish

One kind of animal is responsible for luring thousands of visitors to the Tahoe Sierra—trout. Originally there were only two kinds of trout in our area, the rainbow and the cutthroat, but other species have been introduced and the rainbow has been extensively crossbred. Chapter 5 mentions these trout and their relatives, which collectively are known as salmonids, and it also indicates the lakes in which you can find them.

Some Tahoe Sierra lakes and streams also have nongame fish. In Lake Tahoe there are five species: Piute sculpin, Tahoe sucker, Tui chub, Lahontan redside, and Lahontan speckled dace. The sculpin is particularly interesting. As the female salmonid lays her eggs, sculpins may dart in and eat all the eggs they can. Most eggs are successfully buried, but when the young salmonids emerge from the gravel, many are eaten by the bottom-dwelling sculpins. But as the surviving salmonids grow, the table begins to turn. By the time Tahoe's lake trout reach the 5-10 inch range, about half their diet is sculpin, the other half being invertebrates. Virtually no other fish is eaten. However, when lake trout grow to the 15-20 inch range, they also consume a lot of suckers and chubs. And by the time they surpass 20 inches, their diet is 90% fish, about half of it suckers and a third of it salmonids. Cannibalism is not uncommon.

Amphibians and reptiles

These vertebrates, like fish, are cold-blooded, and hence do rather poorly in mountain environments. If you exclude the lower-elevation South Yuba-Malakoff Diggins area (Chapter 8) and look for these animals in the rest of the Tahoe Sierra, you are likely to find only five species of amphibians and seven species of reptiles.

Two of the amphibians are salamanders. The long-toed salamander measures up to 7 inches and has a row of yellow blotches down its back. The ensatina, which is similar-sized, has some bright orange on its body and a constriction at the base of its tail. You're unlikely to see either unless you actively seek them out in ponds or under logs or leaves.

Top: *western fence lizard and western terrestrial garter snake which has just devoured a mountain yellow-legged frog.* **Bottom:** *a rubber boa, which is safely handled, and a western rattlesnake, which definitely isn't.*

The commonest amphibian is the Pacific treefrog, whose collective, resounding choruses belie their dwarf stature. These fi-1 inch amphibians may be brown or green, but both varieties sport a black eye stripe. Larger, but less common, are the mountain yellow-legged frog, which prefers ponds, and the drab western toad, which enters water only to breed. As an adult, it prefers to forage on land, even in rocky areas.

In the Tahoe Sierra two similar lizards are quite common in dry areas: the western fence lizard and the sagebrush lizard. The fence lizard is about 6-9 inches long and is quite active, especially among brush and rocks. The sagebrush lizard, which is about 5 inches long, is more secretive, usually staying under or close to brush. The males of both species have blue bellies. The northern alligator lizard, which can approach one foot in total length, prefers damper habitats, such as meadows.

The commonest snake is the western terrestrial garter snake, which is found in ponds as well as meadows. In water it may go after frogs or small trout, but then it may also end up a meal for a large trout. In meadows it hunts mostly treefrogs and mice. One of the many species that prey on the garter snake is the mountain kingsnake, which eats—in addition to small snakes—lizards and birds. It is quite a climber. On several occasions while climbing Yosemite Valley's steep walls, I have been upstaged by a kingsnake zipping up a crack.

The blunt-tailed, smooth-skinned rubber boa is one of nature's most docile animals. Like tarantulas, which you can find down in the foothills, this snake is easily and safely handled. One reptile you won't want to handle is the western rattlesnake. While its bite usually is not fatal, don't tempt this snake, but rather give it a wide berth. It wants to avoid a confrontation as much as you do. You are most likely to see it below 6000 feet (i.e., in Chapter 8 lands) in the Tahoe Sierra. I have encountered them among bedrock, on trails, in meadows, under brush, and on forest floors.

Birds

In terms of species, birds greatly outnumber all the other vertebrates. There are roughly 300 species of birds that visit or reside in our area, and that is about five times the number of their nearest rivals, the mammals. They are so successful because by flying they are able to exploit far more varied sources of food inaccessible to most mammals. Additionally, when the Tahoe Sierra becomes snowed under, birds can descend to lower elevations or fly south. Either way, they'll find food. A few, however, "dig in" and actually do quite well during the long, cold winter. The blue grouse, one of these masochists, subsists in the forest deep, eating conifer needles, staghorn lichen, or other paltry food items that most animals wouldn't consider.

The Clark's nutcracker is another permanent resident. During the summer you're almost certain to meet this raucous, oversized gray jay if you are hiking through its favorite habitat, the subalpine forest. Lower down you are bound to meet its equally noisy cousin, the Steller's jay.

Still, most birds make very distinct migrations. One of the commonest and most easily recognized is the dark-eyed junco, which is a small finch with a black or gray neck and head and with white outer tail feathers. Mountain chickadees, with their black cap and black eye stripe, also are very common, but they are far more often heard than seen.

Like invertebrates, birds are too plentiful to present a systematic description of them in a trail guide. Fortunately, excellent guidebooks exist, some of which are listed in "Recommended Reading and Source Materials." I prefer the old standard, *A Field Guide to Western Birds*, by the late (d. 1996) master ornithologist, Roger Tory Peterson.

Mammals

Most of our mammalian species go unseen because they typically are nocturnal and reclusive. Grassy meadows teem with mice, voles, shrews, and moles, while drier slopes attract pocket gophers, hares, and rabbits. Common predatory mammals are long-tailed weasels, badgers, coyotes, and red foxes.

Top: *great blue heron, Canada geese, killdeer.* **Bottom:** *Steller's jay, Clark's nutcracker, mountain chickadee*

Top: *California ground squirrel and golden-mantled ground squirrel.* **Bottom:** *gray squirrel and marmot.*

In shady conifer forests chattering chicka-rees (Douglas squirrels) and their quiet cousins, the northern flying squirrels, harvest treetop crops of conifer seeds. In the lower-montane zone gray squirrels predominate. All are kept in check by martens and predatory birds.

Bear and deer are two large mammals we like to see, though on our own terms. Both can become quite tame and pesky around camp-grounds; both are potentially dangerous. Campgrounds also attract other beggars, such as chipmunks and golden-mantled ground squirrels. Near treeline, these rodents are usu-ally replaced by wilder ones—pint-sized pikas and rabbit-sized marmots.

Finally, there is one group of mammals that mountain visitors can expect to see daily—bats. In the evening you'll see them flitting among or above the trees, harvesting aerial insects. Like shrews, they can, in a few hours, voraciously consume their weight in insects, which thankfully includes a healthy dose of mosquitoes.

Man

The most conspicuous Tahoe Sierra mammal, at least in relatively recent times, has been man. Before the arrival of Europeans, the Maidu people occupied our area's western slopes, usually at the lower elevations. Here, acorns from black, canyon live (gold-cup), and interior live oaks together with sugar-pine nuts were highly prized for flour. One would imagine that the gray-squirrel popula-tion back in those days was smaller than it is today, for these animals competed with, and sometimes served as dinner for, the Maidu. The flour-grinding chore was relegated to the women and children, as was the procuring of ants, grasshoppers, crickets, other insects, worms, other invertebrates, and small game. Men were responsible for catching birds, trout, rabbits, deer, and—after the proper cer-emony—black bears, grizzly bears (now extinct), and mountain lions. Coyotes, wolves (also extinct), vultures, reptiles, and amphib-ians were all avoided, for they were thought to be poisonous.

Maidu villages were located near year-round streams, and each typically had about 10 families and a total population of about 70. The total population of the Maidu people, who were divided into three dialect groups, probably never much exceeded 4000 individuals or 60 villages. Their north and south territorial boundaries were almost identical with the ones that limit the scope of this book. To the west their territory extended down to the higher foothills east of the Sacramento Valley. This valley was occupied by the Wintun, who had much in common with the Maidu, for both groups belong to the same linguistic family, the Penutian. From the Wintun, the Maidu received beads (money), salt, gray-pine nuts, and, in some instances, salmon. In return, they gave the Winton bows and arrows, deer skins, and sugar-pine nuts.

To the east the Maidu territory extended up to, and sometimes beyond, the Sierra crest. Their relationship with the Washoe, who belonged to the Hokan linguistic family, was a hostile one.

The Washoe lived mostly in the fault-dropped valleys east of the Sierra crest, but to them the center of their world was Lake Tahoe. They were a scarce group—3000 individuals at most—who moved with the seasons. A family or group of families would gradually work its way west up toward the Lake Tahoe high country in late spring as snow retreated and certain food came into abundance. In early June, this food was trout plus large suckers, both of which spawned in the creeks that drained into Lake Tahoe. As fish spawning declined, the Washoe ascended mountain canyons in search of game, vegetable food in meadows, and trout in streams and high lakes. On these excursions, they were most likely to encounter the Maidu, who had been working east toward the crest, following in the wake of retreating snowfields.

With the approach of autumn, the Wahsoe returned to the Carson Valley and other east-side valleys. This season was a time of plenty, with the harvest of berries, seeds, and pinyon nuts, followed by rabbit, deer, and antelope hunts. Doves, quail, sage grouse, and rodents were also hunted, but like the Maidu, the Washoe avoided reptiles and amphibians. Their bountiful harvest had to last until spring, when they could harvest wild lettuce, wild spinach, and wild potatoes. The Washoe understood their dynamic environment and were able to totally adapt to it.

The Maidu, on the other hand, modified their environment with almost annual fires,

The Maidu ground acorns in mortar holes

which had the distinct advantage of clearing brush that might hide a lurking enemy. (Fighting was a way of life *between* Maidu settlements as well as with the less numerous Washoe.) This practice also increased the distribution of *Ceanothus,* a genus of aromatic shrubs that sprout profusely after a fire. Since deer often browse on these plants, the size of the herd was increased.

The worlds of the Maidu and the Washoe were little changed by the coming of the Spaniards, who kept to the Coast Ranges and the Central Valley. With the discovery of gold in 1848 came lusty men who destroyed the environment to get rich quick. Maidu forests were logged for mine timbers and for boom-town shanties. Goats and cattle were turned loose in Maidu meadows that had once yielded a rich grain harvest. Professional hunters overkilled animal populations in order to supply mining settlements with food. Gold-bearing gravels washed by high-power monitors (water jets) choked up the rivers and played havoc with the fish. A similar fate lay in store for the Washoe when silver was discovered in the Comstock Lode in 1859. Their world in particular was severely shattered, for they lost not only their land but also their spiritual center, Lake Tahoe.

Right: Backpacker on the Pacific Crest Trail just south of Ward Peak

Part Two   Nine Hiking Chapters

Cliff of quartz-rich sediments, Malakoff Diggins State Historic Park

Chapter 8
South Yuba River and Malakoff Diggins State Historic Park

Introduction

"Gold!" rang out the cry in 1848, as the precious metal was discovered along the American, Feather, and Trinity rivers. By 1849 the Great California Gold Rush was on, and from 1850 to 1862, during the heyday of the rush, annual production averaged 2.64 million troy ounces. (While this amount sounds phenomenal, it really amounts to only 90 tons, which would fit into a cubic box only 64 inches on each side.) California production fell sharply in 1863, and until 1942 it usually averaged ½–1 million troy ounces a year. On October 8, 1942, the U.S. War Production Board issued Limitation Order L-208, closing the nation's gold mines. The order was rescinded in 1945, but the action had gravely wounded the industry, which faced postwar inflation but still got only a fixed price for gold: $35 per ounce. Production slid from 6.2 tons in 1945 to ⅔ ton in 1968, when the government finally deregulated the price of gold. Production continued to fall, despite deregulation, bottoming out in 1971 at about 250 pounds. But then came the 1973-74 Arab oil embargo, double-digit inflation, and speculation in the gold market, which pushed the price per ounce over the $600 level in 1980, and greatly increased production. Prices have since subsided somewhat, but despite a still high price, the gold industry is not as important to the state's economy as it once was.

As the gold industry declined, its maze of mining trails began to disappear. Most of these often steep, utilitarian trails were abandoned or were obliterated by logging roads, reservoirs, or real-estate developments. The few in active use today are sometimes guarded by gun-toting individuals, as are clandestine marijuana plots. Therefore, avoid exploring the foothills' backcountry roads and paths, and instead explore the mining relicts and associated landscapes at Malakoff Diggins State Historic Park and the adjacent South Yuba Recreation Area.

This chapter's first hike, the only trail in it outside these two areas, is nevertheless a part of mining history, for it runs along part of an old mining ditch, one that carried water to the Grass Valley mines. The second and eighth hikes, along the South Yuba Trail, still get their share of modern-day miners. The remaining trails delve into the state park's nooks and crannies. Be sure to stop at the park's museum, in the partly reconstructed mining town of North Bloomfield. This hiking area is relatively close to Nevada City, which is a popular gold-mining town. Every block in this fascinating town exudes history; it is a joy to explore. Numerous shops cater to visitors, as do community events. And finally, compact Nevada City has some excellent restaurants that provide culinary delights.

⊰⊱ 1 ⊰⊱
Independence Trail

Distances:

0.2 mile west to Jones Bar Trail

0.4 mile on trail to South Yuba River

0.4 mile west to South Yuba Overlook

1.1 miles west to Rush Creek

2.5 miles west to Jones Bar Road

2.1 miles east to jeep road

0.3 mile on jeep road to Miners Tunnel

2.3 miles east to Miners Tunnel Overlook

Low/High Elevations: 1440'/1480'

Season: Year-round

Classification; Very easy

Map: 1

Trailhead: Along Highway 49, 6.3 miles west of its split from Highway 20 in Nevada City and 0.6 mile before its bridge across the South Yuba River. Parking for about one dozen cars. Additional parking is available about ⅔ mile farther, along a spur road—a former stretch of Highway 49—which branches from the south end of the highway's new South Yuba River bridge.

Introduction

Becoming independent is a worthy goal for all disabled persons, such as those confined to wheelchairs. Before the 1970s, such persons were rarely, if ever, seen in campgrounds, and were never seen on mountain trails. Today, however, some of Tahoe's larger campgrounds have sites for disabled persons, and several trails are quite suited for them. In this book, these include: Sand Pond Interpretive Trail (mentioned under Hike 14 trailhead), Sierra Discovery Trail (Hike 30), Lake Tahoe Visitors Center Trails (Hike 56), and a loop trail at a Tahoe Rim Trailhead facility (mentioned under Hike 107 trailhead).

This book's first trail, along a part of the defunct Excelsior Ditch, is the nation's first wheelchair trail to be built across rugged terrain. The meaning of its name, Independence Trail, is twofold. First, it gives those confined to wheelchairs greater independence. Second, volunteer work on the trail began in 1976, the bicentennial year of our country's declared independence. On September 30, 1997, this area, together with the Bridgeport area several miles down-river, became a state park.

The Excelsior Ditch, constructed by the Excelsior Mining Company from 1859-1863, transported water from 1863 to 1884 from its intake, about 2 miles up-river from the old Highway 49 bridge, west many miles to hydraulic mining operations in Smartsville, at about 700 feet elevation and about 12 miles west of Grass Valley. Today, a part of it transports hikers, both on foot and in wheelchairs, along its broad, nearly level course. Over about a 5-mile length, it drops, on average, about 8 feet per mile—an amount too small to perceive. The trail can be hiked year-round, although from about mid-November through mid-March an occasional storm may dump snow on it. Nevertheless, it can be hiked even when a few inches of snow are present. An ideal time to hike this route is in the usually balmy months of April and May, when wildflowers put on a lavish display. Some of the species you'll see are illustrated in the next hike's two wildflower plates. Another fine time is from about mid-October through mid-November, when the leaves of deciduous trees and shrubs take on fall colors. Still, the season of greatest use is summer, and then temperatures can soar well into the 90s. Then, the trail still is bearable, because it is almost continuously shaded by conifers and broad-leaved trees. Should you get too hot, you can drive down Highway 49 to the nearby old bridge, closed to motor vehicles, and take a steep path from it down to the inviting waters of the South Yuba River, which on summer afternoons warms into the 70s. From the far side of the bridge a trail starts up-canyon, but it does not provide ready access to the river.

Description

Whether you hike west or east, you have a nearly continuous tree cover, which is desirable on hot summer days, but undesirable on cold winter, spring, or fall days. Additionally, the cover is sufficiently dense that you have very few good views of the scenery. Blocking your view are three species of conifers—Douglas-fir, incense-cedar, and ponderosa pine—plus species of the more-common broad-leaved hardwoods—canyon live oak, black oak, buckeye, laurel (bay tree), and, usually in gullies, big-leaf maple and mountain (Pacific) dogwood. Shrubs include poison oak (shiny leaflets, in threes, green to red), manzanita, and toyon. Ferns include bracken fern, sword fern, and birds-foot fern.

Today the Excelsior Ditch is a mostly flat, dirt-floored path with bedrock comprising the inner side, and a stone wall comprising the outer side. This stone wall varies in height between about 2 and 6 feet, averaging 4, and the Independence Trail sometimes goes along the floor of the ditch, sometimes atop the wall, and sometimes both. Since the west half of the trail was constructed first, it will be described first. (I find both halves equally desirable.)

The trailhead, with its bulletin board and adjacent porta-potties, is quite obvious. Westbound, you walk momentarily south to a crossing under Highway 49. Children and wheelchair-bound travelers have it easy, but most adults have to duck to avoid scraping their heads. The trail winds southwest, and at a bend 0.2 mile into the hike you reach the

Jones Bar Trail. This is a utility trail that initially descends steeply, briefly eases its gradient, then descends all too steeply (up to 30% gradient—at 35% you lose traction) almost to Rush Creek. It then parallels the creek at a moderate gradient 150 yards north down to a suspension footbridge, located immediately below the spot where the Jones Bar Road fords the creek. The shortest distance to the South Yuba River is to skip the bridge and take the road about 90 yards north to a U.S. Geological Survey stream-gaging station. From that vicinity, cautiously climb down sometimes loose rock to water-polished bedrock along the **South Yuba River**. In times of high water the river can be wall-to-wall and over 20 feet deep, but during summer it *usually* is shallow enough for safe swimming. When the water is low and safe, you can walk out on a bedrock rib that almost spans the river, being only several feet short of connecting with bedrock along the north bank. Pools lie both up- and downstream from this spot, and Jones Bar proper lies about ¼–½ mile downstream. To reach it, take the footbridge, walk briefly west along the road to where it

Jones Bar in late summer, when the water is low

starts to climb, then leave it to descend briefly to the river and head down it.

Along the Independence Trail, you contour another 0.2 mile to the roofed **South Yuba overlook**, complete with table, bench, and a fine view down-canyon toward Jones Bar. The trail now heads south, and in about 150 yards you reach Diamond Head, a distinctive, wheelchair-accessible outhouse. Over the next 0.6 mile to Rush Creek, you cross several flume-like structures—they have wooden floors and walls, but certainly are not water-proof, as the original flumes were. They are, after all, meant for transporting people, not water. Easily the largest "flume" is the impressive one that wraps around Rush Creek, crossing above it on a trestle. Immediately after crossing, the Independence Trail gives rise to a boardwalk that contours briefly up-canyon to a view of small falls and pools along **Rush Creek**. From that short boardwalk a longer, wheelchair-accessible one switchbacks down to the creek's bank. From there you can cautiously walk momentarily downstream to the brink of the upper of three falls, each dropping into a tempting pool. Descending to either can be dangerous.

Small falls and pools along Rush Creek

From the boardwalk the Independence Trail continues 150 yards, first as trestle then as canal, over to a second outhouse. In the late 1990s, the wheelchair accessibility essentially stopped here, for although the route ahead to Jones Bar Road was readily hikeable, several spots were difficult or dangerous to those in wheelchairs. Furthermore, there were no special attractions or incentives to continue onward—possibly save one: you can make a 4-mile-long semiloop hike that takes you to both Rush Creek and Jones Bar.

If you've just visited Rush Creek, you contour northward in and out of gullies, reaching after 0.9 mile a fine view up the South Yuba River canyon. You then quickly turn westward and contour 0.4 mile, again in and out of gullies, then reach a conspicuous ridge, from which you contour 0.1 mile south to a shallow gully, where

Author on a superb trestle along the eastbound Independence Trail

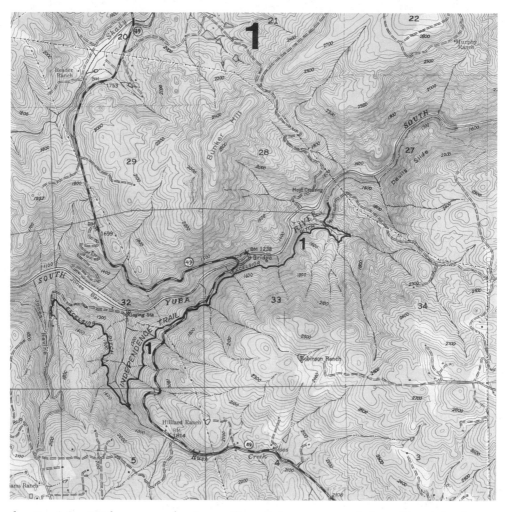

the Excelsior Ditch crosses the **Jones Bar Road**. This road you descend ¾ mile to the footbridge, ramble around the vicinity of Jones Bar and perhaps take in a swim. You then cross the bridge and head up the Jones Bar Trail to the Independence Trail and retrace your steps 0.2 mile to the trailhead. There are two caveats to this route. First, in 1997 the Jones Bar Road was upgraded from a 4WD to a 2WD road, and the public was allowed to drive it. So long as this road is open (and the one across the canyon also descending to Jones Bar is open), you may come upon beer cans, broken bottles, and rowdy people. I hope that with the creation of the new state park, its administrators will close both roads to motor vehicles. The second caveat is that if

it is warm enough for a fine swim down at Jones Bar, you will sweat like a pig ascending the Jones Bar Trail. This is not too much of a problem, because upon reaching the trailhead, you can hop in your vehicle and drive shortly down to the old Highway 49 bridge and jump in the river once again to refresh yourself. On a hot summer afternoon you definitely will not be alone.

Eastbound from the trailhead, the shady Independence Trail contours above Highway 49, and after ¾ mile it curves southeast into an adjacent minor, yet deep gully with a superb trestle across it. The hike to here is worth it just to see this engineering feat. After about 1.2 miles from the trailhead, and about halfway to the Miners Tunnel Overlook, you'll encounter a table with a tree-filtered view of the old Highway 49 bridge. About 0.2 mile beyond it the trail starts a curve east into a hanging side canyon, leaving behind the highway's traffic noise as it does so. Over the next 0.4 mile you contour east then southeast to a gully with a southwest-climbing road, then contour northeast over to a minor gully with a table and piped water. Just ahead to the northeast is the final gully, which holds the main creek, then you contour westward over to a west-descending **jeep road**.

Over your eastbound route you have been oh-so-slightly ascending the Excelsior Ditch, but if you study the topographic map you will see that heading west, *upstream*, to the jeep road, you drop in elevation. In other words, the water flowing along the ditch flows *up* along this stretch. What is going on? Actually, as elsewhere the water flows slightly downhill—it is the map's contours that are incorrect. Producing a map from aerial photographs in a forested area that lacks topographic controls—such as many road junctions whose elevations have been determined from ground surveys—is extremely difficult, and the resulting product inevitably will be full of errors. You can only generalize the elevation of, say, where the bottoms of two gullies meet, and even then you are looking at the tops of the trees in the gullies, and have to estimate their heights. You can easily be off in elevation by tens of feet. Furthermore, the forest canopy hides the smaller gullies. As you will notice when you take the Independence Trail, it meanders far more excessively than the map depicts. If the trail were plotted as it actually exists, it would meander across many contour lines, implying that the Excelsior Ditch ascends and descends many times over the trail's length. There are definite limits to mapping in an undeveloped, forested area!

At the jeep road you can continue 0.2 mile along the Independence Trail to the **Miners Tunnel Overlook** (as far as the completed trail went in 1997), or you can inspect the tunnel firsthand. To do this, head about 0.1 mile down the road, meeting another (on your left) before yours forks atop a shallow saddle. The Miners Tunnel is best view from its up-canyon end, and to reach it, fork right and descend

about 60 yards northeast to where the road dies out and a very steep trail begins. This gets you, in a mere 120 yards down to the river's bouldery floodplain. Start walking west, downstream, along it, and you'll soon reach the **Miners Tunnel**. Hiking through this 300-yard-long tunnel can be risky, so think twice before trying to make it to the far end. That end is reached from the shallow saddle by forking left and descending steeply to a bench, on which you turn left and walk a few paces until the road ends, then carefully scramble down to the river's bank. This is quite a long way in to the tunnel, about 2½ miles. If you were to start from the old Highway 49 bridge, you would reach this end of the tunnel in about ½ mile, although the entire distance would be scrambling from boulder to boulder—a challenging task even when the water is low. Pools exist by either end of the tunnel, although you can find more accessible ones just up- and downstream from the old Highway 49 bridge.

⋘ **2** ⋙

South Yuba Trail, South Yuba Campground east to Missouri Bar Trail

Distances:
0.7 mile to Kenebec Creek spur trail
   0. 5 mile on spur trail to Illinois Crossing
     Picnic and Camping Area
1.5 miles to Overlook Point Picnic Site spur
   trail
2.7 miles to North Canyon spur trail
   0.4 mile on spur trail to South Yuba River
4.2 miles to Humbug Trail
4.6 miles to South Yuba Primitive Camp
6.5 miles to short spur trail
7.9 miles to Missouri Bar Trail
   1.4 miles on trail to trailhead
Low/High Elevations: 1980'/2580'; 3470' to
   Missouri Bar trailhead
Season: March through early November
Classification: Moderate
Map: 2

Trailhead: From the Highways 20/49 split in Nevada City, drive 11¼ miles north on 49 to the paved Tyler-Foote Crossing Road, on the right. Follow it 8.2 miles northeast to North Columbia (no services), and branch right about ¼ mile past its hillside schoolhouse. Now on Grizzly Hill Road you wind 3.1 miles south to a junction (point 2648 on Map 2) with the North Bloomfield Road. If you take a shortcut route, you will also arrive at this junction. From it you descend 0.2 mile northeast on the North Bloomfield Road to the South Yuba Campground spur road. This you descend about 70 yards, to where a spur road veers slightly left from it and parallels the campground's road briefly to a parking area with room for about two dozen vehicles. Note that the North Bloomfield Road takes you 2.4 miles northeast to a junction with the Lake City Road, the route used by those going directly to Malakoff Diggins State Historic Park (Hikes 3-7).

The shortcut route to the South Yuba trailhead (and to Malakoff Diggins) is along a road that leaves Highway 49 immediately west of the Tahoe National Forest headquarters, which is just west of the Highways 20/49 junction. On this sometimes steep, winding North Bloomfield Road (good brakes, no RVs), you go 7½ miles, negotiating hairpin turns, down to a bridge at Edwards Crossing, then climb 1.4 miles to junction "2648."

Hike 2 ends at the Missouri Bar trailhead, so see directions to it under Hike 4, the Missouri Bar Trail.

Introduction

While most of the Tahoe Sierra's high trails are still under spring snow, the South Yuba Trail offers day hikers *and* backpackers a wildflowered landscape in full bloom. During summer the afternoon temperatures are excessive, and you'll get quite sweaty, which makes you likely to attract hordes of pesky flies. Still, mid-July through August is the best time to sample some of the river's many swimming holes, and by getting clean, you'll rid yourself of flies. Other summer activities include fishing, rafting, and gold panning (don't do this at legally staked claims). With autumn come nearly ideal hiking temperatures, nearly

insect-free conditions, and local splashes here and there of fall colors.

By my measurement, the South Yuba Trail is 16 miles long. Hike 2 describes the first half of the trail up-canyon to its midpoint, which is almost exactly at the Missouri Bar Trail junction. Hike 8 takes over up-canyon from there. Logically, one would expect to hike a trail down-canyon, starting high and ending low. However, the eastern, up-canyon trailhead is an inconsequential 50 feet higher than the western one, so you can hike either direction with approximately the same total elevation gain and loss. If you do the entire 16 miles, there are two advantages to hiking up-canyon. The first is that on hot summer days, you can jump into Poorman Creek to cool down and clean off just an easy ¼-mile walk from the eastern trailhead. In the opposite direction, you have a 1.2-mile, 600-foot climb to the western trailhead. The second advantage is that the eastern trailhead is quite close to Washington, a small community in which you can celebrate your achievement with drinks and/or food.

I have broken up the trail into two segments in order to produce two reasonable-length day hikes, each about 9½ miles long, since for many people 16 miles is too long. It is a fine distance for backpackers, and there are several good opportunities to overnight along the river. If you study Maps 2 and 3, you'll notice that there are stretches where the trail is within 100 feet or less of the river, and consequently you might conclude that you can descend to it in dozens of places to reach tempting pools and secluded campsites. Not so. In the vast majority of places, the steep, loose slopes become dangerously steep over the last 20 or so feet down to the river's rocky bench. Regardless of how close the river may appear from a spot on the trail, do not attempt to descend to it unless you can see your *entire* descent route—a 20-foot fall onto a jagged bedrock bench could be fatal. And this caveat brings raises another one. The trail is open to mountain bikes, but there are a number of spots where if you slipped off the trail, you'd fall to your death. Hikers are unlikely to fall, since they can walk these brief stretches slowly and cautiously. Bikers, on the other hand, must maintain a minimum speed to ensure stability.

Description

The first 1.5 miles of trail, which take you to the Overlook Point Picnic Site spur trail, once doubled as a nature trail, for it had numbered posts of the area's more prominent species and features. Unfortunately, the posts and the nature booklets are long gone, but here is a list of plant species you are likely to see. If you have a guide to Sierran trees and shrubs, you ought to be able to identify them. Conifer trees, listed more or less in the order you encounter them, include Douglas-fir, ponderosa pine, sugar pine, incense-cedar, knob-cone pine, and gray pine (once known as Digger pine; also now called foothills pine). Broad-leaved trees include canyon live oak (a.k.a. Maul oak and gold-cup oak), California black oak, California buckeye, mountain (Pacific) dogwood, big-leaf maple, and California laurel (bay tree). Shrubs include poison oak (learn to identify and avoid this one: shiny leaflets, in threes, green to red), mock orange, gooseberry, Mariposa manzanita, barberry, mountain misery, mountain mahogany, hollyleaf coffeeberry, bush monkey flower, toyon, buckbrush, deer brush, and yerba santa. Ferns include wood fern, sword fern, and birds-foot fern. If you hike along this nature trail in spring, you're likely to see blossoming many of the wildflowers shown on plates 9 and 10 in this book as well as mule ears and creeping sage.

During most of the summer and part of the fall, the South Yuba Trail will be dry until you reach Humbug Creek, about 4¼ miles distant. Be sure to bring enough water, which usually is available at the trailhead, or if not, then from one of the spigots in stretched-out South Yuba Campground. From the far end of the parking area, the South Yuba Trail begins by paralleling the campground's descending entrance road for almost 300 yards, down to a trail junction. Here, a spur trail heads briefly west over to the campground's main road, meeting it near the floor of a gully and just southeast of a junction with a narrow road climbing northwest to the campground's upper campsites. Ahead, the South Yuba Trail soon traverses around a low, forested ridge, then descends slightly to Kenebec Creek. If you walk about 35 yards up alongside it, you will get a view of two picturesque cascades, which when flowing, splash down blocky, black phyllite bedrock. This rock and other metamorphosed sediments of Mesozoic and Paleozoic age exist on both sides of the South Yuba River canyon from west of Edwards Crossing, downstream, to our hike's end at the Missouri Bar Trail. From Kenebec Creek we traverse about 260 yards to an old jeep road, down which we descend about 220 yards to the **Kenebec Creek spur trail**.

This side trip is a continuation of the old jeep road. It drops steeply, descending 400 feet in ½ mile to the South Yuba River's Illinois Crossing Picnic and Camping Area. This area is situated atop a level, 30-foot-high bench of pebbles, cobbles, and boulders which are waste products from the Malakoff Mine and other hydraulic mines (see Hike 5). In the mining heyday, the sediments extended about 400 feet across the South Yuba River canyon, and the river flowed atop them. As you can see, most of the sediments have been eroded away, carried downstream to create havoc for past farmers and city folk alike. On the bench and under the shade of live oaks, there are tables for those who like luxurious camping or picnicking. Since this bench is such an easy walk from the trailhead, you might consider carrying a gold pan, for on BLM lands panning for gold is legal. (BLM land extends east through Section 13; Section 18 is on USGS land.) From the bench a trail descends to the nearby riverbank, and a use trail heads downriver toward the lower end of Kenebec Creek.

From the upper end of the Kenebec Creek spur trail, the South Yuba Trail makes an initial ascent, then traverses southeast for ¾ mile to the **Overlook Point Picnic Site spur trail**. Along this stretch you have views south across the canyon toward hydraulic diggings—ancient gold-rich river gravels—which lie on gentle slopes above the canyon's south rim. Many geologists have thought that their bases lie on the floor of a broad, ancient canyon, and that the narrow canyon we see today was cut much later by the South Yuba

South Yuba River canyon at lower end of North Canyon

River in response to major uplift. Actually, our narrow canyon already existed in some form way back then, some 50+ million years ago, and major uplift never occurred again during the ensuing time. What the ancient river did was deposit voluminous gravels, first filling in the river canyon, then spreading gravels on the gentle slopes above the canyon's rims. From the spur trail junction, you descend a few yards to a south-trending ridge, atop which is the picnic site, complete with tables, hidden among live oaks and Douglas-firs. There is no overlook, although several paths descend from the ridgecrest, these perhaps made by hikers in search of a good viewpoint.

Beyond the picnic site's spur trail, the generally forested trail heads north-northeast, climbing a bit and then descending a bit over about 1.1 miles. The trail then descends briefly east to a junction with the **North Canyon spur trail**. Here you are due north of an impressive descending ridge you have seen along your last stretch of trail. This spur trail drops just as steeply as the Kenebec Creek spur trail, but not as long: it drops only 300 feet over 0.4 mile. Thirteen short switchbacks carry you

down to the mouth of North Canyon's creek, which in spring tumbles over an open bedrock bench into the South Yuba River. On this bench in a very scenic part of this river canyon are exposed campsites, which are adequate, but better ones lie just down-river on oak-shaded benches. The river in this vicinity has several swimming holes, one up to 20 feet deep, which are ideal during the summer, when the water's temperature can be pleasantly warm in the afternoon. In spring, however, the temperature is too cold and the current too swift for safe swimming.

About 130 yards past the North Canyon spur trail, the South Yuba Trail crosses springtime-brisk North Canyon creek, then makes a ¾-mile traverse across southwest-facing slopes. Then over the next ½ mile, it traverses south- then southeast-facing slopes, ending with a brief descent east to a junction with the steeply climbing **Humbug Trail** (Hike 3). Here you'll find the Humbug Picnic Site, perched 60 feet above the river. Like the lower Illinois Crossing bench it is composed of pebbles, cobbles, and boulders wasted from the rubble created by hydraulic mining. Back in

Wildflower Plate 9. White, yellow, or pale-pink foothill flowers.
1 Trail plant (white), 2 miner's lettuce (white to pale-pink), 3 alum root (heuchera) (white to pink), 4 white globe lily (fairy lantern), 5 wavy-leaved soap plant (white), 6 yellow star tulip, 7 Hartweg's iris (pale butter yellow), 8 Pacific stonecrop (yellow), 9 canyon dudleya (hens-and-chickens) (yellow to red).

Wildflower Plate 10. Orange, red, violet, or blue foothill flowers.
1 California Indian pink (scarlet), 2 spotted coralroot (red and white), 3 Indian warrior (burgundy red), 4 bush monkey flower (salmon), 5 foothill penstemon (tricolor: magenta / violet / blue), 6 Kellogg's monkey flower (rose), 7 harvest (elegant) brodiaea (rose to violet), 8 bleeding hearts (pink to rose), 9 purple milkweed (reddish purple flowers and stem).

1884, when Judge Lorenzo Sawyer issued an injunction against the dumping of mine debris into rivers, this bench was the bed of the South Yuba River. In the intervening time, the river has carried away most of the tailings so that it now runs clean, but a few debris segments—in the form of conglomerate-rock benches—still remain. Since this bench was built up to its present height in the late 1870s, the live oaks and ponderosa pines growing on it can be no older than that. Before the trees can reach old age (in about three centuries), the bench likely will be eroded away. In the meantime, one can gaze down from its edge into the tempting emerald-green river pools.

From the bench the South Yuba Trail descends steeply to adjacent Humbug Creek, which usually has a bridge across it. The trail then skirts past an inviting but generally shallow South Yuba pool to soon arrive at the outskirts of **South Yuba Primitive Camp**, the largest along the trail. Stretching along a gravel bench for about 180 yards, this camp, complete with picnic tables and an outhouse, can easily hold dozens of backpackers. And beside it is a fine swimming hole to accommodate all of them.

From the east end of the camp the trail climbs briefly but moderately, exchanging Section 14 for Section 13. Over the next mile, which gets you to a seasonal, southwest-descending creeklet, you are apt to see several use paths where hikers have descended 40-80 feet to the river's rocky bench. Should you take one, do so cautiously. If you take one near the aforementioned creeklet, you can then walk about 200+ yards up the bench to an alluring, deep, potholed pool. The trail, unfortunately, climbs above it, and along this stretch the trail briefly traverses steep slopes above a hidden cliff—a slip here would be fatal. The slopes are unstable, and in the near future a stretch of trail could be eliminated, though that would necessitate the construction of a bypass on higher, more stable ground.

After a short traverse, the trail briefly descends moderately to about 30 feet above the river's rocky bench, and here, just within Section 14, are several use paths descending a few yards to it. Just upstream, immediately

within Section 18—USFS land—is a beautiful *rockbar* pool, that is, one with low bedrock ridges extending partway across the pool. In high water they will be submerged; in summer they will offer paths to parts of the pool.

As before, the trail climbs above this tempting pool, and from just within Section 18 we have a fine view of the river up-canyon. About ⅓ mile past it you'll arrive at a **short spur trail**, which switchbacks about 230 yards down to the river's bank. Above this spot is a shallow pool—a poor swimming hole—while below it are bouldery rapids. The site lacks suitable ground for camping. Indeed, its one redeeming quality is that it gives you access to water.

In another ⅓ mile the South Yuba Trail turns from south to east to reach a second spur trail, which is a rough access trail used by a miner who has a legal claim to mine gold in this vicinity. Midway across Section 18, we now head northeast, staying high enough above the river to make a descent to it impracticable and dangerous. The trail leaves the section with a descent almost to the river, and as it curves from east to northeast through the northwestern part of Section 17, it passes two tempting pools. This section is private land, so I discourage camping, even though I saw no signs banning it. Near the section's north edge, about ⅓ mile past the second pool, the South Yuba Trail arrives at the lower end of the **Missouri Bar Trail**, Hike 4. To complete Hike 2, head 1.4 miles up this steep trail—a nearly constant 15% gradient—to its **trailhead**. Fortunately, the route is quite forested, which makes it an acceptable exit even in summer, though not in the heat of the afternoon. Before taking it, consider walking over to nearby Missouri Creek. Walk a few paces down along it to bedrock, then a few paces along it up-canyon east to a rockbar pool, which is an excellent swimming hole. The water among the rockbars can be quite shallow, but adjacent to the westernmost rockbar is a large pool that can be as much as 20 feet deep. This pool is barely within Section 8, which is USFS land.

⊰ 3 ⊱
Humbug Trail

Distance
2.7 miles to South Yuba Trail
3.1 miles to South Yuba Primitive Camp
Low/High Elevations: 2140'/3030'
Season: Early April through mid-November
Classification: Moderate
Map: 2

Trailheads: From the Highways 20/49 split in Nevada City, drive 11¼ miles north on 49 to the paved Tyler-Foote Crossing Road, on the right. Follow it 8¼ miles northeast to North Columbia (no services), and pass the Grizzly Hill Road, which forks right about ¼ mile past the settlement's hillside schoolhouse. In another ¼ mile, before a State Forestry fire station, you leave the Tyler-Foote Crossing Road, and fork right onto the Lake City Road, which winds 3.8 scenic miles southeast to an open-ridge junction with the North Bloomfield Road. You can also get to this junction by going 3¼ miles south on the Grizzly Hill Road, then about 2½ miles northeast on the North Bloomfield Road (see Hike 2's trailhead description).

From the open-ridge junction a road climbs north but you start a fairly level traverse northeast on the North Bloomfield Road, which enters Malakoff Diggins State Historic Park. About 0.8 mile from the junction, immediately after a curve to the right, is the end of Hike 7, the Rim Trail. You then have a glimpse of the park's diggins as you just before you reach a western-access trail to the diggins, which is just after a tight curve to the right, and is about ½ mile past the first right curve, or 1.3 miles from the junction. Then about 250 yards beyond it, at a curve to the left, is the start of the Humbug Trail, Hike 3, almost 1½ miles from the junction. You'll know you missed this trailhead if you reach the conspicuous Diggins Trail, Hike 5, on your left, in 300 yards, almost 1.6 miles from the junction. Other points worth mentioning along the North Bloomfield Road, measured from the open-ridge junction, are: two access trails to the diggins, one at mile 1.9 (to an environmental campsite) and one at mile 2.0 (to a viewpoint); a spur road, at mile 2.5, to a cemetery (start of the Slaughterhouse Trail to the diggins' east access and up to the park's campground); and the Relief Hill Road junction, at mile 2.9, by the park's headquarters.

Introduction
Although this trail is occasionally steep, and in one short stretch potentially dangerous, it is nevertheless worth the effort *in spring* because of its dramatic waterfalls and diverse array of wildflowers.

Description
Just beyond the trailhead you'll reach a creeklet stained rusty orange by the oxidation of iron found in nearby rock deposits. Man, through hydraulic mining, has accelerated this process, and he has stained much of the state-park landscape in more ways than one. Past the creeklet you curve east and follow its waters through a lovely Douglas-fir forest in

Humbug Creek's upper falls

whose shade grow pink bleeding hearts, purple larkspurs, scarlet Indian pinks, and white star flowers (see plates 9 and 10 in the previous hike for the area's common wildflowers). Quickly you come to a bend and start southward down the creek from Malakoff Diggins before you encounter Humbug Creek itself.

Humbug Creek and your route now both wind southward, and you pass a rusty pool followed in a few hundred yards by an algae-choked, rusty spring. In May the dogwoods along this shady stretch of trail blossom with large, white "petals," which actually are bracts that surround tight clusters of small, greenish-yellow flowers. Soon you bridge a tributary creek, which has two nearby environmental campsites. The first is just above the creek, the second is below it, at the end of a 130-yard-long spur trail that begins about 40 yards beyond the creek's bridge. Should you want to stay in one, phone the park at 530-265-2740.

About ¼ mile past the second camp's trail junction, you meet an old road that descends steeply to the point where your trail joins it. The road now descends 0.3 mile to its end at a seasonal creek, encountered immediately beyond a small, round pond on your left. After 50 yards you make a short, steep ascent, curve briefly eastward, then round a ridge, bringing you back to oak- and poison-oak-lined Humbug Creek, which has some tempting pools above the brink of its upper falls. Your trail soon leaves the creek's side, traverses a steep, rocky slope to a small, necessary bridge,

and from it you obtain a spectacular view back at the cascading creek, which jumps from one churning, milky-green pothole to the next via falls ranging up to 50 feet high. Into this southbound stretch of creek below you, a 7874-foot-long tunnel from Malakoff Diggins once spewed its gushing, muddy water. You'll find evidence of sediments carried down the creek when you reach a tailings bench at the junction with the South Yuba Trail, just above the river.

About ¼ mile past the upper falls' view, you pass the small, easily missed, diminutive middle falls. The trail now is relatively close to the creek, and past hikers have marred the slopes with use paths down to a chain of small pools, too small for swimming, but nevertheless refreshing, if brisk. Should you wish to visit any, then leave the trail at an obvious spot where it almost touches the creek's bedrock bank, and head upstream along it. Be aware that just downstream is the brink of the creek's lower falls, and in spring and early summer, when the water flows faster, you could be swept over the brink for a fatal fall.

Having completed 2 trail miles, we now parallel the creek at a distance, making a descent to it uninviting. The descent is easy until just before the end, where you descend very steeply to a junction with the **South Yuba Trail** (see Hike 2). Right beside the junction is the shaded Humbug Picnic Site, which has tables atop a wedge of 60-foot-thick gravels. Back in the mid-1800s, the top of the gravels— the eroded deposits from hydraulic mining—

Lowest rockbar at Missouri Bar

was the floor of the river. From the site you can descend steeply east on the South Yuba Trail to adjacent Humbug Creek, bridge it, then continue a nearly level ⅓ mile east to expansive, linear **South Yuba Primitive Camp**. Complete with picnic tables and an outhouse, it can hold a backpackers' convention, and offers the attendees a fine swimming hole. This hole is best in July and August, when temperatures are highest and the river has slacked off to a safe flow.

⊰ 4 ⊱
Missouri Bar Trail

Distance:
1.4 miles to South Yuba Trail
1.6 miles to swimming hole
Low/High Elevations: 2300′/3470′
Season: Early April through mid-November
Classification: Moderate
Map: 2
Trailhead: See Hike 3 for directions to Malakoff Diggins State Historic Park. Proceed east on the North Bloomfield Road through the park to the Relief Hill Road, immediately before the park's headquarters. Branch right onto it, and drive across Humbug Creek, then up past a spur road on the right before you reach another spur road, on a poorly defined ridge saddle, which is 0.8 mile from the start of the Relief Hill Road. Turn right onto this spur road and drive about 300 yards to an obvious trailhead. Before Memorial Day, the spur road can be quite muddy. Parking is limited but usually is adequate.

Introduction
The Missouri Bar Trail, with a steady, fairly steep descent, takes you down to the South Yuba River in only about ½ hour. This trail is lightly used in spring and fall, and you may have the trail and the river at its end all to yourself. During the summer, however, you may find more people, who descend to the river's fantastic swimming hole.

Description
The trail starts out among black oak, incense-cedar, ponderosa pine, and Douglas-fir. Along shadier parts of the trail, such as those typified by Douglas-fir cover, you may find large banana slugs which oh-so-slowly scavenge the moist forest floor in search of various organic matter—orange peels and mushrooms included! Your essentially viewless, descending route is an obvious one which maintains a nearly constant 15% gradient south-southeast across metamorphic bedrock down to a junction with the South Yuba Trail (end of Hike 2, start of Hike 8). Down here—at Missouri Bar—the river is about 40 yards wide, and even at peak runoff it is usually not more than knee-deep, a feature that certainly pleased old-time miners on their way between the diggins and Nevada City.

Today, however, the attraction is a swimming hole just upstream from the bar. On the South Yuba Trail, walk east over to nearby Missouri Creek, then walk a few paces down along it to bedrock, then a few paces along it up-canyon east to a large, deep pool, which is an excellent **swimming hole**. Although the trail junction is barely within private land (Section 17), the pool is barely within USGS land (Section 8). This pool is adjacent to the westernmost rock rib, or rockbar, which extends partway across the river. Above it are other parallel, closely spaced rockbars among shallow water.

The metamorphic bedrock near the pool is phyllite rather than slate, which is seen downstream. On the South Yuba Trail you can continue east for about 200 yards to another wide, knee-deep river crossing. Just up from this crossing the river narrows somewhat and deepens to 10 feet or more, and in summer offers additional swimming opportunities. To continue east, follow Hike 8.

⊰ 5 ⊱
Diggins Trail

Distance: Indeterminable—
scramble where you wish.
Low/High Elevations: 3000′/3080′
Season: Early April through mid-November
Classification: Easy
Map: 2

Hiller Tunnel's outlet

Trailhead: See Hike 3's trailhead description. There are two trails starting north from the parking area. The one above a creek's west bank goes to the nearby lower end of the 556-foot-long Hiller Tunnel. You want the trail above the east bank.

Introduction

The heart of the North Bloomfield mining district is the Malakoff Diggins, which became a state historic park in 1966. The first gold to be discovered in California was found in the 1770s in the remote Potholes district of southeastern Imperial County. It was, of course, James Marshall's January 1848 gold discovery at Sutter's Mill in Coloma—situated between Auburn and Placerville—that triggered the 49er gold rush to the Sierra. Most of the mining claims were established in a belt that extended from Mariposa—gateway to Yosemite—northward to the Quincy area.

In spring 1851 gold was discovered in the North Bloomfield area by an Irish prospector. He leaked his discovery to other miners in Nevada City, which was an 1849 boom town, and they secretly followed him back to his claim. When they got there, they tried their luck at mining, found nothing, and declared the project a "humbug." Because of this initial bad luck, the shanty community that grew there became known as Humbug, and its creek became Humbug Creek. After several years gold was discovered, and Humbug grew to house a few hundred persons, including the inevitable saloon keepers, gamblers, "dance-hall girls," and merchants. At the

American Hill mining district, which is about 10 miles northeast of their settlement, hydraulic mining of gold-bearing gravels had begun in 1852—the first in California. The following year Humbug's residents adopted this technique and by 1855 hydraulic mining had become the method of choice wherever gold-bearing gravels existed. At a mass meeting held in 1857, the populace decided Humbug was not a proper name for their successful settlement, and they changed it to Bloomfield. There was, however, already a community in southwestern Sonoma county bearing that name, so they changed it to North Bloomfield.

In order to spray vast amounts of high-pressure water against the gold-bearing gravels of the Malakoff mine, reservoirs were constructed, but since this area, like other mining districts nearby, was rather dry, over 50 miles of canals had to be built to divert water from the Bowman Lake area down to reservoirs near the gold fields. In Nevada County as a whole, some 700 miles of canals were built for this purpose. High-pressure water eroded the gravels down into sluice boxes, in which the gold—with a density 19.3 times that of water and about 7¼ times that of its associated sediments—settled to the bottom.

A problem developed over what to do with the remaining sediments, which at the Malakoff mine amounted to a total of about 50 million tons. As profits were pouring in, sediments were pouring out—down the Yuba River. Other Sierra rivers, particularly the Feather, Bear, and American, suffered similar fates. Between 1866 and 1884, the Malakoff hydraulic mine yielded about 3.5 million dollars from its 30 million cubic yards of gold-bearing gravel. The large monitors, or water nozzles, had sprayed out a hole more than 7000 feet long, 3000 feet wide and up to 600 feet deep. The gravels from this mine, and from other nearby mines, brought a great change in the lower course of the Yuba River, particularly along a 16-mile stretch from Smartville down to Marysville. The added sediments built up the river bottom, so that it easily overflowed its banks in times of high water. Not only were farmers' crops ruined by flooding, but an immense amount of fine debris was deposited on the river's plains, covering an area of 25 square miles. These deposits of sand and fine gravel rendered much farm land unfit for cultivation and caused farmers to protect adjacent land by constructing costly levees.

The farmers who were affected took their claims to court in 1884, and in a landmark case, *Woodruff vs. North Bloomfield Gravel Mining Company,* Judge Lorenzo Sawyer issued an injunction against the dumping of mine debris into the Sacramento and San Joaquin rivers and their tributaries—one of the first environmental victories in this country. Other injunctions soon followed, and hydraulic mining all but ended. In its heyday, North Bloomfield could boast of a population of over 1200, but by the time it was considered for incorporation in the state historic park, its population had dwindled to nine.

Hydraulic-mining debris also changed the characteristics of rivers, thereby affecting river-barge transportation. Before the 2200 million tons of sediment choked up rivers, one could travel from Sacramento north 120 miles up the Sacramento River to Red Bluff and south 180 miles up the San Joaquin River to the Fresno area. Hydraulic-derived sediments, carried in flood waters, provided added thrust to scour away the rivers' banks, eroding good farm land in the process, but also leaving the rivers wider when the floods subsided, thereby making them shallower and less navigable. And tragically, the debris buried and obliterated native streamside vegetation.

Description

This trail takes you into the heart of the Malakoff Diggins. Start early if you're hiking it on a hot summer day, for there is little shade in this open pit. At the trailhead is a large sign that gives statistics of the 7874-foot-long drain tunnel engineered by Hamilton Smith, which was begun in April 1872 and completed 30 months later. At present, milky, yellow-brown water trickles from the tunnel. During the mine's heyday, it transported a lot of muddy water and sediments down to Humbug Creek and along it into the South Yuba River. To finance such a tunnel plus the reservoirs and

the many miles of canal needed to feed it required a lot of capital. The miners who worked these diggings weren't independent souls, but rather were company pawns. Except for the first few years, when individuals flocked to the hills in search of placer gold, the extraction of this ore belonged to big business—either in the surface hydraulic mines or in the subterranean bedrock mines, like the ones in the Grass Valley mining district.

Our trail starts north up the east side of a small gully, crossing weathered Paleozoic marine sediments which long ago were metamorphosed to slate, phyllite, and schist. It then tops a low saddle and presents the hiker with a sweeping panorama of the Malakoff Diggins, which are in a 600-foot-thick layer of sediments deposited from about 50 to 30 million years ago by the ancestral Yuba River. The Diggins Trail, if one can call it that, now is an abandoned east-west road along the south side of a large, shallow, muddy pond. Just 40 yards east of your junction with this road, you'll find a 30-yard-long spur trail leading north to the end of the 556-foot-long Hiller Tunnel, which provides an alternate route to the Diggins. (A flashlight is recommended if you take this route. Had you started on a trail north up the west side of the small gully, you would have quickly reached the lower end of this tunnel.). At the pond's southwest end, a footpath begins northwest and gradually curves eastward around the iron rich pond, dying out at its east end. From there, hike wherever you choose.

The pond is not lifeless. Cattails have invaded it, and on them in spring perch male Brewer's blackbirds, each singing a song that proclaims him the master of the adjacent territory he defends against landless males. Along the shore's white, quartz cobbles, the spotted sandpiper lays her eggs, which blend in perfectly with them. Invading the lower slopes above the shore are alders, willows, and ponderosa pines, each species dropping litter, which furthers soil development and aids habitat restoration.

The Diggins resemble a miniature Bryce Canyon both in erosional patterns and in variety of colors. However, in Utah's Bryce Canyon, as in most canyons, the sediments get progressively younger toward the rim, but here, some older sediments stand above some adjacent younger ones. These older gravels were laid down by the ancestral Yuba River, which later cut down through them and then deposited the lower, younger layer of gravels in the cut. At Malakoff Diggins these lower gravels are divided into two colors, the upper being red and the lower pale blue. The gravels are essentially the same in composition, but the blue gravels once lay below the water-table surface, which protected them from exposure to oxygen, while the red gravels got their color from oxidation of the iron in them. It was the blue gravels, the lowest 130 feet of sediments above the Paleozoic bedrock foundation, which contained the most gold. No wonder, then, that the first miners, who worked the uppermost sediments, declared this area "humbug."

✎ **6** ✎
Blair Trail

Distances:
0.9 mile to Clampicnic Area
1.1 miles to Blair parking lot
2.5 miles to trailhead
Low/High Elevations: 3280′/3640′
Season: Early April through mid-November
Classification: Easy
Map: 2
Trailheads: See Hike 3's trailhead description to the Relief Hill Road junction. Your hike will descend to the Clampicnic Area, which is immediately west of this junction, then will continue 0.2 mile up the North Bloomfield Road to the Blair parking lot. You can start your hike at either of these two spots, but I have chosen to start at the Shoot Hill Campground, whose entrance is 0.5 mile past the Blair parking lot. You begin at the Upper Humbug/North Bloomfield trailhead, which starts southeast about 60 yards before camp unit 13; the Rim Trail (Hike 7) starts west about 40 yards before it. Finally, there is one trail not described, but nevertheless shown on Map 2: the Slaughterhouse Trail, which starts

beside camp unit 29. This makes a direct descent for just over ½ mile south along a ridge to an access trail west to the Malakoff Diggins. This trail junction is just 100 yards before the Slaughterhouse Trail reaches the north corner of the town's cemetery, which is mentioned at the end of Hike 3's trailhead description.

Introduction
This trail is a pleasant stroll even on hot summer days, for it is short and shady, and it takes you to an old swimming hole.

Description
Starting in Shoot Hill Campground, we descend southeast on an old road that has been narrowed to a path by encroaching shrubs. Black oak, ponderosa pine, incense-cedar, and Douglas-fir—typical species for this elevation and slope—provide a convenient canopy. Mountain misery locally appears as a sticky, calf-high ground cover, and in summer's heat it fills the air with its subtle aroma. After 300 yards our trail levels and curves to the gully of a seasonally trickling creek. Immediately before it, our trail splits. From here we'll make a loop trip, descending the steeper, creekside Upper Humbug Trail to the Clampicnic Area and returning along the shadier Blair Trail.

During spring our descent is accompanied by the refreshing song of a trickling creek, reached in a few minutes, whose banks are adorned with California Indian pink, wavy-leaved soap plant, lilies, and other water-loving plants. In the conifers, a woodpecker may search for bark insects while a gray squirrel may, after scrutinizing us, resume foraging for ponderosa-pine seeds and black-oak acorns.

After traversing across a drier slope covered with manzanita, we pass behind some buildings of partly reconstructed North Bloomfield, come to a bridge, cross it, and find ourselves in the **Clampicnic Area**, a beautiful, grassy picnic ground dominated by several immense incense-cedars. Across the road stands the silenced Hendy Giant—a 15-foot-long, nine-inch-diameter monitor, which in its day shot down many tons of gravel cliffs with its jets of high-pressure water. After a few steps up the road, we reach Cummins Hall, which serves as the park's headquarters and contains a museum that is open daily from June 1 through Labor Day. A history buff could spend many hours in it and around the settlement's buildings, mentally reconstructing how the town might have looked and what the townsfolk were like back in the 1870s.

A brief walk northeast up the town's road gets us to the **Blair parking lot**. Up a short, closed road we walk to the Blair, which is today a somewhat murky but thoroughly refreshing swimming hole. This hole was the site of early hydraulic mining; later it became a storage reservoir that provided water for one of the monitors at the Malakoff mine. In its deep, milky-green waters swim trout, other fish, and kids. On less crowded days, you may find aquatic garter snakes near or in the reservoir's shallow, vegetated east end. On popular weekends you can expect all the picnic tables, under forest shade, to be occupied.

After taking a last drink from the water fountain, start northeast along the narrow earth dam that separates the Blair from the

A wooden flume

deeply cut gully down which Humbug Creek courses boisterously in the springtime. Leaving the reservoir's shore on a shady path, we follow a ditch that once fed the reservoir, and pass an iron pipe and then a wooden

The Hendy Giant

flume, both used to transport the canal's water across small side gullies. We near the bank of delightful Humbug Creek, then climb up an old road that first curves west up a slope before it curves north and quickly joins a road climbing northeast. We start southwest on this road and descend its westward-curving path 170 yards to a prominent, southwest-descending road. Don't follow it, but continue west on a trail for 120 yards to the park's paved main road, which you cross just 10 yards southeast of its junction with the campground's entrance road.

We start southeast on a path across terrain suitable for large but harmless alligator lizards, then quickly angle northwest over to the upper reaches of Humbug Creek, immediately beyond which we come to the first trail junction we had encountered. From it we make a stiff climb 0.2 mile back to our **trailhead**.

⇜ 7 ⇝
Rim Trail

Distance: 3.5 miles to western trailhead
Low/High Elevations: 3300′/3680′
Season: Early April through mid-November
Classification: Easy to moderate
Map: 2
Trailheads: See Hike 3's trailhead description for the western trailhead, Hike 6's trailhead description for the eastern trailhead, which is our starting point.

Introduction
This trail provides you with an entirely different perspective of the Malakoff Diggins than the Diggins Trail. From mid-May through mid-October, afternoon temperatures can be quite uncomfortable on this often shadeless trail, so during this season, plan to hike the trail—a good one for bird watching—early in the morning.

Description
The trail, starting as an old fire road, curves westward from the campground to some open, grassy slopes, which are subject to ongoing landsliding. Before any hydraulic mining occurred, these once-forested slopes were weathering, mass wasting, and eroding very slowly. In a quarter century, miners created the gaping hole of Malakoff Diggins, and now, over a century later, forest vegetation is still trying to reestablish itself. Once it does, landsliding should be greatly reduced.

We soon cross the first of many creeklets we'll see along this route, which by midsummer are all dry. Growing beside most of them are water-loving big-leaf maples. On drier ground above the first creeklet grow black oaks, incense-cedars, and ponderosa pines, beneath which you'll spot mountain misery, a sticky, somewhat aromatic dwarf shrub with fernlike leaves. Miwok Indians used its leaves to make a tea, which they used to treat various afflictions.

Farther along, we encounter the first of several headward-eroding gullies, each cutting into the route. While each gully's headwall may advance upslope, the lower part of each gully may become stabilized with the growth of shrubs, which help to trap eroded sediments. Beyond it we soon enter an open thicket of manzanita, which attracts an army of bumblebees during May when these plants are in flower, and a variety of birds and mammals in summer, when the fertilized flowers have produced berries. Through this thicket we descend south along a now-rocky route before coming to a level area with ponderosa pines. The rocks and boulders are derived from volcanic flows similar to those at the Sierra crest, which were most active around 16-13 million years ago. In this state park and elsewhere, these andesitic flows buried the gold-bearing gravels of the ancient Yuba River drainage. Had the eastern lands not experienced volcanism, the gravels would not have been buried, and most of the gravels might have been eroded long before any gold-seeking human entered the Sierra Nevada.

The diverse environment of brush and conifers through which we now stroll southwest provides habitat for many animals. The most conspicuous are birds, and here you may see, among dozens of species, robin, dark-eyed junco, California quail, lesser goldfinch, mourning dove, black-throated gray warbler, Steller's jay, mountain chickadee, and several species of sparrows. Each bird species has a specific dietary requirement that is at least somewhat different from that of every other species; in this way, direct head-on interspecific competition is avoided. Instead, competition is *intraspecific*, that is, among members of the same species. A principal mechanism for keeping a population in check—other than predation—is the establishment of territories during mating season—a practice found among other vertebrates besides birds. Only those dominant males who can establish and hold a territory will mate.

Our aromatic route turns south and proceeds down a usually dry creeklet, crosses to a larger, longer-lasting one, leaves it, and then soon descends steeply back to it. We bid farewell to its cloistered grove of incense-cedar, madrone, black oak, Douglas-fir, and ponderosa pine, and hike westward to an open bend, from which we get our first view of the diggins' gravel cliffs. Beyond it we wander through a 10-foot-high manzanita thicket, meet a closed road that descends south, and continue our brief westward, brushy traverse to a forest of ponderosa and sugar pines. Two gullies working headward across our road are passed before we encounter in a deep gully a small outcrop of cross-bedded sandstone, which is part of the gold-poor bench layer of the old gravels.

Our road traverses around the deep gully and emerges on the northwest rim above the large, shallow pond of Malakoff Diggins. Almost immediately a view opens up and we get a sweeping panorama of most of the open pit and its colorful cliffs. Old trees and shrubs grow right up to our rim's edge, indicating that the rim is retreating. Roots protruding from the tops of cliffs together with fallen trees on the slopes below confirm our suspicion. While following the Diggins Trail on the flat below us, one gets the impression that little erosion has occurred since the end of hydraulic mining. Up on the rim, however, we can see that a fair amount has occurred, and by at least three processes. First, heavy rains can send streams of water downslope,

Retreating rim of Malakoff Diggins

which erode the cliffs in bits and pieces. Second, when the upper portions of the steep cliffs get wet from surface water and/or from ground water, small parts of the cliffs are likely to slough off. Finally, if clay is present in sufficient amounts, it can absorb enough water to weaken the cohesion of the gravels and cobbles it binds, and cause a good-sized slump. In several places our road has been eradicated by these slumps, and we can see the debris they deposited on the lower slopes 300 feet below us.

Leaving the Diggins, you commence a traverse through a fairly open field, in which you may see, particularly in early morning, a jackrabbit or a mule deer taking off through the deep brush and past the buckeye trees. Our closed road ends the **western trailhead** beside the park's main road, and you can either retrace your 3.5 miles of route or you can start down the main road. I suggest you descend this road about 0.7 mile to a viewpoint, just after a tight curve to the right, from which a western-access trail descends into the

Malakoff Diggins. Explore them to your heart's content, and then head east from the large pond's south shore for about one mile, over to the eastern edge of the diggins. There you'll meet a junction with an eastern-access trail, which climbs about ⅓ mile east to the Slaughterhouse Trail. On this manzanita-bordered trail partly shaded by an open forest of ponderosa pines, you climb moderately just over ½ mile north up a ridge to the park's campground.

◁⋙ 8 ⋘▷

South Yuba Trail, Missouri Bar Trail east to Washington

Distances
1.4 miles to South Yuba Trail
2.1 miles to Eastern Creek
3.1 miles to Union Creek
4.3 miles to tributary canyon
5.3 miles to Logan Canyon
6.6 miles to spur trail
8.1 miles to McKilligan Creek
8.6 miles to spur trail
9.5 miles to trailhead

Low/High Elevations: 2300'/3020'; 3470' from Missouri Bar trailhead

Season: March through early November

Classification: Moderate

Maps: 2 and 3

Trailheads: Same as the Hike 4 trailhead. If you hike this trail in the reverse, down-canyon direction, you will start at the South Yuba Trail's eastern trailhead. One way to reach this is from Malakoff Diggins State Historic Park. From it, follow Hike 4's trailhead directions 0.8 mile up Relief Hill Road to the Missouri Bar Trail's spur road on a poorly defined ridge saddle. Still on Relief Hill Road, wind eastward 2.9 miles up to a junction just past scattered dwellings that constitute Relief Hill (no services). Ignore the north-climbing road, and wind 6.0 miles eastward, still on Relief Hill Road, but signed Forest Route 36, to the eastern trailhead's short spur road. The last 2½ miles along the route is on rough, but

nevertheless quite drivable, tread. If you miss the trailhead's spur road, you will bridge Poorman Creek in about 200 yards.

A second approach to the eastern trailhead's spur road is through Washington. You reach that small community from the Highways 20/49 split in Nevada City by climbing 13 miles east on Highway 20 to Washington Road. This road is just ¼ mile east of a conspicuous, signed vista point, which offers a view of the South Yuba River canyon. (Washington Road can also be reached from Interstate 80. Leave it about 45 miles northeast of Auburn—or 16 miles west of Donner Pass—and go 14 miles west on Highway 20.) Descend paved Washington Road about 5½ miles to the edge of Washington, where on the left you'll find its post office along a spur road to River Rest Resort. Over the next ½ mile to the South Yuba River bridge, you go through Washington, which has a grocery store, cafe (and tavern), hotel (and tavern) and a few dwellings. From the bridge you go but 0.1 mile east to a junction, and branch left, ascending Washington Road 0.3 mile to a second junction. Gaston Grade Road (Forest Route 21) climbs from here, but you branch west on nearly level Relief Hill Road, which in just under ½ mile becomes signed as Forest Route 36. After about 1.7 miles along from the junction, you'll reach the trailhead's spur road.

Introduction
First see the "Introduction" to Hike 2 for an overview of the South Yuba Trail and some words of caution. Hike 8 is along the eastern half of this trail, but begins first with a descent to it via the Missouri Bar Trail. Along this half are many fine pools, but most are out of reach, lying on private lands. Across these lands the trail climbs high to keep trail users away from riverside private property. You may see some tempting pools, but making a descent to the river is trespassing, is exhausting, and is dangerous. Most users descending the Missouri Bar Trail will either head west on the South Yuba Trail toward the Humbug Trail—this stretch having the best river accessibility, or will head ¼ mile or so east to sample the two swimming holes in the Missouri Bar area. Also, the eastern end of the South Yuba Trail

can get heavy summer use, since the descent from the eastern trailhead is easy, and it takes you, in under one mile, to a short spur trail down to a great swimming hole. Only dedicated hikers will want to do the entire South Yuba Trail.

Description

You begin this route by following Hike 4, which descends 1.4 miles along the Missouri Bar Trail to a junction with the **South Yuba Trail**. Alternatively, you could have taken Hike 2 for 7.9 miles along the South Yuba Trail to this junction, or even have taken Hike 3 for 2.7 miles down the Humbug Trail, and then for 3.7 miles along the South Yuba Trail to this junction. From it you descend 130 yards northeast to Missouri Creek, and if it is a summer afternoon—when the river can warm up into the 70s—you might parallel its east bank briefly out to bedrock along the South Yuba River. Just a few paces up-canyon you'll reach a large, excellent, deep swimming hole situated immediately below the lowest of several bedrock ribs, or rockbars, which project partway across the river. If these are under water,

then the river will be too swift, and swimming here or anywhere else in it will be dangerous.

If you don't take this diversion, then from Missouri Creek you first follow the South Yuba Trail 60 yards southeast to enter the river canyon proper, then start east up-canyon. For about the first 300 yards, the trail is along the edge of a gravel flat, and it is subject to local washouts during very high runoff, as in the flood around New Years Day, 1997. Along the second half of this short stretch you'll pass a second large pool, giving you another opportunity to swim.

The trail then climbs slightly to start a traverse that takes you into the lower reaches of Eastern Canyon, which holds seasonal **Eastern Creek**. Over the next mile the trail exits the side canyon, then climbs eastward, denying you safe, easy access to the South Yuba River. Still climbing, it enters the private land of Section 9 in a gully with steeply inclined, foliated schist. Then in about ¼ mile it swings into short but deep Union Canyon, which has vertically inclined phyllite, a metamorphic rock like schist, but one having experienced less heat and pressure.

A tempting swimming hole among water-polished bedrock

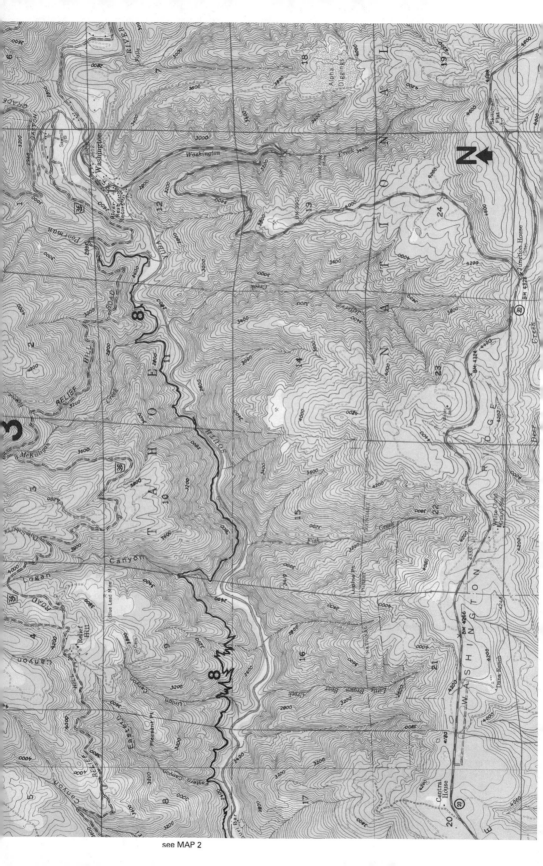

see MAP 2

Easternmost good swimming hole in late summer's low water

From the bridge across **Union Creek** the real climbing begins, which may seem unnecessary—and annoying on a hot day—but the route is high so that trail users cannot descend to private land along the river. We switchback up lower Union Canyon's east slopes, then up the South Yuba River canyon's north slopes, gaining 500 feet to reach the South Yuba Trail's high point at 3020 feet elevation. Fortunately, this ascent is quite shady, as is the vast majority of the trail's length. Generally along the South Yuba River canyon's north slopes, canyon live oaks predominate over black oaks and Douglas-firs, while in side canyons, these false firs predominate. Around the high point, we encounter a few representatives of two species uncommon to the trail, but common higher up: ponderosa pines and sugar pines.

Now we descend over 200 feet, switchbacking down into a **tributary canyon** with a seasonal creek. Over the next mile we first switchback out of this canyon, but thankfully have to climb less than 150 feet, then make a

long, high traverse northeast to **Logan Canyon**. For most of the year you can easily cross its creek, but in high runoff, it may be require fording. On its east bank we enter Section 10, which is USFS land, and we traverse ¼ mile south to a descending ridge, then start a one-mile, gradual descent east down to a junction with a **spur trail**. This descends 50 yards west to the river's gravelly bank, on which you can find one or more small sites for camping. However, in times of high water, some or all may be under water.

From the spur trail the South Yuba Trail climbs briefly east, then traverses about 0.2 mile northeast to where it dips, from where a use trail descends shortly east to the river's rocky bench. Ahead, the main trail in 160 yards first climbs momentarily and then traverses to a gully, where we enter Section 11, which is private land. We climb more, curving from east to north across metavolcanic rock, having a fine view up the river and its canyon before we reach a nearby gully. Another long traverse beneath live oaks and Douglas-firs ensues, and over a stretch of ¾ mile we climb from about 120 feet above the river to about 180 feet above it. Then over the next ¼ mile we head north into the shady confines of a major canyon to bridge its **McKilligan Creek**.

Southward, we make an equally long exit of the canyon, then curve east and have a good view south up 800-foot-deep Jefferson Creek canyon before traversing for a few minutes northeast to a **spur trail**, which switchbacks briefly down to nearly vertical foliated metamorphic rock. Its ragged surface is unsuited for sunbathing, though you can find spots to dive from it into the long, fairly deep pool beside it. When the river is low enough for safe swimming, there should be sandy spots beside it for sunbathing. This is your last good opportunity for river swimming; ahead, the river is quite shallow.

With less than a mile to go, We traverse north across a bedrock cliff—watch your step here—then quickly reach safer ground as we start a traverse east on less steep slopes. As the bedrock gives way to gravel underfoot, we enter Section 12, which is USFS land, and will stay on public land to the eastern trailhead. As you traverse across a broad gravel flat, you are likely to see folks camped out between the trail and the river. Soon we touch the road they drove in on, walk on or beside it for about 20 yards, then leave it to curve north. The road immediately fords Poorman Creek and heads upstream, as do we, but above the creek's west bank. We climb easily north, in 0.2 mile passing a stand of gray (foothill) pines above us—not seen since near the western end of the trail—then curve briefly west. Doing so, we see our last opportunity to cool off: shallow pools of Poorman Creek. Beyond them we start a clockwise traverse and in about ¼ mile reach the South Yuba Trail's **eastern trailhead**, which has a small parking area and an outhouse.

The Sierra Buttes Fire Lookout

Chapter 9
Sierra City and Johnsville Gold Districts

Introduction

Gold was discovered at Sutter's Mill in 1848, and by 1850 frenzied miners were scouring almost every square inch of California's mountain landscape. One mountain area that proved to be quite lucrative was the upper Highway 49 region. This area extended roughly from the Sierra City environs north-northwest to Johnsville, which today is a dormant settlement within Plumas-Eureka State Park.

All the mines were located in a belt of metamorphic rocks, and while there may have been hundreds of mining claims in the 1850s, only two or three dozen eventually brought wealth to their owners. The Sierra Buttes Mine (Map 4, northwest above Sierra City, and near Hike 13), was the granddaddy that lured miners to the area. It extracted about 40 tons of gold, alone accounting for about $20,000,000 of the total $50,000,000 mined in the Sierra City-Johnsville gold districts. The Plumas-Eureka, Jamison, and Four Hills mines, all in the Hike 28 environs, accounted for about $12,000,000. The Monumental Mine, while not particularly productive, did produce, in the 1860s, two monumental nuggets—133 pounds and 158 pounds! Contrast this to milling-grade ore later on, which yielded, on average, about ½ ounce of gold per ton of crushed rock.

Commercial mining all but died with the start of World War I, though the Plumas-Eureka Mine did continue intermittently until World War II. The mining activity never resumed in the postwar years, allowing the creation of Plumas-Eureka State Park in 1959 and then the Lakes Basin and Sierra Buttes recreation areas.

Today, weekend miners still search for the giant nugget or the lost lode, but the area's wealth now lies in its aqueous gems—dozens of mountain lakes. Most of these are in an area bounded roughly by Highway 49 on the south, Gold Lake Road on the east, Plumas-Eureka State Park on the north and the Sierra Buttes-Sierra Nevada crest on the west. The bulk of this chapter's trails lie within this area, which is usually snow-free three or four months of the year. The Eureka Peak Trail, which was described in this book's first three editions, is not included here, because the road to the trailhead is deteriorating to a jeep road. However, because the 1.5-mile trail to peak 7286 is maintained, while the road is not, the route is briefly mentioned under Hike 27's trailhead.

This chapter's first routes, Hikes 9-11, lie in the lakeless, largely viewless canyonlands southeast of Sierra City and Highway 49. The prime attraction, if you can call it that, is the area's longer hiking season, generally from April through November. This extended season permits you to stretch your legs in spring and fall, when the high country is apt to be under snow.

⋞ 9 ⋟
Wild Plum Loop Trail

Distances:
1.2 miles to Pacific Crest Trail bridge over
   Haypress Creek via counterclockwise
   route
1.4 miles to Pacific Crest Trail bridge via
   clockwise route
2.6 miles total, semiloop trip
Low/High Elevations: 4390'/4840'
Season: April through November
Classification: Easy
Map: 4

Trailhead: At the northeast end of Sierra City, leave Highway 49, heading east on Wild Plum Road. In about one mile you reach a parking area on your right, with room for about 10 vehicles. Start here. Had you driven ahead, you would reach, in about 250 yards, a fork, the left branch going to several Forest Service buildings, the right branch bridging adjacent Haypress Creek and entering Wild Plum Campground.

Introduction
This hike is particularly suitable from mid-April to mid-June, when the Highway 49 highlands are still largely under snow. Because it passes through a variety of habitats (mixed-conifer forest, oak woodland, shrub slope, rock outcrop, and stream bank), it offers the hiker in springtime a lavish display of vernal flowers and a large selection of song birds.

Description
From the end of the parking area, start east on a trail that meanders up-canyon between Wild Plum Road and Haypress Creek. After about 280 yards the trail intersects the road to Wild Plum Campground. This spot is 35 yards above the Haypress Creek bridge and 25 yards beyond the road branching left to Wild Plum Forest Service Station. Here we begin our loop trail. You could continue straight ahead, clockwise, but then you would climb a series of switchbacks rather than descend them.

So going counterclockwise, we begin by walking up through the campground, and from its upper end go but 50 yards up a gated

Haypress Creek cataracts

utility road to a branch left. This goes briefly up along Haypress Creek to a small power station. We go straight ahead, climbing moderately above the soon-visible station, and have its powerline as a roadside companion.

About ½ mile from the end of the campground, our road crosses a creek that originates on slopes above Hilda Mine. Just 50 yards beyond the creek you leave the road (Hike 10 continues ahead), and branch left for a short climb to a minor ridge. On it you'll hear but not see Haypress Creek's low, roaring falls, which you can reach by a cautious descent from the ridge. The well-used trail leaves the ridge for a pleasant traverse to a large bridge across Haypress Creek. Here you meet the **Pacific Crest Trail** (PCT), which winds ¼ mile southeast up to the utility road you just left. The Haypress Creek canyon, being V-shaped in cross-section, looks like a typical stream-carved canyon. However, hard as it may be to believe, this stretch of canyon was glaciated, and evidence for this lies just up the PCT. To see it, take this trail about 160 yards east, then 35 yards south, up to some metamorphic bedrock along the west side of the trail. It is polished and striated, the faint striations indicating that the glacier flowed along a bearing of 300°. Additional glacial evidence is found on open slopes above, in the form of granitic boulders, which could have gotten here only through glacial transport.

On the northbound PCT you cross the Haypress Creek bridge, climb momentarily to a flat, then a bit more up to a possibly missed junction. By the mid-1990s, the once obvious eastbound Haypress Creek Trail had fallen into disuse, perhaps because an eastbound road had been constructed on the opposite side of Haypress Creek canyon. Onward, you climb west on the PCT to an adjacent ridge, from which you can take a few steps south for a revealing view of the Haypress Creek gorge and its associated falls. Now with views of dominating Sierra Buttes, we ramble shortly over to seasonally trickling 1001 Mine creek, then in 50 yards leave the PCT (Hike 11 describes the stretch of PCT between here and Highway 49). To complete the loop trail, you start down an array of short switchbacks across somewhat open terrain, which in

summer can be quite hot. At the base of the switchbacks, near the east end of a flat, you'll hear in springtime the muted roar of some impressive cataracts, which you can see by heading a bit south from the trail. To get to the pool immediately below them, switchback briefly down the trail to Haypress Creek, leave the trail, and walk up along the creek's bank.

We complete our loop trail by following the creek downstream, our Haypress Creek Trail skirting south of Wild Plum Forest Service Station about ¼ mile before reaching the Wild Plum Campground bridge. Along this last stretch you'll see myriad boulders transported by the former glacier's powerful stream. From near the bridge, retrace your initial trail segment 280 yards to the trailhead parking area.

⌖ 10 ⌖
Pacific Crest Trail, southeast up Milton Creek

Distances:
1.3 miles to Pacific Crest Trail
2.5 miles to cross Milton Creek
3.3 miles to recross Milton Creek
6.6 miles to Milton Creek canyon viewpoint
Low/High Elevations: 4390'/6510'
Season: June through October
Classification: Moderate
Maps: 4 and 5
Trailhead: Same as the Hike 9 trailhead.

Introduction
Although this route ends with a fine view of a northern Sierra canyonland, it is easily the long way in to that view. If you want just the view, take Hike 40, which is only 3.1 miles, one way, and has but a fraction of the elevation gain. Hike 10 is for those who enjoy hiking and aren't particularly goal-oriented. Though long, this route is mostly a gentle grade.

Description
As in the previous hike, head up through Wild Plum Campground, and from its upper

see MAP 5
see MAP 7
see MAP 6

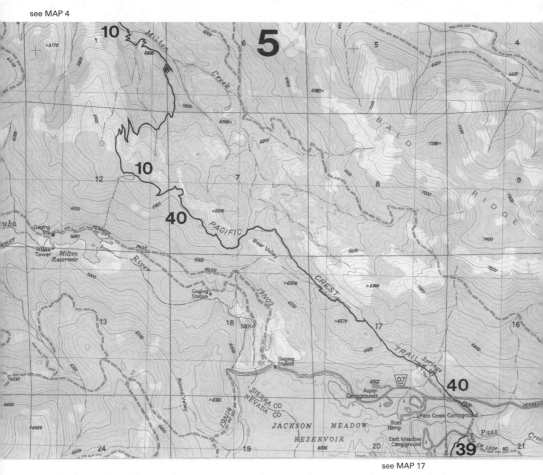

see MAP 17

end climb moderately ½ mile up a gated utility road to a creek, then 50 yards beyond it to a trail junction. Here you leave Hike 9, which branches left, and continue on an easier climb eastward. You may see light-gray granitic boulders here (and just ahead) which clearly look out of place resting on the brownish metamorphic bedrock. They are, having been transported here by the last glacier to descend this drainage. In ⅓ mile the road tops out, and you descend northeast just 90 yards to a junction with the northbound **Pacific Crest Trail** (PCT). Hike 11 describes this trail from Highway 49 southeast to this junction. You continue ahead just 35 yards to a junction with the southbound PCT. Here we leave the utility road and its attendant powerline, both descending to a nearby bridge over Milton Creek (just above its confluence with Haypress Creek) before ascending to a second

small power station, and both then continuing up Haypress Creek canyon.

On the PCT we begin a hike southeast up glaciated Milton Creek canyon. Middle Yuba River glaciers spilled over a divide and down into this canyon, but they performed very little erosion—this glaciated canyon looks just like unglaciated ones. On our trail we pass through a thick growth of conifers, which usually hides the broad creek and muffles its song. In about ¾ mile, we pass just above a check dam and its adjacent, small, concrete, hydrologic structure. Then in just under ½ mile we **cross Milton Creek** on a bridge. After an initial jog north, we switchback up to the crest of a minor intra-canyon ridge, and now on granitic bedrock traverse south easily up-canyon to **recross Milton Creek** on a second bridge. On its south side is an obvious, pleasant campsite.

Umbrella plant (Indian rhubarb) grows along Milton and Haypress creeks

From the bridge a climb begins in earnest, though the PCT has a low gradient, thanks to about two dozen switchbacks. If you're carrying a heavy pack, this is certainly a blessing, but for the day hiker the ascent, and certainly the return descent, can seem unnecessarily long. You negotiate more than half of the switchbacks as you leisurely knock off almost 700 feet of ascent to a saddle on a secondary ridge. You then meander west, in and out of gullies, before ascending longer switchbacks, largely lined with brush. Climbing higher, you have inspiring—and on hot days, perspiring—views of glaciated Milton Creek canyon, and then you contour south to a viewless saddle. A semistagnant lily-pad pond lies immediately south of it, a byproduct of a former glaciation. The Middle Yuba River glacier that excavated the pond's shallow basin was on the order of 900+ feet thick in the vicinity of the river's unseen Milton Reservoir, about ½ mile to the south-southwest.

Robbed of a crest view, you might as well continue on, heading up a shady gully to another viewless saddle, your highest point in elevation. The high point, emotionally, lies just ahead, where the trail descends out to a **Milton Creek canyon viewpoint**. Besides having a commanding view of the canyon, you also spy the sawtooth ridge of the Sierra Buttes, a landmark you haven't seen since you first set foot on the lower part of the PCT. Hike 40 describes the trail from the Jackson Meadow Reservoir environs northwest to this viewpoint.

✥ **11** ✥

Pacific Crest Trail, Highway 49 southeast to Haypress Creek

Distances:
0.3 mile to North Yuba River
1.8 miles to Haypress Creek Trail
2.3 miles to bridge over Haypress Creek
Low/High Elevations: 4580'/4850'
Season: April through November
Classification: Easy
Map: 4

Fishing beneath North Yuba River's bridge

Trailheads East end: same as the Hike 9 trailhead; follow that route to the Haypress Creek bridge. West end: same as the Hike 12 trailhead.

Introduction

The prime attraction of this short piece of Pacific Crest Trail (PCT) is Loves Falls, which is rewarding to anglers and sightseers alike. Few people hike southeast past it, for in summer the traverse can be hot, dry, and fly-infested. However, in March and April, this fairly open hike, lying below snowbound higher trails, can be very enjoyable. Likewise, it can be pleasant in October and November.

Description

From the west trailhead the path parallels Highway 49 northeast, passing a usually flowing spring and an ephemeral seep before reaching the massive bridge that vaults the **North Yuba River**. Here the river has cut a minigorge through resistant Mesozoic-age metavolcanic rocks, and it thunders from fall

to fall, collectively known as Loves Falls. A pool lies at the base of each waterfall, but most of them can be reached only by precarious scrambling. Still, some anglers insist on plying their sport in one or more of these pools, an exceptionally dangerous undertaking when the river runs high.

East from the bridge the trail climbs moderately to a seasonal creek, then eases off for a traverse through a live-oak woodland. This habitat has the invidious characteristic of harboring droves of obnoxious midges, which swarm about you, particularly if you're perspiring, as you're likely to be on summer afternoons. As you advance southeast to a bedrock ridge, you're rewarded with increasingly better views back over your shoulder of the Sierra Buttes. Beyond the ridge, Haypress Creek canyon captivates your attention, and soon you reach a minor ridge, which has a junction with the **Haypress Creek Trail**. The descent from here is described in the last part of Hike 9. You stay on the PCT and take Hike 9 in reverse. Southeastward, you have at least one more fine view of the Sierra Buttes, then one of the Haypress Creek falls—if you take a few steps off-trail before you initiate a descent to the **bridge over Haypress Creek**. Retrace your steps from here. Ahead, the PCT climbs ¼ mile southeast to a utility road, while an older path, also starting from the bridge, winds southwest over to the same road.

Bridge across the North Yuba River

⤳ 12 ⤲
Pacific Crest Trail, from Highway 49 west to Sierra Buttes

Distances:
7.2 miles to Sierra Buttes jeep road
8.0 miles to OHV parking area
9.5 miles up jeep road to lookout and back to OHV parking area
10.4 miles to Pacific Crest Trail
11.3 miles to lower Tamarack Lake
    0.2 mile to upper Tamarack Lake
12.2 miles to trailhead above Packer Lake

Low/High Elevations: 4580′/8591′

Season: July through October

Classification: Strenuous

Maps: 4 and 6

Trailheads: Southeast end: along Highway 49, about 1½ miles northeast of "downtown" Sierra City and 1.0 mile northeast of a road branching east to Wild Plum Campground. Parking on adjacent spur road limited to several vehicles. Northwest end: same as the Hike 15 trailhead.

Introduction
The longest route to the Sierra Buttes Fire Lookout is along a northbound stretch of the Pacific Crest Trail. Few will want to ascend this mostly shadeless, usually dry route; even fewer will want to retrace their steps back down it—a lengthy 17.4 miles, round trip. If you can arrange a shuttle, begin your hike from Highway 49 and end it at the Hike 15 trailhead. Sure, this direction is tougher than north to south, but you'll end your hike with opportunities to jump into three relatively warm lakes (and you'll certainly need a bath regardless of which direction you hike).

Description
The northbound Pacific Crest Trail (PCT) commences northeast from a spur road, and it parallels Highway 49 up-canyon. The first part of this trail section is on a narrow, abandoned road through a forest of black oak, ponderosa pine, and incense-cedar. Mountain misery, a low, sticky shrub, permeates the air with a subtle fragrance as the day's temperature rises. After the PCT bends north onto cooler, east-facing slopes, we meet Douglas-firs and their associated vegetation. About a mile from the start, our sporadically switch-

A virtually shadeless 3¾-mile traverse across Sierra Buttes' south slopes

backing trail leaves noisy Highway 49 and switchbacks relentlessly upward to a flume that today is bone-dry. About ¼–½ mile north lie smooth, brushy ridges, a smaller set within a larger one. These are lateral moraines, largely composed of rockfall which was transported to here by glaciers that descended east from the Sierra Buttes. The early glacier left the outer ridges; the later, smaller glacier left the inner ones.

The existing route 2¾ miles up to the flume has been mostly a forested one, but we leave all trees behind just before the switchbacking ascent tops off, in ¾ mile, on a ridge. From it we have views both up and down the North Yuba River canyon and views up at the east buttress of the Sierra Buttes. Now shrubs line the trail, mainly huckleberry oak, greenleaf manzanita, tobacco brush, and bitter cherry, but also a dab here and there of snow bush and squaw carpet. After weaving around several ridges and gullies and getting saturated with views, we finally arrive, after 3¾ miles, at a saddle and the **Sierra Buttes jeep road**.

If you've got ample water, gear down for the serious grind ahead. Otherwise, first continue a level ¼ mile on the PCT to a profuse alder-lined spring, just below the trail, then return to the saddle. The road first climbs moderately to a switchback, then enters forest cover, lending you much needed shade up the 790-foot ascent to a near-ridge **OHV parking area**. You've climbed but ¾ mile, but you'll swear it's more.

Another ¾-mile ascent to the lookout remains, but the jeep road is better graded and increasingly scenic. This ascent, plus the lookout's views, are described in Hike 16, which is the easiest route to the **lookout**. After your ascent, return to the parking area and continue ahead on Sierra Buttes Trail 12E06. This you'll descend 2.7 miles to its trailhead just above Packer Lake.

The trail at first descends northwest along the Sierra Buttes' ridge, which here is a rim of a glacial cirque. From several spots along it you have stunning views of Young America

Lake. Though only about ¼ mile away, it is nevertheless one of the most inaccessible lakes in the Tahoe Sierra. Lower and farther from you lie the Sardine Lakes and their giant enclosing moraines. Beyond the views you briefly wind among some giant "boulders" of pale blue-green metamorphosed, ancient lava. Next, the trail meanders for ⅓ mile down through a fir-and-hemlock forest where, before late July, snow patches may obscure the blazed trail. The ridge curves northward, and along it your trail descends shortly to a level spot containing a junction with the **Pacific Crest Trail**. Had you not taken the jeep road up to Sierra Buttes but rather had continued north on the PCT, you would have arrived here, after a 1.1-mile traverse. The PCT continues north along the now narrow, almost level ridgecrest, heading 0.9 mile to the Hike 16 trailhead.

On the last part of your descent to the junction, you've gotten vistas of the Tamarack Lakes, which are welcome swimming holes on hot summer days. Your knee-knocking Sierra Buttes Trail heads toward them after first making a switchback down a steep slope. In ⅓ mile your fairly steep route comes to an abandoned logging road. Ahead, your descent is direct and steep, temporarily abating in about ½ mile at a junction above **lower Tamarack Lake**. After your exhausting day, you may not want to take the short road south to **upper Tamarack Lake**. The lower lake, being smaller and shallower, is the warmer of the two. Avoid its grassy west half and swim in its trout-inhabited east half.

Your last leg has been down a jeep road, narrowed over time by encroaching vegetation. Ahead, the jeep road is open to OHVs. Just below the lower lake, you reach a junction. Hike 14, from the Sardine Lakes area, arrives from the east, while Hike 15, ascending from the Packer Lake area, arrives from the north. You descend the latter, usually at a moderate grade, to the ample trailhead parking lot. Packer Lake, just below you, gives you a third opportunity to take a refreshing dip.

⋙ 13 ⋘
Sierra City to Sierra Buttes

Distances:
3.3 miles to Pacific Crest Trail
4.8 miles to Sierra Buttes Fire Lookout

Low/High Elevations: 5188'/8591'

Season: Year round; snow is an advantage
for this hike.

Classification: Strenuous

Maps: 4 and 6

Trailhead: In Sierra City turn north up Butte
Street. Go 0.1 mile up it to paved Sierra Buttes
Road and take it an easy mile west up to a
large flat at the edge of a county dump. Turn
sharply right and follow a graded road 1.4
miles, first briefly east, then northwest. Park
at a junction, about ⅓ mile past a major gully,
with the steep, narrow Sierra Buttes jeep road.
Parking is limited; use nearby turnouts.

Introduction
With 3400 feet to climb, this route seems to be
an uninviting hike. However, when the short
routes to the summit, Hikes 15 and 16, are
snowbound, this route takes on a certain
appeal, and it is grand on a fine spring day,
when some of your route will be snowbound
and you won't have to compete with OHVs.
Furthermore, you can make the upper part of
your descent route an exhilarating glissade.

Description
Winter hikers may have to start their trek
from the large flat at the edge of a county
dump, 1.4 miles down the road. All others
should be able to drive up to the start of the
Sierra Buttes jeep road. You hike ⅔ mile eastward up this shadeless road to its tight bend
west, near a creek that flows until about early
summer. Climbing west, your steady, moderate ascent goes past occasional incense-cedars
and ponderosa pines, which provide convenient, shady rest spots. Along various road
cuts are exposures of blue-green serpentine,
which is the main alteration product of ultra-
mafic rocks, such as the blue-black pyroxene
associated with it. A once-active fault, trend-
ing northwest-southeast, approximately parallels the road below you. Along this fault

these ultramafics, which are remnants of
ancient oceanic, volcanic bedrock, were thrust
upon the surrounding Paleozoic rocks. Once
emplaced, these ultramafics were then invaded by superheated water under intense pressure, which forced water into their crystal
structures, converting the rock to serpentine.

We think of water as being relatively harmless. We can drink it or bathe in it and it does-
n't destroy us. When this same water,
however, is *confined* within rocks and is sub-
jected to temperatures that are several times
greater than its boiling point, it builds up to
tremendous pressures and becomes very cor-
rosive. It then dissolves quartz, gold, silver,
copper, lead, zinc, and a host of other materials and carries them upward away from their
plutonic, subterranean source. As it climbs
farther from the pluton, its temperature—and
hence its pressure—decreases, and the dissolved materials begin to precipitate out. If
dissolved gold is present in the ascending
fluid, it will precipitate out at the same tem-
perature-pressure regime as the silica, which

Stairs to Sierra Buttes Fire Lookout

solidifies to form vein quartz. Hence miners look for quartz veins in the hope they'll find gold in them. Starting tens of millions of years ago, gold from quartz veins in the Sierra was eroded and transported down the North Yuba River. Where its gradient eased, its velocity decreased, and the river dropped its rich, heavy prize along with other sediments. Today, the river still attracts many gold seekers.

The Sierra Buttes mining district is known for its large gold nuggets, and some are still occasionally found. In its heyday, this district produced at least $30 million in gold, but little has been mined since the 1930s. By far the most productive mine was the Sierra Buttes Mine—located ½ mile east of the first major bend in our jeep road—whose gold-rich veins yielded as much as $20 million.

Our 1½-mile open, westward ascent ends at a saddle atop a southwest-descending spur ridge (bottom of Map 6), which separates brushy slopes to the east from forested ones to the north. A conspicuous road goes 0.3 mile along the spur ridge to point 6433, with views down into Ladies Canyon, but our road curves east from the ridge's saddle and in 130 yards reaches a junction with a road contouring northward, bound for the Monarch Mine. We continue briefly eastward, then climb northeast ½ mile through a shady forest—first among white firs, then among red firs and western white pines—to a road intersection at the start of the Sierra Buttes jeep road. So far, our route has been marginally jeep road, but ahead it definitely is an OHV route.

South from the intersection, a road quickly dead-ends. North, it traverses 2.0 miles to another road, which climbs 0.6 mile to the Hike 16 trailhead. Should you take these roads to this intersection, you cut 2.9 miles, each way, off your distance. Winter and spring hikers may miss this intersection, if not the entire jeep road up to it, for both can be under fairly deep snow. The forest, however, is open enough for the snowbound hiker to pick any route. Perhaps the best one is to follow under snowy conditions is to hike up to an obvious saddle immediately north of summit 6924, then climb northeast straight up almost to a ridge, staying near or within the forest's edge.

If you lack snow problems, then take the Sierra Buttes jeep road 0.4 mile steeply up to a saddle crossed by the Pacific Crest Trail, both features lying immediately northeast of a low ridge knoll, point 7179. Be aware that halfway up this steep stretch, the jeep road forks. Keep left, or else you will end up atop the point, not at the saddle. Hike 12, which has progressed 7.2 miles along the PCT from Highway 49, joins our route here. Before continuing upward, if you need water, follow the PCT a level ¼ mile to a profuse alder-lined spring, just below the trail, then return to the saddle.

Your climb ahead is steep, and in ¾ mile you briefly level off at a near-ridge OHV parking area. The Sierra Buttes Trail (Hike 16) climbs southeast to this area, although if it is under snow you won't see it. That doesn't matter. You can't miss the fire lookout unless you are in a whiteout, in which case you shouldn't be up here in the first place. If the ground is snow-free, you have two choices. First, start east up the Sierra Buttes jeep road, which is closed to motor vehicles but not to mountain bikes, or second, start east up the Sierra Buttes Trail, which begins just north of it. This trail for hikers ends about midway up the stretch of jeep road, and you take the road's upper half to the intimidating series of ladders at the base of the **Sierra Buttes Fire Lookout**. See Hike 16 for a description of the lookout's views.

⤞ 14 ⤝
Tamarack Connection Trail

Distances:
1.8 miles to Sardine Lake Overlook Trail
    0.3 mile on trail to overlook
2.5 miles to ridgecrest saddle
3.6 miles to Tamarack Lakes Jeep Road
3.7 miles to lower Tamarack Lake
3.9 miles to upper Tamarack Lake
Low/High Elevations: 5770'/7070'
Season: Late June through mid-October
Classification: Moderate
Maps: 7 and 6

Trailhead: From Highway 49 about 5 miles above Sierra City, drive 1.3 miles west up Gold Lake Road, then branch left onto County Route S621, usually signed for Packer Lake. Take it ¼ mile west to a junction. Here, it turns right, north, but you drive 80 yards straight ahead on the Sardine Lakes Road to a signed trailhead on your right. If there is no available roadside parking, then drive about 0.3 mile up the road to a parking lot at the Sand Pond Picnic Ground and Beach. From it the Sand Pond Interpretive Trail leads southeast along the pond's east edge, then heads east along boggy Sardine Creek lands before looping west and crossing the creek to end by the southwest edge of Sardine Lake Campground.

Introduction

If you're staying in the Sardine Lakes area and want a trail with a lot of views, take this hike, which offers in part a continually changing panorama of the lakes and the Sierra Buttes.

The trail provides a long way in to the Tamarack Lakes, which are better reached by Hike 15. Therefore, most hikers will want to go only 2.1 miles to the Sardine Lake Overlook.

Description

Our Tamarack Connection Trail 12E08 begins as a closed jeep road, which climbs moderately southwest through dense manzanita up to a switchback. From this point we clearly see the sawtooth nature of the Sierra Buttes crest, and we can see that a traverse along it would be impossible without the aid of ropes and climbing equipment. In the foreground lies a favorite summertime swimming hole, Sand Pond. This lakelet owes its origin to mining operations at the Young America Mine, whose large buildings once stood on a gentle slope above Lower Sardine Lake's southwest shore. Higher up on our route, there will be several spots where you'll be able to take a few steps south from the trail and see the rocky, gravelly tailings left by the long-abandoned mine.

Upper Sardine Lake and Sierra Buttes

The mine was a major operation as early as 1885, with a large mill in which ore blasted out of the late-Paleozoic metavolcanic bedrock was crushed to extract its gold, which, over about 50 years, amounted to $1½ million worth. The gangue, or waste material, was then flushed down via a closed conduit to the flat below Lower Sardine Lake, where it was deposited as tailings. In the early 1900s some tailings were removed and were treated by the cyanide process to recover more gold. The depression left by their removal became Sand Pond.

From the switchback, our jeep road heads northeast across brushy slopes, then northwest into white-fir forest to a switchback with a junction. A use road continues ahead, but we turn south and progress up three switchback legs before curving west onto the crest of a lateral moraine and having our first view of both Sardine Lakes. Because most of the moraine is clothed only in brush—chiefly greenleaf manzanita and huckleberry oak—our views up the steadily climbing trail are largely continuous and unobstructed. Occasional Jeffrey pines punctuate the moraine's brushy cloak and some provide us with shady, picturesque, trailside resting spots. Looking southward across Lower Sardine Lake, we see a large lateral moraine the same age as the one we're hiking along.

After about one mile of moraine-crest ascent, we encounter **Sardine Lake Overlook Trail**. This trail, 12E36, descends slightly as it traverses to a switchback with the adjacent **overlook**. This provides a sweeping panorama from the towering Sierra Buttes in the southwest to Upper Sardine Lake below us to Lower Sardine Lake and the Sierran crest lands above us to the northeast. From the switchback an old mining road starts a traverse northeast. Although it tempts one with a shortcut down to Upper Sardine Lake's dam, this route is very abandoned and very dangerous. Return the way you came.

If you're bound for the Tamarack Lakes, you continue southeast moderately up the Tamarack Connection Trail for ⅓ mile, then go a similar distance up short, steep switchbacks to a forested **ridgecrest saddle**. Past glaciers topped this ridgecrest, and directly across the

canyon they were thick enough to spill over the far ridgecrest. Thus, in the vicinity of Upper Sardine Lake, they were *at least* 1200 feet thick, and they must have been very dramatic sights.

Leaving the ridgecrest saddle, the trail switchbacks down to gentler slopes and then undulates and winds past two ponds before heading northwest across a minor ridge and turning southwest to lead ¼ mile over to the **Tamarack Lake Trail**. This is a jeep road, on which vehicles are allowed, and on weekends you may see anglers who have driven this far. The **lower** and **upper Tamarack Lakes** are just ahead and are described in the following hike.

⋙ 15 ⋘
Packer Lake to Tamarack Lakes and Sierra Buttes

Distances:
0.9 mile to lower Tamarack Lake
1.1 miles to upper Tamarack Lake
1.8 miles to Pacific Crest Trail
3.5 miles to Sierra Buttes Fire Lookout
Low/High Elevations: 6260'/6760' to Tamarack Lakes; 8591' to Sierra Buttes Fire Lookout
Season: Late June through mid-October
Classification: Moderate to lakes; strenuous to Fire Lookout
Map: 6
Trailhead: From Highway 49 about 5 miles above Sierra City, drive 1.3 miles west up Gold Lake Road, then branch left onto County Route S621, usually signed for Packer Lake. Take it ¼ mile west to a junction, where S621 turns right, north. You continue 2.7 miles up the county route to a junction by the Packer Lake Picnic Area. The road ahead circles the lake to reach Packer Lake Lodge. The paved road veering left, Forest Route 93, climbs steeply to Packer Lake Saddle, but you take this road a mere 250 yards to a parking area on the right and a trailhead on the left.

Introduction
Like Packer Lake near the trailhead, the Tamarack Lakes provide relatively warm

swimming from mid-July to late August. Like most Sierra lakes, both contain trout, and that is perhaps their greatest attraction. OHVs are allowed on the route to the two lakes, and you are most likely to see them on summer weekends. From the lakes you can hike to the Sierra Buttes, though such a route, while fairly popular is 0.9 mile longer than the Hike 16 route. It also has 750 feet of additional elevation gain, some of it quite steep.

Description

Your route, a jeep road open to vehicles, climbs moderately ¼ mile to a fork, from where a gated road swings east to Duggan Pond and Saxonia Lake. The latter, about one mile east along the road, is a worthy, vehicle-free goal, being fairly deep and trout-stocked. The main route continues straight ahead at a usually moderate grade and in 0.6 mile reaches a junction with Tamarack Connection Trail 12E08 (see previous hike). You veer right on your jeep road, and momentarily arrive at the northwest shore of **lower Tamarack Lake**. Your first view is disappointing, for the west half of the lake is largely knee-deep, little more. The east half, however, is not only swimmable but is deep enough to support a limited trout population.

A larger trout population resides just above in **upper Tamarack Lake**. Just above the lower lake, your jeep road forks, and you take the left road, which also forks, both legs reuniting by the upper lake. The Tamarack Lakes derive their name from the fringe of lodgepole pines that encircles each (as they do

most Sierra lakes). Back in the 1800s, John Muir and his contemporaries called these two-needled, sappy-barked conifers *tamarack* pines.

If you're hell-bent for the Sierra Buttes, take the former jeep road from the fork by the lower lake. Now a wide trail—Tamarack Connection Trail 12E30 (*not* 12E08)—it climbs moderately, affording views across the lakes' basin, then climbs steeply to an abandoned logging road. If you were to follow the road southeast down to its end, and then continue cross-country east-southeast up to a crest saddle, you would discover trout-stocked Young America Lake, which lies 300 feet below the saddle. However, almost everyone continues south from the abandoned logging road, climbing steeply up a trail to a ridge junction with the **Pacific Crest Trail**. From here the Sierra Buttes Trail climbs southeast to the **Sierra Buttes Fire Lookout**. This route, plus the summit views, are described in the next hike.

✦ 16 ✦
Forest Route 93 to Sierra Buttes

Distances:
0.9 mile to Tamarack Connection Trail
1.8 miles to OHV parking area
2.6 miles to Sierra Buttes Fire Lookout
Low/High Elevations: 7012'/8591'

Fishing at lower Tamarack Lake

Season: Mid-July through mid-October

Classification: Strenuous

Map: 6

Trailheads: From Highway 49 about 5 miles above Sierra City, drive 1.3 miles west up Gold Lake Road, then branch left onto County Route S621, usually signed for Packer Lake. Take it ¼ mile west to a junction, where S621 turns right, north. You continue 2.7 miles up the county route to a junction by the Packer Lake Picnic Area. The road ahead circles the lake to reach Packer Lake Lodge. Take the paved road veering left, Forest Route 93, which climbs steeply 1.6 miles to the Packer Lake Saddle—Hike 17's trailhead. Still on F.R. 93, continue 0.4 mile south along a ridge to a junction. Here it switchbacks northwest, and you leave it to continue 0.2 mile south to a second saddle, with trailhead parking for about 10 vehicles.

Introduction

Because this route is relatively short and because it takes you to the best summit views between the Donner Pass area to the south and Lassen Peak to the north, it has become quite popular. Expect dozens of hikers on summer weekends. Seasoned, fanatical hikers can make the ascent in an hour's time, but most hikers will take two. Bring perhaps binoculars, and certainly bring film to capture the summit's airy, top-of-the-world views. To identify prominent peaks, also bring a compass.

Description

Your route, Sierra Buttes Trail 12E06, coincides for the first 0.9 mile with a minuscule stretch of the Pacific Crest Trail, or PCT. For the first half mile, your route is a gated, former logging road. It starts southeast, switchbacks west up to the nose of a ridge, then climbs to the nearby crest. Upon reaching it, the road cuts across it to start a steep descent southeast, intersecting a trail to Tamarack Lakes midway along its length. Now on trail tread, you head south, weaving along an almost level crest, which has a diverse array of wildflowers that grow on or about the phyllite outcrops. These rocks derive their sheen from an abundance of mica minerals, which are planar minerals that form crystals. The crystals became aligned more or less parallel to one another when the original volcanic rock was transformed to metamorphic rock by sustained heat and pressure.

After 0.4 mile you reach a junction where the PCT veers right, traversing 1.1 miles over to a saddle from where Hikes 12 and 13, there united, climb to the Sierra Buttes Fire Lookout. In 0.9 mile, that route joins ours. In just 35 yards we reach a second junction, from where the **Tamarack Connection Trail** veers left. This is Trail 12E30 down to the Tamarack Lakes, Hike 15, then is Trail 12E08 from them over to the Sardine Lakes, Hike 14.

Leaving the junction on our Sierra Buttes Trail, we climb moderately to steeply southeast, staying at or close to the ascending ridge. After about 200 feet of elevation gain, at about 7600 feet, mountain hemlocks begin to swell in rank, creating very shady conditions that keep snow lingering through midsummer. If the trail is snowbound when you hike it, watch for blazes on the trees—though by staying near the ascending ridge, you're bound to reach your goal. On route, you weave among dappled, giant "boulders" of pale blue-green metamorphic rock, then have a heart-throbbing view northeast down the Sardine Lakes canyon. You also spy the lofty lookout, which beckons you onward. Soon you arrive at a small **OHV parking area**. If you have an OHV, you could have continued from your trailhead about 0.6 mile down your road to a road junction, turn left, then traverse 2.0 miles to the Sierra Buttes jeep road. If you drive ¾ mile up it to the parking area, your hike to the lookout and back will be a mere 1.5 miles, versus 5.2 along the Hike 16 route.

Those on Hikes 12 and 13 join us here. Our Hike 16 has two choices to the lookout. The first is to start east up the Sierra Buttes jeep road, which is closed to motor vehicles but not to mountain bikes. The second, for hikers, is to take an obvious trail that starts just north of the jeep road and close to the ridgecrest. This goes 0.3 mile up to a junction along the jeep road, and it is a bit shadier, and a bit shorter (but also a bit steeper) than the part of the jeep road below the junction.

Wildflower Plate 11. Northern Sierra flowers.
1 Nuttall's sandwort (white), 2 silky raillardella (yellow), 3 California helianthella (yellow), 4 plain-leaved fawn lily (white with yellow center), 5 Sierra pincushion (northern Sierra chaenactis) (cream to pink), 6 hot-rock penstemon (pale yellow with red veins), 7 California valerian (white), 8 Sierra primrose (rose with yellow center), 9 skunk-leaved (showy) polemonium (pale blue with yellow center).

On the jeep road we now make a moderate, open, sometimes blustery ascent. Wildflower species not seen below begin to appear. You can't help but notice you're approaching the alpine realm. Trees, the few you see, are diminished in stature, shaven by winter's icy winds. Soon you get an awe-inspiring view of the lookout, perched atop a forbidding cliff like an eagle's aerie. Acrophobics, if they don't get weak-kneed here, certainly do when they confront the airy ladders climbing dozens of steps to just below the **Sierra Buttes Fire Lookout**.

The summit area is so small that the lookout actually projects out into space, and through the iron-grating view deck you stand on, you can look down the nearly vertical northeast escarpment. The deep, glaciated Sardine Lakes canyon to the northeast contrasts strongly with the barely eroded slopes up which the jeep road climbs, and from this virtually everyone (including me in the past) has concluded that the giant Sardine Lakes canyon glaciers performed tremendous erosion. Actually, they didn't. Over the last 2 million years of glacial episodes, the canyon may have been widened by only a couple hundred feet and deepened by a similar amount.

You have far-ranging views. On the distant northwest horizon 76 miles away stands snowy Lassen Peak (10,457'), the southernmost major volcano of the Cascade Range. To the southeast, numerous high peaks dot the Lake Tahoe environs. With compass in hand you can identify Mt. Rose (10,776'), 114°; Mt. Lola (9148'), 126°; and the light-gray Crystal Range of Desolation Wilderness (9983' maximum—Pyramid Peak), about 155°. Round Top (10,381') stands just above and left of the Crystal Range, a hefty 72½ miles from our vantage point, ranking as the southernmost peak in the Tahoe Sierra. Many lower summits and ridges, both near and far, are seen in every direction.

❧ 17 ❧
Pacific Crest Trail, Forest Route 93 north to Deer Lake and Summit Lake

Distances:
2.6 miles to Deer Lake jeep road
   0.3 mile on jeep road to Deer Lake
2.9 miles to connecting trail
   0.5 mile on connecting trail to Deer Lake Trail
   0.8 mile to Deer Lake
4.4 miles to Gold Lake jeep road
   0.1 mile on jeep road to Summit Lake
Low/High Elevations: 7020'/7520'
Season: Mid-July through mid-October
Classification: Easy
Maps: 6 and 8
Trailhead: At Packer Lake Saddle—see the Hike 16 trailhead description.

Introduction
The Pacific Crest Trail along this stretch of the Sierra crest is remarkably level, making it ideal for an easy backpack trip. The most popular destination, Deer Lake, is so close that it is best done as a day hike. Of three possible routes to this lake (Hikes 17-19), this one provides the most views, and takes you to arguably the best shore (least visited, least windy, most photogenic). Most hikers will not want to continue on to Summit Lake. However, a fine backpack trip can be made by combining this hike with Hikes 20 and 27: a relatively long but easy trek along the crest, followed by a descent through Little Jamison Creek canyon, with opportunities to visit up to four of its lakes.

Description
From the crossroads at Packer Lake Saddle, our route, the Pacific Crest Trail (PCT), climbs northeast through a red fir/western white pine forest, taking us quickly to a view of Packer Lake, which lies at the base of our ridge. Soon, shady forest yields to sunny shrubland, and then we cross a jeep road bound for the Wallis Mine. The trail next curves northeast for some more views,

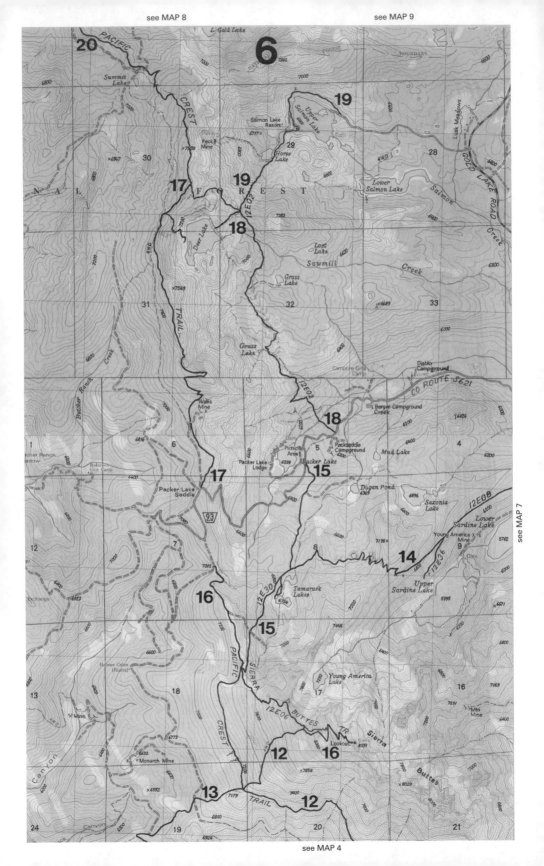

see MAP 7

switchbacks twice, and arrives at the edge of a former clearcut. A two-minute walk north through it to a hemlock-adorned crest saddle saves you ¼ mile of walking. However, the PCT purposely deviates eastward to take you to a rocky point with truly gratifying views.

Although you've hiked but 1¼ miles so far, your minor amount of climbing is essentially done. You next head briefly west, then resume

a northward trek, keeping just west of the ridgecrest. After ¾ mile in this direction, your trail curves right to the ridgecrest, and from it, at a locale just northwest of point 7569 on the map, you have a tree-framed view of alluring Deer Lake. You get additional views as you hike high above its west shore for ⅓ mile to a saddle with the **Deer Lake jeep road**. From the Sierra Buttes north to beyond the scope of the Tahoe Sierra, a jeep road traverses along the crest, and the PCT has adhered close to it. It is drivable, and the occasional hiker may encounter someone in an OHV driving to here, then branching east steeply down the Deer Lake jeep road. In the past, one could drive down to the west shore, but since the 1990s one can drive only half-way down, to a turn-around area. From there, everyone must descend the overly steep, closed jeep road by foot (equestrians will not want to ride down it!). By the shore, the road levels off and continues momentarily south to a spacious campsite near a linear island, just offshore. Jointed bedrock just north of the jeep road offers opportunities to dive into the lake.

Above the lake the PCT traverses 0.3 mile to a second Deer Lake opportunity, the upper end of a **connecting trail** down to it. Being considerably longer, it is much better graded, not a knee-banging descent. It first descends south, then turns abruptly east to soon reach the head of a small, picturesque gully. You descend this, then soon climb south out of it to start an open descent across glaciated bedrock to a junction with the **Deer Lake Trail** (Hike 18). This junction also marks the top end of the Upper Salmon Lake Trail (Hike 19). From here you wind southwest, passing a shallow lakelet midway to the northeast shore of **Deer Lake**. This shore is steep and brushy, so if you want some space for basking or camping, look along the southeast shore.

Back on the PCT at the connecting-trail junction, you walk but a moment to be opposite a small, rocky point, 25 yards to the east. This offers a great view down

Deer Lake, from its west shore

into the Salmon Lakes basin, although you have a similar view just ahead on the trail. Then, just before gaining your first view of Gold Lake, you have a view south of the serrated Sierra Buttes. From the north end of those buttes, the PCT has been adhering faithfully to a crest that many would perceive as the actual Sierra Nevada crest. However, the true crest lies to the east, capped by 8107′ Haskell Peak, almost due east of us, and capped many miles farther southeast along its sinuous backbone by a trio of three 9000+′ summits, Mt. Lola, Basin Peak, and Castle Peak. Unlike our crest, which is metamorphic, the visible Sierra crest is granitic, though its southern half is deeply mantled by volcanic flows and sediments. It is a view which covers a tremendous span of geologic history.

Not far beyond your Gold Lake view, the PCT commences a ¾-mile descent to the **Gold Lake jeep road**. This viewless, partly logged stretch is unappealing, as is small, shallow **Summit Lake**, perched just southwest of a viewless crest saddle just above you. It does, however, have plentiful camping space in its vicinity. Eastward, the jeep road descends to

the west end of Gold Lake, then makes a rutted traverse along its south shore over to a more civilized road near its northeast end. Hike 20 describes the PCT route north from the Gold Lake jeep road.

⇜ 18 ⇝
Deer Lake Trail

Distances:
1.0 mile to first Grass Lake
1.6 miles to trail to second Grass Lake
   0.2 mile on trail to second Grass Lake
2.2 miles to Upper Salmon Lake Trail
2.5 miles to Deer Lake

Low/High Elevations: 6120′/7140′

Season: Early July through mid-October

Classification: Moderate

Map: 6

Trailhead: From Highway 49 about 5 miles above Sierra City, drive 1.3 miles west up Gold Lake Road, then branch left onto County Route S621, usually signed for Packer Lake.

Take it ¼ mile west to a junction, where it turns right, north, then continue 2.4 miles up to Packsaddle Campground. Just within it is trailhead parking. The start of the Deer Lake Trail is about 50 yards back down the county route.

Introduction

A short, popular hike, this trail takes you to deep, relatively large Deer Lake. In addition, two shallow, less visited lakes are easily reached from this trail. With a few hours' effort you can hike to all four Grass Lakes in the Highway 49 region. The first two lie close to our route—the Deer Lake Trail—another is in Lakes Basin (Hike 23) and the northernmost is in Plumas-Eureka State Park (Hike 27).

Description

Leaving the trailhead, we quickly meet and cross several unequal-size creeks that drain Packer Lake and the slopes north of it. By midsummer, only one or two may be flowing. Departing from the lush, streamside vegetation, we begin to climb upward, execute two well-graded switchback legs, and swing past two adjacent lateral-moraine crests. The comfortable underfooting becomes rocky as we curve over to the first Grass Lake's outlet creek, and it remains so almost to the second Grass Lake turnoff. By walking about 100 yards up along the outlet creek, you'll reach

the **first Grass Lake**. You can also reach it by continuing 70 yards up the trail to a switchback, then heading west-southwest briefly over to it. Of the region's four Grass Lakes, this one is the smallest, diminished by invading grass.

From the switchback the Deer Lake Trail climbs first northeast, then northwest, generally across slopes of brushy huckleberry oak. On this ascent you might stop a time or two to admire the Sierra Buttes. Your climb momentarily ends and you walk 35 yards to a **trail** junction on a small flat. From here one can take a short trail east down to the **second Grass Lake**. It is not all that appealing, especially since a strong windstorm in the mid-'90s blew down dozens of large red firs in the vicinity. Larger and deeper than the first Grass Lake, which in late season can be little more than a wet meadow, this grassy-bottomed one is chest-deep, and so is deep enough for humans to swim in, but not for fish. In midsummer the lake warms up too much for trout, and in winter it freezes too deep.

From the trail junction the Deer Lake Trail in about ½ mile first drops into and climbs out of a small cove, then climbs to a boulder-hop of fairly broad Sawmill Creek. If you were to hike cross-country west directly up it, you would reach Deer Lake's outlet in about ¼ mile. A longer but less brushy route is to keep to the trail, which climbs generally moderate-

Deer Lake and Sierra Buttes in June

ly about ¼ mile up to a ridge saddle and the upper end of the northeast-descending **Upper Salmon Lake Trail** (Hike 19). Straight ahead, northwest, a connecting trail climbs about 0.6 mile to the Pacific Crest Trail (Hike 17).

The last stretch of the Deer Lake Trail winds southwest for ¼ mile, passing a shallow lakelet midway to the steep, brushy northeast shore of **Deer Lake**. A use trail circles the lake, and one can head in either direction to find some space for fishing, basking or camping. The best campsites are along the southeast and west shores. At the lake, ice melts rather late, entirely disappearing (in average years) in time for the Fourth of July. However, not until late July does the lake warm enough for pleasant swimming.

⇜ **19** ⇝
Upper Salmon Lake Trail

Distances:
1.0 mile to Horse Lake
1.6 miles to Deer Lake Trail
1.9 miles to Deer Lake
Low/High Elevations: 6510′/7140′
Season: Mid-July through mid-October
Classification: Moderate
Map: 6
Trailhead: From Highway 49 about 5 miles above Sierra City, drive 4.0 miles northwest up Gold Lake Road, then branch left onto the Salmon Lakes Road. After 1.0 mile, you'll see the trailhead, about 70 yards before the Salmon Lake Resort's boat dock.

Introduction
A slightly shorter, alternative approach to popular Deer Lake, this trail provides scenic vistas across the Salmon Lakes basin.

Description
By the Salmon Lake Resort's boat dock there is a phone, which enables you to contact the resort, which lies on the opposite shore. In the past, they have operated a shuttle service (I was offered a free ride). In the future, they

may still offer rides across the lake, although not necessarily for free. Nevertheless, if you want to shave 0.7 mile off your hike up to Deer Lake, you might phone the resort.

The 0.7-mile counterclockwise loop around the north half of Upper Deer Lake is quite easy. On Upper Salmon Lake Trail 12E01 you begin a rocky, moderate ascent up a classic brush slope covered with huckleberry oak, western serviceberry, deer brush, snow bush, manzanita, bitter cherry, and the prostrate subshrub, squaw carpet. The open slopes permit sweeping views. Below you, several picturesque islands, easily reached by short swims from one to another, grow more distant. Upon reaching a flat, your trail commences a moderate descent to the lake's northwest corner. In that vicinity, about 25 yards from the trail, is a rocky viewpoint, which provides a superb view southeast down the lake—reason enough to take the trail instead of a boat.

From the corner the trail heads south along the lake's northwest shore, and it quickly encounters outlying cabins of Salmon Lake Resort. You continue your southbound walk to a crossing of Horse Lake's outlet creek, and just beyond it is the resort's main building. From its far side, start west up a road, which in 0.1 mile climbs along the creek to a short connecting road that bridges the creek to reach additional cabins. Now you turn south-southwest and in a short, gentle climb reach **Horse Lake**. In the early morning calm, this 3½-acre lake is particularly photogenic, when the sunlit, rusty cliffs backdropping the lake are mirrored in it.

Your easy hiking is over. A few short switchbacks lead you up to a sloping bench just south of a creeklet that descends to Horse Lake, seen below. Higher up, your steeply climbing, switchbacking trail offers better views of this lake plus views of Upper Salmon lake and the massive moraine behind it. Note that the moraine isn't that thick; rather, it covers the bedrock ridge with a thin mantle of earth and loose rock. Not too soon you meet the **Deer Lake Trail** atop a saddle, and you follow its last stretch to **Deer Lake**, as described in the last paragraph of Hike 18.

Upper Salmon Lake

⋘ 20 ⋙
Pacific Crest Trail, from Summit Lake north to Trail above Wades Lake

Distances:
4.4 miles to Gold Lake jeep road
  0.1 mile on jeep road to Summit Lake
5.7 miles to first Lakes Basin trail
  1.0 mile on trail to Round Lake
7.8 miles to second Lakes Basin trail
  1.7 miles on trails to Long Lake
9.0 miles to third Lakes Basin trail
  1.8 miles on trails to Long Lake
10.3 miles to jeep road above Wades Lake
10.6 miles to Trail 11E13
11.6 miles to Wades Lake spur trail
  0.2 mile on spur trail to Wades Lake
12.2 miles to Trail 11E11
  0.9 mile on trail to Jamison Lake
  1.1 miles on trail to Rock Lake
13.1 miles to northwest corner of Grass Lake
14.4 miles to Trail 11E13 trailhead

Low/High Elevations: 7050′; 5260′ at Little
  Jamison Canyon trailhead / 7360′

Season: Mid-July through mid-October

Classification: Easy along the PCT; moderate
  along routes up to it

Maps: 6 and 8

Trailheads: If you start at Packer Lake Saddle, see the Hike 17 trailhead. If you start from Summit Lake, you first have to get to Gold Lake. From Highway 49 about 5 miles above Sierra City, drive 6.4 miles northwest up Gold Lake Road to a paved road, on the left, signed for Gold Lake's boat ramp. (If you were to continue 0.6 mile farther, you would reach a junction, from which one road heads southwest over to the nearby corner of Gold Lake, while another one heads northeast, bound for Frazier Falls.) The boat-ramp road winds ½ mile down to a junction, from where the main road angles sharply right over to the boat ramp and adjacent picnicking and camping, while the Gold Lake jeep road continues directly ahead. If you have a high-clearance vehicle, you should be able to drive this, although a 4WD is preferable. This goes about 2¾ miles to a junction on the far shore of Gold Lake, then 1.0 mile up to the Pacific Crest Trail near Summit Lake. This junction is about 300 yards past one with a short spur road up to Little Gold Lake. If you are able to drive to Summit Lake, you then likely have the ability to drive along the crest road that parallels the PCT both north and south of the lake.

Introduction
Although this hike is described from the Gold Lake jeep road northward, my intent is to begin the hike 4.4 trail miles earlier, at the Packer Lake Saddle, which is the start of Hike 17. Hike 20 is the middle leg of a relatively easy 14.4-mile backpack trip from Packer Lake Saddle to the Little Jamison Canyon trailhead. Should you take the spur trails to Wades, Jamison, and Rock lakes, then your total distance will be 17.2 miles, and about 18 miles even if you include a drop to Deer Lake. The first leg, Hike 17, has easy ups and downs, as does the middle leg, and the last leg—the first part of Hike 27 in reverse direction—is a descent.

Description
This hike begins from the intersection of the Pacific Crest Trail with the **Gold Lake jeep road**. (Hike 17 covers the stretch of PCT from the Packer Lake Saddle north to here.) Just southwest of the intersection is a ridgecrest, beside which lies small, shallow **Summit Lake**. It has ample campsites, but these have an overabundance of mosquitoes before about late July. Definitely treat the lake's water before drinking it. North from the jeep road the PCT parallels a crest-hugging jeep road that begins by Summit Lake. The PCT first parallels the jeep road at a distance, then alongside it. Near the north end of the fairly level ridge, a jeep road cuts northeast across the crest and, 1⅓ miles along your hike, you have three route choices. First, you can head a few paces west to the jeep road you've been paralleling and take it ⅓ mile northwest down to Oakland Pond, which is like Summit Lake in water purity and camping potential. About 200 yards past the pond, where the road turns west, a trail climbs moderately north ⅓ mile back to the PCT. Second, you can follow the northeast-heading jeep road, which is the **first Lakes Basin trail** you encounter. The PCT does this for a few yards before leaving it, but you can continue onward along it, the road soon narrows to a trail, 12E34, and later it passes along the west side of a pond. Then 300 yards below it, the trail curves northwest to a

Wades Lake, from Trail 11E13

5-foot-deep-gap. The trail ends at a junction, from which you take a main trail west steeply down to the nearby southeast shore of **Round Lake**. Camping is not allowed in the Lakes Basin, so continue past this lake to Silver Lake, then west above it to Hellgrammite Lake, then west back to the PCT via one of two more trails that connect it with the Lakes Basin. The third route—the least interesting in my opinion—is to take the lakeless PCT.

This route leaves the northeast-bound jeep road in a few paces, then climbs almost to point 7541, switchbacking needlessly several times just south of it. From the switchbacks you get excellent views to the west, particularly of the closer terrain that includes Snake Lake, Little Deer Lake, and Oakland Pond. North of point 7541 you have views down into well-named Lakes Basin, which in the past has harbored past glaciers. Glaciation in the entire Sierra Buttes-Lakes Basin area was quite extensive. From the Sierra Buttes, glaciers descended first northeast to the North Yuba river canyon, and then briefly down it. From the Lakes Basin and the canyons both east and west of it, glaciers extended north down to about the western edge of fault-formed Mohawk Valley.

Steep slopes of granitelike rock prevent us from dropping into the sparkling Lakes Basin. The bedrock here, as along most of our chapter's trails, is metamorphosed volcanic rocks that were erupted along the western edge of North America about 350-400 million years ago. (Today's lands to the west did not exist back then.) At a nearby saddle, our solitary views of the Lakes Basin disappear, and we drop back into forest cover and come to a junction. Had you taken the Oakland Pond route, you'd be climbing northwest to meet the PCT here.

The PCT heads briefly west to a ridge that provides views to the south and west, then enters viewless forest for a traverse almost a mile long. Next, it curves southwest through a shady forest growing on a flat, ill-defined crest that can harbor snow patches into July. Momentarily we meet a former jeep road, now the **second Lakes Basin trail**. this descends 0.5 mile north to a ridge and a junction with Trail 12E30, which traverses east to Hellgrammite Lake. Just north on the ridge is a second trail junction, this one with the third Lakes Basin trail. From this junction, a ridge trail goes 0.5 mile to a third junction, from which you can climb north to Mt. Elwell, descend northeast to the north corner of Long Lake, or descend southeast to the west shore of Long Lake. Both trails down to **Long Lake** are about equally long, roughly ⅔ mile.

The PCT now curves south to a ridge, where you have a view of the Sierra Buttes, then curves west to an excellent point, from where you see Hawley Meadow and mostly hidden Hawley Lake. You re-enter forest again and descend ⅓ mile to a jeep-road crossing at a county-line crest saddle. A spring-fed creek lies 200 yards east along the jeep road, which serves as the **third Lakes Basin trail**. This route goes 0.7 mile east to the just-mentioned second trail junction on a ridge, from which you can take one of two trails down to **Long Lake**. For those who have made excursions through the Lakes Basin, this route is the last one to join the PCT.

Immediately west of the saddle is a diminutive pond that nevertheless has enough staying power to hold water through most, if not all, of the summer. You could camp in this locality. The PCT briefly parallels the jeep road west, then swings north, taking a tortuous route that has to be hiked to be believed. Twice we almost touch the jeep

road, only to veer away, but finally, after 1⅓ miles, we cross it near a high point on the Sierra crest. Leave the PCT at this intersection and take this **jeep road above Wades Lake** northwest to a relatively nearby junction with **Trail 11E13**. Follow this trail, which is described in the reverse direction in Hike 27. This route descends to lateral trails to **Wades, Jamison, and Rock lakes**, and it traverses past **Grass Lake** before descending moderately to the Little Jamison Canyon **trailhead**. Alternatively, you can continue along the PCT, but such an adventure is beyond the northern limits of this book. (The entire trail is covered in a two-volume set, *The Pacific Crest Trail*, by me and others.)

❧ 21 ❧
Round Lake Loop

Distances:
1.9 miles to Round Lake
2.4 miles to Silver Lake
2.9 miles to Cub Lake
3.1 miles to Little Bear Lake
3.2 miles to northwest shore of Big Bear Lake
3.4 miles to northeast corner of Big Bear Lake
4.0 miles to trailhead
Low/High Elevations: 6470'/6850'
Season: Early July through mid-October
Classification: Easy
Map: 8
Trailhead: From Highway 49 about 5 miles above Sierra City, drive 8 miles northwest up Gold Lake Road, then branch left at the Gold Lake Lodge road, which is immediately before the Plumas/Sierra county-line crest. Go 100 yards on it to a parking area.

Introduction
This relaxing trip, an easy morning hike, takes you to five lakes in the southern half of Lakes Basin. Round, Silver, and Big Bear lakes are anglers' favorites, and are also appealing to photographers and swimmers. No camping is allowed in Lakes Basin.

Description
From the parking area take the broad path that parallels the Gold Lake Lodge road,

reaching, in 0.2 mile, a trail that departs for Bear, Silver, and Long lakes. Most hikers turn right here, since this route is the quickest way to most of the five lakes, including Big Bear and Little Bear lakes, which lie 0.4 mile and 0.7 mile from this junction respectively. We'll return along this trail but first will take the long way to these lakes, one that offers views of the lakes we'll visit.

Keeping to the broad Round Lake Trail, a former jeep road, we hike past western white pines and red firs in a forest that is open enough to have a meadowy, wildflowered floor. After a short jog north-northwest we reach a viewpoint, about 0.8 mile from our trailhead, and see justifiably popular Big Bear Lake spreading below us. Those who can't wait can make a cross-country descent about 250 yards northwest to its nearest shore. Those avoiding the temptation to shortcut will continue 0.5 mile on the Round Lake Trail to a beautiful lakelet, a worthy goal in itself. After the snow melts, usually by the Fourth of July, the lake becomes quite warm, and it is deep enough for swimming.

From the lakelet's south end our path soon makes a short climb, circles counterclockwise around a small bedrock mass, and on its far side meets a junction with Trail 12E34. This ¾-mile-long connecting trail starts a steep ascent, which remains so up a ridge, passes through its low cleft, and then presents the hiker with good views of the Lakes Basin. As the ridge eases off, the trail goes through a miniature gap, swings southeast toward a gully and briefly gives one a glimpse of Gold Lake. The trail next turns south and climbs to a small saddle just west of a hidden, rock-rimmed pond, then soon broadens to a jeep road and reaches the Pacific Crest Trail (this junction being the "first Lakes Basin trail" in the previous hike).

Our loop route, however, descends steeply to the southeast shore of **Round Lake**. Mine tailings and mechanical debris, both derived from the abandoned mine above the lake, now fill part of the deep lake's southeastern side. Quartz blasted from the mine's veins is recognizable among the rock fragments in the tailings, and it was in this vein quartz that miners had hoped to find gold. A narrow trail skirts the lake's southeast shore, and on it we reach the jump-across outlet creek. From here our rocky trail makes an open climb northwest above the lake toward the crest of a moraine. Just south of the moraine's crest—and an easy walk west from us—lies a shallow triangular depression that may contain

Fishing in Round Lake

Long Lake and Mt. Elwell, viewed from a ridge above the lake's south shore

water in early season. Atop the moraine crest we start north and immediately see our next goal, **Silver Lake**, before we descend to its east shore. Fringed with lodgepole and western white pines, mountain hemlocks, and red firs, this lake has considerably more appeal than Round Lake, whose shoreline tends to be more brushy and is partly covered with mine tailings. Before August, however, shade-loving mosquitoes may make you prefer Round Lake. A use trail circles Silver Lake, which like all lakes in the Lakes Basin, is heavily fished. The lake's shallow, warm midsummer water invites an enjoyable swim, but by late August the temperature begins to drop and the lake's outlet creek has already dried up. Our trail crosses this east-flowing creek, near which we have a glimpse down-basin at Cub Lake and the Bear lakes, and then we curve over to a junction just above Silver Lake's north arm. Climbing west from here is a trail that soon divides immediately before Hellgrammite Lake. Trail 12E30 climbs toward the Pacific Crest Trail (Hike 20), while Trail 11E14 rambles over to the Long Lake environs and up toward Mt. Elwell (Hikes 23 and 24).

From the Silver Lake junction, our loop trail in about 220 yards first meanders northward, crosses a small flat, and then climbs briefly to a

view of island-dotted Long Lake, which is also wide and deep. Although less than a mile long, it appears larger than it actually is, perhaps because of the stunted growth of the shoreline conifers. Leaving this ridge view, from which the east-dipping strata of Mt. Elwell are readily apparent, we descend east 100 yards to a junction in a small flat that lies between two low crests. The trail going northeast takes you to Long Lake's southeast shore (next hike) before descending to a roadend trailhead above Lakes Basin Campground.

We skip southeast over a low crest and descend to a use trail, which goes about 50 yards south down to circular, shallow **Cub Lake**. Paralleling this lake's unseen drainage eastward, our trail soon crosses just above the north shore of linear, pine-rimmed **Little Bear Lake**. Little Bear and Big Bear lakes are separated by a ridge, and from our trail a well-used path descends about 120 yards to a low, narrow part of the ridge where the two lakes almost touch. The use path then follows the east shore of Little Bear Lake to its end, from where the lake's 40-foot-long outlet creek drains 4 vertical feet down into Big Bear Lake. Little Bear Lake is about 15 feet deep, and is a fine one for swimming. Big Bear Lake, more than four times as deep and six times the size,

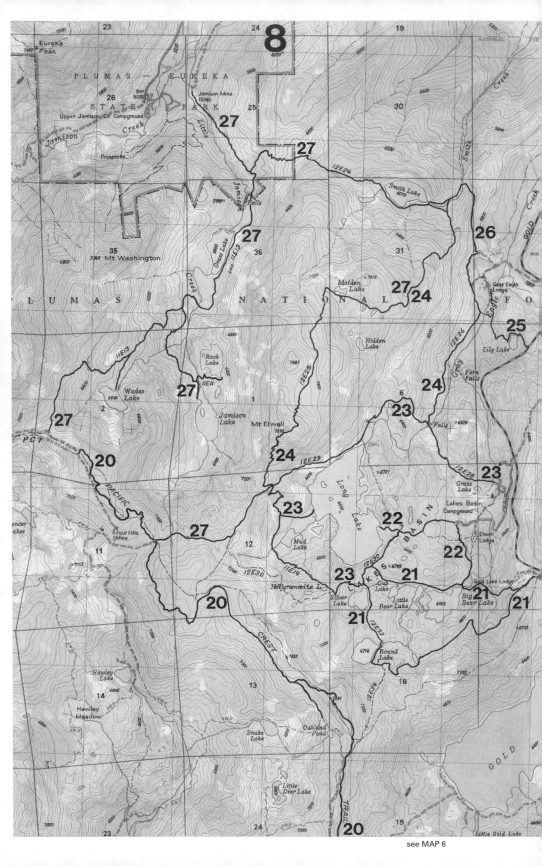

8

see MAP 6

can be a bit cooler, though it still has good midsummer swimming. Along this larger lake's wavy, rocky shoreline, you'll find good spots to fish, and to dive and swim from.

Back at the start of the use trail, from which both Bear lakes are seen, we briefly ascend and then descend to the **northwest shore of Big Bear Lake**, and cross east over a peninsula. Soon we arrive at the **northeast corner of Big Bear Lake** and an adjacent trail junction. Here, Hike 22, which has coincided with our route since the last trail junction, departs northward toward Elwell Lodge and the roadend trailhead above Lakes Basin Campground. We turn south, in 45 yards cross Big Bear's outlet, and then leave this extremely popular, moderately large lake behind as we start down beside its outlet creek.

At first the outlet creek is a flowing pond, but it soon constricts before enlarging into a second pond, which is seen after the trail crosses a ridge above it. Our trail now traverses southeast to a usually dry creek in a meadowy gully. We then ascend eastward, crossing a boggy flat and then arriving at the edge of a cluster of willows and a trail junction. The route straight ahead climbs northeast moderately up to nearby Gold Lake Lodge. Our route veers east, then climbs moderately but briefly to the Round Lake Trail, along which we retrace the first 0.2 mile of our loop route back to our **trailhead**.

⤝ 22 ⤞
Bear Lakes Loop

Distances:
0.5 mile to Long Lake spur trail
0.2 mile on spur trail to Long Lake
1.0 mile to Cub Lake
1.2 miles to Little Bear Lake
1.3 miles to northwest shore of Big Bear Lake
1.5 miles to northeast corner of Big Bear Lake
1.7 miles to trail to Elwell Lodge
2.0 miles to trailhead

Low/High Elevations: 6330'/6670'

Season: Early July through mid-October

Classification: Easy

Map: 8

Trailheads: From Highway 49 about 5 miles above Sierra City, drive 8 miles northwest up Gold Lake road to its county-line crest, then 1 mile farther to the Lakes Basin Campground road. If you're driving south from Highway 89, this junction is almost 6¾ miles up Gold Lake road. The campground road curves south, immediately passing a short spur road down to the campground's Group Camp. Then, 0.4 mile from the Gold Lake Road, you reach a junction, the campground road switchbacking north before curving to a split, each fork ending on a north-south road in the campground's

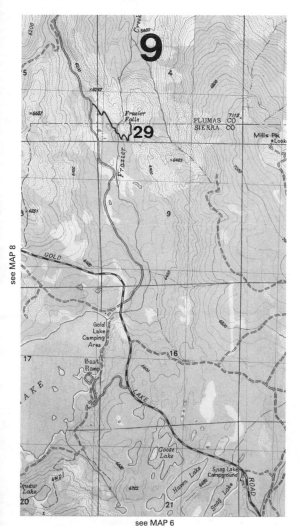

see MAP 8

hub. The Grass Lake Trail starts from an obvious west-side spur on the north part of the road. You, however, ignore the junction with the campground road, continuing south about 250 yards before curving north, then west to a junction with the south-climbing Elwell Lodge Road, 0.8 mile from the Gold Lake Road. You drive ahead a short 0.2 mile up to road's end with trailhead parking for about a dozen vehicles. Two trails start from here: the Long Lake Trail traverses west, while the Bear Lake Trail climbs south.

Introduction

The easiest lakes loop in the Lakes Basin, this hike leads you to four lakes, including one short excursion to giant Long Lake. For those who desire a quick sampling of the Lakes Basin's beauty and charm, this short hike is perfect. No camping is allowed in Lakes Basin.

Description

Walking west on Long Lake Trail 12E30, we immediately cross a creek, then quickly start a moderate climb fro a flat. Doing so, we exchange the shade of white firs and lodgepole pines for fairly continuous sunlight on a more open, brushy slope. Wildflowers often adorn the trail's side, and a short distance up-trail we pass a low, granitelike cliff of metarhyolite, on which rock climbers can brush up their techniques.

Just below the low cliff we cross a wisp of a creek, bordered with lush wildflowers and shrubs. From here we climb to a small flat, shaded by lodgepoles, and on it meet a foot trail. This curves southeast and then progresses eastward, crossing the Bear Lake Trail before descending to the west grounds of Elwell Lodge.

Beyond the foot trail we make a hike shorter than the one we've just completed, ascending almost to a ridge, and we arrive at a junction with the **Long Lake spur trail**. Being very close to the lake, we continue west in its direction, winding up to the ridge and almost immediately dropping to a small bay on the northeast shore of **Long Lake**, only ⅔ mile from our trailhead. At this bay, which is one of the huge lake's readily accessible shores, local residents in the past had obtained permits to keep small fishing boats here. A use trail connects this bay with the lake's outlet, to the north.

After exploring the small bay or perhaps trying your luck at shoreline fishing, backtrack over the low ridge and cruise down to the last junction. From it the main trail climbs southwest and then descends a gully to a trail junction in a small flat. Hike 21, coming from the southwest, descends to this junction, while Hikes 23 and 24 head southwest up from it. You might note that although we're very close to Long Lake's south shore, which

Big Bear Lake

is over 100 feet below us, we can't see the lake at all. A moraine blocks our view north down it, as another moraine blocks our view southeast down toward the Bear lakes. The gully in which our trail descended to this flat separates these two linear products of glacial deposition.

The route for the next 0.7 mile coincides with that of Hike 21, which you should consult for details. Climb briefly southeast over the low, bouldery moraine, descend to **Cub Lake**, and pass the north shores of **Little Bear Lake** and **Big Bear Lake**. At the **northeast corner of Big Bear Lake**, with barely ½ mile left to go, our trail splits from Hike 21, and we descend northward, briefly touching a meander in the lake's outlet creek. Not far beyond this meander is a junction with a **trail to Elwell Lodge**, not far below us. We keep to the Bear Lake Trail, which traverses around a small ridge before descending to our **trailhead**. Midway along this paved stretch, we cross the east-west Elwell Lodge-Long Lake trail, which we had encountered near the start of our hike.

⊰⊱ 23 ⊰⊱
Long Lake Loop

Distances: 0.5 mile to Long Lake spur trail
   0.2 mile on spur trail to Long Lake
0.8 mile to trail to Cub and Bear lakes
1.0 mile to north shore of Silver Lake
1.2 miles to junction near Hellgrammite Lake
2.1 miles to Long Lake spur trail
   0.2 mile on spur trail to Long Lake
2.5 miles to Trail 12E25
3.3 miles to Long Lake's dam
4.3 miles to Trail 12E26
5.1 miles to Grass Lake trailhead
5.7 miles to Long Lake trailhead
Low/High Elevations: 6190′/7020′
Season: Early July through mid-October
Classification: Moderate
Map: 8
Trailhead: Same as the Hike 22 trailhead.

Introduction
All three good access points to the shores of Long Lake are encountered along this route.

You need not, of course, restrict yourself to these three accessed shoreline segments, but rather can investigate cross-country alternatives to virtually untouched shores. No camping is allowed in Lakes Basin.

Description
Hike 22 describes the first mile of the route, which climbs to a Long Lake spur trail, ascends it to Long Lake and then descends, and then climbs southwest above the lake's south shore to a junction with a trail to Cub and Bear lakes (Hike 21). From this junction we climb a bit southwest, then meander south over to a nearby junction with Trail 12E33 above the north shore of Silver Lake. This lovely lake merits at least a brief delay, and if you're trying to maximize your lake visits, you can take Trail 12E33 ½ mile south to hemmed-in Round Lake. Otherwise, scramble westward up a brushy ridge packed with pleasing panoramas that extend across virtually all of the Lakes Basin. Leaving the ridge, our trail now climbs southwest to a junction near Hellgrammite Lake. (Hellgrammites are aquatic, predatory, toe-biting larvae of dobsonflies. These larvae, up to 2 inches long, make excellent trout bait.)

Westward, in 1.1 miles Trail 12E30 first passes above the south shore of this photogenic lakelet, soon passes above a second, which is more of a grassy pond, then passes just below a third, which is more of a wet grassy meadow (dry in late season). From it, rock climbers can scamper ¼ mile upslope to the base of some metarhyolite cliffs. Next the trail tops a flat ridge, and then it plunges down to a gully before climbing moderately to steeply up to a former jeep road. If you were to follow its seldom used stretch south through a forest that has snow lasting well into July, you'd reach the Pacific Crest Trail (Hike 20) in just under ½ mile. North, a short stretch goes to a nearby trail junction. Hike 27, advancing east along a former jeep road to this junction, then continues northeast on a trail about ½ mile over to a junction with our route.

Our loop route climbs northwest on Trail 11E14 over to nearby Hellgrammite Lake. This grassy bottomed, fairly deep lakelet reflects, on tranquil days, the bold cliffs southwest of it. Attaining the high point of the climb before hurtling down toward Long Lake, one may feel compelled—particularly on a hot day—to take a plunge into the lakelet's refreshing water.

Continuing onward, we quickly reach and cross the lakelet's northbound outlet creek, and then descend its rocky gully, pausing momentarily to glance north toward domineering Mt. Elwell, which is the only *real* mountain in the Lakes Basin vicinity. The subsequently metamorphosed volcanic rocks that make up this mass, roughly 350 million years old, appear as distinct layers—which are individual flows of andesite—all dipping northeast.

Our sometimes steep descent northwest enters a red fir/mountain hemlock forest, lessens its gradient, and levels off near the crossing of a major but seasonal creek, which debouches from a striking V-shaped minigorge and empties into chest-deep Mud Lake. Steering clear of the water-saturated westshore meadow, which has been invaded by alders and willows, our trail keeps within the dry confines of red firs before curving north

and then climbing a few yards up a slope to a junction with a **Long Lake spur trail**. This trail briefly ascends, then descends gradually toward **Long Lake**. Once at the shore, the trail veers left, traversing about 60 yards north to bedrock that is suitable for diving off or fishing from. About 250 yards offshore is the closest of several rocky islands. Because the lake is the basin's largest, it is also the slowest to warm up, although it does get into the mid 60s around early August, making a swim at least to the first island feasible.

Backtracking to the main trail, we engage in a moderate ascent northwest up to the edge of some orange-brown metamorphic bedrock, then switchback up through a seasonally soggy, sloping meadow. Above it the trail climbs quite steeply up to a junction with **Trail 12E25** on a small, almost level, tree-dotted bench. Hike 27, which has left the Pacific Crest Trail to traverse first a jeep road east and then a ridge trail northeast to reach this bench, commences a switchbacking route up this trail to Mt. Elwell's summit.

We take Trail 12E29 northeast, which quickly arrives at a gully and starts down it.

Long Lake

The trail then crosses a huge talus slope, from which you have a grand view of the spectacular island-studded lake below you. A steady descent down the unstable talus trail takes you almost to the lake's waters, which lie just beyond a few yards of dense willows and tobacco brush. Now you climb briefly, and then traverse across a brush-covered bench to two very different, cabin-size boulders. The first is smooth, looks granitic, and bears no resemblance to the cliffs above or to the bedrock you stand on. Where did this 100-ton boulder come from? If you've walked along the Pacific Crest Trail—a little over one mile southwest of here (Hike 20)—you'll recognize the mega-boulder as a huge chunk of Paleozoic metarhyolite, which was transported here by the Lakes Basin glacier. Glacier-transported boulders, which are usually smaller than this one, are called *erratics,* and are easy to spot when they rest on bedrock that is quite different in composition.

The rough, second mega-boulder obviously broke loose from the cliffs above. It, too, is a metamorphosed Paleozoic volcanic rock, but its composition is a grade of andesite or basalt. The watermelon-size blocks within its structure bear close resemblance to the blocks in the autobrecciated, much younger lava flows seen near Round Lake on Hike 92, and this large boulder probably had a similar origin.

In 120 yards, just beyond a Jeffrey pine, we come to our third and final approach to the shores of Long Lake—a short spur trail to a small check **dam** at the lake's north end. The shoreline vegetation is open enough for you to scramble around on bedrock to a good fishing site, a swimming area, or a sunbathing slab. You may also note a faint use trail, heading south from the dam, which undulates south above the lake's east shore.

Once back on the main trail, we cross some springs just after our last lake view disappears. These support a seasonal display of colorful wildflowers, which contrast with somber, aged junipers. These slowly growing trees send out roots that seek, and sometimes enlarge, every adjacent crack in the bedrock. Like the wildflowers, a juniper needs soil nutrients and water.

Immediately east of us we see an unmistakable "footprint" of a former glacier—a smoothed-over bedrock knoll. Past glaciers, despite being about 600 feet thick in this vicinity, were powerless to erode this knoll. Closer inspection will reveal that rocks and grit the glacier dragged along its bottom have striated the bedrock in the direction of glacier movement and at best have gouged out only small, angular cavities. Glaciers simply do not have the Herculean excavating powers touted in so many geology texts. Seeking out all nearby cracks atop this glacier-polished knoll are the massive roots of a large Jeffrey pine.

Continuing past it, we begin a descent, immediately negotiate two switchbacks, and then descend across *joint-controlled,* shallow gullies that have been polished by glaciers. Beyond them we skirt the north edge of a grassy meadow, which cradles a lakelet that diminishes greatly by Labor Day. Beyond low bedrock outcrops above the meadow's east edge, we descend northeast down a brushy slope and soon find ourselves momentarily alongside a seasonal creek before we abruptly turn southeast and head for Long Lake's outlet, Gray Eagle Creek. Midway down it, we traverse a small, seasonally spongy meadow, and by a seasonal creek near it far end you may see exposed ground water that had previously flowed through the porous soil. Much of the drainage of a basin, such as Lakes Basin, is accomplished through the ground. The lakes and creeks we see are just surface exposures of ground water.

Lower down, we reach a junction with **Trail 12E26** just 25 yards before Gray Eagle Creek. Both trail and creek descend to Gray Eagle Lodge and its environs (Hike 24 comes up this route). We take Trail 12E28, which crosses the nearby creek. In early season, wide, swift Gray Eagle Creek can be a dangerous ford, especially since the crossing is only 20 yards above where the lively creek turns east and cascades down a rock cliff. Be extremely careful.

Beyond the ford we have an uphill hike rich in verdant growth. Alders and dogwoods rise above thimbleberries, currants, mountain ash, and willows that might hide a lurking coyote. Except in autumn, when it is blazing yellow, mountain dogbane usually goes unseen while ranger's buttons, corn lilies, paintbrushes, and several species of sunflowers add their colors to the greenery. We keep our feet dry in early season by skirting around a boggy meadow rather than slogging through it, then climb up on a ground moraine, which we'll tread upon almost every step of the way from here to trail's end.

After a climb up to a bend in the moraine, we encounter a short spur trail that descends to a shallow, reflective pond overly rich in pond lilies. Curving eastward, we now have a gently undulating path to follow, which takes up past the northern fringe of poorly defined Grass Lake—more of a meadow in late summer. We then bridge its outlet creek near the site of Lake Center Lodge. This was closed by the Forest Service in 1974 and its buildings were removed. While in existence, the lodge's grounds had a grassy lawn beside the creek, and its bank had steps into a part of the creek that had been molded into a swimming pool.

Immediately beyond the bridge across the creek, you reach the **Grass Lake trailhead**, complete with parking and an adjacent picnic area. To get back to your original trailhead, follow the Lakes Basin Campground road south to its end, from which you take a former road, now a trail, first south then southwest over to its terminus opposite the start of the south-climbing Elwell Lodge Road. Here you get on the paved east-west road and hike a short 0.2 mile up to your **Long Lake trailhead**.

⋙ 24 ⋘
Mt. Elwell, from Lakes Basin Campground

Distances:
2.5 miles to Trail 12E25
3.2 miles to Mt. Elwell summit cleft
4.7 miles to Maiden Lake
4.9 miles to Hidden Lake cross-country route
   0.2 mile on route to Hidden Lake
6.3 miles to Smith Lake cutoff trail
6.4 miles to Smith Lake Trail
6.6 miles to Smith Creek Trail

7.2 miles to Gray Eagle trailhead
8.2 miles to Fern Falls spur trail
   0.1 mile on spur trail to Fern Falls
8.7 miles to Trail 12E29
9.5 miles to Grass Lake trailhead
10.1 miles to Long Lake trailhead
Low/High Elevations: 5790'/7750'
Season: Mid-July through mid-October
Classification: Moderate
Map: 8
Trailhead: Same as the Hike 22 trailhead. However, you can end this hike at the Gray Eagle trailhead, which is the Hike 26 trailhead.

Introduction
Unbeatable for Lakes Basin views is a climb to Mt. Elwell's summit area. This loop trip traverses lake, stream, slope, and crest terrains and exposes you to all the species of trees you'll find in the basin. Rock climbers will find numerous opportunities to practice their art, particularly on the south slope of Mt. Elwell. One can shorten the hike by climbing only to the summit and then backtracking, or by leaving a second vehicle at the Gray Eagle trailhead near Gray Eagle Lodge. No camping is allowed in Lakes Basin.

Description
The first half of Hike 23 describes our route up to a junction with **Trail 12E25** on a small flat on the south slope of Mt. Elwell. We go a few yards north-northwest before turning left and diagonaling west-southwest up an easy grade to the mountain's well-defined south ridge, which is usually snow-free by early July. Starting north up a trail, climbers will immediately notice that the massive metavolcanic cliffs ahead, which make up most of the south slope, offer dozens of climbing routes.

At our first switchback, red firs add a photogenic touch to our view of Long Lake, and these trees offer shade along various parts of our steep ascent. Associated with this scattered cover are the trees' usual companions, spiny-seeded chinquapin and lowly pinemat manzanita. About 300 feet in elevation below the top, our trail veers west far enough to present us with views of Jamison and Rock lakes. Now a series of short, steep zigzags confronts

Summit view of Long Lake, Lakes Basin, and the Sierra Buttes

us, and guides us upward. Climbers will find some easily accessible routes just below the peak's southeast summit, and not far above them the trail skirts the base of the peak's northwest summit, which has enjoyable, blocky climbing routes—some of them overhanging.

Very soon we're atop **Mt. Elwell** at a cleft between the two low summits, and discover aromatic tobacco brush thriving up here above the red firs we passed along the trail and the mountain hemlocks we'll soon pass. Both of Elwell's summits are easy scrambles, although harder ways up each are very easy to find. The lower, southeast summit provides the more impressive views, for the entire, glaciated Lakes Basin, dominated by Long Lake, spreads out before you. Beyond Silver and Round lakes lies the deep canyon of unseen Gold Lake, and rising above all on the horizon are the indisputable Sierra Buttes. Elwell's higher, northwest summit looks down on glaciated Little Jamison Creek canyon, whose sides were smoothed and slightly steepened by the ice.

From the top, the shortest way back to the trailhead is to return the way you came. Most people do. Our route, however, completes a loop trip, utilizing the less used trail from

Smith Lake. snow patches just below the summit cleft linger some years till September, and if you are hiking this route in July you could have a route-finding situation waiting for you.

A brief, steep descent northeast leads us over blocks and into the outskirts of a predominantly mountain-hemlock forest—the kind of forest mosquitoes love. Red firs and western white pines soon increase their numbers along our winding, usually descending trail, and just before rounding a ridge, ¾ mile from the summit cleft, and commencing a steeper descent, we pass through a small, sloping meadow. One-quarter mile from the ridge you'll spy a house-sized block off on the right, which certainly will appeal to climbers. It even has a Jeffrey pine on its summit, from which you can rappel or set up a top-rope belay. There are several scramble routes up to its summit that can be done unroped by cautious climbers, and the view from its almost flat top is worth the brief effort. To the northeast and southeast below you lie Maiden and Hidden lakes, and between them, in the middle distance, stands Beckwourth Peak (7255'). Beyond it lies flat, fault-formed Sierra Valley and to its north rise the 8000' peaks of the Dixie and Diamond mountains.

Our trail now descends north, levels off and turns southeast, immediately encountering the shoreline of waist-deep, grass-lined **Maiden Lake**. A thoroughly integrated forest surrounds it, composed of mountain hemlock, red fir, western white pine, and lodgepole pine. Beyond this small lake, an almost level, eastward-winding trail leads us past three lakelets. Between the first and second, you may find a trail sign pointing the way to not-so-hidden Hidden Lake. An essentially **cross-country route**, starting out as a faint trail, departs south toward the lake, which lies 0.2 mile south. **Hidden Lake** is a hemmed-in, green gem, which is good for swimming but not for fishing.

After arcing around the north shore of the second lakelet, we climb above and away from the third, and smallest, lakelet, which dries up before summer's end. We now meander northeastward down a broad ridgecrest which has a mantle of glacial deposits, making it appear to be a lateral moraine. It is shaded by an open stand of red firs, western white pines, and—surprisingly—sugar pines. Foot-long cones, drooping from the ends of long branches, identify this prime-lumber tree (which in the Sierra Nevada has been over-logged in the past, greatly reducing its numbers). Farther down the ridgecrest, our route becomes more brushy and open, and then we curve left, leave the crest, and re-enter forest cover.

Soon we meet a short, east-curving spur trail, which ends at a viewpoint on the crest. From it we see what we just saw a few minutes earlier. Mills Peak Lookout rises above us in the southeast while flat-topped Beckwourth Peak stands in the northeast. Directly across the canyon, the large, linear, east-side, *true* lateral moraine left by past Lakes Basin glaciers is readily apparent. Back on the main trail, we descend a gully northward for about 300 yards to the **Smith Lake cutoff trail**. If you are following Hike 27, branch left onto it to traverse northwest over to campsites on the forested southeast side of nearby Smith Lake. Our route continues north, quickly reaches Smith Creek and immediately beyond it comes to a junction with the **Smith Lake Trail**. The lake's outlet is attained by following the trail west about 250 yards upstream.

We hike downstream, following the creek's damp bank, whose lush vegetation provides a good home and hunting ground for orange-striped garter snakes—harmless unless you're an amphibian, a small fish, or an invertebrate. One way of differentiating the aquatic Sierra garter snake from the terrestrial mountain garter snake is that, when frightened, the former tends to escape into water while the latter tends to hide on land.

Not far downstream, we come to a junction with the **Smith Creek Trail**, and immediately cross multibranched Smith Creek before we leave the shade of red and white firs and top the low crest of a legitimate lateral moraine. An open, steady trail south now guides us down the moraine's brushy, bouldery slope, and we can be thankful we're not engaged in a hot afternoon climb up it. At first, Beckwourth and Mills peaks are visible, but both disappear before we reach the **Gray Eagle trailhead**. You end your hike here if you've left a second vehicle here to shuttle you back to your original Lakes Basin trailhead.

Otherwise, take Trail 12E26—the upper part of the Gray Eagle Creek Trail—which starts a traverse southward across gullied slopes, reaching a junction in ¼ mile with an old trail that descends northeast to the northern grounds of Gray Eagle Lodge. In another ¼ mile the main trail reaches a second junction. If you were to continue east, you would reach Gray Eagle Creek in 65 yards, fording it above a small waterfall. From the east bank the trail continues about 100 yards southeast to the Lily Lake Trail (Hike 25).

From the second junction we continue up Trail 12E26, relishing its easy, almost level, up-canyon climb through a mid-Sierran forest belt of Douglas-fir, white fir, incense-cedar, sugar pine, and Jeffrey pine. About ½ mile from the previous junction we reach a third, with the **Fern Falls spur trail**. Certainly worth taking, this shady trail branching left arcs southeast over to nearby Gray Eagle Creek and briefly follows a chain of pools upstream to 20-foot-high **Fern Falls**—a cascade cutting through a narrow, fern-decked slot.

Beyond this divertissement, our main trail climbs more steeply up to a ducked ridge and crosses it, only to recross it in 200 yards. Before it does so, however, climbers will note tempting routes on the north face of summit 6509, ¼ mile southeast. Our trail heads south, working closer toward this summit, then turns right (southwest) and climbs moderately, though briefly, across a meadowy, sometimes swampy slope. The exposed bedrock over which Gray Eagle Creek tumbles now lies ahead of us. A somewhat-ducked trail up it takes us quickly to a junction with **Trail 12E29**. Here we have a reunion with Hike 23, which has descended this trail to this spot. We follow the last part of this hike's prose, taking Trail 12E28 immediately across Gray Eagle Creek, then on a ¾-mile traverse to a bridge across Grass Lake's outlet creek. Immediately beyond it is the **Grass Lake trailhead**, but to get back to your original trailhead, follow the Lakes Basin Campground road south to its end, from which you take a trail first south then southwest over to its terminus opposite the start of the south-climbing Elwell Lodge Road. Here you get on the paved east-west road and hike a short 0.2 mile up to your **Long Lake trailhead**.

⋙ 25 ⋘
Lily Lake Trail

Distances:
0.2 mile to Lily Lake
0.8 mile to Gray Eagle Lodge
Low/High Elevations: 5920'; 5800' at Gray Eagle Lodge / 5990'
Season: Mid-June through late October
Classification: Very easy
Map: 8
Trailhead: At a long turnout along the Plumas County (north) half of Gold Lake Road, 1.0 mile below the Lakes Basin Campground junction and 0.6 mile above the Gray Eagle Lodge junction.

Introduction
This short trail is a pleasant diversion best suited for an early morning or late afternoon stroll. It also is the start of an alternative route into the Lakes Basin.

Description
On this short, obvious trail, you can wind down to tranquil, moraine-dammed **Lily Lake** in a few minutes' time. White fir, Jeffrey pine, and sugar pine rim this shallow lake, which is named after the large, floating, water-lily leaves so prominent in it. Growing out of shallow water, particularly at the south end, are grasslike bulrushes.

The trail skirts the lake's north and west shores, and then, near its southwest corner, climbs over a low ridge and in 60 yards arrives at a junction. Before the new Gold Lake Road was completed in 1973, a trail from Lakes Basin Campground descended north to here. We angle westward for a brief spurt, then, under a powerline, reach a second junction, from where a trail once climbed to Long Lake. We follow the line north for about ⅓ mile, first climbing over a low ridge, and then ending our walk at a bridge about 100 yards below a small waterfall near the south end of **Gray Eagle Lodge**. About midway along the powerline traverse, you'll see a path that departs northwest, contouring about 100 yards over to a ford of Gray Eagle Creek just above the small waterfall. Across the creek the trail continues 65 yards to Trail 12E26, the upper part of the Gray Eagle Creek Trail, which is described in the last part of the previous hike.

⋙ 26 ⋘
Smith Lake Trail

Distance: 1.0 mile to Smith Lake
Low/High Elevations: 5820'/6090'
Season: Early July through late October
Classification: Easy
Map: 8
Trailhead: From Highway 49 about 5 miles above Sierra City, drive 8 miles northwest up Gold Lake road to its county-line crest, then 2½ miles farther to the Gray Eagle Lodge road. From Highway 89 about 1⅓ miles southeast of

Graeagle, this junction is just over 5 miles southwest up Gold Lake road. Just past Gray Eagle Creek, take a spur road forking right and follow it to its turnaround end. Two trails leave from it, the Smith Lake Trail and the upper part of the Gray Eagle Creek Trail. The lower part of the latter trail is not described here, for it is unappealing for most people. From midway along the spur road it descends 4 miles to Graeagle.

Introduction

Smith Lake is the most accessible lake in this area at which you can legally camp. (The other four lakes with legal camping are mentioned in the next hike.) However, due to the proximity to the trailhead, just a half-hour's hike away, you'd do better to day hike to it, perhaps early in the morning, when the ascent is cool and the trout are biting.

Description

From the trailhead we are confronted with a brushy, largely shadeless, 500-foot-high lateral moraine that stands between us and Smith Lake. Fortunately, our trail doesn't tackle the moraine head-on, but rather climbs gently

north up it, crossing its descending crest ½ mile later at a spot barely 200 feet higher than the trailhead. Now generally in forest cover, we quickly cross multibranched Smith Creek and meet the neighboring Smith Creek Trail, which drops about 1500 feet in 2¼ miles to a loop road bound for Mohawk. We turn left, upstream, and in several minutes pass a junction with Mt. Elwell Trail 12E22, down which Hikes 24 and 27 descend. The first heads down the route we ascended, the second heads west to Smith Lake and beyond. In several more minutes we reach the outlet creek of Smith Lake, and here note a second junction with bifurcating Trail 12E22. Along the lake's south shore are two pleasant campsites, one by the lake's outlet and another just west over a low ridge. Although **Smith Lake** is one of the lowest lakes in the Highway 49 area, it is not one of the warmest, for it is relatively deep and is fed by snowmelt water well into the summer. Therefore, most visitors to this lake may be anglers in hot pursuit of trout.

Campsite at Smith Lake's outlet

⋘ 27 ⋙
Mt. Elwell Loop, from Jamison Mine

Distances:

0.8 mile to Trail 12E24
    1.1 miles on trail to west end of Smith Lake
    1.6 miles on trail to east end of Smith Lake
1.3 miles to northeast corner of Grass Lake
2.2 miles to Trail 11E11
    0.9 mile on trail to Jamison Lake
    1.1 miles on trail to Rock Lake
2.8 miles to Wades Lake spur trail
    0.2 mile on spur trail to Wades Lake
3.8 miles to jeep road above Wades Lake
4.1 miles to Pacific Crest Trail
5.4 miles to jeep road
6.0 miles to Trail 12E29
6.5 miles to Trail 12E25
7.2 miles to Mt. Elwell summit cleft
8.7 miles to Maiden Lake
8.9 miles to Hidden Lake cross-country route
    0.2 mile on route to Hidden Lake
10.3 miles to Smith Lake cutoff trail
10.5 miles to east end of Smith Lake
12.1 miles to Trail 11E13
12.9 miles to trailhead

Low/High Elevations: 5260'/7750'

Season: Mid-July through mid-October

Classification: Moderate if backpacked;
strenuous if day hiked

Map: 8

Trailhead: From Graeagle, a small Highway 89 settlement 1⅓ miles northwest of the Gold Lake Road junction, drive ⅓ mile north to County Road A14, heading west. Drive 4⅔ miles up it to the Jamison Mines spur road, and veer left on it only ¼ mile before A14 bridges Jamison Creek. On the spur road, drive 1⅓ miles up to a large trailhead parking lot among the Jamison ruins.

County Road A14 continues ¼ mile beyond the Jamison Creek bridge to a fork, located near the Plumas-Eureka State Park's museum. For Hike 28 keep right, head through Johnsville (no services) and in almost a mile turn sharply left at a junction, from where you climb ½ mile southwest up a paved road to the park's ski bowl. From the south end of its parking lot, go up a rough, narrow, dirt road, which climbs 1⅓ miles to Eureka Lake. This road is deteriorating into a jeep road, and if you have problems with the first 200 yards, which are among the roughest, turn back. You can walk southwest along the dam to its nearby outlet, and take an old road but 60 yards to the start of the Eureka Peak Trail, which climbs 1.4 miles to peak 7286, not Eureka Peak. The trail is quite obvious, climbing to a saddle, from which peak 7286 is a conspicuous, nearby summit to your left.

A second route to the Jamison ruins trailhead is possible. From the park's museum, drive just over a mile south to Upper Jamison Creek Campground. Just after the campground's main road crosses Jamison Creek, a footpath starts north (left) from the road and takes you ⅓ mile over to the trailhead. Use this route only if you're staying in the campground.

Introduction

In all of the Lakes Basin Recreation Area, there are only five desirable trailside lakes at which you can legally camp: Grass, Jamison, Rock, Wades, and Smith, and this hike visits all of them. In addition to offering camping, swimming, and fishing opportunities, this hike takes you through diverse landscapes and plant communities, and from Mt. Elwell offers you summit views near and far. Climbers will find the recreation area's best climbs along the mountain's flanks, but these are best reached from either the Long Lake or Grass Lake trailhead (Hikes 23 and 24).

Description

Our trail begins at a large parking lot among the ruins of buildings that were the site of a bustle of activity in the late 1800s. From quartz veins in the nearby Jamison mine complex, over $1½ million worth of gold was extracted. These veins rose from a gabbro pluton that intruded the Paleozoic-age volcanic rocks of this locality.

We start up-canyon on an old mining road, which becomes a trail just beyond the last building. Scattered Douglas-firs and other conifers mingle with greenleaf manzanita and huckleberry oak along the lower part of our trail, which parallels Little Jamison Creek, about 100 feet below. Soon we climb moderately to steeply from the creek views and away from forest shade. We ascend across dark bedrock of gabbro, which is rich in pyroxene, olivine, and calcium-feldspar minerals. Our trail leaves this rock as it eases up and curves left to a small flat that has Trail 12E24, bound for Smith Lake. Lying only about 2 miles from our trailhead, this lake is a popular destination, but it is also reached in half that distance and with about one-third the climbing effort from the Gray Eagle trailhead (Hike 26).

Beyond the junction our trail is shaded with incense-cedar, Douglas-fir, white fir, lodgepole pine, and Jeffrey pine. After about ¼ mile of ascent, we reach a short spur trail, which you can take a few paces right to a view of Jamison Falls. Like every other glaciated canyon in the Highway 49 lakes region, Little Jamison Creek canyon has its noteworthy fall, a 60-foot-high, silvery leap into freedom. From the spur trail we have an easy climb, mostly through lush vegetation, to a small canal—the same one we'll see along Smith Lake Trail 12E24—which served operations down at the Jamison Mine. Not far past the canal we arrive at the **northeast corner of Grass Lake**. Campsites along the lake's east shore, which our trail traverses, are small and poor. However, there are two fine ample ones along the lake's west shore. You reach these by taking an obvious trail that first heads along the north shore to the lake's outlet and soon turns southwest. If you were to head north-northwest from the northwest shore on a brushy, cross-country route over a broad ridge, you would reach an unnamed lake in ¼ mile. It is a fine one for swimming, but being hemmed-in by vegetation and rocks, it lacks decent campsites, although minimal ones can be found on a low ridge above its northeast shore.

On our Trail 11E13 up Little Jamison Canyon, we pass by the shallow southern end of Grass Lake, which has aquatic vegetation that attracts ducks, especially those migrating south on the Pacific flyway. Flowing into the south end of the lake as well as into its inlet creek are numerous creeklets. Some are lined with thimbleberry, currant, and gooseberry—

three shrubs producing edible berries—as well as with Bolander's yampah—a large, edible parsley that closely resembles some of its poisonous relatives. On a bench above the lake's south end you can find additional campsites.

As your southbound trail heads for an obvious headwall, which supports hidden Rock Lake above it, you make a sudden bend west. On this tack you traverse an aspen-bordered meadow, then veer northwest, and for 50 yards cross one channel after another. Look for rocks, logs, or whatever to cross this wet ford of not-so-little Little Jamison Creek. Early-season hikers are likely to get their feet wet. Onward, you climb west, then south up to a junction with **Trail 11E11**, which is a rewarding side trip.

This forested lateral trail at first climbs gently, but past the site of a former log cabin it veers southwest and executes several short, steep switchbacks up brushy bedrock benches. Those accomplished, you soon reach the refreshing outlet creek from Wades Lake, which crosses the trail midway up to Jamison Lake. Before you reach Jamison, you have to surmount a low ridge of granitelike metarhyolite, and climbers will certainly spy short crack and face routes up it. On the west slopes above Jamison Lake, climbers will find additional appealing routes, but the east slopes above Jamison, being composed of brown metabasalt or a close analog, are uninviting. Descending the low ridge before **Jamison Lake**, you quickly arrive at the lake's outlet creek, frequented by water ouzels, and cross it 50 yards downstream from the lake's outlet. Just before this crossing, however, a trail splits south to the outlet and the undesirable bedrock campsites not far beyond it. Of all the lakes one passes along this circuit, Jamison probably offers the greatest solitude, for not many hikers go cross-country to the lake's southern shore.

Rather, most cross the lake's outlet creek and follow a brief, winding trail over and across low, glaciated ridges to campsites along the south shore of **Rock Lake**. This aptly named lake is perhaps the most appealing lake along our circuit, and it may well be the finest of the entire Highway 49 lakes region. Photographers will certainly appreciate its beauty, and from selected rocky ledges near its southeast corner swimmers can dive into seemingly bottomless, invigorating water. Contrasting with the depth of this lake is a steep-sided rock island that rises a full 20 feet above the water. Everywhere you turn, you'll find evidence of past glaciers in the form of long scratches, or glacial striations, which were cut by the rock and grit that glaciers dragged along. What makes this lake so attractive is the way the glaciers accentuated the terrain, breaking off blocks of bedrock to create dramatic bluffs. You'll certainly be tempted to linger awhile in this rockbound paradise.

When you return to the main trail, you begin a steep ascent that leads past an outcrop of white, vertically foliated metarhyolite before reaching the **Wades Lake spur trail**. On it you make an easy ¼-mile stroll to the outlet of **Wades Lake**, passing a very good campsite—beneath red fir, lodgepole pine, and western white pine—located on your left just before the lake. This lake, resting in a bowl of greenish-tinted, light-gray metarhyolite, has a shallow north end which slowly gets deeper, allowing the reluctant swimmer to gradually get used to this fairly deep lake's often chilly water.

Back again on the main trail, we start southwest, immediately pass a flat meadow on our right, and engage in a steep ascent up the crest of a lateral moraine, occasionally scented with tobacco brush, before traversing across slopes up to a saddle. A grove of red firs, ascending east to this saddle, obstructs our view west down into glaciated Florentine Canyon, but our sweeping view east toward Mt. Elwell reveals the 4 miles of crest we'll have to circle to reach the peak's two summits. The saddle also marks the boundary between the metamorphic rocks we've just climbed and volcanic ones to be ascended. These rocks—the only geologically young volcanics we'll walk upon in the Plumas-Eureka/Lakes Basin landscape—are autobrecciated andesitic mud flows about 5-10 million years old, and are similar in origin to the flows that are very common south of Highway 50's Echo Summit (see the geology chapter's "Tahoe Sierra

Unnamed lakelet northwest of Grass Lake

volcanism"). We struggle steeply up a ridge-crest made of this material before attaining the Sierra crest, which north beyond the realm of the Tahoe Sierra is mostly volcanic.

On the crest we turn left and climb steeply at first— up a dusty **jeep road**, which parallels the tri-state Pacific Crest Trail, below on our right. Our climb southeast through a field of mule ears and volcanic rocks quickly levels off, and ¼ mile from our trail junction our jeep road intersects the **Pacific Crest Trail** (Hike 20, north end). If you haven't had serious snow problems so far, turn left onto it for a very meandering, forested, 1.3-mile traverse back to the **jeep road**. If you've had snow problems, keep to the jeep road, since it is easier to follow. It soon starts to descend, then in ½ mile passes the Four Hills Mine. Now abandoned, this mine in its day produced $2 million in gold from its quartz veins. A ¼-mile descent south gets you to a junction with the Spencer Lakes jeep road. Down this road, about ½ mile west of you, lie pockets of magnetite, which is a magnetic, iron-rich ore. The composition of iron in these pockets is pretty high, about 40%, but the quantity, estimated at under 5000 tons, is unprofitable to extract. From the Spencer Lakes jeep road junction, you climb ⅓ mile east to arrive at a spot where the Pacific Crest Trail crosses your jeep road. Here, on a broad crest saddle, marked by a small, circular, semistagnant pond, we take the jeep road into the Lakes Basin Recreation Area, and after a few minutes' walk we cross a spring-fed creek, which is your last *usually* reliable water source until Maiden Lake, about 3 miles ahead. Beyond it, we hike a steady ⅓-mile ascent east to a sharp bend where the jeep road turns south, and here meet Trail **12E29**. If you were to continue south along the jeep road, you would reach—in about 70 yards—a junction with Trail 12E30, which rollercoasters wildly east over to Hellgrammite Lake (Hike 23).

On Trail 12E29 we start a traverse north, first on the west side and then on the east side of ridgecrest, and then we briefly contour over to a junction with **Trail 12E25**, bound for Mt. Elwell's summit. Our traverse across the ridgecrest, which exhibits nearly vertical foliation like that of the Wades Lake basin, exposes us to our first good views of the Lakes Basin topography. From the junction we now follow the trail description in Hike 24 up to **Mt. Elwell's summit cleft**, from which we can visit two low summit blocks. Then we descend past **Maiden Lake** and the **Hidden Lake cross-country route** to the **Smith Lake cutoff trail**, which you reach immediately before Smith Creek.

Hike 24 crosses Smith Creek, but our route veers northwest and quickly arrives at a good, large, pine-shaded campsite near the **east end of Smith Lake**. West beyond the campsite over a low ridge lies a second good campsite, which is nestled beside a lively creek lined with alder and dogwood. Our rollercoaster trail west climbs another low ridge, this time over blue-green-gray metavolcanic bedrock, then descends close to the lake's shallow south bay, which is being choked with grasses and rushes. A third ridge climb leads us over to the cascading creek that empties into this clear, green lake. Seeking the creek's life-giving water are alder, dogwood, mountain ash, mountain maple, thimbleberry, and many wildflowers.

West of Smith Lake our trail snakes ¼ mile up to a small notch on a broad, ill-defined saddle, then makes a gradual descent through a forest of red fir and western white pine that also contains sugar pine—an unusual bedfellow for them. Beyond a shallow pond, our trail west drops more steeply and crosses the north-heading, bouldery crest of a lateral moraine midway down to an old mining canal that originates at Grass Lake. A brief descent southwest now takes us to the end of our loop, where we meet **Trail 11E13**. Now back on the main trail, we retrace our steps down Little Jamison Creek canyon to our **trailhead**.

⤛ 28 ⤜
Frazier Falls

Distance: 0.6 mile to viewpoint
Low/High Elevations: 6160'/6210'
Season: Late June through late October
Classification: Very easy
Map: 9

Trailhead: From Highway 49 about 5 miles above Sierra City, drive 7 miles northwest up Gold Lake Road to a junction, from which one road heads southwest over to the nearby corner of Gold Lake, while another, your road, heads northeast. On this *old* Gold Lake Road, drive 2 miles north to the trailhead. Alternatively, from Highway 89 about 1⅓ miles southeast of Graeagle, drive 2½ miles southwest up Gold Lake Road to a prominent moraine crest, where you branch left onto the old road for a 4-mile drive up to the trailhead.

Introduction
Easily the highest falls in the Highway 49 region, this sheet of water continues to impress visitors late into summer. Standing at the viewpoint opposite the perennial falls, you can study the canyon that drops before you and imagine what it must have looked like when an enormous glacier filled it. The falls are best viewed in the morning, when they are fully sunlit.

Description
From the trailhead we start to walk southeast, shaded by firs and pines. Brush becomes more

prominent as we wind around and over low, glacier-polished ridges before coming to Frazier Creek, which is lined with aspen, dogwood, and willow. The dark, blue-gray bedrock over which we walk originally was andesitic lava erupted onto the western North American landscape about 300 million years ago. They subsequently were compressed—causing them to metamorphose—and the compressive forces created the almost vertical stress cracks we see today.

We briefly head up Frazier Creek, then bridge it. Now on the east side, hikers who want to see Frazier Falls up close can leave the trail and parallel the creek to a vantage point just above the falls' brink. Most hikers, however, keep to the short trail, winding among some more low ridges, whose bedrock has been split and intruded with white vein quartz. They then turn north and descend to a fenced-off **viewpoint** directly opposite 176-foot-high Frazier Falls. In the past a sign has indicated that the fall and its cascades have a total height of 248 feet, but the topographic map indicates 200 feet at best. Likewise a sign put the falls 1.9 miles downstream from Gold Lake's outlet, but the distance is 1.7 miles via the meandering creek or 1.4 miles due north via a straight line.

Quibbles aside, this cascade marks the resistant midpoint in a canyon that once contained a 7-mile-long, 800-foot-thick glacier. Originating at the crest above Gold Lake's southwest shore, the glacier had a nonlinear path to follow. Gold Lake, of course, didn't exist back then, although its basin did. About ½ mile beyond the site of its outlet, the glacier was forced to bend northward, and the bend undoubtedly caused crevasses, or deep cracks, to form in the upper 100+ feet of ice. Then, straightening its course, the icy mass traveled less than a mile before it tumbled—in very slow, frozen motion—down the bedrock escarpment that Frazier Falls cascades over today. Just how fast did the glacier cascade over this brink? On the basis of large, present-day glaciers existing in more northern latitudes, we can estimate that the glacier ice might have "fallen" at the rate of about 30 feet per day, or about ¼ inch per minute. This rate of motion would have been barely noticeable

if it were constant. It wasn't. If we had been present, we would have heard the glacier groan as crevasses slowly opened and closed, and ice broke off, fell and was buried under the slow onslaught of ice behind it.

Standing at the viewpoint, you can look down-canyon and see a high lateral moraine that makes up the canyon's west wall. About 20,000 years ago, at the last glacial maximum, a glacier filled this canyon above the moraine's height. Try to imagine what a different landscape this area must have been back then! Only when the glacier began to wane in length and thickness to expose the top of the west wall did this surface receive part of the glacier's rocky load to construct the lateral moraine.

On your way back, note how glacial action, exerting a pressure of 20 tons per square foot, has abraded and smoothed the low ridges you wind along. Still, despite the intense pressure caused by the weight of the thick glacier, erosion by it was minimal. Had erosion been major, the glacier should have carved a deep canyon from the Gold Lake basin down to the base of Frazier Falls. Also on your way back, remember that all the soil and vegetation you see about you have appeared in the last 13,000 years, that is, since the mammoth glacier finally disappeared.

Frazier Falls

Devils Oven Lake and Paradise Lake

Chapter 10
Interstate 80's Recreation Lands

Introduction

This chapter's first two routes, Hikes 29 and 30, are atypical for our area, both being pleasant strolls along wooded nature trails situated at about 4500-5500 feet, where white firs dominate. Each route has a unique characteristic. The first is in isolated Placer County Big Trees Grove, which is the northernmost of a scattering of western Sierra giant-sequoia groves, and it is the only one in the Tahoe Sierra. The second route is just off fairly busy Highway 20, and is on a bedrock canyon floor that has been buried by volcanic deposits. Such deposits can be found on other canyon floors, but they are of interest here, because they help to time the origin of an anomalous bend of the South Yuba River through a resistant ridge. Rivers usually flow down between two ridges, not cut across them.

For the hiker in search of lakes, the Grouse Ridge Recreation Area offers the most lakes for the least amount of effort. Hikes 31-33 in this recreation area take you along trails that visit about 20 lakes and lakelets, and a few more lie not far off these beaten paths. Ones worth visiting include Sanford Lake, early along Hike 33, and some lakes in the Five Lakes Basin, beyond the end of this hike's Sand Ridge Trail.

A smaller lake-blessed area is that of the Loch Leven Lakes, which also includes nearby Salmon Lake. Hike 34 describes trails to all four lakes as well as an alternate route to Salmon Lake. Because the main trail to these lakes is just off Interstate 80, and because this trail is relatively short, the lakes receive heavy use. On summer weekends you can expect to pass dozens of hikers along the trail or at the lakes. To avoid the hordes, you have to go cross-country. Many lakes, lakelets, and ponds exist between the Loch Leven Lakes and the Cascade Lakes, about 4 miles to the east. For example, one possibility is to strike east from High Loch Leven Lake, traversing over to Fisher Lake. This lake and other bodies of water are on fairly open, glaciated, granitic benches that offer secluded camping, often with views. If you are in search of such an experience, obtain a copy of the U.S. Geological Survey's *Soda Springs 7.5'* topographic map. And if you are starting from the Cascade Lakes area, obtain a copy of the Tahoe National Forest map, which updates the roads in that area.

Hike 35 and Hikes 38-41 describe the Pacific Crest Trail, which was built through this area mostly from 1978 to 1982. This trail, which accounts for about 30 of about 80-odd miles of trail described in this chapter, offers views but no significant lakes, except via side trips. Two worth visiting are Paradise Lake, via Hikes 35 and 38, and White Rock Lake, via Hike 38. Be forewarned, however, that White Rock Lake is accessible with OHVs. The Pacific Crest Trail, true to its name, generally stays at or close to the crest, which in the Interstate 80 region is mostly volcanic sediments and broken-up lava flows. These rocks in large part explain the lack of trailside lakes, for in the Tahoe Sierra, the lake basins have been cut by glaciers in granitic and metamorphic bedrock, not in the relatively soft volcanic rocks.

Hike 35, along the Pacific Crest Trail, offers you a chance to visit the most prominent peak in the Donner Pass area, tri-turreted Castle Peak. From where the PCT reaches Castle Pass, an obvious, popular use trail climbs along a ridge to the summit. Near that summit is another popular use trail, which skirts north along a ridge to subdued Basin Peak. Both are worthy goals, due to their exceptional panoramic views of Interstate 80's recreation lands. Finally, several miles north of Basin Peak stands Mt. Lola, the highest summit in these lands. It can be reached via two routes, from a trailhead above the east side's Little Truckee River, Hike 37, or from one near White Rock Lake, Hike 38.

One route deserves special attention: Hike 36 to Devils Oven and Warren lakes. It is one of the most spectacular routes in all of the Tahoe Sierra. However, due to the difficult terrain, this hike lies solely in the domain of the rugged backpacker or mountaineer.

⊰≫ 29 ≪⊱
Placer County Big Trees Grove

Distance: 1.8 miles of trail in the grove
Low/High Elevations: 5190'/5310'
Season: May through October
Classification: Very easy
Map: 10
Trailhead: Leave Interstate 80 just 2 miles northeast of its Highway 49 intersection, as you branch east on the Auburn Ravine Road offramp. Here you'll find a plethora of gas stations, restaurants, and other tourist-oriented amenities. Take the Auburn-Foresthill Road 15½ miles northeast to the Foresthill Ranger Station. In Foresthill, 1.2 miles later, fork right on Mosquito Ridge Road 96 and follow it 24 miles to the Placer County Big Tree Grove spur road.

Introduction

Located about 41 miles from I-80, this grove of giant sequoias is certainly remote for most visitors. However, if you are bound for French Meadows or Hell Hole recreation areas, or for Granite Chief Wilderness (Hike 42), then this grove will be right along your route. This is the northernmost and most isolated grove, lying a distant 55 air miles north of the next grove, in Highway 4's Calaveras Big Trees State Park.

Back in 1876 John Muir had proposed that these sequoia groves—65 of them today, according to the expert, Dwight Willard—are remnants of a once-continuous mid-elevation belt of sequoias. During the Ice Age, Muir believed, major glaciers descended through major canyons, breaking the forest into groves. However, there has never been any evidence for a once-continuous belt. This Placer County grove may be the few surviving remnants of a separate population that migrated west into the Sierra Nevada millions of years ago. But much of this area was not glaciated, so the trees should be more extensive—why aren't they? There are plenty of similar coves in the area, and there should be hundreds, if not thousands, of trees. An alternate hypothesis is that the grove may have originated quite recently, when traveling Indians in the Mokelumne and American drainages, perhaps camping in this area, perhaps dropped sequoia seeds they were carrying, and these gave rise to the grove. This hypothesis would explain why the grove is only here, and not in other suitable, unglaciated sites: no seeds were left at them. Additional evidence for the grove's youthful age is that there are no ancient specimens, that is, ones 2000+ years old. The largest trees are about 10 feet in diameter, and in an ideal site, a sequoia may attain this size within several centuries. There should be really old, giant trees, or downed giants, but there are none. Both lines of evidence suggest a human origin for the grove.

Description

The Forest View Trail, heading left from near a drinking fountain, is exactly what it claims to be: a view of trees and the interesting plant life beneath them, not a view of scenic panoramas. The Big Trees Trail, heading right, has signs that identify trees, shrubs and features, and give the dimensions of the larger sequoias. Since both trails are so obvious, no trail description is necessary. Take the Big Trees Trail first, so that you will recognize some of the species you'll see along the Forest

View Trail. Along the former are numbered posts that correspond to numbers in the Big Trees Interpretive Trail pamphlet, which has a map, and usually is available at the trailhead.

Two trail posts deserve elaboration. The first, number 8, is beside a sequoia that fell back in 1861 or '62. Its trunk is about 154 feet long by up to 10 feet in diameter. Had the trunk belonged to any other species of tree that grows in this grove, it would have long since decayed into oblivion. The bark and wood of the sequoia, however, are very resistant to insect infestation and fungal attack. That this trunk—and the larger Roosevelt Tree trunk near it—has survived over a century is amazing when you consider that the chemical and biochemical processes in this area are quite strong.

Only one other tree, the bristlecone pine, can withstand decay better. Preferring timberline slopes in drier ranges east of the Sierra, this pine has an extremely short growing season—a month or so—and consequently it grows very slowly, producing extremely close-spaced annual rings that are very resistant to all kinds of attack. Until the 1950s, foresters thought that the sequoia was the world's longest-living tree, but not now. The bristlecone pine not only lives longer—about 5000 years versus about 3500 years—but its dead trunks also survive longer. By counting and matching tree rings in both living and dead pines, scientists discovered that some trunks have survived thousands of years; a few pines whose seeds germinated 8000 years ago have their dead trunks lying around today. Since this tree's annual rings reflect precipitation—rings spaced farther apart when there is more of it—scientists have been able to piece together an 8000-year-long climatic history for the Basin and Range province, which includes most of Nevada and adjacent parts of neighboring states.

The second post worth noting, number 10, is for a subterranean stream. Beside it you can look down into some small holes, one or two feet deep, and see water flowing in an underground channel. It is channels like these from which the shallow, far-ranging sequoia roots get the abundant water they require. If you hike both trails in this grove, you'll notice that the sequoias are found only on the lower slopes, which are laced with ephemeral creeklets—signs of flowing groundwater below. Note that the vegetation in the sequoia grove is composed of water-loving species such as dogwood, alder, and azalea, while the slopes above have manzanita. Throughout this small grove you'll see trees found in virtually every one of California's sequoia groves: sugar pine, ponderosa pine, and white fir. Also seen in this locality are scrub tanbark oak, black oak, and Douglas-fir.

One species not seen here and not common in most groves is red fir. However, in the fossil record in sediments east of the Sierra Nevada, ancient sequoias generally associated with the higher-elevation red firs, not the lower-elevation white firs they associate with today. Why this shift in allegiance? There is one sequoia grove in the range that is almost pure red fir, and it provides a clue. This is the Kaweah River's Atwell-East Fork Grove, which is also the highest, extending up to 8800 feet in elevation. It never was glaciated. When glaciers advance across a landscape, they generally erode its soil. Then when they retreat they may leave a thin veneer of deposits, *till*, in which red firs can survive. However, sequoias cannot, for the till does not hold enough groundwater to quench the trees' great demand. I suggest that before major glaciation began some 2 million years ago, sequoias were widespread in the red-fir belt, although they never formed a continuous belt as Muir had proposed. Glaciers then eliminated most of the trees, but the lower unglaciated ones survived, generally among sugar pines and white firs. I propose that today's sequoia groves lie in rather marginal environments instead of in optimal ones.

Sequoia cone, one-half actual size

The present boundaries of the Sierra Nevada's sequoia groves appear to be quite stable; neither expanding nor contracting significantly over thousands of years. However, most of these groves are undergoing a gradual decrease in numbers of sequoias. This decrease has been going on for at least 500 years, so Western man isn't totally at fault—although early entrepreneurs tried to lumber the groves. The sheer bulk of these giants caused them to shatter into useless splinters when they hit the ground, so most of the

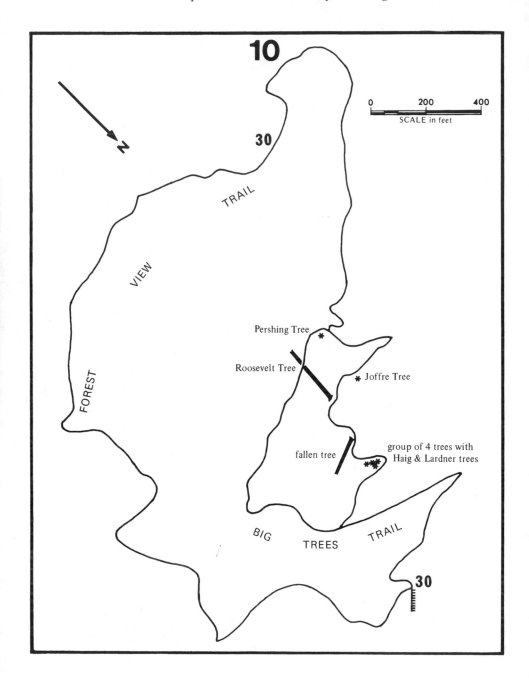

sequoia trees—unlike their close cousins, the coast redwoods—were spared the ax. This Placer County grove was discovered in 1855 by miners who were searching for gold among the quartz veins which infuse marine sediments of the Shoo Fly Complex, deposited roughly 450-400 million years ago, which underlie its fairly deep mineral soil.

It is this moist mineral soil that the sequoia seedling needs to survive, not the mat of drier litter atop it. A survey of three controlled burns in Kings Canyon National Park showed that a year after the fires burned off the litter, there were about 1500 sequoia seedlings sprouting in the mineral soil for every mature sequoia in the burns. In an adjacent, unburned grove, no seedlings sprouted. Today, fire is recognized as a very necessary element to maintain sequoia groves. Burned sequoia litter holds up to three times more water than does unburned litter. Fires also aid seedlings by killing fungi, eliminating some plant competition, and driving off small rodents that feed on the seedlings. Still, mortality is high: only about 30 seedlings per parent survive by the end of the third year.

Once the sequoia grows large enough to develop a good, protective bark, which will eventually get to be over a foot thick, it becomes immune to virtually everything, fire and lightning included. What, then, kills these giants? I suggest that these die due to loosening of their roots by erosion of the soil that supports them. The soils are typically about 3 feet thick, and in this shallow layer the roots radiate

out 100 feet or more from the trunk. Over a 2000-year period, part of this soil can be eroded away, exposing many roots and leaving the tree defenseless against a large windstorm, such as the one in 1861 or '62 that toppled the two giants in this Placer County grove. Unlike short-lived giants such as sugar and ponderosa pines, sequoias do not seem to die of old age. Overuse by people can accelerate erosion, which is why in the Sierra's popular

The Pershing Tree

groves, trees are fenced-in to protect them from the public. Bristlecone pines, such as those in California's White Mountains, just east of the central Sierra Nevada, grow on slower-eroding slopes, and this may increase their longevity. Nevertheless, they too, because of their long lives, are faced with the same problem.

⊰ **30** ⊱
Sierra Discovery Trail

Distance: 0.8 mile for entire loop
Low/High Elevations: 4580'/4630'
Season: Early April through late October
Classification: Easy
Map: 11

Trailhead: Leave Interstate 80 about 45 miles northeast of Auburn (16 miles west of Donner Pass), and head west on Highway 20. In 3.9 miles you come to Forest Route 18 (Bowman Road), signed for Sierra Discovery Trail. (From the Highways 20/49 split in Nevada City, this junction is 24 miles east on Highway 20.) Turn north onto it, and drive ½ mile to the main parking area, on your left, which is immediately past a larger parking area for buses, RVs, and overflow.

Introduction
Like the previous hike, this one is a short nature trail. Actually, it is more than that, for it also introduces you to history and technology: the Nisenan (South Maidu) inhabitants and their way of life, the mid-1800s miners and their canals, and the 1900s PG&E's local hydroelectric project. Just as important, in my opinion, are the lessons learned from the local area's metamorphic and granitic bedrock and from volcanic and glacial deposits, which are not described in the nature-trail signs.

Description
Starting from the trailhead you quickly encounter abundant signs, large and small, which describe the local area's flora, fauna, ecology (how the flora and fauna interact with each other and their environment), and both pre-western and western history. The first

short stretch, on a boardwalk, takes you across a seasonally wet stretch, then you bridge the Bear River, which here is no more than a creek, for its origin lies barely ¾ mile upstream. From the bridge the short trail makes a loop, which you can hike in either direction, although counterclockwise, starting right, is recommended for those in wheel chairs. (There are several short, moderately steep switchbacks which are better descended than ascended.) Along this loop you traverse through a typical white-fir forest, complete with its associated species of conifers and oaks plus an understory of shrubs and herbs.

The loop in the counterclockwise direction first heads north, then northwest to several short switchbacks, which take you down to a road junction. If you took the road, which is not part of the loop, you would climb over to nearby slopes that have developed on the Shoo Fly Complex, which is an assemblage of metamorphic rocks that originally were sediments laid down on the ocean floor roughly 450-400 million years ago. These rocks contrast with those of the Emigrant Gap composite pluton, exposed as a small, dark-gray cliff opposite the main trailhead parking area. This rock, diorite, originally solidified from magma several miles down to form granitic rock about 165 million years ago.

The loop soon turns southwest, and you have a view of a seasonally wet meadow. This is just the eastern part of a very long, broad meadow, which extends about 1¾ miles west to make up the floor of Bear Valley. Quickly you come upon the Bear River and follow it first south then east up to a conspicuous 10-foot-high waterfall—perhaps the trail's most dramatic feature—which is located just below the trail's bridge across the river.

What is important here, in my opinion, is what the river flows over—a lahar. This is a small part of an andesitic mud flow that originated from a volcano near Donner Pass perhaps 15 million years ago. Granitic or metamorphic bedrock likely lies only a few tens of feet beneath the base of this lahar. Over several million years the lahar and later volcanic flows completely buried Bear Valley, for the deposits extend from its floor all the way up to the ridges on either side. The Shoo Fly

Complex does likewise, extending from the floor near the aforementioned road junction northwest all the way up to the north ridge. Bear Valley was just as wide some 15 million years ago, when it began to be buried, as it is today. (Actually, the valley has been wide and flat-floored much longer, based on remnants of rhyolite deposited 33 million years age— see Hike 43.) Contrary to popular geologic thought, it has not been significantly widened by glaciers, which here were at least 1200 feet thick—great enough to top the north ridge. What the glaciers did was remove the volcanic sediments not previously removed by the Bear River. Perhaps the next glacier to advance through this area will remove the last remnant of the lahar, then will be powerless to erode significantly into the underlying resistant bedrock.

Another misconception about past Sierran glaciers is their size. Geologists have stated that their ice surfaces, which transported debris, can be estimated from the highest moraines they left. If you look closely while driving along Interstate 80, especially between Emigrant Gap and the Highway 20 junction,

you will observe that the narrow, linear volcanic ridge is mantled with bouldery glacial deposits—in essence, a lateral moraine. In theory, this bouldery ridgecrest should represent the level of the former glacier's ice surface. It does not. Higher glacial deposits atop the north ridge of Bear Valley dictate that the I-80 ridgecrest must have lain under several hundred feet of ice. Only after the glacier began to wane, and its ice surface lowered sufficiently, was glacial debris left on the ridgecrest.

A final geologic lesson is about the course of the South Yuba River. If you look at this hike's topographic map, you'll note that the river, originating near Donner Pass, makes a conspicuous bend northwest to cut directly through its canyon's north ridge, today flowing through a deep canyon it cut into resistant rock. How did the river do this, and when? Geologists have ascribed this anomalous course to stream piracy. Originally, the hypothesis goes, the Bear River was the major river, and it began east of Donner Pass (before eastern lands subsided), then flowed westward through Bear Valley and beyond. The South Yuba River was a minor river, extend-

Stream-piracy site, viewed from Interstate 80's Emigrant Gap viewpoint

ing headward from the Sierra foothills. But it eventually worked southwest through the resistant north ridge to the Bear River drainage, whereupon this river was diverted, through stream piracy, down the course of the South Yuba River. In the 1990s this hypothesis took on another twist: a geographer said this diversion occurred when a relatively recent former glacier spilled across the resistant ridge and massively eroded through it. As I have said above, the geologic evidence clearly shows—here as elsewhere in the range—that the bedrock topography has changed very little since it was first buried by volcanic deposits, and that glacial erosion here, as elsewhere, has been minimal, so this new hypothesis is not valid.

But the hypothesis of stream piracy appears valid, since the ancestral Bear Valley had to have been created by a major river—today's emasculated river could not have done the job. On the other hand, the ancestral South Yuba River, working headward, would have lacked the ability to cut into the resistant ridge. There is a way out of this conundrum. The ancestral Bear River could be immensely old, having developed in response to major Sierran uplift beginning roughly 160 million years ago. Then later on, volcanism became widespread and voluminous, as it did much later, and the Sierran lands were buried, including the already existing north ridge. The South Yuba River took on a new course across the surface of the volcanic sediments, quickly eroding into them to create a volcanic canyon. The river soon cut down to the buried ridgecrest, but being trapped in a canyon, could not alter its course. Therefore, it cut down through the ridge, bringing about today's drainage pattern. This would have happened before 33 million years ago, and the climates before then were warm and wet, making both weathering and erosion far more intense than they are today. So when did this drainage rearrangement occur? I put it at about 80 million years ago, at the end of this early period of volcanism. So long as voluminous flows and sediments were being deposited, the river drainage would be undergoing rearrangement; it became free to incise only after volcanism ceased.

~≈~ **31** ~≈~
Round Lake Trail to Milk Lake

Distances:
1.2 miles to Island Lake
1.7 miles to Round Lake
1.8 miles to Long Lake
2.1 miles to Milk Lake
Low/High Elevations: 6670'/7010'
Season: Late June through early October
Classification: Easy
Map: 12

Trailhead: Leave Interstate 80 about 45 miles northeast of Auburn (16 miles west of Donner Pass), and head west on Highway 20. In 3.9 miles you come to Forest Route 18 (Bowman Road). Turn right onto it, and after 6.4 winding miles reach a junction with F.R. 14 (Grouse Ridge Road), on the right. Stay on F.R. 18 for 2.1 miles more, to a junction with F.R. 17, also on the right, and immediately past an 8½-mile signpost. Drive 2.1 miles northeast up F.R. 17 to a junction. To reach Lindsey Lake Campground, stay on F.R. 17, which branches left, north, and winds 1.4 miles to a T. Turn right and drive 0.6 mile east up a narrow, rough road (passable for most autos) to the primitive campground. From it the Lindsey Lakes Trail starts a winding route to Rock Lake and beyond (see end of Hike 32 for a trail description).

For Hike 31, keep right at the junction where F.R. 17 branches north, and wind 0.4 mile up F.R. 17-4 to a split, then keep right, and continue 0.3 mile to Carr Lake Campground. Drive through this small, primitive campground to a nearby, obvious parking area on the right, along the shore of Carr Lake. Don't park in the cramped space just beneath the Feeley Lake dam, about 160 yards farther. Leave this for anglers who have to carry their small boats up to the lake.

Introduction

One lake right after another greets the hiker along this short, varicolored, enjoyable route. Because Hike 31 is so short, you'll probably want to do it as a day hike, even though campsites are at every lake. For most hikers, no lake is farther than an hour's walk from the trailhead. From Island Lake you can head north and visit another group of lakes, which are described in the next hike. The Round Lake Trail also provides an alternate way in to Glacier Lake, the Five Lakes Basin, and Beyers Lakes. This route is well suited for hikes in early summer and again in October, when the road up to the Grouse Ridge trailhead may have snow patches or may be quite muddy.

Description

Starting at the trailhead parking area, from where this hike's mileages are measured, we first walk 160 yards east along the last bit of F.R. 17-4—a rough road for cars—to Feeley Lake's outlet creek. At the south end of the lake's dam you'll find the official start of Round Lake Trail 12E26, which originally was a jeep road, though the tread has narrowed with time and parts of it have been replaced with short segments of trail to yield a better route.

We start easily beside Feeley Lake, which is a fairly large, moderately deep, clear lake that in the still of the morning vibrantly reflects the red-brown colors of dominating Fall Creek Mountain. However, by late summer the lake usually drops 5 feet or so, close to its natural,

pre-dam level, and then the shoreline becomes a "bathtub ring." Regardless of which month you visit the lake, you're likely to see anglers hoping to obtain a fine trout.

After about ⅓ mile we leave the shoreline and make a short, moderate climb through a red fir/western white pine forest, top a minor ridge, and quickly arrive at a tranquil, acre-sized, lily-pad lakelet. We jump its outlet creek and parallel first the lakelet's shore and then a seasonally wet meadow's edge, our views north being obstructed by a low bedrock ridge. At the meadow's east end we cross a small gap and are greeted by a pleasant, small lake with a photogenic, lodgepole-covered island. Being mostly waist-to-chest deep, it is a warm lake suited for swimming, but is too shallow to support fish. From just above its southeast corner Crooked Lakes Trail 12E11—Hike 32—branches north.

Keeping to the Round Lake Trail, we quickly encounter a view of the nearby southwest tip of **Island Lake**. Along its south shore you can find some fair campsites. From granitic benches of varying height that border the southeast edge of the lake, one can dive into the cool, deep, refreshing water. Also from these benches one can gaze down toward the lake's bottom, which is 15 feet or more beneath the surface, and see trout.

Feeley Lake (left), Island Lake (center), and Fall Creek Mountain

Farther from the shoreline, the lake attains a depth of 80 feet, which easily makes it the deepest lake in this recreation area.

Island Lake floods most of a narrow, north-south mass of approximately 365 million-year-old andesite lava, which was intruded and metamorphosed in part by granitic rock of similar age, which makes up the lake's east shore. In contact with the metamorphosed rock along the lake's west shore are approximately slightly older marine metasediments and metavolcanics, whose iron-rich content accounts for the red-brown color of Fall Creek Mountain and the adjoining landscape.

From the trail view of Island Lake's southwest corner, we climb east to a north-trending, open bedrock ridge, from which we can see the island-speckled lake below us, and can also see, on the north horizon, the unmistakable sawtooth crest of towering Sierra Buttes, about 13½ miles distant. Leaving the ridge, we descend shortly northeast to a creeklet that drains from Round Lake to Long Lake. If you were to follow the creeklet north, you'd reach the south tip of Long Lake in about 130 yards. Just a few steps beyond the creeklet on the Round Lake Trail you'll spy a footpath. This parallels the creeklet upstream to the nearby west shore of **Round Lake**, with limited space for camping.

If you want to continue onward, stay on the Round Lake Trail (which doesn't visit Round Lake), and make a brief climb to a small gap before making an even briefer descent to the head of a gully. From here, where the trail turns from northeast to southeast, you can head 100 yards down the gully to **Long Lake**. This scenic lake appears to be purposely designed for the best visual effect, for it has a pleasing balance between conifers and granitic benches. The lake's rocky shore, however, precludes spacious camping.

About 150 yards southeast from the Long Lake cutoff, the Round Lake Trail spawns a trail that heads briefly south to the northeast shore of *noncircular* Round Lake. Note that this lake has two outlets, one at the northeast shore and one at the west, and a shoreline trail runs between the two. During midsummer, Round Lake is warm enough for some enjoyable swimming.

From the Round Lake spur junction, we go down the northeast-outlet creeklet a few yards, cross it, and climb rather steeply to a junction below a ridgecrest. Here a footpath starts south, traversing 160 yards over to the northwest corner of shallow, greenish **Milk Lake**. In this vicinity you'll find a fair campsite under forest cover. From it a narrow footpath heads east across slopes densely vegetated with bracken ferns, wildflowers, and shrubs. The trail is barely above the lake's waterline in places, and the thick vegetation at times almost forces you into the lake. By the lake's northeast corner you'll find another fair campsite, the one often used by those who descend from the Grouse Ridge trailhead.

Hike 31 ends at Milk Lake, but from the lake's spur-trail junction, the Round Lake Trail continues east. After a relatively easy ¼-mile climb, it almost tops a shallow saddle at the east end of the previously mentioned ridgecrest. From this locale, a spur trail strikes southwest, quickly vaults the saddle, and then makes a short, steep descent to the northeast corner of Milk Lake. Beyond the spur trail, the Round Lake Trail climbs 120 yards east to its end at a junction, 2.3 miles from your trailhead parking area. Here, on a descending, forested ridge, you meet Grouse Ridge Trail 13E28, which gains 400 feet in elevation in a rather steep, southward climb of ⅔ mile to its trailhead just above Grouse Ridge Campground. Northeast, this trail descends ⅔ mile to a junction with Glacier Lake Trail 13E13. The lake, at trail's end, lies about 2.5 miles farther, and the route to it is described in Hike 33.

<⅔ 32 ⅔>
Crooked Lakes Trail to Penner Lake and beyond

Distances:
1.2 miles to Island Lake
1.5 miles to Hidden Lake
2.4 miles to Crooked Lakes' use trail
3.2 miles to Penner Lake
4.5 miles to Rock Lake

4.5 miles to junction with connecting trail to Grouse Ridge Trail

4.5 miles to junction with Lindsey Lakes Trail

Low/High Elevations: 6670'/6920' to Penner Lake; 7060' to Rock Lake

Season: Late June through early October

Classification: Easy

Map: 12

Trailhead: Same as the Hike 31 trailhead.

Introduction

Penner Lake is a fine goal for the novice backpacker, for it is reached with relatively little effort, yet its setting is more akin to that found in more-remote parts of the Sierra. And those who like off-trail exploration can check out about a dozen lakelets that lie just off the Crooked Lakes Trail. Granted, most are not too appealing, but still a few are quite rewarding.

Description

Follow Hike 31's description 1.1 miles east to your first junction, which is with northbound Crooked Lakes Trail 12E11. You descend a few yards to the southeast corner of a lake that would do well to be named "Little Island Lake." The lake and its island are both little. Because it is quite shallow, it provides relatively warm swimming over most of the summer. Your trail follows the shoreline over to the lake's east corner, from which you have barely a hop, skip, and jump east to the west shore of **Island Lake**. Having an area of 35 acres and a depth of 80 feet, it is the largest, deepest lake you can hike to in the Grouse Ridge Recreation Area (you can of course drive to larger, deeper reservoirs, such as Culbertson and Faucherie lakes). Given its size, Island Lake can hold quite a lot of trout. However, given its proximity to the trailhead, the lake sees a lot of anglers. The lake is also a great one for swimming, though mainly from late July through mid-August, when its temperature is at a maximum.

The trail leaves "Little Island Lake" at its northeast corner, and after you go 150 yards north, you reach a small campsite that is nestled among lodgepole pines just left of the trail. Within a minute beyond it, we almost touch a corner of Island Lake, and if you want to check out tree-ringed **Hidden Lake**, leave the trail here and climb 0.1 mile northwest.

Those keeping to the Crooked Lakes Trail now follow it northeast, and momentarily top a low ridge that juts halfway across Island Lake. Swimmers in particular, take note: you can swim to three islands, or to the east shore, on which you can find "diving platforms" of varying heights. Hiking onward, you may spy a tiny campsite near the lake's northeast tip, and a slightly larger one—on sloping ground—at the tip. From that tip you can usually jump across the lake's outlet creek and then meander over to open benches above the lake's east shore in search of isolated campsites.

Immediately north of Island Lake we drop to a lakelet and walk along its uninviting, lodgepole-and-willow west shore. However, the east shore is quite inviting, at least to swimmers, since it has some good diving *and* sunbathing potential. To reach the east-shore cliffs and slabs, cross the dam at the lake's north end. Also note that a linear lakelet lies about 200 yards east of the cliffs, just over a minor ridge.

Only 120 yards beyond the lakelet, where the Crooked Lakes Trail jogs east a few yards, you'll find a good campsite, whose only liability is that it is too close to the trail for privacy. Ahead, we ramble for ¼ mile, basically northward, through a shady red-fir forest to the first of many Crooked Lakes, this one small, grassy, and unappealing. Three more of similar quality lie out of sight just southeast of the lake.

We continue briefly northward, round a seasonal pond, and then make a short descent northeast. You'll be heading toward a fairly shallow lakelet, but the best of the Crooked Lakes lies out of sight. Immediately before reaching the lakelet, near the bottom of your descent, you should spot a **use trail** that weaves eastward for 150 yards over to a fine campsite above the west end of one of the larger Crooked Lakes. From the campsite you have a fine view east-southeast toward the Black Buttes. And by continuing cross-country southeast from the lake's outlet, you'll encounter three small, shallow lakelets, then briefly east of the last will reach a larger, more inviting one. From its outlet one can head 0.2 mile east and find Grouse Ridge Trail 13E28 along the base of a small hill.

Beyond the Crooked Lakes use trail, you continue past the fairly shallow lakelet and quickly begin a climb, initially northeast, to Penner Lake. Along this 260-foot elevation gain, you're bound to see an attractive, northern member of the Crooked Lakes, which too is a worthy goal. Your climb eases as you curve north and leave views of this lake-blessed area behind. You make a short traverse across a bench to a dumbbell-shaped pond, then conclude your climb with an equally short stretch up to a ridge. Penner Lake spreads out below you.

You start north down the ridge, quickly enter a shallow gully and follow it 120 yards northeast down to its base, then curve left over to the southeast shore of **Penner Lake**. Here you can fish or swim, but you won't find a suitable campsite. The trail wanders northward across barren, metamorphic bedrock and passes a small, shady campsite that is just above a shallow bay. Here you'll see a metamorphic-rock ridge jutting out into the lake,

almost cutting it in two. Were the bay deeper, the ridge would be a good one for high-diving, but such water sport is best at the lake's south end. You'll note that atop the ridge is a monstrous granitic boulder, about 100 tons in weight. This was transported here by a westward-flowing glacier.

From the shallow bay the trail briefly winds along a low ridge, then descends to a moderate-sized campsite by the lake's outlet creek. Just across and down the creek lies a smaller campsite. Here, at the lake's northeast corner, a shoreline trail starts west, while the Crooked Lakes Trail makes an unnecessary climb and descent north to Rock Lake. The former is more interesting, for it gives you fishing and swimming access plus some pleasant views from a gap above the lake's west shore, including a view east-southeast of the rugged Black Buttes.

If you take the latter, you'll be mostly following a former jeep road, which first climbs 160 feet in elevation up a brushy slope to a broad slope with an open red-fir forest. If you're willing to climb an extra 200 feet, continue northwest up to nearby peak 7254 for a

Rock Lake

commanding view of much of the Grouse Ridge Recreation Area. Otherwise, follow the former road down to the east end of **Rock Lake**. You may spot a use trail that curves westward over to a good campsite. About 140 yards past this trail, you come to a junction with a **connecting trail**. This begins near a seasonal pond, and it descends moderately 0.6 mile southeast to Grouse Ridge Trail 13E28. South, that trail makes an uninteresting ascent past Shotgun Lake, which is more meadow than lake, then past the site of former Middle Lake, which now is a meadow with a lot of tree stumps. After 2.3 miles it reaches a junction with Glacier Lake Trail 13E13. North, the Grouse Ridge Trail goes down-canyon 0.5 mile to a junction with an east-descending 0.5-mile-long trail from Rock Lake, then descends an additional 1.3 miles to the west end of a dam across Sawmill Lake.

Finally, after the last 60 yards along the Crooked Lakes Trail, you end at a trail junction that is just northeast of the seasonal pond. The previously mentioned trail that leads east from here descends rather steeply 0.5 mile to the Grouse Ridge Trail. West, the **Lindsey Lakes Trail** goes 3.3 miles to its trailhead. Near the lake's east end are at least two adequate campsites, and two good ones lie along its west shore, between the trail and the lake's dam. The lake is a good one for both fishing and swimming, though usually after mid-August water is let out from the dam, leaving a bathtub ring that becomes quite unsightly, as do some other lakes with dams. Therefore, should you want to visit it, do so before mid-August, when it is quite attractive.

Because Rock Lake via the Lindsey Lakes Trail is only 2.9 miles away, versus 4.5 via the Crooked Lakes Trail, you might consider taking the former trail. Its trailhead directions are described under the Hike 31 trailhead. Briefly, from Lindsey Lake Campground at lower Lindsey Lake, you take a closed road ¾ mile up to a junction just above the north shore of middle Lindsey Lake. This lake has a shallow west lobe, but most of it is deep and inviting. From the junction a jeep road winds ½ mile to upper Lindsey Lake, which is worth visiting, but being hemmed in with bedrock and brush, lacks campsites. Only a low ridge separates the far end of this lake from the south end of large Culbertson Lake. Just ¼ mile past the junction the Lindsey Lakes Trail rounds a shallow lakelet, then in a similar distance climbs to a broad, low ridge. It then descends past private structures above the northwest shore of Culbertson Lake, soon turns west, and quickly comes to a junction. From here a road climbs gently ahead, west, but you take the Lindsey Lakes Trail north to adjacent Texas Creek, boulder-hop or ford it, climb northwest to a nearby low ridge with an old trail descending northwest, then climb briefly north to a gravelly wash. Up this you ascend northeast, reaching a junction 2.6 miles from the trailhead. From here a path goes 150 yards, first east then southeast, over to a spacious campsite by the northwest shore of Lower Rock Lake. The Lindsey Lakes Trail then climbs 0.2 mile northeast to a junction with a west-climbing trail, which is located on a south-heading ridge. You can walk along this ridge and down to the west shore of Rock Lake, or follow your trail east a bit farther for both west-shore and north-shore access.

⊰ **33** ⊱
Grouse Ridge, Glacier Lake, and Sand Ridge Trails

Distances:

0.5 mile on Sanford Lake Trail to Sanford Lake

0.4 mile on Grouse Ridge Trail to Downey Lake Trail

0.4 mile on trail to Downey Lake

0.6 mile on trail to Round Lake Trail

0.2 mile on trails to Milk Lake

1.3 miles on Grouse Ridge Trail to Old Sand Ridge-Glacier Lake trail

1.4 miles on trail to Old Sand Ridge-Glacier Lake trail split

1.9 miles on Old Sand Ridge Trail to westernmost lake in Five Lakes Basin

2.4 miles on same trail to Lake 6992 in central Five Lakes Basin

2.4 miles on Glacier Lake Trail to Glacier Lake

Low/High Elevations: 6940′/7570′ to Glacier Lake; 7428′ to Five Lakes Basin

Season: Early July through early October

Classification: Moderate

Map: 12

Trailhead: Leave Interstate 80 about 45 miles northeast of Auburn (16 miles west of Donner Pass), and head west on Highway 20. In 3.9 miles you come to Forest Route 18 (Bowman Road). Turn right onto it, and after 6.4 miles reach a junction with F.R. 14 (Grouse Ridge Road), on the right. Take this narrow, steep road 5¼ miles up to the Beyers Lake Trail, which you meet immediately before crossing a ridge. About 200 yards beyond it, your road forks, the right branch traversing through primitive Grouse Ridge Campground. You take the left branch, which traverses 0.2 mile just above the campground to a switchback on a descending ridge. This has a short spur road on it with sufficient parking space for a couple dozen vehicles.

Introduction

Sanford, Milk, and Downey lakes are easily less than an hour's hike away, and each is a suitable goal for day hikers, although campsites exist at each. You can visit all three and return to your trailhead in under 4 miles—not a bad day hike. While Glacier Lake and the five Lakes Basin can be reached in about 2 hours' time, each goal is more suited to an overnight hike. With Glacier Lake as a base camp, you can climb the Black Buttes and even drop to the Beyers Lakes. With the westernmost of the Five Lakes as a base camp, you can explore the stark terrain of the Five Lakes Basin.

There is one route starting near the trailhead that is not covered by this guide: the Beyers Lake Trail. This is a combination of the old, southern part of the Grouse Ridge Trail and the reworked Beyers Lake Trail, and it starts from the Grouse Ridge Road immediately before that road crosses the ridge and then splits. What makes the trail unattractive is that it drops steeply for a knee-knocking 1300 feet before temporarily leveling out, dropping a bit more, and then climbing over 700 feet to Beyers Lake. These are major eleva-

tion changes, and the trail is quite a bit more difficult than the recreation area's relatively level, described Round Lake, Crooked Lake, and Glacier Lake trails. Those who want to reach it in a relatively short distance—about 3 miles if they have an OHV—can drive to the end of the 3-mile-long Eagle Lakes jeep road. Even then, they will have to climb about 1400 feet in elevation up the foot trail to reach Beyers Lake. This route begins at the Indian Springs OHV trailhead, which is ¼ mile northwest of the entrance to Indian Springs Campground, just off Interstate 80.

Description

The Grouse Ridge Recreation Area has such an abundance of lakes within its complex, though not difficult, topography that you may want to make an easy hike ⅓ mile up from trailhead to road's end at the Grouse Ridge fire lookout and study the terrain. From it you'll see a much larger landscape, one that extends from Lassen Peak (10,457′), in the north, to the Crystal Range (almost 10,000′) of Desolation Wilderness, in the south.

Our Grouse Ridge Trail, which was once a jeep road like most of the trails in this area, starts down a bedrock ridge and quickly joins a trail from nearby Grouse Ridge Campground. Then, in about 300 yards, we reach a nearly flat spot from which a use trail descended to Sanford Lake. Since the 1990s, another route to it has existed: Sanford Lake Trail 12E31. This obvious trail begins in the campground, descends shortly east to a gully, then makes a clockwise descent from northeast to south down along or near the gully's creek to the north shore of **Sanford Lake**. A use trail winds around the lake's northeast arm to a crossing of the outlet creek. You can then continue south to the southeast arm which, surprisingly, also has an outlet. Of interest to climbers is the 500-foot-high, low-angle cliff immediately south of Sanford Lake. Almost countless climbing routes exist up it, for hundreds of shallow, steep cracks striate this wall of fine-grained diorite. Because the cracks are shallow, however, protection along many routes is quite difficult with climbing nuts.

We keep to the Grouse Ridge Trail and quickly reach a junction with the official

Downey Lake Trail. Like the Sanford Lake Trail, this one is direct, descending a gully to a campsite on a ledge above the southwest corner of **Downey Lake**. This spacious campsite is open, not secluded, although you can find small, secluded sites elsewhere around the lake. But there is a problem: the west shore of the lake is bordered with dense brush while the east shore is bordered with steep, irregular topography. Circumnavigating the lake is an extremely exhausting chore, so if you want to reach its north shore, stay on the Grouse Ridge Trail until later. Like Downey Lake, the smaller lake to its southeast is hemmed in. It is good for swimming, but not for camping. Loney Lake, about ½ mile south of it, looks inviting on the map, but it is a full 500-foot-drop away by a roundabout route—for competent off-trail hikers only.

Just 0.2 mile beyond the Downey Lake Trail our descending ridge route comes to a junction with **Round Lake Trail** 12E26. If you head just 120 yards west down this trail, you'll reach a junction with another trail, which crosses a nearby saddle and makes a brief descent to the northeast corner of **Milk Lake**. For lakes west of Milk Lake, you'll expend less energy if you start east from the Carr Lake trailhead (Hike 31).

Keeping to Grouse Ridge Trail 13E28, you follow a ridge northeast, descending in ⅔ mile to a junction on a broad, level, viewless saddle with the **Old Sand Ridge-Glacier Lake Trail**. From here the Grouse Ridge Trail continues northward. This lightly used, unappealing route descends to the east edge of the Crooked Lakes basin. You can do some interesting lake hunting if you leave the trail here and head west, although these lakes are better reached from Hike 32: the Crooked Lakes Trail. On the trail, you'll quickly pass through a small meadow, then make a gentle descent along a creek to the easily missed site of Middle Lake, which has been a stump-filled, grassy meadow since the shallow lake's dam was destroyed. About ¾ mile beyond this meadow, you'll pass through another meadow, this one holding grassy Shotgun Lake, which is more meadow than lake. Then, in about 270 yards, you'll meet a trail that climbs 0.6 mile northwest to the north end of Crooked Lakes Trail 12E11, near Rock Lake (see end of Hike 32).

Downey Lake

A Black Buttes' view down into the Beyers Lakes basin

Few people will take the above route. Rather, most will choose either Glacier Lake and environs or the Five Lakes Basin. Across the broad, viewless saddle you arc eastward, spying to your right one of many shallow lakelets in the Downey Lake environs. From here you can head south cross-country past several shallow lakelets to the lake's north shore. From rock benches above this shore, you can high dive into refreshing, deep water. Because the lake lies in fairly open terrain and not in a shadowy cirque, it offers a relatively long, warm swimming season. In contrast, Milk Lake and Sanford Lake are often fed by snowfields lasting well into July.

Only a level 120 yards from the previous junction, we arrive at the east end of the broad saddle, where the **Old Sand Ridge-Glacier Lake trail splits**. From here the Old Sand Ridge Trail (formerly Trail 13E13) climbs northeast while the newer Glacier Lake Trail (the current Trail 13E13) traverses east. The older route will be described first. The Old Sand Ridge Trail first almost loops over to touch the Glacier Lake Trail before starting a moderate-to-steep ascent, the gradient hold-

ing until the trail levels off at point 7372, a minor summit on the west end of Sand Ridge. With the 430-foot elevation gain behind you, the rest of the hike is a breeze, sometimes literally, for your ridgecrest route is mostly open. Sand Ridge, which is a low granitic ridge capped with a thick, broken-up andesite flow, is locally clothed with mule ears—a sunflower associated with all of the Tahoe Sierra's volcanic soils. Our pleasant ridgecrest stroll does include some open clusters of red fir, mountain hemlock, lodgepole pine, and western white pine, and between the conifers grow aromatic plants other than mule ears: coyote mint, tobacco brush, and wild parsley.

The largely open vegetation allows us to constantly observe the changing perspectives around us. The serrated Sierra Buttes (8591'), north of us, contrast with the more subdued, hulking mass of much closer English Mountain (8373'), in the northeast, with Faucherie Lake its base. The former summit is constructed of ancient metamorphosed volcanic rocks about twice as old as the other (Devonian vs. Jurassic). Just north of our ridge is well-named Haystack Mountain, whose southern half is granitic and light gray; its mostly hidden northern half, metavolcanic and brownish. To the southeast rise the rugged Black Buttes, composed of diorite—as in the Sanford Lake environs. Diorite is similar to granite in origin and texture, but is rich in dark minerals, such as pyroxene and olivine. In addition to these summits, we can see Sanford and Downey lakes plus Interstate 80, and we can trace most of our route from Grouse Ridge.

From the east end of Sand Ridge we make a short descent to a granitic saddle, from which experienced hikers will have little trouble hiking cross-country ¾ mile southeast up to Glacier Lake, which lies just below a conspicuous saddle in the Black Buttes' crest. From our granitic saddle our Old Sand Ridge Trail makes a short descent northeast to the shallow, trout-planted **westernmost lake in Five Lakes Basin**. You'll find a campsite among a cluster of lodgepole, red fir, and mountain hemlock just above the lake's southwest shore, and from that site a use trail curves first southeast then east over to a campsite above its southeast shore. From that site you can scramble east to a low ridge above the lake's east shore and view some of the lakes of the glacially scoured, naked granite of Five Lakes Basin. Three lakes lie clustered together, and the open descent to the closest one, **Lake 6992**, is easy. It and an adjacent one should have rainbow trout. A fourth lake lies just southeast above these, while a fifth lake, isolated from the rest, lies northeast below the westernmost lake. From the northeast corner of that lake you can view this isolated lake and an obvious descent to it. However, this small lake is hemmed in by bedrock—not an ideal camping situation—and the lake is not stocked.

Those taking the newer, 1980s-vintage Glacier Lake Trail face—before mid-July—an often boggy, mosquito-ridden, viewless route that requires only a bit less energy than did the Sand Ridge Trail when it branched up to Glacier Lake. The first half of the trail is quite flat, then you climb for several minutes almost to the edge of a fairly large, willowy meadow. Immediately right of the trail is a low ridge, clothed with pinemat manzanita, from which

you have an inspiring view of the looming Black Buttes. With this view and a general lack of mosquitoes, this low ridge makes a nice lunch stop.

Just beyond the willowy meadow you skirt a seasonal lakelet, and have a few minutes of contouring before you begin your climb of 500+ feet to Glacier Lake. You end your eastward traverse in ¼ mile, where you cross a creek that originates at the base of the Black Buttes. Now you climb southeast and in just over ¼ mile recross the creek. After an initial start upstream, you switchback, then resume your southeast course for 0.2 mile to the base of point 7547. The trail can be vague as it snakes briefly eastward up talus, then angles northeast across a bedrock ridge and drops to the south edge of a seasonal pond that lies immediately east of point 7547. The final ½ mile of trail is more obvious, unless snowbound, which it can be well into July. It climbs, generally east-southeast, into a red fir/western white pine forest and terminates in a camping area on a bluff that stands above the west shore of **Glacier Lake**. This area can hold about a dozen two-person tents, and on summer weekends you can expect a lot of company. While *all* the natural lakes in the Grouse Ridge Recreation Area owe their existence to glacial erosion, Glacier Lake is the only one that retains an icy chill about it. Being the highest and coldest lake in the area, it's perhaps the only lake you won't want to swim in. And, although it is planted with trout, you may not catch any, due to heavy fishing.

Still, the lake is a scenic site for a base camp. From it you can make a day hike down to the previously mentioned Five Lakes Basin, or you can climb the buttes or explore the Beyers Lakes vicinity. The highest of these dark buttes is reached from the lake by hiking southeast up the steep, matted slope to a conspicuous saddle. From it, a short climb west, which is no more than a scramble, gets you atop summit 8028, and this provides you with a commanding panoramic sweep across many square miles of glaciated lands.

The shallow, warm Beyers Lakes, which are immediately apparent from the saddle, can be reached by a cross-country route that first diagonals east about ½ mile down to a rocky bench with two lakelets, then parallels a usually dry creek southwest then south another ½ mile down to the easternmost lake. Remember that if you drop 1000 feet to these lakes, you'll have to climb back up that same amount. For this reason, I suggest you make this excursion as a day hike—leave your backpack at Glacier Lake.

⋘ 34 ⋙
Loch Leven Lakes Trail

Distances:
2.8 miles to Upper Loch Leven Lake
2.9 miles to Salmon Lake Trail
   0.9 mile on trail to Salmon Lake
3.1 miles to Middle Loch Leven Lake
3.3 miles to Cherry Point Trail
3.9 miles to High Loch Leven Lake

Low/High Elevations: 5800'/6880'
Season: Late June through late October
Classification: Moderate
Map: 13

Trailheads: Leave Interstate 80 at the Big Bend exit which, for eastbound travelers, is 1½ miles east of the Cisco Grove exit. Westbound travelers: this exit is 6 miles west of the Soda Springs exit. On Hampshire Rocks Road (a part of former Highway 40), drive briefly to the Big Bend Visitor Center, which has the Big Bend Campground on its premises. Then ascend 0.2 mile to the start of a curve with an obvious trailhead parking area, on your left, which can hold about a dozen vehicles. The trailhead—for hikers only—is not directly across the road from it, despite one or more use paths starting in this vicinity, but rather lies on your right about 100 yards northeast beyond the parking area. Equestrians should use a spur road about 0.2 mile southwest of this trailhead.

There is a lightly used alternate trailhead. Leave Interstate 80 at the Yuba Gap exit, which is the first one west of the Interstate 80/Highway 20 interchange. From the south side of the exit, go 0.2 mile east, branch right onto Lake Valley Road and follow it south 1.1

miles to a junction with Mears Meadow Road (Forest Route 19). Branch left and take it 4.2 miles east up to a junction with Huysink Road. Branch left and wind 0.9 mile up to Huysink Lake (on private property), then, on a rough tread, 0.7 mile to a sharp curve right. The Salmon Lake Trail starts east from here. Parking is limited to several vehicles at most.

Introduction
The popular Loch Leven Lakes are relatively low in elevation by Sierran standards, and they lie on open benches, not in deep, shady cirques. For these two reasons they become snow-free a month or so earlier than most of the lakes mentioned in this book. In drier years, they may be snow-free even as early as the Memorial Day weekend. Being relatively low, they are among the warmer lakes for swimming. However, being close to Interstate 80 and therefore popular, they attract many anglers, so don't expect good fishing unless you beat the early-season crowd.

Description
From the curve in Hamshire Rocks Road, the 1990s 1.4-mile route to the Southern Pacific railroad tracks is an extra ½ mile longer than the former route, which began on private property. You start south, winding across glacier-smoothed slabs and microgullies, and reaching, in about 0.2 mile, a trail junction. From it a trail descends about 80 yards to a spur road with parking for three vehicles. Equestrians should start here. The main trail strikes briefly east, then winds and climbs southward to a fine view, from a low, trailside knoll, of your South Yuba River lands. Just beyond it you pass a linear, seasonal, stagnant pond, which serves to mark the approximate half-way point to the railroad tracks. Now you traverse over to a descending ridge, from which the old route descends to nearby private land. Over the next ¼ mile, you quickly bridge an alder-lined creeklet, parallel it upstream past bracken ferns, sagebrush, and lodgepoles, then climb momentarily to the Southern Pacific railroad tracks.

Across the tracks lies the Loch Leven Lakes Trail's resumption. It starts westward, but soon tacks southeast. Well-graded switchbacks lead up through a forest of incense-

cedar, white fir, lodgepole pine, Jeffrey pine, and western white pine. Interspersed beneath the shady conifers—particularly near seasonal creeklets—are tall mountain maples and creeping thimbleberries. Above a small hill in the north, we can see through the opening forest a metamorphic landscape in which desolate 7841′ Red Mountain looms above scrubby, reddish-brown Rattlesnake, which itself rises above Interstate 80. About 50 yards beyond this view is a spring that provides water for even late-season hikers. We leave the forest's pleasant, peaceful cover and soon reach Loch Leven Summit, a point on a minor ridge that is our hike's highest elevation.

Down a shrubby slope our trail makes a short, steep descent to the west shore of generally shallow **Upper Loch Leven Lake**. On this shore as well as above the opposite shore are small, fair campsites. Late in the season, this trout-stocked lake becomes somewhat cloudy. The trail first parallels a low bedrock ridge, and on its lake side its slopes are fine for sunbathing or shallow diving into this relatively warm lake. North-south striations on the granitic bedrock of this area indicate that the South Yuba River glacier, flowing westward down-canyon, was thick enough to spill laterally, south across the Loch Leven Lakes benchlands and into the North Fork American River canyon. For it to do so, the glacier near our trailhead had to have had a minimum thickness of about 1500 feet.

Near the pond lilies at the lake's south end is a junction with the **Salmon Lake Trail**. This trail—a good side trip—starts west-southwest, but quickly veers northwest up a low ridge, crosses it and descends slightly to an open swale before winding south-southwest down to a junction near the base of a low, rocky notch. (Had you started from the alternate trailhead, you would have hiked 1⅓ miles east to this junction. This trail offers a shorter way in to the Loch Leven Lakes, and it involves considerably less climbing to reach them.) From the junction you head south through the nearby notch, then descend briefly through a linear gully that disgorges

on the fairly flat bench by the northeast shore of **Salmon Lake**. Climbers will find short cliffs northwest of the lake, which require a half-length rope (25 meters) for safety. Anglers can compete with belted kingfishers that occasionally dart across the lake in search of its smaller trout. The lake is surrounded with brush, not trees, and so is not as aesthetic as the Loch Leven Lakes. Additionally, it lacks adequate campsites.

From the junction with the Salmon Lake Trail, the Loch Leven Lakes Trail quickly crosses the upper lake's ephemeral outlet creek and climbs through a small notch to island-dotted **Middle (formerly Lower) Loch Leven Lake**. Immediately north of where the trail meets this lake, there is a fair-to-good campsite, and from it the trail traverses south, passing a large campsite. As you head along the generally shallow lake's rocky shore, you'll note some tempting slabs, which like those at the first lake are great for sunbathing after a dip in this lake.

At the lake's southwest corner is a junction with the old **Cherry Point Trail**. This trail descends, steeply at times, 2¼ miles to a grassy meadow along a seasonal tributary of Little Granite Creek. Because the total drop to it is significant, about 800 feet, it is not worth your effort except perhaps in mid-October,

Middle Loch Leven Lake

High Loch Leven Lake

when the abundant aspens just north of it turn the canyon gold with color. Onward, the Big Granite Creek Trail eventually descends several miles to the North Fork American River, which at about 3200 feet elevation, represents a very major 3600-foot drop from Middle Loch Leven Lake.

After rounding that lake's southern tip, the Lock Leven Lakes Trail curves northeast, traverses through a narrow, shady gully, crosses its creek, and climbs moderately up to trail's end at **High Loch Leven Lake**. This lake, the shallowest of this hike's four lakes, nevertheless has the clearest water (although as in any stream or lake, Giardia may be lurking). Like the others, it is good for swimming, and it has a beautiful little island from which one can sunbathe on or dive from. The combination of cliffs and conifers that border this heather-lined lake makes it perhaps the most scenic, and its southeast shore has sites that can hold dozens of campers.

⇜ 35 ⇝
Pacific Crest Trail, north to Paradise Lake

Distances:
2.5 miles to Peter Grubb Hut
2.6 miles to Sand Ridge Lake Trail
    1.9 miles on trail to Sand Ridge Lake
6.6 miles to Magonigal Camp jeep road
    1.1 miles on jeep road to Paradise Lake
Low/High Elevations: 7280'/8350'
Season: Mid-July through mid-October
Classification: Moderate
Map: 14

Trailheads: Take Interstate 80's Castle Peak/Boreal Ridge exit, which is the first exit east of the Soda Springs' exit and the first one west of the highway's Donner Summit Safety Roadside Rest Area. From the north side of the highway, drive 0.2 mile northeast up a paved road, then briefly north on a dirt tread to a turnaround spot. Many hikers park here, and this spot is where the above mileages are measured from. Some, however, drive farther, reaching a junction with a right-branching road in about 0.6 mile, while a few, usually in 4WDS, manage to drive an additional 0.9 mile up the rutted jeep road to a small parking area at its end. Doing so cuts 1.5 miles from all of the above destinations. Between the beginning and end of the dirt road are various spots to park. The farther you drive, the less you have to hike. Then again, the farther you drive, the more likely you may get stuck, especially if you are in a low-clearance vehicle. You can also park at the official Pacific Crest Trail's trailhead, mentioned in the next hike. Doing so adds 2.2 miles to all of the above destinations.

Introduction

In the past, the Magonigal Camp jeep road provided access for OHVs to Paradise Lake, although this road now is supposed to be closed to them. Today you are more likely to meet mountain bikers ascending this road or, unfortunately, ascending the Sand Ridge Lake Trail to the Pacific Crest Trail, and then taking it illegally north to that jeep road. Of hundreds of Sierran lakes I've visited, I (subjectively) rank Paradise Lake in my top-ten list.

Description

From the turnaround spot just beyond where the paved road ends, you start your hike up a dirt road that is drivable for many automobiles. In ½ mile the road forks, the right branch descending northeast to a nearby meadow on the floor of Castle Valley. We keep left, and the ascent switches from generally gentle to generally moderate. You'll know you're approaching road's end when the gradient switches to steep. There, you shift into low gear, climbing very steeply 150 yards up a trail—formerly a *real* jeep road—to a junction with the Pacific Crest Trail. In another 100 yards, you top out at Castle Pass.

You have hiked about 1.6 miles to this pass. But if you are on the PCT and have started from the trailhead mentioned in the next hike, you will have hiked about 3.8 miles to it. For the few that do this, follow that hike's description about 1.4 miles to where the Pacific Crest and the Summit Lake trails intersect. The PCT then makes a brief climb west, before turning southwest to descend to the grounds of west-

bound Interstate 80's Donner Summit Safety Roadside Rest Area. Just northeast of its building, the PCT joins a loop trail that circles a lakelet lying immediately west of the building. Walk about 150 yards along this trail to a junction by the lakelet's west shore, where the loop trail turns south. On the PCT you climb west-southwest across glaciated granitic slabs, then soon turn northwest and parallel a major fracture in the bedrock. Beyond it the PCT veers west toward Castle Valley and, staying within tree cover, follows the valley's meadow northwest to a road that descends to it. (This is the same road mentioned in the beginning of this hike.) Onward, the early-season hiker is likely to encounter at least a dozen seasonal streams, some of them quite impressive. And before mid-July you just might get wet feet—and find much of the trail under snow. From the last seasonal stream the PCT curves southwest up to the aforementioned trail junction below Castle Pass.

From Castle Pass you'll see an obvious trail starting north-northeast up a ridgecrest. This popular use trail takes you, in about a mile, up to the west summit of Castle Peak. (This is the easiest and safest one to ascend; mountaineers can tackle the middle and east summits.) The upper part of the trail is quite steep, and you can slip on loose volcanic rubble. Nevertheless, for the careful hiker, the great physical exertion is rewarded with superlative views. Bring a compass and a Tahoe National Forest map to identify the myriad features. One off the map is Lassen Peak, in the northwest, a mighty 98 miles distant, and seen only when visibility is quite good. From Castle Peak another use trail traverses north then northwest along a ridgecrest over to Basin Peak, which also has rewarding views. From the southeast base of the peak, some hikers head north over to the peak's east ridge and descend it to the Devils Oven Lake Trail (next hike). If you are interested only in Basin Peak, the best way to it is to leave the PCT north of Round Valley and ascend its west or northwest slopes.

Round Valley is our next destination, and from Castle Pass we traverse north on the PCT for about ½ mile before commencing a switchbacking descent to the south end of the valley.

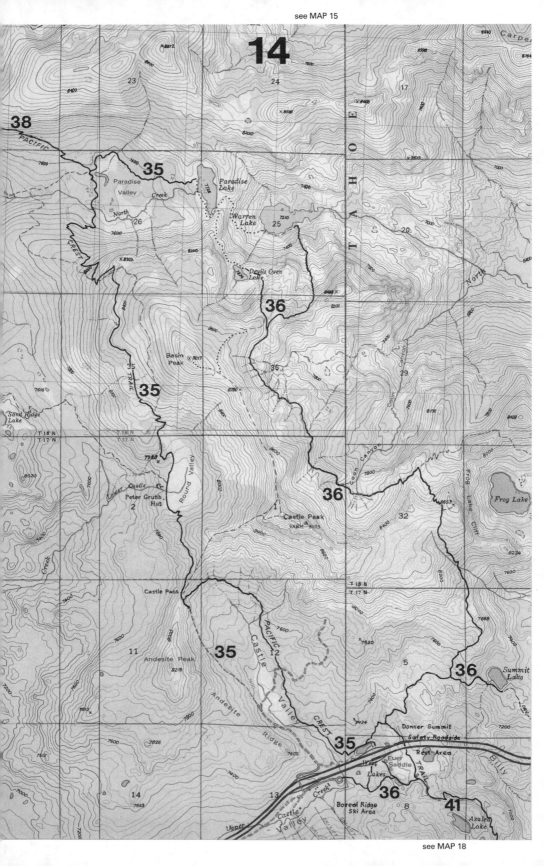

Quickly we reach **Peter Grubb Hut**, which is one of several Sierra Club cabins in the Sierra Nevada. Just southwest of the hut grow some fine specimens of western white pine. When mature, these trees have a conspicuous checkerboard pattern on their trunks, which makes them readily distinguishable. The hut, the pines, and the floor of Round Valley all rest on a granitic bench. Note, across the valley, where the granite gives way to horizontal volcanic flows. Roughly the upper 700 feet of Basin Peak is composed of flows, the upper ones basaltic and the lower ones andesitic. These flows were laid down across a rolling granitic landscape roughly 10 to 15 million years ago. Surveying these flows, late-season hikers have a bonus, for then Basin Peak's slopes turn rusty red as several million lowly Davis' knotweeds don their fall colors. Just past the hut we jump across Lower Castle Creek and come to **Sand Ridge Lake Trail**. This descends ⅓ mile west, traverses 1.0 mile generally northwest to a crossing of a boggy, linear meadow, then climbs ⅓ mile west to a

junction. A spur trail branching left winds up and over to mosquito-prone, shallow **Sand Ridge Lake**—not a worthy goal.

North from the Sand Ridge Lake Trail junction the PCT climbs easily and briefly to the back side of a glacier-smoothed granitic outcrop, which, on the map, is elevation "7920." From it you have westward views of the Sand Ridge environs. Your climb continues, first up along a seasonal creeklet, and then via several switchbacks up to gentler slopes, across which the PCT takes an undulating, generally open, course north. Along it you can leave the trail almost anywhere and through an open subalpine forest you climb about 700 feet in elevation more or less directly up volcanic slopes to the gentle 9017' summit of Basin Peak. It gives you a nearly 360° view of much of the lands covered in this hiking chapter, only slightly higher Castle Peak to the south and Mt. Lola to the north blocking out some of the lands. The nutrient-rich soils it this area support dozens of subalpine-wildflower species, a reward for mountaineering botanists.

Paradise Lake, from granitic cliffs by its south tip. Twenty thousand years ago, this scene lay entirely under glacier ice.

After about a mile of traverse on the PCT, it switchbacks southwest. From this spot you can climb northeast briefly upslope to around the environs of a granitic knoll, "8302" on the map. It has several small patches of glacier-polished bedrock, and when the lighting is right, you can detect faint striations oriented 30°. One would have expected that a glacier originating on the slopes of Basin Peak would have flowed directly downslope, that is, at about 330°. However, the glaciers on both sides of deep North Creek (Paradise Valley) canyon poured voluminous ice into it, filling it up not part way, but to the rim and above. At its maximum the glacier's ice surface was at a minimum elevation of 8500 feet, and from about Paradise Valley it flowed eastward across the Paradise Lake basin down into the North Fork Prosser Creek canyon. (Contrary to what one might expect, glaciers do not always flow away from the Sierran crest; they sometimes flow across it.) This eastward flow diverted the downslope motion of the Basin Peak ice, whence the 30° orientation.

From "8302," hikers can traverse cross-country east along the corrugated topography just above the rim of North Creek canyon to glacially striated and polished knolls above Paradise and Devils Oven lakes. Hikers can start south for a contour counterclockwise on relatively gentle, volcanic slopes high above Devils Oven Lake to the ridge south of and above it, while *skilled* mountaineers can descend north along the west side of an impressive buttress that descends to the southeast shore of Paradise Lake. Although relatively safe by climbing standards, this is a Class 3, somewhat exposed, route that invites serious consequences for the unqualified.

Virtually all readers will keep to the PCT, so from the switchback you make a 700-foot descent into North Creek canyon. You switchback down through a forest dominated by snow-loving mountain hemlocks, and your trail can be snowbound well into July. With all this snow come myriad mosquitoes, and the floor of the canyon, known as Paradise Valley, can be anything but paradise. On the floor you snake northward over to a sturdy bridge across North Creek, then continue to the **Magonigal Camp jeep road**. Note this junc-tion, which is immediately west of a large, boggy meadow. If pursued by mosquitoes on your return trip, you could easily speed past this junction.

Hike 38, which has come 7⅔ miles east along the PCT from the Meadow Lake Road, joins our route here for the last mile to Paradise Lake. Your road, which is often muddy before September, first circles the boggy meadow, then contorts among trees, mudholes, and boulders before diverging into use paths just before the lake. Since the lake spans a broad bench above Paradise Valley, you need not fret over finding it; it's impossible to miss.

While Paradise Valley is paradise for mosquitoes, **Paradise Lake**, or at least its east shore, can be paradise for backpackers (its west shore is mosquito prone and is occasionally approached by OHVs). To reach that shore, round the lake at its south tip, not along the brushy north shore. Just before the south tip you'll hit some bedrock cliffs, but these are quite safely negotiated with a bit of prudent route finding. Look for small campsites along the low, broad, mostly-barren-bedrock saddle above the lake. On it you have a superlative view of Warren Lake, to the east well below you, and you have plenty of slabs for sunbathing after a swim in refreshing Paradise Lake. Lying there, you might see some of the hundreds of glacial striations in the area that are oriented east-west. The orientations of striations on both sides of your canyon clearly indicate that the last glacier flowed east across the Paradise Lake area.

Experienced mountaineers can descend to Warren Lake along a ducked, vigorous—and potentially dangerous—cross-country route. From the low point of the saddle, this route quickly drops to the north end of a granitic bench the size of a football field. The crux is the first 100 yards down from its south end; it's rather steep. Alternatively, experienced mountaineers can head south from the saddle, hopscotching from bench to granitic bench over to tightly confined Devils Oven Lake. However, this stark, lightly visited lake is best approached from the Warren Lake Trail, for from it a use trail down to the lake is much more obvious.

⇜ 36 ⇝
Summit, Devils Oven, and Warren Lakes

Distances:

1.8 miles to Warren Lake Trail
   0.5 mile on Summit Lake Trail to south
     corner of Summit Lake
3.4 miles to saddle
   0.1 mile east to Frog Lake viewpoint
6.2 miles to Devils Oven Lake Trail
   0.5 mile on use trail to Devils Oven Lake
7.5 miles to Warren Lake

Low/High Elevations: 7200′/8653′

Season: Late July through early October

Classification: Easy to Summit Lake; strenuous to Devils Oven and Warren lakes

Map: 14

Trailhead: Take Interstate 80′s Castle Peak/Boreal Ridge exit, which is the first exit east of the Soda Springs′ exit and the first one west of the highway′s Donner Summit Safety Roadside Rest Area. Immediately south of the eastbound lanes′ onramp and offramp, you′ll reach an obvious road which you follow 0.3 mile east to its end at the Pacific Crest Trail′s trailhead parking lot.

Introduction

This hike′s major goal, Warren Lake, is at almost the same elevation as the trailhead. Only a mountain of climbing—over 2000 feet total elevation change in either direction—stands in the way. The hike, then, is not for the weak-hearted. Since most of the Tahoe Sierra′s lakes are considerably easier to reach, why visit Warren Lake? The lake, while interesting, is not particularly outstanding. However, the route to it is. The trail contains a 3-mile rambling traverse of a multifaceted, glaciated basin that is reminiscent of Washington′s North Cascades, conveying a sense of unbridled wilderness not found in most of the Tahoe Sierra.

Description

From the lot, you hike 300 yards eastward to the Glacier Meadow Loop Trail, go ¼ mile up along it, and leave it at a junction. There, just above a shallow, murky lakelet, you make a

200-yard traverse east to a junction with the Pacific Crest Trail. One half mile into your journey, you now go about ¼ mile north along this trail, tunnel under both the eastbound and westbound lanes of I-80, then go a similar distance to a junction with the Summit Lake Trail. On it you climb northeast, crossing two creeklets before paralleling the vertical east side of a minor granitic ridge. You then cross two more creeklets, arc through a crescentic corn-lily meadow, and quickly arrive at a junction with the **Warren Lake Trail**, branching left, north.

Most hikers probably will continue along the Summit Lake Trail. Eastward this leads out to the nose of a bald, descending ridge, proffering a view of I-80 traffic, then it retreats to forest cover. In a couple of minutes you cross the sometimes flowing outlet of **Summit Lake**, then in an equal time parallel the shoreline to arrive at its **south corner**. There are at least three campsites in this general vicinity, although the ambiance is not conducive to a wilderness experience. First, there is the drone of I-80 traffic, a mere ½ mile to the south; and second, the lake is accessible by OHVs. Although the lake is quite shallow along its edges, it nevertheless has a maximum depth of 15 feet, sufficient to maintain its trout population.

Those ready for a workout start north on the Warren Lake Trail, and you immediately begin to climb in earnest. A largely brushy, moderate climb ends as you crest a minor volcanic ridge, carpeted with mule ears, just west of point 7888, a low granitic knoll. Take a breather, walk over to it, and enjoy the scenery. If you look closely, you can see that it has tiny patches of fresh polish, indicating that a glacier flowed across it some 13,000+ years ago. This glacier in its waning stage also dropped some small volcanic rocks that it had incorporated from volcanic slopes above you.

Onward, you traverse around a seasonally wet meadow just north of the knoll, eyeing the lofty Frog Lake point, 800 feet above you, to which you′ll climb. Spurred on, you expend energy proportionally as the trail grades from level to steep. Fortunately, the steep grade persists but ¼ mile, and then on a moderate grade you exchange forest shade for an open field of mule ears, lupines, knotweeds, sidalceas, and other wildflowers. The trail peaks out on an often windblown **saddle** adorned with scattered whitebark pines, western white pines, and mountain hemlocks. From this vicinity an obvious spur trail climbs 200 yards to the **Frog Lake viewpoint**, atop Frog Lake Cliff. The panoramic views from it more than compensate for the minor effort to reach it. Like the low granitic knoll now way below you, this viewpoint also was glaciated. However, the ice was so thin that it did not visibly polish or abrade the bedrock. Its evidence is what is missing: had a glacier swept below either side of the viewpoint, it would have left a lateral moraine along its edge, but none exist; a thin veneer of glacial ice covered all but the Castle Peak-Basin Peak crest. From your viewpoint, note the irregular contact between the layered volcanic rocks of that crest and the underlying granitic rocks. When the volcanic rocks were laid down about 12-16 million years ago, they buried many a granitic valley. Also note the next 3-mile stretch of route across basin slopes. This rambling traverse ends by a far saddle to the northwest of your viewpoint.

With that saddle as a next goal, you switchback down to a ridge junction with a lateral trail from the Frog Lake environs. A brief traverse southwest takes you to a nearby second ridge, from where the rugged terrain ahead is amply spread before you. Before mid-July the route ahead can be smothered in snow, and has over two dozen creeklets to cross. By mid-August, some of the creeklets dry up, and the subalpine wildflowers locally dazzle the eye.

Near the end of your rollercoaster traverse, you cross a low granitic ridge, and at the next, adjacent one arrive at a junction with the **Devils Oven Lake Trail**. This obvious trail north climbs slightly to a level spot on a granitic ridge, from which another use trail begins a climb, first south-southwest then west, up a volcanic ridge. That use trail traverses just above the brink of cliffs of the Devils Oven Lake cirque, while another route, more cross-country than trail, curves from west to south as it ascends the volcanic ridge to the southeast base of Basin Peak. From the level spot on the granitic ridge the Devils

Oven Lake Trail quickly deteriorates into an essentially cross-country route. This is an obvious, curving, descending route, and its steep gradient gets you to **Devils Oven Lake** in short order. Along this 500-foot drop in elevation, you can identify a highly feasible traverse from this lake over to Paradise Lake. Also, if you plan to climb from Warren Lake up to Paradise Lake, assess your potential route.

From the start of the Devils Oven Lake Trail the Warren Lake Trail heads northeast briefly to a crest, cuts shortly across its southern slopes, then crosses it to diagonal northeast down a north-facing slope with long-lasting snow patches to a nearby bench. From this you'll drop 1000 feet on one of the steepest knee-jarring trails imaginable. Constrained by encroaching bedrock, the trail tries vainly to ease the grade with dozens of minuscule switchbacks. By the time you reach several campsites at trail's end, you'll need a well-earned layover day at **Warren Lake**. Less used campsites lie about the lake, particularly along its western half (thickets impede a traverse around the eastern half).

The cross-country climb up to Paradise Lake involves only half as much elevation gain as the trail's steep return route. Consequently, hikers reluctant to retrace their steps up it may be sorely tempted to opt for the cross-country route, which starts at the end of a use trail near Warren Lake's southwest corner. Be forewarned: the ducked route can be hard to follow, and in several places you'll have to use hands as well as feet. This is no route for novices or for hikers with heavy frame packs. If you reach a large bench the size of a football field, you've got the rest of the route made.

⤳ 37 ⤵
Mt. Lola Trail

Distances:
2.1 miles to bridge across Cold Stream
3.1 miles to alternate trailhead
5.3 miles to Mt. Lola
Low/High Elevations: 6620'/9148'

Season: Mid-July through mid-October

Classification: Strenuous

Map: 16

Trailhead: Leave Interstate 80 near the east end of Truckee and drive 14½ miles north on Highway 89 to Forest Route 07 (this junction is 9 miles southeast of Sierraville.) Take this paved road 1.5 miles west to a road branching left. In ¾ mile this starts south to a nearby bridge over the Little Truckee River, then winds east to an intersection of the Henness Pass Road. Turn sharply right onto it and take it 3.0 miles west to a road on the left, which switchbacks south up to private lands, then ¼ mile past it to a spur road diagonaling left. Drive 100 yards up it to the trailhead at its end, where there is parking for about 10 vehicles.

Introduction

Mt. Lola, at 9148 feet elevation, is the highest peak in Interstate 80's recreation lands. To climb to a higher elevation, you would have to visit summits in the the Carson Range, above Lake Tahoe's northeast, east and south shores, or ones in Desolation Wilderness, above its southwest shore. Lola's summit presents far-ranging vistas similar to those from Castle and Basin peaks (Hike 35), which are nearly as high, but the ones from Lola may seem wilder, since you are quite removed from Interstate 80.

Description

The Mt. Lola Trail starts quite uneventfully, climbing a forested route southwest at a reasonable grade for ½ mile up to aspens and mule ears, then curving south in ¼ mile to the mouth of Cold Stream canyon. About ¼ mile up it you'll pass a junction from which an abandoned trail parallels ours south up-canyon. It stays low, close to the stream, while ours is typically about 100 feet above it. Past the junction we begin to parallel a private logging road. At first it is out of sight above us, but the road and our trail gradually converge, eventually touching about 1⅔ mile from our trailhead. They stay close together for about 0.4 mile, to where the trail dead-ends on the road. On it you walk 160 yards up to a **bridge across Cold Stream**, then continue 70 yards farther to your trail's resumption south.

Over the next ½ mile your trail stays within forest cover, tightly confined between the logging road just above and Cold Stream just below. But then it emerges onto the northern end of often saturated Cold Stream Meadow. By skirting just above its west edge, our trail keeps our feet dry. As Tahoe Sierra meadows go, it is on the large size and, with tightly meandering Cold Stream flowing through it, is quite attractive. After about 0.3 mile we leave its southwest end and our trail dead-ends on the logging road. On it we walk 50 yards south to where it angles east to cross the stream. If you could drive up the logging roads to this spot, an **alternate trailhead**, you would cut your energy expenditures in half. However, sections 1 and 29 are on private land, and the roads to this spot may be closed to the public, so don't plan on it. Thus far, your hike has been quite easy, averaging only 7% in gradient. That is about to change; the remaining 2.2 miles average 12%—fairly steep, and in relatively thin air.

Just into the second half of our hike, we at first parallel Cold Stream, quickly boulder-hop a tributary creek, traverse a meadow of willows and corn lilies just beyond it, then climb moderately to a small, corn-lily meadow, ⅓ mile from the alternate trailhead. Over the next ⅓ mile we climb on a lesser gradient to a crossing of Cold Stream, then about 150 yards above it cross a major tributary just before it reaches the stream. Ahead, we climb quite steeply almost 300 yards to a switchback near some Cold Stream cascades. So far in this second half, lodgepole pine, western white pine, and red fir have been the dominant species, but from about the switchback on, mountain hemlocks assume dominance. These trees thrive in areas of deep snow, and if you hike here before mid-July (before August in some wet years), be prepared for a lot of snow.

From the switchback the blazed trail diagonals up slopes, first southeast then east, for 0.3 mile to another switchback, from which it diagonals 0.2 mile southwest to a lengthy ridge, about 4½ miles from our trailhead. Here, above 8500 feet, whitebark pines join the open ranks of mountain hemlocks and western white pines. If you had snow below,

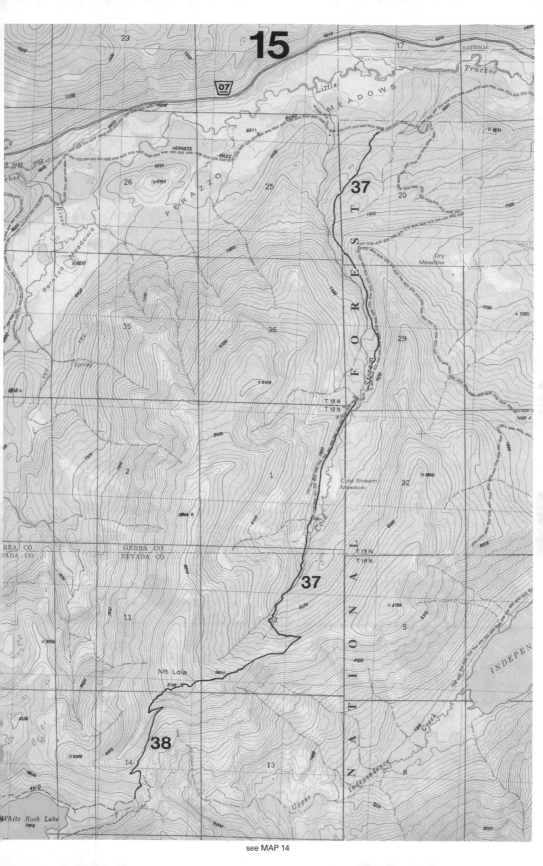

15

you'll have snow above, which generally is not a problem, since the trail ascends directly west up the ridge. The gradient changes from level, to gentle, to moderate, then at a mass of ridge lava, the trail veers right to circle around and above it, and the gradient stays steep along the ridge for the next 200 feet of elevation gain, to where you are just north of a conspicuous lava knoll.

Until about late July or early August, you now confront a short but steep, icy snowbank. I kick-stepped up it in jogging shoes without a problem, but should you slip, you possibly could slide quite a distance northeast downslope. Should you encounter the snowbank, be sure to keep north of the ridge, since to the south, toward the lava knoll, it drops off dangerously steeply. Atop the snowbank you are also atop a nearly level ridge, and can walk over to the lava knoll. The short ascent to its summit is relatively easy, but quite exposed, and for many will not be worth its summit views. Better ones lie just ahead. You briefly traverse the nearly level ridge west to the east base of Mt. Lola's summit block, then ascend steeply for several minutes to reach the highest summit of **Mt. Lola**.

This summit barely exceeds one on a nearly level lava ridge extending just west of true north, or about 345°. With that bearing to orient us, we can begin a counterclockwise scan of the scenery. If you have excellent visibility, you should be able to see snowy Lassen Peak (10,457'), the southernmost major volcano of the Cascade Range, at about a 320° bearing and a hefty 94 miles away. However, on many days, substandard visibility obscures it, and the only prominent peak in the northwest quadrant is then the sawtoothed Sierra Buttes (8591'), in the northwest, a mere 19 miles distant. Closer and to the west rise the summits and ridges of Grouse Ridge Recreation Area, and just north of its northeastern part is English Mountain (8373'), 10 miles distant, the highest summit west of the Sierra crest. To the southwest and at the base of Mt. Lola, White Rock Lake is a conspicuous blue gem among a sea of forest green and granite gray. To the south stand subdued Basin Peak (9017') and left of it, craggy Castle Peak (9103'). Beyond them lies unseen Donner Pass, above which in

the distance, almost breaking the skyline, is Tinker Knob (8949'). Backdropping it on the skyline is a high ridge that serves as the northern boundary of Granite Chief Wilderness. And to its left in the hazy, great distance rise the high summits of Desolation Wilderness. You can then continue your counterclockwise scan over to the southern part of the Carson Range, and see Freel Peak (10,881'), to the south-southeast about 46 miles away, the highest summit in the Tahoe Sierra. Trace the range north to a prominent summit, Mt. Rose (10,776'), lying south of east 25 miles away. Just left but much closer lies Independence Lake, which you've undoubtedly noticed along your ascent. In the hazy distance beyond it lies spreading Stampede Reservoir. Finally, we complete our panorama with views to the northeast and north, where amazingly flat-floored Sierra Valley sprawls below the distant horizon.

⊰≫ 38 ⊰≫
Pacific Crest Trail east to White Rock Lake, Mt. Lola, and Paradise Lake

Distances:
4.6 miles to White Rock Lake jeep road
   1.3 miles on jeep road to east-shore campsites
   1.8 miles to old Mt. Lola Trail
   3.1 miles to Mt. Lola
5.3 miles to White Rock Creek
5.4 miles to new Mt. Lola Trail
   0.7 mile up trail to White Rock Lake
   2.2 miles up trail to old Mt. Lola Trail
   3.4 miles to Mt. Lola
7.6 miles to Magonigal Camp jeep road
8.7 miles to Paradise Lake
Low/High Elevations: 7530'/8110'; 9148' at Mt. Lola summit
Season: Mid-July through mid-October
Classification: Moderate
Maps: 15, 16, and 14

Trailheads: Leave Interstate 80 near the east end of Truckee and drive 14½ miles north on Highway 89 to Forest Route 07 (this junction is 9 miles southeast of Sierraville). Take this paved road 9½ miles west, branch left onto Forest Route 86, and on it drive 6½ miles up to where the Pacific Crest Trail (PCT) crosses the road, and park nearby. This cryptic spot is about 60 yards before your south-climbing road reached the north edge of a nearly level meadow. Should you miss it, you will reach a junction with the White Rock Lake jeep road in 0.2 mile.

Depending on the kind of vehicle you drive, you can reduce the distance to this hike's destinations. On the jeep road, which is 19N11A on the map, vehicles other than stretch limos should be able to go 0.8 mile to a road branching right, which crosses Bear Valley's creek, and then 0.1 mile farther to a second road branching right, the route of the White Rock Lake jeep road. With a high-clearance vehicle, preferably with 4WD, you can drive all the way to the PCT crossing, which shaves 4.6 miles off the above destinations. There are side roads, but the route usually is adequately, if unofficially, marked. In the first ⅓ mile, it descends to Bear Valley's creek, climbs to a road branching left, then quickly reaches a second one left. Ahead, south, you then climb and descend, then after about 1 mile turn east to descend to a granitic bench. On it you negotiate several creeklets and some ruts, then in about another mile curve northeast to start an obvious climb. After about 0.3 mile it heads north for another 0.3 mile, to a curve east, near which you will find the PCT. In early season, this and the two following trailhead routes may have a fallen tree or two across the roads, but by midseason OHVers usually have removed them or sawed through them.

Lacking a 4WD, you can take the aforementioned second road branching right. This goes about ⅔ mile up to a junction, on the right, from which you take a road ⅓ mile to a crest and the PCT (by the "38" hike number in the center of Map 15). Starting here saves 3.1 miles of hiking. The road ahead, descending into Toms Valley, degenerates into a 4WD road before reaching it. Finally, rather than taking the White Rock Lake jeep road across Bear Valley's creek, you can take a road northeast to just below a saddle at the upper end of the valley. This is after about a mile of driving, and just after the road curves south. Starting on the PCT from this saddle saves 2.1 miles of hiking.

Introduction

While most people reach Paradise Lake with a PCT hike north from the Interstate 80 environs, you can also reach it from a less used PCT stretch from F.R. 86, a major road of the Tahoe National Forest. Unless you've got an OHV with which to drive up the Magonigal Camp jeep road to Paradise Lake, the shortest way to it is along this route, starting from one of the alternate trailheads. You can leave the trail to camp at White Rock Lake or to scale Mt. Lola, the highest summit between several Desolation Wilderness peaks, about 40 miles south, and Lassen Peak, about 94 miles northwest.

Description

From Forest Route 86 the southbound PCT begins a few paces down this road than from the northbound PCT (Hike 39). You immediately cross a usually flowing creek, which drains the adjacent meadow, then pass a small outcrop of metamorphic rock. This rock gives way to granitic rock, but you won't see the contact between the two, since a much younger layer of volcanic rocks, roughly 12-16 million years old, covers most of the terrain. You climb through a selectively logged forest of red firs and western white pines, then traverse across open volcanic slopes. Because volcanic rocks decompose to clay soils, this traverse (and most of the route) can be quite muddy when the ground is wet. Note some light-gray granitic boulders, which are certainly out of place here. These were left by a giant glacier which, combined with others, covered nearly all the lands you see. Near the end of your traverse, leave the trail for a brief climb to point 7942 for fine views. To the northwest you see a tree-lined lakelet below you, and distant Sierra Buttes on the horizon.

The PCT now traverses east along a volcanic ridge, almost touching the Bear Valley loop road as it crosses a saddle before turning south to follow a similar ridge. Just ahead, your trail crosses another saddle just above the loop road. This spot is the alternate trailhead that is 2.1 miles along your hike. From it your trail climbs to a precarious point, 8086, which has superb views to the north and northeast—the best such views on this hike's stretch of PCT. Your viewpoint stands at the head of a glaciated valley. From here, glaciers repeatedly flowed 4 miles north-northeast down Perazzo Canyon to a main canyon, through which an 800-foot-thick glacier flowed east along Forest Route 07 almost to Highway 89. Leaving the knobby viewpoint, which is composed of autobrecciated lava, you descend into a forest and in a couple of minutes reach a viewless saddle crossed by a road—a second alternate trailhead, which is 3.1 miles along your hike. If you're starting your hike here and will not be climbing Mt. Lola, consider taking a few minutes to climb up to point 8086 and admire the views.

From the trans-crest road at the saddle, you encounter the first sizable population of mountain hemlocks, which shelter snow, in some years, until September. The tread can be vague, but the trail essentially climbs south for 0.1 mile before contouring southeast. You soon emerge from the dense forest and contour across the head of a boggy, sloping meadow. The contour continues around a low crest point, then you meet a crest saddle, which has your first good views south. On the southeast skyline stands rounded Basin Peak, with three-turreted Castle Peak just to the right behind it. In front of Basin Peak lies straight, deep, granite-walled North Creek (Paradise Lake) canyon.

Below you in the foreground is a meadow, and to reach it, the PCT first switchbacks down profusely gullied slopes to a bend in the **White Rock Lake jeep road** (19N11A), a third alternate trailhead, which is 4.6 miles along your hike. To reach White Rock Lake and/or Mt. Lola, take this road east, which gains about 140 feet of elevation in about ½ mile, then levels out on a broad bench, from which a spur road descends about ¼ mile southeast to relatively isolated camping near the outlet of White Rock Lake. From the junction, the main jeep road makes an equally steep and

short descent to the lake's north shore, then traverses along it to several **east-shore campsites**. These are quite spacious and would be quite popular were they closer to a highway. From them the jeep road climbs eastward 0.3 mile to a junction with a south-heading spur road that quickly dead-ends at a campsite. If you were to walk south upslope for about a minute from that site, you would reach the new (1990s vintage) Mt. Lola Trail, which *ahead* is better graded than the old. Just 0.2 mile past the junction the jeep road ends at the start of the **old Mt. Lola Trail**.

On it you climb almost 1200 feet to the summit, and the first 200+ feet of elevation gain is exceptionally steep. This northward stretch on volcanic rubble is tolerable going up, but is easy to slip on when you are going down. After 0.2 mile, the grade eases dramatically in a shallow gully, and if you look on its opposite (east) slope, you should be able to find the new Mt. Lola Trail among the brush and boulders. (You might take it on your descent, winding down slopes to where it levels off in deep forest, then going cross-country northwest or west to the upper part of the jeep road.)

From the gully, the Mt. Lola Trail curves westward over to a switchback with a view of White Rock Lake, then climbs a well-graded, open-forest stretch that switchbacks again to climb to a narrow ridgecrest. Your last ⅓ mile is steep, climbing brushy, volcanic slopes to the top of **Mt. Lola**. Summit views are described at the end of the previous hike.

If you are bound for Paradise Lake, then from the White Rock Lake jeep road you take the PCT. Ideally, the PCT should have traversed east from the jeep road to the dam across White Rock Lake, then south to a ridge above North Creek canyon, and finally east across slopes to Paradise Lake. Instead, it descends and ascends unnecessarily first across the White Rock Creek canyon then across the North Creek canyon, following an old route. You begin on a winding descent to the nearby, aforementioned meadow. There, the trail generally stays just within forest cover of the meadow's northeast edge and just west of a seasonal creeklet, but halfway down alongside the meadow, the trail enters

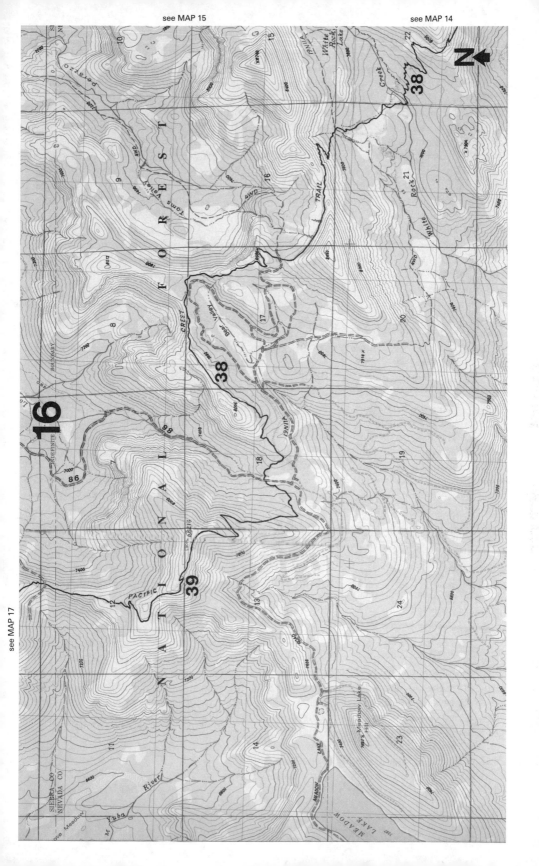

it. When the grass is high, the route may be obscure because of one or more misleading use paths. In a mix of trees and grass, the trail heads briefly east across the creeklet, then south to recross it. It then continues south across the lower meadow and into the forest to quickly arrive at a sturdy bridge across **White Rock Creek**. Should you lose the trail descending through the meadow, you should have little problem spotting the bridge. From the creek's south bank, the PCT heads about 0.1 east upstream to a junction with the 1990s lower stretch of the **new Mt. Lola Trail**.

Northbound PCT hikers would take this route to reach White Rock Lake or the Mt. Lola summit. Since it involves about 100 feet more elevation gain to reach the lake than does the previously mentioned jeep road, most won't want to take it. The trail, however, is pleasant enough, following White Rock Creek, usually at a distance, upstream for 0.7 mile to the dammed outlet of **White Rock Lake**. From there one can traverse to the southeast shore, and leave the trail for a brief walk north to a jutting, rocky, southeast-shore peninsula. There you can find small campsites, and there are some near-shore islands you can easily swim to and sunbathe on. The volcanic-ridge backdrop seen from this peninsula is quite dramatic, and the campsites are quite isolated. Looking at the map, one would think that the peninsula could be easily reached from a traverse south from the lake's east-shore campsites. However, this would entail crossing a wide swath of swampy meadow, which would be okay if you have waterproof boots.

From behind the peninsula the Mt. Lola Trail, which can be snowbound well into July, traverses northeast across lower, mostly viewless slopes, making many minor ups and downs before finally starting a climb below a granitic ridge on the Sierra crest. It gains this ridge on a broad saddle, across which you could walk a few paces northeast for a view of large, linear Independence Lake, about 1000 feet below. The trail then climbs north toward a knoll on the ridge, then traverses northwest around it to dead-end in the aforementioned shallow gully, where you join the **old Mt. Lola Trail**.

From the trail junction along White Rock Creek, the PCT switchbacks up increasingly steep slopes, largely cloaked in a dense, snow-harboring forest. After 1.1 miles you reach a granitic knoll on the descending ridge above the North Creek canyon, which provides you with an excellent view up-canyon. Does this canyon look a little different from most High Sierra canyons? It is lacking one important feature, a headwall. It never existed. What you see here is only the western part of a canyon, for the eastern part has vanished. Back in the late days of the dinosaurs, a river or large stream originated in eastern lands and flowed west down this canyon. Then around 80 million years ago, lands east of today's Sierran crest sank in response to extensional (pull-apart) faulting. Faulting has occurred periodically over millions of years since then, and subsidence of eastern lands still may be occurring on a limited basis today with the area's occasional earthquakes.

In the past 2 million years glaciers have waxed and waned in our landscape, and we can be thankful for them. Locally, they gouged basins in granitic bedrock to give us Paradise, Warren, and Devils Oven lakes. They did little else, despite attaining sufficient size to bury the canyon under ice whose surface was higher than the canyon's rim. About 30-35 million years ago, the canyon was already almost as deep as it is today and perhaps three-fourths as wide.

With one or more of the lakes in mind, we start a 1.1 mile descent on the PCT, quickly enter forest, and finally pass a stagnant pond just before reaching the **Magonigal Camp jeep road**. The pond heralds your entrance to mosquitoland. Apply repellent. Note your junction with the jeep road, for in the past it has been poorly signed (apparently so that dirt bikers won't see it). This road takes you 1.1 miles east up to **Paradise Lake**, whose environs are described in the last part of Hike 35.

⇜ 39 ⇝
Pacific Crest Trail, Forest Route 86 northwest to Jackson Meadow Reservoir

Distances:

1.5 miles to peak 8216
3.2 miles to saddle with road
4.2 miles to just below peak 8166
5.6 miles to just below peak 7986
7.2 miles to minor saddle with road
9.5 miles to recross road at saddle
11.2 miles to East Meadow Campground's entrance road

Low/High Elevations: 7540' (s. trhd.), 6200' (n. trhd.)/8216'

Season: July through October

Classification: Easy (from s. trhd.), moderate (from n. trhd.)

Maps: 15, 17, and 5

Trailhead: South: same as the Hike 38 trailhead. North: see the Hike 40 trailhead.

Introduction

For an excellent view of the Sierra-crest lands between Highway 49 and Interstate 80, take this hike to summit 8216. Since the south trailhead is higher and much closer to this summit than is the north trailhead, it is the logical starting point. On the other hand, the north trailhead is within the popular Jackson Meadow Reservoir Recreation Area, and so the north part of this stretch of Pacific Crest Trail (PCT) is likely to receive more use. Treat your hike from the north trailhead as an open-ended one, hiking south to increasingly better views, but not necessarily hiking the full 9.7 miles to summit 8216 and back again. Midway along this section of PCT, at 5.6 miles, you reach slopes just below summit 7986, from which you obtain views comparable to those from summit 8216.

Description

From Forest Route 86 the northbound PCT heads southwest over to a small meadow, then switchbacks not too far beyond it. We now climb north, and views soon appear, growing better as we ascend through a thinning forest. We switchback over to an adjacent

ridge and climb north up it. Where the PCT leaves the ridge for an open traverse west, you leave the trail for a three-minute climb to **peak 8216**, also known as Lacey Peak.

From the summit you have a 360° panorama of a landscape that in former times was almost entirely hidden beneath glacial ice; only the highest peaks and ridges protruded above it. You'll see, to the north-northeast, shallow, spreading Webber Lake, which lies at the lower end of a glaciated canyon. Above its east shore is a forested gap, through which you see part of giant, flat-floored Sierra Valley. At one time the valley stood much higher, but it collapsed along a fault system about 16-13 million years ago, and since then has been accumulating sediments, which are thousands of feet thick in some places. The valley's flatness is due to past lakes forming in it, and sediments accumulating in them, finally filling the last of them, leaving a flat surface.

Looking 5 miles due east, you'll note Mt. Lola (9148'), a remnant of an old volcano and today the highest peak between Tahoe's Mt. Rose and the Cascades' Lassen Peak. Gently rounded Basin Peak stands in the southeast, joined by triple-turreted Castle Peak, the latter also the ruins of an old volcano. A few miles south of your summit, atop a flat, granitic bench, lie a slew of glacial lakes and ponds. Just right and below them lies man-made Fordyce Lake and, but 2 miles southwest from us, Meadow Lake. Dozens of lakes lie among lands to the west, but most are hidden from view. Our last major landmark, to the northwest, is the serrated Sierra Buttes (8591'). On very clear days you should be able to discern usually snowy Lassen Peak (10,457'), just right of the buttes and about 91 miles away from us.

Leaving the summit, most folks will want to retrace their steps back to the south trailhead. However, if some kind soul has dropped you off at that trailhead and is waiting for you down by Jackson Meadow Reservoir, then you'll have an enjoyable, mostly downhill route to that goal. You begin by traversing a viewful ¾ mile west on the PCT, then round a ridge and descend briefly northeast through a shady forest. If you're going to find snow along your route, it will be

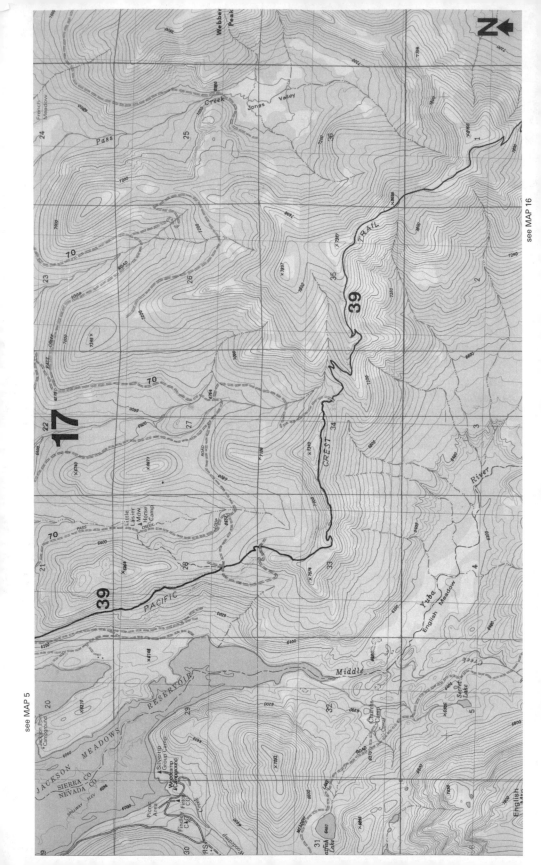

see MAP 5

see MAP 16

here. The descent quickly abates, and you walk north along a ridge to its low point, a **saddle with a road** that crosses over it. Ahead, your only real climb begins—about 450 feet worth—which in under one mile takes you to a crest immediately west of **peak 8166**. A short jaunt up to it tenders views similar to those from peak 8216.

Now the route is essentially downhill all the way to Jackson Meadow reservoir. Views along our descending volcanic crest are plentiful and interesting, though not on a par with those from peak 8166 or 8216. The first 1¼ miles are mostly northwest, but then **just below peak 7986** the trail turns west. After a descent past knobs of autobrecciated (broken) lava, the PCT heads north, descending 0.2 mile almost to a creek that flows through most of the summer. We switchback almost to it a second time, then descend west to a **minor saddle** crossed by a road.

Onward, we climb west just a bit before skirting past autobrecciated lava buttes on peak 7343. Where our descending route finally curves north down a ridge, we enter an area of selective logging, cross a good road, and in ⅓ mile **recross this road at a saddle**. The PCT begins a descent north-northwest, and immediately east of its start is an abandoned road that goes 230 yards along the ridge. Between the two is the start of a sometimes cryptic trail that over the course of ¾ mile first winds along the nearly level ridge, then leaves it for a rocky, occasionally steep, descent to the Pass Creek Loop Road opposite Little Lasier Meadow Horse Camp. If unmaintained, the trail can be rough on horses and hikers alike. Then it may be better to start east from the saddle down the road you've just recrossed, reaching Pass Creek Loop Road in 0.4 mile (water usually available at the creek just to the southeast), then turning left and taking the road 0.7 mile north slightly down to the camp.

Ahead, the descending PCT now diagonals across slopes of metamorphic rocks as we drop ever closer to the northeast shore of spreading Jackson Meadow Reservoir. Nearing the lake, the PCT almost touches a south-climbing road, and if you plan to visit East Meadow Campground, head 0.1 mile down this road to the campground's paved

road. The PCT curves northeast away from the campground, then quickly reaches its paved road only a few yards west of a junction with southeast-heading Pass Creek Loop Road. this junction is our hike's north trailhead. **East Meadow Campground** lies ⅓ mile west along the paved road, and it is perched just above the welcome, fairly warm waters of Jackson Meadow Reservoir, a boaters' Mecca.

❀ 40 ❀
Pacific Crest Trail, northwest from Jackson Meadow Reservoir

Distance: 3.1 miles to viewpoint
Low/High Elevations: 6190'/6450'
Season: Late June through October
Classification: Easy
Map: 5

Trailhead: Leave Interstate 80 near the east end of Truckee and drive 14½ miles north on Highway 89 to Forest Route 07 (this junction is 9 miles southeast of Sierraville). Take this paved road 9½ miles west to a junction with Forest Route 86 (Hikes 38 and 39 start 6½ miles up it), then continue about 5¾ miles west on 07 to a junction on your left with paved Forest Route 70, the Pass Creek Loop Road, which curves over to Jackson Meadow Reservoir's East Meadow Campground. Your trail begins about a minute's walk east on F.R. 07 from the junction. If you don't want to park along this busy road, then park along F.R. 70. Your route, the Pacific Crest Trail, parallels this road, as you'll discover if you walk but a few yards northeast from the road. Hike 39's trailhead lies 0.4 mile along this road, only 40 feet west along the campground's road from where F.R. 70 branches left.

Introduction

If you're vacationing in the popular, boater-oriented Jackson Meadow Recreation Area, you might enjoy this pleasant, easy diversion.

Description

Once you've located where the Pacific Crest Trail (PCT) crosses Forest Route 07, you start an easy climb northwest. Early-season hikers pass more than a half dozen trickling springs, but near summer's end many may be dry. The springs more or less mark the contact between volcanic soils and hidden, metamorphic bedrock. The forest, of white firs and Jeffrey pines, shows signs of former logging as we approach a minor saddle. Descending from it, we see the Sierra Buttes, framed by a linear minicanyon, through which we descend. This steep-walled feature is in itself worth investigating.

A series of short, descending switchbacks take us out of the minicanyon, and then we cross its usually dry creek. Water here may flow underground, for rocks on the southwest wall are marble (the stuff caves are formed in). The rocks on the opposite side are granitic.

Next, we contour across slopes above miniature Bear Valley. Beyond a ridge west of and above it, we traverse northwest, have backward views of Jackson Meadow Reservoir, then cut through a minor gap and make a winding, gentle climb to a shallow crest saddle. Just north of it we reach our **viewpoint**: the Sierra Buttes rise in majesty above deep, mildly glaciated Milton Creek canyon. Ahead

is the upper end of Hike 10, which ends with a ⅔-mile meander along a viewless crest to our viewpoint.

⋙ 41 ⋘
Pacific Crest Trail, I-80 southeast to Hwy. 40

Distance: 3.5 miles to Highway 40
Low/High Elevations: 7020'/7270'
Season: Mid-July through mid-October
Classification: Easy
Maps: 14 and 18
Trailheads: North: Same as the Hike 36 trailhead. South: Same as the Hike 43 trailhead.

Introduction

This 1982 stretch of the Pacific Crest Trail (PCT) passes some small, but nevertheless challenging, granitic cliffs, many of them likely to be crawling with rock climbers on weekends from about July through October. From mid-July through early August, wildflowers are at their peak, which should attract the botanically inclined, though since the terrain is exclusively granitic, the diversity of plant species is quite limited. This hike may appeal

Old Highway 40 and Donner Lake

to day hikers looking for an easy stroll or for a picnic with a Donner Lake view.

Description

The route description begins from the PCT's trailhead mentioned in Hike 36. From here, your hike southward to old Highway 40 is 0.1 mile longer than from the eastbound (south-side) Interstate-80 rest area and 0.2 mile shorter than from the westbound rest area. If you plan to hike for only a few hours, you could start from either. But if you will be out for most of the day, then start from the PCT's trailhead. Alternatively, you could hike northward from old Highway 40. The problem there is parking: there is not much of it where the trail crosses the highway. On a busy weekend literally hundreds of hikers, climbers, and mountain-bikers may park up and down the highway.

Starting from the east end of the PCT's trailhead parking lot, you hike 300 yards eastward on the PCT access trail to a junction with Glacier Meadow Loop Trail 15E32, a nature trail with signs along it. This begins at the eastbound I-80 rest area, specifically, just west of its building, which contains rest rooms. It makes a 0.6-mile counterclockwise loop, which ends near the east side of the building. This loop trail goes about 250 yards southeast to a junction just above a shallow, murky lakelet. From the west side, it goes about 230 yards south-southwest to a junction with the PCT access trail, which you are on, and for ¼ mile you climb eastward to the murky lakelet. From it the access trail continues 200 yards east to a junction with the PCT at the edge of a wet, willowy meadow.

You leave the meadow and curve up a forested swale, passing a small pond just before emerging from forest cover. You immediately approach a shallow gap, on your right, but then switchback down away from it. Ideally, the PCT should have crested the gap, then followed an old path past attractive Azalea and Flora lakes to unattractive Lake Angela. However, these lakes, all on private land, flow into creeks that provide domestic water for the Highway 40 vicinity. The area's residents were rightly concerned about human-transmitted *Giardia lamblia* microor-

Author's daughter on practice slab below School Rock

ganisms possibly getting in their water, so the Forest Service was correct to locate our trail below and east of these lakes.

The PCT heads east along the base of a large granitic knoll, then turns south, heading past its large cliff. Climbing routes up it are definitely inferior to those up the Highway 40 cliffs. You now make a switchbacking descent south, leaving behind most of the I-80 traffic noise. You bottom out near the brush-lined outlet creek of Flora Lake, then traverse a few minutes southeast to a stale pond. Two sets of converging powerlines lie past it, then you switchback up to a second pond, having a view or two of I-80 country along the way. In a few minutes you reach a shallow saddle just northwest of point 7389, which is the top of Grouse Slabs—popular among climbers. From that summit you have this hike's best view of the Donner Pass-Donner Lake landscape.

You next engage a multitude of short, gentle switchbacks, descending near a cliff that

offers more climbing opportunities. You then
cross a flat-floored bowl and arrive at one of
the Donner area's most popular climbing
spots. The trail skirts along the back side of a
practice face, about 50 feet high, known as
Bastille Slab, where beginners learn the trade.
It then skirts along the base of School Rock,
about 200 feet high, where beginners may
encounter their first exposure to considerable
height. Past the climbing rocks, you conclude
on a short stretch blasted out of bedrock, the
trail contouring just above old **Highway 40**.
While not too intimidating to the hiker, one
overhanging wall above the trail would certainly make me nervous if I was on horseback.

Two climbers on School Rock

A Jeffrey pine—one of many giant conifers in Five Lakes Creek canyon

Chapter 11
Granite Chief Wilderness

Introduction

The idea of a Granite Chief Wilderness developed in the 1930s, but a half-century would pass, until, in 1984, the high lands south of Interstate 80 and west of Lake Tahoe's northwest shore finally became official wilderness. the reason for such a protracted "birth" lay in the pattern of public and private ownership of the proposed wilderness. If you were to look at a 1960s or '70s map of Tahoe National Forest, you'd see that much of it was quite discontinuous. Over much of its domain a checkerboard pattern existed, every other township section (each roughly one mile square) being in private hands. Most of this private land belonged to logging-oriented Southern Pacific Land Company, which today is California's largest private landowner. Owning a total area about the size of Los Angeles County or the San Francisco Bay Area, it indeed had a sizable holding, in fact, about 40% more area than the combined total of Lassen, Yosemite, Sequoia, and Kings Canyon national parks.

The checkerboard pattern in the national forests was inherited from a mid-19th century U.S. government policy. To induce the construction of major railroad lines, the government back then donated large tracts of land to railroads along their rights of way, albeit in a checkerboard pattern. Such a land pattern benefits neither Southern Pacific Land Company nor Tahoe National Forest. Consequently, since the 1930s they have gradually traded more and more sections of land. For the Forest Service, this led to the eventual consolidation of the necessary land to create Granite Chief Wilderness. Ongoing trading east of here then led to the creation of Mt. Rose Wilderness in the northern Carson Range (Chapter 16).

The acquisition of private land might have occurred much more rapidly if the Granite Chief terrain had lived up to its name by being largely granitic, as is most of Desolation Wilderness. Instead, it is largely volcanic, and where granitic and metamorphic rocks are exposed, they are often veneered with volcanic soil derived from volcanic sediments up above. And it is this soil which is largely responsible for the area's magnificent forests. It is difficult for a lumber company to give up such prime real estate. Hence, a section often is logged before it is exchanged for a section of National Forest land. This may seem unfair, but living in wood-framed houses, the great majority of us can't complain.

One disadvantage of a volcanic terrain is that it develops lakes only reluctantly. Of the few that do exist in the wilderness, almost all are on granitic or metamorphic benches. For lakes, you'll have to go to Desolation Wilderness. Hiking in Granite Chief Wilderness is largely of two kinds: along open, volcanic ridgecrests and through forested canyon lands. Obviously, the first kind is more scenic, and this chapter offers two exceptionally fine routes: Hike 43, from Donner Pass south to Tinker Knob, and Hike 50, from Barker Pass north to Twin Peaks and the Five Lakes basin. Hike 51 offers an alternate route to Twin Peaks, while Hike 46 offers a short route to the very popular Five Lakes basin. The remaining trails are largely devoid of views, lakes and users, and thus are for those seeking solitude.

⇜ 42 ⇝
Picayune Valley Trail

Distances:
5.2 miles to north end of Picayune Valley
7.7 miles to Trail 15E08
Low/High Elevations: 5600'/7630'
Season: Mid-July through early October
Classification: Moderate
Maps: 19, 20, 22, and 23
Trailhead: First, follow Hike 29's trailhead directions to Placer County Big Trees Grove's spur road. Staying on the main road, Mosquito Ridge Road, or Forest Route 96, you drive about 10¾ miles to the far (south) end of French Meadows Reservoir's dam. Still on F.R. 96, you turn left and pass several recreational facilities before bridging Middle Fork American River, almost 5 miles from the dam. In one mile you pass Ahart Campground, and then in 2 miles reach a junction with a road branching left. You continue straight ahead, on F.R. 51, going 1.4 miles to a junction with Road 15E10, on the right, which is 4.4 miles from the bridge across Middle Fork American River. Ahead, the main road looks like an alluring route out to Soda Springs, but it becomes a jeep road in 1.5 miles and an abandoned road near Forest Hill Divide. On Road 15E10 you go almost ⅓ mile to a trailhead parking area, on the left, with room for about a dozen vehicles. This is located only 0.1 mile before Talbot Campground, which is small and primitive, lying near the union of Talbot Creek with Middle Fork American River.

Introduction

"Picayune" means trivial, but neither scenery, nor the size of Picayune Valley, nor your 2000-foot climb out of it, is. Overall, the climb up the Middle Fork American River canyon to Picayune Valley is an easy one, and most people won't want to continue farther, for the climb out of the deep, steep-walled canyon is strenuous. Along the canyon's route and up at Picayune Valley you can find some fair-to-good isolated campsites. Strong, adventurous hikers can visit the Mildred Lakes or climb Mt. Mildred, these goals requiring a great deal of effort for modest rewards—the wilderness has better lakes and higher summits.

Description

From the trailhead parking area, from which the above mileages are determined, you walk along the road to Talbot Campground, then cross Talbot Creek. From its far (east) bank, you follow the road ⅓ mile to its end. Now on the real Picayune Valley Trail, you traverse across privately owned Section 1 to its east end, where you enter Granite Chief Wilderness.

Now we make a short, moderate climb past white firs, incense-cedars, ponderosa pines, and Jeffrey pines to a notch that separates a low knoll from the canyon's north slopes. A minor descent southeast from the notch takes us down to the start of a gently undulating eastward ascent that parallels the unseen Middle Fork American River for about one mile. By walking south 100-200 yards along the forest's open floor, you can reach this lightly visited section of river and find suitable camping spots. Just after we begin our second, relatively short, moderate ascent, we pass our first usually flowing tributary, then in 0.4 mile cross the Middle Fork, which here makes a short fall into a churning, refreshing pool that supplies us with what may be the best trailside water.

The trail now veers southeast and climbs up to a second low notch, from which we can look north and see a skyline cliff of light-gray granitic rock, this cliff being a spur ridge that was slightly abraded by past glaciers. To the southwest, dark-gray metamorphic cliffs rise above the canyon's floor. Our trail toward Picayune Valley now stays close to the contact between these two very different rock types. From the notch we make a rolling traverse and quickly reach a small, pleasant campsite, which lies among lodgepole pines and white firs between the trail and some nearby small pools on Picayune Valley creek. Our southbound adventure now enters its first field of mule ears, then proceeds through several flowery, wet meadows, which are separated by stands of aspen, cottonwood, alder, and willow.

The sometimes boggy trail tread gives way to a rocky tread as we start our third short, moderate ascent. Near the top, we approach some waterworn bedrock, and here it's worth your effort—at least before August—to walk a few yards west to a view of the creek's 60-foot-high waterfall. Standing here at a rocky brink just before the **north end of Picayune Valley**, we can gaze northward down-canyon and identify three major rock types.

The multihued rocks of the canyon's west slopes originally developed as volcanic sediments, coral reefs, and submarine lavas, which formed on an ocean floor about 350-400 million years ago. Much later, this aggregate was compacted and metamorphosed when it was compressed along the edge of western North America. Much later, magma, which is molten material that solidifies to form granitic rocks, worked upward through the earth's crust in this vicinity about 100 million years ago and intruded into these metamorphic rocks, altering them even further. Some of the magma worked its way to the earth's surface, and erupted sporadically over unnumbered millennia to construct a volcanic mountain range like today's Cascade Range. Over tens of millions of years, that volcanic range was eroded away, together with much of the more-resistant metamorphic rocks, so that today granitic rocks, chiefly granodiorite, make up most of the steep, brushy east slopes of the canyon. Atop both sides of the canyon are dark-brown deposits of andesite that formed about 4 million years ago. These generally loose deposits buried the canyon, but over time gravity, running water, and glacier ice removed most of them, resurrecting the canyon from its volcanic tomb.

If you want a breathless experience, you can make a very steep climb from Picayune Valley to the Mildred Lakes. From the rocky brink with down-canyon views, you quickly enter the valley as you curve around a low knoll and meet a small creekside camp where you enter a stand of aspens. Then in ¼ mile you enter a meadow of lupines, sidalceas, and mule ears, from which you'll see a shallow side canyon west of it. Climb up slopes just south of it. The first 200 feet or so of elevation gain is through dense huckleberry-oak brush, which will stop all but the most determined hikers. Above, the going, though steep, is basically without obstacles. Of the three Mildred Lakes, two are waist-deep ponds, the middle lake being the only one large enough to warrant the title of lake. At about 7950 feet elevation below a snow-harboring slope, the lake can have shoreline snowbanks into July, and by early August will warm up to the mid-60s. This is adequate, but not ideal, for swimming, though after the strenuous climb, you'll probably want to jump in. Fishing may be good, since few people fish the lake, but there are no guarantees. Poor, cramped campsites are another negative factor. Still, should you

Middle Mildred Lake

want to visit the lake, but are not up to bush-whacking and to overly steep slopes, you can take a longer way to the lake. From the end of Picayune Valley, follow the main, wildflower-banked stream west up toward a conspicuous saddle, Heavens Gate, and about ¼ mile before it you diagonal north up variable slopes to the bench holding the lakes. Most folks will be content to avoid the lakes and enjoy Picayune Valley. Some may even continue on the trail toward Whiskey Creek Camp or Five Lakes Creek.

This trail switchbacks up to a saddle just north of an impressive band of deeply grooved andesite cliffs of autobrecciated (broken) lava flows. Climbers will find an abundance of handholds up the two dozen or so deep grooves of these nearly vertical, 200-foot-high cliffs, which require expansion bolts to protect the leader. Leaving the saddle, we follow an ascending crest route that skirts past much lower volcanic cliffs, which for the climber are alone worth the relatively long hike up to them. Nonclimbers may appreciate the interesting composition of these stark landforms as well as the ridgecrest views obtained. On the horizon in the south-south-east, the high peaks of the granitic Crystal Range, in Desolation Wilderness, poke up above the notch that marks the head of Powderhorn Creek canyon.

Our crest route levels off, we enter a red-fir forest, and then we make a short descent to a junction with **Trail 15E08** amid a tremendous field of mule ears that covers the slopes. No single plant in the Granite Chief area so dominates its volcanic slopes as does this aromatic, large-leaved sunflower. Hike 42 ends at this junction, but you, of course, can continue northeast toward Whiskey Creek Camp or southwest toward Shanks Cove, both directions of this trail being covered in Hike 49.

◆ 43 ◆
Mt. Judah Loop Trail and Pacific Crest Trail south to Tinker Knob

Distances:
1.0 mile to Mt. Judah Loop Trail, north end
　0.3 mile on loop trail to use path
　　0.1 mile on use path to summit 7696
　0.7 mile on loop trail to use path
　　0.2 mile on use path to Donner Peak
　1.5 miles on loop trail to Mt. Judah
　2.3 miles on loop trail to south end
1.9 miles to Mt. Judah Loop Trail, south end
2.0 miles to Roller Pass
5.3 miles to spur trail
　0.1 mile on spur trail to Benson Hut
7.1 miles to north ridge of Tinker Knob
　0.1 mile up ridge to Tinker Knob

Low/High Elevations : 7060'/8949'

Season: Mid-July through mid-October

Classification: Moderate

Maps: 18 and 20

Trailhead: Eastbound and westbound drivers both take Interstate 80's Soda Springs exit and drive about 4 miles along former Highway 40 to Donner Pass. Additionally, those down at the west shore of Donner Lake can make a winding climb of a similar distance west to the pass. From the pass drive south 0.2 on a paved road to where it bends west. Here, a pole-line road starts east, reaching in 40 yards a private road, which forks right. Park in this vicinity, which is limited to a few cars at most. Since this area is popular, you may have to park along one of the old highway's turnouts. Do not park in any of the signed "No Parking" stretches.

Introduction

In the entire Tahoe Sierra, perhaps no other stretch of Pacific Crest Trail provides better views than does this hike. Once this route climbs to the crest, it stays at or very near it for over 5 miles, and since the terrain is largely unforested, your views are a cornucopia of optic delight. The route is the epitome of what the Pacific Crest Trail should be. The only drawbacks are lack of realistic campsites and,

18

after the snow melts, lack of water. Plan to day hike this route.

The great majority of people who start south on the PCT stop long before Tinker Knob. Rather, they hike up to the 1990s-vintage Mt. Judah Loop Trail. If you hike up to it, take it, then return to your trailhead, you will do 5.2 miles; more, if you take in the summits of point 7696 and Donner Peak. The loop trail quickly became very popular, and rightly so. Where else can you encounter such awe-inspiring views with so little effort? And for rock climbers, Donner Peak's summit area offers some of the best bouldering to be found anywhere in the Sierra Nevada.

Description

If you are hiking the Pacific Crest Trail (PCT) before mid-July in a typical year, the first ¼ mile can be snowbound. If you have snow problems on this initial stretch, then you can expect more along the east slopes of Mt. Lincoln and in a wooded area north of Anderson Peak. Almost immediately from the trailhead, you enter a 50-yard-long swath of lush vegetation, with wildflowers at their prime in mid-August. Tallest, though not the showiest, of these is alpine knotweed, a head-high, scarce relative of lowly Davis' knotweed, which pervades the volcanic terrain we'll soon see.

You climb a granitic headwall via short switchbacks, which each year accumulate some talus that periodically must be cleared, and soon you have westward views of Lake Mary and northward views of Lake Angela. The latter lies at the headwaters of the South Yuba River. Just west of it rises Beacon Hill, which is composed of a sequence of volcanic deposits. The lowest and oldest is 33-million-year-old rhyolite, and it is in contact with granitic bedrock that comprises the floor of upper Summit Valley. What the rhyolite and volcanic deposits on the valley's south margin demonstrate is that Summit Valley already was broad and flat-floored long before glaciation commenced. Glaciers have only mildly transformed this landscape.

Southbound, we trade view-rich huckleberry-oak scrub on granitic terrain for nearly viewless red-fir forest on volcanic terrain

before we reach a junction with the **Mt. Judah Loop Trail's north end**. Because this trail is so popular, it will be described first. It climbs about 0.2 mile through tree cover to a conspicuous gully that is seasonally colored with a slightly aromatic sunflower, mule ears, which does best in volcanic soil. Look at the volcanic gravels exposed in the gully—they are quite angular, implying that they have not been transported very far from their source, which would have been a long-gone, nearby volcano. Beyond the gully the loop trail quickly levels off on a spot with a **use path to summit 7696**. This goes about 150 yards north-northeast before becoming vague and dying out. From a minor knoll on the northwest corner of a granitic mass that is topped with **summit 7696**, just to the east, you have fine views of the Donner Pass area. To the north-northwest lies Lake Angela, while above loom the turreted summit of Castle Peak. West of the lake, Beacon Hill barely reaches the skyline, and to the west below lies Summit Valley, which holds spreading, shallow Lake Van Norden. If light conditions are favorable, and you look very closely about the minor knoll, you may be able to see faint striations on small patches of glacier-polished rock. The orientation of the striations indicate that a large glacier filling the Sugar Bowl, to your southwest, locally flowed 350° across this knoll. How thick was the glacier in this vicinity? The answer lies ahead.

Backtrack on the use path to the Mt. Judah Loop Trail, take it 70 yards southeast to an old road, now part of the loop trail, and up it climb 0.4 mile eastward to a saddle with a **use path to Donner Peak**. Up here you are unlikely to see any glacial evidence, but on granitic rocks just north of and below the saddle, there are faint striations that indicate glacial ice flowing 330°. For that ice to be thick enough to flow, your saddle must have lain under ice, albeit thin, for there is no evidence of glaciation along an ascent up Donner Peak. The glacial evidence here and elsewhere in the Donner Pass environs indicates that the last glacier to occupy Summit Valley, at 6800 feet elevation, had a thickness on the order of 1000 feet.

If you are careful and are not acrophobic, I heartily recommend that you climb up to the peak's summits. The northeast ascent up one or more vague use paths is relatively safe and straightforward. Reaching the highest of several summits is not. To do that, as you approach the summit area, veer left and scramble up exfoliating slabs to the top of **Donner Peak**. Unless you are an expert climber, do not continue straight ahead northeast to a notch (with a life-threatening drop-off) and then hope to climb cliffs to the left or right summit. A fall from either summit would be fatal, so be careful up there, especially if you've brought along children. The views from the summits are similar, and nearly all encompassing; only Mt. Judah blocks views to the southwest. Your views are similar to those from the knoll near summit 7696, but better, for at 8019 feet you are higher up and you have an "aerial view" of Donner Lake. To the west you again see Lake Van Norden in Summit Valley, but to the northwest you now see linear Boreal Ridge rising above Beacon Hill, and 8219' Andesite Peak behind the ridge and poking above it. to the right of it rules 9103' Castle Peak, the highest summit of the Donner Pass environs. Before 33 million years ago, when enormous rhyolite deposits

originating in the east began to bury our area, Summit Valley was much wider. At the pass, its granitic floor was about 2 miles wide, and the South Yuba River canyon extended an unknown distance up-canyon to an unknown source. Downfaulting over the last 33 million years and concomitant, voluminous volcanism have greatly rearranged east-side drainages and have buried the pre-faulted, formerly high Sierran lands.

For me, the views are rivaled by the uniqueness of the summit area's granitic rock, which is exfoliating on a massive scale into "onion shells" from a few inches to a foot or so thick. The exfoliation shells are fairly horizontal, and the fracture between shells provides climbers with a narrow, horizontal crack ideal for holds. On your visit, you are quite likely to meet one or more climbers relishing the dozens of short, vertical routes in the small summit area. Safety-minded climbers can use a half-length top rope for the longer routes.

Return to the Mt. Judah Loop Trail and make a switchbacking climb southward up its open east-side slopes to its namesake. In about ¾ mile you gain the crest at a minor saddle of your north-trending volcanic ridge, then hike about 300 yards south to its high point, 8243' **Mt. Judah**. Although this summit is not as photogenic as that of Donner Peak, its views, subjectively, are better, for they are farther ranging. To the northwest you see now familiar Summit Valley and its attendant, winding Southern Pacific railroad tracks. Beyond both is a light gray landscape, where barren granitic bedrock has been stripped of its soil and overlying volcanic sediments by former glaciers. Behind it lies the Sierran crest, and left of both, to the west, is a dominating, solitary, two-face ridge. To us, 7841' Red Mountain presents a red, metamorphic face. From crest lands far to the north,

View southeast toward Anderson Peak

it presents a gray, granitic one. To the east you see the now familiar Donner Lake and its winding Southern Pacific railroad tracks. It traverses the lower slopes of Schallenberger Ridge, which blots out most of Truckee. Behind the ridge lies flat, expansive Martis Valley, an area of historic faulting. Behind it, one summit rises above the Carson Range crest on the skyline. This is volcanic 10,776′ Mt. Rose, which is the third highest peak in the Tahoe Sierra, ranking behind granitic 10,881′ Freel Peak and 10,823′ Jobs Sister, the pair above the south side of unseen Lake Tahoe. The southern part of the Carson Range, which contain these two summits, is largely unseen, for it is blocked in part by a ridge extending south from 8383′ Mt. Lincoln, to our southwest. That ridge contains the rest of our route, the PCT to pointed 8949′ Tinker Knob. Just right of it is a closer destination, blocky 8683′ Anderson Peak.

From the Mt. Judah summit, its namesake loop trail begins a switchbacking descent southward, and near the upper part of it you have a view southwest across the Sierran crest into the North Fork American River's Royal Gorge. Midway along your ¾ mile descent, you switchback at an impressive knob of autobrecciated lava—lava that fractured as it was in the process of solidifying. You saw smaller samples near the summit. You then begin to enter forest cover, which stays with you down to the **loop trail's south end**. From here you can take the PCT northward down to the trailhead or southward up to Tinker Knob.

Those intent on reaching Tinker Knob might adhere to the PCT all the way, saving the Mt. Judah Loop Trail, taken in reverse, for their return trip, should they find the time and energy to do it. From the north end of the Mt. Judah Loop Trail, one mile from the trailhead, the PCT first crosses under a Sugar Bowl ski lift in 90 yards, then reaches an old road in 140 yards. This is an alternate start for the loop trail, one you might take if you have been encountering a lot of snow. In a red-fir forest you climb easily south 0.3 mile to an alder-lined seep, from which you may see a use trail departing southwest. This goes briefly over to the top of another Sugar Bowl ski lift. Ahead, the PCT climbs easily southeast over to a nearby gully, which exposes metamorphic bedrock, then it arcs southward up to the **Mt. Judah Loop Trail's south end**. Just beyond, you enter a mountain-hemlock-shaded saddle, **Roller Pass**. From it you can take a path 90 yards east to a brink. It was here that the ill-fated 1846 Donner Party used winches to haul their wagons up the brink.

From the pass the PCT climbs south briefly up the crest to a fairly level spot, where you are beside a jeep road that you could take to the summit of Mt. Lincoln. The summit separates private land on the west from Forest Service land on the east. Although you're a mile from Mt. Judah, your views are very different, for you see much land to the west and south that was hidden from that summit. You can look straight down the North Fork American River, which has cut a mammoth canyon. In its deepest section, Royal Gorge, the river lies over 4000 feet below its north rim, Snow Mountain. Obviously, the river has been cutting through this metamorphic terrain for a long, long time.

The PCT traverses across Mt. Lincoln's gullied, steep east slopes, and when snow-covered, this stretch could be dangerous. Ahead, you enter Section 33, which is largely private land, but you also begin a relatively easy, generally open, Sierran crest jaunt. You switchback down to a crest saddle, then have a long, though easy, near-crest ascent to point 8043, just within Section 34. From it you descend just a mite, then climb slightly to a switchback with a photogenic pinnacle of autobrecciated lava—a definite challenge for climbers. Its short east side is about 40 feet high; other sides, higher.

Ahead, you switchback almost to the top of Section 3's point 8210, and near it have a splendid view of hulking Anderson Peak, the next major goal. This is composed of dipping lava flows, which are about all that is left of a former volcano. In front and just left of the peak is somewhat forested point 8374. Part of the vent of the volcano lies immediately east of this point, and the vent marks the location of the volcano's center. This volcano apparently was active a few million years ago, late in the period of the range's east-side down-faulting.

After you traverse past point 8374, you reach a long saddle, from whose south end climbs a very conspicuous **spur trail**. This heads very steeply south directly up a ridge to a spot holding **Benson Hut**. When I visited it, two signs presented a conflicting message: "No trespassing" and "Available for public day use or as emergency shelter." If you are caught in an emergency, use it; otherwise, don't. About 250 yards past the spur trail the gently climbing PCT passes a less conspicuous one which climbs east to the hut. The trail then rounds Anderson Peak's northwest, west, and south slopes. Where the trail makes a short jog, you can leave it and climb breathlessly northward for about 10 minutes up to the obvious summit. This is for peak baggers only, since its views are very similar to those along the trail.

Dwarfish, drought-tolerant, subalpine wildflowers now line our crest route southeast toward Tinker Knob, which was once part of the conduit of an old volcano. Just before the knob the trail veers east from the knob's **north ridge**. From this point you can climb south cross-country, carefully up to the highly fractured summit of **Tinker Knob**, which you'll reach in 5-10 minutes. Inspecting the terrain seen from today's summit, you view a volcanic landscape that has undergone major transformation. In its death throes several million years ago, much of the volcano would have been blasted away. Over the ensuing time, mass wasting, stream erosion, and glacial erosion removed additional volcanic material, exposing the underlying granitic and metamorphic bedrock. Among the more prominent landmarks is Mt. Rose, standing high above Lake Tahoe's north shore. To the south rises aptly named Granite Chief, devoid of volcanic rock. It is one part of the old granitic-and-metamorphic landscape that escaped burial by successive episodes of volcanic eruptions over the last 33 million years. You'll see, in the distant south, the snowy, granitic Crystal Range, which forms the backbone of Desolation Wilderness. In the west lies a deep gash in the landscape, Royal Gorge. Compare this canyon to the shallow South Yuba River canyon, in the Donner Pass vicinity, from where you began your hike.

❧ 44 ❧
Squaw Valley to Tinker Knob

Distances:
3.8 miles to Pacific Crest Trail
5.3 miles to Painted Rock Trail
8.0 miles to summit of Tinker Knob
Low/High Elevations: 6240′/8949′
Season: Mid-July through mid-October
Classification: Strenuous
Maps: 21 and 20
Trailhead: From Interstate 80's Highway 89 exit in western Truckee, drive about 8½ miles south up 89 to the Squaw Valley junction. If you're coming from Lake Tahoe, this junction is just over 5 miles down 89 from the major junction by Lake Tahoe's outlet at Tahoe City. Drive 2.2 miles up Squaw Valley Road to a fire station, on your right, which is immediately before the ostentatious Olympic Village Inn. No trailhead parking area is set aside, so check at the fire station for the best place to park.

Introduction
The best route to Tinker Knob is along the previous hike. However, the Squaw Valley route to Tinker Knob offers relatively secluded camping along the upper reaches of the North Fork American River canyon. Rock climbers may want to go only 2½ miles up the trail, to

Tinker Knob, from the Pacific Crest Trail

an assortment of moderate-to-difficult climbs up small, granitic cliffs.

Description

From the east (right) side of the Squaw Valley Fire Station, our Granite Chief Trail 15E23 starts a climb up-canyon. After a few minutes you come beside a chorusing creek, lined with aspens and cottonwoods, and you parallel it about 90 yards to a junction. Upstream, a trail continues toward one of Squaw Valley's many chair lifts. We turn right, climb away from the creek, and with elevation cross a seasonal creeklet before reaching the edge of an opening that is carpeted with leafy, aromatic mule ears. Here, about a mile from your trailhead, a conspicuous trail comes in on the right. Be sure on your descent to bear left at this junction. From the opening we recross the seasonal creeklet and start a climb up sloping, granitic benches. Below these benches the midsummer hiker will see quite a diverse display of wildflowers, thanks in part to a wealth of minerals supplied by volcanic soils derived from volcanic rocks above. On the sloping benches, however, a former glacier removed

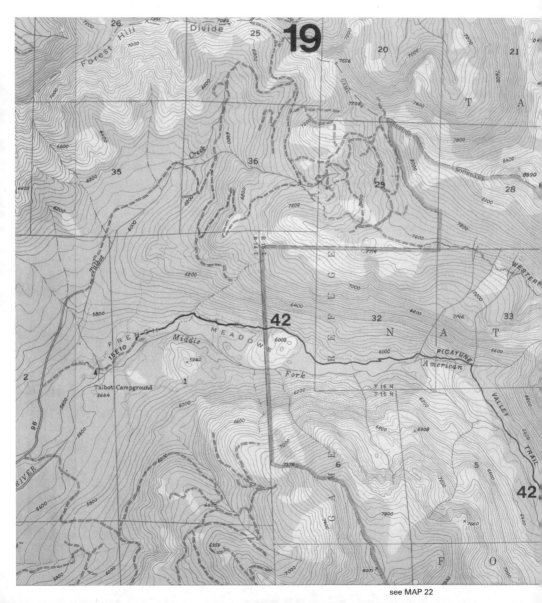

see MAP 22

see MAP 18

see MAP 19

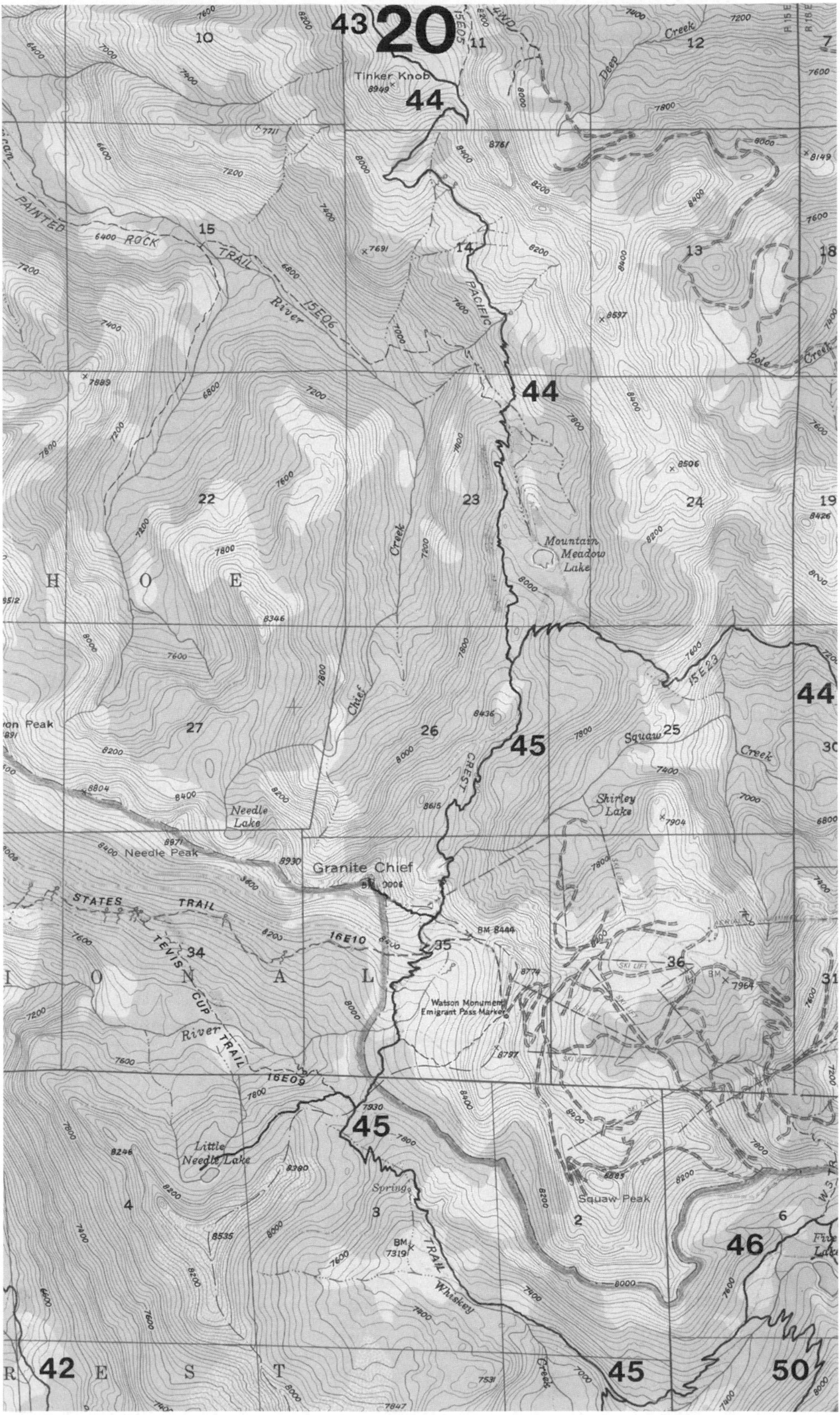
20
43
44
45
46
42
50
Tinker Knob
8949
PAINTED ROCK TRAIL
River
15E06
15E05
4WD
Deep Creek
PACIFIC CREST
Chief Creek
Mountain Meadow Lake
H O E
Needle Lake
Needle Peak
Granite Chief
STATES TRAIL
TEVIS CUP TRAIL
River
16E10
16E09
15E23
I O N A L
Watson Monument
Emigrant Pass Marker
Squaw Creek
Shirley Lake
SKI LIFT
Little Needle Lake
Spring
Squaw Peak
Whiskey TRAIL
Creek
Pole Creek
R E S T

see MAP 21

see MAP 23

all the soil, and very little new soil has formed in the ensuing 13,000 years.

From the benches you have views of the spreading Squaw Valley ski complex, and more views of it lie ahead. As long as you're looking in that direction, note the trail's route. On your descent you might lose the trail across this barren bedrock. With elevation, Lake Tahoe comes into view, and then we curve into a side canyon with a refreshing creek. Better views appear as we climb southwest up to a set of major, sloping benches with cliffs up to 50 feet high. Rock climbers: routes here are fair to good.

Beyond the last, polished, striated bench, we turn our backs on the Squaw Valley developments, cross and recross a persistent creeklet, and then enter a forested, hanging side canyon. Near its upper end a trail segment once climbed north up to a close-by crest saddle and then descended briefly to nearby Mountain Meadow Lake. However, that lake and its surroundings are on private land, which also doubles as a University of California Ecological Study Area. Consequently, our trail to Tinker Knob was rerouted so now it soon switchbacks up to a junction with the **Pacific Crest Trail**, immediately east of a south-climbing ridge.

Here we turn north, then cross the crest at a nearby saddle, and soon our high route opens up and offers us views south toward Granite Chief, southwest toward Needle and Lyon peaks, northwest down the North Fork American River canyon, and north across the canyon toward our goal, Tinker Knob. The views actually improve as we get lower, and then we leave the crest and switchback down to a junction with **Painted Rock Trail 15E06**, 1½ miles after the previous junction. This old route, climbing 3¾ miles up from the old Soda Springs, was described in the original edition of *The Tahoe Sierra*. However, by 1983 the roads to the trailhead had become so plastered with NO TRESPASSING signs that I felt compelled to strike this public trail from the book.

On the PCT we descend to the nearby headwaters of the North Fork American River, then climb around and over granitic outcrops, reaching a bowl with water and a campsite in ⅔ mile. About ⅓ mile past this bowl, the trail enters a larger one, with more-spacious camping on a waterless flat below the trail. Beyond the bowl you contour past two usually flowing springs and then, in ¼ mile, switchback for a sustained 0.6-mile climb to Tinker Knob saddle. Sharp-crested ridge 8761, just south of us, divides the impressive panorama we have to the south and east. Descending north is Cold Stream Trail 15E05, whose lower part crosses private land.

Tinker Knob looms above us to the west, so we head ⅓ mile west on the PCT to where it starts to drop northwest along the Sierra crest. Leave the trail and climb south carefully up to the highly fractured **summit of Tinker Knob**. The summit's main views are described at the end of Hike 43.

⇚ 45 ⇛
Squaw Valley to Granite Chief, Little Needle Lake, and Whiskey Creek Camp

Distances:
5.2 miles to east ridge of Granite Chief
   0.4 mile on use trail to summit of Granite Chief
5.4 miles to Western States Trail
6.0 miles to Tevis Cup Trail east
6.6 miles to Tevis Cup Trail west
   0.7 mile on trails to Little Needle Lake
8.7 miles to Whiskey Creek Trail
   0.4 mile on trail to Whiskey Creek Camp
Low/High Elevations: 6240′/8550′ at ridge; 9006′ on Granite Chief's summit
Season: Late July through early October
Classification: Moderate
Maps: 21, 20, and 23
Trailhead: Same as the Hike 44 trailhead.

Introduction
This rugged, varied hike visits the highest lands of the granite Chief Wilderness. Its last goal, Whiskey Creek Camp, can certainly be reached more easily, and those in a hurry should instead take Hike 46 to it. The adventuresome can leave Hike 45's main route and make visits to Granite Chief, Needle, and

Lyon peaks, and to Needle and Little Needle lakes—all lying in the cool, subalpine realm. Note that you can *greatly* reduce the amount of initial climbing by taking Squaw Valley's aerial tramway and then hiking about a mile up to the Watson Monument at Emigrant Pass. Doing so cuts your distance by about 4 miles and the amount of climbing to Granite Chief ridge by about 75%.

Description

The first 3.8 miles of Granite Chief Trail 15E23 up to a near-saddle junction with the Pacific Crest Trail (PCT) are described in the previous hike. From that junction we head south, initially up a broad, gentle ridgecrest, then along its eastern slopes. At first we traverse beneath granitic cliffs that are laced with veins. Just beyond them we get views of Squaw Valley and Lake Tahoe, which continue as we climb through a forest that is increasingly rich in mountain hemlock. Along this usually ascending traverse, one sees plenty of short cracks on the cliffs, which would tempt the rock climber were they closer to the trailhead.

We cross a small flat, covered with gruss (granitic gravel), just before we descend momentarily to the eastern edge of a fragile, subalpine meadow, which harbors the headwaters of Squaw Creek. Rising above it is the northeast face of Granite Chief. We cross the creek, briefly skirt the meadow's edge, and then climb on short, steep switchbacks toward a ski-lift tower on the **east ridge of Granite Chief**. The PCT reaches the windswept Sierra crest immediately east of the tower, and if you've successfully carried a backpack up to here, you can celebrate, for now almost every step of the way to Whiskey Creek Camp is downhill.

Only a few paces down, and just before the Granite Chief Wilderness boundary, you'll meet two trails. Left, a trail arcs southwest, climbing moderately in just over ⅓ mile to the Watson Monument at Emigrant Pass. If you've taken the aerial tramway, you'll follow a road one mile up to the shallow pass atop a high ridge, then take this trail to our junction. To the right of our PCT, a use trail climbs a similar distance to the **summit of Granite Chief**. Being steep and unofficial, this trail has

several variations, for hordes of hikers in the past have taken different descent routes down the shrubby slopes. In 1994 the Forest Service was going to construct a summit trail in order to keep hikers on one path, thus minimizing impact on native vegetation. However, part of the trail would have been across dynamited bedrock. The most economical way to drill holes for dynamite is with a *motorized* rock drill, which is illegal in a wilderness. Using a hand-held star drill (hit with a sledgehammer) would have been tedious and expensive, but would have been legal. Ultimately, the Forest Service decided to delay construction indefinitely, so the vegetation still suffers.

Atop the summit, Granite Chief offers worthy views. To the southeast is relatively close-by, flat-topped Squaw Peak, standing high above Whiskey Creek. Farther away and right of the peak are the Twin Peaks, and right of them are the distant, often snowy peaks of Desolation Wilderness. To the left of Squaw Peak is much of the Squaw Valley Ski Area plus some of Lake Tahoe. Tinker Knob is a prominent point on the northern skyline, and left of it in the distance are peaks of the Donner Pass area, the highest one being triple-turreted Castle Peak. finally, under a mile west of us is Needle Peak, a closer point that is bound to tempt peak baggers.

Should you be so tempted, descend west to a nearby saddle, then traverse the south slopes of a crest summit to a second saddle, this one above Needle Lake. It would be hard to find a colder lake in the entire Tahoe Sierra, for this lake can be mostly or partly snow-bound well into August, when virtually every other lake has warmed to the 60s or low 70s. From the saddle, you're confronted with a headwall, and can go around either side. With a lot of exertion, but not much exposure, you'll reach the base of Needle Peak. If you're looking for the easiest route up it, head for its west side and cautiously scramble up it. Should you try the steep east side, use extreme caution and/or a rope. Views are similar to those from Granite Chief, except that Lake Tahoe is largely obscured.

Back on the PCT near Granite Chief's east ridge, we reach, after about brief descent, a snowmelt creeklet, and then in a similar dis-

Little Needle Peak above Little Needle Lake

tance intersect the **Western States Trail**. East, it goes 0.2 mile to the Sierra-crest saddle, where it meets the previously mentioned trail to Emigrant Pass. West, it fluctuates wildly for 1⅓ miles over to a junction with the Tevis Cup Trail. this stretch, constructed by horsemen in the 1980s, was apparently built without any forethought, since the steep ups and downs are random and have nothing to do with topography or obstacles.

Onward, we have an open, switchbacking descent to the minuscule headwaters of Middle Fork American River. You'll find a well-used campsite just above its south bank, and a few yards past it is a junction with part of the old **eastbound Tevis Cup Trail**, which climbs rather steeply 0.6 mile east to Emigrant Pass.

From the junction our PCT winds through forest down to a saddle that separates the American River and Whiskey Creek drainages. Here is the **westbound Tevis Cup Trail**. Just 100 yards northwest down this trail, by the edge of a meadow, one sees a use trail climbing west-southwest upslope. After ⅔ mile this trail crosses the north outlet of **Little Needle Lake** (there is also a west outlet). The trail then dies out at a small campsite on a ridge above the lake's northwest shore. If you continue cross-country southwest, you'll find a second campsite near the west outlet.

The Tevis Cup Trail continues beyond the Little Needle Lake use trail, crossing the

American River in about 0.7 mile, then climbs, in 0.6 mile, all too steeply, to a junction with the previously mentioned Western States Trail. United as one, the trail in 0.8 mile first traverses springy slopes, then drops to a spur ridge—the top of the wilderness' most prominent granitic cliff. Serious climbers can camp among red firs atop the ridge, getting water from the last spring they passed. But climbers aren't the trail's main users. Each year, a grueling foot race is run along this course, starting in Squaw Valley and ending 100 miles west. And, since 1955, equestrian groups have annually made a similar trek, some starting as far east as Carson City and ending in Sacramento. West from the granitic ridge, the trail fluctuates madly to avoid dense alder thickets, and along this stretch one can do some exceptionally fine botanizing. The author mapped the trail all the way to a primitive road, as shown on Maps 19 and 20, but since the user enters private property from the east edge of Section 29, he discourages the trail's use.

From the American River/Whiskey Creek divide the PCT heads south over to a nearby flowery—although often boggy—meadow, then switchbacks down forested slopes to the headwaters of Whiskey Creek. Soon views open up as we descend into one of the Sierra's largest fields of mule ears. On the floor of a hanging valley we approach Whiskey Creek and some small campsites that are hidden under the dense cover of trees beside it. We parallel the usually unseen creek east to where the valley floor drops off sharply; then views soon reappear, down-canyon toward the obvious, closely spaced summits of Twin Peaks.

After a 0.6-mile traverse across mostly scrubby slopes, we come to a shaded junction with the **Whiskey Creek Trail**. On it we switchback for a few minutes down to Whiskey Creek, above whose west bank one finds **Whiskey Creek Camp**. The spacious camp, with bunkhouse, storage shed, and a roofed stove, was popular with equestrians. The structures are now in poor shape and are off-limits, and camping within 250 feet of them is prohibited. Head west or north 100-200 yards to find comfortable, legal sites.

⊰⊱ 46 ⊰⊱
Five Lakes Trail to Five Lakes Basin and Whiskey Creek Camp

Distances:
1.8 miles to northernmost lake
1.9 miles to Five Lakes Trail
   0.2 mile on trail to westernmost lake
   0.3 mile on trail to southernmost lake
2.0 miles to W S Trail
2.6 miles to Pacific Crest Trail
4.0 miles to Whiskey Creek Trail
   0.4 mile on trail to Whiskey Creek Camp

Low/High Elevations: 6560'/7600'

Season: Early July through mid-October

Classification: Moderate

Maps: 21, 20, and 23

Trailhead: From Interstate 80's Highway 89 exit in western Truckee, drive about 10 miles south up 89 to the Alpine Meadows Ski Area junction. If you're coming from Lake Tahoe, this junction is just under 4 miles down 89 from the major junction by Lake Tahoe's outlet at Tahoe City. Drive 2.1 miles up Alpine Meadows Road to the Five Lakes Trail, on the right, which is opposite a junction with the

upper end of Deer Park Drive. Park along either side of Alpine Meadows Road.

Introduction
Ascending this wide, well-graded, popular trail, you can reach the Five Lakes basin in only an hour's time, leaving many hours to fish, swim, explore, or relax around these lakes. Due to extremely heavy use, camping is prohibited at these lakes. Whiskey Creek Camp, a favorite among equestrians, is an easy 2¾-mile descent farther.

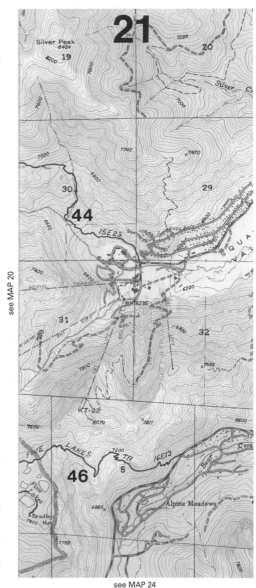

see MAP 20

see MAP 24

Description

We start west among volcanic talus, derived from the andesite cliffs above us, and hike up past dense stands of scrubby huckleberry oaks beneath a scattered cover of Jeffrey pines and white firs. Rounding a broad ridge, we can look south toward the upper canyon, whose slopes support the ski lifts of mostly forested Alpine Meadows. Our dusty Trail 16E13 becomes a gravelly one as volcanic rocks give way to granitic ones, some of them stained reddish by iron oxide from weathered minerals. A few switchbacks through dense brush transport us higher up the slope, and then we arc southwest to a switchback on a weathered granitic ridge. From it we can look east, back the way we came, and see the clear contact between the medium-gray young volcanic rocks and the lighter, much older granitic bedrock west of them.

After passing stunted Jeffrey pines and some western white pines that struggle in the shallow soils of this dry granitic ridge, we climb moderately northwest. The grade then eases, and we arc west across brushy slopes, then climb up to the east boundary of Granite Chief Wilderness, at the edge of a stand of red firs. Our path quickly levels off, and from where it curves from southwest to west, a faint use trail descends 70 yards to the **northernmost lake** in the Five Lakes Basin. This lake, visible from the main trail, is a shallow, grassy body of water dotted with granitic boulders.

After a few minutes' walk beyond the use trail, we come to the **Five Lakes Trail**, branching left, which definitely is more heavily used than the trail ahead. We take this trail, which in 250 yards bifurcates just above the basin's **westernmost lake**, which is the largest and the most popular. A short trail west goes to the north shore, while a longer trail south goes above the northeast shore. It quickly branches, one branch descending toward the lake's east corner, while the other heads east over to the adjacent, **southernmost lake**. In early season, before the water level drops, this lake is actually an eastern lobe of the westernmost lake. Seasonally draining into the north and southeast corners of this "lobe" are creeklets from two of the basin's other lakes, which can be reached by heading up the creeklets.

If you want to camp or get away from the crowd, continue on toward the Whiskey

Squaw Peak and the westernmost of the Five Lakes

Creek Camp environs. From the Five Lakes Trail junction, start west and in a minute reach a junction with the **W S Trail**. This climbs north to a nearby crest, then descends into Squaw Valley to meet the Western States Trail. This starts east of Highway 89, crosses the Truckee River, climbs west across Squaw Valley's south slopes to Emigrant Pass, then intersects the Pacific Crest Trail near Granite Chief (see Hike 45).

Moving on, we soon cross a creek fed by snowfields on the east slopes of volcanic Squaw Peak. Next, we traverse southwest, then descend south, heading past meadowy lands to reach a junction with the **Pacific Crest Trail** (PCT). Hike 50, originating at Barker Pass, traverses along the Sierra crest, passing Twin Peaks before switchbacking down to here. On the PCT, which over the next 1.4 miles is an upgrade of the old trail to Whiskey Creek Camp, we head southwest down-canyon across generally open, picturesque slopes that offer both dry-land and wet-land floral displays. After dropping about 250 feet in elevation the trail curves west and soon arrives at a junction with **Whiskey Creek Trail** 16E06. On it we switchback several times before winding down to nearby Whiskey Creek. Just above its west bank lies **Whiskey Creek Camp**, which has a former bunkhouse, storage shed, and a roofed stove. These historic structures are now in

poor shape and are off-limits, and camping within 250 feet of them is prohibited. Therefore, head west or north 100-200 yards to find comfortable, legal sites. You'll find a junction at Whiskey Creek Camp, and Hike 48, from Diamond Crossing, climbs north to this junction, while Hike 49 climbs west from it.

⇜ **47** ⇝
Powderhorn Trail to Diamond Crossing

Distance: 4.0 miles to Diamond Crossing
Low/High Elevations: 6000'/7820'
Season: Mid-July through early October
Classification: Moderate
Maps: 26 and 23

Trailheads: Leave Highway 89 opposite Kaspian Beach, at a junction with Barker Pass Road (Forest Route 03). This junction is 4.3 miles south of the major junction by Lake Tahoe's outlet at Tahoe City, and only 0.4 mile north of overhanging, roadside Eagle Rock, which in turn is about 4 miles north of Tahoma. Drive 2.3 miles west on Barker Pass Road to a junction, from which Road 15N38 continues ahead to an OHV staging area. You curve left on your paved road to quickly cross Blackwood Creek and then make a 4.7-mile

A cliff of columnar lava

climb to the Sierra crest. Here, the pavement ends, and you'll find the start of the Ellis Peak Trail, on your left. The peak and adjacent Ellis Lake are more easily reached along an OHV route beginning from Miller Meadows (Map 27). From the crest you descend just under ½ mile to the Barker Pass PCT Trailhead, from where Hike 50 starts north; Hike 75, south. Still on the main road, traverse 1.6 miles to a sharp curve left in the road at a minor, but deep, gully. The Powderhorn Trail begins from the gully's west (far) side. Roadside parking is limited, but use is light.

Introduction

Within the area covered by this book, past volcanic eruptions buried much of the lands near the Sierra crest. Today, many volcanic deposits still remain on that crest and on crests descending west from it. Soil creep and stream erosion have carried weathered, *nutrient-rich* volcanic particles down slopes and onto valley bottoms, where there have developed luxuriant forests. As one would expect, most of the stream drainages with such forests have been heavily logged. One exception is the Five Lakes Creek drainage, which has been only slightly logged. If you want to view an old-growth forest with a minimal imprint by man, take this trail down to Diamond Crossing, and if time and energy permit, also Hikes 48 and 49. Those who descend to the crossing are rewarded with solitude and with one of the best series of swimming holes to be found along any creek in the Tahoe Sierra.

Description

By a gully carved from loose volcanic rocks, our Powderhorn Trail 15E15 climbs initially southwest before switchbacking north for a short climb to a nearby broad saddle surrounded by red firs and western white pines. This area was selectively logged, and then the saddle briefly served as a trailhead parking area before major storms closed the road to it. From the saddle you descend a steep, former logging road ¼ mile to its switchback, and there find the start of trail tread. In the head of the Powderhorn Creek drainage, heavy snow in some years can hide the trail until early August, and if the road has some snow patches on it, you may want to keep to the road

rather than take the trail, which is bound to have even more snow. The trail descends all too steeply down slick-when-wet volcanic slopes and past mountain hemlocks, crossing the headwaters of Powderhorn Creek about 160 yards before reaching the lower stretch of the road. On it you walk about 35 yards northwest to the trail's resumption, and descend just over 200 yards to the southern boundary of Granite Chief Wilderness.

The area of former logging is now behind you, and pristine forest lies ahead. On a generally moderate grade we descend north and soon exit the forest to enter natural "clearcuts." The fractured volcanic rocks and sediments high above us eventually become unstable—usually when heavily laden with snow—and a rock-and-snow avalanche ensues, mowing down all the vegetation in its path. You can tell by the height at which the myriad trees have been snapped just how much snow lay on the ground when each avalanche occurred: the parts of tree trunks lying under the snow were unharmed. Also you can tell by the orientation of the snapped trunks the source area of each avalanche. Some trunks lie upslope, indicating that an avalanche originated on the opposite side of the canyon, descended to the floor, and then flowed upslope to mow down our trailside trees. Elsewhere, trunks lie downslope, indicating that an avalanche originated high on our side of the canyon. If you look closely in this area, you'll notice at least one cabin-size boulder that fell from cliffs above us. The texture of this and others is characteristic of the autobrecciated lava flows above us. Large boulders can have a wide assortment of smaller, angular boulders that range up to several feet in diameter.

Beyond the avalanche area the trail bends northwest and soon arrives at the lower edge of a talus slope composed of lava blocks, which were derived from a cliff of columnar lava, which is every bit as dramatic as those seen at Devils Postpile National Monument—and higher. Without too much effort you can scramble up to its base to be really impressed with the size of these columns.

The trail again enters forest cover, although the species tend to be increasingly white firs (and some incense-cedars) as we descend at a usually moderate grade to lower elevations. In about ½ mile, we have a view down at nearby Powderhorn Creek at the site of a large landslide. Additional landsliding will take out a small stretch of trail, which then will have to be rerouted a bit higher. After another ½ mile we enter a level meadow, which is rich in grass in early season, in corn lilies and yampah in late season. We start west through it, then turn north, and leave the meadow to boulderhop nearby Powderhorn Creek, with an adjacent campsite. Early-season hikers may find the creek 10 yards wide and more than a boulderhop. North, you walk about 300 yards to reach the outskirts of open **Diamond Crossing**, and Hike 48 continues the route description north from here.

From a junction in this sloping meadow, a lightly used trail descends west, reaching Five Lakes Creek in about 0.4 mile. In early season it can be a 20-yard-wide, very wet ford. On the creek's west bank you'll find a good campsite, but more-secluded ones that are just as good or better can be found by spending a few minutes looking upstream or downstream.

Alternatively, from the junction you can diagonal northwest to quickly reach the lower stretch of Bear Pen Creek and find an additional possible site or two. More importantly, just upstream from where this creek joins Five Lakes Creek is the lower end of a very impressive inner gorge with a chain of swimming holes. The lower pools are easily reached, since they are separated by short rapids, but higher up the pools are separated by waterfalls. You can walk northeast up the rim of the inner gorge and view these pools, which even for climbers are quite difficult to reach. Best to look but don't touch—you wouldn't want to be carried over a waterfall.

~> 48 <~

Diamond Crossing to Whiskey Creek Camp

Distances:
0.2 mile to Bear Pen Trail
   2.8 miles on trail to Bear Pen
2.5 miles to Big Spring Trail
   0.6 mile on trail to Big Spring
2.8 miles to Shanks Cove Trail
4.8 miles to Whiskey Creek Camp
Low/High Elevations: 6050′/6940′
Season: Mid-July through early October
Classification: Moderate
Map: 23
Trailhead: None; see introduction.

Introduction

This hike, north up Five Lakes Creek to Whiskey Creek Camp, takes off from Hike 47's Diamond Crossing. From that hike's trailhead, the camp lies a distant 8.8 miles away via the west-side route. Like Hike 45, this route is certainly a long route to the camp. Most travelers will reach it via Hike 46. Hike 48, however, continues Hike 47's traverse through an uncut, old-growth forest, and the route offers secluded camping. Of great interest to me is the giant size of many of the trailside trees and wildflowers. This area seems conducive to maximum growth.

Description

Hike 47 describes the route to Diamond Crossing, which is a large, usually dry meadow with a trail junction. From it we climb gently northeast on Five Lakes Creek Trail 15E31 through the meadow for 200 yards to its edge, where there may be several tall, Jeffrey pines. These were stately in the 1980s, but then a 6-year drought ensued, and perhaps because of it, they died. Eventually they will topple, most likely in a wind storm.

Just 150 yards into the forest we come to a junction with **Bear Pen Trail** 16E26. If you follow this moderately climbing trail 2.8 miles east to its end, you'll reach the **Bear Pen**, which is a small, meadowy cove, surrounded by mountain hemlocks, at the upper end of a

Five Lakes Creek near Diamond Crossing

feet, reaches 5-6 feet. Just beyond the seasonally wet area we pass some mammoth Jeffrey pines, which stand out among the smaller, far-more-common red firs. Note the chartreuse-colored staghorn lichens growing profusely on these firs (and note that they grow very poorly on the pines, which are largely devoid of them). The lichens grow down to within a few feet of the ground, this lower limit more or less marking the depth of the average winter snowpack.

We next cross Grouse Canyon's sizable creek, doing so within sight and sound of Five Lakes Creek. In ¼ mile we jump across a spring-fed creek, then in ½ mile come to a junction with the **Big Spring Trail**. This ascends nearly due north at a mostly gentle grade, reaching **Big Spring** in 0.6 mile. If it is not obvious, look for it just west of and below the trail by the south edge of a meadow. As at the Bear Pen, this vicinity is a good one for secluded camping, and a spacious campsite lies among lodgepole and Jeffrey pines immediately west of the spring. The trail ahead is abandoned. Formerly, it traversed 0.2 mile northwest through the meadow to a junction, from where it once continued north, while another, lightly used trail headed southwest over to nearby Five Lakes Creek. From the creek over to nearby Trail 16E17 this lightly used trail is quite obvious.

From the Big Spring Trail junction the main trail winds 400 yards west to Five Lakes Creek, which is likely to be a wet ford in early season. Later on, you jump across on large boulders or use a fallen tree, if available. On the fairly level terrain near the creek you should be able to find secluded campsites.

From the creek we walk 170 yards west to a junction with ascending **Shanks Cove Trail** 15E11, which is described in the opposite (easy) downhill direction in Hike 49. Those on it join us here for the remaining 2.0-mile easy-to-moderate climb north to Whiskey Creek Camp. We begin initially northeast up Trail 16E17, soon almost touching Five Lakes Creek,

boxed-in canyon. By the meadow's north edge, you'll find a campsite just east of trickling, alder-lined Bear Pen Creek. This reclusive site is only 4½ miles due west of Lake Tahoe's busy shoreline Highway 89, but because it is hemmed in on three sides by steep, 1000-foot-high walls, it feels like it is in the middle of nowhere.

On Trail 15E31 we go 150 yards to cross Bear Pen Creek immediately east of its miniature gorge. We then climb up to the east side of a nearby metamorphic knoll, and here you can leave the trail to climb across its south slopes over to a view of Five Lakes Creek's very impressive inner gorge. Beyond the knoll we soon enter a meadowy stretch, which can be quite boggy in early season. However, by August the soil is reasonably dry and the wildflowers have achieved their maximum height. Here the tall larkspur lives up to its name, growing 7 feet tall, and the arrow-leaved senecio, which usually tops out at 3-4

Granite Chief Wilderness

then veer from it to climb, then almost level out, 0.6 mile from the last junction, at a fork in the trail. The right branch strikes northeast, and is the aforementioned lightly used trail that momentarily reaches Five Lakes Creek. This can be crossed on large boulders and/or logs, and from the opposite bank this lightly used trail dies out by adjacent Big Spring 's meadow.

The main trail jogs initially northwest and almost immediately enters a meadow with cottonwoods. Just beyond it your trail parallels Five Lakes Creek for ¼ mile, giving you your last opportunity for secluded camping. You then leave the creek's side, paralleling it at a distance as you climb north for ¾ mile moderately up to a low ridge, just beyond which is a flat holding **Whiskey Creek Camp**. From a trail junction by the west end of the camp, you can head west or north for campsites. No camping is allowed within 250 feet of the camp's three small structures.

⇔ 49 ⇔
Whiskey Creek Camp-Shanks Cove Loop

Distances:
1.5 miles to Picayune Valley Trail
3.4 miles to Grayhorse Valley Trail
   0.4 mile on trail to packers' trail
      0.3 mile on trail to campsite
3.8 miles to packers' trail
   0.6 mile to packers' camp
6.4 miles to Five Lakes Creek Trail
8.4 miles to Whiskey Creek Camp
Low/High Elevations: 6350'/8080'
Season: Mid-July through early October
Classification: Strenuous
Maps: 23 and 22
Trailhead: None. Start from Whiskey Creek Camp, which is the end point of Hikes 45, 46, and 48.

Introduction
If you've got an extra day at Whiskey Creek Camp and are up to an energetic day hike, take this loop. It circles in a counter-clock-

wise direction, challenging you with the diffi-cult stretches of trail first, while you are still fresh. However, this section up to crest views is also the most rewarding. Cross-country afi-cionados can extend the route, making a top-of-the-world excursion over to the remote Mildred Lakes. Those looking for isolated camping will find sites at the end of two later-al trails plus additional sites along Five Lakes Creek between Whiskey Creek Camp and the Shanks Cove Trail.

Description

This loop route begins and ends at a trail junc-tion in Whiskey Creek Camp. A level traverse west leads us past a large, obvious campsite, about 100 yards from the camp's three small structures, and then we hit a small, steep slope. Short switchbacks take us to a gentler slope above, colored and scented by mule ears. Beyond it, our Trail 15E08 climbs steeply once again, entering a forest of red firs and western white pines. Midway up our 680-foot climb to an east-descending ridgecrest, we encounter an alder-lined, usually flowing creeklet, which gives us an excuse to rest. Before September, this is the last fairly dependable water before an isolated camp-site, almost 4 miles farther.

Once on the fairly open ridgecrest, we have another excuse to pause, for we have a panorama that extends from Granite Chief, north of us, southward along the ridgecrest andesite flows that cap Squaw, Ward, and Twin peaks. A low ridgecrest notch to the south is the saddle over which the Powderhorn Trail crosses. Looking through the Five Lakes basin notch, we can see the dis-tant, broad, saddle-shaped summit of Mt. Rose (10,776'), the third highest of the Tahoe Basin peaks.

We ascend our ridgecrest briefly , then make a descending, westward traverse through one of the Sierra's largest fields of mule ears (a larger one is crossed in Hike 46). This 40+ acre spread of large-leaved sunflow-ers saturates our visual and olfactory senses. Characteristic of, but not limited to, slopes of dry, volcanic soils, mule ears tend to grow in almost pure stands, shading out the shorter competition. By late summer they die back,

and then a smaller aromatic plant, the coyote mint, may become more obvious.

After rounding a forested slope, we tra-verse through a second large field of mule ears and come to a junction, near a shallow gully, with the **Picayune Valley Trail**. This makes an initial ascent, then traverses 0.6 mile west to a conspicuous crest saddle before dropping into Picayune Valley (Hike 42). From the initial ascent you could walk cross-country upslope for several minutes to a close by, minor, crest saddle, which offers you a view down into this 1000-foot-deep valley.

Beyond the trail junction we descend through a red-fir forest to an open, sometimes wet cove below an impressive array of deep, vertical grooves that striate a huge cliff of vol-canic deposits above us. Were this deeply grooved rock more solid and closer to the trail-head, it would attract rock climbers. Leaving the cove, we begin a three-stage, 920-foot climb, first past red firs, then we scramble up as it climbs very steeply to an east-descending ridgecrest. The last bit of this ascent is on bare volcanic rock, and the trail's tread may disap-pear. Should you slip here, you could slide tens of feet. With the first stage behind, you take the trail west up the steepening ridge, climbing about 150 feet higher before leaving it. Doing so, you have a short, precarious tra-verse on bare volcanic rock, and a slip could result in a very dangerous slide down a steep slope. (If you hike this loop in the opposite direction, the route is more cryptic and the chance of slipping greater.)

With the short traverse behind, you com-plete the second stage by first climbing past some grotesque formations before the trail eases up and soon reaches an east-west sad-dle. Here, above the head of Picayune Valley, we can gaze down into it as well as admire the rugged scenery surrounding it. Bordered by brown metamorphic rocks on its west slope and light-gray granitic rocks on its east slope, this valley sits deep beneath the dark-gray andesite flows that cap the two ridges above its slopes (see Hike 42 for a geologic interpre-tation). From this viewpoint we begin our third stage by climbing southwest on a more moderate grade through a forest of hemlock and pine to a long north-south saddle. From it we can see—due west of us—Johnson Monument, which is a large, isolated, severely overhanging volcanic block atop a narrow pedestal. In the northeast, Mt. Rose again projects its broad summit above the deep Five Lakes basin gap.

To reach Johnson Monument, Mt. Mildred, or the Mildred Lakes, cross-country explorers should leave the trail just before the north end of the long saddle, head northwest across flat-topped summit 8109, then descend, steeply at first, to a saddle separating Picayune Valley, to the north, from Grayhorse Valley, to the southwest. To reach the Johnson Monument requires work, for you have to traverse almost a mile from the saddle, crossing brushy, rubbly slopes. Your saddle offers a view southwest down heavily logged Grayhorse Valley, a hanging valley that obscures a view of Hell Hole Reservoir, about 1800 feet below it. To get a glimpse of that reservoir, you'll have to climb to the summit of Mt. Mildred.

Only peak baggers can justify this 650-foot climb. Others climb just a bit, then leave the crest for a traverse northwest to the base of steep slopes beneath Heavens Gate, which is the saddle immediately north of Mt. Mildred. A scramble up to the saddle will earn you a view of French Meadows Reservoir. Then by keeping just below the base of steep slopes, you can reach Mildred Lakes in about a ¾-mile traverse north. The middle lake is deep enough for a brisk swim, while the north and south lakes are mere ponds. Camping space is very limited, but the isolation of these lakes does offer you a true wilderness feeling.

Most of this hike's few travelers won't take the side trip just described. They continue south on the long saddle with a view of the Johnson Monument to a trail fork. To the right, the **Grayhorse Valley Trail** descends almost 0.4 mile southwest to a junction, from which a **packers' trail** traverses ¼ mile south to a verdant, spring-fed gully. Just 60 yards past it is an isolated **campsite**, beneath mountain hemlocks, in a miniature hanging valley. From this trail's junction, the Grayhorse Valley Trail 15E11, heading down a shallow gully, switchbacks down to its trailhead at a bend in a former logging road. (To drive to this trailhead, see Hike 42's trailhead directions to the far—south—end of French Meadows Reservoir's dam. Still on F.R. 96, you turn left and take it ¾ mile east to a junction with F.R. 48. Take this winding road up to Chipmunk Ridge, then briefly down into South Fork Long Canyon. Just past its creek, about 4½ miles from F.R. 96 and about 2½ miles before a junction with a road to Hell Hole Reservoir, leave F.R. 48 for a 6-mile jaunt to the trailhead. In the late 1990s the road was not in very good shape, so check first with the Foresthill Ranger Station to see how drivable it is.)

From the south end of the long saddle, 3.4 miles along the hike's basic loop, we branch left and make a switchbacking descent toward Shanks Cove. About midway down to it, after completing a 300-yard-long switchback leg southeast, we meet a sometimes easily missed junction with a **packers' trail**. This oscillates southward, eventually climbing in about ½ mile to a willowy, seasonally boggy meadow. The trail skirts between the meadow's east edge and a low outcrop, then climbs momentarily to a 1914-vintage **packers' camp**. This large, very isolated camp, among mountain hemlocks and beside a spring, is close to the base of a talus slope created by large blocks falling from an adjacent cliff. If you make it to this picturesque spot, you'll see that the cliff still is in the process of falling apart, some enormous blocks being ready to break free at any time. The camp, however, is not threatened.

From the junction with the packers' trail, the Shanks Cove Trail first executes short, steep switchbacks eastward, then jogs briefly north before commencing a steep descent east toward Shanks cove. When we arrive at this almost level cove, which stands apart from most others in the wilderness in that it is completely forested, we cross a rhapsodic creek, then on our Trail 15E11 we parallel its cascading course over a winding route down metamorphic bedrock. Where the gradient decreases, we recross the creek, ⅔ mile downstream, and parallel its trout-inhabited waters east through lodgepole forest down to a flat where we meet **Five Lakes Creek Trail** 16E17. To complete our loop, we follow the last part of the previous hike 2.0 miles up this trail to arrive at **Whiskey Creek Camp**. Welcome home.

❧ 50 ❧
Pacific Crest Trail, Barker Pass north to Twin Peaks and beyond

Distances:
4.9 miles to south ridge of Twin Peaks
  0.4 mile cross-country to west summit
8.3 miles to Ward Peak maintenance road
11.4 miles to upper Five Lakes Creek Trail
14.0 miles to Alpine Meadows Road

Low/High Elevations: 6660'/8420'; 8878' atop Twin Peaks

Season: Early July through mid-October

Classification: Moderate

Maps: 27, 24, 23, 20, and 21

Trailhead: See the Hike 47 trailhead for directions to Barker Pass.

Introduction
Twin Peaks provide good views of Lake Tahoe, and the easiest way to their summits is from Barker Pass, north along the Pacific Crest Trail, which along this hike also coincides with the Tahoe Rim Trail. Most of the route to the south ridge of the peaks is viewless, so if you want additional views, you can continue north beyond the peaks. That stretch of the PCT/TRT has almost continual, inspiring views. Then after a major descent you can head northeast up an easy route to Five Lakes for a refreshing swim and follow it with an easy downhill hike to the Hike 46 trailhead. A vehicle shuttle is required.

Description
From the trailhead along Forest Route 03 at Barker Pass, we start west, up the southern slopes of Barker Peak, and have views of past logging operations in and around the Barker Creek basin, to the south of us. In a short while we top a ridge and view Lake Tahoe to the east and two small volcanic buttes, our immediate goals, to the north. Traversing toward them, we have views southeast, of Barker Peak and, above and left of it, a ridge sweeping up to Ellis Peak. Both are part of the same series of andesitic lava flows. When we reach the two buttes, our southeast panorama

now contains metamorphic Dicks Peak, 14 miles away, standing on the skyline above Barker Peak. Our two blocky trailside buttes are climbable, although I climbed the closer one unroped only with some trepidation. Its twin is an easier scramble, and it offers the hiker additional Tahoe views. Rock climbers, armed with ropes and assorted gear, will find its 280-foot, nearly vertical east face exceptionally challenging.

Leaving the buttes and concomitant views, we descend on the Pacific Crest Trail (PCT) into a shady forest of mountain hemlock, western white pine and, soon, red fir. Past seasonal springs we reach a nearly level camping area along the headwaters of North Fork Blackwood Creek. Onward, we descend for another ½ mile and then, 3 miles from our trailhead, start a ½-mile traverse north. Having lost about 400 feet of elevation since we left the buttes, we now have to make it up, which we do on a series of switchback legs of varying gradients, almost to the Sierra crest.

North of Twin Peaks you meet a stretch of classic crest-hugging PCT

The Pacific Crest Trail traverses southeast across open slopes toward Twin Peaks

Just about every hiker will resent this drop and gain (except those camping by the creek), but there is method to the trail's "madness." We round a crest knoll, point 8434, and about 100 yards later, on the north side of an even smaller knoll, see why the trail goes where it does. To the southwest is a knife-edge lava ridgecrest, across which a trail would have been difficult to build and, with snow, deadly to traverse. In this vicinity you have excellent views in almost all directions, so relax and enjoy them before you make a final push to Twin Peaks.

When you're ready to continue, head ¼ mile north along the wilderness-boundary crest to where the trail begins a gently descending traverse. Here, on the lower **south ridge of Twin Peaks**, the Tahoe Rim Trail (TRT), ascending southwest from Tahoe City, is slated to join the PCT in either late 1998 or '99 (see more about this trail segment under Hike 51). Here also you begin a cross-country ascent to the summits of Twin Peaks, starting initially up the south ridge. The gradient increases as you approach the base of a lava knoll, and you leave the ridge, veering left (north) and climbing steeply up behind it. You then see the easy, obvious route up to the **west summit of Twin Peaks**.

Although you barely need to use your hands to reach the west summit, you'll need to use them a lot to reach the east summit. From the saddle separating the two summits, you can cautiously scramble directly up to that summit, though this route may be too intimidating for some folks. You can find eas-

ier routes by traversing east along the peak's south slopes. Do note that all routes up to the east summit (8878') require caution, since all are fairly steep and loose rocks abound.

Regardless of which summit you climb, the views are quite similar. You'll see, to the north-northwest, a prominent ridge with about five major summits. The central one is unmistakable Needle Peak (8971'), with Lyon Peak (8891') west of it and Granite Chief (9006') east of it. West of this ridge is subdued Mildred Ridge (north summit is 8509'), while east of it is a ridge topped by Tinker Knob (8949'). Below it lies closer, spreading Ward Peak (8637'), from which the broad, glaciated Ward Creek canyon swoops east to Lake Tahoe. You'll note Mt. Rose (10,776') rising above the lake's northeast end and the Freel Peak massif (10,881') rising above its southeast end. Desolation Wilderness monopolizes the southern horizon, with Mt. Tallac (9735') readily identifiable. Finally, if you're on the west summit of Twin Peaks, you'll have a five view west down into adjacent, deep Bear Pen Creek canyon. From the pointed east summit, which is the solidified conduit of a former volcano, this view is largely obscured by the blocky west summit. When you're ready to descend, retrace your steps if you're returning to your trailhead. If you're continuing north toward Ward Peak and Five Lakes, make a descent more or less down the northwest ridge to a saddle immediately east of a prominent knob, 8521 on Map 24. The PCT is about 130 yards below the saddle.

A southward panorama from near two small volcanic buttes. Barker Peak is in the left mid-ground, with the Ellis Peak ridge left of it and with Dicks and Jacks peaks above and right of it. Immediately right of them is pointed Pyramid Peak, capping the south end of the Crystal Range.

You don't have to climb Twin Peaks to get good views, for plenty lie ahead along the PCT. From the south ridge of Twin Peaks your trail traverses below the west peak, regains the crest just beyond knob 8521, and then stays on or very close to it for the next 4 miles. Classic crest views prevail. Early on this crest traverse you see massive, columnar lava flows on the flanks of Powderhorn and Little Powderhorn canyons, to the southwest. These flows dwarf those of the more famous Devils Postpile, south of Yosemite National Park. Beyond peak 8522, which is a remnant of a lava flow perched high above Grouse Canyon, you pass beautiful, trailside hexagonal columns like those at Devils Postpile. As you head north toward Ward Peak, note how the lava flows dip away from deep Ward Creek canyon, to the east. Perhaps about 5 million years ago a sizable volcano stood above the canyon, but today all we see are parts of its western flank. Our trail nearly tops Ward Peak, and just northwest of the summit our PCT closely approaches the **Ward Peak maintenance road**. On it you can descend to Alpine Meadows Ski Area.

Past our view of non-alpine Alpine Meadows, our trail, which has been mostly on volcanic rocks since Barker Pass, completes its crest traverse on older rocks, first metamorphic and then granitic. Beyond the last crest knoll the trail begins a 900-foot descent, switchbacking 16 times down to Five Lakes Creek. Those adept at cross-country hiking can leave the trail at the ninth switchback, traverse on a slight descent north for a minute or two, and then arrive on a crest about 100 feet above the westernmost of the Five Lakes. If you adhere to the PCT, you walk about 150 yards beyond the creek to the **upper Five Lakes Creek Trail**. Head about ¾ mile northwest up this trail to a junction with a short, heavily used, southbound trail that descends to the westernmost lake, which offers fine swimming from mid-July through mid-August. Then follow the first part of Hike 46 in reverse 2.6 miles down to the Alpine Meadows Road.

⟜ 51 ⟜
Twin Peaks, via Stanford Rock Trail

Distances:
4.3 miles to Stanford Rock
6.3 miles to east Twin Peak
6.5 miles to west Twin Peak
Low/High Elevations: 6440'/8878'
Season: Early July through mid-October
Classification: Moderate
Map: 24
Trailhead: From the major junction by Lake Tahoe's outlet at Tahoe City, drive 2¼ miles south on Highway 89 to William Kent Campground, then about 250 yards farther to the first road west, Pineland Drive. Take this 0.4 mile to a junction with three roads, where you curve left onto Twin Peaks Drive (the main route—follow the yellow center line), which in about 0.1 mile becomes Ward Creek Boulevard, and on it you continue west through lower Ward Creek canyon for 0.9 mile to a creekside turnout on your left—your trailhead—at the start of Road 15N35.

Introduction

This is a longer route than the previous hike to Twin Peaks, and it has about twice as much elevation gain, so why take it? Well, the first 4.9 miles (the bulk of the route) is along an old road that is recommended for mountain-bike use. By using a mountain bike, you can reach the summit in under 2 hours, if you're in shape. But many hikers and bicyclists prefer to go only up to Stanford Rock, which by itself is a rewarding goal. Indeed, if you're staying at William Kent Campground, you're close enough to the trailhead (1.5 miles away), that you needn't drive to it. However, the climb to both Twin Peaks and back to the campground is a hefty 16 miles, which is nevertheless not a bad day hike for strong hikers or bicyclists.

Starting perhaps as early as late 1998, or more likely in 1999, there will be an alternate route up to the Twin Peaks—a stretch of the Tahoe Rim Trail (TRT). This will begin from the next left-branching road, 15N62, which is 0.7 mile past the start of Road 15N35 toward Stanford Rock and 2.1 miles from Highway 89. Between the two roads (¼ mile before Road 15N62) is right-branching Paige Meadows Road 15N60, which first climbs to the meadows then descends toward Tahoe City. Another stretch of the TRT may follow this road exactly or may parallel it. In 1997 and 1998 the Stanford Rock Trail and this Road 15N60 provided access to an already constructed segment of the TRT that begins from the Tahoe City trailhead, the start of Hike 112. That hike's trailhead description tells you how to get from the major junction by Lake Tahoe's outlet at Tahoe City to the trailhead. To get to lower Ward Creek canyon from the major junction, first head 0.6 mile south on Highway 89 to Granlibakken Road and then head 0.3 mile west up it to Rawhide Drive, which is just before Granlibakken Road curves left. Go 300 yards south up Rawhide Drive to its end at Bonanza Drive, where the dirt road up to Paige Meadows begins. Part of this road is closed to motor vehicles but not to hikers and bicyclists.

The stretch of TRT from Ward Creek Boulevard up to Twin Peaks will be almost the same length as the Stanford Rock Trail and will involve about the same amount of elevation gain. However, this new stretch will have one advantage: it will offer backpackers and equestrians camping opportunities along Ward Creek. On the other hand, these trail users will miss many views obtained from Stanford Rock Trail, the current Hike 51.

Description

The Stanford Rock Trail begins as old, closed Road 15N35 (formerly 15N47), which first dips to cross adjacent Ward Creek, then keeps right at an immediate road branch. From it you climb briefly upslope through a logged area, then climb east at a moderate grade. Just before you cross a crest, you meet a blocked-off route—an old road—that provides access to your route from roads above Highway 89. From the crest you have views of Lake Tahoe as you traverse brushy slopes, but soon you turn west. The road climbs back up to the crest, switchbacks away from and then back to the crest, and then quickly comes to a junction. Here, about 1.8 miles from the trailhead,

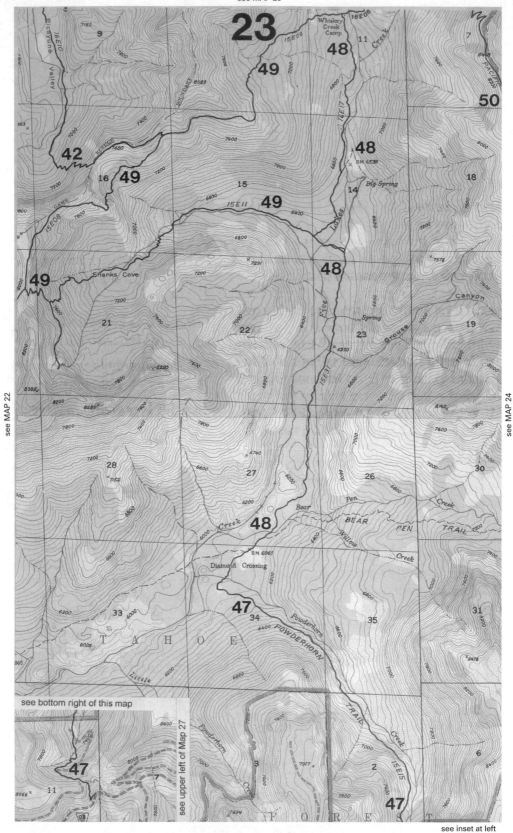

see MAP 22

see MAP 24

23

Whiskey Creek Camp

16E08

15E08

15E17

48
11

49

50

7

42
49
16

48
BM 6539
14
Big Spring

18

15

49
15E11

48

Shanks Cove

49

21

22

23
Spring
Grouse
Canyon
19

15E3

Five Lakes

28

27

26

30

Bear Pen
BEAR PEN TRAIL

48
Creek

Willow
Creek

BM 6061
Diamond Crossing

33
T A H O E

47
34

35

31

POWDERHORN

see bottom right of this map

Powderhorn Creek

TRAIL

15E15

Creek

47
11

7

3
7977

2

6

47

F O R E S T

see upper left of Map 27

see inset at left

see MAP 21

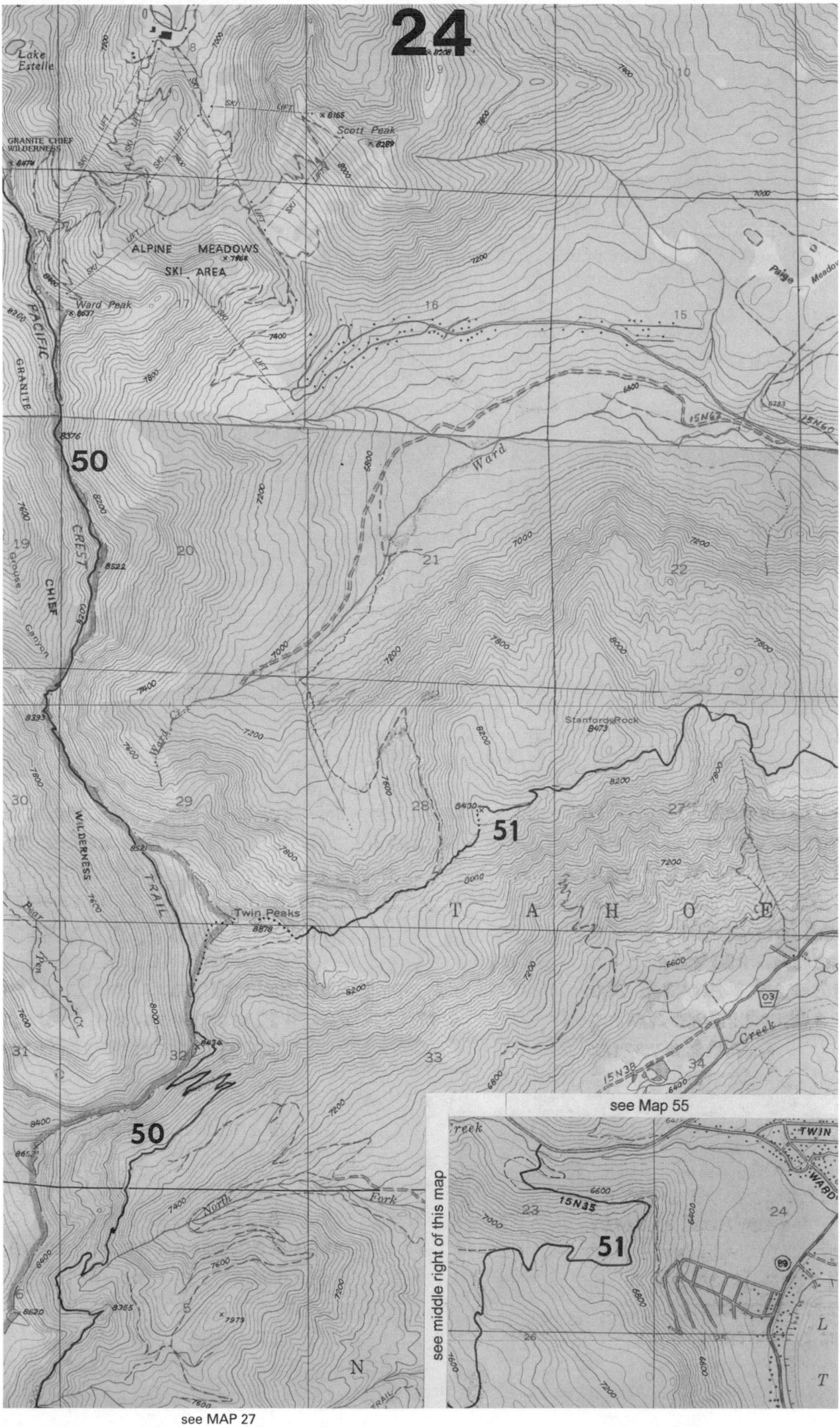

24

see MAP 55

see inset below

Lake Estelle

GRANITE CHIEF WILDERNESS

Scott Peak

ALPINE MEADOWS SKI AREA

Ward Peak

Paige Meadow

50

PACIFIC CREST CHIEF

GRANITE

Grouse Canyon

Ward

Stanford Rock

51

WILDERNESS

TRAIL

Twin Peaks

T A H O E

Creek

50

North Fork

N

see MAP 23

see MAP 27

see Map 55

see middle right of this map

Creek

TWIN

WARD

51

L

T

a minor road continues right, but you keep left, quickly curving south. You have another Tahoe view just before a meadow, then another one after it, where you approach the brink of deep Blackwood Creek canyon. Now you climb easily and shortly northwest to a junction with another minor road, then traverse shortly southwest almost to the brink of a prominent gully. From the brink, atop a lava cliff of "shaley" rock, you have a fine view up Blackwood Creek canyon toward Barker Pass.

Ahead the road is steeper, and you've got to be in good shape to bicycle farther. You climb to the gully's head, where you'll meet a steep shortcut road that eliminates a switchback. Most folks will take the slightly longer route, keeping left, and will quickly rejoin the shorter route just before once again touching the main crest. You now climb moderately-to-steeply 0.3 mile southwest, then 0.1 mile northwest, to where the gradient slackens as the road turns west-southwest. Here, virtually everyone will leave the road and continue about 250 yards west upslope, then will go an equal distance northwest across the top of an ancient lava flow to the brink of a cliff—**Stanford Rock**. Clockwise, you see, starting in the southwest: Twin Peaks, Ward Peak, Needle Peak and adjacent Granite Chief, Tinker Knob, the top of the Truckee river canyon, and the north half of Lake Tahoe. Stanford Rock would be a good place to practice rock climbing, were it not so far from the trailhead.

To regain the old road, just traverse southwest, keeping left and below this vicinity's highest point (which has poor, tree-blocked views). Back on the road, you descend to a nearby saddle, then make a brief climb west up to a flat-topped ridge where, at its west end, the road dies out. Here, at a fine rest stop, you have an inspiring view of Twin Peaks, just a mile away, plus a panorama of upper Ward Creek canyon. When you're ready to move onward, make an open, slightly descending cross-country traverse 0.1 mile south to where you'll reach the top of a southwest-descending crest. Following it, you'll quickly locate a footpath that winds rather steeply down it to a saddle. Climbing up to it will be a new stretch of Tahoe Rim Trail,

which basically follows old Trail 16E07. This was quite abandoned in 1997 and in local spots virtually impossible to follow. When the new stretch is completed in 1998 or '99, its main difference will be the inclusion of several long switchback legs to make the climb from the canyon floor up to the saddle more bearable. The stretch, as proposed in 1997, is shown on Map 24, and it will provide an alternate route down from Stanford Rock, allowing you to make a loop trip rather than a repeat of the route you ascended. If you arrive at the saddle via Hike 51 and do not find a *good* trail descending from it, then don't attempt to descend a marginal trail. Until it is reconstructed, the descent to the floor could be hazardous, and the on-and-off cross-country where the old route's tread has disappeared would be frustrating.

Bound for Twin Peaks, you leave the saddle and parallel a crest west-southwest toward the summits. The crest gives way to amorphous, hemlock-clad slopes, which become steeper with elevation. You regain the crest after ⅓ mile, then have a steep ascent to the top of a southeast-descending ridge. When the Tahoe Rim Trail through here is completed, this short ascent may be replaced with a couple of switchbacks to keep the gradient to 15% or less. The top of the ridge is a volcanic dike. Your goal, east Twin Peak, is congealed lava that formed in the throat of an ancient volcano. Lava, upwelling from below, exerted enough pressure to cause a vertical fracture in the volcano, which was intruded with lava, and much later was eroded, revealing this dike. In 1997 the old trail basically ended here, but the new Tahoe Rim Trail will start a traverse through a field of mule ears by the upper end of the dike, then will reach the Twin Peaks' south ridge and briefly descend it to the Pacific Crest Trail.

You reach the east summit by an obvious route, though it should be attempted only by competent hikers/mountaineers lacking acrophobia. Others should traverse below the east summit and over to the west summit. To reach the east summit, continue up through the field to the crest and follow it to the top. A cliff-edge footpath hugs the precipitous crest, and a fall from it could certainly be fatal.

Therefore, don't feel compelled to take this route; you can always traverse west and then scramble up boulders and bedrock to the top of **east Twin Peak**. Regardless of how you ascend steep slopes to the summit, use caution, for there is plenty of potential for dislodging rocks. To reach the other Twin Peak, you can descend directly to the saddle separating them. this descent route starts out quite intimidating, but quickly becomes easier. The walk up the back of **west Twin Peak** is a piece of cake. Views from both summits are described near the end of the previous hike.

Lake Tahoe, view from the Rubicon Trail

Chapter 12
Southwestern Lake Tahoe Basin

Introduction

Lying between Lake Tahoe and Desolation Wilderness is a stretch of Highway 89 terrain, some in private hands, but the rest in Sugar Pine Point, D.L. Bliss, and Emerald Bay state parks and in the USFS Lake Tahoe Basin Management Unit's Fallen Leaf Lake recreation area. These public lands are immensely popular during summer, as any would-be camper in search of a campsite can tell you. If you are lucky enough to procure a site, you can spend some time relaxing in or hiking through this area. In winter this area is particularly popular with cross-country skiers.

Sugar Pine Point State Park, the northernmost park, has a fine Lake Tahoe beach along the park's east-side day-use area. Starting from the park's campground, west of Highway 89, is this chapter's first route, Hike 52, which is easily the longest, taking you 7½ miles up to Lost Lake. You'll find swimming at this lake considerably warmer than down at Lake Tahoe, and certainly far less crowded.

D.L. Bliss State Park is very popular, for from its campsites you can walk down to its two beaches: Lester Beach and Calawee Cove Beach. From Calawee Cove, Hike 53 heads south past several miles of shoreline, staying high above Lake Tahoe for the first 2 miles, before approaching Emerald Point, the mouth of Emerald Bay. Trail users can try rather frigid swimming around here in Lake Tahoe, or swim in its appendage, Emerald Bay, which is usually several degrees warmer.

Emerald Bay State Park, which shares a boundary with D.L. Bliss State Park, also offers a beach route, Hike 54, down to Vikingsholm, at the head of Emerald Bay. Because this route is short, it is very popular, as you can judge from its often overflowing trailhead parking lot. The trail is short enough that some folks carry down air mattresses, inflatable rafts, and beach chairs.

Hike 55, to Cascade Creek Falls, starts immediately south of Emerald Bay State Park. You won't reach a beach, but you'll reach a scenic viewpoint, which is a good spot for a picnic.

East from the Cascade Lake environs lie Lake Tahoe's south-shore beaches: Baldwin, Kiva, and Pope. Just south of these lies Fallen Leaf Lake, which is separated from Lake Tahoe by a few low glacial moraines. During some earlier times, this lake was, like Emerald Bay, an appendage of Lake Tahoe. Today, Fallen Leaf Lake nudges out Donner Lake as the Sierra Nevada's second largest *natural* lake. The largest, of course, is Lake Tahoe. The chapter's remaining routes, Hikes 56-58, offer hiking suggestions in this Fallen Leaf Lake area. Most folks, however, will probably spend time relaxing at Tahoe's beaches or boating in either Tahoe or Fallen Leaf.

❧ 52 ❧
General Creek Trail to Duck and Lost Lakes

Distances:
3.2 miles to Lily Pond Trail
    0.3 mile to Lily Pond
5.3 miles to uppermost General Creek crossing
7.3 miles to Duck Lake
7.5 miles to Lost Lake

Low/High Elevations: 6290′/7700′

Season: June through October for creek, mid-July through mid-October for lakes.

Classification: Easy along creek, moderate to lakes

Map: 28

Trailhead: From where Highway 50 leaves Highway 89 in South Lake Tahoe, drive 18¼ miles north on 89 to the entrance to General Creek Campground. Immediately past an entrance station (day-use fee required), branch left and head briefly east to the first parking lot on your left. Park in this eastern lot near its south edge. If you're coming from Tahoe City, drive 9¼ miles south on 89 to the campground entrance.

Introduction
In Sugar Pine Point State Park, lower General Creek is flanked by two main trails, giving visitors many access points to the creek. Backpackers will find Lost Lake quite rewarding, for it is warm as Sierra lakes go. It even has a huge granite slab on which you can sunbathe. Leave your pets at home, since they are not allowed on the park's trails.

Description
Take a paved bike path east along the south edge of the park's eastern parking lot, and in 60 yards reach a dirt trail branching south. On this trail you skirt along the perimeter of giant General Creek Campground, soon turn west, and then stay along the rim of a minor gorge cut by the creek. We pass campsites on our right and paths down to the creek on our left, then leave the rim for a quick junction with a closed road coming 0.1 mile from its start opposite campsite 150. If you happen to be

camping at or near this site and begin your hike from it, then you can subtract 1.1 miles from all of the above distances.

Now on the one-lane closed road, we strike a level ¼ mile southwest to a junction with a second closed road, and are confronted with a choice of two equally long routes to upper General Creek, Duck Lake, and Lost Lake. The north-bank route is shadier and wetter, and before mid-August can have a mosquito problem. However, its vegetation is more diverse, and it is the shortest way to Lily Pond.

If you take the north-bank route, you'll hike ¾ mile along your closed road, passing midway along this stretch a glade with ferns and thimbleberries. Just before reaching General Creek, the road dies out in a lupine field, and a trail takes its place. This trail, becoming narrow, rocky, and quite winding, goes a shady mile southwest to a junction immediately past a gully. From it you can ascend the ⅓-mile-long **Lily Pond Trail** to the south shore of **Lily Pond**, which for all but serious nature lovers is not worth the effort.

Lost Lake, view from its peninsula

The terrain is boggy and, through July, the mosquitoes are bad. This shallow pond nurtures yellow pond lilies, and it also supports a healthy crop of tall bulrushes. Like all of the park's species, these two plants are protected, although Indians formerly ate both. The bulrush in particular was highly desirable. One would eat the green shoots raw, or wait until autumn and make flour from the plant's roots. Its seeds, too, could be crushed and eaten. Furthermore, the stalks were useful for weaving bed mats and similar articles. From the junction with the Lily Pond Trail, the north-bank route turns southeast and winds 100 yards to the south-bank route, the junction lying at the fringe of an aspen grove.

The south bank route, mostly a road, begins by first crossing General Creek. Use a nearby footbridge to keep your feet dry. Back on the road, you then quickly reach another road. Eastward, this goes 1 mile to Highway 89, opposite the state park's entrance to its Lake Tahoe shoreline day-use area (which has additional hiking opportunities). We go westward and parallel usually unseen General Creek upstream, passing granitic boulders dropped by a melting, retreating glacier. Soon we enter a long, thinly forested flat, which offers views of the two huge lateral moraines that border our creek valley. Their ridges are about 500 feet above us, and the glaciers that left them were at least 500 feet thick. The views disappear after about a mile of southwest hiking as we enter a thick, shady forest and soon bridge General Creek. Beyond it the road rapidly diminishes to a trail, reaching the aspen-grove junction about 0.4 mile beyond the creek. In early season this path can be quite soggy, and then you'll want to take the north-bank route.

From this junction we head south on a sometimes poor tread, which in ¼ mile improves as the trail turns westward, climbing to drier terrain. Jeffrey pines, lupines, and mule ears now line much of the trail, each species producing a pleasant, though often subtle, aroma. (Walk up to a large pine and stick your nose in a bark furrow. Smell like butterscotch? vanilla?) Beyond the state-park boundary, we're in for an easy 1/-mile climb through National Forest lands, which offer the

first camping possibilities. We then make our **uppermost crossing of General Creek** immediately below a lovely triangular pool and now, briefly on private land (the south half of Section 27), climb a steep, rocky, ducked route to a closed jeep road. The road, which is just within National Forest land, winds 250 yards west to General Creek and thence back onto private land. We, however, start east, then immediately curve south, crossing the creek from Duck and Lost lakes in 0.8 mile, then recrossing it in an equal distance.

About 230 yards past the second creek crossing you'll come to an old logging spur left that drops 100 yards south to lodgepole-fringed **Duck Lake**, which is shallow enough to wade across. The main road curves right, climbing up to a second spur road, this one dropping north 200 yards to beautiful **Lost Lake**. Although past logging is evident along the main road to these two lakes, a swath of trees ringing each lake was spared the ax. You'll find a large campsite by Lost Lake's knobby south-shore peninsula and more-secluded ones along the path that circles this fine swimming lake.

❧ 53 ❧
Rubicon Trail to Emerald Bay

Distances:
0.1 mile to Rubicon Point
0.3 mile to lighthouse
3.1 miles to Emerald Point
3.6 miles to Emerald Bay Boat Camp
4.4 miles to Vikingsholm
Low/High Elevations: 6230'/6580'
Season: Late May through mid-September
Classification: Moderate
Map: 32
Trailhead: From where Highway 50 leaves Highway 89 in South Lake Tahoe, drive 11 miles north on 89 to the entrance to D.L. Bliss State Park. If you're coming from Tahoe City, drive 16½ miles south on 89. Take the park's road 2.4 miles down to its end. Halfway down this road, just 0.2 mile past the entrance station, is a small parking area, an alternate trail-

head. From it one trail heads 100 yards east to the Rubicon Trail, while another one 60 yards north of it begins a crest route north to the road's end.

Introduction

Lester Beach and Calawee Cove beaches are the prime attractions for the hundreds of campers who nightly crowd the park's five campgrounds. A few campers may visit "balancing rock" along the park's short nature trail, but even fewer hike the Rubicon Trail south to either Emerald Point or to Emerald Bay's Vikingsholm beach. Secluded shorelines await those who take this scenic trail. Pets are not allowed on this trail.

Description

Just a few paces from the trailhead the Rubicon Trail reaches a junction. Branching right, a newer trail makes a switchbacking ascent 0.2 mile to a junction, from where you can traverse 70 yards southeast to the spur trail down to the lighthouse, mentioned below. Onward, the newer trail continues 0.8 mile, winding up and down a forested crest to a trailhead midway along the park's road. With poor views and sparse wildflowers, this trail is for those wanting exercise.

From the north end of this newer trail the Rubicon Trail makes a 150-yard, almost level traverse to the back side of **Rubicon Point**. From here you may see one or more use trails descending east to Tahoe's shore. One of them descends to the base of Rubicon Point, from where bathers can dive into the lake's chilly water. The water warms to the low 60s by mid-September, just when the state park is about to shut down.

We leave the back side of Rubicon Point, ascending shady, steepening slopes. Fortunately, a protective rail is present on the steeper slopes, for a slip there could be fatal. Just before the trail turns briefly west, you'll spy the old lighthouse, a small wooden structure resembling an outhouse, perched at the brink of a cliff about 60 feet above our trail. Where the trail bends west, you have dramatic views from atop a precipitous point just east of the trail. The east face of this point plus the nearby overhanging pinnacles together offer challenges for roped rock climbers. From its back side the point is a safe, easy climb, and you can gaze into Tahoe's deep, deep-blue depths. In 1970 you could see objects as much as 100 feet down, but by the mid-'90s you could see them only about 70 feet down. The

From the shallow entrance to Emerald Bay the 1955 rockslide stands out well on the flank of north Maggies Peak

clarity should not decrease much more, thanks to many stringent measures taken to restrict nutrient flow into the lake, which will reduce the algal growth rate.

Climbing briefly west, our route passes some trailside pinnacles and immediately meets a trail that climbs 70 yards steeply to a small flat and a junction with a newer trail. From here a spur trail descends 40 yards very steeply to the **lighthouse**. At one time it must have commanded quite a view, but today tall conifers block it.

On the Rubicon Trail we now climb gently south, heading toward usually unseen Mt. Tallac, the most prominent peak above Tahoe's west shore. We see it, and most of Lake Tahoe, from a large trailside boulder found where the trail turns from south to southwest. Continuing on, we quickly reach two former roads about 25 yards apart. They unite in about 65 yards, then lead 35 yards to the park's road. From that alternative trailhead the lighthouse is ⅔ mile away, whereas it is only ⅓ mile from the Rubicon trailhead.

The Rubicon Trail now briefly climbs through a dense forest of white firs. These are so closely packed that they have shaded out huckleberry oaks, which once thrived when sunlight was more abundant. In this viewless forest we start a one-mile descent to Tahoe's shoreline. About ⅓ mile down it you may notice a former burn, on your right, where charred fir snags have been replaced with tobacco brush. Given time, these aromatic bushes will be overshadowed by firs.

A pair of switchbacks offer us a fine lake view, and they mark the approaching end of our descent. Just past them we meet the first of several use trails that descend to the bouldery shoreline. Here, 2 miles from the trailhead, you have your first easy access to Lake Tahoe since Rubicon Point. In the next ¼ mile you pass about a half dozen access trails, then climb briefly to a spring-fed creeklet, the only lasting, trailside flow between our trailhead and Emerald Bay. A short, moderate climb takes us to a point with a great lake view, then we take short switchbacks down almost to the shoreline. Next we climb a low rise to tiny, tranquil Bonnie Bay, ideal for swimming (if

indeed the cold water can be considered ideal).

About 150 yards southeast from the bay the trail forks. The main branch, termed the Bypass Trail, climbs over a low terminal moraine, first south and then southwest, to reach the northwest corner of Emerald Bay in just over ¼ mile. A less-used tread starts east to a small cove, then parallels Tahoe's shore ⅓ mile over to **Emerald Point**, from where a more popular tread parallels the bay's north shore ½ mile over to the Bypass Trail. The mouth of Emerald Bay is extremely shallow, so much so that when Lake Tahoe lowers its level by 5 feet, one can boulder-hop halfway across the bay's mouth, getting a spectacular view up-bay of the rugged glaciated scenery. Had the last glacier occupying Emerald Bay dropped just a bit more of its transported rockfall debris, we'd see "Emerald Lake," like similar Cascade and Fallen Leaf lakes south of it. Emerald Point is a good vantage spot to study two enormous lateral moraines that flank the bay. These are deposits left on slopes by former glaciers. Above the bay's far end is a huge scar, which is the result of a December 26, 1955 rockslide. It was caused by the construction of Highway 89 across a steep, unstable slope.

From where the Emerald Point's trail rejoins the Bypass Trail the bay is easily accessible, and the shallow water is fine for late-summer swimming. Now hiking southwest on the Rubicon Trail, we soon enter forest shade and see notable representatives of white fir, Jeffrey pine, incense-cedar, and sugar pine. On a slope carpeted with bracken ferns our trail levels and we pass some of the tallest willows to be found in the Sierra Nevada. You'll recognize these 40-foot-high Scouler willows by their pale gray, aspen-like bark.

Leaving the willows behind, we descend 100 yards to an old road, and join it for 120 yards, to where a trail goes to a nearby, conspicuous public pier. We continue 35 yards more on the road, then leave the now-paved road where it starts to climb from the bay. In this vicinity we are in the heart of the **Emerald Bay Boat Camp**, which continues southwest above the bay for another 230 yards. This spacious campground is also open to hikers. If you want to hike to it, park at the Eagle Falls trailhead (Hike 77), walk briefly north on Highway 89, and then descend a road to the paved road (Hike 54). Then take either it or the shoreline Rubicon Trail northeast to the camp.

From the paved road the Rubicon Trail starts as a broad path, but soon narrows as it descends to the bay to skirt beneath the campsites. Just beyond the last site you make a short climb to a low ridge, from which an old road ascends to the paved one. Our trail stays just above the shoreline, departing briefly from it only to climb behind Parson Rock, about ½ mile past the public pier. A use trail goes out to the rock, giving the avid photographer one of the best views of Emerald Bay. Swimmers, usually walking northwest from the Vikingsholm beach ¼ mile away, find the rock a nice hunk of granite to dive from. Past it our shoreline trail heads over to a popular beach near the **Vikingsholm**, described in the next hike.

⋘ 54 ⋙
Vikingsholm Trail to Emerald Bay

Distances:
0.8 mile to Emerald Bay, west shore
0.9 mile to Vikingsholm
1.1 miles to Eagle Falls
Low/High Elevations: 6230′/6630′
Season: Late May through mid-September
Classification: Easy
Map: 32

Trailhead: From where Highway 50 leaves Highway 89 in South Lake Tahoe, drive 9 miles north on 89 to a large parking area, on your right. This area is just ¼ mile past Eagle Falls Picnic Area's parking lot entrance. If you're coming from Tahoe City, drive 18½ miles south on 89. Lock your car, for thefts are all too common here.

Introduction
Lake Tahoe's beaches attract throngs of sunbathers, and the beach on the west shore of

Emerald Bay is no exception. However, because it is the only Tahoe beach in this book's area that you have to hike to, it is less congested. Limited trailhead parking, which is usually full on summer weekends, also limits the number of Emerald Bay visitors. Most Lake Tahoe visitors would agree that this bay is the most scenic stretch of shoreline to be found along all of the mammoth lake.

Description
The route is simple: follow a closed road down to Emerald Bay. By the start is a low knoll, which provides you with a commanding view of Emerald Bay as well as of the deep canyon to the southwest. Huge glaciers repeatedly descended this canyon, but barely eroded it, and in the bay, Fannette Island stands as testimony to glacial impotence. (When basal glacial ice meets an obstacle such as this, it melts, flows around it, and refreezes—not a process that erodes rocks.) The glacier surfaces were at least as high as the moraines they left, and therefore may have been about 700 feet thick. This was enough to bury the low knoll under ice, but only thin, stagnant ice. Hence during the last glaciation, old, foot-deep solution pockets were not planed away, nor was the bedrock polished smooth.

Before making your 400-foot drop to Emerald Bay, be sure to leave your pets behind—but not in a vehicle where they might expire in the summer heat. The closed road drops ⅔ mile to another one, from which you descend 120 yards south to where a trail heads past a former gardener's cottage down to the nearby beach of **Emerald Bay**. Swimmers will find the bay's water very cold until early August, when it climbs into the low 60s and stays there until mid-September, when the park generally closes. Perhaps the two weeks after Labor Day are best, for the crowds have diminished and Lake Tahoe typically has dropped a couple feet, creating a sandy beach not enjoyed by earlier visitors. After another 110 yards on the road, you meet a second trail, which heads over to the **Vikingsholm** as well as to the beach. It is usually open daily for tours from about July 1

The Vikingsholm

through Labor Day, and then weekends until the park closes.

The road then goes past outhouses, on the right, and also curves over to the Vikingsholm. Along this curve, the Eagle Falls Trail starts west. On it, cool, lush vegetation gives way to brush-covered slabs moments before you reach **Eagle Falls**. Eagle Falls are roaring when Emerald Bay State Park opens in May, and they continue to do so well into July.

This area is for day-use only. However, about ¾ mile northeast of it is a camp open to both boaters and hikers. You reach it by a road or by the shoreline Rubicon Trail, which is described in the opposite direction, in the previous hike.

⋙ **55** ⋘
Cascade Creek Fall Trail

Distance: 0.7 mile to Cascade Creek Fall
Low/High Elevations: 6800'/6910'
Season: Mid-June through mid-October
Classification: Easy
Map: 32
Trailhead: See the Hike 77 trailhead.

Introduction

Cascade Lake, which unfortunately is mostly on private land, is confined between two giant, 500-foot-high lateral moraines. You get fine views of this lake as you're switchbacking on Highway 89 up or down the lake's western moraine, and you'll see a voluminous waterfall plummeting toward the lake. This fall, like Emerald Bay's well signed Eagle Falls, is easily approached by trail. The fall and the southwest shore of Cascade Lake are on National Forest land.

Description

From the trailhead parking area immediately above Bayview Campground, you branch left on the Cascade Creek Fall Trail, avoiding the Bay View Trail, which starts straight ahead. You head southeast for a 110-yard climb to a brushy crest of a lateral moraine, then head 150 yards southwest along it. From the crest you next have a ½-mile footpath across steep slopes to the brink of the fall. Because all but the start of the path is across either brushy or rocky slopes, you have almost continual views of Cascade Lake and Lake Tahoe. Your descending, brushy traverse turns into a climb up rocky slabs, upon which the trail dies out. To reach the brink of **Cascade Creek Fall** is easy, but be careful as you approach it, since a slip over the brink would certainly be fatal. This spot is a fine one for a picnic, since the views rival those from the brink of Eagle Falls, above Emerald Bay, and here you don't have the crowds. Photographers take note: don't hike before mid-morning, or else most of your shots will be into the sun. From the vicinity of the falls a surprising number of backpackers head cross-country up Cascade Creek to Snow and Azure lakes, but the route is vague and it can be dangerous in spots, so it is not described here.

⋘ **56** ⋙

Lake Tahoe Visitors Center Trails

Distances:
Smokey's Trail, 0.1 mile
Forest Tree Trail, 0.2 mile
Rainbow Trail, 0.6 mile
Lake of the Sky Trail, 1.0 mile
Tallac Historic Trail, 1.3 miles
Low/High Elevations: All trails lie between 6235 and 6300 feet.
Season: Late May through late October
Classification: Very easy
Map: 32
Trailheads: All but the last trail begin at the Lake Tahoe Visitors Center, whose paved access road leaves northbound Highway 89 only 150 yards west of the Fallen Leaf Road. This southbound road, in turn, lies 3.1 miles west of the junction where Highway 50 leaves Highway 89 in South Lake Tahoe. Opposite this road is a northbound one, which quickly splits, the left fork to a parking lot for Tallac Point visitors, the right fork to a parking lot for Kiva Beach and Tallac Historic Trail users.

Introduction

A plethora of foot, bike, and horse trails lace the Fallen Leaf/South Shore Tahoe/Camp Richardson area. Hike 56 covers only five of these, which basically are nature trails for hikers only. If you're staying in this area for a spell, you may want to take one or more of them, especially the Rainbow Trail, along which you can get an underwater view of trout.

Descriptions

Smokey's Trail
This extremely short trail, starting immediately south of the Visitors Center, shows you how

to set up a safe campfire. Young children may be interested in this trail. Certainly, they should learn proper campfire procedures.

Forest Tree Trail
A broad path just east of the Visitors Center curves northwest over to adjacent Lake of the Sky Amphitheater. You go but 30 yards on it, then branch right onto the Forest Tree Trail, for a short loop through a fairly open Jeffrey-pine forest that is understoried with bitter-brush and sagebrush. The former blooms in early summer, producing a cinnamon odor. The latter blooms in late summer, but its leaves always produce a subtle odor. Squeeze one of its light-gray-green leaves and smell your fingers. The Jeffrey pine also produces an odor, which is noticeable on warm days. Stick your nose in a bark furrow and smell the tree's "butterscotch" resin, an aroma lacking in the superficially similar ponderosa pine.

Rainbow Trail
Easily the Visitors Center's most popular route, this trail begins just past the center. It loops around a grassy, willowy marshland, which is quite a change from the nearby Jeffrey-pine forest. Midway along this trail is the enlarged 1997-vintage Stream Profile Chamber, a partly sunken viewing room. Through its plate-glass windows you can view and photograph several species of trout that swim in a pool fed by a channel diverted from Taylor Creek. For best photographic results, visit this site in mid-day, since you'd be shooting into the sun in the early morning and into shadow in late afternoon.

Lake of the Sky Trail
Like the Forest Tree Trail, this one starts by the amphitheater. From that open structure it continues north to Tallac Point, with many Tahoe views, including one to the west of the large

A trout viewed from the Stream Profile Chamber

Wildflower Plate 12. Tahoe Basin flowers.
1 Macloskey's violet (white), 2 mountain (bitter) dogbane (Indian hemp) (white to pink), 3 vari-leaved (virgate) phacelia (dusty white to greenish brown), 4 narrow-leaved (Torrey's) lotus (yellow top, white bottom), 5 slender tarweed (gumweed) (yellow), 6 meadow (Canada) goldenrod (golden yellow), 7 large-flowered (grand) collomia (salmon), 8 Oregon (spicate) checker (pink), 9 giant (great) red paintbrush (rose-red).

lateral moraines hiding Cascade Lake and Emerald Bay. From the point you head ¼ mile east along Kiva Beach, then branch right and walk south to your trailhead. About ⅓ of the way, you'll cross a parking lot, which also serves as a trailhead. Signs along this trail deal with water quality, geology, and wildlife.

Tallac Historic Trail

This route starts from the Kiva Beach parking lot's north end, traverses ¼ mile west to the previous route, and then heads north briefly to Kiva Beach. You then walk ½ mile east along the beach, taking in the Tallac Museum and wandering among some old estates. The museum is open only for the summer season, during which you can take a guided tour of the estates. After exploring the historic buildings, head back to the parking lot, which is about 200 yards southwest from the museum.

Starting from the Visitors Center, you can put together a scenic and historic 2.0-mile route. Follow Lake of the Sky Trail north to Tallac Point, next head east to the museum and the estates, from the museum head southwest, cross the Kiva parking lot and continue southwest to your trailhead.

⪻ 57 ⪼
Fallen Leaf Lake Trails

Distances:
Variable
Low/High Elevations: 6360′/6420′
Season: Late May through late October
Classification: Very easy
Maps: 32, 35, and 36
Trailheads: For the Fallen Leaf Lake trail system there are several possible trailheads, although only two will be mentioned. From where Highway 50 leaves Highway 89 in South Lake Tahoe, drive 3.1 miles west on 89 to southbound Fallen Leaf Road. Take it about ½ mile to the entrance to Fallen Leaf Campground. By its entrance station you'll see a detailed map of the campground's layout. Part of the Fallen Leaf Lake trail system, a part formerly known as the Moraine Trail, begins

at a small parking area opposite campsite 74 and ends at site 85. This loop route provides campers with lake access. Noncampers should use one of two trailheads. Either use one along Fallen Leaf Road ¼ mile south of the campground's entrance, or one along Cathedral Road. The latter road leaves Highway 89 about ½ mile west of the Fallen Leaf Road junction (and about 150 yards west of the highway's crossing of Taylor Creek). The trailhead is just past a sharp curve right and just before the back side of Camp Concord, above and right of the road.

Introduction

The Fallen Leaf Campground and its associated trail system offer a diverse array of trees, shrubs, and wildflowers, especially the latter, of which there are dozens of species. A small fraction of this area's flowers appears on Plate 12, while most of the others appear on Plates 1-8. For most campers, however, the major attraction won't be wildflowers but rather Fallen Leaf Lake, and they will take the various trails to access its northern shores. At the lake one can swim and sunbathe, though the heaviest use probably is by anglers.

Description

Most campers take a loop trail, formerly known as the Moraine Trail, to reach the north shore of giant Fallen Leaf Lake. Once at the lake, anglers can fish along the shore, but they are not allowed to do so from the lake's dam. From the dam's west end, one principal trail heads about ½ mile down the lake's outlet creek, Taylor Creek, meeting a northwest-heading, 100-yard-long spur trail just before it dies out at a meander along the creek. That trail goes over to a small trailhead parking area ⅔ mile up Cathedral Road. From the dam's west end, another principal trail heads south along the northwest shore of Fallen Leaf Lake, crossing the low crests of two recessional moraines before reaching, in about ½ mile, a small-but-conspicuous bay. Along its south shore and its east end, Sawmill Point, are some picnic tables. From this vicinity you can take a road's-end loop south briefly to a trail that goes about 100 yards to the foundation and chimney of what was once a sizable place. Use trails can lead you astray to this spot, which marks the end of a maintained trail. Southward is an unmaintained, lakeshore use trail.

Noncampers interested in reaching the lake's north or northeast shores should start from the trailhead about ¼ mile south of the Fallen Leaf Campground's entrance road. Parking for several vehicles lies on each side of Fallen Leaf Road. From the west-side parking area, a horse trail starts northwest while the Fallen Leaf Lake Trail starts

Upper Angora Lake attracts summer-weekend crowds

southwest. Both climb to the crest of a moraine. The latter goes about ¼ mile southeast along the crest as well going briefly northwest before dropping to the northeast shore of Fallen Leaf Lake and quickly meeting the horse trail.

⋘ 58 ⋙
Fallen Leaf Lake to Angora Lakes

Distances:

0.5 mile to Lower Angora Lake (from Angora Lakes parking lot)

0.8 mile to Upper Angora Lake (from Angora Lakes parking lot)

0.9 mile to Angora Lookout (via Clark Trail)

1.4 miles to Lower Angora Lake (via Fallen Leaf-Angora trail)

1.7 miles to Upper Angora Lake (via Fallen Leaf-Angora trail)

Low/High Elevations: 7220'; 6410' from Fallen Leaf trailhead/7470'

Season: Early July through mid-October

Classification: Easy from Angora Lakes parking lot; moderate via trail from Fallen Leaf

Map: 35

Trailheads: From where Highway 50 leaves Highway 89 in South Lake Tahoe, drive 3.1 miles west on 89 to Fallen Leaf Road, on the left. For the principal trailhead (the only one

with parking), take this road 2.0 miles south to Tahoe Mountain Road, turn left, and drive 0.4 mile up it to a fork. Angle right and drive 1.8 miles up Angora Ridge Road 12N14 to Angora Fire Lookout (great views), then 1.0 mile south to the large trailhead parking lot for Angora Lakes, which are reached by hiking up a closed road.

Hike 58 takes a longer way to Angora Lakes, one up the Clark Trail and then down the Fallen Leaf-Angora Trail. To reach the Clark Trail, take Fallen Leaf Road 4.5 miles south from Highway 89, to where it curves west over to the highly developed south shore of Fallen Leaf Lake. Here it turns left, south, and you briefly ascend it to the first road on your left, which you take to its nearby end and the start of the Clark Trail. Fallen Leaf Road continues 0.4 mile ahead, looping up through the development over to the major, north-branching entrance road, on your right, to the Stanford Sierra Camp. The Fallen Leaf-Angora Trail heads south from here. Be aware that there is no trailhead parking at either of these two trails. The described hike is for those staying in the Fallen Leaf-Stanford Sierra Camp area. All others should use the first trailhead, which provides the shortest route to the Angora Lakes.

Introduction

This "hike" is actually composed of three separate ways to reach popular Angora Lakes. Combined, they make a 4.4-mile semiloop route that is best suited for those staying in the Fallen Leaf area or at Stanford Sierra Camp. This route ascends the Clark Trail, follows the Angora Ridge Road to a large parking area, heads up to the Angora Lakes and returns to the parking area, then descends the Fallen Leaf-Angora Trail, ending ½ mile west of the Clark trailhead. Most hikers, however, will take the shortest way to the Angora Lakes, up a closed road from the large parking area.

Description

From the end of a short residential road, we begin a stiff climb up the Clark Trail. Half way up it the gradient moderates, the forest cover of white fir thins, and Jeffrey pine together with huckleberry oak, chinquapin, and manzanita become more predominant, allowing us views across Fallen Leaf Lake toward Lake Tahoe. High on the slope, the seductive aroma of tobacco brush above lures us on to the crest, where the trail ends, just south of 7290' **Angora Lookout**. Angora Lookout, lakes, and peak were named for the herds of Angora goats that were pastured in this vicinity by

Cooling off in Upper Angora Lake

Nathan Gilmore, an early stockman who discovered Glen Alpine Springs.

From the lookout you obtain a commanding view of the southern Tahoe basin. High above it in the east you see an ancient, granitic massif capped by 10,881' Freel Peak, highest in the Tahoe Sierra, just barely nudging above its close relative, 10,823' Jobs Sister, immediately northeast of it. To the southeast lies Upper Truckee canyon, in which the last glacier left 10 recessional moraines as it retreated up-canyon. Each moraine consists of a collection of rocks and debris left by the leading edge of a glacier when it temporarily halted its retreat. To the south, more icy evidence exists in the form of two cirques, on the north and east flanks of Echo Peak. Unseen beyond its southeast ridge lie the popular Echo Lakes. Directly west of and above us is Cathedral Peak, which is the steep-sided, lower southwest flank of Mt. Tallac.

At the foot of Mt. Tallac and beyond, north of us, stand some imposing lateral moraines. Impressive though they are, they are a mile shorter and 400 feet lower than the mammoth moraine we're on. About 20,000 years ago a glacier spilling down Glen Alpine canyon and one down the Upper Truckee canyon both overtopped our lookout, suggesting each was about 1000 feet thick. Logically, such glaciers *should* have tremendous erosive power, but that is not so. Our huge moraine isn't 1000 feet thick; it merely mantles a buried bedrock ridge. Furthermore, the floor of Fallen Leaf Lake was not deeply scoured by glaciers. Before Lake Tahoe existed, both Glen Alpine Creek and the Upper Truckee River descended into the large Tahoe basin. After the lake formed, sediments accumulated above its south shore and buried these two valley floors.

After absorbing all the views you can, follow Angora Ridge Road south one mile to an extended parking area. From here in a broad gully, your route back to Fallen Leaf Lake climbs northwest over a low saddle. To reach the Angora Lakes, merely hike up a gated road starting from the south end of the parking area. Up it you climb moderately to **Lower Angora Lake**, with private cabins, then continue on the road to **Upper Angora**

Lake. Here you can rent boats from Angora
Lakes Resort, buy snacks at its small store, or
bask on an adjacent, attractive beach. A lucky
few actually get to stay in the resort's few
rental cabins, which can be booked a year or
more in advance. Hikers who've brought
along their fishing rods will find both lakes
stocked with trout. Swimmers may traverse
the talus of the east shore to reach some good
diving rocks above the south shore of this
deep lake. Virtually all of our area's lakes have
at least one bedrock bench from which you
can dive into the lake. Here they range up to
50+ feet. However, I caution all would-be high
divers: *do not exceed your ability*—at least one
fatality has occurred, not to mention injuries.
Don't let peer pressure tempt you into risky
dives.

Returning to the parking lot, you climb to
a nearby saddle, and then descend the forested Fallen Leaf-Angora Trail—with several
verdant oases of lush vegetation—steeply
down to eventually pass the west side of a
small church just before ending by a road
junction with the Stanford Sierra Camp's
entrance road.

An unnamed tarn lies below the northwest face of Pyramid Peak

Chapter 13
Desolation Wilderness, west side

Introduction

This book's star attraction is compact Desolation Wilderness, which is certainly northern California's most accessible wilderness. Via Highway 50, it's just a 3½-hour drive from the San Francisco Bay Area, a 2-hour drive from Sacramento, and a few minutes' drive from South Lake Tahoe. This roadless area averages 12½ miles long by 8 miles wide, and it can be traversed in any direction by a strong hiker in a day or less. Because it is so compact and readily accessible, it is too crowded to be considered a wilderness in the strict sense of the word. Although the 1964 Wilderness Act stipulates that wilderness areas should be pristine havens for solitude, don't expect to find solitude unless you hike before or after the summer season, hike off-trail on summer weekends, or hike at least several miles on trail on summer week days. And pristine it's not: dozens of lakes have low dams, and into the 1990s several hundred cattle have been allowed to graze all of the west-side lands in late summer. (Until 1988, they also were allowed to graze in Rockbound Valley and the lands above it, which include Doris, Lois, Schmidell, Leland, Horseshoe, and 4-Q lakes.)

Although the Forest Service limits the number of backpackers to 700 per day, they currently place no limit on the number of day hikers. Wilderness permits are required for both types of visitors, and those caught without them are usually cited (*see Chapter 3's section on Wilderness Permits*). With all these visitors treading the trails and splashing or fishing in the lakes, Desolation Wilderness is neither desolate nor wild; rather, it's best viewed as a mountain playland, an extension of the Lake Tahoe recreation scene. Some may lament that the wilderness is overused. It is and it is not. Very popular Lower Twin Lake, out of the Wrights Lake Recreation Area, can receive over a hundred visitors on a busy summer day; some other lakes, less, but still a dozen or more. But to keep things in perspective, one should realize that in this 63,691-acre wilderness, only the lake shores (100-foot-wide zone) and trail corridors (10-foot-wide zone) are heavily used, and they constitute less than 1% of the total wilderness area. This means that more than 99% wilderness is essentially devoid of humans, although a few occasionally do leave the trails to go cross-country. In short, there is plenty of solitude in the wilderness for those who are willing to seek it.

What attracts hikers to this readily accessible, triple-crested wilderness? Its Crystal Range, which is the prominent, granitic, light-gray crest you see when driving east up Highway 50, averages only 9500 feet in elevation, and the two crests east of it are even lower—hardly a match for central California's High Sierra. But where else can you find 130 lakes, about 90 of them named, packed into only 100 square miles of mountain scenery?

To describe the whole wilderness and its trails leading into it would make a very large chapter. Consequently, the area has been divided into two parts, Chapter 13, covering trails west of the Sierra crest, and Chapter 14, covering those east of the crest. In each chapter the routes are arranged from north to south. In Chapter 13 some routes don't enter the wilderness: Shadow Lake Trail (Hike 60), Bassi Loop Trail (Hike 61), and trails to Pearl Lake (Hike 62), Barrett Lake (Hike 63), and Bloodsucker Lake (Hike 70). Technically, the

Shadow Lake Trail briefly switchbacks through a small segment of the wilderness, but nevertheless for this trail and the others mentioned, you won't need a wilderness permit. On the other hand, these hikes are inferior to most of the Desolation Wilderness trails in terms of scenery and ambiance.

⋘ 59 ⋙
Loon Lake Trail to Camper Flat

Distances:
3.7 miles to spur trail
    0.4 mile on trail to Pleasant Campground
5.0 miles to second broad saddle
    0.3 mile cross-country to Lake Winifred
6.1 miles to Buck Island Lake
6.7 miles to Rockbound Lake
8.2 miles to Fox Lake
8.3 miles to Rubicon Reservoir
11.7 miles to AAA Camp
13.5 miles to McConnell Lake Trail
13.6 miles to Camper Flat
13.8 miles to Blakely Trail
Low/High Elevations: 6410'/7210'
Season: Late June through mid-October
Classification: Easy to moderate
Maps: 25, 30, and 31
Trailhead: If you plan to enter the wilderness (Rockbound Lake and beyond), be sure to get a wilderness permit. The best place to get one is at the Eldorado National Forest Information Center, on Camino Heights Drive about 5 miles east of Placerville. From this center continue 17 miles east up Highway 50 to its bridge across the South Fork American River and in 100 yards reach the Crystal Basin Recreation Area turnoff, Ice House Road, on your left. (Westbound drivers: this junction is about 27 miles west from Echo Summit.)

Your road, paved all the way to the trailhead, climbs 9 miles to Ice House Resort. Farther north, your Forest Route 3 passes the Crystal Basin Ranger Station as well as spur roads to Union Valley Reservoir's campgrounds. After a 13-mile winding course from

the resort you reach the Loon Lake Road, branching right. Still Forest Route 3, you take it 4½ miles to a fork. Left, a road goes 3¼ miles over to Loon Lake's far dam. You branch right and go 0.4 mile to an entrance to a horse camp. Equestrians start from a trail at its end and should add 0.4 mile to the above trail distances. Immediately past it is a pay site, which has a map of the vicinity. Just past it, the road branches again, boaters going left, hikers and campers going right. You curve briefly counterclockwise past a group camp, then reach a third branch. Old campsites lie along it. You keep right and drive briefly to newer campsites, on your right, and a newer group camp, on your left. Just past them you enter the trailhead parking lot, *usually* with wilderness permits available.

Introduction
For easy hiking in Desolation Wilderness, you can't beat this route. The 13.8-mile route has only minor ups and downs and, if you hike to its end, you'll gain only 800 feet in elevation. In late June and early July, when most of the Desolation Wilderness lakes are still frozen or just thawing, the seven lakes along this route provide good fishing and brisk swimming.

Description
Beginning at the far end of the trailhead parking lot, the Loon Lake-Trail goes but 60 yards to a junction with a trail from the horse camp. This trail circles the south and east sides of the Loon Lake camping complex, midway encountering a southern extension of the Loon Lake Trail. It first descends 0.3 mile to South Fork Rubicon River, parallels it downstream for 0.2 mile, then crosses it (rock-hop or ford) to start a meandering 2-mile course southward to roads which, in a similar distance, take one to the Van Vleck trailhead (next hike). Unless you are simply out for exercise, you will probably want to avoid this lakeless, viewless route.

From the junction just above the parking lot, our trail goes 160 yards to another junction, this with a 150-yard-long feeder trail ascending northeast from the far end of the old-campsites section of the multi-bodied Loon Lake Campground. Ahead, our trail first heads north, then traverses northeast and

Pyramidal Guide Peak rises above Loon Lake's "Pleasant Lake" arm

generally parallels the lake's visible shoreline, usually keeping about 100 yards distant. About ½ mile beyond the campground the trail almost touches the lake, and then it soon traverses around a 15-foot-high boulder perched on a trailside granitic outcrop. This glacier-transported boulder is considerably larger than others nearby, though hardly a record. The largest I have seen is near the south base of the Dardanelles, in the Stanislaus River drainage. It is roughly 45 by 20 by 20 feet, and weighs over 1000 tons.

Beyond these boulders the trail soon bends east-northeast for a mile-long, fir-and-pine-shaded traverse that passes a seasonal creeklet soon after your first glimpse of Brown Mountain. This summit stands about ½ mile southeast, and it may be the remnant of a small, basaltic volcano. Glaciers removed its looser rock, and topped it at least once, as evidenced by the granitic rocks left behind on its summit.

About 2½ miles from the trailhead we climb to a ridge, whose northwest extension almost divides the lake in two. Before 1967,

when the new dam was completed, this ridge separated Pleasant Lake from Loon Lake. As we make an eastward traverse, we see possible brushy descent routes to the shoreline, these in the direction of bald-topped Guide Peak, which juts prominently skyward behind the lake. Continuing eastward, one has good views ahead toward a saddle, between two unnamed peaks, in which lies Hidden Lake.

After the traverse we momentarily turn south into a gully to cross its creek, then turn north and gradually descend to an abandoned road that descends to the east arm of Loon Lake. We make a short climb north up this closed road to a roadcut blasted out of bedrock, exposing a thick, light-colored vein, or dike. From it we can look southwest across the lake to its dam and the hills beyond. At the shoreline below us is a hidden cove visited by boaters. In ¼ mile our road reaches a gully and begins a moderate climb west. Here you can take a 0.4-mile **spur trail** to **Pleasant Campground**. Just before one reaches the actual campground, one has to leave the gully and cross northwest over a low ridge. The campground, which has tables, stoves, and an outhouse, is primarily for boaters, and a fee is charged for overnight stays. Consider a day visit to this area to fish or swim along the shore.

Back on the closed road again, we climb northwest to a ridge, then follow it east up to a broad saddle, leaving views of the Loon Lake terrain for those of the gentle Sierra crest. Northeast of and not far below the trail lies a linear, seasonal, lily-pad pond. About 100 yards beyond it you should see the western arm of **Spider Lake**, to which you could descend. Campsites lie about the sprawling lake, and don't be content with the first vacant one you spy. About ¼ mile farther southeast on our road you reach a low ridge on which you could also descend directly to near the lake's shallow south arm. This route, one of several possible, begins just as you reach a long, straight stretch of road. Just before this route junction you could have begun a cross-country route southwest ½ mile up relatively open slopes to the Hidden Lake saddle. Onward, we walk about 0.4 mile on our road,

Lake Winifred

first gently down, then gently up to a **second broad saddle**. From it an easy ⅓-mile cross-country jaunt southwest takes one over a low ridge and down to campsites beside tranquil **Lake Winifred**. For real seclusion, try visiting one of the lakelets or ponds lying south of this lake.

Most hikers will instead continue along the road, which from the broad saddle makes a long, steady, rocky, one-mile descent southeast, crossing a seasonal cascading creek just before reaching a curve east. Along that short curve is a trail intersection, which can be easily missed if unsigned. In 70 yards the road reaches shallow, rocky **Buck Island Lake** and then climbs ¼ mile southeast back up to the trail (which also goes the same distance to end at the road). In late summer the lake's level can be low and its shoreline desolate. Little water flows from its dammed outlet; rather, the water flows through a tunnel down to Loon Lake, which, like Rockbound and Rubicon reservoirs upstream, is part of Sacramento's water supply system. After Labor Day, Loon Lake loses much of its water, its waterline dropping 30-35 feet by early October. From the trail intersection just above Buck Island Lake the northbound trail goes ½ mile to the lake's dam and just beyond it to the Wentworth Jeep Trail, which, after 1½ miles, approaches the north shore of Spider

Lake. Past off-highway vehicles have so impacted parts of this jeep trail that in many places it has been eroded down to bedrock.

If camping at Buck Island Lake looks unappealing when you visit it, due to OHVers, then head into the nearby wilderness. From the trail's end at the road at a bend just above the lake's south shore, take the closed road east, which quickly climbs into Desolation Wilderness and soon traverses over to nearby **Rockbound Lake**. With the addition of a low dam, this lake has been deepened, making it quite appealing before the water drops in late summer. As your road curves southeast above this lake, look for small campsites under the sparse tree cover by its south shore.

Near the lake's inlet the road dips into forest cover to quickly reach Highland Lake creek, which has an adjacent campsite. Generally you can rock-hop this wide, attractive creek, then you continue on the road but 180 yards, to where it is blocked off. On your right is a tortuous trail, which you take for 0.3 mile before rejoining the road. This trail segment exists to bypass the "new Rubicon River," up to 15 yards wide, which seasonally gushes from the lower end of a tunnel draining Rubicon Reservoir. On the road you climb about 110 yards to a saddle overlooking **Fox Lake**, which lies 250 yards to the north. From here, competent off-trail hikers can strike south, quickly attaining a broad ridge, eventually leaving it to parallel Highland Lake's creek up to the Highland Lake Trail, and then taking that up to the lake (last paragraph of Hike 65).

As your road starts down from the saddle, you can leave the road and make a quick, fairly easy cross-country descent to this tempting lake. On a small island—a peninsula in late summer—several lodgepoles grow beside two large, dark erratics, which are boulders left behind by the last glacier to descend this canyon. Glacial striations mark the direction of its flow.

From the saddle the road descends ¼ mile to a trail junction above the northwest lobe of Rubicon Reservoir. Now on the Rubicon River Trail we momentarily cross above the reservoir's ¼-mile-long outlet tunnel, then meander south, paralleling the west shore of shallow **Rubicon Reservoir**, which turns into an unattractive mud-and-boulder flat late in summer. We leave this reservoir as the trail curves east, then climb ¼ mile up to two stagnant ponds on a large bench. After a momentary descent the trail climbs ½ mile south to a ford of wide, shallow Rubicon River. To keep your feet dry, try boulder-hopping it about 100 yards downstream.

If you'd like to visit Lake Zitella, you can take a cross-country shortcut up to it. Rather than ford the Rubicon, climb more or less south-southwest up slopes. Half way up, you'll reach a forest on a flat bench and a brushy, short, steep escarpment, which can be climbed unroped (*use caution!*) by several routes. Above, you'll find hiking relatively easy if you stay 100-200 yards from the creek rather than keeping close to it. Cross the creek just below the obvious bench that holds the unseen lake.

Those staying on the trail cross the Rubicon and then start south along low-angle exfoliation slabs, in 300 yards reaching a long, shallow river pool. Just past it you nearly touch the river again, then soon curve east for a ⅓-mile climb upriver to a lodgepole flat, abounding with bracken ferns. Curving across the flat, the trail goes to nearby Phipps Creek, crossing it at the south end of a shallow, wide pool. Now, in a ¼-mile segment, the trail makes a brief, steep climb, then winds south to where ducks mark a 200-yard traverse west to lodgepole-shaded **AAA Camp**, perched on a bench above the Rubicon. By it the river cascades into a 10-foot-deep pool— brisk, but excellent for diving, cooling off, or just frolicking.

With the Camper Flat area as this hike's goal, we wind southward from the AAA Camp junction, first across the back of a broad, glacially polished ridge, then along the base of its east slopes. Along this undulating stretch a master joint (major fracture in bedrock) lies about 100 yards east of the trail.

Erratic on Fox Lake's island

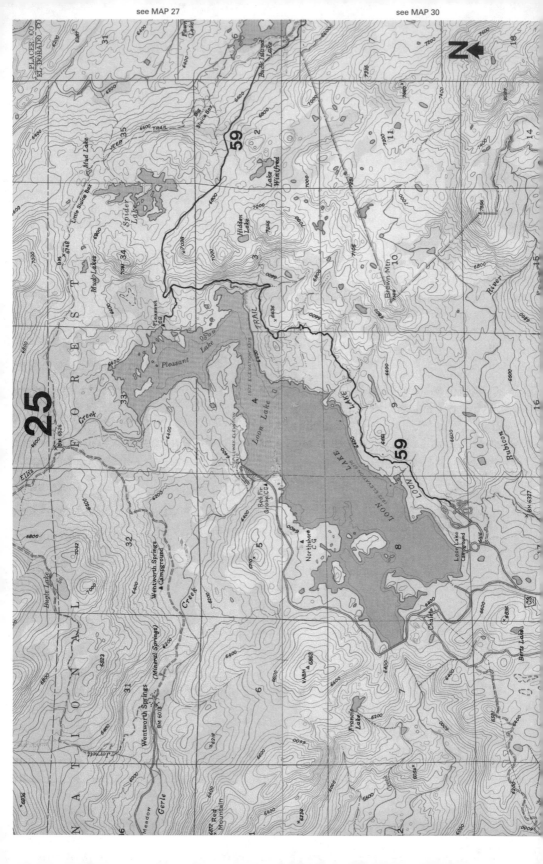

N

26

60

60

60

61

61

61

Tells Peak

Forni Lake

Shadow Lake

PEAK

FORK

RED

TRAIL

HIGHLAND

TRAIL

ELDORADO

NATIONAL

Landing Strip

LOON LAKE TRAIL

Fork

South Fork

POISON

Poison Hole

Chipmunk Bluff

Stone Cellar

Water Tank

Van Vleck Ranch

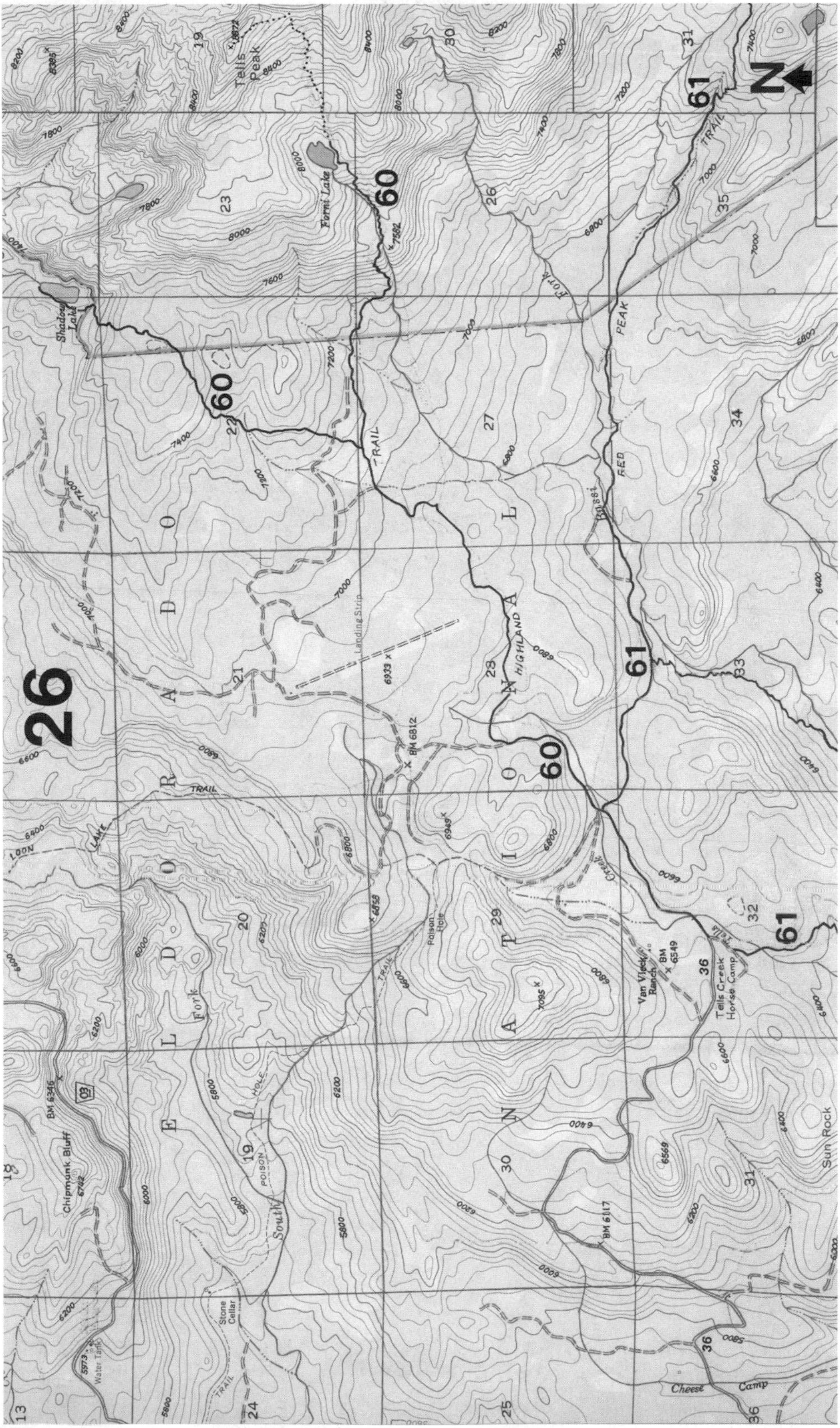

Tells Creek Horse Camp

Sun Rock

Cheese Camp

BM 6812

BM 6817

BM 6549

BM 6345

6948

6945

6933

7782

27

51
Barker Peak
8166
7

Barker Pass
JEEP
03
7782
75

Middle Fork
03
9
7400

10
Lake Louise
8200

Ellis Peak
8740
Ellis Lake
8200
Knee
8394
8400

Sierra
8271
8519
ELLIS
PEAK
Divide
TRAIL

18
7904
17
16
15
7400

F O R E S T

75
14N20
Cothrin Cove
7600

Bear Lake
7800
North Miller
Cr
TRAIL

Buck La
8224

75
6708

19
PACIFIC
Barker

20
21
22
7127
JEEP

75
6820
BM 7108
Miller
Meadows
Sierra Divide
7115
Miller Lake
7400

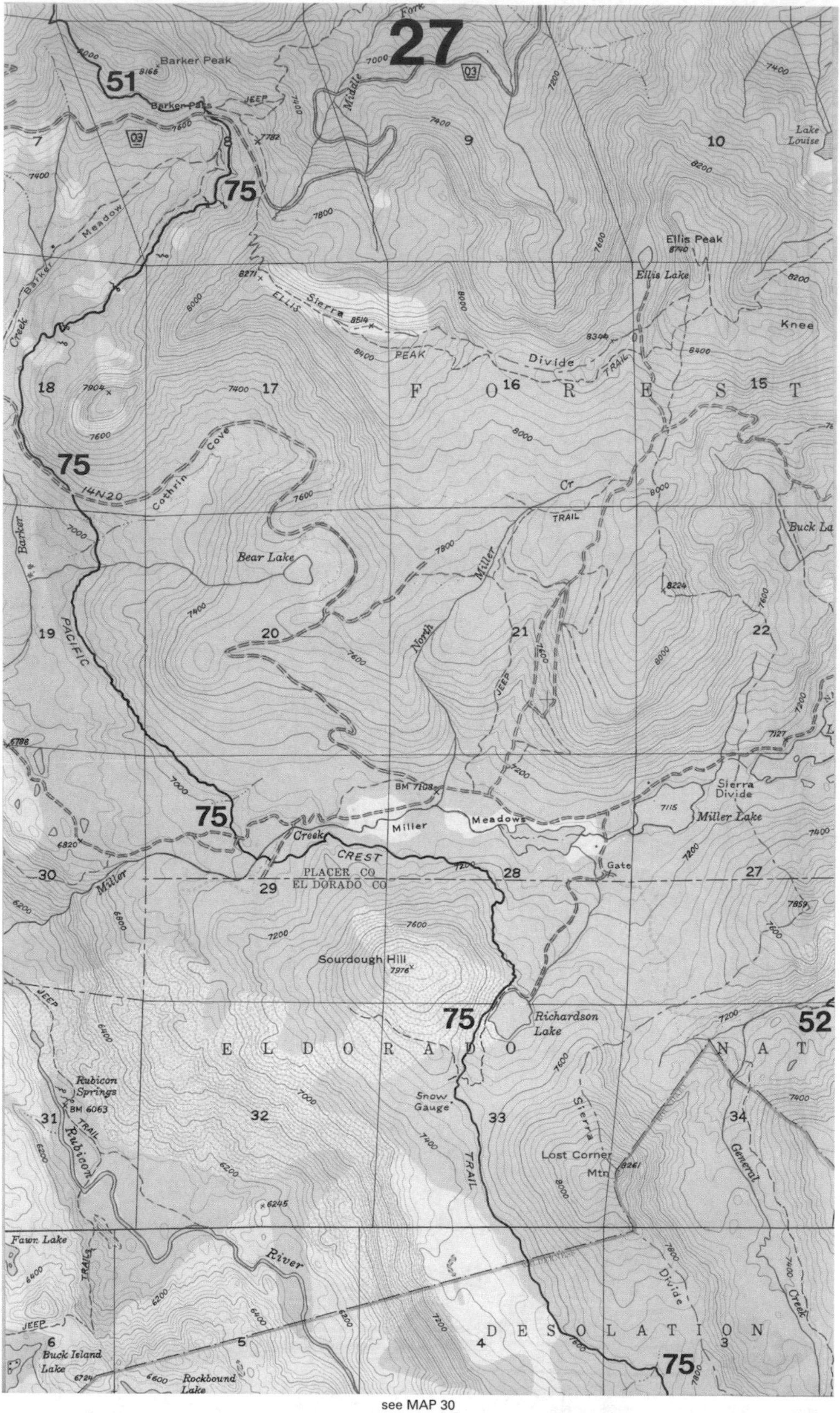

30
Miller
Creek
CREST
PLACER CO
EL DORADO CO
29
28
27
Gate
7859

75
Sourdough Hill
7976
Richardson Lake
52
NAT

31
Rubicon Springs
BM 6063
Rubicon Trail
JEEP

ELDORADO
32
Snow Gauge
33
Sierra
34
7400

Lost Corner Mtn
8261
8000

6245
General

Fawn Lake
River
Divide

6
Buck Island Lake
6724
5
Rockbound Lake
4
D E S O L A T I O N
3
75

About ½ mile past the junction you climb southwest to a crest saddle, then drop along a somewhat brushy gully to the nearby river. For ⅓ mile you parallel it up-canyon, noting several large, shallow pools. At a lodgepole thicket where the river bends, you ford it or possibly log-cross it. In this area the trail may be hard to find if hikers have been striking paths up and down the river looking for a dry crossing. If you're on the right track, which starts southeast, you'll reach the north edge of a stagnant pond in about 80 yards. Just ¼ mile past it the trail reaches the Rubicon. Following it gently up-canyon, you pass two of its large, emerald-green pools, the second one at the base of a small cascade. Optimal swimming (still brisk!) is in late afternoons in August.

After a few minutes' walk past the second pool, you meet the **McConnell Lake Trail**. If you've got a couple of days to spare, you might make the 4-Q, Horseshoe, McConnell, Leland, Schmidell lakes loop and perhaps even take in Lake Zitella and Highland Lake. All these lakes, which are usually mosquito-ridden and chilly before early August, are described in Hike 65.

Just 70 yards past the McConnell Lake Trail our trail meets Lake Schmidell creek. If it is too high and wide to jump across, look for a log crossing. Past its east bank we slog through a damp meadow, usually very alive with vibrant wildflowers and pesky mosquitoes, then arrive at a spacious campsite at **Camper Flat**. Here you'll find a shallow Rubicon River swimming hole that begs you to linger. About 250 yards beyond this area you'll note a spur trail going west 30 yards to a cold, seeping, rust-stained mineral spring. In 70 more level yards you meet the **Blakely Trail**, this hike's end. From here you can travel southwest up to Lake Schmidell (Hike 65), south up-canyon to Lake Aloha (Hike 66), or

Pool at AAA Camp

east up to the Velma Lakes (also Hike 66). This last option begins from another trail junction 100 yards south of the Blakely Trail. No camping is allowed along this 100-yard stretch or along a 100-yard stretch south of that junction. From it, anglers head briefly up the Rubicon River to fish from its open, granitic slabs. These also are great for sunbathing adjacent to one of the river's brisk swimming holes.

** **60** **
# Highland and Shadow Lake Trails

Distances:
0.7 mile to Red Peak Trail route
1.3 miles to Highland Trail
3.1 miles to Shadow Lake Trail
    1.7 miles on trail to Shadow Lake
4.6 miles to Forni Lake
5.4 miles to saddle above Forni Lake
    0.6 mile cross-country to Highland Lake
5.8 miles to Tells Peak

Low/High Elevations: 6500'/7540' to Shadow Lake; 7940' to Forni Lake; 8872' to Tells Peak

Season: Mid-July through mid-October

Classification: Moderate

Maps: 26 and 30

Trailhead: See the Hike 59 trailhead directions to Ice House Resort. Then your road, Forest Route 3, passes the Crystal Basin Ranger Station as well as spur roads to Union Valley Reservoir's campgrounds. The northernmost one is Yellowjacket Campground, on a spur road branching left, and on Forest Route 3, you drive north 1.6 miles past its spur road to a curve left, and a junction with Forest Route 36. Turn right and follow this paved road eastward, passing several spur roads before descending to a road, branching sharply right, after 5.4 miles. Straight ahead, the main road descends 150 yards to a gated crossing of Tells Creek. You turn sharply right and drive about 150 yards to a conspicuous parking area for the Van Vleck trailhead (no wilderness permits available). This holds about one dozen vehicles. Ahead, this road

winds briefly through primitive Tells Creek Horse Camp, where you could find additional parking spots. Along it about 70 yards southwest from the parking area, the Bassi Loop Trail, on the left, begins a descent south to nearby Tells Creek.

Introduction
The Van Vleck trailhead is one of the most isolated and least used in the vicinity of Desolation Wilderness; consequently the trails starting from it usually are lightly used. The scenery viewed along the trails is subdued, not dramatic, and Forni Lake has poor campsites. Above, hikers can climb to a saddle and then climb Tells Peak, which provides rewarding views. Also from the saddle, skilled mountaineers can descend cross-country to stark Highland Lake, also deficient in campsites, but abounding in scenery. This mountaineer's route to the lake, about 6 miles in length, is less than half as long as a trail route beginning in the popular Wrights Lake area (Hikes 64 and 65). This hike also has an optional route to Shadow Lake, just outside Desolation Wilderness and the lowest and warmest of this hike's three lakes. It is visited by equestrians, some staying at a fairly large horse camp on its north shore.

Description
Mileages are based from the trailhead parking area, even though no trail begins from it. Get back on F.R. 36, descend 150 yards to Tells Creek, and continue about 0.6 mile leisurely up your now gated road to a junction with the **Red Peak Trail route**. This route, branching right immediately before a recrossing of Tells Creek, begins as a road, and is described in Hike 61.

Immediately past Tells Creek, Road 13N22 branches left, bound for the Crystal Pack Station. Still on Forest Route 36, we climb northeast along the edge of a meadow, then turn north for a short, moderate climb. The road then stays level for 0.1 mile before starting another moderate climb. At that point we leave the road, forking right on the **Highland Trail**. This begins with an arc around the north part of a sloping meadow, then from it makes an easy traverse 0.4 mile east to a ridge of hundreds of giant boulders, up to 20+ feet, transported here by most recent, receding Bassi Fork glacier. Just after skirting along the edge of the bouldery ridge, the trail curves north along the west edge of a usually boggy meadow, then traverses across it for about 130 yards. If you find the trail vague, sight along an 80° bearing to the far side of the meadow, and head for that point.

Ahead, the trail climbs about 0.3 mile northeast before arcing northwest over to an abandoned road. Up this you climb 0.2 mile northeast to a junction where your road begins to curve northwest. Here you take a road east, immediately crossing a creeklet, then immediately reaching the resumption of trail tread. Ahead, your abandoned road quickly dies out. We begin an eastward climb across a meadow, but this one is different from the others. It is dry, is developed from volcanic deposits—not from the pervasive granitic bedrock—and supports large-leaved sunflowers, mule ears. On this open, eastward climb, with views south across subdued terrain, you encounter the **Shadow Lake Trail**.

This trail climbs moderately north 200 yards up open slopes to an east-west road, then climbs briefly at a steeper gradient through an open red-fir forest. Ahead, it makes a viewless traverse north to an alder-lined gully, crosses it, then climbs, sometimes steeply, generally northeast to a bench. Here, among red fir, mountain hemlock, and western white pines, you arrive at the south end of a shallow, seasonal lake. Late-season hikers will find only a grassy meadow—a shadow of the former lake. Nevertheless, it is not Shadow Lake, which lies ahead. You skirt along the east shore of the seasonal lake, wind northward across the bench, then descend, steeply at first, down to fairly open, glacially polished and striated, granitic bedrock. From it you descend in a couple of minutes to the southwest shore of **Shadow Lake**, with its small, fair, gently sloping campsites. From here the trail continues along the west shore to the lake's north end, which has a very ample packer's camp with a pleasing view of the lake.

Beyond the junction with the Shadow Lake Trail, the Highland Trail climbs gently eastward 0.4 mile to a creeklet, then enters Desolation Wilderness before reaching a second, nearby creeklet. This flows through a boggy meadow, which you skirt eastward along its south edge. Past it, the trail steepens to moderate, but unfortunately only briefly so, for it quickly becomes a very steep ascent, taking you 300 feet higher up bouldery, brushy slopes before momentarily abating to cross Forni Lake's outlet creek. Ahead lies an equally long, equally steep trail. The trail, however, is ill-defined, in essence cross-country. It climbs 200 vertical feet alongside the creek before switchbacking briefly south to a viewpoint, then winds upslope before traversing north over to the nearby outlet of **Forni Lake**. Hemmed in with vegetation, the lake is not particularly photogenic. Surrounded by slopes and, on its west side by a large-block moraine, it has fair camping at best. A small site lies about 100 yards east of where the trail meets the lake. Another lies just north of where the trail begins a climb east from the lake. What you will hopefully find here is solitude.

Above the lake, the trail is quite difficult to follow, especially your descent from the features above. As you are climbing eastward, be aware of two problems you will face. First, essentially the entire east shore and slopes above it are covered with dense, lush vegetation. Be sure you end up along the south side of it to reach the lake's southeast shore, or else face a bushwhack. Second, there are short drop-offs above and more-sizable ones lower down. If you lose the diaphanous "trail" on your descent, you will probably have to negotiate a safe route around one or more of these.

Your goal is a **saddle above Forni Lake**, a very obvious feature attained after a 700-foot ascent. If you are bound for Tells Peak, you can veer north up open slopes before reaching this saddle, but doing so robs you of a stunning view down into the deep cirque harboring Highland Lake. From the saddle, the cross-country route down to the lake is perfectly obvious. While this route is the shortest way to the lake, it is also potentially the most dangerous. With a heavy pack, you can easily sprain an ankle if you are not careful on the steep descent. Only *competent* cross-country hikers should attempt a route down the

32°-steep slope across bedrock and large-block talus to **Highland Lake**. Campsites along the lake's shore are small and should be avoided. Look for better ones on the broad, openly forested ridge just north of the lake, or on the spacious bench below and north of it. It is quite exposed, but this is not a problem in good weather. Regardless where you camp, you will probably find yourself between a rock and a hard place.

Rather than descend to the lake, from the saddle or just before it you can head northward cross-country up to nearby, obvious **Tells Peak** (8872′), which provides a 360° panorama of this part of the Tahoe Sierra. Here, on the northernmost summit of the Crystal Range—the granitic west ridge of Desolation Wilderness—you see part of Highland Lake below you to the east, and above it, on the distant skyline Jobs Sister (10,823′) and Freel Peak (10,881′), about 20 miles away, and just to the left of closer Mt. Tallac (9735′). To its right, southeast, and closer are the summits of Dicks Peak (9974′) and Jacks Peak (9856′). The next right is McConnell Peak (9099′), a mere mile away, its

proximal bulk blocking most of the Crystal Range. Continuing our clockwise scan, we see, to the south-southwest, glacially scoured, naked-bedrock ridges and gentle domes, the highest summit being the dome of Twin Peak (7576′). Its slightly closer, steep-sided twin is fraternal at best, and just above its left side rises Slick Rock (7242′). Right of all is a sliver of Ice House Reservoir. To the southwest, well beyond Forni Lake, lies spreading Union Valley Reservoir and its unattractive fire-ravaged backdrop. More attractive is Loon Lake, to the northwest, surrounded by glacially scoured lands. Just in front of the lake and left of its constriction lies Brown Mountain, a resistant mass of basaltic lava not removed by glaciers. Above it and well behind the lake are the right-facing Red Cliffs of metamorphic McKinstry Peak (7933′).

To its right to the north-northwest, and closer, is conical Guide Peak (7741′), and east of Loon Lake lies Spider Lake. Just right of it and due north of us lies Buck Island Lake, while just right of it lies larger Rockbound Lake. This reservoir is located on a bench about 400 feet above the floor of the Rubicon

Highland Lake and Rockbound Valley

River canyon. When the canyon's last glacier was at its maximum about 20,000 years ago, it was about 1600 feet thick, which was enough to slightly overflow across the broad saddle you see behind the reservoir. Similar-sized Rubicon Reservoir lies up-canyon from it, nestled in a granitic topography laced with long, straight fractures, or joints. Finally, above this landscape we see a wedge of Lake Tahoe, and the northern part of the Carson Range behind it, capped by volcanic, 10,776' Mt. Rose.

⪻ 61 ⪼
Red Peak and Bassi Loop Trails

Distances:
1.5 miles to Bassi Loop Trail
   3.4 miles on loop trail to trailhead
1.9 miles to Red Peak Trail
2.2 miles to Bassi Fork Big Silver Creek
6.3 miles to Lake No. 3 spur trail
   0.4 mile on spur trail to Lake No. 3
6.5 miles to Lake No. 4 use path
   0.2 mile on use path to Lake No. 4
6.8 miles to Lake No. 5
7.4 miles to Lawrence Lake spur trail
   0.2 mile on spur trail to Lawrence Lake
      0.5 mile to Lake No. 9
      0.6 mile to Top Lake
   0.2 mile cross-country to Lost Lake
7.6 miles to Barrett Lake

Low/High Elevations: 6500'; 6190' at Upper Bassi Ranch site/8270'

Season: Mid-July through mid-October

Classification: Easy to moderate

Maps: 26, 29, 30, and 33

Trailhead: Same as the Hike 60 trailhead.

Introduction
The main destinations of this hike are the lakes below Red Peak. These receive more visitors from the Wrights Lake area, who take Hike 63 to them. The first 3½ miles of our main route, the Red Peak Trail, are across lowlands that before August tend to be very mosquito-prone. Therefore, you might take this hike in August, when OHVs are allowed on

the Barrett Lake Trail, an old jeep road. You won't find any along the Red Peak Trail, which provides a less used, more serene approach to the lakes.

The Bassi Loop Trail connects to the Red Peak Trail, but is a longer way to the lakes. However, the first 2 miles make an easy day hike, taking you to a very scenic stretch of Bassi Fork Big Silver Creek.

Description
As in the previous hike, you take F.R. 36 150 yards down to Tells Creek and continue about 0.6 mile leisurely up to a road junction with the Red Peak Trail route, branching right immediately before a recrossing of Tells Creek. East, your road climbs easily ½ mile to a broad saddle, then descends slightly over ¼ mile to a junction with the upper end of the **Bassi Loop Trail**. It makes up 3.4 miles of the 5.0-mile loop; your 1.5-mile road route to this junction makes up most of the rest, and 0.1 mile between the two routes' starting points account for the remainder.

The Bassi Loop Trail is a full 2 miles longer to the above destinations if you start from the trailhead parking area, and so it is not worth taking. However, on your return, when your pack is a bit lighter, it may be, since in this direction there about 400 feet of net descent but only 300 feet of net ascent. This switchbacks briefly down to the Bassi Fork, which you quickly leave to traverse a flat of lodgepole pines and red firs. This soon gives way to an open, brushy descent past huckleberry oaks and open slabs down again to a second flat, about 1.0 mile along the trail. From here onward you might find isolated, creekside camping. In 0.2 mile you might see a spur trail heading over to the creek, then just beyond it, a packer's camp. Just beyond that, at about mile 1.3, you come alongside the start of a very scenic stretch of Bassi Fork. This stretch is a worthy goal, so the 2.1-mile hike to it will be described in the opposite direction.

Just beyond the trailhead parking area in the Tells Creek Horse Camp, the Bassi Loop Trail leads south briefly to alder-lined Tells Creek, which you should be able to log-cross or boulder-hop. If it is a raging torrent, then the larger Bassi Fork, your destination, will be

The Bassi Fork of Big Silver Creek

more so, and could be dangerous for wading or swimming. About 1.0 mile along your mostly descending hike, you reach a junction with the Sun Rock Trail. It may not be signed, so on your return be sure to keep right at this split in order to arrive back at your trailhead. Ahead, you have a 0.7-mile traverse east, the second half across unsigned Upper Bassi Ranch property, to a bend north. You are now alongside the Bassi Fork, and can see east, across it, the ranch's derelict structures. Northward, you climb about 300 yards before leaving the unsigned property. This climb, and that ahead, is a ducked route across granitic slabs, and it can be vague in spots. Over the next 0.3 mile you can leave the trail at any time to investigate broad Bassi Fork's alternating generally shallow pools and usually mild rapids. The open slabs are ideal for sunbathing, and the erratic-strewn, naked-granite slopes across the creek make a complimentary backdrop.

Those on the Red Peak Trail route at the upper end of the Bassi Loop Trail continue their eastward trek, approaching Bassi Fork in about 0.2 mile, then doing so again in another 0.2 mile. Here your road curves north, and the real **Red Peak Trail** begins. Before August this trail across a meadow-and-forest flatland can be boggy, and then you may want to take the slightly longer road route, first north then east, over to a junction with the trail beside broad **Bassi Fork Big Silver Creek**. Unless a fallen tree provides a dry crossing, head 100–200 feet upstream and look for a suitable boulder-hop. Once across, you start up the road, which soon narrows to a trail, then traverse through an open, meadowy lodgepole forest to the Desolation Wilderness boundary. The same vegetation persists for 0.3 mile, then begins to change as you commence a 2.8-mile-long, 1400-foot ascent to a junction near Lake No. 3. This begins easily enough in a gully, but steepens with elevation, leaving it near its upper end to switchback up an adjacent, minor ridge. Near the highest switchback you cut across huckleberry-oak slopes, and can pause to take in a view west across the gentle topography you have traversed. Ahead, a moderate-to-steep ascent soon abates, then your trail drops slightly to a major tributary of Bassi Fork, which can be boulder-hopped just downstream. Just before the crossing, about 4.7 miles from the start, one could head ¼ mile south cross-country up to a nearby, broad saddle to find, just below it, an unnamed lake on a bench that offers a panoramic view of western and southern lands, dominated by Twin Peaks, about 2½ miles to the southwest.

From a low granitic outcrop by the tributary crossing, you are almost halfway up the Red Peak Trail's major ascent, and are at the mutual boundary of the Loon Lake and Rockbound Valley 7.5' quadrangles (Maps 26 and 30). Here, western white pines and mountain hemlocks have joined the red firs, and become increasingly more common above. For too short a time, we have a respite from our ascent, then face a partly moderate, partly steep climb to a recrossing of the tributary, now not very major, and 1¼ miles above the last crossing. One short climb, a steep one, gets us to the lip of a small, hanging gully, near whose upper south end we meet a **spur trail**, which goes 0.4 mile to **Lake No. 3.** Southwest 50 yards from the junction, the Red Peak Trail crosses a minor saddle and descends 0.2 mile to a broader one, from which a **use path** descends 0.2 mile northwest to **Lake No. 4.** Ahead, the Red Peak Trail winds southeast past **Lake No. 5**, which is reached in about the same distance via Hike 63. Ahead, all destinations are shorter by that hike than by this one. Your trail next descends southward to a short **spur trail** traversing northeast upstream to nearby **Lawrence Lake.** Above it, one can climb cross-country to either **Lake No. 9** or **Top Lake.** From the spur-trail junction, one can also contour southwest cross-country over to a bench holding **Lost Lake.** The Red Peak Trail then exits the wilderness to quickly terminate at the Barrett Lake (Jeep) Trail. Directions to all these lakes, as well as descriptions of them, appear in Hike 63.

⪡ 62 ⪢
Wrights Lake to Pearl Lake

Distances:
0.6 mile to Beauty Lake
1.8 miles to Jones Fork Silver Creek
2.6 miles to Rupley Jeep Trail
4.7 miles to Pearl Lake
Low/High Elevations: 6860'/7350'
Season: Mid-July through mid-October
Classification: Moderate
Maps: 33, 29
Trailheads: If you plan to *backpack* in the wilderness (Hikes 63-69, 71), be sure to get a wilderness permit. The best place to get one is at the Eldorado National Forest Information Center, on Camino Heights Drive about 5 miles east of Placerville. From this center continue 17 miles east up Highway 50 to its bridge across the South Fork American River and in 100 yards reach the Crystal Basin Recreation Area turnoff, Forest Route 3 (Ice House Road), on your left. (Westbound drivers: this junction is about 27 miles west from Echo Summit.) Your paved road first climbs 9 miles to Ice House Resort, your last chance for food and supplies, then continues 1½ miles farther to Forest Route 32. Turn right and take this paved road 9 miles, first passing Ice House Reservoir's three campgrounds, then finally reaching a junction with Forest Route 4 (Wrights Lake Road). The lower part of this road, which begins 36 miles up Highway 50 from Placerville (and 8 miles down from Echo Summit) was permanently closed in 1997, after heavy rains caused major damage. Those taking Hike 71, turn right and drive 1.8 miles to Lyons Creek, then 0.1 mile farther to a spur left, parking for the Lyons Creek Trail. Day users can *usually* get a wilderness permit up at Wrights Lake.

For those taking Hikes 62-70, turn left onto Forest Route 4 and drive 1.8 miles up to a spur road on your right, which leads into the Wrights Lake Horse Camp and at its south end has the start of Hike 70 to Bloodsucker Lake. Just 0.2 mile past this spur road is the Wrights Lake Information Kiosk. Day users can get wilderness permits here or at trailheads, which are needed for Hikes 63-69. Overnighters must get their permit elsewhere—see Chapter 2's section on wilderness permits.

For Hikes 62-67, branch left (northwest) immediately past the kiosk and in ¼ mile reach an obvious Rockbound trailhead parking area, on your left. If you were to continue ⅓ mile farther, you would reach Dark Lake. The limited parking there is for the lake's users, *not* for hikers.

For Hikes 68 and 69, branch right (east) immediately past the kiosk to immediately cross Wrights Lake's outlet and pass its nearby campground, then wind past homes to a fairly large Twin Lakes trailhead parking area, on your right. The actual trailhead lies 90 yards farther, down at the road's end.

For Hikes 62-69, you could start from other trailheads in the Wrights Lake area, as well as from the northwest or southeast section of Wrights Lake Campground, and each start would give you a different distance to a given point.

Introduction

Isolated from other Silver Creek lakes is lightly visited Pearl Lake, which lies at the base of geologically interesting, instructive, exfoliating granitic slabs. An incentive for camping at or near it is that you don't need a wilderness permit.

Description

Starting opposite the upper end of the Rockbound trailhead parking area, our Rockbound Pass Trail makes a brief climb to a broad, glaciated bedrock ridge and winds north atop it ½ mile to tree-ringed **Beauty Lake**. Large granitic boulders, left by a melting glacier some 14,000 years ago, form miniature islands that add charm to this lake. From here a trail descends south-southeast ⅓ mile to homes by the northwest corner of Wrights Lake. After strolling 70 yards north along

Exfoliation slabs above Pearl Lake

Beauty Lake's west shore, we leave the main trail to branch northwest over a nearby gap in a low moraine ridge, and then descend 250 easy yards west to the Barrett Lake (Jeep) Trail. OHVs are allowed on this area's jeep trails from about late July onward.

We start north on the jeep trail, approach the east edge of a pond in 15 yards, and soon descend past the west edge of a larger one, which has grasses and pond lilies. We quickly bottom out to make a fairly level, seasonally muddy traverse ⅓ mile north to a fair campsite, shaded by red firs and lodgepoles, on the east bank of **Jones Fork Silver Creek**. Where the road crosses the creek, the ford can be up to 15 yards wide, but upstream you can find a boulder hop.

Our road leaves the creek and the forest cover, climbs northwest, and provides us with a view of Rockbound Pass and the adjacent Crystal Range. Soon we reach a wet meadow, rich with wildflowers. Here, in Mortimer Flat, the road splits. For Pearl Lake, take the left fork. This **Rupley Jeep Trail** climbs ¾ mile through a viewless forest to a broad, equally viewless saddle, then descends north ¼ mile to the northeast edge of a meadow. Where the road turns west to start a climb, the Red Peak Stock Trail formerly began a wildly fluctuating 1.5-mile climb to the Barrett Lake Trail. From here onward lies private property of the Rupley Ranch.

The Rupley Jeep Trail next climbs briefly up to a morainal ridge rich in granitic boulders, then descends to a ford of alder-choked Big Silver Creek, which drains the Pearl Lake basin. Beyond the creek we walk about 100 yards west, then follow a spur road northeast ½ mile up glacial sediments to **Pearl Lake**, which lies on Forest Service land. Like almost every lake in the Wrights Lake area, as well as those in adjacent Desolation Wilderness, this lake has a low dam, here built to stabilize summer streamflow and to provide a better year-round habitat for fish. Because the lake's water is semistagnant, get fresh water just to the south, at a spring-fed creek.

On the south shore is a fair campsite overlooking the lake's shallow waters, which in the morning reflect the somber, exfoliating slabs above the northeast shore. *Exfoliation*

occurs in granitic bedrock because it originally solidified several miles down under pressures on the order of a thousand times more than at the surface. When the overlying material is gone, shells of depressurized granite pop off. Glaciers greatly accelerate the rate of exfoliation, because the Sierra's thick glaciers persisted for thousands of years, adding pressure to the underlying bedrock, and then they rapidly melted away, causing rapid depressurization. Consequently, lots of post-glacial exfoliation occurred, resulting in abundant talus. In contrast, the Sierra's unglaciated granitic lands generally lack talus, for exfoliation occurs so slowly that the resulting rockfall blocks decompose to gravel before they can accumulate to form a mass of talus.

⫷ 63 ⫸
Wrights Lake to Barrett, Lawrence, and Top Lakes

Distances:
5.9 miles to Barrett Lake
6.1 miles to Lawrence Lake spur trail
  0.2 mile on trail to Lawrence Lake
    0.5 mile cross-country to Lake No. 9
    0.6 mile cross-country to Top Lake
  0.2 mile cross-country to Lost Lake
6.7 miles to Lake No. 5
7.0 miles to Lake No. 4 spur trail
  0.2 mile on trail to Lake No. 4
7.2 miles to Lake No. 3 spur trail
  0.4 mile on trail to Lake No. 3
Low/High Elevations: 6860'/8270'
Season: Mid-July through mid-October
Classification: Moderate
Maps: 33 and 30
Trailhead: See the Hike 62 trailhead.

Introduction
The Barrett Lake Trail, which is an old jeep road, provides access to an area partly in westernmost Desolation Wilderness that has over a dozen lakes and ponds. This hike describes routes to eight lakes, from popular Barrett Lake to lightly visited Lake No. 9. Just above Barrett Lake is Lawrence Lake, one of

our area's more dramatic lakes. Above it is Top Lake, a unique bilobed lake whose water level is two feet higher at its east end than at its west end. And geologically interesting Lake No. 3 provides the start of a cross-country route across the Crystal Range.

Description

If you go no farther than Barrett Lake, you won't enter the wilderness and won't need a permit. Be aware that every summer OHVs use the jeep road up to Barrett Lake, but only after the roads have become quite drivable. Generally OHVs are allowed from about late July onward, so to avoid motorized recreationists, hike before then. From about late July onward, you can also avoid them by taking Hike 61 up to this hike's lakes.

The previous hike describes the first 2.6 miles to a junction with the Rupley Jeep Trail in Mortimer Flat. You continue up the Barrett Lake Trail, which first ascends a little canyon above the flat, then curves north up to a low ridge. Your jeep trail next fords a wisp of a creek before attaining an open slab from which you'll obtain a panorama of the Crystal Range to the east and southeast. From this vantage point the prominent Wrights Lake and Lyons Creek moraines are very obvious as lateral moraines, whereas close up, their forest cover and their minor irregularities tend to camouflage their shape. Beyond this open slab the jeep trail climbs to a marshy, forested flat, curves east across it, and turns northward up a ridge. This we eventually cross, and then climb steeply up to a saddle and the start of a ridgecrest trail, the Red Peak Stock Trail. Through 1987 this was used to drive cattle over the crest of the Crystal Range and into the heart of Desolation Wilderness. Looking gentle and safe where we see it, this trail becomes, one mile east, a steep, potentially treacherous route. Also, about ½ mile up the driveway a southeast-trending, 1¾-mile-long trail, 16E11, formerly cut across it, linking the Barrett Lake Trail with the Rockbound Pass Trail, passing two shallow lakelets on its way to Willow Flat. Higher up, the tread of the seldom used stock trail disappears, and the route becomes hard to follow—treat it as a challenging cross-country route.

From the ridge the Barrett Lake Trail makes a steep, 0.2-mile descent to a small meadow with a muted creek, this just 30 yards north of the site of former Trail 16E11's northwest end. Across the creek we make a brief, braking descent, then recross its cascading segment. We cross it once more as the jeep road skirts along the east edge of a logged-over meadow being invaded by lodgepoles. Just past the turn of the century this plot was sold by the Barrett family to the University of California at Davis, which set up an experimental station here and tried to improve the local herds through selective breeding. From this site we climb, steeply in places, to a broad saddle, on which our jeep road diminishes to a trail. After a short, sunny, gravelly descent we reach the swift Barrett Lake outlet creek, a boulder hop. Now we follow a gully that in places becomes a shallow chute, and in ¼ mile the jeep trail ends at an enormous, flat campsite, under shady red firs, occupying most of the west shore of **Barrett Lake**. This site would hold a large Boy Scout troop with room to spare, and the lake's coves and diving rocks, together with its shallow rock-slab pools below its low dam, would keep all the kids active and content.

Beyond Barrett Lake we take the Red Peak Trail, which doesn't go to the peak. This begins as a pack trail, first climbing steeply 0.1 mile to the wilderness boundary, then steeply up another 0.1 mile to a trail junction by the cascading Lawrence Lake outlet creek. Now with law-abiding OHVers staying behind at Barrett Lake, we branch right for an easy creekside climb to a fair campsite near the northwest end of the waist-high dam across **Lawrence Lake**. Cross the dam and take a footpath past a small rock island to Top Lake's outlet creek, which announces itself 150 yards before entering the beautiful, symmetrical lake by cascading 50 feet down a glistening rock slab. To the east is the higher but less spectacular cascade of the outlet creek of **Lake No. 9**. A ½-mile walk up along either creek will get you to less used campsites at these two lakes.

A side trip to **Top Lake** is particularly rewarding. Perched at the lip of a cirque, it seems to sit on top of the world, and the

Top Lake has a naturally terraced east end

backpacker who sets up camp here enjoys panoramic sunsets that are hard to match anywhere. The lake has a peninsula that almost divides it in two. The most amazing aspect of the lake, however, is its naturally terraced east end, where water is ponded up as much as 2 feet higher than at the west end. Thick clumps of grass and heather are progressively invading the lake, building dikes and trapping sediments. More vegetation grows upon them and ponds up the water level.

For more lake hunting, return to the Red Peak Trail junction. If you contour ¼ mile southwest from it, you reach a bench holding **Lost Lake**, probably the least visited of the Red Peak lakes. This linear lake is deep enough for swimming laps and, like the other wilderness lakes along this trail, it has a population of brook trout. Keeping to the trail, you climb steeply north 0.2 mile to a forested ridge, then make a short descent to a meadow in which you pass three seasonal ponds, all on your right. Flowing from the last of these, as well as from a soggy meadow, is a small creek we must cross before it enters **Lake No. 5**. This lake is a haunt of spotted sandpipers, who build nests in the dense grass along the water's edge. If you want to camp at this

serene lake, do so on the west shore, a dry, rocky moraine from which you obtain tree-framed views down the glaciated slopes to the west.

Beyond the lake we climb to a saddle, where our trail turns abruptly right. The ducked path straight ahead leads 0.2 mile northwest down to unappealing, semistagnant **Lake No. 4**, which is too shallow for trout. Our trail climbs north-northeast up an open, bedrock slope to a narrow ridge. If not well marked, this stretch can be missed. The correct route goes through a shallow gap in the narrow ridge and continues 50 yards beyond it to a junction. See Hike 61 for a description of the route from the Van Vleck trailhead up to this junction.

With Lake No. 3 as the last goal, we leave the Red Peak Trail just beyond the narrow ridge and hike northeast through a swampy meadow, head between a rock pile on the left and the main rock slope on the right, and curve northward up to another wet, spongy meadow through which flows the tiny outlet creek from Lake No. 3. Small though it is, this creek can support good-size trout. Across the creek we head northwest toward the base of a moraine at a point 30 yards west of the creek's cascade. Now it's just a short climb up to **Lake No. 3**, whose relative isolation from Wrights Lake rewards you with relatively pristine lakeside campsites beneath a cover of mountain hemlock and lodgepole and western white pines. Those wishing to spend a few days here might make a relatively easy cross-country day hike northeast to the saddle between Red Peak and Silver Peak, and then descend to the Leland Lakes.

Hikers content to relax at lovely Lake No. 3 might take note of the arc of boulders near its outlet, which make up a recessional moraine—one formed behind a glacier's terminal moraine. Lake No. 3 stands out from others in that it has a clear recessional moraine behind the more amorphous one found at the lake's outlet. Many Sierra lakes appear to be dammed by such recessional moraines, but actually it is the bedrock beneath the moraine that is damming them. When you return to surprisingly shallow Wrights Lake, you might walk north along the west shore of this surprisingly shallow large lake and see how many recessional moraines you can identify.

⤜ **64** ⤛
Wrights Lake to Lakes Lois and Schmidell

Distances:
0.6 mile to Beauty Lake
1.8 miles to old Rockbound Pass Trail
2.3 miles to Tyler Lake Trail
4.6 miles to Maude Lake
5.9 miles to Rockbound Pass
6.2 miles to Lake Doris
6.4 miles to Blakely Trail
7.3 miles to Lake Lois
7.8 miles to Red Peak Stock Trail
8.4 miles to McConnell Lake Trail
8.6 miles to Lake Schmidell
Low/High Elevations: 6980′/8530′
Season: Late July through mid-October
Classification: Strenuous
Maps: 33 and 30
Trailhead: See the Hike 62 trailhead.

Introduction

Some visitors will want to go only as far as Maude Lake, either as a day hike or as an overnight hike. Unfortunately, when too many people linger at Maude Lake, it is likely to metamorphose to "Mud Lake." It is one of the more popular trailside lakes reached from Wrights Lake. Sturdy day hikers can perspire up to Rockbound Pass for well-earned vistas before returning on their 11.8-mile route. If you go beyond the pass, you'll probably want to make your trek a backpack trip. Weekend backpackers usually venture only as far as Lakes Lois or Schmidell, leaving the more-distant lakes (Hike 65) to those with more time.

Description

As in the previous two hikes, we take the Rockbound Pass Trail briefly up to a broad, glaciated bedrock ridge and wind north atop it ½ mile to tree-ringed **Beauty Lake**. We head 70 yards north along its west shore, to where a trail (Hikes 62 and 63) branches northwest over a minor gap. Then we curve eastward about 250 yards, exit north through another gap and, just east and up from it, meet a trail fork. Right, a trail descends eastward to the Twin Lakes Trail (Hike 68). We go left to wind 300 yards northeast up to another trail fork in a shallow, forested ridge saddle, from which a lightly used trail descends northeast to the old Rockbound Pass Trail. Rather than drop, only to climb again, we take the newer trail, which weaves along both sides of an irregular ridge, providing views both east and west. In about 0.9 mile we rejoin the **old Rockbound Pass Trail**.

By taking a shorter trail route beginning from the Twin Lakes trailhead, near the northeast tip of Wrights Lake, you can shave 0.5 mile off all the destinations beyond this junction, including distances to destinations mentioned in Hikes 63-67. From that trailhead this alternate route first crosses a prominent bridge over the lake's inlet creek. From the bridge's far side, a use trail heads west to north-shore homes, while your trail heads first northwest, then north, staying within forest cover to avoid a seasonally swampy meadow. Here Ed Wright grazed his dairy cattle from 1850 to 1900, and cattle still graze once it

Lakelet and Lake Doris, from just below Rockbound Pass

dries out. After 0.4 mile your trail, now widened to a road, meets a short trail eastbound for the Twin Lakes Trail (Hike 68). In about 15 yards your road starts a curve west and meets a spur road. If you continued west about 90 yards, you would reach a trail that climbs west to Beauty Lake. You take the spur road north, the start of the old Rockbound Pass Trail, and over ⅓ mile it quickly narrows to a trail and then reaches a junction with a trail that climbs southwest to Beauty Lake. Keeping north, you can enjoy the nearly level tread for ¼ mile, then make a generally moderate climb ⅓ mile to a ridge junction with the 0.5-mile-longer new Rockbound Pass Trail.

Ahead, the route is unchanged, and we climb northeast, first shortly up the ridge, then below and north of it to reach, in about ½ mile, a junction in a small, shady flat. From here the **Tyler Lake Trail** (Hike 67) climbs, surprisingly, to Gertrude Lake.

Our Rockbound Pass Trail branches left, crosses several snowmelt creeklets, soon enters Desolation Wilderness, then climbs moderately-to-steeply ½ mile north through a thinning forest to a seasonal pond atop a saddle. Now our trail makes an equally long and steep descent across brushy slabs to a boulder crossing of Jones Fork Silver Creek 1¼ miles below Maude Lake. Beyond the crossing our rock-lined route ascends largely barren, low-angle, glacially polished and striated slabs upon which rest numerous erratic boulders left by a melting glacier some 14,000 years ago. Along the massive slab's sparse fractures grow junipers, lodgepoles, and other plants that can get a roothold.

We cross a low, minor ridge, parallel it north, and enter the thicket of Willow Flat, which besides willows has bracken ferns, corn lilies, and aspens. A short, bouldery, creekside ascent leads to a shady lodgepole flat, where we jump across the seasonal creek just below its rush down a polished ramp. We make a shady ascent 200 yards to within several yards of the forest's abrupt north edge, from where abandoned Trail 16E11 once traversed westward over to two shallow, unappealing lakelets before intersecting the Red Peak Stock Trail and ending at the Barrett Lake (Jeep) Trail (Hike 63).

Climbing toward Maude Lake, our trail leaves forest shade behind as it switchbacks up a barren slope, traverses northeast above Silver Creek's inner gorge, and then makes a short descent to a pond. Immediately above it lies **Maude Lake**. Campsites abound, many illegal, around this overused lake. Swimmers who venture out in its relatively warm, shallow water can attest to the muddy character of the lake's bottom, which may have prompted someone to remove the *a* in a former *Maud Lake* sign (in the 1990s the spelling changed from "Maud" to "Maude").

Ahead lies a 900-foot elevation gain to Rockbound Pass. This is not a major gain by High Sierra standards, but it is for Desolation Wilderness. For some the ascent is intimidating because you almost always see the stark pass looming up before you, and because its dwarf trees make it look higher and farther away than it is. Our trail to the pass was built around 1918, after an early heavy October storm of the previous year almost decimated a herd of cattle then grazing in and above Rockbound Valley. Joe Minghetti, a hired hand on the Blakely Ranch but formerly a Swiss stone mason, was commissioned by the Forest Service to build the trail so that there would be an escape route for the cattle when they had to be quickly evacuated. The trail was not to exceed 15° in grade, but as the hiker soon finds out, in places it does.

The climb from Maude Lake starts out through a sloping meadow, which is boggy for most of the summer, and then goes steeply up slopes abundant with huckleberry oak, western service-berry, and wildflowers. The trail's switchbacks—short and steep—are characteristic of old, pre-recreation standards, when trails were made as steep as the stock would bear. After the last set of switchbacks we reach a small flat with several large junipers growing on and

near it. From this welcome rest spot you can appreciate the progress you've made, and can enjoy views of the nearby head of your canyon, of Maude Lake in the middle distance, forested lands beyond.

Also in sight are three granitic plutons, originally formed several miles below the earth's surface. Long ago each of three light-density molten masses worked its way up through existing rock until it finally cooled to form a solid mass, a pluton. On the wall opposite you, from north to south, the three plutons are rusty orange, dark gray, and light gray, and their respective compositions are granite, diorite-gabbro, and probably granodiorite.

Beyond the junipers you almost stroll up to sometimes windy **Rockbound Pass**, with its weather-beaten, dwarfed mountain hemlocks and lodgepole and whitebark pines. Typically snowbound through late July, the trail from this pass switchbacks northeast down toward Lake Doris, passing both red mountain heather and white heather. Note that not only are their flowers different colors, they are differently shaped, and the former has needle-like leaves while the latter has scale-like ones. Both grow in prime-mosquito areas—something to think about should you ever camp near them. Among hemlocks growing above the lake's north shore is a fair

Fishing at trout-stocked Lake Lois

campsite. After briefly touching the east shore of shallow **Lake Doris**—the turf here sometimes painted yellow with buttercups and marsh marigolds—the trail climbs a few feet, then makes a brief descent to a junction. From here the Rockbound Pass Trail descends 1½ miles east down to Rockbound Valley (see Hike 66).

Our trail, the **Blakely Trail**, descends northwest to immediately cross Lake Doris' outlet creek, then makes a scenic traverse north, offering us panoramas to the east. It passes just above one lakelet and then skirts two ponds on a low, broad saddle, and quickly reaches an east finger of **Lake Lois**. This lake rests in a basin mostly of dark diorite-gabbro bedrock, although its southern part and the lower cliffs above it are varying hues of marine sandstone that was metamorphosed through repeated, compressive forces acting on the area.

Popular Lake Lois and its neighbor one mile to the northwest, Lake Schmidell, both bear the brunt of weekend backpackers. At each you'll find many sites that are within 100 feet of the shore and very few that are more than 100 feet away. Imaginative backpackers can find additional, isolated sites on small, level benches east and north of Lake Lois. This lake's southeast corner, although often only 50°F in mid-August, attracts some who like to do brisk high diving—up to 20+ feet—into its very deep water. Those who just like to swim will find its isolated east finger 10° warmer. The lake is stocked, but given its high usage, don't count on a trout meal.

Paralleling the east finger, the rocky trail winds over to the outlet creek, crosses its low dam, heads briefly west along the north shore, and then climbs north ⅓ mile to a ridge, where it meets the **Red Peak Stock Trail** (Driveway). This trail, not used by cattle since 1987, climbs 1¼ miles to a high, but shallow, gap on the Crystal Range crest. It then descends about 2¾ miles, making a dangerously steep drop lower down as it approaches the Barrett Lake (Jeep) Trail (Hike 63). The former stock driveway is a longer and scenic route back to Wrights Lake that is best left to competent hikers who can navigate where stretches of trail tread are absent.

From the stock-trail junction we make a fairly steep descent northwest through an open forest, almost touching a small creek before reaching a junction with the **McConnell Lake Trail**, just above unseen **Lake Schmidell**. To reach its campsites you could hike northeast 200 yards down a trail to a pond, then 250 yards northwest up another trail to the lake's dammed outlet. A good campsite lies just north, above the lake's northeast shore. An easier way to reach the lake and it's more popular campsites, which are perched on a mountain-hemlock-and-lodgepole-shaded bench above the southeast shore, is to walk due north 100 yards from the junction. This shore has bedrock slabs that are good for diving into the relatively water, for basking on, or for admiring the local scenery.

⋖≓⋗ 65 ⋖≓⋗
Wrights Lake to Horseshoe Lake, Lake Zitella, and Highland Lake

Distances:
8.4 miles to McConnell Lake Trail
9.8 miles to lower Leland Lake
10.6 miles to McConnell Lake
10.8 miles to Camper Flat
11.8 miles to Horseshoe Lake and Highland Lake Trail
12.0 miles to 4-Q Lakes (via Camper Flat)
12.3 miles to Lake Zitella
13.5 miles to Highland Lake
13.9 miles to 4-Q Lakes (via McConnell Lake)

Low/High Elevations: 6980'/8530'

Season: Late July through early October

Classification: Strenuous

Maps: 33, 30, and 31

Trailhead: None. Start from the McConnell Lake Trail junction above Lake Schmidell.

Introduction

This backpack trip is an extension of the preceding hike, offered to those who are willing to put forth the effort to visit less used lakes in one of the more remote parts of Desolation Wilderness. From Rockbound Pass onward,

Red Peak (right) stands high above Horseshoe Lake

the trip averages about one lake per mile and gives backpackers plenty of opportunities to select a campsite. Those fortunate enough to have the time to visit every lake mentioned in this hike will log almost 30 miles, and should allow at least four days to properly savor the route's many delights.

Description

The previous hike describes the first 8.4 miles to a junction with the **McConnell Lake Trail** above the southeast shore of unseen Lake Schmidell. This junction is the start of a 9.6-mile loop that, clockwise, visits lower Leland Lake, McConnell Lake, Horseshoe Lake and its Highland Lake Trail junction, 4-Q Lakes, Camper Flat, and Lake Schmidell. The first part of this loop, along the McConnell Lake Trail, reaches the Highland Lake Trail junction in only 3½ miles. This part is the shorter, and the more scenic and popular, way to the junction, and so will be described first.

The McConnell Lake Trail leaves the junction above Lake Schmidell and first traverses southwest to a cascading creek. You boulder-hop it, then make a scenic though taxing ascent to a shallow saddle on the granodiorite ridge above Lake Schmidell's talus slopes. The Leland Lakes quickly come into view as we make an equally steep descent north

toward the upper lake. Avoiding this lake's grassy east shore, our trail swings northeast a bit, dips through a boggy meadow, and then descends to the southeast corner of **lower Leland Lake.** Since its lakeshore campsites are off limits, you might look for a site on land between the two Leland Lakes. Camping here is definitely inferior to that at Lakes Schmidell and Lois.

Leaving the lower lake, we descend alongside its pleasing outlet creek, cross it in a forested flat, and continue briefly northwest to the forest's edge. Watching for ducks—both the rock kind and in late season the live ones—we follow a path that arcs around the west shore of a marshy pond, **McConnell Lake.** Most campers will avoid it, so the few that linger in the environs are likely to have solitude. Leaving its soggy meadow of grass and heather behind, we reach a low ridge, head through a few yards of brush, and then descend an open slope northwest to the base of an imposing granodiorite wall, which would provide challenging ascents to any climber willing to haul in ropes and gear.

A prominent low-angle waterfall glides down the middle of this wall, and just after crossing its creek on level ground, one can sometimes encounter route-finding problems. If you do, look for ducks that mark the route

see MAP 26

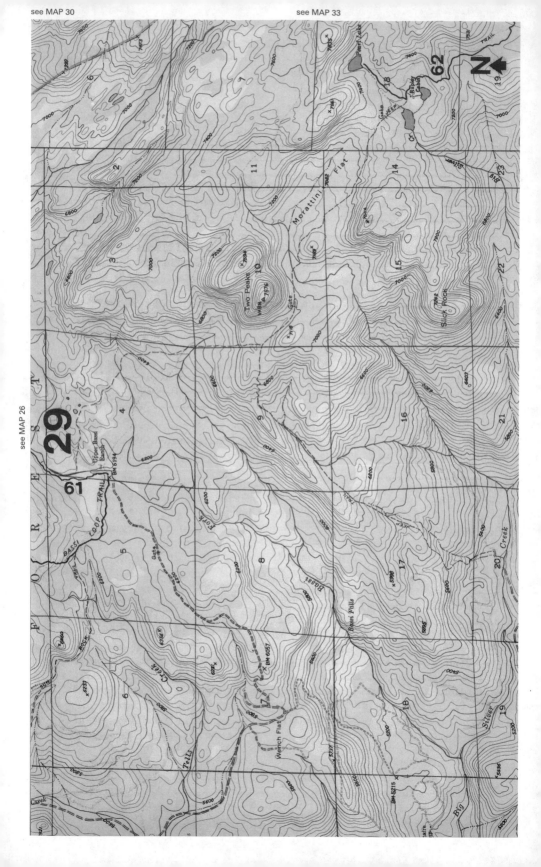

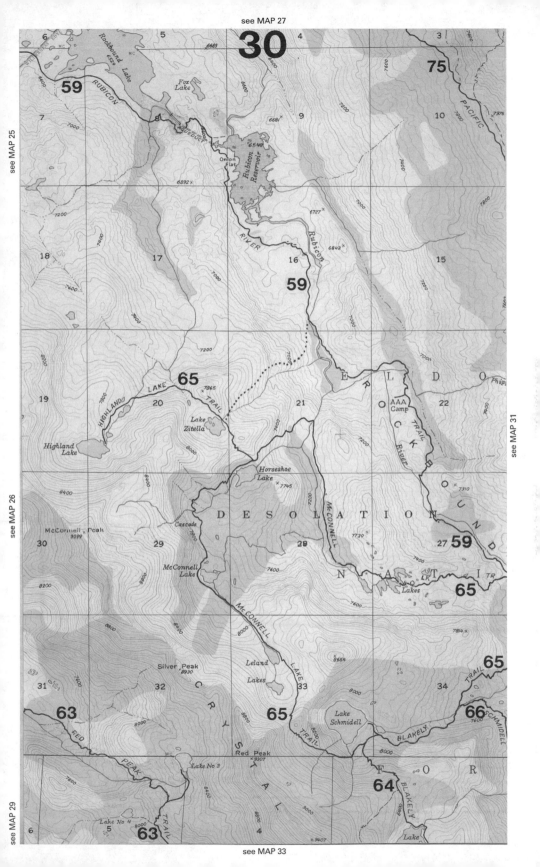

30

75

59

see MAP 25

see MAP 31

see MAP 26

see MAP 29

6
5
4
3

Rockbound Lake
Fox Lake
RUBICON
AQUEDUCT
7
8
9
6681 x
Onion Flat
6548
Rubicon Reservoir
10
PACIFIC

59
6892 x
RIVER
Rubicon
6727 x
6842 x
16
15

59

E L D O

R O C K

7865
HIGHLAND LAKE TRAIL
Lake Zitella
21
AAA Camp
River
22

19
20
Highland Lake

Horseshoe Lake
7745
B O U N D

D E S O L A T I O N
McConnell
7739
7310

McConnell Peak
9099
Cascade
McConnell Lake
29
29
27
59
N A T I
LK
Lakes
65

30
8554
Silver Peak
8930
Leland Lakes
McConnell LAKE TRAIL
33
34
TRAIL
65

31
32
Lake Schmidell
66
SCHMIDELL

63
RED
CRYSTAL
65
BLAKELY
8000

PEAK
Red Peak
9307
TRAIL
64
BLAKELY
F O R

Lake No 3
7600

6
5
Lake No 4
8000
4
9407
Lake

63

31

76

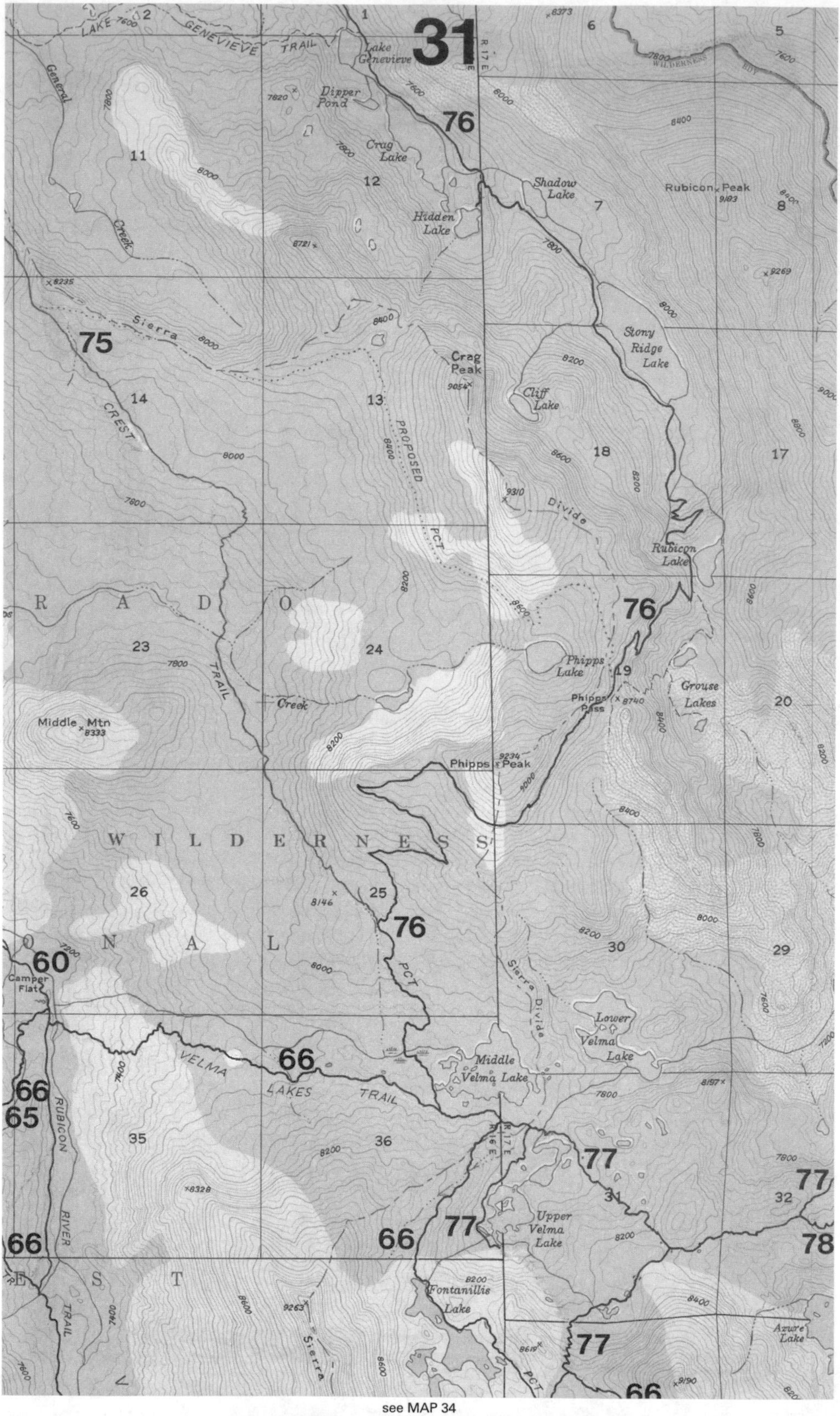

see MAP 30

see MAP 32

LAKE GENEVIEVE TRAIL
Lake Genevieve
Dipper Pond
7820
Crag Lake
Hidden Lake
8721
General Creek
11
12
6373
6
5
WILDERNESS
Shadow Lake
7
Rubicon Peak 9183
8
9269

75
Sierra
CREST
14
13
Crag Peak 9054
PROPOSED
PCT
Cliff Lake
Stony Ridge Lake
8200
18
17
9310
Divide
Rubicon Lake

R A D O
23
24
Creek
Middle Mtn 8333
76
Phipps Lake
Phipps Pass 8740
Grouse Lakes
20
Phipps Peak 9234
19

W I L D E R N E S S
26
8146
25
76
30
29
8200
8000

O N A L
60
Camper Flat
Sierra Divide
Lower Velma Lake
8157

66
65
VELMA LAKES TRAIL
66
35
36
8328
Middle Velma Lake
77
31
77
32
77
78

66
RUBICON RIVER TRAIL
77
Upper Velma Lake
8200
Fontanillis Lake
9263
66
77
Azure Lake
8619
9190

see MAP 31

see map 36

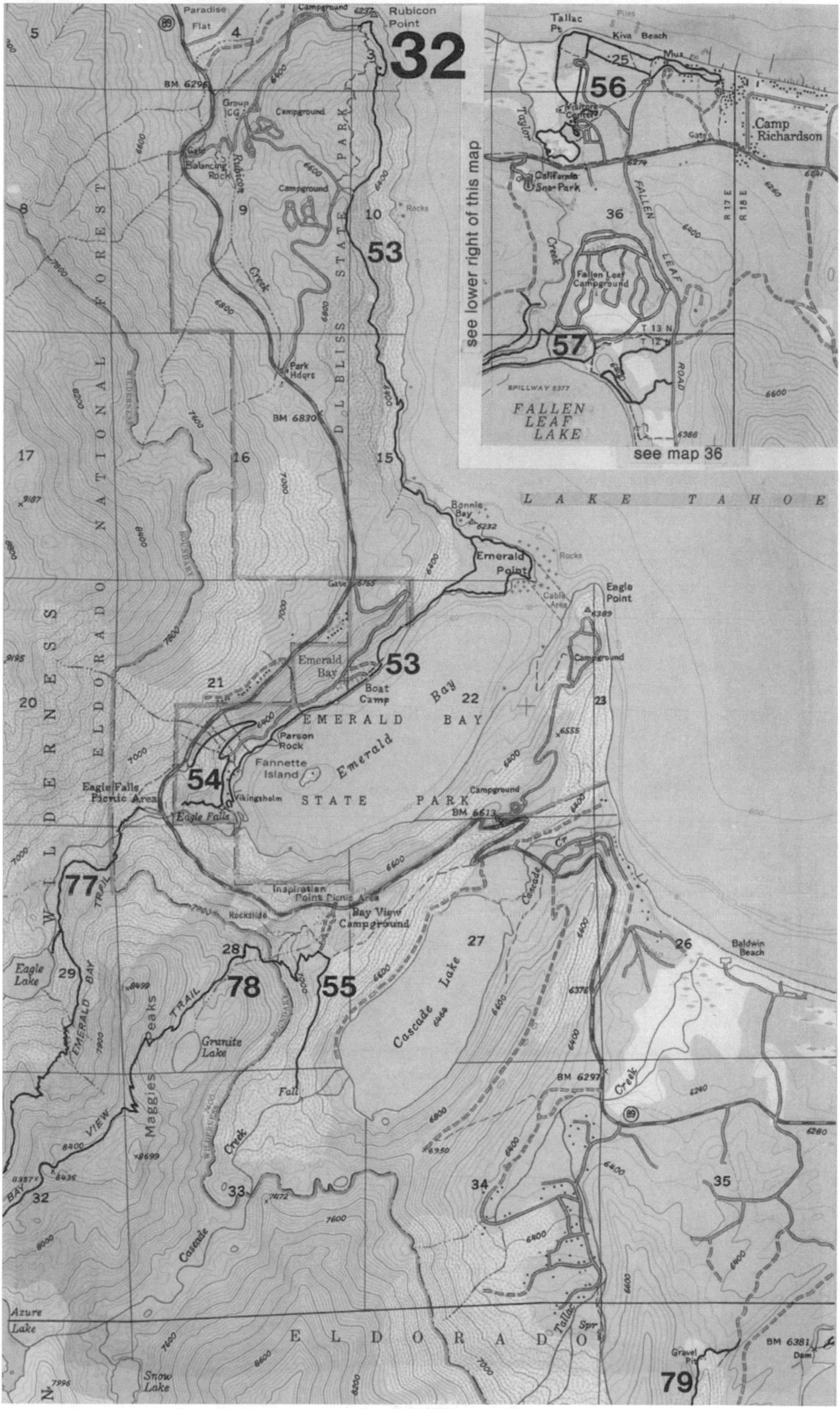

see lower right of this map

see inset above

up and down a low slab. Then just beyond it, where the trail climbs over another low slab to a gully with a trickling creek, contour east 100 yards, descend slightly to another short traverse, this one northeast, then top a low, rocky ridge. Several short switchbacks lead down to an alluvial flat on which lies shallow **Horseshoe Lake**, speckled with rock islands. Although you may not find a legal campsite along the lake, you can find many legal ones on the small flats of the low ridge southeast of the lake. Being quite open, the ridge provides campers with very scenic, panoramic views.

Just above the northeast corner of Horseshoe Lake is a junction with the **Highland Lake Trail**. Before describing it, this guidebook now will describe the long, counterclockwise way to this junction.

This generally viewless route first drops 200 yards to the pond below Lake Schmidell's outlet creek, staying on the Blakely Trail as it makes an eastward, heather-lined descent— muddy and mosquito-ridden usually through mid-August—to a crossing of the outlet creek. Immediately beyond this it reaches a lateral, the Schmidell Trail, for those traveling to upper Rockbound Valley, Mosquito Pass, and Lake Aloha. Beyond this junction you make

an equally long, but drier, descent to a second crossing, then in ⅓ mile reach a junction on a bench above the Rubicon River. One hundred yards south of this junction a trail fords the Rubicon and then climbs east to Middle Velma Lake and over to Lake Tahoe's Highway 89 (Hikes 66, 77 and 78).

Start north along the Rubicon and in 70 yards reach a spur trail west to a cold, rusty, seeping mineral spring. After a few minutes' winding walk north, you reach broad, level **Camper Flat**, where beside a good, if brisk, Rubicon swimming hole is a campsite. Bearing westward through a lush meadow, you reach your last crossing of Lake Schmidell's outlet creek. If necessary, look for a log to cross it and then reach in 70 yards, near open slabs lining the Rubicon, the McConnell Lake Trail. This west-climbing trail skirts several stagnant ponds before reaching the first small lake of the relatively warm **4-Q Lakes**, this one about 40 yards northwest of the trail (an orphaned 4-Q Lake lies south of the trail, just on the other side of a short, low, broad ridge.) Just ¼ mile beyond it is the second 4-Q lake, across which you must "walk on water." Two peninsulas almost cut the lake in half, and you cross the shallow, 40-foot strait via rocks and/or logs.

Vegetation grows along linear master joints above Rockbound Valley

Lake Zitella and its low-angle cliff

Beyond the lake crossing the trail curves over to the west shore of this lake, touches upon the north shore of adjacent lake number three, and then makes a brief climb to a stagnant, bush-fringed pond, where you often do have to walk on the water to follow the trail. Most hikers keep their feet dry by going around and above the pond's edge and then rejoining the trail, which climbs a few paces before descending southwest to the fourth lake, subjectively the best. In the fairly open forest in the 4-Q Lakes area, there are plenty of small bedrock benches ideal for an isolated camp.

From the north end of the fourth lake the ducked route goes along the lake's outlet-creek gully, first descending moderately northwest through red-fir stands, then it eases its grade and descends north through alternating lodgepole-pine stands and huckleberry-oak scrub. Nearing the end of this 1.4-mile descent, we find ourselves often walking along glaciated granodiorite slabs. Watch carefully for ducks. Our trail crosses the creek just 20 yards above a narrow chute you can jump across. In this vicinity you can find rocky campsites whose hardness is more than compensated for by their isolation and by the nearby views north down the Rubicon River's canyon, Rockbound Valley.

Now climbing west, you watch for ducks to minimize your effort. The often faint trail climbs steeply up a slope, staying about 100-200 yards north of Horseshoe Lake's outlet creek. The route reaches a ridge above that lake, and leaving views behind, you follow ducks for about 50 yards west down to the **Highland Lake Trail** junction, mentioned earlier.

To visit Lake Zitella and Highland Lake, take this trail, which climbs steeply up a gully. Above it you diagonal left up more-open slabs, from which you have a backward glance at photogenic Horseshoe Lake and its dramatic backdrop, the spine of the Crystal Range. Notice how the trees on the granitic slopes beyond the lake are concentrated along *master joints*, which are major fracture lines in this otherwise very resistant rock. Our 200-foot ascent tops out at a saddle, from which the trail ahead to alluring Lake Zitella descends ¼ mile to this shallow lake's outlet creek. Just before crossing it, look northeast across Rockbound Valley. If the master joints above Horseshoe Lake weren't obvious, hopefully the ones on the opposite canyon wall are unmistakably clear.

Relatively shallow, slightly cloudy **Lake Zitella** is one of the warmest cirque lakes in the wilderness, its temperature rising into the low 70s. It is an excellent swimming hole, with plenty of shoreline slabs and rock islands to bask on. In the shallow water, yellow-legged frogs, unlike trout, are sometimes abundant. Several campsites exist above the west half of the lake. Above the lake is a low-angle cliff that provides easy routes for rock climbers.

Those seeking isolation can now begin an arduous route to Highland Lake. The northwest-bound trail climbing from Lake Zitella's north shore is simple enough, but from the saddle above it, the trail makes an extremely steep descent—almost an uncontrolled slide at times—down a gully. Despite its steepness, it is not very exposed and not very dangerous. This steep route exists because a cliff prevents a traverse west. At the base of the cliff the route turns west and begins to climb. At this point one views an obvious, open, cross-country route, spread out below, descending to either Rockbound Lake or Rubicon Reservoir (Hike 59).

Hiking toward Highland Lake, watch for ducks that mark the open rock-slab ascent to a crossing of Highland Lake creek at the lip of a cirque, then traverse 150 yards southwest to the northeast shore of a rockbound lakelet. From it the trail makes a winding, ducked ascent in the same direction up to a ridge that is just north of a tiny, photogenic lakelet, whose waters are aerated by several cascades splashing into it. After a momentary descent, we make a short, steep ascent to a shelf, which we follow briefly south to icy, trout-stocked **Highland Lake**. Being the wilderness' most remote lake by trail, it has the *potential* for solitude. But being rockbound, its has only small campsites that are best avoided. Look for better ones on the broad, openly forested ridge just north of the lake, or on the spacious, open, bedrock bench below and north of it.

<&> **66** <&>
Wrights Lake to Lake Aloha and Velma Lakes

Distances:
6.4 miles to Blakely Trail
8.6 miles to Lake Schmidell
9.6 miles to Schmidell Trail
10.6 miles to Rubicon River Trail
11.7 miles to Rockbound Pass Trail
12.1 miles to China Flat Public Camp
14.8 miles to Clyde Lake spur trail
   0.3 mile on spur trail to Clyde Lake
15.4 miles to Mosquito Pass
16.4 miles to Pacific Crest Trail at Lake Aloha
17.1 miles to Heather Lake
18.2 miles to Susie Lake
18.8 miles to lateral trail to Glen Alpine Trail
19.3 miles to Glen Alpine Trail
19.9 miles to Trail 17E09
   0.2 mile on trail to Gilmore Lake
22.2 miles to Dicks Pass
23.9 miles to saddle north of Dicks Lake
24.1 miles to Dicks Lake spur trail
   0.1 mile on spur trail to Dicks Lake
26.0 miles to Velma Lakes Trail
26.3 miles to junction above southwest
   Middle Velma Lake
28.6 miles to Blakely Trail
29.8 miles to Schmidell Trail
39.4 miles to Rockbound trailhead

Low/High Elevations: 6980'/9380'

Season: Late July through early October

Classification: Strenuous

Maps: 33, 30, 31, 34, and 35

Trailhead: See the Hike 62 trailhead.

Introduction

This lengthy hike explores the heart of Desolation Wilderness. In the process of traversing the Sierra Nevada highlands, you'll cross three mountain passes, each usually snowy through late July (sometimes longer), and will visit a dozen lakes, of which only Clyde Lake is not heavily used. To avoid possible crowds at the other lakes, start your hike on Monday and end it on Friday. You'll log about 39½ miles for the complete semiloop trip; about 40½ miles total with side trips to Clyde, Gilmore, and Dicks lakes.

Description

As in Hike 64, climb to Rockbound Pass, then descend briefly to Lake Doris and its nearby junction with the **Blakely Trail**. Here, if you continue down the Rockbound Pass Trail to Rockbound Valley (which is 7.9 miles from your trailhead), you'll shave about 3.8 miles off the described route. To maximize your exposure to lakes, our hike, which begins with the last part of Hike 64, follows the Blakely Trail past Lake Lois, over a ridge, then down to a junction with the McConnell Lake Trail, from which you head over to nearby **Lake Schmidell**. Plan to spend your first and last nights at either lake.

From the junction of the Schmidell Lake spur trail, you then continue down the Blakely Trail, immediately passing a trailside pond. Your trail, likely to be muddy and mosquito-ridden through mid-August, descends eastward to Schmidell's creek, crosses it, and immediately reaches an important junction with the **Schmidell Trail**. Here you'll begin and end a lengthy loop, which is 20¼ miles long if you don't make any side trips.

Branch right onto the Schmidell Trail, which immediately recrosses the creek, winds downstream, and then climbs ¼ mile southeast to a minor ridge. From it a former, unnecessary trail once veered left to descend to the floor of 8-mile-long Rockbound Valley. We

continue ahead, ½ mile south down to the floor and reach the **Rubicon River Trail**. North, it descends 1.2 miles to a junction with a trail descending 2.2 miles west from Middle Velma Lake, which we'll take later on. Note that the 1.2-mile stretch along the Rubicon River Trail offers some isolated camping for those willing to leave the trail and scout for sites near the river's bank.

Our hike, however, heads south, up-valley, and we first cross several branches of the Lake Lois outlet creek. Then we meander onward, and after many twists and turns we cross the Lake Doris outlet creek. Only ¼ mile farther we join company with those descending the shortcut route, the **Rockbound Pass Trail**. In about 300 yards our southbound trek presents us with the first of three Rubicon River crossings, this one up to 15 yards wide. Before late season, when the flow is much diminished, you will have to ford the stream if a downed log is unavailable. Ahead, you go almost ¼ mile to where you can see, just off to your right, **China Flat Public Camp**. It is beside "Lake Rubicon," a long, broad stretch of river that stays wide (and deep enough for swimming) even in late season. It owes its origin to a resistant bedrock rib across the river, forming a natural dam. This site is an ideal base camp for anglers, and also is the logical first-night camp for those who have taken the shortcut route.

Many islanded Lake Aloha, from trail above its north shore

Onward over the next ¼ mile we start south, head southwest through a meadow, China Flat proper, and reach the Rubicon's lodgepole-lined east bank. In this vicinity are additional camping possibilities. The river here is wide, and as before, will be a wet ford if a downed log is unavailable. Along the west bank you ascend gently south, crossing many creeks as you parallel the Rubicon, which is largely unseen due to the thick, lush vegetation. Hidden campsites as well as hidden fishing holes await those willing to search for them. One mile from the second Rubicon ford, we come to the third, where the river is up to 7 yards wide. To keep your feet dry, go a few yards downstream and cross a narrower stretch via large boulders. By the east bank you'll find the last good campsite until the north shore of Lake Aloha.

You now climb south through an open forest of red fir, mountain hemlock, western white pine, and lodgepole pine, reaching, in just under a mile, a spur trail. This strikes 100 yards east to swampy Jacks Meadow, which hosts willows, heather, and mosquitoes. One-third mile farther, we hit another **spur trail**, this one descending ¼ mile down a large-block talus slope to **Clyde Lake**. Although lower and smaller than upcoming Lake Aloha, this cirque lake is much colder, usually reflecting a snowfield across its protected waters until well into August. the steep walls above three of its sides perpetuate a sense of chill in this glacier-carved head of Rockbound Valley. In addition to the steep trail and the bleak environment, a lack of good campsites is another argument for not visiting the lake. It does, however, have some positive features: it is isolated and it is stocked with golden and brook trout.

From a seasonal creek by the start of the Clyde Lake spur trail the Rubicon River Trail climbs out of forest cover and up past seeps with ferns, columbines, larkspurs, monk's hoods, and corn lilies. With unrestricted views north down Rockbound Valley we head up the rock-blasted trail to broad **Mosquito Pass**, just over ½ mile beyond the spur trail. On the far side of the pass we make a short switchbacking descent through a sparse stand of mountain hemlocks, entering expansive,

glacier-resistant Desolation Valley, whose flat floor is now occupied by Lake Aloha. This shallow lake, created to supply hydroelectric power to the people of Sacramento, is easily the largest lake in Desolation Wilderness—at least before late summer. After Labor Day it can shrink appreciably, to only a fraction of its maximum size.

From where the switchbacks end we quickly come to a long, grassy flat, which has suitable campsites. About 7½ miles from Lake Schmidell this flat makes a scenic second night's stop. After a ½-mile traverse east along Lake Aloha's picturesque north shore (before September, that is!), you reach the lake's north tip, and meet the very popular **Pacific Crest Trail**. We'll hike north about 10 miles along it, and for this entire stretch the PCT coincides with the unofficial Tahoe-Yosemite Trail, or TYT, the two splitting into separate routes about a mile north of Middle Velma Lake. It also coincides with the official Tahoe Rim Trail north to Twin Peaks (Hikes 50 and 51). All the lakes along this stretch are heavily impacted by too many campers using illegal, shoreline sites. Along Hike 66 you will probably camp at one of these lakes, and if so, please look for sites at least 100 feet away from its shore.

From the northeast corner of Lake Aloha, which has a 2-foot-high retaining wall to prevent it from spilling over the actual Sierra Nevada crest into Heather Lake, our PCT descends east, giving us views of the Freel Peak massif, lording it over Lake Tahoe's southeast shore. A switchback takes us to a delicate 20-foot-high waterfall just above the northwest shore of deep **Heather Lake**, ¾ mile below Lake Aloha. Near a large red fir and the fall's creek is an adequate campsite. Our trail leaves Heather Lake at its low dam, climbs a low, barren ridge, and descends to a cove on the southwest shore of heather-ringed Susie Lake, which is also ringed with illegally close campsites. Should you want to camp at this heavily impacted lake, you might consider looking for a site on the open bedrock lands just southwest of the lake. There also are good, but overused campsites on a small bench 70 yards down its outlet creek.

On the PCT we cross the outlet creek of **Susie Lake**, follow the rocky tread over a low

Dicks Lake, from saddle near Dicks Pass

ridge, pass two stagnant ponds, and descend to a flowery, swampy meadow, which has a **lateral trail to the Glen Alpine Trail**. It is part of Hike 83, which along with the Glen Alpine Trail proper are the quickest ways in to our hike's 20-mile loop. Other reasonably short routes to it begin at Echo Lake (Hike 87), Bay View Campground (Hike 78), and Emerald Bay (Hike 77).

The PCT, now all uphill 3.4 miles to Dicks Pass, first switchbacks ½ mile northeast up to a junction with the southeast-descending **Glen Alpine Trail**. Northwest, trail tread goes to Half Moon and Alta Morris lakes (Hike 82), nestled on a broad basin floor that offers relatively isolated camping. Beyond this intersection the PCT switchbacks up past junipers to a junction with Trail 17E09, which ascends ¼ mile to good campsites above the south and east shores of orbicular Gilmore Lake. This lateral (Hike 81) then continues 1¾ miles up to Mt. Tallac's summit, which gives you perhaps the best view of Lake Tahoe you'll ever see.

As we start west up toward Dicks Pass, we get a peek through the lodgepole forest at Gilmore Lake, and then we ascend steadily northwest, climbing high above the pale-brown metavolcanic-rock basin that holds Half Moon and Alta Morris lakes. Lake Aloha plus Susie and Heather lakes also appear. Lodgepoles, mountain hemlocks, and western white pines are soon joined by whitebark pines, the harbinger of treeline, as we

approach a saddle east of Dicks Peak. From it a fairly popular use trail heads up a ridge to the rusty peak's summit.

Rather than descend north from the saddle, our trail climbs ¼ mile east up alongside the ridgecrest in order to bypass the steep slopes and long-lasting snowfields that lie north of the saddle. Our trail reaches **Dicks Pass**, an almost level area with clusters of dwarfed, wind-trimmed conifers. Here at 9380 feet, we are on the highest trail pass in Desolation Wilderness, and we get far-ranging views both north and south.

Ducks guide us across Dicks Pass, the boundary between metamorphic rocks to the south and granitic rocks to the north, and then we descend on hemlock-lined switchbacks, rich in thick gravel from the deeply weathered bedrock. After descending northwest 1.7 miles beyond the pass, we reach a trail junction on a **saddle north of Dicks Lake**. Hike 78, from Highway 89's Bay View Campground, climbs up to meet us here. We descend south 0.2 mile to a **spur trail**, on which one can descend 100 yards to **Dicks Lake** and head over to popular campsites along its north shore and east peninsula.

From the spur-trail junction we follow the PCT northwest down to a large tarn with a good campsite. Soon we descend a gully to a small cove on Fontanillis Lake's east shore and parallel this shore northwest to the outlet creek. Legal, enjoyable campsites are absent beside this lake, although by making a nominal effort, one can start at either its south or north end and head over to sites on open benches above the lake's long west shore. We leave this rockbound lake at its outlet creek, and over the next 1.0 mile we first traverse north to a shady ridge, and then descend part way along its crest. We then curve left, jump a creek and descend another ridge to a junction with the **Velma Lakes Trail** just above the south shore of Middle Velma Lake. Hike 77, from a trailhead on Highway 89 above Lake Tahoe's Emerald Bay, joins us here. Only 70 yards northwest on this trail, which coincides with the PCT, we get a good view of Middle Velma Lake, and here you may want to descend to campsites near the lake's shore, which are about the best you'll find north of Gilmore Lake. On weekends this lakeshore is crowded, since it is readily accessible from Emerald Bay. You can swim out to and drive from the lake's rock-slab islands, which are also good for sunbathing. The other shores are less visited.

Westward, we traverse briefly on the Velma Lakes Trail, which does quadruple duty, also being the routes of the PCT, TRT, and TYT. Then only 35 yards beyond a creeklet we reach a **junction above the southwest corner of Middle Velma Lake**, where we leave the PCT/TRT/TYT. Continuing on the Velma Lakes Trail, we head west through a dense forest, which thins as we lose altitude. After about 1½ miles, where the trail jogs from northwest to southwest, we find a short spur trail, which departs north to a placid pool at the base of a rock slab. We next make an open descent southwest, with views up and down glacier-scoured Rockbound Valley, cross an alder-bordered creeklet in ¼ mile, then conclude our descent in thickening forest cover, reaching the broad Rubicon River in ½ mile. You can find isolated camping by heading briefly cross-country up-canyon on barren, glacier-scoured slabs. Where the trail crosses the Rubicon, you may face a substantial wade before late July. Above its west bank you meet the Rubicon River Trail, and no camping is allowed on the stretch 100 yards south from this junction. You walk north on the trail to the **Blakely Trail**, located near the

south margin of Camper Flat. No camping is allowed on this 100-yard-long stretch between the two trail junctions. To complete Hike 66, first make a winding, shady 1.2-mile ascent to the **Schmidell Trail**, where you complete your 20-mile loop. Then retrace your footsteps for a mile up to Lake Schmidell for possibly your last night's stay in the wilderness, and retrace your first 8.6 miles out to the **Rockbound trailhead**.

⋙ 67 ⋘
Wrights Lake to Gertrude and Tyler Lakes

Distances:
2.3 miles to Tyler Lake Trail
3.8 miles to Gertrude Lake
3.9 miles to Tyler Lake
Low/High Elevations: 6980′/8220′
Season: Mid-July through mid-October
Classification: Moderate
Map: 33
Trailhead: See the Hike 62 trailhead.

Introduction
Two photogenic subalpine lakes climax this moderate hike. Despite their somewhat easy accessibility, they remain relatively unvisited, perhaps because hikers prefer lower, closer lakes or else backpack into the lakes beyond Rockbound Pass. If you are in good shape, lower your environmental impact by making this route a day hike. You can cut your distances by 0.5 mile if you start from the Twin Lakes trailhead on an alternate route described early in Hike 64.

Description
The first 2.3 miles coincide with the first part of the Rockbound Pass Trail (Hike 64) to a junction in a small, shady flat. From here we follow the **Tyler Lake Trail** to its end at, surprisingly, Gertrude Lake. Climbing east above the flat, we quickly enter Desolation Wilderness as we follow this ducked trail up slabs and a gully to a viewpoint, from where we can trace the outlet streams of Umpa and Twin Lakes flowing—sometimes cascading—

Gertrude Lake

over open, glaciated slabs on their way down to Wrights Lake. Our trail drops briefly to a flat, then climbs north steeply up a brush-lined gully to a forested, shallow saddle on a ridge. Beyond it the trail parallels an ephemeral creeklet and then climbs steeply north above it, becoming faint before reaching another ridge. From a shallow saddle, it enters a hemlock forest, with an ankle-deep pond, then makes a fluctuating traverse northeast. Blazes and ducks guide our route across snow-fed creeklets, and then we make a steep, bouldery ascent to a short spur trail, which descends a willow-choked gully 125 yards to Tyler's grave. A local ranch hand, he froze to death in a November 1882 snowstorm while trying to round up cattle. Along a 0.2-mile ascent bisected by Tyler Lake's creek, our trail becomes faint before reaching **Gertrude Lake**. Short on campsites but long on scenery, this shallow lake has a photogenic balance of shoreline slabs and spaced conifers.

To reach our trail's namesake, backtrack to its creek and parallel it up open slabs to **Tyler Lake**. Only a few scattered pines and hemlocks provide shade at this slab-happy lake,

which lies in an alpine setting. Exposed but legal campsites lie above its rocky east shore.

⪗ 68 ⪘
Wrights Lake to Twin and Island Lakes

Distances:
0.4 mile to Twin Lakes Trail
1.4 miles to Grouse Lake Trail
2.7 miles to Lower Twin Lake
3.1 miles to Upper Twin and Boomerang lakes
3.3 miles to Island Lake

Low/High Elevations: 6950'/8150'

Season: Mid-July through mid-October

Classification: Moderate

Map: 33

Trailhead: See the Hike 62 trailhead.

Introduction

Because these attractive lakes lie so close to Wrights Lake, they receive heavy use. Therefore, to minimize your impact at these lakes, please make day hikes to them rather than camp overnight at them, for they aren't that hard to hike to. Although the lakes are close together, each has its own special attributes.

Description

Three trails leave from the road's end by the east arm of Wrights Lake. One begins west along the arm and eventually bifurcates, one branch going to an amphitheater and to the southeastern Wrights Lake Campground, the other going to the lake's dam. Another trail crosses a prominent bridge over the lake's inlet creek. From the bridge's far side, one branch strikes west along the lake's north shore while another goes first northwest then north to a road from which the *old* Rockbound Pass Trail still begins an ascent. The third branch—yours—meanders northeastward, keeping just within forest cover to avoid a swampy meadow just to the west. After 0.4 mile of easy walking, you reach a junction with the **Twin Lakes Trail**. This starts northwest around the base of sloping bedrock, then quickly tacks to start a winding course west

over to the road that gives rise to the old Rockbound Pass Trail.

From the junction we take the Twin Lakes Trail for a climb quite steadily northeast, often being within hearing distance of Grouse Lake's outlet creek. After a mile of climbing, you reach a junction with the **Grouse Lake Trail**, which is described in the next hike.

Keeping on the Twin Lakes Trail, we branch left (north) and immediately cross Grouse Lake's seasonal outlet creek. We next climb north up quite open glacier-polished slabs, then bend northeast for a curving ascent moderately up additional slabs. Soon the trail vaults north over a minor ridge, then traverses northeast before climbing east along Twin Lakes' outlet creek. From a boggy area crossed on large-block stepping stones, we make a short climb northeast to **Lower Twin Lake**, whose outlet creek the trail crosses about 40 yards below a waist-high dam. You may find it more convenient to cross immediately below the dam. Before you cross, however, you might want to stop at the lake's south shore and rest a while or swim and dive from rocks along this fairly deep shore. Anglers

Lower Twin Lake

Boomerang Lake

will find the lake stocked with brook and rainbow trout. Rainbow were first introduced in 1904 by Joe Minghetti, a local hand, who eventually stocked most of the lakes in the Wrights Lake Recreation Area. Today many of these lakes receive yearly plantings.

From the dam the trail parallels the lake's west shore to a gully at its northwest corner, from where you could climb west to a low nearby ridge for views and then descend to compact Umpa Lake. But with Boomerang Lake in mind, we stick to the Twin Lakes Trail, which is now faint and rocky. It climbs northeast from the gully, passes through a 10-foot-deep notch, then reaches **Boomerang Lake**, on whose north shore of the southeast arm one can dive from 12-foot ledges into the lake's often cold, deep water. By descending southeast cross-country, you can quickly reach the north shore of **Upper Twin Lake**, which is merely 2 feet higher than its sibling. Glacier-polished, gently sloping slabs separate the twins, and in this vicinity lie fair campsites.

After passing between Boomerang Lake and its eastern satellite, the Twin Lakes Trail climbs above the northern tip of a small, linear lake, fed by a seasonal snowfield and by two longer-lasting, narrow cascades from Island Lake. In a brief climb we reach **Island Lake**, a fairly large, rock-island lake whose shores are nearly devoid of trees. Although tall, dark-gray diorite-gabbro cirque walls lend a stark beauty to this subalpine lake, it is not as popular as the Twin Lakes, with their border of sparse trees. At Island Lake you may find more gulls or ducks than backpackers. From this lake accomplished mountaineers can strike northwest over a saddle and descend to Tyler and Gertrude lakes (Hike 67), or strike southeast for a more arduous ascent of Mt. Price, which at 9975 feet is only 8 feet lower than the wilderness' highest, Pyramid Peak.

⊰≳ 69 ⊰≳
Wrights Lake to Grouse, Hemlock, and Smith Lakes

Distances:
2.1 miles to Grouse Lake
2.6 miles to Hemlock Lake
3.0 miles to Smith Lake
Low/High Elevations: 6950'/8700'
Season: Mid-July through mid-October
Classification: Strenuous
Map: 33
Trailhead: See the Hike 62 trailhead.

Introduction
Three subalpine lakes, each with its own special qualities, are the highlights of this trip. From Smith Lake, the highest of the three, you have one of the best views of the Wrights Lake and Crystal Basin recreation areas. Camping is quite poor at all three lakes, so plan to do this route as a day hike.

Description
Follow the previous hike 1.4 miles to a junction with the Grouse Lake Trail, which in former days was named the Hemlock Lake Trail. In about 100 yards this northeast-climbing trail enters Desolation Wilderness, following a ducked route up granitic slabs into an open forest and to a gravelly flat. The trail turns southeast and then starts to climb more gradually, but soon it becomes steep, and after a brief traverse to cross a creek, it continues steeply but briefly up to a moraine at the outlet of **Grouse Lake**. This lake, fringed with rocks, meadow, red mountain heather, and Labrador tea, is a very pleasant lake to linger, particularly after the rather arduous climb. Its shallow, clear water invites a swim. Nearby campsites, on sloping ground above its northeast shore, should be avoided; better sites exist above the far shore, and you can reach them with a use trail that circles the lake. Be forewarned that before early August this locality teems with mosquitoes.

From the far shore, past hikers have taken an easy cross-country route southward up to a low point on the ridge above the lake, perhaps to discover what is the secret of Secret Lake. It is unique, but not in a pleasing way, for it is entirely circled by *superabundant* large, granitic blocks (of interest to geologists), negating the possibility of camping. Indeed, circling this small lake is a very arduous task. Additionally, the lake leaks, its water apparently seeping through a moraine dam, causing it to drop considerably over the summer. As such, it is unsuitable for trout, and it is one of the wilderness' few named lakes that is not stocked.

From Grouse lake we have a steep climb north up a low ridge with glacial deposits plus a longer ascent northeast up a rocky slope to tiny **Hemlock Lake**. This is named for the mountain hemlocks that border its south shore. Its small size is compensated for by a dramatic exfoliating cliff above its north shore. You can find a campsite or two near the lake, but they are not desirable.

From this lake you can make a cross-country hike over to the Twin Lakes vicinity. From the north shore, you start a traverse briefly west, then traverse northwest just above an alder-lined creeklet. (If you go too low, you have to fight your way through the alders.) Onward, you head northwest, dropping as you traverse slopes over to a nearby, descending ridge. Walk west down it until you feel comfortable with descending north on slabs and slopes to the Twin Lakes Trail.

From Hemlock Lake its namesake trail climbs moderately, but shortly southeast, then just above a forested flat starts a steep climb of short switchbacks. Large blocks abound, and on many you can sit and enjoy the scenery.

Grouse Lake

Soon you reach **Smith Lake**, which at 8700 feet is almost at treeline. Its steep, confining slopes, most having snowfields that last well into the summer, also retard tree growth. Nevertheless, a small stand of lodgepole and western white pines thrives above the lake's northwest shore. From a rocky spot near the lake's outlet we can view the Wrights Lake and Crystal Basin recreation areas and identify Wrights Lake and Dark Lake below us and Union Valley Reservoir in the distance. This is the only lake from which you can get such expansive views of these two areas. No adequate camp site exists at the lake.

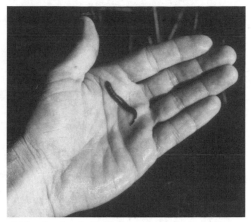

A Bloodsucker Lake leech

⋙ 70 ⋙
Wrights Lake to Bloodsucker Lake

Distances:
0.7 mile to bypass trail
   1.6 miles on trails to Lyons Creek Trail
1.8 miles to Bloodsucker Lake
Low/High Elevations: 6910'/7430'
Season: Mid-July through mid-October
Classification: Moderate
Map: 33
Trailhead: See the Hike 62 trailhead.

Introduction

For those who have seen leeches only in the movies, this hike is an eye-opener. It is also an alternate approach to upper Lyons Creek, Lyons Lake, and Lake Sylvia.

Description

From the Wrights Lake Horse Camp at the south end of the parking loop, begin south on a short trail segment. After 0.1 mile the trail angles left and drops to a nearby boulder hop of Wrights Lake's South Fork Silver Creek. A use trail begins east, soon curving north to head up the creek before dying out just before the Wrights Lake Campground. Hopefully, this trail will be extended to it, providing campers with a direct route to Bloodsucker Lake. At the boulder hop, we take the main trail, which starts down the creek's east bank, then top the crests of two low recessional

moraines before topping the crest of a third. This one has a road heading westward down it. Our route ahead is now a generally closed road, which first traverses 200 yards east to a fourth moraine, this also having a road, which descends south. Deposits such as these moraines allow us to map the former extent of glaciers. From here former glaciers descended several miles southwest to near the east end of Ice House Reservoir.

From the road junction we continue 230 yards east on a gentle ascent to a junction with a **bypass trail**. In almost 0.7 mile it first crosses several streams then climbs to a junction with the Bloodsucker Lake Trail. Northeast, in just under ½ mile this first descends slightly and briefly to a meadow, seasonally rich in wildflowers and mosquitoes, then climbs moderately to the closed road at Bloodsucker Lake. Southeast, the Bloodsucker Lake Trail in almost 0.9 mile first passes in 200 yards a seasonal lakelet, soon crosses a broad ridge, makes a steep ½-mile descent to a boulder-hop of Lyons Creek, and climbs momentarily east through a meadow to a junction with the **Lyons Creek Trail**. This alternate route—the bypass trail and the southeast-heading segment of the Bloodsucker Lake Trail—is only 0.3 mile longer to Lake Sylvia and Lyons Lake than is the principal route (next hike), although it involves about 400 feet of extra elevation gain, each way. Still, if you are staying in the Wrights Lake area and don't want to drive to the Lyons Creek trailhead, this alternate route is worth taking.

At the start of the bypass trail, our road to Bloodsucker Lake curves northeast and starts a moderate climb. In ¼ mile we cross a creek originating at Secret Lake (mentioned in the previous hike), then climb 0.4 mile to a switchback on a ridge, from which one could descend briefly south to Bloodsucker Lake's outlet creek. In about ¼ mile, after ascending the ridge and leveling out, we cross that creek and then momentarily reach a junction with the Bloodsucker Lake Trail. Thirty yards southeast on the road is a campsite, not far from the shore of **Bloodsucker Lake**. This lake is *not* conducive to camping, for the knee-deep lake's water is questionable at best.

Blue Mountain, with the Crystal Range as a backdrop, adds to the scenic beauty of the lake, but its main attractions are the bloodsuckers—yes, leeches—up to 3 inches long. (You may have to stir the water with your hand to find them.) It seems that the only aquatic species that could serve as hosts for these leeches are yellow-legged frogs, of which there are many. In the absence of frogs, however, the leeches could survive on many of the lake's smaller arthropods, for blood is not essential for their subsistence. Just how the leeches got here in the first place is a puzzling question; none of the other shallow lakes in this guide's area seem to have them. Perhaps one or more were carried up to that environment in relatively recent times by some unfortunate or unsuspecting host. Those interested in aquatic invertebrates will find this lake a well-stocked field laboratory.

The shallow notch above Lake Sylvia

⋙ 71 ⋘
Lyons Creek Trail to Lake Sylvia, Lyons Lake, and Pyramid Peak

Distances:
2.0 miles to Bloodsucker Lake Trail
    1.3 miles on trail to Bloodsucker Lake
4.9 miles to Lake Sylvia
5.0 miles to Lyons Lake

Low/High Elevations: 6710'/8380'; 9983' at summit

Season: Mid-July through mid-October

Classification: Moderate to lakes, strenuous to summit.

Maps: 37 (inset at bottom), 33, and 34

Trailhead: See the Hike 62 trailhead.

Introduction
The several meadows along this trail will reward wildflower lovers, while at least three sets of creek pools will please others. However, the main attractions are two subalpine lakes, which by early August can be suitable for swimming. Mountaineers can use either lake as a base camp to ascend three of the wilderness' loftiest summits.

Description
From the parking area we immediately pass a gate and walk almost 0.4 mile along a closed road to its end. From its southeast side the Lyons Creek Trail climbs gently eastward. Where the trail almost touches the creek, a short spur goes over to a set of shallow pools among granitic slabs. We then pass many seasonal tributaries, as well as several meadows, before reaching the site of Lyons at the edge of another meadow, which like the others presents the best wildflowers in July. Just as our trail climbs east to leave this meadow, the **Bloodsucker Lake Trail** cuts west-northwest to Lyons Creek, which is boulder-hopped. This alternate way up to **Bloodsucker Lake** is 3.3 miles long overall, versus 1.8 miles overall for Hike 70, and hence for most is not worth taking.

From the Bloodsucker Lake Trail junction, the Lyons Creek Trail climbs comfortably for

Wildflower Plate 13. Desolation Wilderness flowers.
1 common camas (blue-violet to purple), 2 branched (racemose false) Solomon's seal (white), 3 lesser star tulip (white to pale-violet), 4 Newberry's (alpine) gentian (grayish white), 5 mountain sorrel (brownish red), 6 Jessica's stickseed (blue with white center), 7 one-sided wintergreen (whitish), 8 large-leaved (blue-pod) lupine (violet to blue), 9 Bolander's locoweed (milkvetch) (pale yellow).

1.4 miles to a spot just beyond the Desolation Wilderness border, where you can take a short spur northwest to a second set of slab pools, deeper than those near the trailhead. Then, climbing up open, granitic slopes, you have your first view of Pyramid Peak, and you reach a third set of pools just before crossing lodgepole-lined Lyons Creek. After 200 yards east from the crossing, you reach a junction. The branch east quickly reaches and then traverses a 50-yard-long swath of creeks, which is usually boggy through mid-July, then climbs ¼ mile to shallow, placid, trout-inhabited **Lake Sylvia**. Although this 8050' lake lacks impressive views like those found along the Lyons Creek Trail, it does have some large, good campsites, under a canopy of shady conifers, and in early August a swim can be fairly warm. This locale is a good base camp for a climb up Pyramid Peak, which towers almost 2000 feet above the lake. To reach it, first scramble up to a shallow notch above the lake. This stretch can pose problems due to some loose rocks and, in early season, ice and snow. The rest of the climb is obvious. Summit views, however, are somewhat disappointing since Lake Tahoe is largely hidden from view.

Back at the junction east of Lyons Creek, the left fork climbs north steeply up an open granite slope, affording us views of the often snowbound lower northwest face of Pyramid Peak. The steep ascent ends quickly, and we reach scattered hemlocks near a forebay, which is 3 feet lower than dammed 8380' **Lyons Lake**. Small, minimal campsites lie about the lake; Lake Sylvia's sites definitely are better. (Mountaineers may find it necessary to make a base camp at either lake, but to lessen human impact, most visitors should day hike to them.) Like Lake Sylvia, Lyons Lake is fringed with red mountain heather and Labrador tea. Conifers, however, are much more scarce, and the setting is stark and different from that at Sylvia. For experienced mountaineers Lyons Lake is a good base camp for the twin summits of Mts. Price and Agassiz. Both harbor alpine wildflowers, although mountaineering botanists rarely visit their summits.

⋘ 72 ⋙
Horsetail Falls Trail to Lake of the Woods, Lake Aloha, and Pyramid Peak

Distances:
1.3 miles to base of lower Horsetail Fall
1.8 miles to Avalanche Lake
2.0 miles to Pitt Lake
2.4 miles to Ropi Lake
3.5 miles to Lake of the Woods
4.9 miles to Lake Aloha, southeast corner

Low/High Elevations: 6110'/8120'; 9983' at summit

Season: Mid-July through mid-October

Classification: Strenuous

Maps: 37, 34, and 35

Trailhead: From the Highway 49 junction in Placerville, drive 5 miles east up Highway 50 to the Eldorado National Forest Information Center, get your wilderness permit there, then continue 35 miles up the highway to the settlement of Strawberry. Finally, drive an additional 1 ⅔ miles to Twin Bridges, with a store and post office. About 200 yards past it you bridge Pyramid Creek and immediately find parking for about two dozen vehicles. (Westbound drivers: this parking area is 6¾ miles west from Echo Summit.)

Introduction
Twin Bridges is an understandably popular trailhead, for the trail from it provides the quickest route to the Desolation Valley lakes. An official trail exists only to the wilderness' boundary, and beyond that the route essentially is cross country. This is the only dangerous route described in this book, and it would not be described at all were it not an official way into the wilderness. Supposedly a number of hikers have fallen to their deaths trying to reach Desolation Valley.

Description
If you need a guidebook to stay on route, you shouldn't be on this sketchy trail. Consequently, the directions for it are intentionally very brief. Also, if you haven't hiked it, don't do so alone—you might have to be rescued.

The official path starts along the west side of Pyramid Creek, although you may find one or more use trails. You quickly leave the creek near its bend east, then rejoin it ½ mile later and follow it 250 yards northwest through open forest to another bend, then 160 yards north to the wilderness boundary, in a shady fir grove. About ½ mile past the boundary your first real route-finding problems begin, and if you can't find the trail, turn back; it gets worse ahead. After about 200 yards of climbing up an increasingly steep tread, you reach a vantage point from which you can look down-canyon and identify the canyon's huge east-wall lateral moraine. You can also study nearby **lower Horsetail Fall**, often roaring as it plunges 100 feet into a splashing pool. This vantage point is on ice- and water-polished, gravel-covered, sloping bedrock. In other words, it's very slippery. One could easily slip and plunge on a one-way trip into the lower fall's rocky gorge.

The trail, if you can call it that, veers away from the lower fall and starts west steeply up open slabs. In several places you'll probably have to use your hands as well as your feet. And you'll have to use good judgment in route finding. (In the past, one or more possible routes have been marked with ducks and/or with paint.) High above the lower fall the route bends north and diagonals up a talus slope before cutting 80 yards east to a small flat just above the brink of upper Horsetail Fall. The view from the flat *almost* justifies this arduous ascent, and from it you can now identify the canyon's west-wall moraine, which isn't nearly so spectacular as its multistage east-wall counterpart. It's hard to believe that a glacier descending Pyramid Creek filled the canyon at least to the crest of these 900-foot-high moraines.

With danger behind you, drop briefly north from the small flat, then parallel Pyramid Creek 200 yards up to small but scenic **Avalanche Lake**. Your route to Ropi Lake is now essentially cross-country. About ¼ mile beyond Avalanche Lake you approach relatively unappealing **Pitt Lake**, and near its northern end you must make a decision. To get to Lake of the Woods, you'll have to cross Pyramid Creek, and this is best done before

Horsetail Falls

you reach Ropi Lake—if you want to keep your feet dry. Therefore, start looking for suitable boulders and/or logs on which you can cross the creek.

The principal cross-country route stays along the creek's west bank as it climbs ⅓ mile to the outlet of **Ropi Lake**. From here, one can head west to nearby Toem Lake or, above it, to Gefo Lake. For solitude seekers, isolated lakelets and ponds lie on naked granite to the south of these. A fast way to Lake Aloha is to climb north from Toem or Gefo, passing Pyramid and Waca lakes. You can also start from Ropi Lake's northeast shore and ascend Pyramid Creek, passing a chain of lakes up to Lake Aloha's principal dam.

If Pyramid Peak is your goal, make a climb west from Ropi Lake past Toem Lake to Gefo Lake. From it several routes are possible, for the slopes are not too steep. You can diagonal due south up to the peak's southeast ridge, reaching it at roughly 8600 feet; or you can climb west up either side of the Gefo Lake inlet creek and then briefly up to the ridge. From it you diagonal west up to the peak's south flank, then climb straight to the bouldery summit. Its views, however, are

Pyramid Peak above Ropi Lake

somewhat disappointing since Lake Tahoe is largely hidden from view.

From the east arm of snag-infested Ropi Lake, an official trail starts a climb to Lake of the Woods. This trail ascends east-northeast ⅓ mile up a joint-controlled gully, crosses a tiny, seasonally boggy flat, then continues on an easier grade ¼ mile east to Lake of the Woods' outlet creek. This it follows 200 yards upstream to a crossing that can be hard to find for those *descending* this trail. From the crossing you head east just past the south edge of a small, stagnant pond, then immediately turn north to begin a ¼-mile climb to a low ridge damming extremely popular **Lake of the Woods**. This lake's shores abound with campsites, the better, more private ones being found along its west shore. If you camp here, be sure you do so *at least* 100 feet from the shore—200 feet is better. For example, camp on small, flat bedrock benches located on gentle slopes just west of the lake and just north of Frata Lake. That lake, located about 200 yards west of Lake of the Woods' outlet, is shallow but still is deep enough for pleasant swimming in its slightly cloudy water.

At the lake's northwest corner, which is nearly a mile by trail from its outlet, take a trail that starts a climb northwest, reaching a popular trail to Lake Aloha in less than ½ mile. Just 60 yards down it you reach a junction above a southeast arm of shallow, sprawling **Lake Aloha**. From here a popular *de facto* trail branches left and embarks on a ¾-mile course over to the lake's 20-foot-high dam. Relatively warm in August and dotted with islands, the part of the lake near the dam is a justifiably popular swimming area. On barren granitic benches to the south of the lake you can make a camp.

◈ 73 ◈
Ralston Peak Trail to Ralston Peak

Distances:
2.5 miles to prominent spur ridge
3.4 miles to open ridge
4.0 miles to Ralston Peak
Low/High Elevations: 6500'/9235'
Season: Mid-July through mid-October
Classification: Strenuous
Maps: 37 and 35

Trailhead: From Twin Bridges, mentioned in the previous hike's trailhead description, drive 1¼ miles up Highway 50 to Camp Sacramento, on your right, and Sayles Flat, on your left. (Westbound drivers, this spot is 5¾ miles west from Echo Summit.) Park on the flat if there is no room at the trailhead. To reach it, head 200 yards up an old, paved road to a chapel. Immediately beyond it the road curves sharply right, and the trail begins from it.

Introduction
You'll command excellent views, both nearby and far-reaching, from the summit of Ralston

Peak. From it you can study the different characteristics of Desolation Wilderness, the river canyons to the west, the Carson Range to the northeast, and the Freel Peak area to the east. You can reach Ralston's summit by the overly steep Ralston Peak Trail or by moderately graded trails from Echo Lake (Hike 86). On the plus side, that hike's trailhead is 1000 feet higher; on the minus side, it is 2.9 miles longer. However, you can cut 2.5 miles off it by taking the Echo Lakes water taxi, thereby making it the easier of the two routes. The Ralston Peak Trail may appeal only hikers wanting a physical challenge and to those who want to avoid the crowds of the Echo Lakes-Lake Aloha Pacific Crest Trail thoroughfare.

Description

From the road's sharp curve your trail begins by switchbacking up through a white-fir forest that shades the slopes of a giant lateral moraine. The trail almost tops the level crest of the moraine but chooses instead to parallel it for about 200 yards before actually reaching it. From this spot you can gaze northwest at pointed Pyramid Peak, which stands high above 900-foot-deep, glaciated Pyramid Creek canyon below you. To the southwest lies the nearly vertical northwest face of Lovers Leap, which has dozens of difficult climbing routes up it. Hikers can easily reach the summit of this face by taking the 1.2 mile-long Lovers Leap Trail that begins in Camp Sacramento, opposite this hike's trailhead. The camp is for Sacramento residents, but anyone can drive in and day hike to the summit. It is quite thrilling to look down and see a climber or two, complete with high-tech climbing paraphernalia, although it is more thrilling to ascend any of these difficult climbing routes. At the trail's start you can borrow a nature pamphlet that identifies common trailside plants, the numbers in the pamphlet keyed to numbered trailside posts found along the first half of the route.

Along the Ralston Peak Trail just before and after the Lovers Leap viewpoint you may see one or more faint trails climbing up to yours. These start from a Seventh Day Adventist Camp in Pinecrest. Now you face a steep-to-very-steep 1350-foot open climb up weathered granitic rock that is largely covered with huckleberry oak, manzanita, and some chinquapin. A 60-yard-long spur trail marks the 500-foot point. Continued steep climbing up short switchbacks for an elevation gain of 450 feet brings us to an eastward traverse, along which we pass a trickling spring. A few more short, steep switchbacks are negotiated, and then the gradient eases as we climb to a **prominent spur ridge**, covered with an open stand of red firs and western white pines. From it a brief initial descent speeds us on our way along a ⅓-mile traverse northwest across a meadowy slope.

Just after our traverse turns into a moderate climb, we encounter two small but usually profuse springs, each with its associated cluster of corn lilies—telltale indicators that water is nearby. Beyond them a steep, ducked ascent brings us up to a generally **open ridge** that has clusters of mountain hemlocks. From it we can look northwest down at Lake of the Woods, below us, and beyond at island-dotted Lake Aloha, which has a backdrop of the metamorphic masses of Jacks and Dicks peaks. Pyramid Peak is the prominent granitic guardian above Aloha's southwest shore.

Hike 74 continues the description ahead, north. You, however, with the bulk of the climbing behind you, complete it by following an amorphous tread east up the open ridge to Ralston Peak's northwest descending ridge. On it you may locate a faint, ducked tread, which you take southeast up to the ice-fractured quartz-monzonite summit rocks of **Ralston Peak**. At its foot lie Tamarack, Ralston, and Cagwin lakes, and to their east and below them lie Upper and Lower Echo lakes. Above the canyon beyond them are the granitic summits of the mostly unglaciated Freel Peak massif, the closest and tallest peak being 10,881′ Freel Peak.

Perhaps the most instructive view from the summit is one north toward Fallen Leaf Lake, barely visible, and Lake Tahoe, immediately beyond it. Our view is framed by the metamorphic mass of Mt. Tallac, on the left, and the granitic mass of Echo Peak, on the right. From our vantage point, the lower southeast slope of Mt. Tallac *appears* to be almost level, and it forms a conspicuous bench from which canyon walls drop steeply to Fallen Leaf Lake (see photo). Conventional wisdom has it that the deep canyon between the two peaks was carved by glaciers. Actually, in resistant rock, which abounds in our guidebook's area, glaciers are virtually impotent at deeply eroding the landscape. However, during the last 2 million years of repeated glaciation, rockfall has been much greater than in earlier times, and the glaciers have transported a tremendous amount of rockfall debris. This has accumulated in places to form giant lateral moraines. But the amount of debris in any moraine is considerably less than one might expect, since granitic bedrock ridges lie just beneath the deposits, and they make up most of the volume of these landforms.

From Ralston Peak one can hike ½ mile southeast cross-country quite easily along a ridge for a view down at Cup Lake, which, unlike any other lake in our area, sits in a deep hole. Could glaciers excavate such a small, deep hole? Ralston's southern slopes are, at best, minimally glaciated. Perhaps the circular basin is a meteorite-impact crater. It is the same diameter as a 140-foot-deep impact crater 2½ miles southeast from and above Lower Twin Lake (south of Bridgeport). You decide. Is there glacial evidence (moraine, polish, striations) or is there meteorite evidence

(impact-fractured rock)? From the ridge saddle just west of Cup Lake you can make a relatively rapid descent by heading west, diagonaling steeply down across open slopes for about ⅔ mile to the prominent spur ridge, mentioned earlier.

⊰ 74 ⊱
Ralston Peak Trail to Lake of the Woods and Ropi Lake

Distances:
3.4 miles to open ridge
4.8 miles to Lake of the Woods Trail
5.4 miles on trail to Lake of the Woods
7.1 miles on trail to Ropi Lake
Low/High Elevations: 6500'/8870'
Season: Mid-July through mid-October
Classification: Strenuous
Maps: 37 and 35
Trailhead: Same as the Hike 73 trailhead.

Introduction
Justifiably popular Lake of the Woods, with its islands, coves, bays, and good campsites, is a fine subalpine lake for pure relaxation, and is stocked with trout. Ropi Lake, below and beyond it, serves as a base camp for forays up

Lake of the Woods and Lake Aloha, from open ridge at Hikes 73/74 split

and down Pyramid Creek as well as for an ascent of Pyramid Peak—the highest peak of the Crystal Range. Its ascent is described in Hike 72. Since all these attractions are more easily reached by Hikes 72 and 87, Hike 74 is only for those who want to take in Ralston Peak's summit views. Visiting it will add 1.3 miles to the total length of the hike. It is best visited on the way out, for you start out quite a bit higher than from your trailhead, your pack will be a bit lighter, you will be a bit more in shape, and you will be somewhat acclimatized from an overnight stay among the lakes in Desolation Valley.

Description

Follow the previous hike up to the **open ridge** overlooking Lake of the Woods. Ahead, you take the trail down a short, steep, north slope, which is usually buried under snow through early August. The trail may be temporarily lost in a small subalpine meadow, boggy from the snowmelt, but it can be located in a stand of hemlocks and pines visited by Clark's nutcrackers. These large, gray, vociferous cousins of the lower-elevation jays feed primarily on pine-cone seeds, which at this elevation would be those of the thin-barked, five-needled, whitebark pine. From this conifer stand a spur trail climbs ⅔ mile south to the summit of Ralston Peak.

A northward descent takes us down a gully toward a bench on which there is a pond, with plenty of water-loving wildflowers on the gentle slope above it. We then curve around a flat to a smaller pond, on a saddle, and then start a climb northward up a low knoll. Near its top we obtain a pine-filtered view east of the Echo Lakes and of the Sierra beyond. then we descend to another saddle, where we meet the **Lake of the Woods Trail**, just west of and above Haypress Meadows. This trail descends ⅓ mile east before reaching a junction with the Pacific Crest Trail. If we

were to continue north from this saddle on the Ralston Peak Trail, we would reach, in ¼ mile, a second junction with the Pacific Crest Trail (see Hike 87).

Since we're going to Lake of the Woods, we turn left and follow the trail westward. This switchbacks across mostly open, wildflowered, viewful slopes down to the northeast corner of **Lake of the Woods**. Here you can take a shoreline trail ¼ mile west to the northwest corner, from where it climbs generally northwest to a broad saddle, then descends briefly to the Lake Aloha Trail, the junction being 60 yards before another junction just above the southeast tip of Lake Aloha. From Lake of the Woods' northwest corner a use trail heads south 300 yards to "land's end' on a rocky, forested peninsula that separates the warm, island-cluttered west arm from the main lake body. Several good-to-excellent campsites are on this large peninsula, and more campsites are near the arm and near the lake's southwest shore.

From the northeast corner of Lake of the Woods, our trail to Ropi Lake contours the wetter, more forested east shore for 0.6 mile and then descends to a nearby, forested flat. On it you head west along the south edge of a small, stagnant pond, then immediately cross Lake of the Woods' outlet creek and follow it south. the creek curves westward, as does our ducked trail, and we reach a tiny, swampy flat at the base of a small summit ¼ mile south of the lake that serves as a constant landmark. From the flat we hike west along the summit's south slope down a joint-controlled gully, then immediately beyond it we arrive at the southeast arm of shallow, snag-infested **Ropi Lake**. Campsites can be found near its rocky, sinuous shore, and although they and the lake aren't the best, they serve as a base for further exploration of the lakes in this basin. See Hike 72 for a brief list of options, including an ascent of Pyramid Peak.

Dark, metamorphic Dicks Peak looms above granite-lined Middle Velma Lake

Chapter 14
Desolation Wilderness, east side

Introduction

Since the introduction to Chapter 13 describes Desolation Wilderness in some depth, there is no need to repeat that information here. Be aware, however, that to enter the wilderness you'll need a wilderness permit—the how, when, where, and why of it being mentioned early in Chapter 3.

The east side of Desolation Wilderness differs from the west side in at least two ways: 1) the routes tend to be more popular, and 2) about half of them have Lake Tahoe views. The latter, however, is not the cause of the former; these routes are more popular simply because their trailheads are more accessible. It would be very subjective to say that the east-side scenery is better than its counterpart; I rate them equal.

As in Chapter 13 this chapter's hikes are arranged from north to south. The first route, Hike 75, is a very long, almost viewless way in to the heart of Desolation Wilderness. Furthermore, it has an undesirable stretch which should have been rerouted back in the 1970s, but never was. Strike two. the only redeeming factor that precludes it from being omitted is that it is part of the popular, tri-state Pacific Crest Trail. The stretch of PCT that constitutes Hike 75 is not scenic, although it has the potential to be so if it is relocated to the crest and up to Phipps Pass.

Hike 84 is another questionable hike, not due to lack of scenery, but rather to its severity. This exceptionally scenic route to the summit of Echo Peak is certainly the harder of two routes; Hike 85 is definitely easier, if less scenic. Other than Hikes 75 and 84, the chapter's other hikes are highly recommended.

⇒ 75 ⇐
Pacific Crest Trail, Barker Pass south to Richardson and Velma Lakes

Distances:
4.3 miles to McKinney-Rubicon Springs jeep road
6.2 miles to Richardson Lake
10.3 miles to high point
13.8 miles to Tahoe-Yosemite Trail
14.9 miles to Velma Lakes Trail
15.2 miles to Middle Velma Lake
19.6 miles to Eagle Falls trailhead
Low/High Elevations: 6960'/8120'
Season: Mid-July through early October
Classification: Moderate
Maps: 27, 30, and 31

Trailheads: See the Hike 47 trailhead for directions to Barker Pass. Alternatively, you can start this hike farther south, along the McKinney-Rubicon Springs jeep road. Reach it from the major junction by Lake Tahoe's outlet at Tahoe City by driving about 7½ miles south on Highway 89 to County Road 3013 (a.k.a. 14N34 and McKinney-Rubicon Springs jeep road) in Chambers Lodge. From where Highway 50 leaves Highway 89 in South Lake Tahoe, drive about 20 miles north on Highway 89 to this junction. More precisely, southbound drivers will find this junction 0.1 mile past a bridge over McKinney Creek, and northbound drivers will find it about 1.5 miles past the General Creek Campground entrance (Hike 52). On the road, drive 2.1 miles to McKinney Creek, then 0.2 more to the signed McKinney Creek OHV Staging Area. If you have a 4WD or an OHV, you can continue 2.6 miles west to a junction, just beyond trout-stocked Miller Lake, and if bound for Richardson Lake, drive 1.0 mile up a jeep road to it, where you will find the Pacific Crest Trail.

Introduction

This route is along a stretch of the Pacific Crest Trail, which also doubles as a stretch of the Tahoe Rim Trail. Although not difficult, it is certainly the long way in to Desolation Wilderness. You reach its north boundary about 1 mile beyond Richardson Lake, this lake being a worthy goal. This hike requires a shuttle, leaving a vehicle at the starting trailhead and another at the ending trailhead. However, you can get by with one vehicle by taking a public bus along Highway 89. Hike south along the Pacific Crest Trail to Middle Velma Lake, descend to Emerald Bay, then take the bus north (be sure to first check the bus schedule). To reach the Barker Pass trailhead, you'll have to hike 7½ miles and climb over 1500 feet—quite an effort. If you use public transportation, it is better to start from the alternate trailhead, for to reach the McKinney Creek OHV Staging Area you'll have to hike only 2.3 miles and will gain only about 400 feet.

Description

For the long way in to Richardson Lake, start from the Pacific Crest Trail/Tahoe Rim Trail's Barker Pass trailhead. Southbound on the PCT/TRT, you immediately cross Forest Route 3, soon curve south, and soon begin to meet springs and creeklets, some active throughout the summer. For 1½ miles you make a winding traverse southwest, generally through forest, but sometimes across meadow. Near the end of your gently descending traverse you cross a sloping meadow whose north edge is demarcated by a spring-fed creek. Just ¼ mile past this meadow you come within a stone's throw of the Bear Lake road (F.R. 03.4, formerly 14N20). You can drop to it and follow it about 200 yards west over to Barker Creek, with abundant camping space frequented by OHV campers. This is useful information only if you are hiking in the opposite direction and may be looking for a final night's camp. The PCT parallels the road for ⅓ mile before crossing it. Bear Lake, although shallow, is pleasant enough, and can be reached by a 2-mile walk up the Bear Lake road. There, expect OHV campers.

Just ⅓ mile past the Bear Lake road the PCT crosses Bear Lake's reliable outlet creek, and then it traverses 1½ miles through viewless forest to a crossing of the **McKinney-Rubicon Springs jeep road**. This heads 4.5 miles east to the McKinney Creek OHV Staging Area, your hike's alternate trailhead. Beyond the jeep road you quickly reach usually flowing Miller Creek, of questionable purity, then in 100 yards cross a lightly used road. Your next, winding 1¾ miles are through a forest that is so dense you could lose your bearings. You circle Sourdough Hill and at last come upon the north corner of **Richardson Lake**. Those who have started their hike from the McKinney Creek OHV Staging Area join

Metamorphic Dicks and Jacks peaks and the granitic, snowy Crystal Range

us here, having walked 3.6 miles up to it, then 0.1 mile northwest to the PCT. This alternate route shaves 2.5 miles off the distances from Barker Pass and saves only about an hour's walking. Along the northeast shore of shallow, relatively warm, trout-stocked Richardson Lake are spacious campsites. Because OHVs can drive up here, you may see one or more of them at the tree-rimmed lake, especially if you arrive here on a weekend after mid-July, when the snow typically has melted.

From the lake's north corner the PCT climbs south, paralleling a jeep road ½ mile up to a forested saddle. A glacier flowing down the Rubicon River canyon overtopped this saddle by about 80 feet when it was at its maximum about 20,000 years ago. To do this, the glacier must have had a thickness of about 1450 feet. From the saddle the PCT goes but 200 yards to pass a nearby snow-depth indicator, standing in a small meadow just below the trail. After about a ½-mile traverse you reach a large, flat, bedrock bench just west of the trail, which is almost devoid of trees. The isolationist will find plenty of open space for usually dry, relatively mosquito-free camping. Along the west edge of this bench you have visual command over many miles of glaciated Rubicon River canyon scenery.

Ahead lies mosquito land before mid-August. Unfortunately, by the time the mosquitoes subside, the creeks ahead dry up, and your route from Richardson Lake to Middle Velma Lake can be waterless. You begin by ducking into a shallow, often soggy bowl, then climb out of it you reach a short, dry, open stretch and can take a breather, beside a few junipers. Here you have some more views of Rubicon River country plus metamorphic Dicks and Jacks peaks and granitic Crystal Range. In a couple of minutes you pass a monstrous trailside Jeffrey pine, armed with threatening, pendulous limbs, then you stroll ½ mile farther, mostly close to a broad, fairly level crest, to where, just after you climb from a crest saddle, you may see a junction with the abandoned General Creek Trail. Ahead, you traverse southward, again mostly close to a broad, fairly level crest, but after ⅔ mile start a short, moderate climb up to your hike's **high**

point. From it a 40-yard-long spur trail heads southwest to some rocks from which you can see Rubicon, Rockbound, and Buck Island reservoirs down in the deep Rubicon River canyon.

The PCT now leaves the crest lands, dropping 200 feet to a boggy meadow, and just beyond it passes northeast of a 50-yard-long seasonal pond. You then ascend a shallow gully with a narrow meadow running along it, cross a forested spur-ridge saddle, then descend gently to the outlet of a small, seasonal pool, situated just below a rock slab. Beyond you descend to glacier-polished granodiorite slabs just north of Phipps Creek. You can camp here, but when the creek is flowing, the mosquitoes will be abundant. Over the next 1.5 miles the PCT makes a long climb to an almost imperceptible spur ridge, then briefly descends a shallow gully to quickly reach the **Tahoe-Yosemite Trail** (next hike). Ahead the PCT winds down forested slopes, negotiates a seasonally muddy traverse across Middle Velma Lake's swampy outlet, then reaches the lake's southwest arm. Onward you quickly reach a junction with the **Velma Lakes Trail** just above the lake. West, this trail descends to Camper Flat (Hike 66). East, this trail, also doubling as the PCT and TYT, traverses 0.3 mile to a junction above the south shore of **Middle Velma Lake**. Just 70 yards before this junction, you have a good view of the lake and may want to descend to popular campsites near its shore. From the junction follow Hike 77 in reverse 4.4 miles out to the **Eagle Falls trailhead** along Highway 89 above Emerald Bay.

⇜ **76** ⇝
Tahoe-Yosemite Trail, Meeks Bay to Velma Lakes

Distances:
4.6 miles to Lake Genevieve
4.9 miles to Crag Lake
5.7 miles to Hidden Lake
5.9 miles to Shadow Lake
6.3 miles to Stony Ridge Lake
8.1 miles to Rubicon Lake

9.1 miles to Phipps Pass
12.0 miles to Pacific Crest Trail
13.1 miles to Velma Lakes Trail
13.4 miles to Middle Velma Lake
17.8 miles to Eagle Falls trailhead

Low/High Elevations: 6239'/8880'

Season: Late July through mid-October

Classification: Moderate

Maps: 28 and 31

Trailhead: From where Highway 50 leaves Highway 89 in South Lake Tahoe, drive 3.2 miles northwest on Highway 89 to the Lake Tahoe Visitor Center. Get your wilderness permit here, then continue 13¼ miles on Highway 89 to a closed road just 230 yards past the Meeks Bay Campground entrance. If you're driving from Tahoe City, follow Highway 89 south 2.2 miles to the William Kent Visitor Center, get your wilderness permit, and then continue 8¾ miles to the trailhead, just 250 yards past Meeks Bay Resort. Park where you can find space anywhere along the highway. This trailhead usually has wilderness permits for *day users.*

Crag Peak rises high above Hidden Lake

Introduction

This relatively easy backpack route is along the subdued, northernmost part of the Tahoe-Yosemite Trail, which rewards you, starting 4½ miles in, with one lake right after another. Those who choose to take another trail down to Highway 89 should then be able to ride a bus back to the trailhead. First verify that these public buses are running between South Lake Tahoe and Tahoe City.

Description

The Tahoe-Yosemite Trail, or TYT, starts west along a gated road and takes us through a forest of white fir, incense-cedar, and lodge-pole, ponderosa, and sugar pines. After 1⅓ miles our road nears the upper end of a grassy swamp, on the left, and here a trail branches right. Ahead, the road ends in ⅓ mile at the site of former Camp Wasiu. On the trail we climb moderately for 0.4 mile up to a seeping trailside spring, and then continue up a gentler gradient to Meeks Creek. Its banks abound in wildflowers, thimbleber-ries, and bracken ferns as well as alders and willows.

Our ascent now becomes almost negligible as we progress southwest, enter Desolation Wilderness, and parallel the usually unseen creek along a large, mostly forested flat. We hike through the south edges of three dry meadows that sprout variable amounts of lupine and mule ears, and offer possible camping near their border. Beyond the last one we parallel the creek up a moderate ascent, then reach a second forested flat. Up here red fir, Jeffrey pine and western white pine have replaced their lower-elevation look-alikes: white fir, ponderosa pine, and sugar pine. Incense-cedar was the first to drop out, but a somewhat similar tree, the juniper, will be seen on exposed rocky bench-es above. Lodgepole pine—an inhabitant of several vegetational, climactic, and soil zones—remains with us.

We angle south gently down to a bridge across Meeks Creek, this locality having pos-sible camping. Now we climb moderately up a path that arcs east into a shady, moist, red-fir-forested cove rich in vine maple, currant, thimbleberry, and fireweed. Then, winding

A brave jump into Rubicon Lake's cold, clear water

southwest up the cove's south slope, we soon arrive at a much drier, more open ridge, a good resting spot from which we can just barely see Lake Tahoe. Now we climb southeast for a short, pleasant stretch beside cascading Meeks Creek as we hike up to shallow, relatively warm **Lake Genevieve**, lowest of the Tallant Lakes. In 1895, California's Fish Commission authorized the stocking of these lakes with Great Lakes Mackinaw fingerlings. When fully grown, these trout top 30 pounds. They migrated down Meeks Creek into Lake Tahoe, grew, and were eventually blamed by Tahoe fishermen with destroying Tahoe's native cutthroat trout. Since all large trout cannibalize smaller trout, the Mackinaws weren't the only culprits. Besides, unrestricted commercial fishing had been going on for decades, first to feed the mining populations in western Nevada's silver mines, then later to supply more distant markets, and very little effort had been put into restocking the lake. (In like manner, the forests were mowed down to provide mining buildings, and then the razed slopes were abandoned.)

Along Lake Genevieve's northeast shore you may see the old Lake Genevieve Trail striking northwest toward the lake's outlet. It rambles 2 miles over to General Creek. In the early days of the Pacific Crest Trail (the 1970s), a stretch of that trail's route descended the old General Creek Trail. However, with the rerouting of the PCT, both of these old trails fell into disuse.

There are campsites around Lake Genevieve, some even with a good view of dominating 9054′ Crag Peak, but since most of them are within 100 feet of the lake, you should move upstream and quickly reach larger, more appealing **Crag Lake**, beyond which Crag Peak rises in all its granitic glory. Like Lake Genevieve downstream and Stony Ridge Lake upstream, Crag Lake has a low dam. Along its northeast shore are environmentally incorrect trailside campsites. Secluded, more appropriate sites exist along the lake's opposite shore. Just west of the lake's outlet lies hidden, trout-stocked Dipper Pond.

Beyond Crag Lake your trail quickly guides you to a boulder-hop of Meeks Creek, and then you encounter a spur trail on a ridge just beyond it. This trail descends to shallow **Hidden Lake**, nestled near the foot of Crag Peak. Climbers wishing to climb moderately difficult Class 5 routes up its 400-foot northeast cliff should consult Carville's guide, mentioned under "Recommended Reading and Source Materials."

From the Hidden Lake trail junction, we climb up the ridge, a lateral moraine, and then curve east to another ridge, this one being a recessional moraine. Behind it lies shallow **Shadow Lake**. Given enough time, all lakes face extinction, since in the Sierra Nevada most accumulate sediments (mostly pollen and dust) at a rate of about ½-2 feet per one thousand years. Over the last 13,000 glacier-free years, sediments have filled the lake to such an extent that water lilies have invaded its southern half. Close behind them in the marshy water are water-loving grasses and wildflowers. Pursuing them on mucky soil are currants and alders. In time the lower half may become a meadow, while the upper half may sprout lodgepole pines and mountain hemlocks. However, before this happens, a glacier—like dozens of previous ones—will advance down the Tallant Lakes canyon, obliterating sediments, soil, and vegetation.

Leaving this swampy lake behind, we hike up a moderately graded trail that momentarily becomes steeper as it climbs alongside Meeks Creek, whose water is tumbling in cascades and rapids down a granitic gorge. Above the gorge we reach **Stony Ridge Lake**, largest of the Tallant Lakes. Here, the best campsite of many available may be the one above its north end, just across a low dam. Our trail contours the long, southwest shoreline, briefly crosses some mafic rocks, and fords several wildflower-bordered creeks. The dark, mafic bedrock is similar to granitic bedrock in that it was intruded from below up into overlying rocks that have since been eroded away. It differs in that it is much richer in iron and magnesium—hence the darker color.

At the lake's southwest corner we cross and immediately recross the lake's inlet creek, proceed south along the west edge of a boggy meadow, and then, near an impressive, low-angle cliff of granodiorite, start up a series of well-graded switchbacks, bounded by two tributaries. After almost reaching a steep, churning cascade, we turn onto the last switchback, climb southwest, and get hemlock-framed views below of Stony Ridge Lake and its damp meadow. We soon curve south into a little willow-lined creek cove, bordered by steep, vertical-jointed cliffs. Now a short climb southeast past a tiny tarn takes us to the west shore of **Rubicon Lake**. Dammed by a ridge of resistant bedrock, this lovely lake is the highest of the Tallant Lakes. Because they

form a line of "beads" along the creek that connects them, they are called *paternoster* lakes, after their resemblance to beads on a rosary. Fairly close to the water is a good campsite under mountain hemlocks and lodgepole pines. The lake's water is nippy, reaching at best into the low 60s, but a tempting rock just off the west shore beckons one to jump into the invigorating, clear water. After you climb out to bask atop this rock, you can peer over its edge and watch trout swimming lazily below.

Above the lake's south end we reach a junction with an unmaintained trail that descends ⅓ mile to the Grouse Lakes, which are a bit stagnant, and then 15 yards beyond the junction we top a saddle. The TYT then switchbacks up to a granodiorite outlier, just beyond which we can look back at it and see how joints really control its angular shape. We pass a small gully, snowbound as late as early August, then reach a switchback. Before climbing any farther, you might rest under a juniper or pine and enjoy the view in the southeast. Looking beyond the north end of Fallen Leaf Lake, we see Tahoe Mountain immediately above it, and from its slopes a long, level ridge—debris left by glaciers—extends southwest. Although this ridge, a glacial moraine, towers up to 900 feet above the lake, that doesn't mean these deposits are 900 feet thick. If we were to tunnel into them, we would find granitic bedrock beneath these *surficial* sediments.

A switchback leg north takes us higher up the joint-controlled rocks, and then our trail climbs moderately southward and crosses a gully just before skirting above **Phipps Pass**, the shallow saddle on your left. Just beyond the pass, the trail almost tops a crest on your right, and from it you could drop 320 feet in elevation down a steep slope to isolated camping near cold, circular Phipps Lake.

The route ahead, except for a few trivial gains, is all downhill. Our trail traverses granitic slabs and boulders along the southeast slope of Phipps Peak, named after General William Phipps, who settled along his ("the General's") creek near Sugar Pine Point. We encounter a spring, then swing around to the peak's open south slope, from which we can see the Velma Lakes in the gray, granitic basin below, and the rusty, metamorphic summit of Dicks Peak towering above it. The contact between the two rock types is clearly evident.

On the TYT we curve northwest, re-enter an open forest of mountain hemlocks and lodgepole, western white, and whitebark pines, perhaps pass some raucous Clark's nutcrackers flying from tree to tree, and then come to within 30 yards of a ridge. Our route now descends southwest, then traces three long, well-graded switchback legs down to a junction with the Pacific Crest Trail. Along this descent we thrice cross a trickling creek and we pass many large red firs. Some of the older firs, now in the process of decay, have had their rotting trunks excavated by busy pine martens—larger cousins of the weasel—who chase down ground squirrels, which might also nest in these rotting trunks.

At the junction, we're only about a mile from and 200 feet above Middle Velma Lake, so we head down to this swimmer's paradise. The trail makes a moderate, generally viewless, descent to the lake's outlet creek, which all too often gets hikers' feet wet. The acres of soggy soil found in this forested flat prove to be a fantastic breeding ground for mosquitoes. Before August you'll want to scamper south along the trail trying to evade the pesky critters. After skirting past the southwest arm of Middle Velma Lake, you climb briefly to a junction with the Velma Lakes Trail. West, this trail descends to Camper Flat (Hike 66). East, this trail, also doubling as the PCT and TYT, traverses 0.3 mile to a junction above the south shore of the **Middle Velma Lake**. Just 70 yards before this junction, you have a good view of the lake and may want to descend to popular campsites near its shore. From the junction follow Hike 77 in reverse 4.4 miles out to the **Eagle Falls trailhead** along Highway 89 above Emerald Bay.

❧ 77 ❧
Emerald Bay Trail to Eagle and Velma Lakes

Distances:
1.0 mile to Eagle Lake Trail
   0.1 mile on trail to Eagle Lake
2.5 miles to Bay View Trail
3.1 miles to lateral trail
   0.9 mile up lateral trail to Pacific Crest Trail
      0.2 mile on trail to Dicks Lake spur trail
         0.1 mile on spur trail to Dicks Lake
4.2 miles to Upper Velma Lake Trail
   0.3 mile on trail to Upper Velma Lake
4.4 miles to Middle Velma Lake
4.9 miles to Fontanillis Lake (via Dicks Lake)
5.2 miles to Fontanillis Lake (via Middle Velma Lake)

Low/High Elevations: 6580'/8500'

Season: Mid-July through mid-October

Classification: Strenuous

Maps: 32, 31, and 34

Trailhead: From where Highway 50 leaves Highway 89 in South Lake Tahoe, drive 3.2 miles northwest on Highway 89 to the Lake Tahoe Visitor Center. Get your wilderness permit here, then continue 5.6 miles on Highway 89 to the moderately large but often overflowing parking lot of Eagle Falls Picnic Area, immediately past Eagle Creek. If you're driving from Tahoe City, follow Highway 89 south 2.2 miles to the William Kent Visitor Center, get your wilderness permit, and then continue 16½ miles to the picnic area. This usually has wilderness permits for *day users*. Lock your car, for thefts are all too common here.

Introduction
Despite its difficulty, the trail up Eagle Lake canyon is one of the most popular in the Tahoe region, for it takes you, in a few hours' time, to the Dicks Lake-Velma Lakes area. By making a loop through this area you pass at least five lakes and one lakelet, all good for swimming or camping.

Description
At times incorrectly signed the Eagle Falls Trail (the falls are *east* of Highway 89), our trail makes a brushy ascent southwest up-

canyon, climbs past a vertical cliff, then bridges Eagle Creek. The bridge could easily support horses and their riders, but this trail is for hikers only; equestrians must use the Bay View Trail (next hike), which has equestrian trailhead parking. From the bridge our footpath cuts across the base of a blocky talus slope, climbs up to a bench, and enters Desolation Wilderness as it swings west to a second bench, on which lie erratic boulders transported down-canyon by a glacier. From this bench we can look northeast down at Emerald Bay and out to the Carson Range above Tahoe. Beyond the bench we cross a small lodgepole flat, round a low headwall, and parallel Eagle Lake's outlet creek. Shortly we reach another flat, shaded by white firs and Jeffrey pines. We now make a brief ascent, see the creek's rapids, and catch a glimpse of **Eagle Lake** as we reach a well-used spur trail that goes 200 yards over the bedrock to the lake. This picturesque lake is hemmed in by granitic cliffs, which along with cliffs you

Eagle Lake

passed down-canyon, attract talented rock climbers. (See Carville's guide, mentioned under "Recommended Reading and Source Materials.") Nonclimbers can relax, photograph, or fish at the lake.

Beyond this lake the Emerald Bay Trail climbs steeply to a saddle and a junction with the Bay View Trail. On this strenuous climb, aromatic tobacco brush, drab huckleberry oak, and needle-tipped snow bush dominate the vegetation. This section is a bad one for wearing shorts, due to the brush, or for carrying a large backpack, due to the steepness. Starting up it, we first pass under the towering cliff of North Maggies Peak, then arrive at a gully, shaded by pines and firs, that has a trickling creeklet. Short, steep switchbacks lead up the gully's west side and higher up we arrive at a barren slab to a small flat with lodgepole pines. Our trail traverses its west side for 50 yards before climbing south-southwest up to and through a clump of alders, arriving at the base of an outcrop. After an initial 30-yard climb west along this base our trail, which can be indistinct over the last ¼ mile, becomes obvious, and we climb south steeply up a slope and then traverse to a rocky bench on the west ridge of South Maggies Peak. These two similar, pointed peaks, popular conversation for 19th century Lake Tahoe boaters, were named not for Maggie but for her breasts. Back in those days, the two peaks' names were more explicit. (Today, Wyoming's Tetons survive unchanged because the name is French, and therefore not offensive.)

A short, steep switchback leg takes us down from the bench, and then we make a traverse high above a large pond overgrown with grass and pond lilies. Along the trail we find, in an alder thicket, a trickling spring, which is the last dependable water until Velma Lakes creek, about 2 miles ahead. Beyond the spring we switchback up to an ephemeral creek, cross it, and climb a gradually easing slope to a saddle on which we meet the **Bay View Trail** (next hike). From here we traverse west, pass two ridgetop ponds, and then make a ½-mile traverse past brush and bedrock almost to a saddle. Here, near a small, seasonal, ankle-deep pond, is a

Swimmers at Middle Velma Lake

junction with a **lateral trail**, from which you can start and end a 4.2-mile-long, clockwise loop to Dicks, Fontanillis, and Middle Velma lakes. The lateral trail first traverses ½ mile southwest, passing four more ponds—these being larger—before reaching a lakelet worthy of a lunch break or a refreshing swim. Ahead, the trail continues southwest for 250 yards, then makes a steep ¼-mile climb south to a crest junction with the **Pacific Crest Trail**. This you can then take ¼ mile south down to a spur trail that drops 100 yards to the northwest shore of **Dicks Lake**. See Hike 66 for more details about this lake and about the more-remote **Fontanillis Lake**.

From the lateral-trail junction we're taking the more-popular Velma Lakes Trail. We leave the junction by the ankle-deep pond as we climb northwest 50 yards to a slightly larger pond atop a broad saddle, and then descend a convoluted ¾ mile more or less in the same direction to a shallow, unnamed Velma lake, on the left. Don't camp at tempting shoreline sites, but rather farther back. When you reach its wide outlet creek, you may have to walk just upstream to find a dry crossing. If you were to go downstream 0.4 mile cross-country, preferably along the creek's northwest bank, you would reach Lower Velma Lake. This receives a lot less use than its trailside sisters and, being bedrock-lined, it has fewer mosquitoes. From the outlet creek our Velma Lakes Trail climbs 100 yards to a junction with the **Upper Velma Lake Trail**. By hiking south ⅓ mile on a trail from here, you can reach the north end of **Upper Velma Lake**. It is unique in having a grassy, semistagnant pond nestled on its bedrock island.

Only 180 yards past the Upper Velma Lake Trail junction, our westbound trail meets the Pacific Crest Trail, which descends one mile from **Fontanillis Lake** and 2 miles from **Dicks Lake** to here. We take the trail about 70 yards northwest, to where it curves west. Here you'll see **Middle Velma Lake**, and you can leave the trail for a quick descent to it. On weekends this lakeshore is crowded, for it has inviting water that tempts hikers to swim out to, dive from, or sunbathe on one or more of the lake's rock-slab islands. Rainbow trout also lure anglers to this sprawling lake. Popular campsites lie about here, more-remote ones above the more-distant lakeshores.

☜ 78 ☞
Bay View Trail to Granite, Dicks, Fontanillis, and Velma Lakes

Distances:
1.1 miles to Granite Lake
2.7 miles to Emerald Bay Trail
4.5 miles to Dicks Lake
4.6 miles to Middle Velma Lake
4.7 miles to Upper Velma Lake
5.1 miles to Fontanillis Lake via Dicks Lake
5.4 miles to Fontanillis Lake via Middle
  Velma Lake

Low/High Elevations: 6910'/8440'

Season: Mid-July through mid-October

Classification: Strenuous

Maps: 32, 31, and 34

Trailhead: From where Highway 50 leaves Highway 89 in South Lake Tahoe, drive 3.2 miles northwest on Highway 89 to the Lake Tahoe Visitor Center. Get your wilderness permit here, then continue 4.5 miles on Highway 89 to Bayview Campground, on your left. (Southbound drivers: from Tahoe City follow Highway 89 south 2.2 miles to the William Kent Visitor Center, get your wilderness permit, then continue 17½ miles to Bay View Campground. This campground is one mile southeast of Eagle Falls Picnic Area.) Drive through the campground to a parking area which holds about three dozen vehicles. Don't park in the campground's sites. This trailhead usually has wilderness permits for *day users*.

Introduction
Like the previous hike, this one provides access to the Dicks Lake-Velma Lakes area. Which hike should you choose? If you are on horseback, there is no choice, for horses aren't allowed on the Emerald Bay Trail. To its debit the Bay View Trail is 0.2 mile longer and has perhaps about 100 feet of additional elevation. But to its credit this trail has a better tread and, while fairly steep, is certainly better graded. It also has better views, and its off-highway trailhead is probably less likely to attract thieves. Along either route day hikers can

Lightly used Lower Velma Lake spreads out below Phipps Peak

reach a fine lake after only about a mile of walking.

Description

From the trailhead parking area the Cascade Creek Fall Trail branches left while the Bay View Trail starts straight ahead. On it you climb moderately through a dense white-fir forest with a chinquapin understory, then switchback up to a sharp bend in an old jeep road. Now you immediately enter Desolation Wilderness as you follow the closed jeep road northwest up to the top of a ridge of weathered granodiorite bedrock. By walking a few paces north, you'll obtain a tree-framed view of Emerald Bay, its bedrock Fannette Island, and Lake Tahoe.

Your route ahead is now a trail that climbs southeast alongside Granite Lake's trickling, alder-lined outlet creek. Also along it you find water-loving wildflowers, including Bolander's yampah, or olaski, as the Miwok Indians called it, who ate the roots of this wild carrot. Don't pick this plant because, first, it is illegal to do so, and second, there are some poisonous wild carrots that closely resemble it. The sensuous aroma of tobacco brush heralds our approach to moderately large Granite Lake. Your trail climbs above this lake, and you can leave the trail where you feel most comfortable to do so, dropping briefly to it. You'll appreciate the relatively warm water—up to 70°F—of clear **Granite Lake**. A broad moraine lies at its north end, and the lake's outlet flows along bedrock beneath it. Due to its proximity to Highway 89, the lake should be day-use only.

Beyond this lake the Bay View Trail climbs 1.6 miles over Maggies Peaks and down to a junction with the Emerald Bay Trail. In a nutshell, this switchbacks high above Granite Lake, traverses gentle slopes below forested South Maggies Peak, then weaves a contorted ½-mile route down to a junction with the **Emerald Bay Trail**. See the previous hike for directions to **Dicks Lake**, **Middle Velma Lake**, **Upper Velma Lake**, and **Fontanillis Lake**.

79

Mt. Tallac Trail to Floating Island Lake, Cathedral Lake, and Mt. Tallac

Distances:
1.7 miles to Floating Island Lake
2.5 miles to Cathedral Lake
4.6 miles to Mt. Tallac
Low/High Elevations: 6480′ / 9735′
Season: Mid-July through mid-October
Classification: Strenuous
Maps: 32 and 35
Trailhead: From where Highway 50 leaves Highway 89 in South Lake Tahoe, drive 3.2 miles northwest on Highway 89 to the Lake Tahoe Visitor Center, whose entrance is just 150 yards west of Fallen Leaf Road. If you're going to Floating Island Lake or beyond, get a wilderness permit here (they usually are also available, *for day hikers only,* at the trailhead). Westward, you bridge Taylor Creek in ¼ mile, then in another ½ mile reach a signed intersection. From here most folks drive ½ mile north to Baldwin Beach, but on a paved road you head south, branching left in 0.4 mile, then keeping right at a quickly reached second fork. You then drive ½ mile to a parking area with space for at least a dozen vehicles.

Introduction

Like Hike 81, this one takes you to Mt. Tallac's summit, but it does so in fewer miles. Two small lakes—one of them unique—are passed along your way up this route, which has more views but fewer campsites than does Hike 81. Hence it is best done as a day hike.

Description

You start among Jeffrey pines and sagebrush, climb 120 yards up an old road to a blocked-off fork, veer right, and reach an old gravel pit. The gap here offers a glimpse of the structure of a glacial moraine, which is largely composed of unsorted boulders in a gravel matrix. Beyond the pit we're now on a trail, climbing south up a shallow gully that lies between two lateral moraines. The east one was left by the last glacier to occupy the basin now filled by Fallen Leaf Lake. The west one probably was deposited by the same glacier, earlier in its history. A larger, unseen moraine lies west of it, this one terminating just south of the major bend in Highway 89. We'll cross that moraine near Floating Island Lake.

Starting toward that lake, we make a moderate climb south, the gradient rapidly reducing to gentle. In ⅓ mile we crest the moraine, which is largely cloaked in huckleberry oaks and greenleaf manzanitas on its east slopes and in white firs and Jeffrey pines on its west slopes. Our first views are stunning, but better ones lie ahead as we traverse south. After a ½-mile walk we drop away from the crest, being saturated with views of Fallen Leaf Lake, Lake Tahoe, and the Freel Peak massif. We enter another intermorainal gully, then make a rocky ascent across the earlier moraine, the ascent yielding to a brief traverse into a red-fir forest. Under deep shade we make a short, steep climb south up almost useless switchbacks, then level off just inside the Desolation Wilderness boundary by the north end of shallow **Floating Island Lake**.

In 1890 this unique lake was noted as having a 20-foot-diameter floating mat of grass and shrubs, whence the name. In more recent times there have been several floating, grassy mats, and more mats are ready to slough off from the lake's soggy northwest shore. It's a mystery why mats slough off at this lake and not at any other, for in all other respects this lake seems quite ordinary. Anyway, mats do slough off here, replacing older mats that break up. Therefore chances are very good that you'll see at least one island floating in this lake. Conifers ring this lake, denying space for a legal campsite.

Climbing toward Cathedral Lake, you leave Floating Island Lake and parallel its inlet creek to a nearby gap. From it an essentially cross-country route—formerly a trail—traverses south 0.2 mile to a trail from Fallen Leaf Lake. We head southwest up our trail, lined with wildflowers, currant, service-berry, sagebrush, and other shrubs we've seen, and soon come to a saddle immediately west of a little rocky knoll. From its juniper-covered summit, free of mosquitoes, we can relax and take in a panorama that includes most of Lake Tahoe, some of Fallen Leaf Lake, and beyond it the granitic summits of the Freel Peak massif.

Mt. Tallac's summit area, now visible, beckons us onward, so we make a brief descent to Cathedral Creek, cross it, and meet a trail from Fallen Leaf Lake. This descends, excessively so in one stretch, 1.0 mile to a junction about 130 feet above the lake's west shore. From there a trail heads ⅓ mile south to the private grounds of Stanford Sierra Camp, while in the other direction it heads ⅔ mile north to the Fallen Leaf Tract summer homes. There's hardly any space to park at this north trailhead, and the hot, steep nature of this trail to Cathedral Lake makes it the least desirable route to Mt. Tallac.

Just a few minutes' hiking past the trail from Fallen Leaf Lake, our trail from Floating Island Lake

Floating Island Lake

reaches **Cathedral Lake**. Named for its proximity to Cathedral Peak, which is not a peak but rather a cliff on Tallac's southeast ridge, this mostly shallow lake does support a few trout. Its water is clearer than that of Floating Island Lake, and swimming is fair along its south shore. As at the previous lake, legal campsites are hard to find. A path of sorts skirts the lake's west and south shores, from which one can climb a chaotic jumble of huge talus blocks for a view of the Tahoe scenery.

However, better views are at Tallac's summit, so make a very steep climb 200 feet above Cathedral Lake to a trail segment with water usually running along it. Bordered with monkey flower, forget-me-not, larkspur, fireweed, thimbleberry, and other water-loving plants, this short stretch is an excellent place to take a lunch break, since it may be your last dependable source of water. Beyond it the trail climbs steadily and steeply up the sloping floor of a cirque toward its headwall, which usually has snowfields well into August. Several trails, formed on talus through continued use, try to avoid most of the snow. The correct route has a switchback leg that climbs *south* up to the top. Once on it we have great views east, south, and west—a taste of what's to come.

We leave the edge of Tallac's southeast ridge as we hike northwest up an increasingly steep trail bordered by currant, gooseberry, snow bush, spiraea, and sagebrush. Also, clusters of western white, lodgepole, and whitebark pines speckle the slope. Near the 9000' level, the brush diminishes and wildflowers become more predominant. At about the 9400' level you may see an abandoned trail going directly downslope, leading unwary descending hikers astray. Finally, in just over 200 yards, we reach a junction with the trail from Gilmore Lake (Hike 81). Here, ¼ mile below the summit, one can enjoy a breather while taking in a view of the lakes and ponds below, and can identify circular Gilmore Lake in its cirque to the southwest, Susie Lake on a bench beyond it, and Lake Aloha along the east base of the granitic Crystal Range.

There being now only 200 vertical feet to climb to the summit, we first head east to a weatherbeaten clump of conifers, which makes a good wind-protected emergency shelter, but is no place to sit out a lightning storm. You should not attempt to climb to this summit—or any summit—if a storm is impending. We now follow a rocky route, first northeast to the brink of a dangerously steep avalanche chute, then diagonally northwest for the last few steps to the pointed summit. Most panoramas from any high summit are spectacular, but those from dark, metamorphic **Mt. Tallac** are exceptional. Because it stands so close to Lake Tahoe, it offers a view of almost the entire lake, and we can study the major currents that swirl about in it. Standing above Tahoe's northeast end is andesite-capped Mt. Rose, which at 10,776 feet is the basin's third highest peak. Along the east shore rise the granitic western slopes of the Carson Range, which remain unglaciated because they lie within a rain shadow cast by the Sierra crest above Tahoe's western shore. The western crest receives 70-90 inches of precipitation annually, whereas the eastern crest receives only about 30-40 inches.

Along the lake's south shore are the readily visible Tahoe Keys, which together with the highrises stand out in this basin as a monument to man's economic exploitation of a unique high-mountain lake basin that should have been a national park. Southeast of this shore rise 10,881' Freel Peak and 10,823' Jobs Sister, ranking first and second among the basin's peaks. In the distance to the southeast is the 10,000' ridge near Carson Pass. To the south rises granitic Echo Peak, and beyond it Ralston Peak, the unseen Echo Lakes lying between them. West of Ralston Peak is Pyramid Peak, the high point and south end of the Crystal Range.

Of much interest are the huge, linear, lateral moraines that border Emerald Bay, Cascade Lake, and Fallen Leaf Lake. With crests as high as 900 feet above adjacent basin floors, the crests of these moraines indicate the *minimum* thickness of the glacier that filled the basins. The Tahoe basin must have been an extremely impressive sight some 130-200,000 years ago. During that time large glaciers from Squaw Valley, and from Pole Creek north of it, periodically dammed Tahoe's outlet and raised the lake's level. And then glaciers from the Upper Truckee River canyon and from every canyon along the lake's west shore north to its outlet reached the lake, spalling icebergs into its frigid, deep water.

~ 80 ~
# Glen Alpine Trail to Grass Lake

Distances:
1.6 miles to Grass Lake Trail
2.6 miles to Grass Lake
Low/High Elevations: 6540'/7240'
Season: Early July through mid-October
Classification: Easy
Map: 35
Trailheads: Hikes 80-84 start near Glen Alpine Creek, and since all of them enter Desolation Wilderness, you'll need a wilderness permit. The most convenient place to get one is at the Lake Tahoe Visitor Center, whose entrance is on Highway 89 about 150 yards west of Fallen Leaf Road. (This road is 3.1 miles northwest on Highway 89 from the junction in South Lake Tahoe where Highway 50 branches northeast from Highway 89.) With permit in hand, drive 4.5 miles south on Fallen Leaf Road, then 0.4 mile west through Fallen Leaf Lake's south-shore development to a junction with a road which branches right to immediately bridge Glen Alpine Creek before ending at Stanford Sierra Camp. Continue ahead 0.4 mile farther up the main road to the sometimes cryptic start of the Tamarack Trail, Hike 84, which begins 300 yards before the road bridges cascading Glen Alpine Creek. If those taking this hike can't find a roadside parking spot by this trailhead, they should park at the Glen Alpine trailhead parking area, spread out just beyond the bridge. Those taking Hikes 80-83 park there, where there usually are wilderness permits for *day users*.

Immediately beyond the bridge is the moderately large Glen Alpine trailhead parking area (for Hikes 80-83), which usually has wilderness permits for *day users*. Park here if

you can't find a roadside spot by the trailhead.

Introduction
An easy day hike, this route leads to a rock-bound lake with a dramatic cascade on the cliffs beyond it. Its fairly warm water is just right for a midsummer afternoon swim. Being so close to the trailhead, the lake has developed vegetation, sanitation, and soil problems due to overuse. Hence if you feel you absolutely must camp at Grass Lake, do so with minimum impact (no fires; carry out *all* wastes).

Description
From the Glen Alpine trailhead parking area you walk west about 1.1 miles on a closed road past private homes to where a trail begins just beyond Glen Alpine Springs. Nathan Gilmore discovered these mineral springs—high in bicarbonate, chloride, sodium, and calcium—while looking for his stray cattle in 1863. They were then gushing at about 200 gallons an hour. In the late 1870s Gilmore began bottling the carbonated water, which soon achieved a reputation, and he developed Glen Alpine Springs into a very popular resort.

Our first ½ mile of trail tread is up the Glen Alpine Trail, which soon climbs southeast about 200 yards before climbing west up a rocky, joint-controlled gully. You make a switchback south out of the gully, curve around a low ridge, and walk west again to a small, waist-deep pool with a tiny fall splashing into it. Just beyond it, on a flat immediately before the trail bends northeast as it starts a switchbacking climb, we arrive at a junction with the **Grass Lake Trail**. From here, head a few yards west, jump across Gilmore Lake's outlet creek, which here is part of the Desolation Wilderness boundary, and follow the trail southwest up a brushy slope to reach a grassy pond that is an overflow of Glen Alpine Creek. The best spot to cross this creek is at some rapids below the pond, where water flows east down a small, granitic, 20-foot-high **V** gorge.

Beyond this crossing our trail winds almost up to the outlet creek of Lake Lucille. You may see an older trail that still climbs southwest to it before curving northwest to Grass Lake, but our trail curves north, passes northwest through a **V** trough, and then curves southwest and descends through another one. Joint control certainly expresses itself in this granodiorite bedrock. Just beyond the second trough our trail meets the older trail, and 100 yards farther we are at the southeast corner of shallow **Grass Lake**. The trail continues 0.2 mile to a shallow bay, passing several campsites located too close to the shoreline to be legal. For legal camping, continue westward.

Lining the south shore are some metavolcanic rocks, below which is the lake's deepest water. Here, an eight-foot-high rock bench makes an ideal platform for diving into the lake's fairly clear water, which warms up into the high 60s. These brown rocks contrast strongly with the gray, joint-controlled granitic ones that dam the lake's east end. Fishing is poor because the lake is relatively small and is heavily fished. However, what may be lost in the way of a trout dinner is compensated for by the lovely lakeside surrounding, including a silvery cascade from Susie Lake that splashes down the cliff northwest of us.

Grass Lake

⇜ **81** ⇝
Glen Alpine Trail to Gilmore Lake and Mt. Tallac

Distances:
1.6 miles to Grass Lake Trail
3.5 miles to Pacific Crest Trail
4.2 miles to Gilmore Lake
6.0 miles to Mt. Tallac

Low/High Elevations: 6540'/9735'

Season: Early July through mid-October

Classification: Moderate to lake, strenuous to summit

Map: 35

Trailhead: See the Hike 80 trailhead description.

Introduction
Of all the significant peaks you can climb by trail, Mt. Tallac is the closest one to Lake Tahoe's shore. Consequently, your lake view is truly exceptional, and it is highlighted by the dramatic, linear, prodigious lateral moraines that border Emerald Bay, Cascade Lake, and Fallen Leaf Lake. Gilmore Lake, along your ascent route, is an ideal spot to rest or camp before making the final push for the summit.

Description
Follow Hike 80 1.1 miles on a closed road to the Glen Alpine Trail, then ascend it 0.5 mile to a junction with the **Grass Lake Trail**. Over the next 1.6 miles we switchback north up a brushy, open-forested granitic slope, where frisky golden-mantled ground squirrels scamper about. Re-entering forest shade, we soon come to an alder-lined, step-across creeklet, then continue upward and onward to Gilmore Lake's outlet creek, which one must have to ford in early summer. Just 30 yards beyond its crossing, we reach a signed trail fork. Both forks climb to the Pacific Crest Trail, which also doubles through most of Desolation Wilderness as the Tahoe-Yosemite Trail. Those on Hike 83 fork left, those on Hikes 81 and 82 fork right. Taking the right fork, we make a ¼-mile ascent up a rocky path, climbing steadily above a shallow tarn below us to a juniper-flat intersection with the

Wildflower Plate 14. Desolation Wilderness flowers, continued.
1 Three-leaved lewisia (white with pink stripes), 2 western spring beauty (white to pale-pink), 3 (longhorn) steer's head (pale pink), 4 Sierra saxifrage (whitish with yellow center), 5 water-plantain buttercup (yellow), 6 rosy sedum (kingscrown) (burgundy red), 7 shaggy hawkweed (yellow), 8 hawksbeard (yellow), 9 Douglas' catchfly (campion) (white to lavender).

Gilmore Lake and Mt. Tallac

Pacific Crest Trail, or PCT. From here Hike 82 continues straight ahead to Half Moon and Alta Morris lakes.

On the PCT we switchback north up mostly open slopes for 0.6 mile, passing large, rusty-barked junipers, and having views south to shallow Grass Lake and southwest to rockbound Susie Lake. Just before the trail comes alongside Gilmore Lake's cascading outlet creek, you catch a glimpse of granite-lined Lake Aloha in the southwest. Veering slightly away from the creek, we reach an almost level junction in an open lodgepole-pine forest. From here the PCT turns west and continues its climb to Dicks Pass (Hike 66).

We, however, head north, upstream, and in 200 yards reach a trail junction. To reach Mt. Tallac or the east shore of **Gilmore Lake**, you cross the outlet creek; to reach its south shore head briefly up the outlet creek. Campsites near the outlet at the lake's southeast shore are overused, so if you want to camp at the lake, use ones above the south and east shores. In the entire Sierra there is hardly a lake more circular than this one, and it is amazing that it doesn't bear the name *Round Lake*, especially when you consider how many noncircular lakes in the Sierra do bear this name. Instead, it was named to honor Nathan Gilmore, a local settler from 1863 onward, who in 1877 stocked this lake with 20 black bass. It later was stocked with lake, brook, and rainbow trout, but now is stocked only with rainbow trout.

From just above the southeast shore our trail to Mt. Tallac climbs steeply, first northeast and then north, heading up through a rapidly thinning forest of lodgepole and whitebark pines and crossing three flower-lined creeklets. As the last of the snow is melting, these creeklets and associated seeps can be densely speckled yellow with a myriad of buttercups, which are shown on Plate 14. Other wildflowers which appear on this plate can also be plentiful, but the smaller ones—the lewisia and steer's head in particular—are easily overlooked. Interested botanists will also want to consult Plates 11, 13, 15, 16, and 17, all dealing with high-elevation wildflowers.

Our path becomes drier as we hike to within 150 yards of a 9000-foot-high saddle, then switchback east up the grass- and sagebrush-lined trail. About 200 feet below the summit we meet the **Mt. Tallac Trail**, which has climbed past Floating Island and Cathedral lakes (Hike 79). The last part of that hike describes the final ¼-mile ascent plus the views you'll see from the summit.

⋙ 82 ⋘
Glen Alpine Trail to Half Moon and Alta Morris Lakes

Distances:
4.8 miles to Half Moon Lake
5.5 miles to Alta Morris Lake
Low/High Elevations: 6540'/8150'
Season: Late July through mid-October
Classification: Moderate
Maps: 35 and 34
Trailhead: See the Hike 80 trailhead description.

Introduction

Situated on the corrugated bedrock floor of an immense cirque, Half Moon and Alta Morris lakes see relatively little use despite their accessibility; they are bypassed for lakes in more demure settings along the highly popular Pacific Crest/Tahoe-Yosemite trail. Within this cirque basin you're almost guaranteed to find a suitable, isolated campsite.

Half Moon Lake

Description

Follow the first paragraph of the previous hike 3.5 miles up to the juniper-flat intersection with the Pacific Crest Trail, from where you continue straight ahead. Our trail starts a contour northwest, then arcs west across a small, forested bowl. Leaving the bowl, we climb to a low ridge and see Susie Lake, nestled in her metamorphic bed. On the skyline, Pyramid Peak stands at the south end of a long stretch of the granitic Crystal Range. Leaving this viewpoint, we descend slightly into a shallow gully, go up it, cross a low ridge bordering it, and then traverse a lodgepole flat and a mucky-banked creeklet flowing through it. Next we climb up the southwest slope of yet another gully and soon approach a chest-deep pond, on the left. After passing two smaller ponds on the right, which support pond lilies and other aquatic vegetation, we come to a grass-lined pond with a campsite on its northeast shore. Since this site is within 100 feet of the shoreline, it is off limits, so if you want to camp in this vicinity, try above the south or west shore.

From a low ridge immediately beyond the last pond, we see clear, appropriately named **Half Moon Lake**, which occupies almost the entire width of the huge cirque lying between Jacks Peak and Dicks Pass. Not only is this the largest cirque in Desolation Wilderness, but it is also the deepest, and the lake is hemmed in on three sides by a dark wall of steep rock that averages 1300 feet high.

The trail makes an undulating traverse across a meadowy talus slope of metamorphic rock that borders the lake's north and west shores. In some places the trail is boggy; in others it is indistinct and somewhat overgrown with willows. Eventually you'll reach a fairly large campsite, nestled under pines and hemlocks, on a bench above the northwest shore of **Alta Morris Lake**. This lake, perhaps the most scenic cirque lake in the wilderness, rests above the southwest corner of Half Moon Lake, and it can be approached by a more direct, drier, cross-country route.

Starting this route when you first see Half Moon Lake, head west and stay on the rocky bench above its south shore. On the map this route looks almost level, but in reality you ascend and descend a number of small, glacier-smoothed gullies. Midway across your washboard traverse you'll cross Half Moon's outlet creek, which cascades into a clear, linear, grassy-bottomed lakelet that is nice to camp near. Continuing west toward the dark rusty-brown metamorphosed sandstone-and-mudstone east buttress of Jacks Peak, you walk across buff-colored metamorphosed conglomerate that contrasts strongly with it. Soon you reach one or more small, semistagnant ponds and, just beyond them, the northeast bench above Alta Morris Lake. Trout fishing, hopefully, will be good at both lakes.

≪ 83 ≫
Glen Alpine Trail to
Susie and Heather Lakes
and Lake Aloha

Distances:
3.7 miles to Pacific Crest Trail
4.3 miles to Susie Lake
5.2 miles to Heather Lake
6.1 miles to Lake Aloha
Low/High Elevations: 6540'/8120'
Season: Mid-July through mid-October
Classification: Moderate
Maps: 35 and 34
Trailhead: See the Hike 80 trailhead description.

Introduction

This route takes you up to large, shallow Lake Aloha, which is probably the most popular lake in Desolation Wilderness. By arriving at its scenic northeast shore, however, you avoid most backpackers, who generally camp at its south shore. Rockbound Susie Lake, two-thirds of the way up to Aloha, is a favorite lake of many backpackers, and for late-season excursions it is a well chosen goal, because much of Aloha dries up after Labor Day.

Before then, both Susie and Heather lakes may be too crowded—at least on weekends—to suit your fancy.

Description

Follow Hike 80 1.1 miles along a closed road, then 0.5 mile up to the Glen Alpine Trail junction, then follow Hike 81 1.6 miles up to a signed trail fork just beyond Gilmore Lake's outlet creek. The right fork climbs to a junction with trails to Dicks Pass, Mt. Tallac, and Half Moon Lake (Hikes 66, 81, and 82). We take the left fork, which over 0.5 mile makes an initial climb west, traverses through a lodgepole forest past four water-lily ponds, and then descends westward to join the **Pacific Crest Trail**. Here, at the upper end of a boggy meadow, you can identify an abundant variety of wildflowers—after mid-August, when the mosquitoes aren't pestering you to death. Identified by their aromas are swamp onion, lupine, and coyote mint. Also look for tiger lily, corn lily, buttercup, columbine, ligusticum, paintbrush, senecio, yarrow, and daisy.

Ahead, we pass two stagnant ponds, climb over a low ridge, and find bedrock-rimmed Susie Lake lying before us. Precious little flat space for camping is to be found here, although on a weekend many backpackers

Susie Lake and Dicks Peak

33

63

64

66

Lake No 5

RED PK TR

8500

8000

Lots TRAIL

Lost
Lake

Lawrence
Lake

Lake No 9

9354

8800

Lake Doris

TRAIL

9331

8600

8400

Rockbound
Pass

TRAIL

Barrett
Lake

Top Lake

8400

90

8
7609

9

ROCKBOUND PASS

Univ Calif
Cow Camp

7800

8400

DRIVEWAY Spr

8400

8800

RANGE

x 9/63

LAKE

RED PEAK

7600

STOCK

7800

7600

Maud
Lake

8400

9400

8800

17

16

7778

7400

Willow
Flat

Silver

Creek

7600

Gertrude
Lake

Grave

Tyler
Lake

8400

BARRETT

7200

Fork

Silver

7800

7600

21

67

7984

8000

9925

Island
Lake

63

Jones

7200

LAKE

931

62

Mortimer
Flat

Creek

20

7800

7200

Fourth
of July
Flat

7200

7600

TYLER

8000

Umpa
Lake

TRAIL

Boomerang
Lake

Twin
Lakes

8600

68

9000

LEXDE

Silver

4254

7400

LAKES

7800

8000

Fork

7000

Hemlock
Lake

931

29

64

28

LAKE

HEMLOCK

8600

8000

69

Smith
Lake

Jones

62

Beauty
Lake

Gate

TWIN

Grouse
Lake

8600

8600

Dark
Lake

Wrights
Lake

Parking

7400

Secret
Lake

Parking

7000

7200

7000

Blue Mtn
8772

8400

Old Campground

32

SPILLWAY
6911

RS

Wrights
Lk CG

33

34

7655

16E13

70

6963

Creek

7200

7400

71

Bloodsucker
Lake

70

7600

34

see MAP 33

see MAP 35

66

RUBICON

China Flat

Rubicon

VALLEY

Divide

PACIFIC

Dicks Lake

6

Sprs

5

Kalmia Lake

RIVER

River

TRAIL

Jacks Mdw

Mosquito Pass

Jacks Peak
9856

Dicks Peak
9974

Sierra

Fall

x 9579

Dicks Pass

66

7

82

Half Moon Lake

Alta Morris Lake

CREST

HALF

MOON

8242

18

17

Susie Lake

TR

66

CREST

83

PACIFIC

20

7800

Heather Lake

66

8400

Clyde Lake

Island Lake

CRYSTAL

LAKE

ALOHA

Divide

PACIFIC

Lake Le Conte

Cracked Crag
8781

87

CREST

TRAIL

SPILLWAY
8116

87

Mt Price
9975

ISOLATION RANGE

Mt Agassiz

WILDERNESS

DESOLATION

American Lake

29

8383

Smith Lake

9250

Lyons Lake

Waca Lake

Channel Lake

32

VALLEY

Pyramid Lake

Desolation Lake

71

Lake Sylvia

Pyramid Pk
9983

71

Gefo Lake

Town Lake

Osma Lake

Pyramid Cr

74

Ropi Lake

72

Pitt Lake

T 12 N
T 11 N

see MAP 32

35

see MAP 34

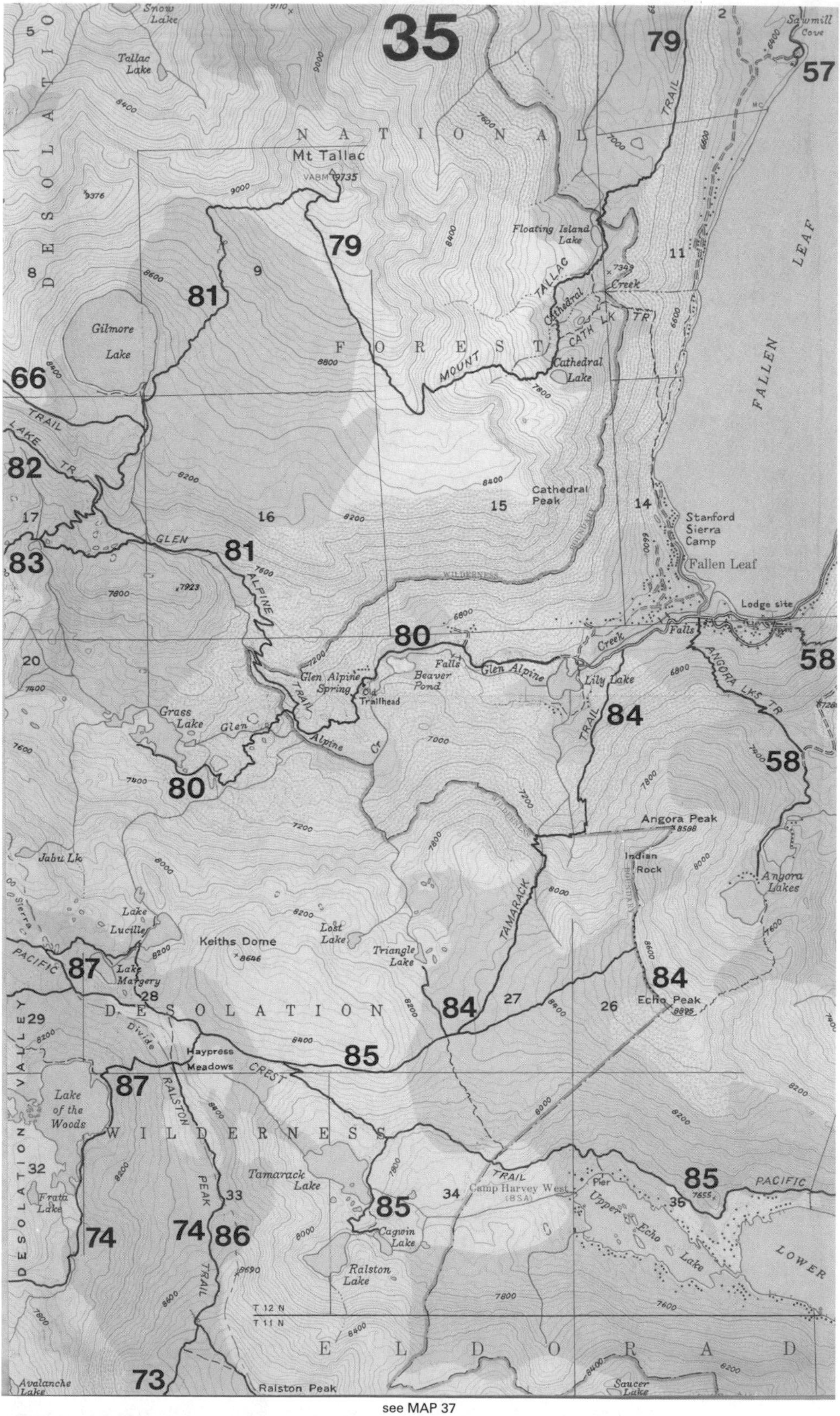

see MAP 36

see MAP 37

Snow Lake
Tallac Lake
Sawmill Cove
Mt Tallac
VABM 9735
Floating Island Lake
Cathedral Creek
DESOLATION
NATIONAL
FOREST
MOUNT TALLAC
Gilmore Lake
Cathedral Lake
Cathedral Peak
Stanford Sierra Camp
Fallen Leaf
FALLEN LEAF
Lodge site
Falls
WILDERNESS
Glen Alpine Spring
Beaver Pond
Falls
Glen Alpine Creek
Lily Lake
Trailhead
Grass Lake
Glen
ANGORA LKS TR
Jabu Lk
Angora Peak
Indian Rock
Angora Lakes
Lake Lucille
Keiths Dome
Lost Lake
Triangle Lake
Echo Peak
Lake Margery
DESOLATION
Haypress Meadows
CREST
TAMARACK TRAIL
PACIFIC CREST TRAIL
DESOLATION VALLEY
Lake of the Woods
WILDERNESS
Ralston Peak
RALSTON PEAK TRAIL
Frata Lake
Tamarack Lake
Camp Harvey West (BSA)
Pier
Upper Echo Lake
PACIFIC
LOWER
Cagwin Lake
Ralston Lake
T 12 N
T 11 N
ELDORADO
Avalanche Lake
Ralston Peak
Saucer Lake

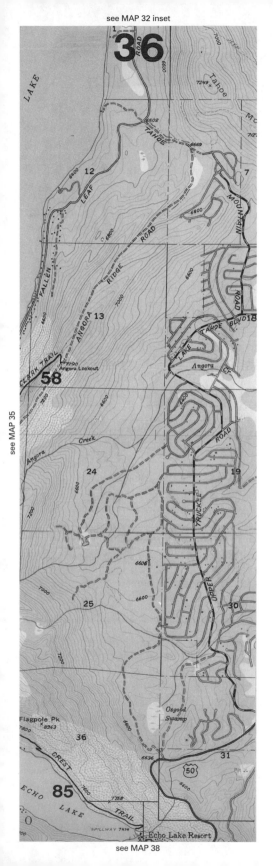

may try to do so. Head south to soon reach the outlet creek of **Susie Lake**. Along it a spur trail descends 70 yards to a small bench, which has suitable campsites. From the outlet your route then rounds the lake to a cove along its southwest shore, from which it leaves the multihued environs for a short climb over a barren ridge to **Heather Lake**. After you skirt Heather Lake's north shore, you'll find an adequate campsite near a large red fir by an inlet creek. We cross this creek, climb a bit to a switchback by the creek's 20-foot-high waterfall, then with a bit more effort top out at the northeast corner of **Lake Aloha**.

From a junction at this corner the PCT heads southeast, while the Rubicon River Trail (part of Hike 66) heads west. Along the latter you'll find campsites with fine sunrise views across the lake—before mid-September, that is. Soon after the Labor Day weekend, the lake is drained to fill other reservoirs lying closer to Sacramento, so from about mid-September onward you see a desolate lake bottom—the rumpled floor of Desolation Valley. This draw-down does allow, however, cross-country routes across the lake where midsummer hikers would have to walk on water. The move conventional route along the seasonally giant lake's northeast shore is described, in a northward direction, in Hike 87.

⋙ 84 ⋘
Tamarack Trail to Triangle Lake and Echo Peak

Distances:
2.3 miles to flat saddle with trail intersection
2.7 miles to Triangle Lake
3.6 miles to Echo Peak
Low/High Elevations: 6520′/8895′
Season: Mid-July through mid-October
Classification: Strenuous
Map: 35
Trailhead: See the Hike 80 trailhead description.

Introduction

Almost every ascent to a mountain's summit provides the climber with far-ranging, panoramic views. This hike up a primitive trail to the Echo Peak ridge and summit area certainly is no exception, but in addition it routes your return trip past Upper Angora Lake, which is an ideal relaxing site after your arduous climb. The Tamarack Trail is definitely the hard way up to Triangle Lake and Echo Peak. However, for summer residents or visitors in the Fallen Leaf Lake area, it is an appropriate route, for one does not have to drive all the way up to the Echo Lake trailhead. For these people, a hike part way up the trail may be rewarding. The wildflowers along the ascent in midsummer are so abundant that the amateur botanist may feel fulfilled even if he or she never makes it to the top.

In early summer the Tamarack Trail may be too dangerous. Before mid-July, start from the Echo Lakes trailhead and follow Hike 85 up to the Triangle Lake saddle and then east to Echo Peak. Hike 84's descent route is safe, but it is so steep that few would want to climb up it. It is, however, the shortest way to the top, only 2.0 miles from the Angora Lakes parking lot (see Hike 58's trailhead directions).

Description

Starting on metamorphic bedrock with granitic boulders transported here by a glacier, the trail enters an open forest of white fir and lodgepole and Jeffrey pine, with a rich substory of aspen, alder, willow, vine maple, tobacco brush, currant, and spiraea. Beyond a low knoll we get a view of Mt. Tallac's dark back side, then enter a shady forest. Now a steep ascent begins, but thirst on this climb can be slaked at a number of refreshing creeklets, each with its own population of water-loving plants, including thimbleberry, columbine, monk's hood, and bracken fern. Less common is pinedrops, and rare is snow plant, these having, respectively, orange and red stems. Lacking chlorophyll, they obtain nutrients mostly from soil fungi.

The grade eases and the forest opens as we approach a second knoll, from which we can look west-northwest at the two brownish-red metamorphic summits of Jacks and Dicks

peaks. Near us is a huge, 20-foot-high orange-and-gray block of metamorphic rock in contact with granitic rock that intruded it about 90 million years ago. Beyond it we are soon climbing up steep switchbacks through an overwhelming amount of vegetation. Finally emerging from this jungle, we make a short traverse west to a relatively barren flat on which a few hardy junipers survive. From here we have an inspiring view of most of Fallen Leaf Lake and part of Lake Tahoe beyond it. Now also visible is Mt. Tallac's rusty summit. Just above our flat is an exposed campsite, relatively close to a long-lasting snowfield, and both are just inside the Desolation Wilderness boundary.

For many, this is as far as they may want to ascend, because now a short, climbing traverse west brings us to a *dangerous creek*, about 1.1 miles into our route, that we must jump across. Should you slip, you're likely to go over the brink of a very steep cascade. Short, steep switchbacks up a path gloriously lined with wildflowers take us to a safe recrossing of the creek and to some good rocks to stop at and rest, from which one can photograph the magnificent canyon and lateral moraines to the north.

Refreshed, we climb steeply up the wild-flowered east bank of the creek, cross it after a 250-foot climb, then continue up an increasingly easy grade that eventually levels off. Here we see a panorama from Lake Tahoe past Tallac, Dicks, and Jacks summits to barely showing Pyramid Peak, in the west-south-west. From this vicinity, adept hikers can start a cross-country jaunt west to Triangle Lake, saving ½ mile. Along a nearly level stretch of trail the forest now is an open one of juniper, western white pine, and mountain hemlock, and on slopes grasses, sedges, sagebrush, and drought-resistant wildflowers grow. An easy stroll next takes us down to a **flat saddle with a trail intersection**. To the north, the Triangle Lake Trail descends about 0.4 mile to **Triangle Lake**; south, it descends to the Echo Lakes; west, the Tamarack Trail traverses to the Pacific Crest Trail (see Hike 85 for more details about the lake and the trails to it).

To climb Echo Peak, retrace your steps 85 yards east-northeast to where your trail turns left, northeast. From there you start east up an unofficial use trail. This quickly curves northeast, and one basically just ascends directly upslope. The topography and vegetation are so amenable to cross-country travel that you need not attempt to look for a trail. You climb through an open forest that now includes whitebark pine, then eventually reach the rocky northwest ridge of Echo Peak.

Here it behooves you to walk 130 yards north to the brink of the ridge, from where you not only see everything you might have seen from the Angora Lookout (Hike 58), but also have a better perspective of it all. Very conspicuous is Mt. Tallac's preglacial, almost flat erosion surface, which has remained little changed over millions of years. Conventional wisdom has it that the deep canyon below it was carved by glaciers. Actually, in resistant rock, which abounds in our guidebook's area, glaciers are virtually impotent at deeply eroding the landscape. Dated, ancient lava flows on the slopes and floors of glaciated Sierran canyons allow one to reconstruct ancient canyons. Doing so shows that they had already attained their "glacial topography" some 30 million years before the first major glaciers ever entered them. Glaciers merely accentuated the features of the preglacial topography, and on slopes and ridges deposited a veneer of transported rockfall to form the moraines.

From where we reached the northwest ridge, an easy, ducked route southeast takes us to granitic, potholed **Echo Peak**, which gives us an additional panorama, one of the Crystal Range to the south and west. On the southeast horizon near Carson Pass stand Stevens and Red Lake peaks, respectively 10,059 and 10,063 feet, with hulking Round Top, to their right, overtopping them at 10,381 feet. Like every other Tahoe peak, ours has its resident golden-mantled ground squirrels, which may search through your pack, should you leave it for a minute.

Descend the way you came, or else descend to Upper Angora Lake. To do that, start east from the summit on a ducked use trail through gruss, which is an accumulation of feldspar and quartz crystals that have broken off weathered granitic rock after the dark minerals disintegrated and freed them. The use trail soon starts a descent on a very steep, minor northeast ridge of Echo Peak, and then it continues down a gully so rich in gruss that you can almost ski down it. Large backpacks are definitely not recommended on this very steep descent. Several short-switchback routes descend northeast down this gully and merge on a flat 300 feet above the lake. Midway down the very steep gully someone long ago placed a facetious sign, *Caution— Maximum Speed 25 Mi.*

From the flat, descend northwest very steeply down another gully to Upper Angora Lake's southeast corner. Here you can traverse west to a rock slab above the south shore, where you can sunbathe or dive into water that is deep for a lake its size—48 feet. High benches serve as high-dive platforms, but in the past there have been injuries and at least one death, so be careful. The trail from the southeast corner consists of a traverse across a large-block talus slope to the lake's outlet, then a walk northwest to Angora Lakes Resort. From here follow Hike 58's description down to a trailhead on Fallen Leaf Road, then hike southwest 0.4 mile up the road to your original trailhead.

⋘ 85 ⋙
Echo Lake to Tamarack and Triangle Lakes and Echo Peak

Distances:
3.6 miles to spur trail
    0.2 mile on spur trail to Tamarack Lake
    0.5 mile on spur trail to Ralston and
      Cagwin lakes
4.3 miles to Tamarack Trail
5.1 miles to flat saddle
5.5 miles to Triangle Lake
6.4 miles to Echo Peak
Low/High Elevations: 7420′/8895′
Season: Early July through mid-October
Classification: Easy to Tamarack, Ralston, and Cagwin lakes; moderate to Triangle Lake and Echo Peak
Maps: 36 and 35

Trailhead: From the Highway 49 junction in Placerville, drive 5 miles east up Highway 50 to the Eldorado National Forest Information Center, located on Camino Heights Drive. Get your wilderness permit there, then continue 41 miles up to Johnson Pass Road. (Westbound drivers: this road is 1¼ miles west from Echo Summit.) This road climbs 0.6 mile east to a junction, where you turn sharply left and take the Echo Lakes Road 0.9 mile north to a large parking area, most of it on the south side of the road. Park here, *not* down at Echo Lake Resort. The southbound Pacific Crest Trail, not described in this book, starts from the smaller north part of the parking area. The northbound trail starts from Lower Echo Lake's dam, where day users *usually* can get wilderness permits. To reach this north trailhead, take a short steep trail northwest down to it, starting from the west end of the north part of the parking area.

Introduction

The trail from Lower Echo Lake to Lake Aloha may be the most heavily used one in the wilderness. Its popularity is due in part to its accessibility—just off Highway 50—to nearby summer homes and summer camps, and to the trail's relative ease. At 7420 feet the trailhead is about 800 feet higher than other wilderness trailheads, hence the hiker has that much less elevation to gain. Also, hikers who take the Echo Lakes water taxi can subtract 2.5 miles from the above mileages, making the routes to Tamarack, Ralston, Cagwin, and Triangle lakes a one-hour hike (or less) for most, and the route to Echo Peak a two-hour hike.

Description

To save 5.0 miles of round-trip hiking, take the Echo Lakes water taxi, operated by Echo Lake Resort. Since Pacific Gas and Electric Company owns the top 12 feet of the lake (because they've dammed it that high), they can lower the water by that amount, and by mid-September they usually do so. Then the lake reverts to its natural, upper-lower pair of lakes, and the taxi goes only to the peninsula separating the two lakes. You'll still save 3.4 miles, round trip. The first part of Hike 85 is on a minuscule segment of the 2650-mile

Pacific Crest Trail, which extends from the Canadian border to the Mexican border. On our hike this PCT segment also coincides with the Tahoe-Yosemite Trail, or TYT, and with the Tahoe Rim Trail, or TRT.

We begin by crossing Lower Echo Lake's dam, make an initial climb east, and then head west on a sparsely treed, rollercoaster trail. The trail soon traverses below some prominent granodiorite cliffs. These and others above the Echo Lakes offer climbers about 100 routes, almost all imaginably difficult for the non-climber. Climbers will find many routes described in Carville's guide, mentioned under "Recommended Reading and Source Materials."

Beyond the prominent cliffs the trail switchbacks twice and then climbs high above lakeshore summer homes. Scattered Jeffrey pines give way to thick groves of lodgepoles as we descend toward the lower lake's northwest shore. We then traverse to a rusty, granitic knoll, round it to forested slopes above Upper Echo Lake, and continue westward. The tree cover is thick enough to blot out any possible view of the public pier at which the water taxis land, and use trails down to the lake may add to the confusion. If you've taken the taxi, you'll know which trail to take back. The proper trail should be signed, and it descends 90 yards to a public phone near the pier. Phone the resort (659-7207) if you want a boat ride back.

Beyond the pier's trail you climb a rocky tread up open slopes of slightly metamorphosed quartz monzonite and quickly reach a junction with a faint trail. The dark inclusions you've been seeing in the rocks over the last stretch are blocks of rock that were broken off and incorporated into rising magma that later solidified to form a pluton. The Triangle Lake Trail is a shortcut to Triangle Lake, climbing steeply ¾ mile north to a saddle, then descending to the lake. If unsigned, this northbound trail can be easily missed. It begins just 20 yards past a small bend that has conspicuous junipers growing on it and 70 yards before you enter an obvious, small grove of lodgepole pines. This route also provides the shortest way to Echo Peak, described below. If you take this shortcut trail, you can subtract 1.3 miles from the above distances.

Onward from the Triangle Lake Trail, we ascend 0.6 mile, then our PCT rounds a bend, passes through a dynamited, 5-foot-high trail cut, and in 40 yards reaches an obvious junction with a **spur trail**. From here the PCT continues to climb, while the ducked spur trail descends south over barren bedrock to **Tamarack Lake**, largest of the Ralston Peak basin lakes and, like the other two, fringed with mountain hemlock and lodgepole and western white pine. From the south tip of this shallow lake you can either head south on a ducked route directly over a low ridge and descend to the north shore of moderately deep **Cagwin Lake**, lined with red mountain heather and Labrador tea. Or you can follow a primitive trail southwest over the west end of the ridge and down to deep **Ralston Lake**, which is totally surrounded by steep slopes. Because these three lakes are so close to the trailhead, they are heavily used, and consequently the Forest Service prohibits camping at them.

From the spur-trail junction, the PCT climbs to a tiny creeklet in a gully, then follows two switchbacks up to a bedrock bench and a junction with the **Tamarack Trail**. On it you make a nearly effortless traverse east across a slope predominantly colored with paintbrush and sagebrush, and you pass occasional junipers and view the changing perspective of the Ralston Peak basin lakes below and the peak above. Then make a brief climb to a ridge and a new panorama suddenly appears. To the east you get an aerial view of both Echo Lakes and the Sierra beyond; to the west looms Pyramid Peak above Haypress Meadows; to the south you have a detailed inspection of the basin lakes below; and to the north you even see a bit of Lake Tahoe beyond Angora Peak. Most of the crest of the Crystal Range, northwest to around Rockbound Pass, is visible in one sweeping glance. After you have taken in this grand panorama, continue onward, descending ⅓ mile to a broad, **flat saddle**, where you intersect the northbound Triangle Lake Trail you had met earlier.

Take this trail northward, first through a meadow then across ducked quartz-mon-

Pond lilies in placid Cagwin Lake

zonite bedrock above the lake, and have an excellent view of Mt. Tallac and its southern slopes. After 40 yards down the jagged bedrock, drop a few yards east to a creeklet and follow a duff trail down to the shallow, grassy south end of **Triangle Lake**. From good diving rocks above the lake's northwest shore one can look down into the water and see trout swimming lazily in this deep arm of the slightly cloudy lake. Small, fair campsites lie in nooks among the ice-fractured rocks above the lake, but since the lake is so close to the trailhead, one should only day hike to it. In a cirque just ¼ mile west of this lake lies trout-stocked Lost Lake, which receives much less visitation.

Those who want to climb **Echo Peak**, 1.3 miles east of the flat saddle above Triangle Lake, follow a trail about 85 yards east-northeast to where it turns left, northeast. From there an unofficial use trail starts east. Hike 84 has a description of this route and the summit's views.

⊰⊱ 86 ⊰⊱
Echo Lake to Ralston Peak

Distances:
4.7 miles to Haypress Meadows
4.9 miles to Ralston Peak Trail
6.9 miles to Ralston Peak
Low/High Elevations: 7420'/9235'
Season: Mid-July through mid-October
Classification: Moderate
Maps: 36, 35, and 37
Trailhead: Same as the Hike 85 trailhead.

Introduction
See the Hike 73 introduction.

Description
As in Hike 85, if you take the Echo Lakes water taxi, you can subtract 2.5 miles from the above mileages. First, follow that hike 4.3 miles up to a junction with the eastbound Tamarack Trail, then just under 0.4 mile beyond it you meet the **Lake of the Woods Trail**. Leave the Pacific Crest Trail by forking left, and skirt past Haypress Meadows on a short climb southwest to a ridgecrest intersection of the **Ralston Peak Trail**. While most hikers continue down to Lake of the Woods, you stick to the ridgecrest. Your rocky route, climbs south over a ridgecrest knoll rather than around it, giving you views of Tamarack, Ralston, Cagwin, and Echo lakes to the east, and Lake of the Woods, Lake Aloha, and a gaggle of Desolation Valley lakes to the west.

Just beyond the knoll is a saddle with a seasonal pond, from which you traverse quickly past a more lasting one, then climb, steeply at times, up through a hemlock forest. Before August this ascent can be quite snowy. About 1⅓ miles from the Lake of the Woods Trail you enter a small subalpine meadow, in which the trail can be easily lost. A snowfield, often lasting into August, lies above the boggy meadow's south side, and it can obscure the route. You climb southeast steeply up a bowl to an open ridge, which to its west has clusters of mountain hemlocks. You continue climbing southeast to the obvious summit of **Ralston Peak**, whose views are mentioned in Hike 73.

⊰⊱ 87 ⊰⊱
Echo Lake to Lake of the Woods and Lake Aloha

Distances:
4.7 miles to Lake of the Woods Trail
   0.6 mile on trail to Lake of the Woods
   2.3 miles to Ropi Lake
4.9 miles to Lake Lucille Trail
   0.2 mile on and off trail to Lake Margery
   0.3 mile on trail to Lake Lucille
5.3 miles to Lake Aloha Trail
   0.5 mile to Lake Aloha, southeast corner
6.1 miles to Lake Aloha, east shore
6.6 miles to use trail
   0.1 mile to Lake LeConte
7.5 miles to Lake Aloha, northeast corner
Low/High Elevations: 7420'/8430'
Season: Mid-July through mid-October
Classification: Moderate
Maps: 36, 35, and 34
Trailhead: Same as the Hike 85 trailhead.

Introduction
Most backpackers starting from Echo Lake set either Lake Aloha or Lake of the Woods as their primary goal. If they take the Echo Lakes water taxi, they can subtract 2.5 miles from the above mileages. Then, only lightly visited Clyde Lake, on the far side of Mosquito Pass, is more than 5 miles (a couple of hours) away. And there are over a dozen lakes—mostly between Lake Aloha and Ropi Lake—that can be reached by easy cross-country hiking. Furthermore, this hike's main thoroughfare is part of the Pacific Crest, Tahoe-Yosemite, and Tahoe Rim trails. No wonder the Echo Lake trailhead is so busy. While most hikers won't proceed past Lake Aloha, those on the PCT/TYT/TRT do. Since the PCT goes on to the Canadian border—certainly beyond the scope of this book—you might be more prudent to take the TYT, which ends at Lake Tahoe's Meeks Bay. The TRT circles the lake, and is described in this guidebook. Where one TRT hike ends, you merely consult the next referenced hike.

Description

First follow Hike 85 4.3 miles on the PCT/TYT/TRT up to a junction with the Tamarack Trail. Now with almost all of the climbing behind you, regardless of your destination, you climb a bit higher in just under 0.4 mile to meet the **Lake of the Woods Trail**. If you're bound for that lake or any of the Desolation Valley lakes except Lake Aloha, fork left here. You skirt past Haypress Meadows and in 0.2 mile have a ridgecrest intersection of the Ralston Peak Trail. Hike 86 follows this trail south, but most hikers switchback 0.4 mile down to the northeast shore of **Lake of the Woods**. To minimize your impact on this popular lake, camp away from the shoreline, preferably at least 200 feet from it. See Hike 74 for the route down to **Ropi Lake**, and Hike 72 for routes to other lakes.

About 300 yards past the Lake of the Woods Trail, our hike's main thoroughfare, the PCT, reaches the north end of the Ralston Peak Trail. This climbs 0.2 mile south to the crest intersection of the Lake of the Woods Trail. Just 150 yards farther on the PCT, we reach the popular **Lake Lucille Trail**, forking right. This descends 150 yards to a trailside pond, from which you can head cross-country 200 yards northwest to the east shore of **Lake Margery**. If you keep to the sometimes soggy trail, you'll reach **Lake Lucille** in ¼ mile. At its northwest shore you'll find a small peninsula, almost an island, which is a good relaxing spot for lunch. Enriched with food and thought, and perhaps a view from the end of this lake down upon Fallen Leaf Lake and Lake Tahoe, you can follow the Lake Margery Trail up the northwest side of that lake's outlet creek. Pausing at this shallow, rock-dotted lake, you may see backpackers traversing high above it on the Pacific Crest expressway. Like Lake Lucille, Lake Margery has very limited camping potential if you camp away from its shore.

If you keep to the PCT, you'll log just over ½ mile between the Lake Lucille and Lake Margery trail junctions. About ⅓ mile west along this stretch, you'll meet the **Lake Aloha Trail**. Many hikers take this ½ mile down to the **southeast corner of Lake Aloha**. Approaching this corner, you'll pass a connecting trail from Lake of the Woods just 60 yards before another lateral branches left. This one winds ¾ mile over to Lake Aloha's 20-foot-high dam, at a popular swimming area when there's water in this reservoir. The great bulk of Lake Aloha is less than 10 feet deep, and after Labor Day the lake's water level drops sufficiently to create a desolate wilderness. Lake Aloha owes its existence (and Desolation Valley owes its desecration) directly to P.G.& E. and indirectly to California's burgeoning population.

If you're a purist and want to adhere to the PCT/TYT/TRT all the way to Lake Aloha, then continue northwest from the Lake Margery Trail, which starts its eastward course from the south tip of the westernmost of three shallow, nearly attached ponds. After 0.6 mile you'll reach a trail junction above the **east shore of Lake Aloha**. You can find good, legal camps between this junction and the one by the southeast corner, a 0.6-mile hike south along the east-shore trail.

The next stretch of PCT passes hundreds of dead lodgepole snags, the lasting reminders of the forest that grew here before the floor of Desolation Valley became Lake Aloha. The

Lake Lucille

lake is so shallow, one wonders if it holds enough water to justify its existence. When the lake drops just 5 feet, you can wade across it in several places. At its height the lake is a swimmer's paradise, for there are hundreds of rock islands you can reach. Should you want to swim in it, come here between mid-July and mid-August, when the water is warm enough and the lake is full.

Soon our trail takes us alongside a fairly clear, chest-deep lakelet, on our left, which like Aloha, warms up to the mid-sixties in midsummer. Walking 150 yards beyond it, we reach a gully, up which our trail seems to head. This gully holds a **use trail** to nearby, chilly, rockbound, trout-stocked **Lake LeConte**. This diversion provides you with a view of two high summits, Jacks and Dicks peaks.

A snowbank, often lasting through July, can obscure the correct PCT route, which makes a brief climb southwest from the gully before traversing northwest again. We now traverse along a nicer, snag-free section of Lake Aloha, and then reach its northeast cor-

ner, which has a two-foot-high retaining wall to prevent the lake from spilling over into Heather Lake, below us to the east. Climbing just a few yards beyond the wall, we meet a junction from where the PCT descends first north and then east to Heather Lake. Here, at the **northeast corner of Lake Aloha**, Hike 87 ends. Note that although you are surrounded by mountains, you are standing on the actual crest of the Sierra Nevada, which runs along the low dam. East, water flows down to Lake Tahoe, then out to Nevada. West, water drains from Lake Aloha out to the Pacific Ocean.

If you plan to continue onward, then consult the last half of Hike 66, which first climbs past Clyde Lake and over Mosquito Pass to your junction, then continues past Heather, Susie, and other lakes to Middle Velma Lake, which is about 17¼ miles from your trailhead. Meeks Bay is another 13 miles farther, and you achieve that objective by following Hike 76 in reverse. By traversing west from your junction, you can find additional, less-used campsites above the north shore of Lake Aloha.

Lake LeConte, Jacks Peak

An Echo Lakes panorama, from the eastbound lateral trail.

Round Top (left) and the Sisters, from Trail 17E47 one-half mile below Round Top Lake

Chapter 15

Dardanelles Roadless Area and northern Mokelumne Wilderness

Introduction

Upper Highway 50 is a dividing line between two obviously different landscapes: granitic Desolation Wilderness, to the north, and volcanic lands, to the south. In this chapter we investigate the latter. Among most of this landscape's trails the hiker is confronted with dark, volcanic cliffs, ridges, and peaks—some very impressive. Who would forget a campsite view of towering volcanic palisades above Round Lake's east shore, or a lake-hopping hike along the base of Round Top, the eroded core of a former volcano?

But although the hiker is left with the distinct impression that this landscape is largely volcanic, it's not. It is largely granitic. Our impression is due to the fact that the light granitic bedrock is almost everywhere overlain by dark, volcanic rocks. The area's streams, avalanches, and former glaciers have covered much of the granitic basin lands with a veneer of volcanic sediments, thereby hiding much of the granitic bedrock. Furthermore, these sediments decompose to soils that usually produce luxuriant forests, so the hiker, surrounded by trees, doesn't really notice the geology. And, it might be added, because the hiker typically is laboring uphill toward a lake, he or she couldn't care less. However, the hiker, upon reaching the lake, can relax and enjoy the views, which usually include volcanic cliffs, ridges, or peaks. The granitic nature of the basin lands escapes notice, for a green forest mantle enshrouds them.

The observant hiker, however, might notice one interesting feature about this seemingly volcanic landscape: every single lake in it lies in a *granitic* basin. You see none in a volcanic basin, although Round Lake superficially appears to be in one, althougly granitic bedrock lies beneath it. For a glacier to excavate a basin, the bedrock must be highly fractured in a local area. Where it is solid, glaciers hardly abrade it; where it is highly fractured in a local area, glaciers quarry out that local area to form a basin. Volcanic rock, on the other hand, is in our area mostly composed of relatively horizontal, less resistant beds of volcanic sediments and flows. Glaciers, flowing over such beds, plane them away, one layer after the other.

This chapter's first seven routes, Hikes 88-94, deal with trails in the Dardanelles Roadless Area. This "proto wilderness" is roughly triangular in shape, its north edge extending from Lovers Leap east to Echo Summit, and beyond to Luther Pass. The two other sides converge on Carson Pass. Hikes 88-90 are unappealing to most hikers (other than botanists), the first two providing very long routes in to Showers Lake. Hike 90, the Hawley Grade Trail, is basically for history buffs and mountain bikers. The remaining Dardanelles Roadless Area routes are deservedly popular, taking you to Dardanelles, Round, Meiss, and Showers lakes, each in a unique setting.

One trail in this roadless area that is not included in this chapter is the Lovers Leap Trail. Nevertheless, it is briefly described in the first paragraph of Hike 73's route description, and it is shown on Map 37. This trail traverses across granitic terrain very similar to that found in Desolation Wilderness, just north of it. Likewise, Hike 95, the Lake Margaret Trail, which starts from Highway 88, appears to be a granitic transplant from Desolation Wilderness. The trail is easy and the lake is enjoyable.

The last four routes, Hikes 96-99, enter a northern, 1984 addition to Mokelumne Wilderness. This addition is dominated by the eroded ruins of an extinct volcano, Round Top. From it a high, volcanic crest extends west, and I have drawn the Tahoe Sierra's southern boundary along this crest, although Hike 98 does extend beyond it, down past Fourth of July Lake and then east up Summit City Creek canyon. For most hikers the braking descent to this lake coupled with the rigorous ascent from it do not justify a visit.

Three Mokelumne Wilderness lakes do justify a visit: Winnemucca, Round Top, and Emigrant lakes. Frog Lake, which you pass along Hikes 98 and 99, has frogs and about enough water to wash the trail dust from your legs. All four are subalpine, and therefore too chilly for enjoyable swimming. Their average elevation is 8945 feet. Compare that to the average elevation of the four highest *peaks* in Granite Chief Wilderness—8954 feet.

The northern part of Mokelumne Wilderness is quite spectacular, being perhaps the most photogenic area in the Tahoe Sierra. In botanical terms, it is also spectacular, having, mile for mile, the greatest number of species. This is particularly true along the chapter's last hike, whose chief attribute is its flora.

If you plan to spend the night in the wilderness during a period lasting from about the Memorial Day weekend through all of September, then you'll need a wilderness permit—see Chapter 3 for details. Day hikers don't need permits.

⟨⟩ 88 ⟨⟩
Sayles Canyon and Bryan Meadow Trails

Distances
4.8 miles to Pacific Crest Trail (via Bryan Meadow)
5.6 miles to PCT (via Sayles Canyon)
11.3 miles for complete Sayles Canyon/Bryan Meadow semiloop trip

Low/High Elevations: 6880'/8700'

Season: Mid-July through mid-October

Classification: Moderate

Maps: 37 and 38

Trailhead: See Hike 73's trailhead directions to Sayles Flat, opposite Camp Sacramento's entrance, and from there drive 0.5 mile up Highway 50 to a curve and quickly reach a road, branching right. Take this road, which immediately bridges the South Fork American River, and from an adjacent **T** you turn right and follow the road 0.5 mile to a small parking area at road's end.

Introduction
There are at least 10 trail routes in to Showers Lake. The Sayles Canyon Trail and the Bryan Meadow Trail are the two longest and, in my estimation, the least scenic. These trails, which climb appreciably, will appeal to only a select few, such as equestrians, who let their horses do the walking, and botanists, who may hike only part way.

Description
Starting among red firs and lodgepole, western white, and Jeffrey pines, we hike under a cool, protective forest cover whose floor is adorned with a variety of colorful wildflowers. After a 0.4-mile ascent we reach a road's end turnaround loop. This road starts in the Sierra at Tahoe ski area, shown on Map 37.

From the upper end of a parking loop the Sayles Canyon Trail continues climbing through a shady forest. You then ascend a

Pyramid Peak, from Sayles Canyon Trail

bouldery, rocky tread southeast to scrub-vege-
tated granodiorite slopes and, before curving
east around a low glacial moraine, can glance
back and see Pyramid Peak towering above
barely visible Horsetail Falls. Curving east
between the moraine and a creeklet alongside
it, we quickly reach a junction with the Bryan
Meadow Trail, almost 1.2 miles from our trailhead. We'll be returning down this trail.

After crossing the creeklet, we soon come
to an alder-lined Sayles Canyon creek tribu-
lary that descends from Bryan Meadow.
Rather than ford the shallow creek where the
trail does, head just upstream to a boulderhop
crossing. Here, under lodgepoles, you'll find a
nice, flat campsite near the creek's north bank.
Beyond the ford our verdant pathway climbs
southeast up the stepped canyon floor, at
times almost touching Sayles Canyon creek.
We pass some large boulders—up to 20 feet
high—then traverse through a meadow largely overgrown with willows, alders, and corn
lilies before we ford lushly vegetated Sayles
Canyon creek. We then tread a moderately
graded stretch of trail 0.4 mile east up to the
northwest corner of grassy Round Meadow.
Near the meadow's north edge, the trail starts
out along the south side of a clump of willows, heads east-southeast to a quick crossing
of trout-inhabited upper Sayles Canyon creek,

and then diagonals east-northeast toward
some corn lilies. Beyond them it reaches
slopes at the forest's edge, from which the trail
upward is blazed and ducked. Mosquitoes,
abundant through mid-August, make this
damp meadow an undesirable camping area
in early and mid-season.

On a trail that is bouldery at first, we
ascend north moderately up past red firs and
lodgepole pines, parallel a linear corn-lily
meadow eastward, climb steeply north, and
make a long, relatively gentle climb southeast
before curving east up to a saddle. Here we
encounter the **Pacific Crest Trail**, which also
coincides for some distance with the unofficial
Tahoe-Yosemite Trail. Hike 89 continues south
from this junction for 3½ miles, reaching
Showers Lake's east-shore campsites.

Tracing the Pacific Crest Trail northward
for just under one mile, we climb to a low
summit, which has weathered boulders but
no views, then we gradually descend through
an open forest of mountain hemlock and
lodgepole pine, cross a mucky slough that
annually sprouts a magenta field of blazing
shooting stars, and reach a trail junction at the
upper east end of **Bryan Meadow**. Here the
Pacific Crest Trail, Hike 89, turns east.

An old trail once cut straight down Bryan
Meadow, and today a use trail still goes 50

see MAP 38

see upper inset

37

73 Ralston Peak

73

73

3

x 9155

Cup Lake

Talking Mtn

8826

8600

2

Bech

River

BM 712

Horsetail Falls

RALSTON

PYRAMID

HORSETAIL FALLS TR

PEAK

Creek

TRAIL

Tamarack

Creek

Pinecrest Camp

Chapel of Our Lady of the Sierras

Sayles

Camp Sacramento

SKI LIFT

72

73

8

9

10

11

Phillips

American

NATIO

7582 x

Gate

7290

Aspen

Creek

7377

Sierra at Tahoe

SKI LIFT

Twin Bridges

50

17

16

15

14

8852 x

South Fork

Bryan

Creek

F O R E

BRYAN   MEADOW

TRAIL

22

23

88

88

Sayles

SAYLES

CANYON

Canyon

TRAIL

26

Round Meadow

88

see upper left edge

see bottom of Map 33

Pyramid Cr

Lovers Leap Campground

Lovers Leap 6994

8

17

7944

errry

see bottom of Map 33

70

4

5

E   L   D

3

Silver

Fork

Dry Lake

8

7162 x

7100

71

9

LYONS

Lyons (Site)

CREEK

Lyons

TRAIL

3

6915

x 7100

10

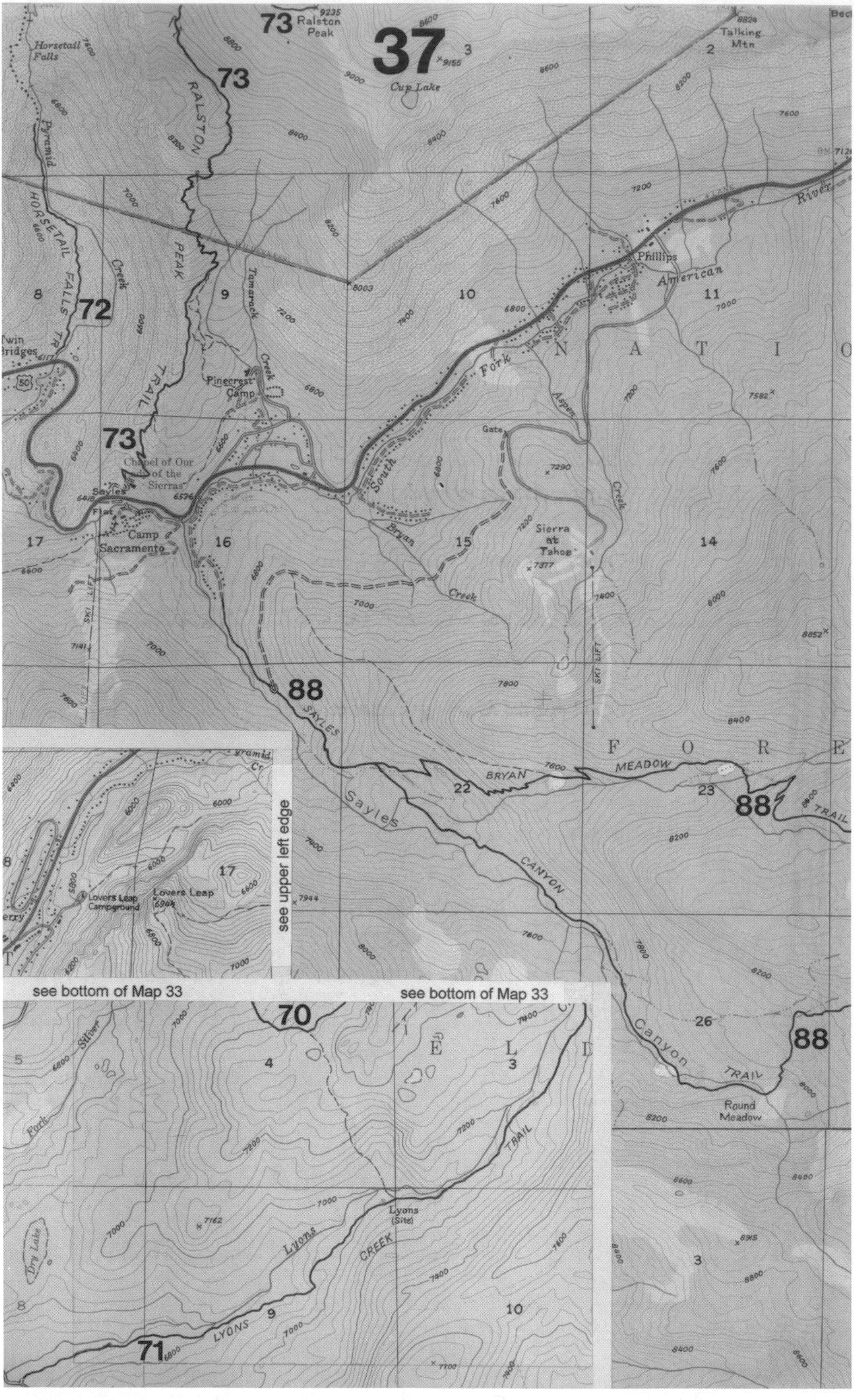

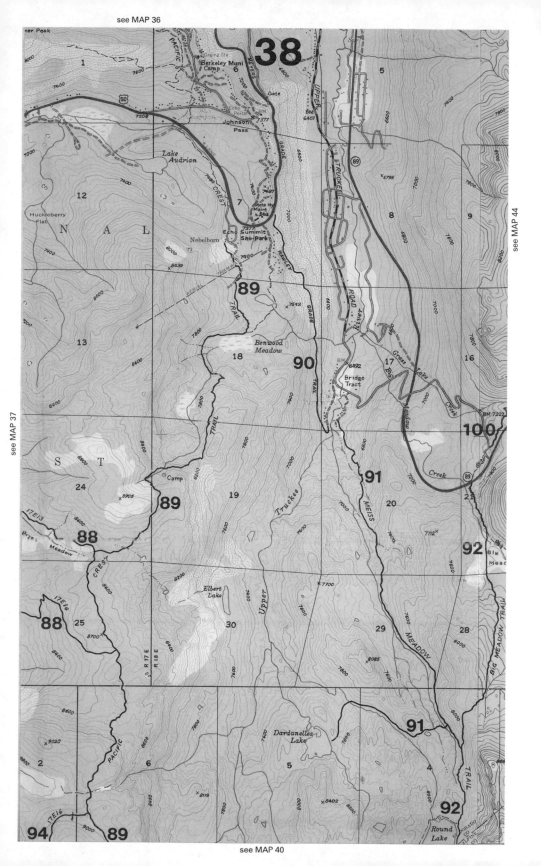

see MAP 36

see MAP 37

see MAP 44

see MAP 40

yards west down to a small, poor campsite amid a cluster of lodgepoles. Our Bryan Meadow Trail begins north, but quickly curves west to a gully, and then parallels the north edge of Bryan Meadow. In a number of spots we walk along the meadow's thick soils, rich in humus and clay. Both hold a lot of water. The clay likely is eroded from volcanic sediments on slopes northeast of and high above the meadow. The result is a richer profusion of plant species than would be found growing in nutrient-poor granitic soils.

Beyond the meadow our trail traverses a slope while paralleling Bryan Meadow's creek, below us. The trail here is drier, for the slope has a typical cover of *gruss*—the chunky, residual quartz and feldspar crystals that are left behind after most of the dark minerals of granitic bedrock decompose and erode away. We descend a ridgecrest, switchback down its more-forested north slope, ford several branches of a creek, and then curve westward as we descend to a fairly large, forested flat. At the west end the creek tumbles down a steeper slope while our trail switchbacks down a sloping meadow. It then goes left and descends via more switchbacks through more-open forest down to the Sayles Canyon Trail, on which we retrace our steps to the trailhead.

⤜ 89 ⤛
Pacific Crest Trail, Echo Summit south to Showers Lake

Distances
1.0 mile to Benwood Meadow
3.9 miles to Bryan Meadow Trail
4.8 miles to Sayles Canyon Trail
6.4 miles to Trail 17E16
8.3 miles to Showers Lake
Low/High Elevations: 7380′/8990′
Season: Mid-July through mid-October
Classification: Moderate
Maps: 38 and 40
Trailheads: Drive up Highway 50 nearly to Echo Summit. The Pacific Crest trailhead is

near the start of Echo Summit Sno-Park's Road, which begins 0.3 mile west of Echo Summit. Just 100 yards along it is parking for about a dozen vehicles. For an alternate trailhead, drive 200 yards east of signed Echo Summit, turn south on a narrow spur road and follow it ⅓ mile to its end, with parking for several vehicles.

Introduction
Like the previous hike this one is a long way in to Showers Lake, and may appeal most to equestrians and botanists. The route's greatest users, however, may be neither, but rather long-distance hikers doing part or all of either the Pacific Crest Trail or the unofficial Tahoe-Yosemite Trail. From the heart of Desolation Wilderness south to the Carson Pass area, these two trails share the same tread.

Description
From the trailhead parking area, the northbound Pacific Crest Trail, or PCT, stays near Highway 50 for 0.7 mile, and along this stretch it eventually parallels an alder-lined creek down to a road that bridges it. If you were to take that road about ½ mile west-southwest to a creekside road, then ¼ mile up it, you would reach trout-stocked Lake Audrian. North from Highway 50, the PCT winds 1.3 miles over to the Echo Lake trailhead (Hike 85). The Pacific Crest Trail, both north to Echo Lakes and south to Showers Lake, is also the route of the Tahoe-Yosemite Trail and the Tahoe Rim Trail.

We, however, want the southbound PCT, and to find its trailhead we walk south along the Echo Summit Sno-Park's road to the end of its parking loop. Immediately south of it is a loop road, from which you should see—by mid-July, when it should be snow-free—the PCT start an ascent south up an open ski slope. This trail quickly bends southeast, and you take it up to an old road, which has ascended from the southeast part of the loop road. Up the old road you pace off 120 yards, then branch left on trail tread. The PCT tread should be obvious, but if not, it is where the road turns from south-southwest to southwest and increases its gradient. Now you traverse just under ½ mile south, almost to the northeast edge of Benwood Meadow, where you'll meet an older trail coming from the alternate trailhead.

This trail, 0.3 mile shorter than the main route, begins at a small flat just west of a cluster of summer homes. It winds southward along a boulder-lined path atop a mammoth moraine that towers up to 1100 feet above the Upper Truckee River's canyon floor. Soon the trail descends past a lily-pad pond, to the west, and crosses its southeast-flowing outlet creek. The pond resembles so many others one sees in the glaciated High Sierra, but

Granite-rimmed Showers Lake

it is quite distinct in its mode of origin. Instead of forming behind a recessional moraine, as many have, this pond was dammed between two lateral moraines. The huge Upper Truckee canyon lateral moraine blocked the creek's drainage eastward and another lateral moraine extending east from the north edge of Benwood Meadow blocked its drainage southward, thereby ponding up the creek. On the low Benwood Meadow moraine you traverse southwest and, just after spying the meadow, join the Pacific Crest/Tahoe-Yosemite trail.

Benwood Meadow is a popular goal among botanists, for it is readily accessible, and it contains a diverse array of native species. The PCT fortunately avoids this fragile environment, circling around its west edge on somewhat drier, forested terrain. You then climb a brushy, rocky slope, cross a creek feeding the unseen meadow, and climb to a nearby switchback. Starting briefly west, you get your first view north of Lake Tahoe. Turning south, you climb ¼ mile to a shallow gap, having several more lake views along this moderate ascent. You next climb slopes up through an open forest, the terrain characterized by granitic outcrops and giant boulders.

About ½ mile past the gap you reach a crest saddle, which yields your route's best view, of the Upper Truckee River basin. Murky Round

Lake, at the base of a volcanic palisade, is one of the most identifiable features. Just right of it and about a mile closer to you is Dardanelles Lake, which is nestled at the foot of a granitic cliff. Rising on the skyline between the two lakes is flat-topped Red Lake Peak, which at 10,063 feet nudges out Stevens Peak by 4 feet to be the basin rim's highest point. Stevens is above and just left of Round Lake. Note how thick the volcanic deposits are in this area, roughly 2000 feet from Stevens Peak down to the Round Lake environs. These deposits, which are mostly andesitic, locally were episodically erupted from about 20 to 5 million years ago, and they eventually buried most of the Upper Truckee River basin. Over time, first streams and then glaciers removed most of the fairly erodible deposits from the basin, exposing its granodiorite landscape once again, little changed from what it had been at the time of burial.

Before moving on, note two more landmarks, both to the south-southeast. The first is the basin rim's low point, a saddle above the river's headwaters. Through this saddle the PCT climbs south, heading for the Mexican border, about 1080 trail miles away. Just to the right of and beyond the saddle is Round Top, the glacier-gouged remains of an ancient volcano, which at 10,381 feet is the highest peak between Highways 88 and 4.

Showers Lake, due south on a high, granitic bench, is unseen.

Beyond the viewpoint you skirt along the base of some intimidating granodiorite cliffs as you climb southeast. Just past them you reach the jump-across Benwood Meadow creek and above its west side can spy a small flat near the east bank. This is the site of "Six Pack Camp," in which you can pack six campers. Ahead, we climb rather steeply southwest to a lovely cove beneath a conspicuous dark cliff of volcanic rocks. Now we cross a sparkling creeklet that drains from the melting snowfield clinging to the upper slopes, then begin a reasonable ascent southeast to the gentle volcanic summit's forested east shoulder. Then we descend southwest on volcanic soils which, due to their porosity, are much drier. Flowers of mule ears and lupines, both with unmistakable, though subtle, scents, thrive in these soils. We get a brief view of peaks to the southeast but then submerge under the forest's cover once again as we descend, sometimes steeply, on granitic soils to a ravine with a tiny creeklet.

A short, easy climb west now takes us to a thickly cloaked saddle above Bryan Meadow, which has fair-to-poor campsites along its fringe. (You would do better to make a dry camp along our ridge.) Descending about 200 yards west to the meadow's east edge, we reach a junction from which the **Bryan Meadow Trail** (Hike 88) curves north. Should you need water, take this trail to the creek flowing from the lower end of the meadow.

Our Pacific Crest/Tahoe-Yosemite trail turns south, and after climbing 100 feet of elevation in that direction, we can see Pyramid Peak, *the* prominent summit of the granitic Crystal Range, on the northwest skyline. Through an open forest of mountain hemlock and lodgepole pine we now complete our easy climb to a low, viewless summit, then momentarily drop to a crest-saddle junction with the **Sayles Canyon Trail** (also Hike 88).

From the saddle our trail meanders along the broad crest for about ½ mile, then crosses a seasonally soggy, small meadow with a snowmelt creeklet. A rocky ascent of 300 feet gives way to a descent of 100 feet to a shallow crest gap. From it a faint use trail strikes east

250 yards down a linear meadow to a camp with a fine view, just beyond the meadow's far end. To the west, a similar tread descends 330 yards to the upper edge of a large meadow, then angles at 330° for 130 yards to a camp among a cluster of lodgepoles. Both camps usually have water nearby through July.

Climbing 0.2 mile from the gap, we reach a near-crest junction with **Trail 17E16**. This eventually descends to Schneider's Cow Camp, and is described in Hike 94. Our route traverses southeast for ⅓ mile, then drops steeply, but briefly, south into a broad, glaciated basin. With volcanic flows and sediments above us and granitic bedrock below, we make an undulating traverse across the basin, always staying close to the contact between these two rock formations. While hiking this stretch, you might observe how each differs in kinds and abundance of plants, in soil production, and in the shape of the landscape. You may also note that volcanic-rock formations tend to have more streams and springs while granitic ones have the lakes. The first observation is true because many volcanic rocks are very porous, and can store water underground for year-round runoff, while granitic rocks are impervious, their water supply being stored in seasonal snowfields or briefly in shallow, gravelly soils. The second observation is true because the glaciers in this area were able to remove the loose volcanic sediments and carve basins in underlying, fractured granitic bedrock. Lakes then formed in these hollows when the glaciers receded. Volcanic rocks, being less resistant, are more easily planed smooth or removed by glaciers, and hence hollows (and therefore lakes) rarely develop.

Our glaciated basin traverse takes us just beneath a precarious, overhanging volcanic point, beyond which we descend to where a use trail skirts southeast across willowy slopes that lie south of Showers Lake. For horses, this shortcut route is okay, but for hikers, the mire of mud negates the time saved. The official trail heads northeast through a gap in a linear wall of granodiorite that hides **Showers Lake**—a stone's throw—from us. Due to the obtrusive bedrock, the trail drops steeply down the lake's outlet creek, only to climb equally steeply up its other side to the lakeshore. However, in late season, you *might* be able to avoid this effort by fording, rock-hopping, or log-crossing the creek by the lake's outlet. Once across, you reach lakeside campsites shaded by mountain hemlocks, western white pines, and lodgepole pines. If you camp here before early August, be prepared for abundant mosquitoes.

⇔ 90 ⇔
Hawley Grade Trail

Distance:
1.9 miles to Highway 50
Low/High Elevations: 6520'/7370'
Season: Late June through late October
Classification: Easy
Map: 38

Trailhead: From where Highway 89 branches south from southwest-climbing Highway 50, drive southwest ⅓ mile on 50 to Upper Truckee Road, found immediately before a KOA Campground. Drive 3¼ miles south up this gently climbing road to where it curves left to bridge the Upper Truckee River. Immediately before it does so, you branch right on Road 1110 and take this short spur road past Bridge Tract homes almost to its boulder-blocked end, finding parking space for two or three vehicles about 50 yards before the end.

Introduction
Along the Hawley Grade you relive a bit of California's history by ascending the first wagon road to be built across the central Sierra. Hawley's Grade was a short-lived but key link in a trans-Sierra route to Hangtown and Sacramento. By 1850 Hangtown—today's Placerville—had become the unofficial capital of northern California's gold-mining region, and two years later a route of sorts was built from it to Johnson Pass—¾ mile north of today's Echo Summit—from where it dropped into Lake Valley. Drop it did, so steeply in fact that block and tackle had to be used to haul westbound wagons up it. An alternative grade had to be found.

A route over Luther Pass, to the southeast, was surveyed in the winter of 1854 for the purpose of providing a wagon road to Sacramento and Hangtown that would be better than Johnson Pass and also shorter and easier than the primitive Carson Pass route. That spring, Asa Hawley established a trading post in upper Lake Valley near a part of the Upper Truckee canyon's wall that quickly became known as Hawley's Hill. Construction soon began on a grade that would be gentle enough to safely accommodate wagons. Financed by private interests, this route—Hawley's Grade—was completed in 1857, making it the first conventional wagon road to cross the central Sierra. Combined with a recently constructed Luther Pass segment, this grade fast became *the* route to take. In 1858 El Dorado and Sacramento counties improved western segments of this largely-one-lane toll road, making it far superior to the higher, longer-snowbound Carson Pass route to the south.

Timing couldn't have been better, for in 1859 silver was discovered in the Comstock Lode at Virginia Town, today's Virginia City. Traffic was reversed on this road as a flood of miners from California's gold fields scrambled east over this toll road to try their luck at or near Virginia Town. Alas, even as Hawley's Grade was constructed to channel westbound miners and pioneers into California's Mother Lode country faster than was possible along the Carson Grade, so too were plans made to convey miners and others east to the Comstock by a faster route. By the summer of 1860, a wagon-and-stage toll road—abandoned today—had been constructed down Meyer's Grade, then east to climb over Daggett Pass, situated above Tahoe's southeast shore. Hawley's Grade, briefly a shortcut that siphoned traffic from the Carson Pass route, now became the longer, unprofitable toll road.

Description
From the boulders that today block the road, we start our hike up this historic grade by walking south about 100 yards, to where the road bends sharply and commences its climb to Echo Summit. From this bend, if you

choose, you can first follow a trail 50 yards south to the tumbling waters of the Upper Truckee River. The road quickly reduces to a trail and we soon encounter a tangle of alders, bushes and wildflowers that take advantage of the preponderance of springs and creeklets in this area. Beyond them we're on a narrow road again with more spacious vegetation. Scattered Jeffrey pine and other conifers break the monotony of the slope's mantle of huckleberry oak, and in shady spots bracken fern, thimbleberry, and dogbane ("Indian hemp") add variety. In October the leaves of this diminutive hemp turn a bright yellow, making the plant one of the more conspicuous species. After the first fall frost, Indians would collect its stems in order to make string, which would be used for basket weaving and for bowstrings.

Midway along the ascent we reach our first good view north, then enter a gully down which a creek from Benwood Meadow and a pond north of it falls and cascades, splashing on the large boulders we must cross. Although our path across this gully is partly washed out, we have little difficulty crossing, and from its north side we can look back and see the tall volcanic cliffs that loom above Round Lake. Soon we get a glimpse of Lake Tahoe and spy trucks struggling up Highway 50's present Meyer's Grade. We can also see that the forested valley below us has been transformed into a suburb of South Lake Tahoe.

Our views of Lake Tahoe improve as we climb steadily north, but soon we veer west into a forest of white fir and Jeffrey pine and lose the views. Replacing them are the undesirable noise from traffic on Highway 50, which we're rapidly approaching, and the highly desirable aroma of a spread of tobacco brush. You can follow Hawley's Grade all the way to Highway 50's embankment, but this shoulderless highway is dangerous to walk along. When you see this embankment you can instead climb west up a shady gully and reach **Highway 50** at its junction with a narrow road leading south to the start of the Benwood Trail, Hike 89's alternate start. Most hikers, however, will retrace their route back to its trailhead.

⋖≥ 91 ⋖≥
Meiss Meadow Trail to Round and Dardanelles Lakes

Distances:
2.7 miles to Dardanelles Lake Trail
   1.3 miles on trail to Dardanelles Lake
3.5 miles to Round Lake
Low/High Elevations: 6520'/7820'
Season: Mid-July through mid-October
Classification: Moderate
Map: 38
Trailhead: See Hike 90's directions to a bridge over Upper Truckee River. Drive across the bridge and immediately turn right on Road 1111. Take this spur road ¼ mile, passing Bridge Tract homes before you come to a trailhead, which has parking for two vehicles, about 35 yards before a gate across the road.

Introduction
Since Hike 92 gets you to Round Lake and Dardanelles Lake in less distance and in less elevation gain, many hikers will skip Hike 91, particularly since trailhead parking is very limited, and there may not be any on summer weekends. Though longer and starting lower, this hike up the lower half of the Meiss Meadow Trail does have favorable attributes. It is much less used, and therefore more peaceful, it usually stays within earshot of a spring-fed stream, and wildflowers are more abundant.

Description
This trail starts in a shady forest whose floor and slopes are adorned with a variety of colorful wildflowers. The trail starts to climb immediately from the left side of the road, and quickly reaches large boulders of a talus slope, which it traverses, and then it climbs steeply through the forest up to a more open, minor ridge. Here we contour toward a trickling creek, and make a steep ascent alongside it, then cross it just before topping a not-too-evident second minor ridge. Ahead is a third rise, but it is shorter and less steep than the first two, and the trail eases off and approaches a tributary of the Upper Truckee River. We make a relaxing stroll upstream beside this alder-

and willow-lined creek, but then must climb moderately again as we reach a section of rapids. Eventually our ascent comes to a junction with the **Dardanelles Lake Trail**, situated in a predominantly red-fir stand of conifers that also includes Jeffrey, western white, and lodgepole pines. The main trail continues south-southeast 0.2 mile gently up to a second junction at the more popular Big Meadow Trail (Hike 92), which climbs south 0.6 mile to **Round Lake**.

Cliff-bordered south shore of Dardanelles Lake

If Dardanelles Lake is your goal, veer southwest on its trail and ascend 30 steep yards toward the creek you've been paralleling—but first note the strange, 10-foot-high boulder you've seen downstream. This boulder broke off from the impressive volcanic palisade that towers above Round Lake. The cluster of smaller volcanic rocks that make up the large boulder you see are just a biopsy of one of the large volcanic mudflows one would see on Hike 92, which elaborates about these flows.

The spring-fed creek receives its water from subterranean channels that flow through the volcanic rocks downstream from Round Lake, ⅔ mile south of us. Across the creek the trail traverses a broad, low slope, first passing a second Round Lake creek, larger than the first, and then a lily-pad pond. After a quick descent, the trail reaches a third Round Lake creek, which leaves a dam at the lake's northwest corner and tumbles down a narrow, curving canyon. At one point these outlet creeks are almost a mile apart before finally merging only 200 yards upstream from our trailhead.

Our creekside journey downstream soon takes us past an aged patriarch—a 7-foot-diameter juniper—then past many creekside willow thickets to a ford of this creek. We tread across some low, glacially polished granodiorite slabs, and then climb southward on a ducked trail up a straight, easy, joint-con-

trolled gully leading to rock slabs above the east shore of **Dardanelles Lake**. From its south shore rise the steep granodiorite cliffs of summit 8402, which, for climbers, are the reward of this long ascent. Nonclimbers will have to admit that the cliffs do add to the beauty of this shallow lake, which in midsummer warms to 70 degrees or more, making it ideal for swimming. Fishermen can try to catch a tasty trout dinner. Late in the summer the lake's water becomes slightly cloudy, making it less attractive. Fair-to-good campsites exist among scattered junipers and lodgepoles on slabs bordering the east and northwest shores.

⇐⇒ 92 ⇐⇒
Big Meadow Trail to Round, Dardanelles, and Meiss Lakes

Distances:
0.6 mile to Big Meadow
2.5 miles to Meiss Meadow Trail
   1.5 miles on trails to Dardanelles Lake
3.1 miles to Round Lake
4.6 miles to Meiss Lake (via west route)
4.9 miles to Meiss Lake (via Meiss Meadow Trail)
5.4 miles to Pacific Crest Trail

Low/High Elevations: 7200'/8070' to Round Lake

Classification: Moderate

Season: Early July through mid-October

Maps: 38 and 40

Trailhead: From Echo Summit, Highway 50 drops into the Lake Tahoe basin, reaching a junction with Highway 89 in 4.0 miles. Drive about 4½ miles south up this highway to the start of a long curve left, then another ¾ mile along it to where it straightens out and you turn left onto an old road. (If you are driving northbound on Highway 89, this junction is about 3.3 miles west of Luther Pass.) This road descends quickly to the signed Tahoe Rim Trail's Big Meadow Trailhead facility. The Big Meadow Trail begins from the bottom parking loop. If you continue down the old road (former Highway 89), you'll pass by primitive campsites of the Luther Pass Overflow Camping Area.

Introduction

Because it has volcanic and granitic soils in various stages of development, the Upper Truckee River's uppermost basin supports approximately 300 species of wildflowers, shrubs, and trees, and it supports a similarly diverse invertebrate fauna. The Big Meadow Trail is the most popular trail into this lake-dotted, volcanic-rimmed basin, which offers

climbers some interesting routes. Most hikers go to Round Lake, the basin's largest lake, which strong backpackers can reach in about an hour. This route is part of the Tahoe Rim Trail, connecting that trail's lengthy traverse of the Carson Range crest lands with the Pacific Crest Trail's lengthy traverse of the Sierra Nevada crest lands.

Description

From the bottom parking loop our trail goes 240 yards to Highway 89, which you cross. Then you make an initial ascent south toward Big Meadow Creek, jog east, and then perspire southeast up an increasingly steep slope of weathered, glacier-dropped granodiorite boulders. Near the top of the climb you pass through a stock gate and *may* meet a lateral trail just before you arrive at the north end of grassy, well-named **Big Meadow**. The lateral, bound for Scotts Lake, takes 2½ miles to reach it. Most of this lake lies on private land. Just within the north fringe of Big Meadow, beyond a clump of willows, our trail curves slightly right (southwest) and fords trout-inhabited, jump-across Big Meadow Creek.

Beyond the creek crossing, our path turns south again and we make a very flat traverse before we enter forest cover again, in a cluster of mature lodgepoles that trespass into the southeast corner of the meadow. Now our path winds south up a lodgepole-covered slope, which also is cloaked with clusters of red fir in some places and with open patches of mule ears and sagebrush in others. Near the top of our climb the grade eases and the trail swings southwest, passes through a barbed-wire fence, leaving cattle-grazing land behind, and soon begins a moderate descent from a broad, forested saddle.

On the fairly steep slope of volcanic rubble that we descend, the trees aren't as densely packed as were

The Dardanelles, which are volcanic cliffs, tower over Round Lake

those along our ascent, so we can survey the basin we are entering. At the base of a prominent granodiorite cliff one mile west lies shallow, unseen Dardanelles Lake; above and beyond both stands a volcanic ridge, usually laced with snow and composed of many flows that are discernible by the naked eye. At the base of the massive volcanic cliffs ahead lies our unseen destination, Round Lake.

After passing some fine specimens of Jeffrey pine, whose deeply furrowed bark emits a butterscotch odor that permeates the warm air, we meet the Meiss Meadow Trail, which has climbed up a tributary of the Upper Truckee River. A gentle 0.2-mile descent along its aspen-covered banks will take you to a junction from where a 1.3-mile-long trail branches west to **Dardanelles Lake** (see Hike 91). We continue south, climbing up, down, and around on hummocky terrain of volcanic mudflow deposits and blocks. Our trail, now over fine-grained volcanic soils, is considerably dustier than the coarser-grained granitic soils we started on. Several minutes before we reach a flat above Round Lake's northeast shore, we pass one large mudflow block that has a 5-foot-long granitic boulder cemented into it, indicating that the mudflow must have packed a lot of power to have lifted this 2-ton boulder.

Arriving at the northeast shore of **Round Lake**, we see it is different from all the other lakes of this guidebook's hikes. Bordered by volcanic deposits along its north, east, and south shores, the lake is brownish-green in color due to super-fine volcanic particles held in suspension. Since you'll probably not want to drink this water, hike 170 yards along the lodgepole- and cottonwood-lined east shore and obtain water from a trickling creek. Fair campsites are scattered about the northern half of the lake, the southern half generally being too vegetated and swampy. Perhaps the best site is at the lake's outlet. From the northeast corner, follow a narrow path west past Jeffrey pines, junipers, sagebrush, mule ears, and buckwheat to a small campsite on a granodiorite bench just west of a head-high dam. Beneath red firs and lodgepoles you can take in superb sunsets that set the towering volcanic palisade east of you ablaze with color.

Just east of this campsite is a small cove in which you can enjoy a refreshing swim. *Fishing, however, is forbidden in the Alpine County part of this basin.*

If you want to hike up to shallow, boulder-dotted Meiss Lake, you can reach it from Round Lake by two routes. The first is to start from the northwest campsites and follow a use path south along the west shore of Round Lake. At this lake's southwest corner you'll find more campsites, these shaded by lodgepoles growing on a flat bench above the lake. From this bench a faint use trail climbs south a short mile to **Meiss Lake**. The second route to Meiss Lake is to hike south from Round Lake on the Meiss Meadow Trail. After one mile you reach a meadowy area with a conspicuous, entrenched creek. Leave the trail just before it crosses this creek and head cross-country ½ mile west to **Meiss Lake**. This second, slightly longer, route is preferable if you are carrying a heavy pack, for its terrain is easier than the first. Meiss Lake is one of the warmest in the Tahoe area, for it is very shallow. Indeed, you can wade across it—too shallow for trout. If you use the lake's campsites—along its west shore—expect plenty of mosquitoes until early August. For many decades the Upper Truckee River lands above Round Lake, particularly around Meiss Lake, were cattle country, but in 1992 the Forest Service banned cattle in order to restore the meadows, the fisheries, and the environment in general. However, holders of grazing permits would like to see the lands reopened, and in some future year you may again find cattle up here.

Back near the creeklet dropping to Round Lake's northeast shore, the Meiss Meadow Trail passes an enormous block that, like so many others there, has broken off from the vertical-to-overhanging cliffs above. Climbers who like to go bouldering will find this an ideal block to climb. Since some routes are overhanging and others are as long as 40 feet, and since the holds aren't always secure, a top rope is desirable. More daring climbers may want to try the potentially dangerous deep fissures on the vertical cliffs above.

These mudflow cliffs are part of the Mehrten Formation, which is an assortment of andesitic flows and deposits that here are up to about 2000 feet thick. From 26 to 5 million years ago thick andesitic lava flows sporadically poured from various Sierran volcanoes that probably resembled those of today's Oregon Cascades, and they covered an area from Sonora Pass north to Lassen Park and beyond. The *autobrecciation* of flows—the self-fracturing of a flow's rocks by its own movements—was responsible for the overwhelming quantity of *lahars,* or volcanic mudflows, which characterize the Mehrten Formation. A lahar flows when an accumulation of fragmental debris becomes saturated with water. The extensive autobrecciation of these andesite flows produced a very abundant supply of fragments, "food" enough to feed hundreds of lahars like the ones that compose the 1000-foot-thick wall above Round Lake. Streams and then glaciers have removed most of the lahar deposits that once filled the southern part of the Upper Truckee River basin.

From Round Lake, those on the Tahoe Rim Trail continue south about 2+ miles on the Meiss Meadow Trail to the **Pacific Crest Trail** and turn right. North, this trail is also the route of the Tahoe-Yosemite and Tahoe Rim trails; south, of the Tahoe-Yosemite and Meiss Meadow trails (Hike 93).

≪≫ **93** ≪≫

Pacific Crest Trail, Carson Pass north to Showers Lake

Distances:
2.9 miles to Meiss Meadow Trail
  1.1 miles on and off trail to Meiss Lake
  2.1 miles on trail to Round Lake
3.5 miles to third Truckee River crossing
  0.5 mile on use trail to Meiss Lake
5.1 miles to Showers Lake
Low/High Elevations: 8350′/8790′
Season: Mid-July through early October
Classification: Moderate
Maps: 41 and 40
Trailhead: Drive on Highway 88 to a curve with a parking lot, just 0.2 mile west of the parking lot at Carson Pass. This pass is about 100 miles from Highway 99 in Stockton and about 20 miles from Highway 50 in the Lake Tahoe Basin.

Introduction
This walk along the Pacific Crest Trail presents the hiker with a very scenic route to Showers Lake, the highest lake in the Upper Truckee River basin. The lake is a worthy goal in itself, but even if it were not, the hike to it across a glaciated volcanic landscape would justify the effort. The country traversed along this hike is among the Sierra's best for subalpine botanizing. Side trips include visits to Meiss and Round lakes.

Description
From the trailhead at the northwest corner of the parking lot, first climb southwest and then round a ridge to make an undulating traverse northwest past junipers and occasional aspens to a gullied bowl. Both tree species release subtle scents, though these usually go unnoticed by the hurried hiker; they are often masked by the stronger scents produced by mule ears and sagebrush. After winding in and out of several gullies, you follow short switchbacks north, then traverse west to a junction with the Meiss Meadow Trail. Starting opposite a Woods Lake road junction 0.9 mile west of Carson Pass, this old trail climbs steeply to this junction in 0.5 mile, versus 1.3 miles for the scenic, leisurely PCT. In 110 yards your north-climbing trail tops a pond-blessed saddle. In early season this shallow pond looks quite fresh, but with time, stock muddy its water. It's probably best not to drink the water regardless of its clarity. The saddle is a good place to rest and admire the view to the south, dominated by Round Top (10,381′) and flanked on the east by Elephants Back (9585′). Former glaciers grew outward from Round Top, and a giant one advanced over our drainage divide and eroded a hollow in our saddle, which filled to become the pond.

The saddle is the logical spot to start a 1½-mile-long, 1300-foot-ascent cross-country up to Red Lake Peak. Work east up an ascending ridge, then veer north when the gradient gets too steep. This gets you around an auxiliary

Shallow, warm Meiss Lake and Stevens Peak's broad 9700' outlier

ridge summit, located about ½ mile southwest of Red Lake Peak. As you skirt around this summit, the route to the top becomes quite obvious. The top abounds in resplendent vistas, which encompass three major basins: Upper Truckee River, to the west; West Fork Carson River, to the east; and Caples Creek (which feeds into Silver Fork American River), to the southwest. The relatively gentle slopes below the peak's summit rival those of Mt. Rose, Stevens Peak, and the Freel Peak massif in diversity of alpine cushion plants. However, the soils they grow in are incoherent and therefore readily erodible. So whether you're botanizing or just up there for the lofty views, take care not to disturb these diminutive plants. The summit area and the route to it are the easiest access to abundant, truly (not marginally) alpine flora in the Tahoe Sierra. (You can reach alpine flora with slightly less effort by ascending Hike 97 toward Round Top, but the ascent is past far fewer species.) Should you attempt Red Lake Peak, wear a hat, dark glasses, and sunscreen, for the ultraviolet radiation up there can be quite intense, and be prepared for strong winds.

With most of the climbing behind us, the PCT, whose route coincides with the Tahoe-Yosemite Trail, now leaves the saddle to make an easy traverse ⅓ mile north along former jeep tracks to a junction. From here we angle left and descend tracks to a campsite by the infant Upper Truckee River, which we jump across. Fishing is prohibited in this stream, its

tributaries, and Meiss and Round lakes. We now have an easy descent northwest, then pass through a gate, recross the river, pass through a second gate and in a moment reach a fork. From here, near cabins in giant Meiss Meadow, the **Meiss Meadow Trail** heads 2.1 miles to large, slightly cloudy **Round Lake**, then 0.2 mile along its east shore to its northeast corner (see Hike 92). You can follow this trail over a low, broad ridge, reaching a lodgepole-fringed meadow in 0.5 mile. From it you can then leave the trail and head cross-country 0.6 mile northwest down gentle slopes to the southeast shore of shallow, warm **Meiss Lake**.

Our main trail, the PCT, continues northwest, passing another tread in ¼ mile, this one going to the meadow south of Meiss Lake. Just before we meet our **third Truckee River crossing**, we see the lake, and immediately before the ford a use trail provides the hiker with an easy ½-mile meadow traverse to **Meiss Lake**. The meadow, which in the past was often dotted with cattle, is often damp if not downright boggy, particularly near the south end of the lake, and until early August this wet environment nurses a multitude of mosquitoes. Before mid-August take the cross-country route from the Meiss Meadow Trail northwest to Meiss Lake. From mid-August through mid-September this chest-deep lake is ideal for swimming, and if cattle aren't reintroduced, for peaceful relaxation.

After jumping across the Upper Truckee River for the last time, we head northwest along a meadow's edge and, just before crossing a shallow gap, may see a faint use trail, on our left, which comes 2.1 miles from Schneider's Cow Camp (Hike 94). Just beyond the gap we descend north to a pond, and resume our lodgepole-and-meadow traverse. Our route soon curves left for an increasingly steep ascent to a broad crest. As we start a descent from it, we meet a second, and official, trail from Schneider's Cow Camp, 2.0 miles distant (also Hike 94). After a brief descent we reach campsites along the east shore of granodiorite-bound **Showers Lake**. An old horse trail still traverses northwest across willowy slopes south of the lake, but the slopes are very muddy, and hikers should avoid it. If you continue north past the lake, follow Hike 89, which is described in the reverse direction.

⋖⋟ **94** ⋞⋟

Schneider's Cow Camp to Showers and Meiss Lakes

Distances:
2.1 miles to Showers Lake
2.9 miles to Meiss Lake
5.7 miles to Showers Lake (via long route)
Low/High Elevations: 8340'/9200'
Season: Late July through mid-October
Classification: Strenuous along short route
Maps: 40 and 38
Trailhead: From Highway 99 in Stockton drive about 97 miles northeast up Highway 88 to Caples Lake Resort, above the north shore of Caples Lake. Continue 0.9 mile past the resort to a paved road, on your left. (Westbound drivers: this road is 3.0 miles west of Carson Pass.) Take this road ¼ mile to the Caples Lake Maintenance Station, and immediately past it turn right and drive up a graded road. Before August it can be muddy in several places, mostly in the first half-mile stretch. After 1¼ miles you pass waterless Schneider Camping Area, on a broad ridge to your left, then continue 0.4 to a gate and a road fork. Park here.

Introduction

The shortest trail to Showers and Meiss lakes starts from near Schneider's Cow Camp. Ironically, this trail hasn't gotten much use in the past. The trail to Showers Lake has a short section along which you obtain one of the most expansive views to be seen anywhere in the Tahoe area.

Description

From the fork in the road past Schneider's Cow Camp, you can start two routes to Showers Lake. The longer route starts by going up the road you drove in on, which quickly becomes a jeep road. The shorter route, which will be described first, starts by the east side of the road fork. This trail climbs 230 yards east to a barbed-wire gate, then climbs at a gradually steepening pace through cow country. Lodgepole stands give way to open spaces, which seasonally abound with many species of wildflowers. You leave most of the cows behind as you switchback steeply up to a crest saddle, passing a few whitebark pines before reaching it. Only 1.1 miles from the trailhead, this view-packed saddle is a worthy goal in itself. And for even better views you can go easy cross-country along the crest, either ¼ mile northwest to peak 9325 or, preferably, ¼ mile southeast to peak 9422. From the saddle you see Meiss and Round lakes to the northeast, and above them see the volcanic palisades of the Upper Truckee River basin. To the left of these cliffs stands a distant granitic massif with 10,881' Freel Peak, the highest peak of the Tahoe Basin rim. The view to the southwest includes the volcanic palisades above Kirkwood Creek, but Caples Lake and Round Top remain hidden.

From the saddle you gently climb 85 yards to a junction. From it a use trail drops 0.9 mile east down Dixon Canyon to the Pacific Crest Trail (which here also coincides with the Tahoe-Yosemite Trail route). It is generally easy to follow, but the last 200 yards to the PCT are vague, bearing 110°. If you take this short trail, you won't have any trouble finding the PCT, but study this locale so you can find your trail if you plan to return along it (you may want to follow the last part of Hike 93 to Showers Lake). On the PCT this "junction" is about 180 yards south of a pond and 360 yards northwest of an Upper Truckee River ford. From the east side of that ford you can follow an often wet use trail ½ mile north to **Meiss Lake** (see Hike 93).

From the junction just beyond the crest saddle, the left trail climbs briefly and then descends, usually at a moderate grade. Before Showers Lake comes into view, stop and admire the astounding views, which are among the best in the whole Tahoe area. You can see from 10,776′ Mt. Rose, above the north shore of Lake Tahoe, southward to 11,398′ White Mountain, about 4 miles north of Sonora Pass. This 70-mile panorama includes, northeast to southeast: granitic Freel Peak, relatively close Stevens and Red Lake peaks, and very distant Highland and Arnot peaks—all above 10,000 feet. Lower prominences rising above the end of Upper Truckee River canyon are Reynolds Peak, the Nipple, peak 9381 and, on the far right, broad-topped Elephants Back. Your panoramic views continue to a cluster of mountain hemlocks, by which you have the first view of your goal, Showers Lake. Distant Mt. Tallac, in eastern Desolation Wilderness, appears just above this lake, and to its left are the two summits of Dicks and Jacks peaks, in the heart of that wilderness. The isolated peak west of them is Pyramid Peak, the sentinel

lording it over the southwest border of the wilderness.

The short descent to Showers Lake is rubbly and excessively steep. It's bad enough when dry, but after a storm, or when snow-patch-dotted in early season, you'll really slip and slide down this trail segment. Then, it's better to take the longer, alternate route. The steep descent moderates just before you reach the PCT, along which you have only a couple minutes' walk to campsites along the east shore of subalpine **Showers Lake**. If you camp here before early August, be prepared for abundant mosquitoes. This lake is one of the cooler lakes to be found in the Tahoe area, and most people will find swimming in it acceptable only in August, a couple of weeks after nearby snow patches have melted.

If you have a heavy pack or are on horseback, you may not want to make the steep descent to Showers Lake. For variety, hikers might plan to take the longer route to the lake, and then, with lighter packs, climb out via the shorter route just described. From Schneider's Cow Camp the longer route starts northwest up a jeep road, quickly passes a gate, and almost ½ mile from the start crosses a seasonal creek. About 40 yards past it you come to a trail, which you ascend steeply north. The trail rapidly swings left, and on an easier

Red Lake Peak (left), Elephants Back (far right),and the Upper Truckee River basin

grade you climb west with views south to Caples Lake and Round Top mountain.

About one mile from this hike's start the trail bends north, enters forest shade, and climbs to a nearby early-season creeklet. You cross it, parallel it upstream, climb to a subordinate crest, and then drop to a small flat. Staying close to the contact between volcanic rocks above and granitic ones below, you traverse north-northwest for ½ mile, passing two closely spaced springs midway to a trail fork. From here an old trail goes left, descending ¼ mile to die out on a broad ridge. Our trail briefly climbs north, then traverses east below the slopes of Little Round Top. Along this traverse you'll get a couple of views of Pyramid, Jacks, and Dicks peaks. From a reliable creek the trail angles north and contours 0.4 mile to an enormous trailside mountain hemlock, on your left—among the largest you'll find anywhere. About 90 yards past it you enter lands of the *Fallen Leaf Lake* 15' quadrangle (Map 38) and momentarily receive additional views of the three Desolation Wilderness peaks seen earlier. Our Trail 17E16 then curves east, drops to a spring-fed creeklet, and reaches the PCT in 200 yards. From here you follow the last part of Hike 89 south 1.9 miles to campsites along the east shore of **Showers Lake**.

If you're not ready to join the weekend crowd at Showers Lake, then descend about 300 yards north on the PCT to a saddle. From it a faint, discontinuous path strikes east 250 yards down a linear meadow to a camp with a fine view, just beyond the meadow's far end. To the west, a similar tread descends 330 yards to the upper end of a large meadow, then angles at 330° for 130 yards to a cow camp among a cluster of lodgepoles. Both camps are seldom visited, at least by humans.

⋘ 95 ⋙
Lake Margaret Trail

Distance:
2.3 miles to Lake Margaret
Low/High Elevations: 7480'/7740'
Season: Mid-July through mid-October
Classification: Easy
Map: 39

Trailhead: This is along a short spur road on the north side of Highway 88, about 95 miles east of Stockton and 5 miles west of Carson Pass. More specifically, it lies 0.5 mile east of Kirkwood Meadows road and 0.2 mile west of the base of Caples Lake's west dam, where there is a large parking area for lake users and for those taking the Emigrant Lake Trail (Hike 96). Parking on the spur road is limited to about 10 vehicles.

Introduction

Lake Margaret Trail 17E46 takes the hiker, in about an hour's time, to a lovely lake in a granitic, hemmed-in setting. For rock climbers this lakes is an ideal place for a base camp. In the entire Tahoe Sierra you won't find another backcountry lake with such an abundance of good climbing routes up solid rock.

Description

After a minute's walk northwest along a minor, rather open ridge, you turn right and drop to a small, seasonally damp flat. This can be prolific in both wildflowers and mosquitoes, and more of these environments lie ahead. You exit to a dry bench, then wind down to the south fork of Caples Creek, which you either log-cross or rock-hop, at least before late summer, by when the creek bed is typically dry. Heading north, you skirt the base of a granitic knoll, ignore a trail heading east along its north base, then in a swampy meadow bridge the major north fork of Caples Creek.

Northward, you immediately pass the east edge of a low granitic outcrop, which has been polished and striated by one or more west-trending glaciers. From it you jog momentarily northeast, then climb a brushy ¼ mile to a narrow pass. Here it's worth your time and effort to scramble east up some smooth granitic slopes, just above the trail, for a 360° view. If you site on a 300° bearing, which is roughly the course of your unseen path, you'll see a broad, low gap, about a mile beyond unseen Lake Margaret. Although this gap in the canyon wall stands about 800 feet above the Caples Creek canyon floor, it nevertheless was too low to contain a major glacier advancing down-canyon. Past glaciers spilled north through this gap into the Strawberry Creek drainage, at least one burying the gap under more than 200 feet of ice. From your vantage point the views to the south are the most impressive, particularly of the gaping Kirkwood Meadows canyon, whose steep-sided walls reveal layer after layer of volcanic sediments and flows.

Back on the trail you skirt past a minor pond, then just north of and above it start down a ducked route across bedrock to a larger grass-lined pond. You quickly cross its seasonal outlet creek, only to recross it about 200 yards downstream. In a minute you approach a more substantial creek, follow it a bit downstream, veer away, and then cross it just after rejoining it. You continue 150 yards downstream, heading toward an overhanging cliff, then switchback and climb steeply up brushy slabs, skirt through a shallow notch, and behold tranquil **Lake Margaret.** From its south corner a *de facto* trail circles around the lake's east and north shores, ending near the lake's outlet. I prefer the shorter, rougher cross-country route above the west shore to reach this outlet.

You'll find two campsites—one quite spacious—near the east shore, two more near the northwest shore. Swimming is recommended, for the lake's small bedrock islands are tempting goals, and from the lake's southeast shore, you can dive from heights up to 10 feet. The lake is surrounded by slabs and cliffs, which offer rock climbers many possible routes, generally about 50 feet long. However, one cliff, 300 yards above the northeast shore, requires a full-length rope. Nonclimbers can scramble up easy routes to one of the lake's adjacent knolls and witness a Sierran sunrise or sunset.

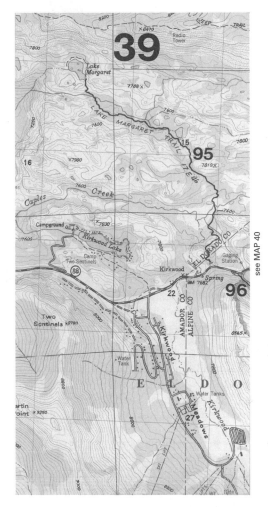

◅ 96 ▻
Emigrant Lake Trail

Distances:
2.2 miles to Caples Lake's south end
4.2 miles to Emigrant Lake
Low/High Elevations: 7770' / 8600'
Season: Mid-July through mid-October
Classification: Moderate
Maps: 39, 40, and 42

Trailhead: At the base of Caples Lake's west dam—see the Hike 95 trailhead. If you plan to camp overnight in Mokelumne Wilderness, first obtain a wilderness permit at the Amador

Ranger District Office, in Pioneer, or at the Carson Pass Information Center up at the pass.

Introduction

Another writer lauded Emigrant Lake as one of the most beautiful in the area. Perhaps this is why it is so popular. Of all the Chapter 15 backcountry lakes I have visited, I have found only Round Lake to be more popular. Visiting Emigrant Lake on an unseasonably cold mid-summer weekday, he found this lake, which is set in a deep, stark, often snowy and windswept cirque, a chilling experience. However, the slopes above the lake's east shore were resplendent with wildflowers which, in my biased view, mitigated the otherwise bleak setting.

Description

The first 2¼ miles of Emigrant Lake Trail 17E18 are extremely easy, for the trail never goes more than 50 feet above the shore of Caples Lake. Many anglers hike only along this stretch, dropping to one or more small coves along the adjacent shore to fish for trout. Our shoreline route, through a generally shady forest, certainly contrasts with the open forest along the reservoir's north shore. Our shore is more luxuriant because its soils were derived from nutrient-rich volcanic sediments of the largely unseen volcanic cliffs and slopes above us.

After only about ¼ mile into your route you pass a snowmelt creeklet that drops over a 10-foot-high cliff. Note here that the cliff is composed of *stratified* volcanic sediments—ones that were laid down by a stream. When we look at an array of volcanic sediments, such as the giant palisades in the distance above Caples Lake Resort, we tend to think these layers were laid down rapidly, due to eruption after continual eruption. Actually, the volcanic rocks in this chapter's area originated as lava flows or their sedimentary derivatives, being constructed over the last 5-20+ million years. During that vast amount of time, erosion, not eruption, was the basic element transfiguring the landscape.

When you reach an open area strewn with granitic boulders, you'll be midway along your shoreline trek. Near the far edge of this opening you may see an old EMIGRANT ROAD sign, although all evidences of its tread are absent. A few aspens herald forest cover, under which you walk a mile to near the **south end of Caples Lake**. Here a path goes 80 yards out to the water's edge, at which you'll have some nice views plus some shoreline slabs for sunbathing or fishing.

Alongside the lake, the trail has served as the Mokelumne Wilderness boundary, but now you enter the wilderness proper as you leave the lake's south tip. After a couple of minutes you pass through a small meadow, which grows a crop of corn lilies and arrow-leaved senecios, and here you enter prime mosquito country. Before August you can expect their humming chorus to serenade you all the way up Emigrant Creek. About 0.6 mile past the meadow you come to a junction with a trail that climbs a steep ¼ mile southwest up to a Kirkwood Meadows ski-lift-maintenance road. From the south end of that road one could continue south on a trail into the heart of the wilderness, but that

Chilly, windswept Emigrant lake

subalpine landscape, the location of many lakelets, is largely beyond the scope of this book. Trails from the Silver Lake area offer easier routes into this region.

Just 0.1 mile past the junction and a little over 3 miles from the trailhead we rock-hop Emigrant Creek and discover a noticeable increase in trail gradient, in mountain hemlocks and, before August, in snow patches. Switchbacks keep the gradient within reason and, just beyond a cascading distributary of Emigrant Creek, we're treated to northward views. These disappear as we climb westward to Emigrant Creek proper, up which our trail's finale is an easy, if marshy, stroll. The trail dies out along the brushy east shore of **Emigrant Lake**. Instead of hiking onward, cross the creek just below the lake's outlet and head past an assortment of camps to the conspicuous peninsula. From it you can fish or sunbathe (which is necessary after a frigid dip) and have a find spot for admiring the surrounding scenery.

⋘ 97 ⋙
Woods Lake to Round Top Lake and Round Top Summit

Distances:
1.4 miles to Winnemucca Lake by Trail 18E06
2.1 miles to Round Top Lake by Trail 17E47
2.3 miles to Round Top Lake by Trail 18E06

Low/High Elevations: 8210' / 9410'; 10,381' to summit

Season: Late July through early October

Classification: Moderate to lakes, strenuous to summit

Maps: 40, 41, 42, and 43

Trailheads: Drive up Highway 88 toward Carson Pass. Eastbound drivers leave this highway just 1.2 miles after they pass a junction with a road to the Caples Lake Maintenance Station, the junction being above Caples Lake's northeast shore. If you miss the Woods Lake turnoff, you have a second chance, 0.9 mile later. This is the turnoff westbound drivers take, which is 0.9 mile west of Carson Pass. Eastbound drivers traverse a

paved road (the *old* Highway 88) 0.8 mile to another junction, while westbound drivers descend a dirt road 0.5 mile to it. This descent to the junction offers overflow campsites when the Woods Lake Campground is full.

From the junction you drive almost 0.2 mile south up a paved road to a trailhead parking area that is immediately before Woods Creek. If you are going in overnight, then park here and hike ⅓ mile up an east-bank trail to Winnemucca Lake Trail 18E06. If you are day hiking, you can drive 0.4 mile up the road and park in the lakeside picnic area. Trail 18E06 begins 50 yards before the start of the picnic area's loop road.

For Trail 17E47 follow the same procedure. To reach its trailhead, hike about 90 yards north from the Trail 18E06 trailhead to the start of the one-way road through Woods Lake Campground. Walk west 0.2 mile up to campsite 12 to find the trailhead a few yards past it, on your left.

All of the above mileages are calculated from the start of Trail 18E06. If you are beginning from the start of Trail 17E47 (no parking here), then subtract 0.2 mile. If you hike up the east-bank trail to Trail 18E06, then add 0.3 mile. If you hike from the same parking area up to the start of Trail 17E47, then add 0.2 mile. This assumes you walk ¼ mile up the Woods Lake Road to the north end of the campground's one-way road, then go 320 yards up to this road.

If you plan to camp overnight in Mokelumne Wilderness, first obtain a wilderness permit at the Amador Ranger District Office, in Pioneer, or at the Carson Pass Information Center up at the pass.

Introduction
Two of the Tahoe Sierra's most photogenic lakes lie only an hour's hike away: Lake Winnemucca via Trail 18E06 and Round Top Lake via Trail 17E47. Round Top Lake, at 9350 feet, is the highest lake in the Tahoe Sierra. From it you can climb, with a lot of effort, to the Round Top summit in another hour. This peak, surpassed in height only by Mt. Rose and the Freel Peak massif, offers unsurpassed didactic views for tens of miles in every direction. Because the features along this hike are

40

89

94

93

94

94

94

93

93

93

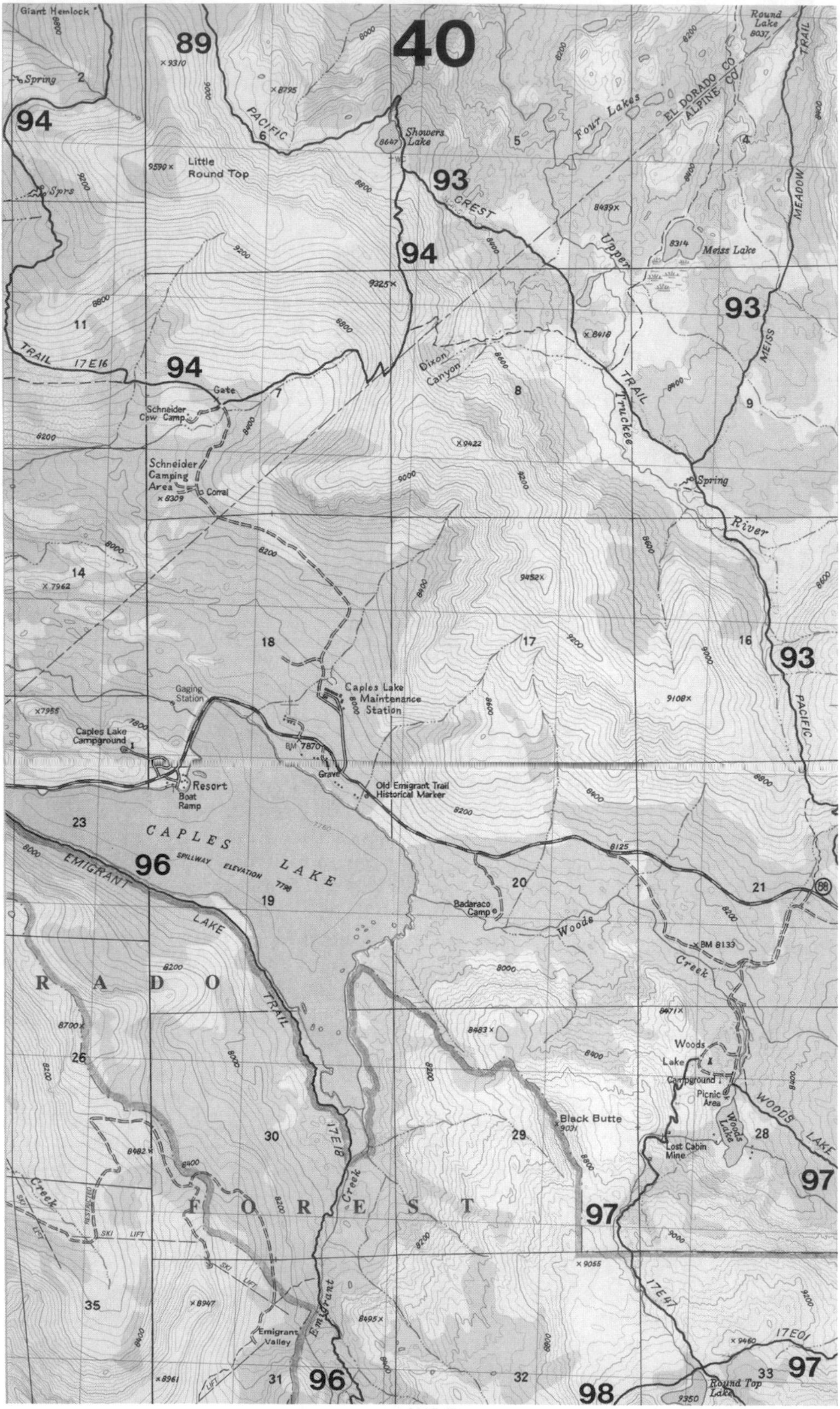

see MAP 39

see MAP 41

Giant Hemlock

Spring

Little Round Top

9310 ×

× 8795

Showers Lake
8647

Four Lakes

Round Lake
8037

EL DORADO CO
ALPINE CO

MEADOW

9590 ×

PACIFIC

CREST

Upper

Meiss Lake

8314

8439 ×

TRUCKEE

MEISS

8418

TRAIL

TRAIL

17 E 16

Gate

Schneider Cow Camp

Dixon

Canyon

8

9422 ×

Spring

River

9452 ×

9108 ×

PACIFIC

Schneider Camping Area

8309 ×

Corral

7962

14

18

17

16

Gaging Station

Caples Lake Maintenance Station

7955 ×

Caples Lake Campground

BM 7870

Resort
Boat Ramp

Grave

Old Emigrant Trail Historical Marker

96

23

CAPLES

LAKE

SPILLWAY ELEVATION 7798

19

Badaraco Camp

20

21

98

BM 8133

Woode

Creek

EMIGRANT

LAKE

RADO

8700 ×

26

8693 ×

6471 ×

Woods
Lake

8982 ×

TRAIL

30

17 E 18

Creek

29

Black Butte
9031

Campground

Picnic Area

Lost Cabin Mine

WOODS

LAKE

28

97

97

Creek

SKI LIFT

35

8947 ×

SKI LIFT

Emigrant Valley

Emigrant

Creek

8495 ×

9055 ×

17 E 47

31

96

32

98

17 E 01

9460 ×

Round Top Lake
9350

33

97

8961 ×

F O R E S T

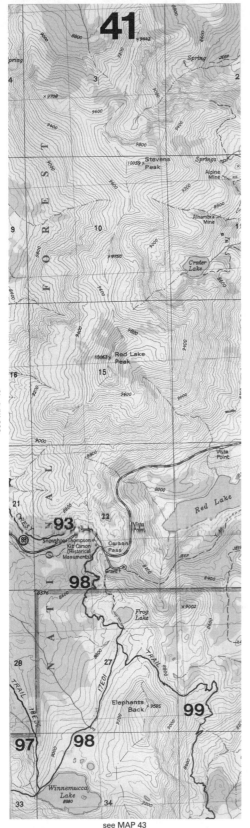

so readily accessible, you should day hike rather than backpack to them. The lakes, which do attract campers, are both near treeline, and consequently they have fragile environments that can't withstand the impact of heavy use. Under no condition should equestrians camp at them.

Description

From Woods Lake you can make a 4.4-mile loop to Winnemucca and Round Top lakes by starting up either Trail 18E06 or Trail 17E47. By taking in Round Top peak, you add about 2.0 miles to your loop. The advantage of a loop is that you of course get to see more terrain. I recommend ascending Trail 18E06 since it is better graded.

Winnemucca (formerly Woods) Lake Trail 18E06 begins by immediately bridging Woods Creek, down whose east bank runs a cutoff trail from the Woods Creek parking area. Climbing southeast, we meet this 0.4-mile-long trail after a minute's walk, then continue in the same direction, having a glimpse or two of Woods Lake, seen through hemlocks, lodgepoles, and western white pines. About ½ mile from our trailhead we hike along a creeklet and its attendant wildflower garden, then reach an old arrastra, which is a circular floor of stones about 10 feet across. Usually a mule would drag a large stone round and round it, the stone pulverizing smaller, ore-laden stones, enabling a miner to extract the gold and silver.

Beyond this historic artifact the forest thins appreciably, the ground cover transforming to one of sagebrush and wildflowers. Along this ⅔-mile open stretch up to Winnemucca Lake, a botanist can have a field day identifying dozens of wildflowers. This hike's Plate 15 has a fraction of this area's wildflowers. For additional high-elevation species, consult Plates 11, 13, 14, 16, and 17.

Our moderately climbing path, which has paralleled the lake's outlet creek at a short distance, enters Mokelumne Wilderness about ⅓ mile before ending at a junction with Tahoe-Yosemite Trail 17E01. Here, beside **Winnemucca Lake**, you'll see broad, rounded Elephants Back, about a mile to the northeast. From its easily attainable summit, straddling the Sierra Nevada crest, you have excellent views to the east and west, plus one capital view southwest of dark, massive Round Top.

Westbound on the TYT we cross the lake's outlet in 70 yards, the outlet's gravelly, saturated soil seasonally highlighted with diminutive mountain monkey flowers and alpine shooting stars. Climbing west, all but late-season hikers are likely to encounter snowfields. The open route, however, is quite obvious, and in ⅔ mile we crest a shallow gap in a granitic ridge. Notice up here—the high point if you don't climb Elephants Back or Round Top—how the freezing winter winds have cropped the whitebark pines down to shrublike stature. Their asymmetrical growth reveals the direction of the prominent winds.

You now have an easy descent 300 yards to Round Top Trail 17E47, which intersects the TYT by the northeast corner of **Round Top Lake**. With clusters of whitebark pines adorning its northwest shore, the lake is relatively wind-free, and is a fine spot for a lunch break. However, if you plan to climb Round Top, then eat lightly. To climb to its summit, which you should attempt only in good weather, you should have brought along several items: dark glasses, a cap or hat, sunscreen, and a windbreaker. The first two are very useful in protecting your eyes from the intense ultraviolet radiation you'll receive on this exposed climb.

Starting southeast from the lake, you're almost bound to see some sturdy green gentians, which can grow to chest height by late season. After you climb 0.4 mile up a narrow tread, it switches from granitic to volcanic and your gradient switches from steep to *very* steep. You're now in the alpine realm, though alpine wildflowers are relatively scarce due to the rubbly nature of the steep slopes. The rubble is just enough to make us backslide on our ascent, but not deep enough to comprise a scree slope. Consequently, on your way down, instead of "skiing" down the rubble you'll have to cautiously pick your way.

Before August, snow can cover most of the upper trail, which appears to be heading for the broad saddle separating Round Top from the East Sister. Actually, the trail dies out before the saddle, and you climb cross-

country not to the saddle, but left of it, to a small but obvious notch in Round Top's descending ridge. Once on the ridge you climb up its back side, staying close to the crest, until you reach a false summit. For most hikers, this is far enough. The true summit, only a few feet higher, blocks your views to the east, but then, that direction is the least photogenic.

Between the two summits is a small, steep-sided cleft, which perhaps separates the brave from the wise. Were it not for the rubbly nature, the descent into this minor cleft would be quite safe. As matters stand, if you slip on the loose rock, you could find yourself plunging down a steepening slope and into an avalanche chute—almost certain death. From the cleft, don't tackle the true summit head-on, but instead descend a few yards south before taking a curving route of least resistance northeast to the small summit. I found this ascent from the cleft considerably less intimidating that the descent into it.

From the summit you have, on a clear day, an extremely far-ranging 360° view. If you look due east along Round Top's descending ridge-crest, you'll see Markleeville Peak (9415'), 5½ miles away, which lies 1½ miles north of Jeff Davis Peak (9065'), which is a miniature Devils Tower that challenges the best of climbers. (If you've got a Markleeville 15' quad map, then subtract 75 feet. This is quite some discrepancy. Usually the peak elevations in the newer 7½' quads agree to within several feet of the elevations of the older 15' quads.)

Scanning counterclockwise, you next see, above Winnemucca Lake, domelike Hawkins Peak (10,023'), which is all that is left of the throat of an ancient volcano. Looking above Elephants Back (9585'), you barely see the top of Pickett Peak (9118'). The latter is, like your summit, the core of an ancient volcano, while the former is a dome of andesite lava. Carson Pass is the broad, obvious gash in the Sierra crest, beyond which lies spacious Hope Valley. Sierra-crest glaciers coalesced to form a mammoth glacier that flowed north down this valley and, unable to make a sharp turn east down the West Carson Canyon, part of the glacier continued to flow 1½ miles straight ahead, climbing about 400 feet in the process.

This huge glacier, which received some of its impetus from Round Top's north-slope glaciers, was thick enough to spill west over Luther Pass. Hope Valley, therefore, was buried under about 800 feet of glacier ice (see the geology chapter's glacier map).

Above Hope Valley stands Freel Peak (10,881') and its entourage of 10,000+' peaks, the highest summits of the Carson Range. Between the crest of that range and the Sierra Nevada crest lies the Lake Tahoe Basin. Part of this basin, which includes the Upper Truckee River drainage, can be seen to the north. Geologically speaking, Lake Tahoe is quite young, faulting and volcanism older, and the bedrock landscape (granitic and metamorphic features) much older, as discussed in the geology chapter. On clear days you can see a high peak north of the lake's northeast shore. This is Mt. Rose (10,776'), a respectable 46 miles away. Scanning westward, you'll readily identify pointed Mt. Tallac (9735') above Tahoe's west shore and, above the east shore of Caples Lake, Pyramid Peak (9983'), which is steeper-sloped than Tallac. Between the two lies the bulk of Desolation Wilderness.

Closer to us beneath that high country lies the broad Caples Creek basin, which, from about 80 to 30 million years ago, was a granitic landscape. But ensuing eruptions interred this landscape in a volcanic sepulcher, and there it lay until perhaps a few million years ago, when streams removed some of this overburden to resurrect the bedrock. Then beginning about 2-2½ million years ago, wave after wave of glistening white glaciers stripped away additional amounts of dark volcanic sediments. These glaciers were truly monumental. The latest ones filled the Caples Creek basin almost rim to rim, entombing the floor under as much as ¼ mile of glacier ice. In a 2½-mile-wide cascade, they crevassed eastward down upon the equally giant Hope Valley glacier. In the Carson Pass area the glaciers have been thick enough at times to spill over into the Upper Truckee River basin, this basin itself the breeding ground for enormous, north-flowing glaciers that spilled laterally west over Echo Summit and into the South Fork American River drainage. Westward, down the Caples Creek basin, the giant glaciers spilled laterally north into this

Snow-robed Round Top and whitebark-pine-bordered Winnemucca Lake

Wildflower Plate 15. Subalpine flowers.
1 Woolly senecio (butterweed, groundsel) (yellow), 2 California Jacob's ladder (low polemonium) (violet to pale-blue with white center), 3 alpine paintbrush (dull-yellow to purple-green), 4 mountain monkey flower (yellow), 5 Lewis' monkey flower (pink), 6 showy penstemon (red-violet to blue), 7 western blue flax (pale blue or violet), 8 green gentian (monument plant, giant frasera, deer's tongue) (pale green flowers and stem), 9 fringed lungwort (streamside bluebells) (blue or pink)

same drainage, overflowing a low pass you see above the north shore of Caples Lake. During glacial times your summit, surrounded by a sea of ice, would have presented a viewer with a scene of indescribable beauty. Despite the mammoth size of past glaciers, they were relatively impotent at eroding the area's resistant, granitic bedrock. On a small scale, they locally smoothed and plucked the bedrock, but today's glaciated bedrock canyons are little deeper or wider than their ancestral, pre-volcanic canyons.

Returning momentarily to present time, we continue our counterclockwise scan. A sinuous volcanic ridge, to the west, separates the Caples Creek basin from the granite-walled Summit City Creek canyon. Averaging about 2000-2500 feet in depth, it is about twice as deep as the Caples Creek basin. Like that basin, this canyon had achieved most of its width and depth before the first glacier flowed down it. Its past glaciers were not solitary, but rather were tributaries originating from the northern edge of a *mer de glace*—a sea of glacial ice. Repeatedly, these seas buried the broad, relatively flat Blue Lakes area to the southeast. From this 8-mile-long, trans-Sierra crest plateau, glaciers flowed in all directions: north down the West Fork Carson River drainage (Hope Valley), northeast down the East Fork Carson River drainage (Charity and Pleasant valleys), southwest into the North Fork Mokelumne River canyon (in effect, a 10-mile-wide glacier), and west over a "minor" ridge into the headwaters of Summit City Creek canyon.

And there was another *mer de glace* nourishing the Summit City Creek canyon glacier. During the last glaciation, this one covered about 60 square miles of rolling uplands from the volcanic peaks above unseen Silver Lake south to Mokelumne Peak (9332'), 10 miles southwest of us. From this peak, which easily stands over 4000 feet above the floor of the canyon, the east edge of the *mer de glace* stretched 8 miles north, to Emigrant Peak (9763'), which is 2 miles to our west-southwest. This 8-mile-wide stretch of glacier ice flowed into the canyon, and helped to bury the canyon under about 3500 feet of ice. Now that's awesome!

From the summit and its instructional views, *carefully* retrace your steps back down to Round Top Lake, from where you decide what course to follow. You can backtrack, you can head over to Fourth of July Lake (Hike 98), or you can continue straight ahead down Trail 17E47.

By and large, Trail 17E47 is a joy to descend. Its fairly steady grade averages 11%, which is steep enough to propel us forward effortlessly but not so steep so as to require a braking, knee-knocking effort. Hikers ascending this trail will find it a bit too steep, particularly up here in this rarefied air. We start an open, scenic descent northwest, usually staying a short distance from Round Top Lake's outlet creek. Black Butte, at first insignificant, grows formidable as we approach it. Above it stands the roof of the Crystal Range, topped by Pyramid Peak. Backward glances aren't bad either. If anything, they're more impressive, particularly in mid- or late afternoon, when Round Top and The Sisters cast photogenic shadows on their north-slope snowfields.

After ¾ mile you make a short, steep descent and turn northeast, entering a mountain-hemlock forest that lies just north of the Mokelumne Wilderness boundary. Hemlocks have a propensity to sustain snowfields, so don't be surprised to find snow here in August. This snow can cover the bend in the trail and even our adjacent creek, particularly in early season, leading unsuspecting hikers astray.

A ¼-mile, sometimes steep and rocky descent through the hemlock forest gets you down to a second right-angle bend. Here, where the trail turns northwest, you'll find a good-sized camp, on a small flat. A snowmelt creeklet provides water through most of the summer. Of all the campsites you may see along Hike 97, this is the only one which is suitable for equestrians.

In 130 yards we reach the start of a jeep road, where Trail 17E47 becomes the Lost Cabin Mine Trail. On our right is an old mine shack, "landscaped" with red elderberries. this bush, with foul-smelling leaves, produces a myriad of red berries in late season, but unlike the tart but tasty berries of its lower-elevation, taller cousin, the blue elderberry, these berries are mildly poisonous.

On the road we quickly reach a creekside meadow, which is backdropped by now-hulking Black Butte. While the butte appears large, it is but a petty remnant of the extensive volcanic sediments that once buried the Caples Creek basin. Just past the meadow, Round Top Lake's outlet creek has cut into our jeep road. Onward, we briefly enter forest shade and descend steeply to Lost Cabin Mine, which we reach immediately after crossing the creek. This mine was worked on and off from perhaps the 1860s or '70s until 1962, producing a recorded 132 troy ounces of gold, 375 ounces of silver, 917 pounds of copper, and 3,832 pounds of lead. All this came from 196 tons of ore extracted from some faulted quartz veins.

From the mine you have an uneventful, winding, somewhat open descent ½ mile down to Woods Lake Campground. If you're parked at the lake's picnic area, turn right and walk 0.2 mile to the main road, then head south on it. If you're parked by the overnighters' trailhead, turn left and walk 320 yards to the main road, then head north on it.

⊰⊱ 98 ⊰⊱
Tahoe-Yosemite Trail, Carson Pass south to Fourth of July Lake

Distances:
1.2 miles to Frog Lake
1.3 miles to PCT/TYT junction
2.5 miles to Winnemucca Lake
3.4 miles to Round Top Lake
5.2 miles to Fourth of July Lake
6.3 miles to Summit City Canyon junction
9.4 miles to Forestdale Divide
Low/High Elevations: 8590' at trailhead; 8170' at Fourth of July Lake; 7440' at Summit City Canyon junction/9410'
Season: Late July through early October
Classification: Moderate
Maps: 41, 40, 42, and 43

Trailhead: Beside the Carson Pass Information Center, which is at the south end of a long turnout at Carson Pass. The Highway 88 pass is about 100 miles from Highway 99 in Stockton and about 20 miles from Highway 50 in the Lake Tahoe Basin. During the summer months, when the center is open, those planning to camp overnight in Mokelumne Wilderness can obtain a wilderness permit at it.

Introduction
Along this route you visit two scenic, sub-alpine lakes of the upper Caples Creek basin. In addition, you have the opportunity to visit Fourth of July Lake, although the steep drop to it—over 1000 feet—makes it a questionable objective. Rather than ascend from it the way you came, you can continue to descend to the floor of the Summit City Creek canyon, then take a better graded route out, one that climbs to Forestdale Divide before descending to your trailhead. Such a loop trip is 14½ miles long.

Description
From the south end of the parking lot and by the west side of the Carson Pass Information Station, you start south on the Pacific Crest/Tahoe-Yosemite trail, which leisurely winds and climbs to a junction just south of and above aptly named **Frog Lake**. Until about 1990, an older segment of the PCT/TYT began south from the old, abandoned Highway 88 and climbed up to Frog Lake then traversed along its west shore to our junction. It did so in only 0.6 mile, half the distance of our newer route, but its overly steep ascent was grueling. Much of Frog Lake is shallow, and when by midsummer its water-line drops a couple of feet, the lake has a conspicuous, unsightly, muddy bathtub ring. With this ring of muddy shore, the lake looks too shallow to support trout, but with a maximum depth of 27 feet, it can do so quite effectively. Anglers, however, may have to wade out in shallow, muddy water to cast effectively for trout.

If you walk over to the Sierra's crest, which is barely above the lake's east shore, you'll get a view north-northeast down into Hope

Valley. U.S. Geological Survey maps depict a fault running, almost literally, right below your feet, heading north down a gully toward Red Lake, the east-side lands being down-faulted. The fault, however, is suspect, as are so many along the east-side of the Sierra crest (see Geology chapter). During the last 2 million years, glaciers repeatedly advanced down from Round Top and across your site, joining forces with a coexisting Hope Valley glacier, which sometimes flowed up onto the gentle slopes at the north end of the valley, below the Freel Peak massif.

Both the lake and our junction are just within the Mokelumne Wilderness, and from the junction we traverse a mere 230 yards to the **PCT/TYT junction**, where the two long-distance trails split to go their separate routes. From a junction just north of and above Middle Velma Lake in central Desolation Wilderness, they have had one solitary tread for about 35½ miles, and they won't rejoin until just within Yosemite National Park, about 81 miles via the PCT tread and about 86 miles via the TYT tread.

We continue straight ahead on the TYT, across an open landscape of sagebrush which is sporadically punctuated with clusters of lodgepole and whitebark pines. Snowy-robed Round Top, the ruins of an ancient volcano, acts like a giant lodestone, drawing us ever nearer.

Along this stretch, indeed, for the next 3 miles, you're likely to pass many mountain snowberries. With relatively small, drab leaves, these waist-high shrubs are easily ignored, particularly since most of the time they lack both flowers and berries. The flowers are small, tubular, and pinkish—nothing special—but the berries are white, whence the name "snowberry." No other shrub in the Tahoe Sierra produces white berries. While mildly poisonous, they may nevertheless be sampled by northward-migrating black bears, who use the TYT. Such bears, tagged in Yosemite National Park, have been found as far north as Desolation Wilderness!

After we do a mile of easy walking, chilly though photogenic Winnemucca Lake comes into view. For an interesting diversion leave the trail at this point, traverse ¼ mile east,

passing above the north shore of a sunken pond, then climb northeast a little over ½ mile to the summit of Elephants Back. The views you obtain are second only to those from Round Top (Hike 97), which requires a great deal more effort. You also get your best possible view of the irregular Red Lake-Forestdale Divide escarpment.

For secluded camping, try the broad, tree-less crest notch above the east shore of Winnemucca Lake. It tends to be windy, but then, so are the popular, cramped site along the lake's northwest shore. However, from your solitary site you can experience a glorious Sierra sunrise. In this area, above the east shore, you may possibly find some molybdenite, which is a mineral that occurs locally in the granitic bedrock. Its crystals are quite small, flat, and colored silvery gray, with a hint of blue. With it you're likely to find another mineral, pyrite, also known as fool's gold.

By the west corner of **Winnemucca Lake** we meet Trail 18E06 and now join Hike 97 for 0.9 mile as it climbs up often snowy, granitic slopes to a notch in a treeline divide, then drops to nearby **Round Top Lake**. Here you meet Trail 17E47, which descends to Woods Lake. It also continues up toward Round Top, whose summit is the apex of Hike 97. This strenuous but superlative side trip is highly recommended—for competent mountaineers.

Continuing along the Tahoe-Yosemite Trail, we make a ¼-mile-long traverse west above Round Top Lake's north shore, passing several small, windswept campsite among the whitebark pines, then curve south on a ½-mile traverse to a crest divide. From here proficient cross-country hikers can make an easy off-trail hike to Emigrant Lake. You first traverse about one mile west to a notch that is immediately southeast of the map's point 9020. From that notch the ⅓-mile, 420-foot drop toward the lake's outlet is perfectly obvious.

For the botanically inclined the descent to Fourth of July Lake is a sheer delight when the wildflowers are blooming. For most others, it is a sheer drop. The grade, averaging 20%, is too steep and often too bouldery; consequently you'll be scrutinizing the underfooting instead of the dozens of trailside wildflower species. Down at **Fourth of July Lake**, camping space is limited by either too many willows or two steep slopes. The few good sites are along the east shore, between the trail and the lake's outlet creek. Due to relatively heavy usage here, you should, for ecological reasons, consider camping down along Summit City Creek.

Most of the 1.4-mile descent to the canyon floor is across open slopes that are liberally covered with huckleberry oaks, greenleaf manzanitas, snow bushes, and bitter cherries—very Sierran. The snow bush, not to be confused with snowberry, is a mis-named shrub that has little to do with snow. Due to its rigid, sharp-pointed branch tips, this sometimes trail-encroaching shrub is bane for hikers dressed in shorts. Because your descent is treeless, you have abundant views up and down the canyon. Within a stone's throw of **Summit City Creek**, you meet a lodgepole-shaded **junction**. To continue down-canyon along the Tahoe-Yosemite Trail, consult Thomas Winnett's "bible" guide to that trail. It's only about 135 miles to Tuolumne Meadows.

Instead of climbing 2.5 miles back up your route, you can climb 3.1 miles up the canyon to the Forestdale Divide. Along Trail 18E07 the ascent is fairly steady, averaging a moderate 9% grade. About 45 yards up this route you'll spy a small camp, on the right, then in 120 yards will come to a junction with Trail 18E21. This heads 2 miles up the canyon, climbing 1200 feet before topping an "intra-canyon" divide, then heads 1 mile down to Upper Blue Lake, which is about 450 feet below the divide.

Keeping left at the trail junction, you soon leave lodgepoles behind in exchange for red firs and western white pines. About half way up, just a few minutes beyond your climb up a ¼-mile-long switchback, the forest recedes below you and you have your first good views up and down the glaciated canyon. Sierran brush is your almost constant trailside companion over most of the next ¾ mile, interrupted midway by a wildflower garden around a trailside spring. Here, alpine knotweeds grow to head height.

Beyond another switchback sagebrush takes over as the dominant plant, though as we climb north toward Forestdale Divide, wildflowers and open ground become increasingly prominent. After another switchback you cross often snowy slopes and soon intersect the Pacific Crest Trail. Ahead, your hike ends in 130 yards, where the Blue Lakes Road crosses **Forestdale Divide**. To return to your trailhead, follow the next hike in reverse.

⋖⋗ 99 ⋖⋗
Pacific Crest Trail, Carson Pass south to Forestdale Divide

Distances:
1.3 miles to PCT/TYT junction
5.1 miles to Forestdale Divide
Low/High Elevations: 8590' at trailhead; 8280'/9060'
Season: Late July through early October
Classification: Moderate
Maps: 41 and 43
Trailhead: Same as the Hike 98 trailhead.

Introduction
Offering often-bathtub-ringed Frog Lake and several troutless ponds, this route is not an angler's favorite. Furthermore, due to constraints imposed by the topography, the trail, although well engineered, drops and climbs too much to suit most hikers. Therefore, it is used primarily by long-distance Pacific Crest Trail hikers who, to stay on route, must hike this taxing stretch. But it should also appeal to botanists since, according to my determination, it has more wildflower species, mile for mile, than any other trail in the Tahoe Sierra.

Description
See the previous hike's first three paragraphs for the route to the **PCT/TYT junction**. Southbound on the Pacific Crest Trail, you branch left and make a meandering ⅓-mile ascent to the Sierra crest, crossing it just north of dome-shaped Elephants Back. From the

96 **42** 98 97

Round Top

Thimble Peak
9905x

The Sisters 10/53
10095 x

8600

Emigrant Lake 8590

Fourth of July Peak
9536 x

Covered Wagon Peak x 9565

8200

2

8800

x 9020

9000

8800

x 9798

5

4

8600

7800

17 E 01

see MAP 43

Emigrant Peak 9763 x

8980 x

Corrie Lochan

Fourth of July Lake

8164

17 E 01

Scout Carson Lake
x 9002

9250

9000

x 9607

Creek

9

7

M O K E L U M N E   W I L D E R N E S S

8600

Ridge

Horse

Canyon

PACK

7800

7200

Summit City

7200

8600

x 9434

x 8408

TRAIL

9006 x

9100

7800

14

Telephone Gu

7000

7800

8200

9400

see map 41

99 **43**

x 9016

9400

Round Top 10381

9942 x

8600

Divide

8400

West Fork

Swansea

9600

4

3

9000

9200

8600

x 9492

18 E 07

7800

1

x 9776

8600

PACIFIC

8600

98

Creek

18 E 21

8600

8600

Lost Lakes x 8772

8800

see MAP 42

M O K E L U M N E   W I L D E R N E S S   E L D O R A D O

9

City

Summit

10

7600

8600

Spring

x 8902

8600

CREST

8800

TRAIL

12

8400

Devils

11

8600

Corral

7800

Upper Blue Lake Campground

LAKES

9626 x

8600

8200

ROAD

Upper Blue Lake

SPILLWAY ELEVATION 8136

9646

8400

Creek

8200

Damsite C G
Boat Ramp

WC

Middle

east side of the Sierra crest you can see your goal, the Forestdale Divide, only 1.8 air miles away. Snaking down into and then out of the intervening basin, the PCT takes 3.6 miles to reach it. On this trail you start a rather steep descent, and before August the tread can lie beneath snow. When the snow is iced over, the traverse across it is rather touch and go, and you might prefer instead to voluntarily fanny-slide down to a small pond. From it you can walk briefly southeast up to a small notch at the base of the Sierra crest escarpment.

Next you walk across a brushy granitic ridge, which is alive with wild buckwheats, sagebrush, and other plants that seek dry, gravelly soil. From the ridge's far end, you initiate a moderate descent with multitudinous views. Examining the trailside vegetation along your descent, you'll note one new species after another popping up to greet you. Once, while hurriedly traversing the 3.6-mile stretch across the basin to beat the setting sun, I nevertheless noted over 60 wildflower species. Just think how many more you'll find if you've got the time! (Over 500 plant species have been identified in the Carson Pass area.)

Approaching the basin's floor, we first wind among some granitic outcrops, then briefly descend to cross one of Forestdale

Creek's snow-fed creeklets. Now the climb begins, first up beside the creeklet, then up a switchbacking ascent to a second one. Your trail levels just before reaching a third creeklet (early-season hikers may pass more). If you were to go just upstream, you'd reach a pond—the first of five in this subalpine basin. Not far beyond the creeklet you'll reach a tiny pond and, off to your right, will see another one, equally small. The second one of these you circle, then you approach a fourth, somewhat larger, but only knee-deep, and hardly anything to rave about—unless you're a frog. And frogs we can use, for the mosquitoes, as one could predict, are seasonally fierce. Your trail approaches the Blue Lakes Road—here a jeep road—then turns southwest and climbs above the fifth pond, the only one large enough to qualify as a lakelet. You could camp near it if you're prepared to stave off the mosquitoes.

Beyond the ponds you switchback through a thinning subalpine forest, climbing about 200 feet in elevation before you crest the **Forestdale Divide**. In a couple of minutes you intersect Trail 18E07, which is described at the end of the previous hike. To continue onward along the PCT, consult my **Pacific Crest Trail** (Volume 1: California).

Red Lake Peak looms over the PCT/TYT junction, just south of unseen Frog Lake

Cow camp on Upper Truckee River

Difficult climbing routes lie up the north face of Jobs Sister

Chapter 16
The Carson Range and
Lake Tahoe's North Rim

Introduction

To most earth scientists the Carson Range may be little more than an appendage of the northern Sierra Nevada. It is, however, respectable in its own right, with dimensions very similar to those of southern California's San Bernardino Mountains. The Carson Range splits from the Sierra Nevada proper at Carson Pass, then arcs gracefully northward past Lake Tahoe, ending indistinctly just south of Interstate 80's borderline town of Verdi, about 57 miles north.

The range is very old, becoming the entity it is today perhaps around 80 million years ago when, during one or more episodes of faulting, the crust of the earth hereabouts was stretched and crustal blocks subsided. The Carson River's valleys, east of the range, came into being, as did other east-side basins and valleys such the Mono Basin and Owens Valley. Likewise, the Truckee River's valley came into being, but *sans* Lake Tahoe. The lake is a geologically young feature, brought about when, roughly 4 million years ago, faulting was reactivated in the river's drainage, accompanied by volcanic eruptions. The outpouring of lava constructed a dam across the river valley, and over time Lake Tahoe ponded up behind it. It is this massive accumulation of lava that today makes up the north-rim lands of the Lake Tahoe Basin.

The rocks of the Carson Range are very similar to those of its western counterpart, lands along the Sierra Nevada crest. Both are dominated at their north and south ends by volcanic rocks, with mostly granitic rocks in between. but when you compare the granitic Desolation Wilderness landscape with the granitic central Carson Range landscape, you see quite a difference. This is due mainly to the *rain shadow* cast by the high ridges of Desolation Wilderness. Most storms approach the Sierra from the west, and they unleash most of their precipitation—usually snow—as they rise up the western slope, because air cools as it rises, and the colder the air is, the less water vapor it can hold. By the time a storm has worked its way from the Sacramento Valley, near sea level, 9000 feet up to the Sierra crest, its air mass has cooled about 30° Fahrenheit and its water-vapor capacity has been halved. Half of its water vapor has been converted to precipitation. When the storm reaches the Carson Range, it is carrying much less water, and as a result this high country receives only about half the precipitation received by Desolation Wilderness.

How does this precipitation difference affect landscape development? During the Pleistocene epoch, or "Ice Age," snowfields covered Desolation's uplands and were the source of huge glaciers that scoured out loose bedrock on lands east and west of the ridges. With considerably less precipitation than its counterpart, the Carson Range spawned glaciers only at its high-elevation north and south ends. While admirable in size, these glaciers were no match for the giant Sierra-proper glaciers, and only one sizable lake basin was created through glacial erosion—that of Star Lake (Hikes 101 and 102).

The central Carson Range was unscathed by glaciers, though during the Pleistocene epoch it probably had some very decent snowfields. Because it was not scoured by glaciers, its soils were not removed. Whereas most of Desolation's soils—where they exist!—have formed from glacial deposits left when glaciers finally retreated about 13,000 years ago, the central Carson's soils never were eroded in the first place. The range has had soils for tens of millions of years. Over this time, soil creep, landsliding, and stream erosion have removed soils, but the soil cover has continually been replenished by newly weathered fragments of bedrock.

An advantage of old, deep soil is that it *can* hold more water than do new, discontinuous patches of soil in Desolation. While most creeks are rapidly drying up in Desolation after the snow melts, the creeks in this area may still flow, since abundant water *can* be stored in deep soil. I stress "can" because in actuality, much of the Carson Range is quite dry. There are at least two reasons for this. First, slopes often are fairly steep, and on such slopes soil creep—the downward movement of grains—occurs sufficiently fast so that a thick soil never develops; the steeper the slope, the faster the soil creep, and the thinner the soil. Second, lying in a rain shadow, the range's plants receive less precipitation, so the density of trees, shrubs, and herbs is less. Where vegetation is dense, as in the Sierra proper, plants can hold soil creep to a minimum. Furthermore, where vegetation is dense, a lot of plant litter accumulates, which can retard soil creep, but perhaps more important, the litter can be converted to humus. This humus in the soil can retain a lot of water. The Carson Range's granitic soils are mostly grains of quartz and feldspar, and water flows easily among the grains. Therefore, only on gentle slopes or canyon bottoms, where granitic soils are thick, are you likely to find perennial streams.

In this chapter, the great bulk of trail miles is along the Tahoe Rim Trail. Because this "TRT" has been constructed mostly along ridge crests and on steep slopes beneath them, much of the trail is waterless once the snow melts. In mid- and late summer, you may walk 5 or more miles between water sources, although even in many waterless stretches, water is relatively close at hand. But to obtain it, you may have to drop 200-500 feet below the trail, going as much as ½+ mile out of your way.

Old trails, which dominate in the Tahoe Sierra, often were built as steep as horses and other stock animals could safely manage. The horses struggled, not their riders. The TRT, in contrast, is a modern trail with a minimal amount of steep, usually short, sections. These mostly occur where the topography has prevented the construction of a more reasonably graded section. Overall, the TRT is a joy to hike because it generally is level or has only a gentle or moderate gradient. Therefore, it attracts not only hikers, but also joggers. Residents or visitors in the most densely built-up part of the Lake Tahoe Basin, Stateline and South Lake Tahoe, can drive east up Highway 207 to Daggett Pass, and jog either south (Hike 102) or north (Hike 103) along several generally easy miles of the TRT. It is hard to say which stretch of the trail is the most scenic, although the one between Highways 50 (Spooner Summit) and 431 (Mt. Rose Summit) (Hikes 106 and 107) arguably contains the best views of Lake Tahoe. That judgment may have to be revised when the stretch west from Highway 431 is completed (Hike 109), for it will have a multi-mile stretch of nearly continuous lake views. Westward and southwestward along the descending north rim of the Lake Tahoe Basin, the lands are mostly forested, and views are fewer and inferior. Consequently, the TRT along it (Hikes 110-112) is not that rewarding. Mountain bikers are likely to be the primary users.

The idea of the TRT originated with Glenn Hampton, a Forest Service recreation officer who was transferred to the Tahoe area in 1977. Hiking the trails back then, he wondered why there was no single, continuous trail following the rim above the lake. In 1980 he attended Utah State University to study public-recreation management, and the major project he chose was "The Tahoe Rim Trail—A Hiking Adventure." From this seminal work came the start of actual TRT construction in 1983. The west-rim was already completed, for the TRT was aligned along the existing Pacific Crest Trail. In the early and mid '80s, the trail was being built by hikers and equestrians, who had intended their kind to be the trail's sole users. Little could they realize that by the '90s the main users on the new trail segments constructed in the Carson Range and across the north-rim lands would be mountain bikers. Just as the trail has proven to be well suited for joggers, it has proven to be almost optimal for mountain bikers, who today are the principal users.

They also are principal users on this chapter's only hike that is not part of the TRT: the gated road up North Canyon to Marlette Lake and beyond (Hike 105). This may be the most popular route in this chapter, and one of the most popular in the entire book. On a beautiful summer day you may encounter one or two dozen hikers and several dozen bikers. Rivaling it for popularity is the climb to the summit of Mt. Rose (Hike 108). On a beautiful summer day you may encounter several dozen hikers and—along the lower part of the route, where bikes are legal—a dozen or more bikers. Mt. Rose is the highest Tahoe Sierra summit reached by an official trail. The area's two slightly higher summits, Freel Peak and Jobs Sister (Hikes 101 and 102), are reached partly by cross-country ascents.

The lower part of the Mt. Rose Trail will probably double as a stretch of Tahoe Rim Trail along the segment from Highway 431 west to Martis Peak. This will likely be the last segment to be finished, and officers of the Tahoe Rim Trail organization see 2001 as the year of completion. While I hope this 150-mile-long trail will come to pass, I can remember that when working on the trail back in 1984, some of us optimistically believed it would be completed in 1990. The trail still needs all the volunteers it can get, and perhaps a hike along a part of it will motivate you to join a work crew. For information on how you can help (with time and/or money), contact the Tahoe Rim Trail, Inc. at P.O. Box 4647, Stateline, NV 89449 (phone: 702-588-0686).

⊰⊱ 100 ⊰⊱
Tahoe Rim Trail, Highway 89 north to Armstrong Pass

Distances:
2.0 miles to Tahoe Rim lateral trail
   0.6 mile on lateral trail to alternate trailhead
4.4 miles to Saxon Creek Trail
5.6 miles to divide between Freel Meadows
6.5 miles to Hell Hole viewpoint
9.4 miles to Armstrong Pass
Low/High Elevations: 7300'/9440'
Season: Early July through mid-October
Classification: Moderate
Maps: 38, 44, and 45
Trailheads: The primary trailhead is the Tahoe Rim Trail's Big Meadow Trailhead facility, which is the same as the Hike 92 trailhead. An alternate trailhead is located along Highway 89 at the west end of the large, flat

Grass Lake meadow, which is about 1.8 miles west of Luther Pass and about 1.5 miles east of the Big Meadow Trailhead. Park along the south side of a curve in the highway, then walk about 130-150 yards east to the start of a west-climbing trail along the north side of the highway.

Introduction
Although the views along this route aren't too frequent or spectacular (except perhaps at the Hell Hole view), the well-graded trail is a pleasant hiking or riding experience. You can camp in the Freel Meadows environs, which is a good place for an isolated base camp from which you can explore the adjacent crest, its plants and animals, and its views.

This segment of Tahoe Rim Trail (TRT), one of the first to be constructed, was completed in 1987. It began at what is now the alternate trailhead, which back in the early '80s was the start of the now abandoned

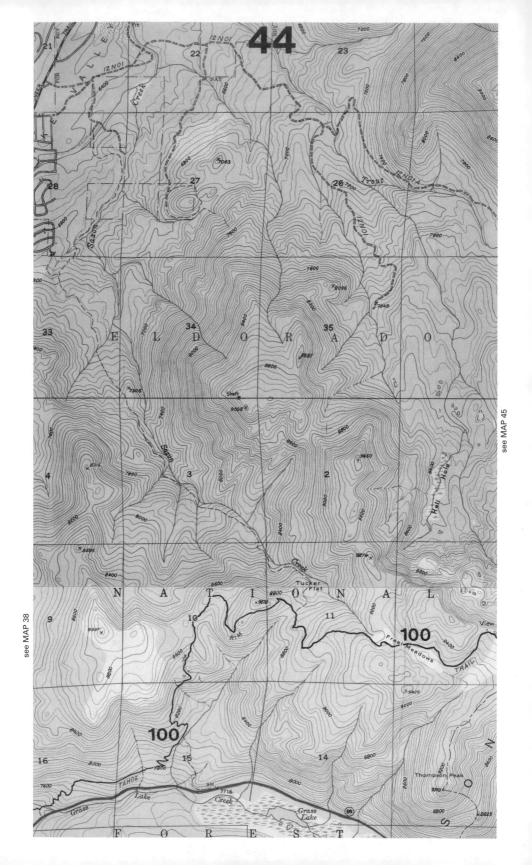

see MAP 45

see MAP 38

see MAP 44

45

101

100

Trimmer Peak

Star Lake

Jobs Sister

Freel Peak

101

EL DORADO CO
ALPINE CO

RANGE

Fountain Place

Creek

TRAIL

RUN

Fountain Face

NATIONAL FOREST BOUNDARY

101

Horse Meadow

T 12 N
T 11 N

TAHOE

Armstrong Pass

100

Willow

NATIONAL FOREST BOUNDARY

T O I Y

Creek

100

see upper right of this map

Jobs

Spring

RANGE

Jobs Peak

101

Willow

Creek

13

Dangberg Camp...

see upper right of this map

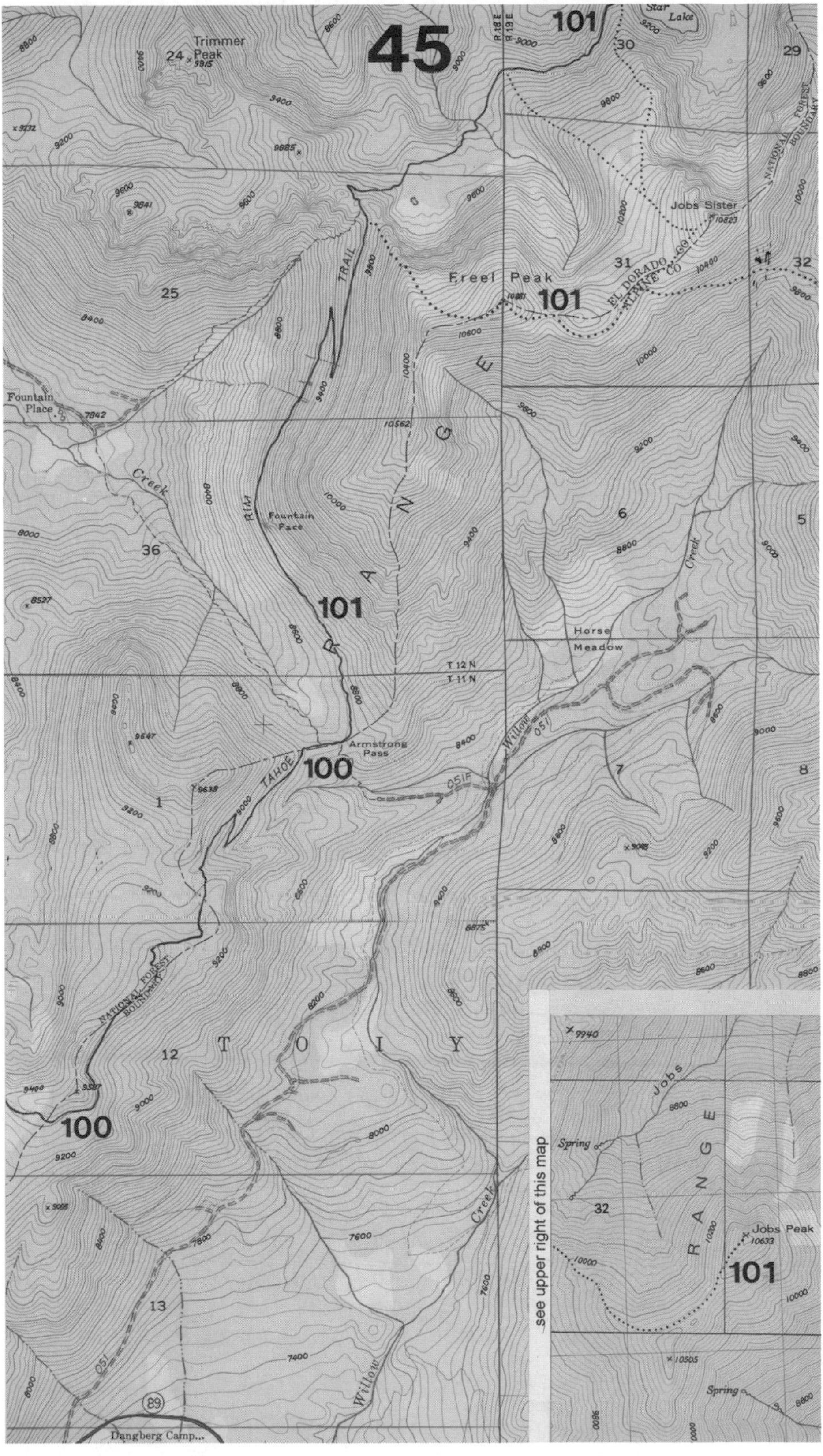

Author's wife working on the TRT in 1984

Tucker Flat Trail. Back then, TRT volunteers expected to build an entirely new trail segment from the Pacific Crest Trail in the Upper Truckee River drainage, traversing north along the west slopes of Red Lake, Stevens, and Waterhouse peaks to this trailhead. However, with trail construction on all TRT segments going slower than expected, this time-consuming route was rejected in favor of a connecting trail that would unite the existing Big Meadow Trail with the revamped Tucker Flat Trail. Today, if you hike the TRT in its entirety in a clockwise direction, then from the Big Meadow Trailhead you first take the Big Meadow Trail (Hike 92) south up to the Pacific Crest Trail, then head north on it for about 50 miles (Hikes 93, 89, 85, 87, 66, 75, 50) before leaving it at Twin Peaks (Hike 51).

Description

The entrance to the Tahoe Rim Trail's Big Meadow Trailhead facility is just off an old road, former Highway 89, and from this entrance you pace off 100 yards along that road, curving first right, then left. At the left

curve is the actual TRT trailhead for your hike, and the above mileages are measured from it. You begin along an abandoned road, which in 90 yards yields to trail tread. Your winding, ascending trail parallels unseen but definitely heard Highway 89 northeast about 0.4 mile up to another abandoned road, on which you turn left and ascend briefly up it to the resumption of trail tread. To get away from the highway's traffic noise, this connecting segment of the TRT now switchbacks, climbing about 250 feet, then making a 0.6-mile traverse through a forest of white firs and Jeffrey pines almost to a creek. The TRT again switchbacks and climbs up the creek an additional 250 feet to the **Tahoe Rim lateral trail**, which from the opposite creek bank makes a rather direct, 10% average-gradient descent to the TRT's alternate trailhead. If you start from it, you can subtract 1.4 miles from all but the first of the above distances.

From the junction the TRT heads briefly up along the creek, then veers west to wind 200 feet higher to a mule-ears meadow before starting an ascending traverse north. This takes you ¼ mile to a creeklet that flows beneath giant boulders. Here and just above you have views southeast through Luther Pass to 10,023' Hawkins Peak, 7½ miles distant. Its steep-sided summit, and that of Pickett Peak below it and 2 miles closer, are volcanic plugs. These plugs were formed in conduits through which former volcanoes had expelled their lava. When the action finally subsided, these conduits became choked with andesitic lava. Over a few million years much of each volcano was dissected by erosion, exposing the resistant plugs.

From the creeklet you climb briefly but steeply northeast up to a small flat, on the left, upon which you could camp. For water, continue about 100 yards north along the TRT to an aspen-lined, spring-fed creeklet, which flows below a row of giant boulders. From this reliable creeklet, ¾ mile above the lateral-trail junction, you climb past red firs, with the creeklet's meadow on your left, and cross a nearby secondary ridge. Just 200 yards beyond it you reach a viewless saddle on a major ridge. Here, about 3.2 miles from the main trailhead, you could set up a dry camp, although snow should be available on nearby north-facing slopes until August.

Staying just southeast of the actual crest, you climb 0.3 mile northeast up gravelly slopes that support clusters of pinemat manzanitas. Their lowly stature belies the extent of their impressive root system, as my wife and I found out while constructing a short segment of the trail through here back on August 25, 1984. From a broad, very shallow gap on the crest, the trail climbs up and around peak 9078's southern slopes, offering some views before descending shortly to a saddle and a junction with the **Saxon Creek Trail**, beginning northeast. This trail was passing into oblivion before the construction of the TRT, but now it is resurrected, and sees use primarily by macho mountain bikers, who labor south several miles up it to our junction. Beginning southwest, the Tucker Flat Trail once plunged directly down slopes to Highway 89. Although you may see a faint tread at the saddle, be forewarned that the tread fades away, and then you face a rugged, knee-knocking descent.

Once again we climb, first winding southeast and then heading east to a ridge near western Freel Meadow. Here we have our first glimpse of Freel Peak, above the meadow, and of Lake Tahoe, beyond Saxon Creek canyon. Rather than head over to the meadow, which has a creek flowing through its lower part, our trail climbs east above it, ducks into a wild-flowered cove cut into a patch of volcanic rock, then winds eastward to a broad, forested, almost level **divide between the western and eastern Freel Meadows**.

Next we climb above the eastern meadow's north edge, soon crossing a sloping meadow rich in mule ears, lupines, and paintbrushes. The mule ears in particular are very abundant, growing in volcanic soil, their favorite substrate. The patch of volcanic rock here is the second along our route. After crossing the meadow's

wisp of a creek, we're back on granitic terrain, traversing southeast. From where the trail bends northeast across bouldery slopes, we have our best view so far. The snowy south end of the Carson Range, capped by Stevens and Red Lake peaks, lies to the south-southwest, while a cluster of 10,000+' peaks lies to the southeast. Hawkins Peak, seen earlier, is the closest to us, followed to the right by distant Silver and Highland peaks, each appearing as a double summit and both near Highway 4's Ebbetts Pass, then intermediate-range, pyramidal Raymond Peak. In the foreground about 200 feet below your trail is a meadow, near which you can establish an isolated camp. Obtain water near the meadow's lower end.

A totally different panorama awaits you after you climb ⅓ mile northeast to a crest saddle. Here, just a few yards north of the trail at the **Hell Hole viewpoint**, you have the hike's best view, which includes deep, glaciated Hell Hole canyon in the foreground, Lake Tahoe beyond it, and the Tahoe Sierra's highest summit, 10,881' Freel Peak, above the canyon's east wall. Flanking Freel is the second highest peak, 10,823' Jobs Sister, which is separated by a fairly deep saddle from the fourth highest peak, 10,633' Jobs Peak.

You traverse 100 yards east to another, nearly identical Hell Hole viewpoint on the crest saddle, then veer southeast and traverse across volcanic slopes, the third patch along our route, these vegetated with sagebrush, mule ears, angelica, and lupine. These slopes

Western Freel Meadow

quickly yield to granitic ones as our ridge and trail veer from east to northeast, and we find ourselves very high above the floor of northern Hope Valley. From our vantage point the vehicles on Highway 89 are mere specks. The slopes ahead become increasingly bouldery, so the trail keeps low while swinging north around peak 9587. Vegetation now consists of lodgepole, whitebark, and western white pines, the forest open enough to offer dramatic views to the east and southeast.

Soon we regain the crest and from it see 10,381′ Round Top, to the south above the Carson Pass environs, plus the distant 10,000+′ peaks to the south-southeast above unseen Highway 4. From Round Top and the highlands south of it mammoth glaciers periodically flowed north toward us, the last two so thick that they spilled west over Luther Pass. A lobe from each of these glaciers flowed east down the West Fork Carson River canyon, but another lobe flowed north, directly ahead through Hope Valley, ascending 400 feet in 1½ miles before finally coming to a halt directly below us (see glacier map in Chapter 5).

Along the nearly level crest we stroll northeast for ¼ mile, our shoes squishing into the deep gruss (granitic gravel) as we pass occasional bedrock outcrops. The crest then begins to descend, taking us with it, though soon we curve north, kicking up the deep gruss as we descend through an open forest to a crest saddle. The TRT actually traverses east of the very broad saddle, descending north along the east side of a low knoll to immediately reach the upper end of a northeast-draining gully. The trail then makes a well-graded descent ¼ mile north to a switchback, above which is a small cliff that makes rock climbers drool. It is quite fractured, thereby offering multiple routes, but more important, it is peppered with dark inclusions, which being resistant, offer dozens of holds. The cliff is easily top-roped, and can be reached by trail in about 1.3 miles from the next hike's trailhead, below Armstrong Pass.

With that goal in mind, we first switchback 230 yards south down the TRT, then descend moderately northeast across forested slopes to the west edge of the broad pass. If you study Map 45, you may realize that the pass and the lands just north of it are a typical glacial landscape: broad-floored and steep-walled. However, there is no evidence that it was ever glaciated. Contrary to popular belief, especially among Sierra geologists, the Sierra Nevada has quite a number of *unglaciated* canyons that are U-shaped in cross profile.

We start east across a ridge and quickly meet Trail 18E09, descending northward toward the Fountain Place. The lowest part of this locally indistinct trail and the upper part of the road to its trailhead are on private land, so the trail should be avoided. About 150 yards farther east on the ridge, we reach **Armstrong Pass** proper, from which a lateral trail descends 0.4 mile to the next hike's trailhead. See that hike for a description of the Tahoe Rim Trail north to Star Lake. If you are backpacking and want to camp near Armstrong Pass, consider doing so down at the trailhead, since there is both space and water.

◁◈ 101 ◈▷
Tahoe Rim Trail, Armstrong Pass north to Freel Peak, Jobs Sister, and Star Lake

Distances:
0.4 mile to Tahoe Rim Trail at Armstrong Pass
1.4 miles to Fountain Face
3.4 miles to trail's highest point
   1.0 mile cross-country to Freel Peak
   2.0 miles cross-country to Jobs Sister
   3.5 miles cross-country for Freel Peak-Jobs Sister loop
5.3 miles to Star Lake
Low/High Elevations: 8420′/9730′; 10,881′ at Freel Peak; 10,823′ at Jobs Sister
Season: Early July through mid-October
Classification: Trail, moderate; summits, strenuous
Maps: 45 and 46
Trailhead: From either Highway 50 or Highway 88, drive up Highway 89 to Willow Pass Road (Forest Route 051). This branches

north from the highway just 0.8 mile east of signed Luther Pass, this junction being 1.8 miles northwest of the Highways 88/89 junction down in Hope Valley. Take F.R. 051 2.6 miles to a bridge across Willow Creek, then 0.9 mile farther to a bridge across its tributary. Immediately beyond it is a junction with F.R. 051F, branching sharply left. On it you quickly bridge Willow Creek, climb steeply to a fork, keep right, then drive to a turnaround at road's end, 0.5 mile from F.R. 051.

Introduction

In the past, access to Star Lake was difficult due to private lands lying in the way. However, with a road system constructed close to Armstrong Pass, coupled with the 1993 completion of the Tahoe Rim Trail between Highways 89 and 207, this subalpine lake—at 9100 feet, the highest trout-inhabited lake within the Lake Tahoe basin—has become as accessible as most Desolation Wilderness lakes. Another bonus of the trail is that its highest point comes to within about 1200 vertical feet of the Tahoe Sierra's highest summit, Freel Peak. Strong hikers can make the mile-long cross-country ascent up to it in about an hour, can head over to the area's second highest summit, Jobs Sister, and then can descend to the trail for a mile or less traverse on it over to Star Lake. Peak baggers can also climb Jobs Peak, the fourth highest summit in the Carson Range. Finally, rock climbers can test their leading skills on the Fountain Face, a half-hour's walk from the trailhead. Alternatively, they can head south from Armstrong Pass for a similar distance to one or more challenging cliffs (near end of previous hike) that are best done with a top rope.

Description

Your route to nearby Armstrong Pass is a no-nonsense, steep lateral trail, which averages a 15% gradient as it climbs, with the aid of a few short switchbacks, generally northwest to the Tahoe Rim Trail at 8310′ **Armstrong Pass**. Northbound, the trail mildly rollercoasters for ¾ mile, dipping in and out of gullies and passing scattered junipers before commencing a serious climb toward the northwest ridge of Freel Peak. Ascending slopes dominated by sagebrush and drought-resistant wildflowers,

the trail quickly offers views. They include one of Desolation Wilderness' Crystal Range, topped in the south by 9983′ Pyramid Peak, lying almost due west. Directly ahead, you see a looming cliff, the **Fountain Face**, whose base the trail skirts. It has several prominent crack routes plus many potential face routes. The cracks, while good for jamming, are relatively poor for protection; consequently, use pitons or a top rope.

Views improve as your trail climbs past the cliff, and you see, about 1100 feet below you, a lush meadow near unseen Fountain Place. In 1859 silver was discovered in Virginia Town's (today's City) Comstock Lode. In that year Garret Fountain started grazing beef cattle and milk cows along the headwaters of Trout Creek, including in the meadow, and he thought that Armstrong Pass might provide a faster route for the miners who were leaving California's Mother Lode in droves and scrambling east, via Luther Pass, to the Comstock Lode. In 1860 he built a way station, Fountain Place, hoping to profit from the passing traffic. Armstrong Pass, however, never became a popular route, for the Comstock Lode mine operators financed the construction of a road over Daggett Pass, 8¼ air miles north of Freel Peak. No buildings remain standing at the Fountain Place today, but the cattle remain.

As the TRT curves from north-northwest to north, it enters a very open forest, sagebrush and views both abounding. About 1.6 miles from Armstrong Pass we encounter the first of several reliable, flower-lined creeklets, just within a denser forest. Those taking Hike 101, who are only 2.0 miles along it, won't need to tank up, but others on the previous hike probably will. These creeklets offer the first reliable trailside water since the Saxon Creek headwaters in western Freel Meadow, about 5.7 miles earlier. From the first creeklet the trail climbs ½ mile to a switchback with an unobstructed view across your side canyon toward some imposing cliffs. These are highly broken up, making them unappealing to climbers, as also would be the approach to them.

After a 0.3-mile climb south, the TRT resumes its northward course, climbing 0.7 mile to a high, minor saddle with nearby,

A pinnacle on Jobs Sister

windswept whitebark pines. You are at 9730 feet, the **Tahoe Rim Trail's highest point**. Indeed, you are above all but a handful of the highest summits in Desolation Wilderness. Within that wilderness, just one trail climbs this high, the one to the summit of Mt. Tallac, seen in the west-northwest, above the southwestern part of Lake Tahoe. Although you are quite high, you can nevertheless be intimidated by the hulking mass of Freel Peak rising about 1150 feet above you. A far better view of the lake awaits you at its summit.

To attain the summit, leave the trail here, or just a bit earlier, heading over to the base of a steep, though reasonably safe, north-descending ridge. For the first half of your ascent, you generally stay just west of the actual ridgecrest, switchbacking as often as necessary to

ease its atrocious average grade of about 45% (25°). After about 400 vertical feet of ascent, the gradient abates, and soon you can head east across the ridgecrest to gentler, but nonetheless steep, gravelly slopes, often snowy in early summer, which lie above treacherously steep ones of a cirque. The remaining route to the summit is obvious. Of course, if the weather is looking threatening, don't even attempt this ascent, for there is no place to hide, should a lightning storm break loose. Along this rigorous ascent, which is breathtaking due both to a surplus of views and to a shortage of oxygen, you'll note that the whitebark pines have been getting progressively shorter and bushier in stature, dwindling eventually to knee-high specimens. This dwarfed form of trees is called *krummholz*, which is German for "twisted wood." The ascent is also breathtaking because you have to slog upward through deep, coarse sand, known as *gruss*. This is abundant in the Freel Peak massif due to intense freeze and thaw of water at these high elevations. The process pries chunky quartz and feldspar crystals from the granitic bedrock.

When at last you reach the summit of **Freel Peak**, you have all the Tahoe Sierra lands lying below you, and can make a 360° survey—to the tune of an incessant hum from our summit's microwave tower. Like many high peaks outside wilderness areas, this one now serves modern civilization. In the south is a ribbon of Highway 88; in the west-southwest beyond Echo Summit is the South Fork American River canyon. Unmistakable Pyramid Peak, seen many times earlier on, looms above the Echo Lakes to your west. In the northwest the slopes of dark, metamorphic-capped Mt. Tallac descend to Lake Tahoe's shoreline. Above the lake's northeast corner stands volcanic-capped Mt. Rose, whose summit, at 10,766 feet, is third highest in the Tahoe basin, ranking below only Freel Peak and Jobs Sister. Viewing the latter, you can identify two parallel, massive quartz veins that paint its west slope white with rocky "snow." To the right of this summit and 2 air miles from us stands Jobs Peak, at 10,633 feet a bit shorter in stature than his sister, and ranking fourth among the area's highest peaks. Lake Tahoe, of course, is the main feature that captures the eye. This deep, blue gem seems to be too large to be in so high a basin; one almost expects it to overflow into the lower, dry desert to the east.

Atop the summit grow small clumps of whitebark pines, here only knee-high, and in this vicinity one sometimes sees mountain bluebirds and rosy finches. The bluebirds dart swiftly after insects wafted up here by updrafts, while the finches pursue ground insects and spiders as well as seeds of alpine plants.

You can return the way you came, but with Jobs Sister a tempting, easy mile away, you might as well bag its summit. Past a minor ridge summit, skirted on either side, is a long, broad, barren ridgecrest saddle, about 10,500 feet in elevation, from which one could head cross-country east for about 0.6 mile, diagonalling down across grussy, openly forested slopes to another broad saddle, about 650 feet lower, which separates Jobs Sister from Jobs Peak. Then from the saddle, you climb about 1.4 miles to the peak. For most, this route is not worth the effort, and hence is not mentioned under "Distances," but for peak baggers, it is. You cross the saddle and climb up a relatively easy ridgecrest almost to peak 10505. (If you go too low, you'll have to diagonal up some slopes of very loose gruss.) You then curve northeast and stay close to the crest all the way to the windswept summit. Although the topo map shows your whole route to be through a forest, this "forest" is so low that you stand above it, for the whitebark pines are wind-cropped shrubs. The summit views overall are inferior to those of Jobs Sister.

With that goal in mind and if the weather still is not threatening, head up an open, obvious route to the summit of **Jobs Sister**. It rewards you with views to the east equal to those of Jobs Peak; views to the north, west, and south equal to those of Freel Peak; and a view down its north face, which is far higher and steeper than those of Jobs and Freel peaks. And it has on the floor of its deep cirque the liquid gem of Star Lake. To reach it, return to the Tahoe Rim Trail. This you do by

Star Lake

descending cross-country west, then northwest, to broad gentler slopes. The preferred, though longer, way is to continue northwest, staying fairly close to the edge of a canyon between Freel Peak and Jobs Sister. Alternatively, you can head north across the gentler slopes to a ridge that descends north to the outlet of Star Lake. This, descent, a real knee-knocker, is as steep as your initial ascent toward Freel Peak.

Those not climbing any summit start a descent from the high, minor saddle, the TRT's highest point. You drop to an adjacent, minor saddle, and from this vicinity see High Meadows, almost 2000 feet below you, and above it, the ponderous mass of 10,067' Monument Peak. After a nearby switchback, you head east toward Jobs Sister, descending almost to the floor of a Freel Peak cirque. This contains a pond, waist-deep when full, which provides a very uninviting, bleak, camping environment. After a brief traverse northward, you descend moderately northeast to a brisk creeklet, jumping across it just above its audible cascades. Just beyond it the TRT crosses a small flat suitable for camping. Up here, almost 4 miles from Armstrong Pass, you are still sufficiently high that the forest is quite open, offering no protection when the wind blows. From it you traverse briefly north (those descending from Jobs Sister meet us here), then make a long, counterclockwise traverse across the bowl of the Cold Creek headwaters. Along it you will encounter numerous chunks of vein quartz that have weathered from the western slopes of Jobs Sister and have, over time, traveled via soil creep downslope to their present locations.

After ½ mile, the trail reaches the ridge descending north from Jobs Sister (the alternate descent route), and follows it down to the outlet of **Star Lake**. You can find tiny, poor campsites along this last stretch, but they are greatly inferior to those above the lake's north shore. These not only are roomier and have better lake access, they offer a lake setting backdropped by the imposing north face of Jobs Sister. Being the highest lake within the Tahoe basin, the lake is not warm. Under optimal conditions, it warms to the low 60s at best. Lakes lying in high, granitic basins are supposed to be crystal clear, but Star Lake is mysteriously murky. You can see about 5 feet down through the water, which is sufficient to spy a trout or two. Star Lake, at 9100′ elevation, is not quite the highest one in the Lake Tahoe basin. Mud Lake, in the Mt. Rose vicinity in the northern part of the Carson Range, is, at 9239′. It, however, is more the size of a lakelet, and as its name implies, it is not attractive, nor does it harbor fish.

⋘ 102 ⋙
Tahoe Rim Trail, Highway 207 south to Star Lake

Distances:
1.8 miles to South Fork Daggett Creek
3.6 miles to Mott Canyon creek
4.7 miles to stateline
5.1 miles to powerline saddle
7.7 miles to Cold Creek tributary
8.8 miles to Star Lake

Low/High Elevations: 7500′/9110′

Season: Late June through mid-October

Classification: Easy to moderate, depending on distance

Maps: 47 and 46

Trailhead: From Highway 50 near Lake Tahoe, drive 3.2 miles east up Highway 207 to

Daggett Pass. From it head south 1¼ miles up Tramway Drive to a fork, branch left onto one-way Quaking Aspen Lane, and descend briefly to the base of the Stagecoach ski lift. Park beside the obvious trailhead.

Introduction
Of all this guide's sections of Tahoe Rim Trail, this may be my favorite, even though it does not have the dramatic views found along the segment of TRT between Highways 50 and 431. This hike abounds with inspiring, although not superlative, views, equally divided between those of the Carson Valley, in the first half of the hike, and those of the Lake Tahoe basin in the second half. And except for two short, unavoidably steep stretches, the trail is amazingly well engineered—an absolute pleasure to hike.

Description
Because the lands of the Daggett Pass area are private, not governmental, the construction of a continuous trail through it became impossible. For those taking the trail entirely through the Carson Range, they will walk on about 3½ miles of roads between this hike's trailhead and that of the next hike. The southbound Tahoe Rim Trail begins among private land, and is constrained by it to make a steep, direct, 0.3-mile climb up a ski-lift gully to a road-traversed saddle. Now just within the Toiyabe National Forest, you walk about 80 yards south on a road to the trail's resumption. It immediately curves east to begin a well-graded climb through a forest of western white pines and red firs to a switchback. Here, ¾ mile into your hike, you have views of Carson Valley to the east, the Kingsbury Grade to the northeast, the crest lands of the Carson Range to the north, and a bit of Lake Tahoe to the northwest. Today's grade is a modern version of a more challenging route constructed by David Kingsbury and John McDonald back in 1858-1860.

In just over ½ mile, the TRT climbs west, then south, offering us glimpses of Lake Tahoe before reaching a second saddle. Then, over the next ½ mile, it descends slightly to step-across **South Fork Daggett Creek**, encountered just beyond a ski lift. Next, we traverse briefly to a nearly level area on a

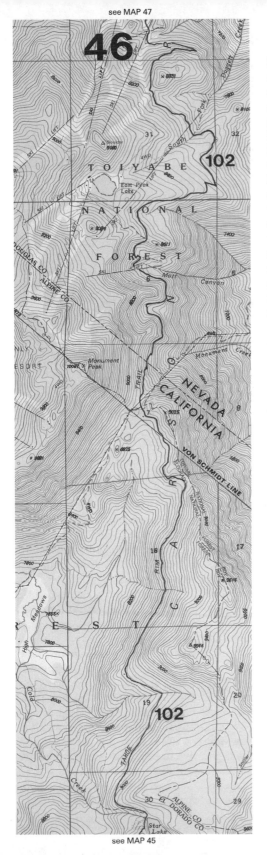

broad, northeast-descending ridge, suitable for camping. (Northbound trekkers should be aware that the TRT between Highways 207 and 50 lacks reliable water.) Just south of the possible camping area, the TRT passes within 20 yards of granitic boulders, from which you have a fine view of Carson Valley. The trail next climbs gently 0.4 mile south to a switchback, then switchbacks moderately up to an east-descending ridge. This it crosses, and westbound, the vegetation changes, fairly shady eastern slopes of red firs and western white pines give way to fairly open, steeper, southern slopes of Jeffrey pines. Early on this new tack, you have your first view of steep-faced Jobs Sister and spreading Freel Peak, while closer by you confront the enormous mass of Monument Peak.

After ½ mile the trail resumes its southern course, soon reaching a saddle on a minor ridge. Here is our only other steep stretch, and steep it is: you descend a ski-lift maintenance road having a 20% gradient. Thankfully, the descent is short, and 85 yards past a switchback, we leave the east-dropping road for traversing trail tread. In about 150 yards we arrive at step-across **Mott Canyon creek**. This is just before a ski lift, and on a forested flat by its base you could set up a fine camp.

From the creek the trail traverses ¼ mile eastward through the amphitheater of upper Mott Canyon, then climbs briefly south to enter a smaller bowl. At that bend, you have both a view southwest across openly forested slopes to the summit area of 10,067' Monument Peak and a view east across a broad swath of the Carson Valley. The granitic rock of the peak and adjacent lands solidified within the earth's crust about 90 million years ago, and at the time of the Sierra's last uplift, about 75-65 million years ago, at least part of the upper rock would have been exposed through erosion. A granitic landscape then evolved over 30-40 million years of warm, wet climate, achieving a look similar to today's landscape some 33 million years ago, when the climate changed. Carson Valley, a down-faulted trough already existed at the time of uplift, but in the last few million years renewed faulting has caused the western part of the valley to sink, placing it within a rain shadow and thus in a high-desert climate. This western tilting of the Carson Valley block has caused the north-flowing Carson River to migrate laterally westward. Consequently, today the river does not flow through the center of the valley, but rather flows close to its down-faulted western edge.

High-desert vegetation exists at our viewpoint, the most prominent species being the drab-colored curl-leaf mountain-mahogany. However, it exists up here not due to a prominent rain shadow, but because the local soils are very thin, and once the snow melts, very little water is available for use almost half the year. Well below us lies the site of a 1990s burn. The trees were sufficiently plentiful to provide enough fuel for a widespread fire, one hot enough to cause thin layers of granitic bedrock to exfoliate. It may be surprising for many to discover that fire may be the most effective process at slowly—very slowly!—dismantling the Carson Range.

Progressing toward Star Lake, you traverse in and out of the smaller bowl, carpeted with pinemat manzanitas, climb gently south through an open forest, then soon curve westward to enter Monument Creek canyon, easily recognized by the powerlines ascending it. The trail quickly curves south and equally quickly reaches a short switchback, and your grade up to the head of Monument Creek canyon switches to moderate. In about 200 yards the trail reaches another short switchback. Midway between the two you reach the **stateline**, and climb south from Nevada into California. Approaching (but not reaching) 9000 feet elevation, you can get quite breathless in this rarefied air. Fortunately, the climb to the broad, rather amorphous **powerline saddle** is not long. Views from it are not great, but they are after a brief walk south to a bedrock outcrop, immediately west of the trail. Standing on it, you can follow the powerlines down to the northern edge of High Meadows, over 1000 feet below you. You can also hurl a rock southwest over to the invisible Von Schmidt state-boundary line of 1873.

W. A. Von Schmidt, with the U.S. Coast and Geodetic Survey, was to survey the California-Nevada boundary south along the 120th meridian of longitude to the 39th parallel of latitude, then survey a straight line southeast to the Colorado River at the 35th parallel. A tall order. Von Schmidt began his southward surveying near Verdi, along today's Interstate 80. Back in 1873 it had a railroad station with a telegraph. With that instrument he was able to synchronize his timepiece with that in an astronomy station in San Francisco, whose longitude was precisely known. With that information, he could quite accurately locate the 120th meridian, which lay about ½ mile west of Verdi. A problem was that the line ran through Lake Tahoe; it is quite impossible to set mileposts in the 1200-foot-deep lake. Worse, the boundary change to a southeast direction occurred within the lake. Another problem lay where the line intersected the Colorado River. This boundary had been surveyed earlier, back in 1860, before the railroad and its telegraph line existed, and Von Schmidt discovered that in the intervening 13 years the intersection point had moved 1½ miles, thanks to some major meandering. His line proved to be inaccurate, so from 1893-95 and 1898-99, the boundary was officially resurveyed, and it stuck. But it is not accurate. The surveyed 120th meridian, where it intersects the north shore of Lake Tahoe, lies ¼ mile west of the true location. Oh, for a Global Positioning System back then! That, however, would not have helped the boundary between California and Arizona, surveyed down the middle of the Colorado River. The boundary line is fixed; the river is not. Politicians hadn't realized that one should not put boundary lines on meandering rivers, but rather should put them on the rim of a mountain range. Had that been done, Lake Tahoe would have laid entirely within California (Nevada politicians lacked the political clout).

With Tahoe and rim on our minds, it is time to continue south along the Tahoe Rim Trail. Views of the Carson Valley now are gone, but ones of looming Jobs Sister and Freel Peak urge us onward. Our hike is very easy, and unless you survey it, you won't be sure, after 1.4 miles from the powerline saddle, if you've gained or lost a few feet in elevation (you've dropped slightly along a 1% gradient). Although you traverse to this point across amorphous, variably forested slopes, it

Southern Lake Tahoe Basin and Crystal Range of Desolation Wilderness

nevertheless is easy to recognize. At it you look in a line of sight directly along a 2-7-mile stretch of westward-oriented powerlines. Beyond it rises much of the highland mass comprising Desolation Wilderness. To get our first glimpse of Lake Tahoe, so far blocked by Monument Peak, a minor summit on a major ridge, we contour about 0.2 mile south to a conspicuous large-block gully, then an equal distance beyond it. Red firs and western white pines generally prevent panoramic views, and these species persist for almost ½ mile, to where, on a broad, west-descending ridge, we meet an impressive western juniper. Now we climb gently southeast across open terrain to a diminutive **Cold Creek tributary**, which nevertheless flows throughout most of summer. By its south bank lies a small camp.

Virtually everyone would pass this up for ones at Star Lake, which lies 1.1 miles ahead. Most of the distance is along a moderate ascent, one well forested, but nevertheless still offering views of Lake Tahoe. Once again the trail veers southeast for a climb across relatively open slopes, and you'll see. This descends to the private lands of High Meadows. From the junction the Tahoe Rim Trail descends in 90 yards to the outlet creek of **Star Lake**. The lake and its environs are discussed in the last paragraph of the previous hike.

⇜ 103 ⇝
Tahoe Rim Trail, Highway 207 north to South Camp and Genoa Peaks

Distances:
5.4 miles to Road 14N24
6.2 miles to lateral trail to Road 14N32
   0.8 mile up jeep road to Genoa Peak
6.7 miles to South Camp Peak

Low/High Elevations: 7760'/8818' at South Camp Peak; 9150' at Genoa Peak

Season: Late May through late October

Classification: Moderate

Maps: 47 and 48

Trailhead: From Highway 50 near Lake Tahoe, drive 2.9 miles east up Highway 207 to North Benjamin Drive, 0.3 mile before Daggett Pass, and turn left. After 0.3 mile, your road ahead becomes Andria Drive, which you take through a development to its end, a signed trailhead on the left, 1.9 miles from the highway. Ahead, Road 14N32—an alternate, less inviting route to South Camp and Genoa peaks—begins a steep climb north up a dry gully.

Introduction

The Tahoe Rim Trail north from Daggett Pass is mostly viewless, and generally where views exist, they are only fair. The two exceptions are along the trail's mile-long traverse of

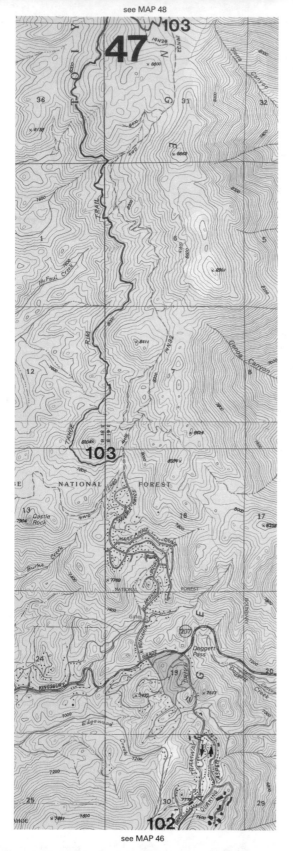

South Camp Peak, which is a high plateau with excellent views of Lake Tahoe, and on the summit of Genoa Peak, which offers 360° views that include the lake, the Carson Range, and desert lands to the east.

Description

Except in early season, when melting snow lies about and feeds ephemeral creeklets, this entire route is dry. If you are going to do the entire hike, bring along a liter of water; if it is a hot day, bring two. Backpackers hiking north through the entire Carson Range should first obtain water at George Brautovitch Park, located along Andria Drive 0.8 mile north of Highway 207. The Tahoe Rim Trail begins in Burke Creek's headwaters gully, which lacks both water and a creek bed. Lying in the rain shadow cast by the Sierran crest above Lake Tahoe's west shore, the Carson Range receives relatively little precipitation. Our part of the range was not glaciated, so its soils and sediments were never removed, and they can be relatively thick. Unfortunately for us, the relatively little water that falls on this range flows through gravel, not down a bedrock-lined creek bed. Consequently, if you do need water, you usually will have to descend a half mile or so down any promising gully, dropping about 400-500 feet in elevation.

Our trail climbs west, and in ¼ mile offers a fair view of southern Lake Tahoe and one, to the southwest, of Castle Rock. In another ¼ mile our TRT reaches a broad, low saddle, from which a use path heads west to a low knoll with poor views through its trees. The TRT then begins a winding, 4.6-mile traverse north, dipping into and climbing out of creekless gullies, and between each each two it usually offers poor-to-fair lake views, impaired by a moderately dense growth of red firs, western white pines and Jeffrey pines. Just 0.4 mile along this traverse, as you approach the dry headwaters area of a

Lake Tahoe, from 8818' summit of South Camp Peak

south fork of McFaul Creek, you cross a bike path. Mountain bikes are legal on your stretch of the TRT, which is great if you like this sport, but upsetting if you are a hiker in search of solitude, for bikers seem to be this trail's primary users. The traverse north ends as we start to curve east around a nose, from which we contour southeast ¼ mile to the floor of a broad gully, the waterless headwaters of Lincoln Creek. Just across its nearly level floor the TRT crosses **Road 14N24**.

A shorter of two ways to the top of Genoa Peak is to take this road, first south then east, 0.3 mile up to a junction with Road 14N32 (Genoa Peak Road), then from that junction go cross-country directly upslope for about 0.7 mile to the top. However, those interested in the most direct way would not have taken the TRT, but rather from its trailhead would have begun on Road 14N32 and would have followed it 3.7 miles to the road junction, saving 2.0 miles.

From the crossing of Road 14N24, the TRT switchbacks briefly eastward up slopes, then climbs about ⅔ mile north to a switchback just below an obvious saddle. Your trail goes briefly east, and almost at the saddle, veers north. Here you meet a 50-yard-long **lateral trail to Road 14N32**. If you walk just 40 yards south on this road, you will meet the start of a jeep road, the longer way up to Genoa Peak. This climbs quite directly southeast up to **Genoa Peak**, which offers a 360° panorama.

From the lateral trail the TRT begins a 200-foot gain in elevation to the highest of several summits along the western edge of a plateau of South Camp Peak. Midway up our ½-mile-long northward ascent, the trail passes immediately east of an andesite outcrop, which offers a viewpoint. Then higher up, at the open, 8818' summit of **South Camp Peak**, it reaches a similar outcrop with similar views. Most of Lake Tahoe spreads below you, only its southeastern part hidden behind a granitic ridge. In the distant north stands the Carson Range's third-highest summit, 10,776' Mt. Rose. In the distant south stands, from left to right, a cluster of its other high summits, 10,633' Jobs Peak, 10,823' Jobs Sister, and 10,881' Freel Peak, ranking respectively fourth, second, and first. Freel is partly obscured by 10,067' Monument Peak, ranking fifth, and barely beating out Stevens and Red Lake peaks, at the south end of the range, by several feet. Much closer to us in the southern direction is 9150' Genoa Peak, which though lowly, is quite imposing due to its proximity.

The volcanic rocks of that peak and of our South Camp Peak are mostly andesite and dacite, but some lighter-colored rhyolite is present, and all are very old. These formed mostly or entirely during the Jurassic period, a span of time from 208 to 140 million years ago. All then were exposed to regional metamorphism, perhaps around the end of the Jurassic period, when the early Sierra Nevada experienced severe compressive forces. Contact metamorphism, operating on a smaller scale, may have occurred about 90 to 85 million years ago as rising, hot magma intruded this bedrock and locally altered it before cooling to form the widespread granodiorite exposed in most of the Carson Range today.

⇚⇛ 104 ⇚⇛
Tahoe Rim Trail, Highway 50 south to South Camp and Genoa Peaks

Distances:
1.3 miles to first vista trail
 260 yards up trail to south end of summit 7811
3.1 miles to second vista trail
 100 yards up trail to summit 8120
5.1 miles to northwest edge of South Camp Peak
5.9 miles to South Camp Peak
6.4 miles to lateral trail to Road 14N32
 0.8 mile up jeep road to Genoa Peak
Low/High Elevations: 7150'/8818' at South Camp Peak; 9150' at Genoa Peak
Season: Late May through late October
Classification: Moderate
Map: 48
Trailhead: Along Highway 50 at Spooner Summit, which is 0.8 mile east of the Highways 28/50 (Spooner) junction. Park at the summit's Spooner Picnicking Rest Area.

Introduction
This route is shorter than the previous one to South Camp Peak, and one need not hike all

the way to its actual summit. About a 5-mile walk south up to the northwest edge of the plateau-like peak offers Lake Tahoe views that rival those from Snow Valley Peak, a farther destination mentioned in the next two routes. This route usually is waterless, so be sure you carry enough. In the past, water has been unavailable in the rest area, so don't count on filling water bottles there.

Description
The Tahoe Rim Trail starts from the south (far) edge of the Spooner Picnicking Rest Area. It first switchbacks briefly southward up slopes, then traverses westward to a switchback. Now, ½ mile into your hike, you begin a fairly direct route southward past white firs, Jeffrey pines and shrubs such as tobacco brush, chinquapin, and greenleaf manzanita. After gaining about 550 feet of elevation above your trailhead, you traverse a volcanic flat to shortly reach your **first vista trail**. This short route initially climbs northeast, then heads to the **south end of summit 7811**, from where you have a fair view east toward desert lands, and a better one west toward Desolation Wilderness lands above the southwest shore of Lake Tahoe.

Back on the TRT, you are now sufficiently high that greenleaf manzanitas have been replaced with pinemat manzanitas and white firs with red firs. About ½ mile past the first vista trail, and just past an ascent through an extensive field of mule ears, you momentarily top out at a minor 7800' volcanic summit, from which you have good views of the north and west shores of Lake Tahoe. You then soon curve east and make a fairly level traverse over to a road that crosses a low, broad saddle with a nice view north toward Snow Valley Peak. About 40 yards southeast, the TRT crosses the road's east spur, then turns south to traverse along the lower slopes of Duane Bliss Peak. In about 0.4 mile you reach an abandoned road, which, if you were to follow it southeast over a low saddle, would in ¼ mile reach a lodgepole-fringed meadow with a nearby pond. In spring it has water, and then this spot is suitable for camping.

Ahead the TRT climbs 0.4 mile south to the **second vista trail**, which in about a minute's

Lake Tahoe and its basin's north rim, from northwest edge of South Camp Peak

walk takes you to **summit 8120**. This offers a view east down Water Canyon to the Carson Valley, plus nice ones north along the crest of the Carson Range and northwest across Lake Tahoe.

Just west past this second vista trail, you pass the 5k mark along the north slope of a minor knoll—joggers on a 10k run turn around here. Beyond it we drop briefly to a saddle crossed by Genoa Peak Road 14N32. Now you begin an 800-foot ascent to the summit of South Camp Peak. You should be high enough to get Lake Tahoe views, but trees usually obscure the views. As you climb higher through a red fir/western white pine forest, you start to see mountain hemlocks, which become quite common by the time you start a westward climb, after 1⅓ miles of ascent. In ¼ mile you reach the **northwest edge of South Camp Peak**, and have your best lake views so far. But save the film, for by walking about 100 yards southeast up the trail, you get even better views. The features seen from it are described in the previous route, and you see them several times more as you continue up to an andesite outcrop immediately west of the trail near the 8818' summit of **South Camp Peak**.

Ahead, you're following Hike 103 in reverse, descending ½ mile south almost to a **lateral trail to Road 14N32**. This short trail goes about 50 yards southeast to a spot where the road crosses a broad saddle. Just 40 yards south on the road you will find the start of a jeep road, which climbs southeast to 9150' **Genoa Peak**. This is the only one along your hike that provides a truly 360° view: east to

desert lands, west to Lake Tahoe, and north and south along the Carson Range.

⋙ **105** ⋘

Spooner Lake to Marlette Lake, Marlette Peak, and Sand Harbor Overlook

Distances:
2.8 miles to North Canyon Campground
  1.4 miles up trail to Tahoe Rim Trail
3.8 miles to Snow Valley Peak jeep road
  1.2 miles up jeep road to TRT
  1.6 miles up jeep road to Snow Valley Peak
4.7 miles to road junction above southeastern Marlette Lake
  1.4 miles on lakeshore road to lake's dam
5.9 miles to jeep road
  0.4 mile to TRT
6.4 miles to road junction with TRT intersection
  0.3 mile on TRT to Marlette Peak Trail's south end
    0.6 mile on trail to viewpoint
    1.3 miles on trail to TRT
  0.5 mile on TRT to Marlette Peak Campground
  1.2 miles on TRT to Marlette Peak Trail's north end
  1.5 miles on TRT to ridge trail south
    0.1 mile on trail to viewpoint
  2.2 miles on TRT to Sand Harbor Overlook Loop Trail
    0.6 mile on trail to Sand Harbor Overlook

Low/High Elevations: 6950'/8157' to Marlette Lake; 9214' to Snow Valley Peak

Season: Late May through late October

Classification: Moderate to Marlette Lake, strenuous to Sand Harbor Overlook

Maps: 48 and 49

Trailhead: Along the east shore of Lake Tahoe, take Highway 28 south to the Lake Tahoe Nevada State Park's entrance road, which is 1 mile north of the Highways 28/50 (Spooner) junction and 12¼ miles south of the Highway 431 junction at the western outskirts of Incline Village. Take the entrance road past the entrance station to the second of two parking areas.

Introduction

In my opinion, the Sand Harbor Overlook rivals the Mt. Tallac summit (Hike 79) for the best Lake Tahoe view that one can get from a trail. The overlook is atop a precipitous slope situated less than one mile from the lake's shore, versus a full 3 miles for Tallac. Sure, that higher summit offers breathtaking views of Emerald Bay and Fallen Leaf Lake, but it also presents sprawling south-shore development, including Nevada's high-rise casinos. Is the overlook view worth a 19-mile round-trip trek? This is quite a day hike, although as mentioned under the description, you can do this route as an overnight backpack trip. The Marlette Peak viewpoint, which also is one of the lake's best views, is somewhat more man-

ageable, being about 14½ miles, round trip. And the hike just to Marlette Lake is a worthy trip in itself, although you will meet a lot of mountain bikers along it.

Description

Mileages are measured from the second (northern) parking area in Lake Tahoe Nevada State Park. From its northeast edge a broad path descends northeast almost 0.1 mile to a road junction that is just below and west of Spooner Lake's dam. We start on the obvious North Canyon road, quickly cross the lake's outlet creek, and parallel a meadow's edge northward. As we approach the mouth of the canyon, sagebrush gives way to white firs, lodgepole pines, and Jeffrey pines, and soon we see our first aspens, which are very common as far as Marlette Lake, though are generally sparse throughout most of the Tahoe Sierra. Just 0.7 mile from our starting point, we pass a cabin, on the left, situated near the north end of the meadow, and then in 0.2 mile cross North Canyon's aspen-lined creek.

Our closed road recrosses the creek 0.4 mile upstream, then parallels it on a usually gentle grade 0.6 mile farther, to where you'll note a gap in North Canyon's west wall. This gap is seen immediately before the road curves right and you get your first view of treeless Snow Valley Peak. On your ascent you may have noticed that North Canyon's creek seemed rather small, given the size of

Marlette Lake and Lake Tahoe, from a ridge viewpoint north of Marlette Peak

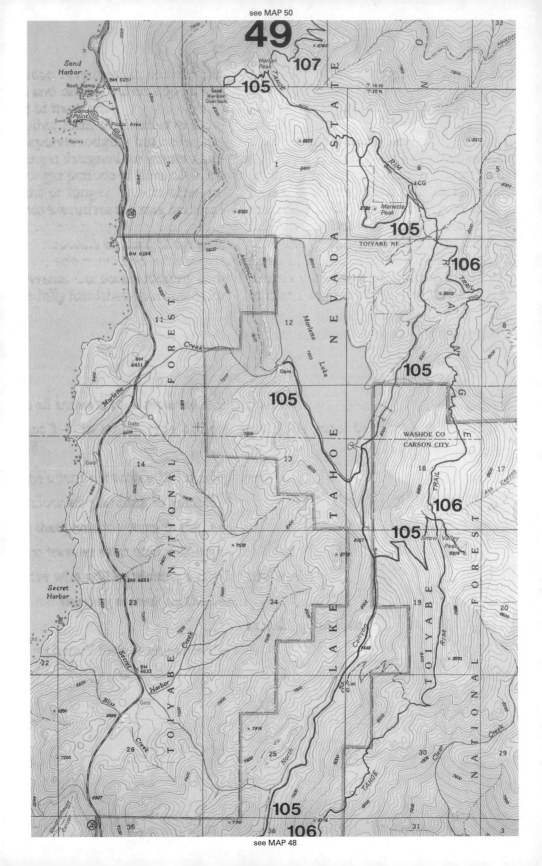

49

the canyon. The answer lies here, at the gap. A tributary of Secret Harbor Creek, eroding headward, cut through the canyon's west wall, so that today most of upper North Canyon's drainage flows through the gap, with only a little water flowing south. This is a case of *stream piracy*, or stream capture. These are uncommon in the Sierra Nevada, but fairly common in some drainages along the San Andreas fault system, in western California. I haven't seen any captures *in progress* anywhere else. The ones I've seen have happened or are about to happen.

Just after we get our first Snow Valley Peak view the road's first red firs appear, and not much farther, the last white firs disappear. About 0.9 mile past that view we come to a junction with a trail, and about 45 yards up it is the **North Canyon Campground**. Here you'll find a small, 1997-vintage cabin and an adjacent campsite complete with a fire ring. Water is available from the creek, among aspens just west of the road. (To camp here or at Marlette Peak Campground, you need to contact park rangers or call park headquarters at 702-831-0494.) If you were to continue up this moderately graded, fir-and-pine-shaded trail, you would reach the **Tahoe Rim Trail**, along which you could hike north to the Snow Valley Peak jeep road. Taking this route to that junction is almost one mile longer than via the North Canyon route. Nevertheless, the stretch of TRT is rich in views, so if you plan to visit the peak, you might consider returning south along the TRT and then west down the connecting trail to the North Canyon road.

On that road we cross North Canyon's creek in ¼ mile, doing so in the south end of a scenic, fairly large meadow. At its north end our road, which has been easy until now, takes on a moderate grade, and then a steep one—which separates the macho mountain bikers (who pedal up it) from the rest (who walk their bikes up). The gradient abates at a junction with the gated **Snow Valley Peak jeep road**. Right by the gate you'll hear the canyon's spring-fed creek, which is piped beneath the jeep road.

If you're game for exceptional views, start up the jeep road, which switchbacks up brushy slopes with ever-improving views.

Just before you reach a crest saddle, you come to a spur road at the final switchback. Even if you're exhausted, make the effort to follow it 100 yards up to a viewpoint which, in my opinion, equals or exceeds the view from Snow Valley Peak: Marlette Lake spreads naked below you, backdropped by the somber volcanic crests and peaks of the Mt. Rose area, while the northern part of Lake Tahoe evokes wonder at its swirling surface currents.

Just beyond the spur road is a saddle with a crossing by the **Tahoe Rim Trail**. If you've climbed this far—about 850 feet elevation gain up the jeep road—you might as well make the 250 feet elevation gain up it to 9114' **Snow Valley Peak**. The summit area, unfortunately, is gently sloped, and its apex is occupied by a microwave relay tower. Thus, to get views in all directions, you'll have to wander about. Besides having lake views, you also see sprawling Reno, in the distant north, and its high-rise casinos.

If you've brought a Tahoe-area map along, you should be able to identify some of the major features. Clockwise from Reno, you scan the eastern valleys, noting Washoe Lake, Carson City, and Carson Valley. From the valley a major canyon—the route of Highway 50—swoops up to the crest of the Carson Range. Near its southern end rises the range's highest mass, the Freel Peak massif, with the area's first, second, and fourth highest peaks. Scanning westward, you'll note the high, often snowy peaks of Desolation Wilderness, with Tahoe's Emerald Bay lying at their base. Meeks Bay, to the west-southwest, is harder to spot, though it lies at the mouth of the first major canyon north of Emerald Bay. Northward, you'll scan past four major canyons before spotting Tahoe's outlet, the Truckee River canyon. From the lake's outlet the Tahoe rim rises, then drops to Brockway Summit, and then rises to a culmination of the area's third highest peak, Mt. Rose. About the only prominent feature you don't see is relatively close-by Marlette Lake.

On foot, you can be back to the North Canyon road in about ½ hour. On it you quickly crest a deep cleft, an 8157' pass. North Canyon road has been following a fault up to this cleft, from which both road and fault continue north to Marlette Lake and beyond. Along the road you quickly have a view of the lake, and you pass a number of roadside springs along your ¾-mile-long, gentle-to-moderate descent to a **road junction above southeastern Marlette Lake**. To immediately reach the lake, take the short road west down to it. Those bound for Marlette Peak and the Sand Harbor Overlook Loop Trail take the main road north. First, however, the book will describe the route to the lake's dam.

On the main road south, known as the Flume Trail, you begin a clockwise hike around the lake. You first descend slightly to the lake's south shore where, just south of the lake and your road, you'll see a fish-spawning station for cutthroat trout, and fishing is strictly forbidden (yes, rangers drive the roads). Camping too is forbidden.

The road along the lake's southwest shore is nearly level and is fairly shaded with red firs, western white pines, and lodgepole pines. However, one possible annoyance to early-season bikers is one or more encounters with downed trees. The road ends just beyond a cut through a bouldery bedrock ridge and just before the **lake's dam**. The toe of the ridge is a fine spot for diving into the lake, which in midsummer warms to the mid and upper 60s. Marlette Lake is really shallower than one would guess from the way granitic slopes plunge to its west shore. Most of the lake is quite shallow, and its deepest spot, by the dam, is only 52 feet. A dam, just 26 feet high, was constructed back in 1873, ponding up Goodwin Lake, lying in a presumably fault-formed basin. This was quickly raised 11 feet just 3 years later, then in 1959 was raised to its present height. At roughly 350 acres Marlette Lake provides quite a lot of domestic water to Carson City.

Back at the lake's east-side junction, those bent on superb views start north along a road. For the first ½ mile the road traverses through a well-watered aspen grove, and along this stretch you have access to the lake's southeast shore. But soon your road begins a ¼-mile climb, mostly steep, to a crossing of a willow-lined creek. Your road briefly parallels it upstream, and should you want some water,

be aware that this year-round creek is your last opportunity. Above the creek the road climbs generally on a steep gradient to a junction with a **jeep road**. This traverses, first southeast then northeast, 0.4 mile to the **Tahoe Rim Trail**.

On the main road you reach a conspicuous viewpoint after about a minute's walk northwest. From it you see parts of Lake Tahoe and Marlette Lake; far better views lie ahead. Your road traverses a bit, then descends slightly to a broad, amorphous flat, on which you reach a **road junction with a Tahoe Rim Trail intersection**. To reach the Marlette Peak Trail you can either start northwest along a road, then quickly leave it for a road that climbs steeply to the trail, or you can take the TRT.

I prefer trail tread to jeep tread, so he recommends the latter. This starts north, crossing a water pipeline midway to some slopes, up which the trail climbs northwest. Upon topping a minor crest, you quickly reach a junction with the **Marlette Peak Trail's south end**. Take the trail. In 90 yards you intersect the aforementioned jeep tread, which ends at the TRT about 0.2 mile north.

On the Marlette Peak Trail you start initially northwest, but from a switchback make a clockwise climb moderately up to a bouldery **viewpoint** on the peak's southwest ridge. The view is incredible. All of Marlette Lake spreads below your feet, as does most of Lake Tahoe. Although your viewpoint lies west of the Carson Range's crest you nevertheless can look east across the broad flat and see desert ranges. To the south-southeast rises relatively close Snow Valley Peak, and the distant views you get from your viewpoint are similar to those from that peak, whose views were described earlier in this hike. Mountain bikes are allowed up to the viewpoint, but not beyond it, for the first half of your ⅔ mile trail north to the TRT is quite bouldery. Along this trail you traverse mostly across volcanic terrain, although the actual summit of Marlette Peak, not much above you, is granitic, indicating that it was not buried by eruptions that occurred in this vicinity about 13-16 million years ago. Your continuous Lake Tahoe views end when your trail climbs briefly to the Carson Range crest, and they are replaced with desert-lands views until trees obscure them as you approach the **Tahoe Rim Trail**.

If you don't take the Marlette Peak Trail (perhaps saving it for your return trip), then from its south end you take the nearly level TRT northwest 0.2 mile, paralleling the jeep tread just above you, until it turns abruptly to descend to your trail opposite the **Marlette Peak Campground**. This is situated on a gently sloping, broad ridge, and it has tables and an outhouse but alas, no water. Should you camp here, be sure you've filled your water bottles at the previously mentioned willow-lined creek, about 1.3 miles earlier.

From the campground you've got to climb back to the Carson Range crest, and the first 0.4 mile is a viewless ascent northwest through a forest of mountain hemlocks and red firs. Your trail then curves north and climbs briefly across open slopes of mule ears to a bend, from which you have excellent views northeast to Washoe Lake and beyond it to Reno. From the bend you next make a short climb southwest to a junction with the **Marlette Peak Trail's north end**. You then continue to climb, first north then west, up to the Carson Range's locally volcanic crest. Here you find a junction with a **ridge trail south**, which quickly ends at a **viewpoint**. Its views are similar to those from Marlette Peak's viewpoint: you see most of Marlette Lake, the northern slopes of nearby Marlette Peak, and considerably more of the desert lands to the east.

From the junction you soon skirt just west of a granitic knoll, then cross the range's crest to begin a 0.6-mile forested traverse. Roughly midway along it, volcanic rocks yield to granitic ones, and this is reflected in the soils, which in turn influence the vegetation. In particular, granite-derived soils retain less water, so water-loving mountain hemlocks are absent. At the end of your traverse you arrive at a junction with the **Sand Harbor Overlook Loop Trail**. On it you take a series of short switchbacks up to the 8830-foot crest of Herlan Peak, the ascent tiring because of: 1) their steepness, 2) your many miles of hiking to this vicinity, and 3) the thinner air at this altitude. From the crest your trail descends gravelly slopes, first northwest then south-

west, to a fork. Here begins a short loop of the loop trail. Take either fork down to a quick junction, from which a 45-yard-long spur takes you to the trail's fabulous, frighteningly exposed **Sand Harbor Overlook**. From this viewpoint you are quite safe, but you certainly won't want to go clambering around its brink—a slip likely would be fatal. Sand Harbor, more than 2400 feet below you, is so close that you can see vehicles in its parking lot as well as along Highway 28. You also see virtually all of Lake Tahoe plus the southern half of Marlette Lake. Views of the desert lands to the east are absent, but you see virtually all of the Lake Tahoe Basin's rim. This includes most of the Carson Range from the Freel Peak environs in the south to the Mt. Rose environs in the north, the forested north rim west of Mt. Rose, and the Sierra Nevada crest from the Carson Pass environs north through the Desolation and Granite Chief wildernesses to the Donner Pass environs. To get a better view of the lake and its basin, you'd need an airplane.

Lake Tahoe Nevada State Park's greatest attraction is its fine beach at Sand Harbor

⪻ 106 ⪼
Tahoe Rim Trail, Highway 50 north to Snow Valley Peak, Marlette Peak, and Sand Harbor Overlook

Distances:
4.2 miles to saddle with a lateral trail
    1.4 miles to North Canyon Campground
    and North Canyon road
5.8 miles to Snow Valley Peak jeep road
    1.2 miles down jeep road to North Canyon
    road
    0.4 mile up jeep road to Snow Valley Peak
8.8 miles to second jeep road
9.1 miles to Marlette Peak Trail's south end
    0.6 mile on trail to viewpoint
    1.3 miles on trail to TRT
9.3 miles to Marlette Peak Campground
10.0 miles to Marlette Peak Trail's north end
10.3 miles to ridge trail south
    0.1 mile on trail to viewpoint
11.0 miles to Sand Harbor Overlook Loop Trail
    0.6 mile on trail to Sand Harbor Overlook

Low/High Elevations: 6950'/8157' to Marlette Lake; 9214' to Snow Valley Peak

Season: Late May through late October

Classification: Moderate to Snow Valley Peak, strenuous if day hiked to Marlette Peak and beyond

Maps: 48 and 49

Trailhead: Along the east shore of Lake Tahoe, take Highway 50 north up to Spooner Summit, which is 0.8 mile east of the Highways 28/50 (Spooner) junction. Alternatively, from Incline Village along the northeast shore of Lake Tahoe, take Highway 28 south to the junction. At the summit, park along the north side of the road, opposite the Spooner Picnicking Rest Area.

Introduction
Like the previous hike, this one takes you to the summit of Snow Valley Peak. Since it is almost a mile longer and usually is waterless, why take it? There are at least four reasons. First, it is better graded—its tread generally is an easy or moderate ascent. In contrast, the previous route is gentle for about the first 3

miles, then is moderate-to-steep to the summit. Second, it is a trail, not a road. Third, the North Canyon road gets heavy use by mountain bikers; the trail, less. And fourth, being a part of the Tahoe Rim Trail, it stays close to the lake basin's rim, offering more views. If you were to hike all the way to the Sand Harbor Overlook, taking in Snow Valley and Marlette peaks along the way, your round-trip distance would exceed 24 miles—quite a day hike. Keeping only to the TRT, the round-trip distance to the overlook still would be 23.2 miles. Fortunately you can make a backpack trip out of this hike, overnighting at Marlette Peak Campground, 9.3 miles along the TRT. Leave your backpack in this vicinity, then with perhaps just a fanny pack, hike around Marlette Peak and beyond to the Sand Harbor Overlook, then return to the campground and head back out.

Description
For about the first ½ mile of the Tahoe Rim Trail you traverse northwest on an old road. Near a minor summit the road continues northward, but you branch right, northeast, on trail tread, circling around the west and north slopes of a minor summit to a switchback. The TRT now snakes northward and upward along the forested, generally viewless Carson Range crest. Several good views do exist. At about 1.4 miles you encounter the first; at about mile 2.1, a second, both offering views east. Then at about mile 2.8 you reach a spur trail, and by taking it about 100 yards south to a vista point, located about 1000 feet higher than your trailhead, you have your first good view of part of Lake Tahoe and of the Sierra Nevada crest lands above the lake's west shore. Over the 1.4 miles you have a mostly gentle, mostly viewless ascent northeast, crossing several crest saddles before coming to one with a **lateral trail**. This switchbacks down to the **North Canyon Campground** immediately east of the **North Canyon road**. Just west of it is the canyon's reliable creek. The 700-foot drop along the trail's 1.4-mile length won't be worth the effort unless you are a backpacker and need a legal site within Lake Tahoe Nevada State Park. (To camp here or at Marlette Peak Campground,

Wildflower Plate 16. Carson Range flowers.
1 Silver-leaved phacelia (cream), 2 Recter's rock cress (white to pale-pink), 3 flat-seeded rock cress (white to pink), 4 Copeland's owl clover (pink to red), 5 Nuttall's linanthus (white with yellow center), 6 granite gilia (white to violet), 7 frosty-leaved buckwheat (yellowish), 8 western peony (rusty brown with yellow-and-green center), 9 Brewer's lupine.

you need to contact park rangers or call park headquarters at 702-831-0494.)

The TRT leaves the lateral trail by first traversing east, offering you a good view of the Kingsbury Grade, then switchbacking over to west-facing slopes of the south ridge of Snow Valley Peak. Northward, you have unobstructed views of the Lake Tahoe Basin, although a parallel ridge to the west of the TRT conceals the lake's eastern lands. As you climb higher on your northward trek, tobacco brush yields to sagebrush as the dominant shrub. Beneath the actual summit of Snow Valley Peak, the TRT levels off and you contour ¼ mile to a junction with the **Snow Valley Peak jeep road**. Most hikers will take this closed road southeast up to nearby **Snow Valley Peak**. Its summit views are described in the previous hike.

Ahead on the TRT, the traffic is much less. You briefly climb up to the Carson Range crest, cross it, and descend across west-facing slopes which offer abundant views of Marlette Lake. The crest then jogs east, as does the trail, passing scattered whitebark pines before crossing a minor crest saddle and starting a switchbacking descent north. Western white pines and red firs increase in number, and your views—west, north, and east—diminish in quality and number. About 2.0 miles beyond the Snow Valley Peak jeep road, your crest route arrives at a minor gap that has a junction with a **second jeep road**. Unless you are carrying a large amount of water, you will want to follow this trail 0.2 mile southwest down a gully, to where the trail bends northwest. From there, continue about 200 yards down the gully to find spring-fed water.

Retrace your steps and continue on the TRT, which leaves the minor gap by taking the jeep road about 140 yards east. Trail tread begins northeast, but it quickly starts a traverse west before commencing a winding, forested descent to a broad, amorphous flat, on which you reach a **road junction**. This is the same spot as the previous hike's "road junction with a Tahoe Rim Trail intersection." From this spot, follow that hike to reach the **Marlette Peak Trail**, the **Marlette Peak Campground**, and the **Sand Harbor Overlook Trail**.

⇜ 107 ⇝
Tahoe Rim Trail, Highway 431 south to Twin Lakes and Sand Harbor Overlook

Distances:
2.3 miles to spring-fed creeklet
7.1 miles to major saddle
8.4 miles to Tunnel Creek road
8.9 miles to eastern Twin Lake
11.0 miles to Sand Harbor Overlook Loop Trail
   0.6 mile on trail to Sand Harbor Overlook

Low/High Elevations: 7860'/8830'

Season: Late May through late October

Classification: Moderate to Twin Lakes, strenuous if day hiked to Sand Harbor Overlook

Maps: 51, 50, and 49

Trailhead: From Incline Village along the northeast shore of Lake Tahoe, drive 6.5 miles up Mt. Rose Highway 431 to the trailhead for the Ophir Creek Trail and the southbound Tahoe Rim Trail. These start on the same closed road on your right, opposite a private road on your left, which goes to Incline Lake homes. Do not block the private road. To reach the Mt. Rose trailhead for Hikes 108 and 109, continue northeast up Highway 431, driving through Tahoe Meadows. In 0.8 mile you reach a parking area and facility (restrooms, displays, wheelchair-accessible loop trail). Just 0.4 mile beyond it, you reach a gated road, on your left, the trailhead for the Mt. Rose Trail and northwest-bound Tahoe Rim Trail. Park on either side of the highway, but do not block the gated road. The entrance to the Mt. Rose Campground lies ¼ mile up the highway, and the Mt. Rose Highway's summit is 100 yards beyond it.

Introduction

Like the previous hike, this one goes to the Sand Harbor Overlook, reaching it in exactly the same distance. Which one is better? The answer is subjective. The previous hike offers side trips to Snow Valley and Marlette peaks, plus dramatic views of Marlette Lake. This one offers more east-side views plus a visit to

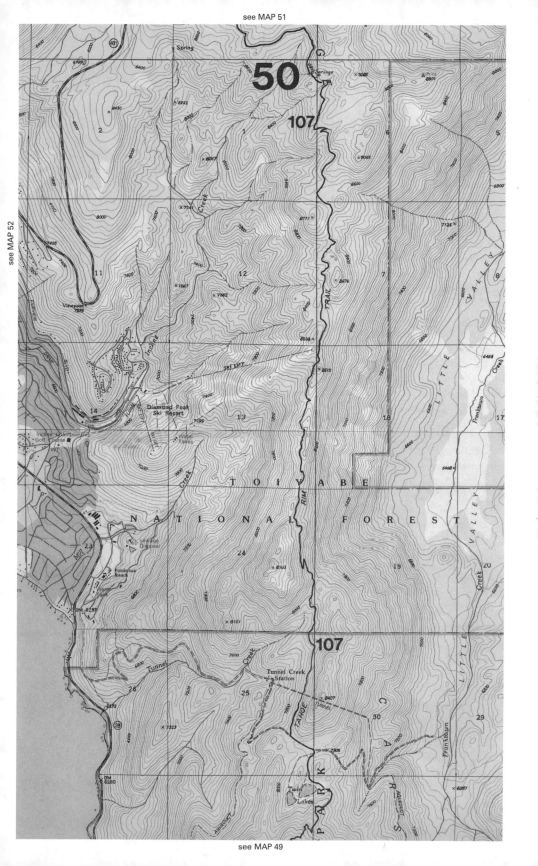

a pair of natural lakes. Both hikes are worth your consideration.

Description
The Tahoe Rim Trail begins along the Ophir Creek Trail, which is a former road. This starts east through a lodgepole-pine forest, then curves southward and traverses momentarily along an edge of Tahoe Meadows before arriving at a nearby junction only 0.4 mile from the trailhead. The Ophir Creek Trail continues east to three shallow, man-made lakes, descending past Upper and Lower Price lakes in about 2½ miles and past Rock Lake in another 1 mile. It then ends in Davis Creek County Park, along Highway 365, after about 2½ miles. The total drop, at over 3400 feet, is quite substantial.

We take the TRT, which for the most part has relatively modest ascents and descents. Starting south, we begin our first ascent, a forested climb to a ridge about 250 feet above us. On it a road crosses the TRT, and by walking south on the road a few yards you get your first view of Lake Tahoe, 1.2 miles into your trek. From the road crossing the TRT starts southeast on a former road spur, quickly narrowing to trail width. In just under ½ mile of contouring through an open forest, we pass barely above a saddle with a small granite-block knoll just south of it. If you were to walk about 100 yards over to it, you would

receive a fine view of most of the Lake Tahoe Basin. However, even better views lie ahead.

Over the next ¾ mile the TRT contours, first east then south, to a reliable **spring-fed creeklet**. Especially in early hiking season, you'll see other flowing creeklets hereabouts. The southernmost one flows down a shallow gully, and just beyond it, atop a minor ridge, is a good campsite among an open stand of whitebark and western white pines. From the ridge the trail heads briefly east to a larger gully, then parallels it southwest about 200 yards downstream. In early summer water may flow where the trail crosses the gully, but by late summer you'll have to go 100–300+ yards down the gully to obtain water. Be aware that here, about 2½ miles into your hike, is your last reliable water until the Twin Lakes, almost 6½ miles farther. In drought years these may dry up in late summer, so if you are hiking in such a year, check with the Lake Tahoe Nevada State Park headquarters at Sand Harbor (702-831-0494).

Ahead, you gradually descend south as the TRT traverses across slopes from one minor saddle to the next. The forest is quite open in places, offering you views of Lake Tahoe scenery. About 3.8 miles from the trailhead, just beyond a broad-crest area with old selective logging, you cross a saddle and immediately have your first view of desert scenery. A significant 3600′ below you lies Washoe Lake,

View east toward Washoe Lake and adjacent desert lands

Northern Lake Tahoe, Stateline Point, and Crystal Bay

at 5029' elevation, with irrigated lands just west of it, New Washoe City just east of it, and above all the virtually naked Virginia Range, capped by 7456' McClellan Peak. The range is mostly treeless, partly because it lies in the rain shadows cast by the Sierra Nevada and Carson Range crests, and partly because miners in the great 1859 Comstock Lode silver rush eventually razed the sparse forest for lumber, mine timber, and firewood. The lake is one of the few natural, permanent lakes in the Basin and Range province of the western United States; most of the basins in this desert landscape receive inadequate precipitation to support a year-round lake. However, during the last Ice Age, more than 90 such lakes existed, thanks to cooler temperatures (less lake-water evaporation) and to large, glacier-fed streams.

Until now, the forest of red fir and western white, whitebark, and Jeffrey pines has had a floor mostly of abundant pinemat manzanita, but as we drop in elevation southward, we soon encounter bush chinquapin and then its common associate, tobacco brush. By flirting with the Carson Range crest, the TRT presents us with alternating west and east views. About 5.1 miles into our hike we skirt just below the top of Diamond Peak Ski Area's uppermost ski run, which is quite conspicuous from a small crest saddle just south of it. This offers us a view not only of Washoe Lake, but also of sprawling Carson City, which will become more prominent as we progress south.

Over the next ¼ mile we have inspiring views of Lake Tahoe lands, then briefly curve southeast to a narrow saddle, at 8300', with a good view east. From here the trail climbs a bit to traverse ½ mile south on west-facing slopes, then from a saddle it traverses ½ mile south on east-facing slopes to a sudden viewpoint with sweeping views. From it begins a "modest" descent across steep, open slopes, dropping about 300 feet, with the aid of rather steep switchbacks, to a crossing of a **major saddle**. You have been on Forest Service lands to here, and can camp anywhere on them. About 100 yards south you enter Lake Tahoe Nevada State Park, and no camping is allowed from this border south until the Marlette Peak Campground (mentioned in the two previous hikes). It is unfortunate that currently the park does not allow camping at fishless Twin Lakes, whose shallow basin is an ideal site. Consequently, unless the camping ban is lifted, backpackers should plan to camp at the major saddle. Obtain water by descending about ¼ mile from it southwest to the headwaters of Tunnel Creek. Here, you are 4.5 miles from this hike's final goal, the Sand Harbor Overlook.

From the saddle we traverse south 1.2 miles across the upper, forested slopes of the Tunnel Creek drainage, and drop slightly to a prominent saddle with the well-used **Tunnel Creek road**. The TRT heads east-southeast 0.2 mile down this road to a junction with a minor road. On it you arc about 80 yards south to an intersection of another minor road. From this point the second road climbs west-southwest then heads south over a saddle and down to the nearby western Twin Lake. The TRT route, however, keeps to the first road, which climbs, first southwest then south, to a saddle, and in 50 yards diverges left from the road. It briefly parallels the road south, then swings east to parallel the northeast shore of **eastern Twin Lake**. Unlike *virtually* all of the other *natural* lakes mentioned in this guidebook, the Twin Lakes do not owe their origin to glaciers excavating shallow basins. Lake Tahoe is one exception, ponding up behind a lava dam. The Twin Lakes may owe their origin to down-faulting, since a fault is believed to run along the west edge of the lakes' shallow basin. But the fault may be no more than a linear fracture—a master joint—which would have essentially no displacement. Could these shallow lakes have formed without glaciers or lava dams or faults? Perhaps. Long ago today's basin may have been essentially flat, but over time it may have become shallowly excavated as strong winds, occasionally whipping east over the Carson Range crest for countless millennia, gradually removed the basin floor's decomposed granitic bedrock—*gruss*, or gravel.

The TRT skirts southeast along a broad, low, open, gravelly divide, along which a campground could be established, should the state park choose to do so in the future. Immediately ahead lies this hike's only significant climb, a 750-foot switchbacking ascent up to the north slopes of Peak 8706. The ascent is forested, which is great if you are toiling up it on a warm day, yet it is open enough in spots to yield views north along the Carson Range. The highest peak seen is dark, volcanic, 10,776' Mt. Rose, and just right of it and somewhat closer is light, granitic, 9698' Slide Mountain (the site of the slide is quite obvious). Just right of it and farther away is the metropolitan Reno-Sparks area, which you see by looking north-northeast down Franktown Creek's Little Valley. It supposedly has formed through down-faulting, but again, the fault is questionable. Straight, broad-floored valleys like this one exist in unfaulted lands of the southern Sierra Nevada, and their origins are

due to tens of millions of years of weathering under ancient, warm, wet climates.

From Peak 8706 your trail descends briefly to a broad, viewless flat, then makes an equally brief ascent to a junction with the **Sand Harbor Overlook Loop Trail**. This short-but-steep trail and the views obtained from its terminus, the Sand Harbor Overlook, are described in the last paragraph of Hike 105.

⪦ 108 ⪧
Mt. Rose Trail

Distances:
2.5 miles to road junction by Tahoe Basin rim saddle
3.3 miles to perennial creek
4.5 miles to saddle west of Mt. Rose
5.9 miles to summit of Mt. Rose
Low/High Elevations: 8840'/10,776'
Season: Mid-July through early October
Classification: Moderate
Map: 51
Trailhead: See the Hike 107 trailhead.

Introduction
Mt. Rose is the Tahoe Sierra's third highest peak, its summit being about 100 feet lower than Freel Peak, and about 50 feet lower than the runner up, Jobs Sister (see Hike 101). And Mt. Rose is the only 10,000+' peak with a path all the way to the top. This hike is short enough and starts high enough that the summit can be easily climbed and descended in half a day. Because the trailhead and summit are so readily accessible, the route is quite popular, and on warm, sunny days, dozens of hikers may ascend it. Because the summit is located north of the Lake Tahoe Basin rim, some of the lake is hidden, and so the view is not so grand as from, say, the Sand Harbor Overlook or from Marlette Peak. Desert views are expansive, although dominated by the sprawling Reno-Sparks metropolitan area. And if you are fond of wildflowers, this hike is for you, for on no other Tahoe Sierra peak can you see such a diverse array of alpine flora.

Description

The first 2½ miles of route are an easy climb up a gated service road to a saddle. You start up toward it through an open forest of lodgepole pines, which tap water in the fairly deep soil of weathered granodiorite the road initially is built upon. Soon, Lake Tahoe and Desolation Wilderness peaks rise over the ridges south-southwest of us, while peaks of the Virginia Range—parent of the Comstock Lode—rise above the framed view through Ophir Creek canyon to the southeast. Along the easy walk, pleasing aromas from sagebrush, mule ears, coyote mint, and lupine at times complement your visual experience.

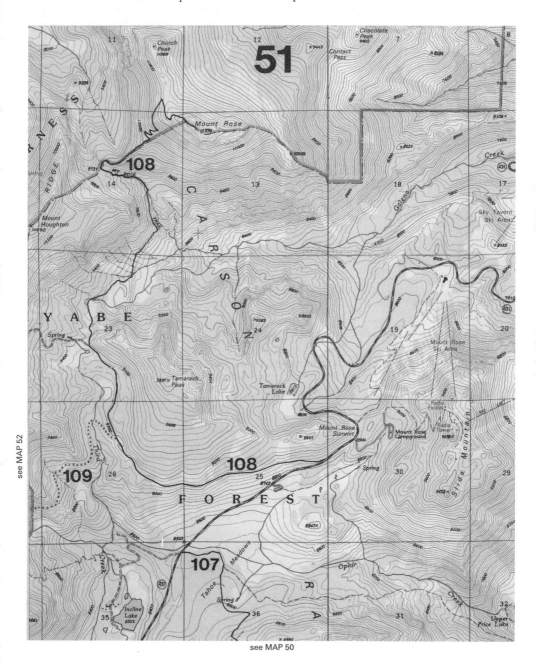

see MAP 52

see MAP 50

Where the road makes a noticeable curve right, about 1 mile from the trailhead, its road cut reveals an anatomical vignette of the volcanic rocks you now tread upon. These layered rocks are not horizontal, rather, they slope down to the east. (Geologists say they *dip* eastward.) A short walk west therefore takes one across increasingly older volcanic rocks, although all are probably about 12-16 million years old. From east to west you pass through a reddish brown autobreciated (self-fractured) lava, then a 2-foot-thick buff-colored tuff layer, which is the consolidated product of ash that was explosively ejected from a volcano. Next you pass through a brown-gray andesite flow, which rests on a small exposure of weathered granodiorite that initially may have formed beneath a landscape some 90 million years ago, eventually being exposed through erosion perhaps 5-20 million years later.

Your closed road soon curves northwest, leaving behind views of Lake Tahoe and the Incline Lake development, below you. A northern (red-shafted) flicker or a Clark's nutcracker might be seen flitting from tree to tree, the flicker in search of bark insects, the nutcracker in search of seeds from lodgepole and whitebark pines. Then after a ½-mile of gentle ascent you approach a meadow, and from it make a moderate ¼-mile climb to a minor divide that dams a snowmelt pond, below, which for a brief period is the mating ground for myriad treefrogs. Immediately beyond it is a **road junction by a Tahoe Basin rim saddle**.

You leave your service road and fork north (right) immediately over the saddle, taking either a trail or the adjacent road, which quickly join. The road winds down to a nearby meadow, and heads north through it to some trees at its northwest end. You take a brief trail segment that cuts north right through it to rejoin the longer road. Near the reunion, a clump of corn lilies signals the presence of a roadside spring emanating from the porous andesitic soil. To the southeast we can look head-on at the fantastically eroded, deeply grooved cliff of easily eroded autobrecciated lava.

Your road descends northeast from the spring, first paralleling overhead powerlines,

then bending more northward and crossing a flat with a small, curving ridge at the brink of an east-facing slope. Just north of this flat's whitebark pines is a creek, and our road winds steeply down to it in about 270 yards, narrowing to a trail. For late-season hikers this **perennial creek** is your last reliable source of water.

Continuing beyond the creek, you go north on a trail that traverses a bouldery slope and crosses several seasonal creeklets that last well into summer. Wildflowers abound, particularly lupine, tall larkspur, paintbrush, coyote mint, mule ears, arrow-leaved senecio, and angelica. Shrubs are represented by sagebrush, currant, elderberry, and willow. To the east you can look well past the ski lifts and see distant desert ranges.

Ahead, the trail climbs moderately northeast, and then at a ridge bends northwest and climbs moderately to steeply up the slope of a deeply incised gully. After gradually leveling off, the trail fords the gully's creek, which usually flows through late August, then it climbs along the northeast bank all the way up to a **saddle west of Mt. Rose**. Here, among some weather-beaten whitebark pines, you meet the boundary of Mt. Rose Wilderness, which from the saddle heads east up a ridge to the summit. You do likewise, and from about here onward you might watch for alpine vegetation (see this hike's Plate 17 plus Plates 11 and 14-16). Now is the time to put on a hat and/or dark glasses, for the intense

Summit of Mt. Rose

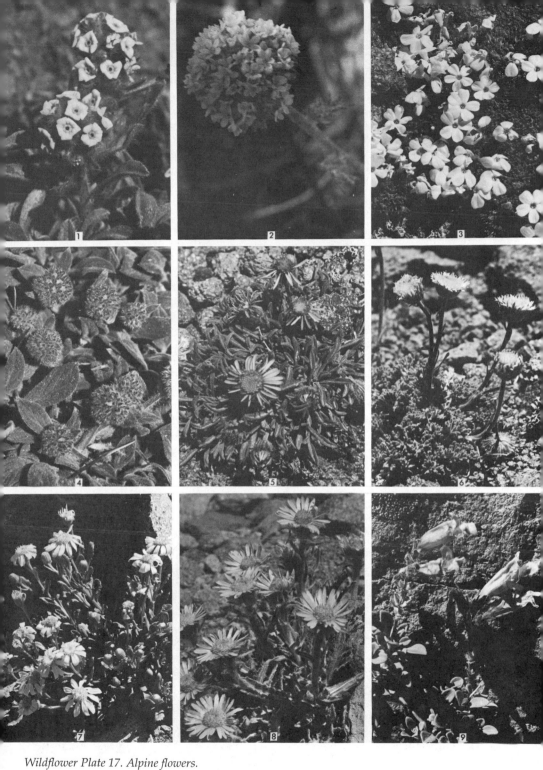

Wildflower Plate 17. Alpine flowers.
1 Dwarf cryptantha (white), 2 ballhead ipomopsis (white), 3 Coville's phlox (white to pink), 4 timberline phacelia (white to violet), 5 cushion stenotus (violet rays, which sometimes drop off, with golden disk), 6 cut-leaved daisy (same as 5), 7 Fremont's senecio (yellow), 8 alpine gold (yellow), 9 Davidson's penstemon (red-violet).

ultraviolet radiation up here can cause minor injury to your eyes. The trail ascends along the crest of the narrow, autobrecciated-lava ridge over toward the dark, volcanic hulk of Mt. Rose, from where you get a superb view northwest down the glaciated canyon of Bronco Creek and see large Stampede Reservoir flooding valleys among some low hills north of Interstate 80.

From your start up the deeply incised gully, you have climbed about 800 feet to the west slopes of Mt. Rose. The climb ahead, although it looks intimidating, is no greater. You begin a switchbacking ascent up the west slopes of Mt. Rose, and your views improve as the whitebark pines become fewer in number and shorter in stature. Soon you can see three reservoirs down-canyon to the northwest which, left to right, are Prosser Creek, Boca, and Stampede. On September 12, 1966, an earthquake of magnitude 5.4 cracked Prosser Creek Reservoir's dam, demonstrating that the Tahoe area still has some active faults. To the south you see Lake Tahoe, the Carson Range, and Desolation Wilderness. By the time you approach a crest extending north from Mt. Rose, you are above treeline, though you may see occasional whitebark pines, cropped by the wind to knee-height. Up here you now see Donner Lake in the west and the unmistakable ribbon of highway called Interstate 80. You now climb southeast up the summit block of Mt. Rose and for the first time see the Reno-Sparks area and the desert lands beyond it. Now it's only a few minute's walk to the summit register atop **Mt. Rose**.

From the summit you can look due south beyond the nearby volcanic edifices and trace the granitic backbone of the central Carson Range, which separates the Lake Tahoe Basin from the Nevada desert. Structural geologists would classify the basin as part of the westernmost border of the Basin and Range province, which extends east across Nevada into Utah, for like the basins in that geologic province, the Lake Tahoe Basin is faulted down between two mountain blocks. Geochemists and geomorphologists, on the other hand, would classify the basin as part of the Sierra Nevada, for it is largely granitic rock, and its glaciated, adjacent crests are continuous with

similar glaciated crests of the Sierra Nevada. Botanists would classify the basin as Sierran, but the basin's east ranges have a good share of juniper, sagebrush, mountain mahogany, and other high-desert species. As for Mt. Rose, its inhospitable summit supports only the most hardy species, cushion plants.

From the summit you see, near the southern part of the Carson Range, Jobs Peak, Jobs Sister, and Freel Peak, these ranking fourth, second, and first among the Tahoe Sierra's highest peaks. On their summits, as on Mt. Rose, the thickness of the air you breathe is a full one-third less than that at sea level. West of them stand several dark summits of the Carson Pass area. Continuing a clockwise sweep, you spot pointed Pyramid Peak. Contrasting with it is the dark, metamorphic summit of Mt. Tallac. Turning toward the west-northwest, you'll see the Sierra Buttes, whose sawtooth crest, above Boca Reservoir, is a hefty 42½ miles away. But this distance pales in comparison to the Lassen Peak summit, seen above the east shore of Stampede Reservoir and lying a whopping 115 miles away. However, don't expect to see it except on very clear days.

⊰⊱ 109 ⊰⊱
Tahoe Rim Trail, Highway 431 west to Martis Peak

Distances:
Approx. 1.7 miles to Tahoe Rim Trail-Mt. Rose Trail split
Approx. 1.9 miles to Third Creek
Approx. 3.2 miles to Ginny Lake
Approx. 3.9 miles to Western States Trail
Approx. 4.5 miles to 9340' saddle
Approx. 5.2 miles to saddle above Mud Lake
Approx. 5.5 miles to trail's high point
Approx. 6.4 miles to rejoin the Western States Trail
Approx. 7.1 miles to slopes below Rose Knob
Approx. 8.6 miles to slopes below Mt. Baldy
Approx. 9.1 miles to California-Nevada boundary
Approx. 9.7 miles to trail junction
Approx. 10.8 miles to 8430' saddle

Approx. 11.3 miles to road crossing
Approx. 11.7 miles to second road crossing
Low/High Elevations: 8370′/9450′
Season: Mid-July through mid-October
Classification: Moderate
Maps: 51, 52, and 53
Trailhead: See the Hike 107 trailhead.

Introduction

The segment of Tahoe Rim Trail extending from Highway 431 west to the vicinity of Martis Peak is not likely to be completed until about 2002, if then. Nevertheless, even today it is quite hikeable by following the Western States Trail. This trail, which like other old horse trails is excessively steep in spots, begins on private land of the Incline Lake development. Until the Tahoe Rim Trail is completed, you can avoid the private land by first ascending the Mt. Rose Trail and then traversing cross-country for about 2 miles over to the old trail. The 4-mile traverse past Rose Knob Peak, Rose Knob, and Rifle Peak offers more views of Lake Tahoe than does any other comparable stretch of trail in the area.

Description

Because the Tahoe Rim Trail segment has not been completed, the following description is tentative, whence the approximate mileages listed above. The dotted parts of the route shown on the maps do not exist. What actually will be constructed will be different, although not significantly so. The route I have mentally constructed is one that is neither excessively long nor excessively steep.

As in the previous hike, you start by climbing gently up a gated road—the Mt. Rose Trail—to a noticeable curve right, about 1 mile from the trailhead, then soon curve northwest. Where the road dips slightly to cross a minor gully, about 1.7 miles from the trailhead, is the locale where the **TRT may split from the Mt. Rose Trail**. Alternatively, it may split as much as 0.4 mile north up the Mt. Rose Trail. Assuming the first site, which minimizes trail construction, the trail, if optimally designed, would descend slightly for about ¼ mile to a crossing of **Third Creek**, your first reliable source of water. The route then would contour first south, then east over to the sloping floor of a cirque developed in granitic

A small natural bridge among dipping lava flows

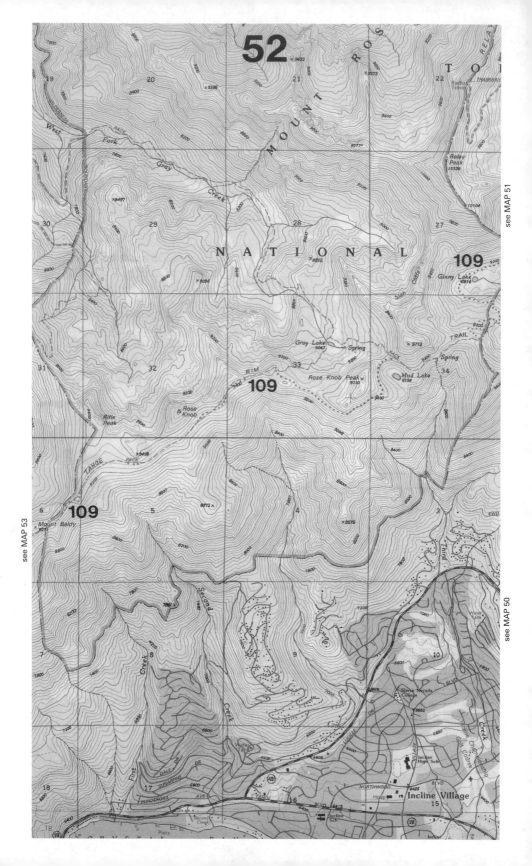

see MAP 51

see MAP 53

see MAP 50

MOUNT ROSE

TO

Radio Tower

TRAMWAY

Relay Peak
10338

10104

NATIONAL

109

Ginny Lake
8916

Slab Cliffs

TRAIL

Gray Lake
9043

Spring

9772

Spring

PACK

Mud Lake
9239

Rose Knob Peak
9710

109

RIM

Rose Knob

Rifle Peak

TAHOE

PACK
9498

8672

109

Mount Baldy
9211

8575

Second

Creek

Way

Third

Water Tank

Incline

7200

Sierra Nevada College

8682

Water Tank

First

DALE DR

SUGARPINE

PONDEROSA

AVE

Incline High Sch

NORTHWOOD

BLVD

Hosp

Incline Sch

Incline Village

431

TAHOE

BLVD

6412

28

West Fork

Gray

Creek

9422

9373

9977

9206

8497

9054

8812

CRYSTAL

BAY

Piers

Second Creek

bedrock. Ahead, the route would head south across gentle slopes, then turn west to cross steep ones over to gentler slopes above **Ginny Lake**, nestled on the floor of a granitic cirque. At just under one acre in size, it is more lakelet than lake. If camping is allowed at it (the lakelet feeds the Incline Lake development), you will have a truly wild setting. Located in an east-facing bowl with a dramatic volcanic cliff at its head, this site hides you from development you've seen early on your hike.

Your next goal is the broad, obvious saddle directly south of Ginny Lake. The slopes up to it are gentle enough for you to walk cross-country steeply, but safely, up to it. The TRT, however, is slated to take a gentler route, climbing moderately to the **Western States Trail**. At present this trail climbs too steeply for hikers, so switchbacks likely will be added, although not necessarily similar to those shown on the map. The existing trail crosses the windswept **9340' saddle** then traverses ⅓ mile across openly forested, volcanic slopes to a spring, and a similar distance to a **saddle above Mud Lake**. This traverse offers your first views of Incline Village way below you and Lake Tahoe beyond.

The Western States Trail drops steeply from the saddle, reaching acre-size Gray Lake in 0.6 mile, then climbing a similar distance back to the volcanic north rim of the Lake Tahoe Basin. The TRT, however, will cross the saddle, and will arc about ¼ mile south to what will likely be the **trail's high point**, at about 9450', situated on the southeast ridge of Rose Knob Peak. Even without the trail, this is easy cross-country. For the next 3+ miles you will have an open traverse that will provide almost continuous views of Lake Tahoe and its basin. Nowhere else on the entire Tahoe Rim Trail is there such a long stretch of lake views. By ascending Rose Knob Peak's southeast ridge, you can easily reach its summit for 360° views. Until the TRT is constructed, you'll want to head up to the summit to avoid a traverse across the peak's steep, rubbly south slopes. The descent west from the summit is easy, and you'll aim for a long ridge saddle just west of it. From there you and the TRT traverse northwest over to **rejoin the Western States Trail**. From here westward, the TRT

route will coincide with this existing trail all the way to a road on the east flank of Martis Peak. However, the old trail's short steep stretches likely will receive switchbacks to lessen the gradients. Again, the switchbacks actually constructed may not match those I've drawn on the map.

The Western States/Tahoe Rim trail makes a high, mostly open, long traverse across **slopes below Rose Knob and Mt. Baldy**, one that offers not only lake views, but also views east and west along the basin's north rim. Note that its upper part is volcanic—derived from andesitic lava—but most of the slopes below you are granitic. For tens of millions of years a granitic ridge has extended west from the Carson Range, although not so far west as to create a Lake Tahoe Basin. The Upper Truckee River was free to flow north through "Tahoe Valley" and then flow undammed northward until voluminous eruptions of lava in the last several million years built up a west half of the north rim, damming the river and creating the lake. On the TRT, you will not see granitic rocks up close—or set foot on them—until south of Barker Pass (Hike 75), midway along the west rim above Lake Tahoe.

From the west end of Mt. Baldy, your trail descends northwest along an open ridge. For about ¼ mile you have views north, west, and south, then around the **California-Nevada boundary**, you encounter trees and soon are submerged within forest cover. Along the route ahead you will have lake views, but you won't get good views until you reach the west rim of the Lake Tahoe Basin, and even then, these views will be few and far between.

From the boundary the Western States Trail drops too steeply along the northwest ridge, and the Tahoe Rim Trail will definitely need switchbacks to make the grade acceptable. Just before the ridge drops to a saddle, the trail turns southwest and descends briefly to a **trail junction**. From here a lateral trail descends about ¼ mile to the upper end of Road 16N33, which the TRT crosses later on, in the next hike. The TRT continues ahead, northwest, adhering close to the crest of the forested, volcanic ridge, and after about a mile turns west for a short descent to a viewless **8430' saddle**. The Western States Trail descends west too steeply, and so this short descent will have to be rerouted. From the saddle the trail arcs westward across gentle slopes, vegetated with red firs and western white pines, over to a **road crossing** just south of and below a broad, viewless saddle. When I mapped the completed TRT from Brockway Summit up to the Martis Peak environs in 1990, the trail shortly ahead was flagged, but not constructed. The trail first parallels the road southwest, which descends about 270 yards to a junction with a spur road east. It then parallels the road about 110 yards southwest to another road junction, then traverses along the main road for about ¼ mile to a **second road crossing**, this one on the gentle south ridge of Martis Peak. Here, Hike 109 arbitrarily ends. To reach the Martis Peak Lookout, consult the last paragraph in Hike 110.

⇔ 110 ⇔
Tahoe Rim Trail, Highway 267 northeast to Martis Peak

Distances:
1.2 miles to spur trail
   0.3 mile up trail to summit 7766
1.8 miles to Road 16N33
2.4 miles to Road 16N32
3.9 miles to viewpoint
4.3 miles to south-ridge road
4.9 miles to Martis Peak Lookout

Low/High Elevations: 7020′ / 8656′

Season: Mid-July through mid-October

Classification: Moderate

Map: 53

Trailhead: From Kings Beach at Lake Tahoe, drive north then west up Highway 267 toward Brockway Summit, reaching the Tahoe Rim Trailhead, along Forest Route 56 on your right, in 2¾ miles. Should you miss it, you will cross Brockway Summit in ½ mile, and then start a descent northwest toward Northstar and Truckee. The segment of Tahoe Rim Trail bound for Martis Peak begins 100 yards up F.R. 56. The segment bound for Watson Lake (next hike) begins from the south side of Highway 267 at the start of F.R. 56.

Introduction
Although most of this hike is across generally viewless, somewhat logged lands, it does have its merits. In only 1.5 miles you can reach a fine summit with good views in most directions. In just under 4 miles you can reach an excellent view of the Lake Tahoe Basin, and finally, at hike's end, you can reach the Martis Peak Lookout, with ranging views to the north and west.

Description
From F.R. 56 (a.k.a. Road 16N56), the Tahoe Rim Trail climbs initially west through a selectively logged forest predominantly of white fir with minor amounts of Jeffrey pine. After ¼ mile, the trail switchbacks, and after two more tacks and another ¼ mile, it climbs east, maintaining a fairly steady 10%, no-nonsense gradient. Since the trail ascends moderately steeply up south-facing slopes, you won't want to make this hike on a hot afternoon. The TRT climbs increasingly away from the din of Highway 267 traffic, and after a mile, it curves north and levels off to soon reach a westbound **spur trail**.

For great views take this short, fairly steep trail up out of the forest and past tobacco brush, huckleberry oak, and chinquapin to **summit 7766**. This summit is the high point of an andesite-lava ridge, which is vegetated with brush, pine, and fir. The stand of trees is open enough for inspiring views. To the south is a fine view of Lake Tahoe, while to the northwest are views from Truckee west up to Donner Pass, dominated by turreted Castle Peak. A ridge to the north of the summit blocks views in that direction. You can see this hike's principal goal, Martis Peak, rising fairly symmetrically in the northeast, about 1000 feet above us and almost 2½ air-miles away.

From the spur-trail junction, the TRT descends northeast along a fir-clad crest, first dropping slightly to an abandoned road, then traversing briefly to a south-winding road, and 30 yards past it crossing a southeast-traversing road. Northwest, it goes 300 yards to Road 16N33, which our trail climbs 160 yards northeast to cross. Eastbound, **Road 16N33**

see MAP 52

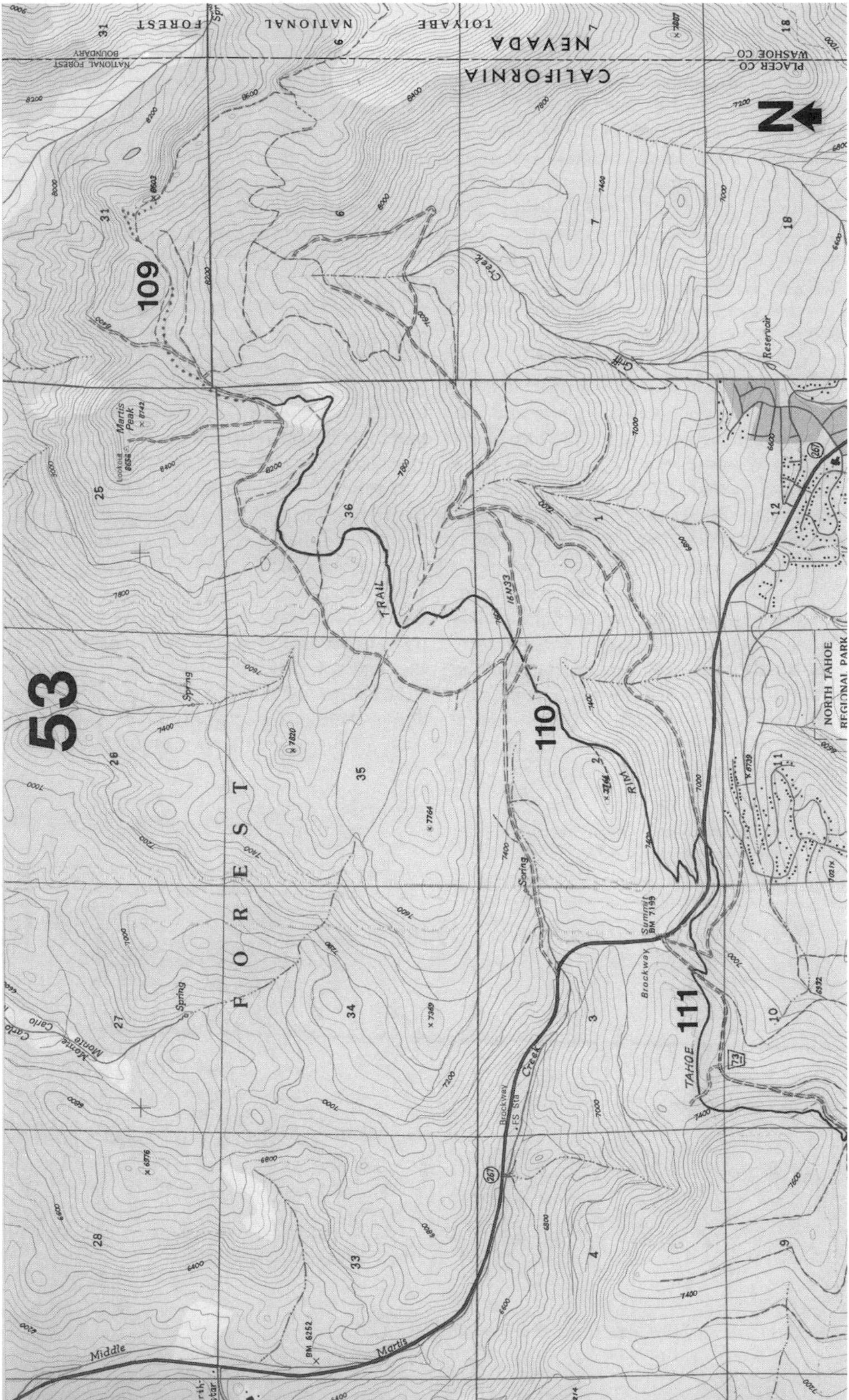

see MAP 54

winds and climbs about 3⅓ miles to a short trail that climbs to the Tahoe Rim Trail. The TRT takes a better route to that junction. Westbound, Road 16N33 makes a straight descent to Highway 267 in just under 1½ miles, reaching it about ½ mile north of and below Brockway Summit. Because the area traversed along your hike is prime lumber country, it is laced with roads, so you can expect to see or hear motor vehicles, especially 4WDs, SUVs, and pickups.

From Road 16N33 the TRT makes an easy climb northeast through a brushy, somewhat open forest co-dominated by white and red firs. It then turns north, and midway along this tack crosses a road before reaching a major one, **Road 16N32.** Lodgepole pines, which have been infrequent to here, are locally common in this vicinity, but we leave them as we climb ¼ mile east-northeast up to "tobacco road." When the flowers of the abundant tobacco brushes are in bloom, the air is filled with their aromatic, sensuous fragrance. On this road you pace 80 yards east to find the resumption of trail tread. Your TRT first parallels the road east, then quickly starts a curve north for a climb up through an extensive field of mule ears. From it you can see Lake

field of mule ears. From it you can see Lake Tahoe and its basin.

At the upper end of the field you intersect another road, then climb north through a forest of red firs and mule ears before curving east to climb to yet another road. On it you ascend for 140 yards, then branch right from it where it curves left, northeast, to climb steeply. Our TRT tread climbs east briefly but moderately up slopes of "shalely," broken, lava to the southern end of Martis Peak's south ridge. Here, at almost 8300 feet in elevation, you have your hike's best **viewpoint.** Located due north of the center of Lake Tahoe, this high viewpoint offers you views of almost all of Lake Tahoe and almost all of the rim that surrounds it. You have uninterrupted views clockwise from southeast to south to west. From Stateline Point, which protrudes from the north shore of Lake Tahoe, cleaving that shore into Agate Bay, on the west, and Crystal Bay, on the east, you can look beyond the latter and identify Sand Point protruding from the lake's northeast shore. Above it stands 9214' Snow Valley Peak, the highest summit above the east shore. Farther south along the crest of the Carson Range is 9150' Genoa Peak,

Sierra crest and Tinker Knob, from trail north of Painted Rock

rising just above a high plateau, South Camp Peak. The lake's two highest summits, 10,823' Jobs Sister and 10,881' Freel Peak, both 30 miles away, rise above the southeast corner of the lake.

Continuing our clockwise scan, we see 10,059' Stevens Peak, 38 miles away, beyond the south shore of Lake Tahoe and near the southern end of the Carson Range. Just west of that peak and just beyond that range stands 10,831' Round Top, which is nearly due south of us a distant 42½ miles away. Closer lies Fallen Leaf Lake, along Tahoe's south shore. Just west of it rises 9735' Mt. Tallac, which from our viewpoint lies above Cascade Lake and Emerald Bay. As you scope north along the west shore, and then past it, you see, respectively, Twin Peaks to the southwest, Tinker Knob north of it, and the Donner Pass environs in the west, in the distance above our north-rim lands.

From the viewpoint the TRT turns north to climb up Martis Peak's south ridge, and after ¼ mile reaches a road where it crosses the now-broad south ridge. Our trail parallels this **south-ridge road** for almost 200 yards, then crosses it as it begins to drop slightly north. From here you can follow the next hike in reverse over to the Mt. Rose Highway. Most hikers, however, may head over to the Martis Peak Lookout. Rather than backtrack on the south-ridge road, just head cross-country northwest across the broad ridge over to a road and follow it ½ mile north up to the **Martis Peak Lookout**. This is easily reached by OHVs and mountain bikes, so this lookout probably gets more riders than hikers or equestrians. It provides views similar to those already seen, but now you have additional views north down to the Truckee River lands and beyond them of Prosser, Boca, and Stampede reservoirs.

⋙ 111 ⋘
Tahoe Rim Trail, Highway 267 southwest to Watson Lake

Distances:
0.7 mile to first crossing of Forest Route 73
2.0 miles to second crossing of Forest Route 73
3.2 miles to lightly used road
4.0 miles to Forest Route 74
4.8 miles to spur trail with viewpoint
6.6 miles to Watson Lake
Low/High Elevations: 6920'/7780'
Season: Mid-July through mid-October
Classification: Moderate
Maps: 53 and 54
Trailhead: See the Hike 110 trailhead.

Introduction
This is the shorter of two trail routes to Watson Lake, both along the Tahoe Rim Trail. Because one can drive to this lake, it lacks a wilderness aura. It is, however, the only natural lake to exist in the totally volcanic lands of Tahoe's north rim. The principal hikers to it are likely to be those planning to do all of the Tahoe Rim Trail or hikers looking for exercise. The route to Watson Lake has only one good view of Lake Tahoe; there certainly are shorter trails to equally good or better views.

Description
From the south edge of Highway 267 opposite the start of Forest Route 56, the Tahoe Rim Trail begins this segment with a traverse west along a former one-lane road. The route at first is through a selectively logged, somewhat open forest of mostly Jeffrey pines. Soon the old road begins to climb, and equally soon we leave it, just before it rejoins the highway. Now on trail tread our route traverses over to a nearby descending road, then climbs briefly to our **first crossing of Forest Route 73** (a.k.a. Mt. Watson Road 16N73). This begins at nearby Brockway Summit and also goes over to Watson Lake. When these lands and the TRT are somewhat snowbound in late spring and early summer, this easy-to-follow road is a suitable alternate route, one that maintains a more constant elevation. The lingering snow patches on the road are insufficient for snow-

see MAP 53

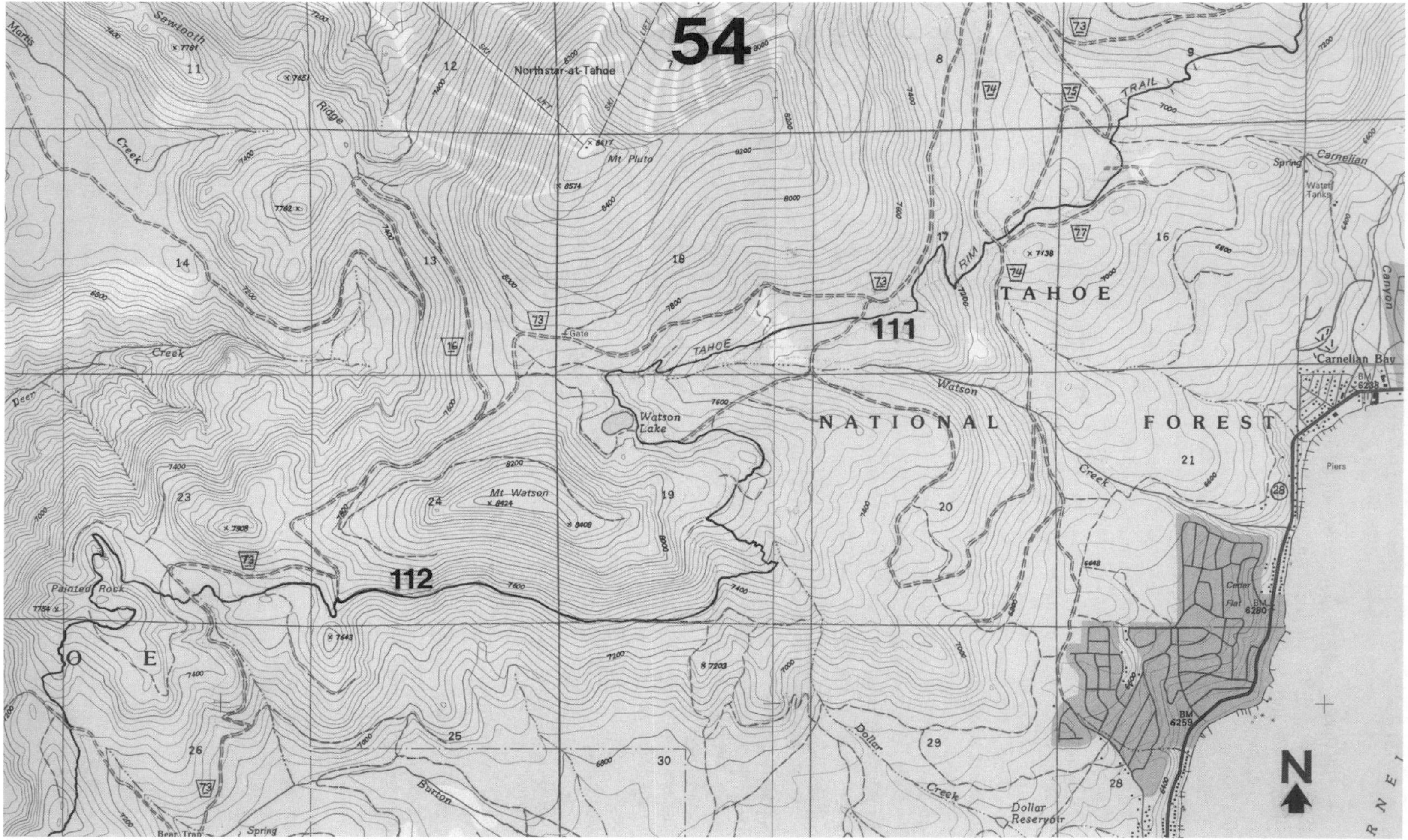

see MAP 55

Watson Lake

mobiles, yet are sufficient to block OHVs. Be aware that after the snow melts, there is no reliable trailside source of water until you reach your destination, Watson Lake.

We climb slightly above F.R. 73 to parallel it ½ mile west across forested, gentle slopes to a minor road, then curve south to climb to an ascending, abandoned road. After taking a few steps along it, we resume trail tread south for a minor, quick descent to a **second crossing of Forest Route 73**, immediately east of its junction with F.R. 73J. Whereas the road traverses west to a saddle, then south toward Watson Creek, the TRT heads more or less southwest toward it, dropping many hundreds of feet, only to regain them on its climb back toward the road. We begin this descent and ascent by first heading south down a shady ridge, which has east-facing bluffs. Along it we have a view of Lake Tahoe, then soon, ¼ mile from the road, angle west. Our trail tread soon ends at an arrow-straight, abandoned road, which takes us ¼ mile down to a resumption of the trail tread and the start of a moderate descent to an east-trending, grassy, abandoned road. On a lesser gradient the TRT winds south 330 yards to a **lightly used road**. Just 20 yards west from this cross-

ing is a junction, and both the west and north branches are segments of F.R. 75. East the lightly used road goes 1.0 mile, gradually increasing its gradient, then turns south for a moderate, 0.6-mile descent to Carnelian Woods Avenue, which gently descends 0.4 mile to Highway 28 in Carnelian Bay. Dropping only 700 feet in 2 miles, this is the shortest route to civilization along the entire TRT (except, of course, where the TRT route heads through the Tahoe City environs).

From the lightly used road the TRT drops south a few feet more to a nearby grassy meadow, where it bottoms out at this segment's lowest elevation before climbing to a nearby west-heading road. It then climbs easily southwest through a selectively logged, predominantly red-fir forest, crosses west over a broad, minor divide, then heads briefly southwest up to a crossing of F.R. 75. This crossing is only 70 yards north of the Roads 75/77 junction, which in turn is only about 90 yards northeast of the Roads 75/74 junction. From there F.R. 74 heads north about 1 mile to F.R. 73 and south to others that descend to Highway 28 in Cedar Flat, about 2½ to 3 miles distant. More importantly, should you desperately need water, you can get some at Watson

Creek, which F.R. 74 crosses in 0.7 mile from the junction. From the crossing of F.R. 75 the TRT climbs 110 yards southwest to a minor divide traversed by **Forest Route 74**.

Ahead we face a 350-foot elevation gain to the top of a lava escarpment, reached via moderately graded switchbacks. The top of the escarpment is a broad lava flow, and upon attaining it, the TRT encounters a **spur trail** that heads 90 yards east to a viewpoint. Take it, since it reaches the only worthwhile view along this entire hike. It offers a view of the Lake Tahoe Basin, one that includes Carnelian Bay below you and Agate Bay to its east, along the lake's north shore and bordered on its east side by Stateline Point. The relatively high ridge above the actual shoreline point is volcanic, as is all the land we've traversed. In contrast, Stateline Point is granitic, and it is the southernmost extension of a granitic ridge that extends west from the Carson Range, seen in the distance. From about 20 million years ago until about 2 million years ago, intermittent, voluminous outpourings of lava resulted in the burial of most of the granitic ridge and in the construction of today's volcanic north rim of the Lake Tahoe Basin.

Although you've gained over 500 feet since the trail's low point, you still have over 300 to go before you reach Watson Lake, situated in a glacier-excavated basin only a few feet below this hike's high point. From the spur-trail junction you head a level ¼ mile west, crossing an old road midway to a Fire Protection Road, beside which vehicles have camped. If you need water, descend this road ⅓ mile to usually reliable Watson Creek.

You continue to traverse for 0.4 mile, over to a crossing of a minor road ascending north through a mule-ears meadow, then you continue 0.5 mile to where you almost touch sometimes dry Watson Creek. From there your trail tread turns north to reach an abandoned road just above, along which you climb gently west for ¼ mile. You then leave the road, heading south immediately across the minor, often dry, headwaters bowl of Watson Creek, then rounding the east end of a minor ridge to arrive at **Watson Lake**. You may find an isolated camp or two along its north shore, although the real camping area is along its

south shore. Ordinary vehicles can drive from Brockway Summit west along F.R. 73 to a junction on a very broad saddle just northwest of the lake. They may continue eastward on a road that goes 0.7 mile down to the south shore of the lake, but only OHVs will be able to drive the whole way.

Six-acre Watson Lake holds the distinction of being the only lake in the Tahoe Sierra to lie wholly upon volcanic bedrock. All other natural lakes in this region lie either upon granitic or metamorphic bedrock, and almost all of them originated through glacial excavation of shallow basins. (The exceptions are the Twin Lakes and the precursor to Marlette Lake, in the Carson Range.) The former glaciers that originated on the northeast slopes of 8424' Mt. Watson to excavate Watson Lake's basin didn't get too far beyond it, stopping in the upper part of the Watson Creek drainage. These glaciers originated at elevations comparable to those in canyons along Lake Tahoe's west shore, such as the Ward Creek and Blackwood Creek canyons. But while the former glaciers in those canyons and in the ones south of them reached the lake, spewing icebergs into it, the Watson Creek glaciers did not, since they lay in the rain shadow of the Sierra Nevada crest, and hence received less precipitation. Small as the last glacier was, it nevertheless was similar in size to today's high-elevation glaciers, which are barely holding on in the central Sierra Nevada.

⋙ 112 ⋙
Tahoe Rim Trail, Tahoe City north to Watson Lake

Distances:
2.8 miles to cross good road
3.4 miles to point 7572
4.4 miles to Truckee River canyon viewpoint
5.0 miles to saddle crossed by one-lane road
6.0 miles to road crossing in Burton Creek
   headwaters
7.1 miles to Painted Rock saddle
8.1 miles to Forest Route 73
9.0 miles to start of traversing road
10.8 miles to end of traversing road

11.4 miles to bedrock ridge viewpoint
12.5 miles to Watson Lake
Low/High Elevations: 6300'/7850'
Season: Mid-July through mid-October
Classification: Moderate
Maps: 55 and 54
Trailhead: From the major junction by Lake Tahoe's outlet at Tahoe City, drive 0.2 mile west on northbound Highway 89 to the first road on your right, Fairway Drive, and head 0.2 mile up it to the Tahoe Rim Trail's Tahoe City trailhead, opposite the city's Fairway Community Center.

Introduction
This is the longer of two trail routes to Watson Lake, a destination also accessible by roads. Most of this trail route is through a selectively logged forest that offers only several good views. Day hikers may want to hike only about the first third of this route, the 4.4 miles up to a Truckee River canyon viewpoint; beyond it the views are not of sufficient quality and number to justify the effort. Therefore, the trail users going the full 12.5 miles to Watson Lake most likely will be those planning to do all of the Tahoe Rim Trail. (In the counterclockwise direction, the next stretch of TRT is found under Hike 51.) If you plan to hike all the way to Watson Lake, then be aware that after the snow patches disappear in early- or mid-July, the entire route between the trailhead and the lake is very likely to be dry. If you are backpacking on a warm August day, you may have to carry a gallon of water to last you to the lake; twice that, if you plan to camp before it.

Description
After a short climb southwest, the Tahoe Rim Trail jogs to climb ⅓ mile north to a second jog, from which you have a good view of Lake Tahoe. In another ⅓ mile of ascent you cross a road, which climbs northwest up to a seasonally wet, sloping meadow. Onward, you climb initially steeply, then your ascent becomes easy as you parallel a usually unseen, good road westward through a mostly white-fir forest to a minor road. Southwest, it goes about 210 yards to the good road. Now, 1.2 miles from the trailhead, the TRT starts a climb northwest up an amorphous ridge clothed in red fir, sugar pine, and white fir. After a short switchback leg west, the TRT climbs northeast briefly to the top of a lava outcrop, and among

View west up Bear Creek (Alpine Meadows) canyon to Five Lakes Saddle

its brushy huckleberry oaks we have a fair view of Lake Tahoe. Just beyond it and 1⅔ miles from the trailhead our trail jogs west, and we climb a rocky tread up the crest of a well-defined ridge that turns north at about mile 2.0. Just ¼ mile up it we have our first real views to the west and southwest, seeing,

respectively, the ridge above Squaw Valley and the ridge including Twin Peaks.

Slightly higher, the TRT climbs north on broken-up, platy lava of our soil-deficient ridge. Trees are sparse, due to the lack of deep soil to hold seasonally abundant snow melt. Consequently, shrubs locally dominate, especially huckleberry oak and greenleaf man-

see MAP 54

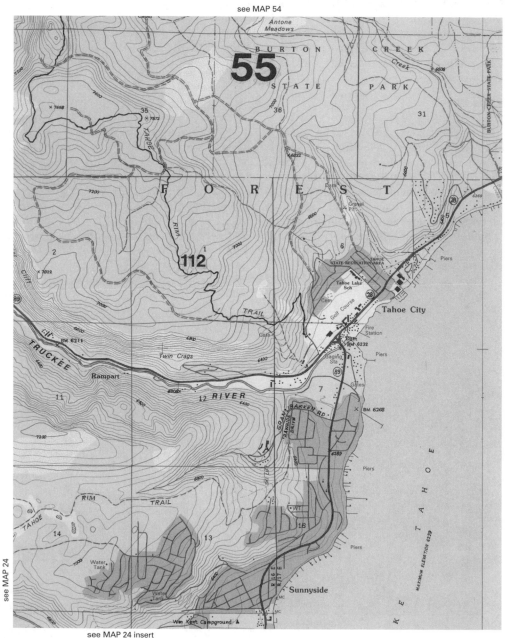

see MAP 24 insert

zanita, although as we near the end of our northward ascent, we encounter our first chinquapin. Just above, mat manzanita predominates on the floor of an open red-fir forest growing on a broad crest. Up here we **cross the good road** we had originally paralleled west. Our mostly gentle ascent continues through a selectively logged forest, first northwest, then north, up to a minor gap immediately west of **point 7572**. This gap, at about 7550 feet, marks the end of our climb to the Lake Tahoe Basin rim, for ahead the trail will for the most part stay confined between 7400 and 7800 feet.

For views, carefully climb up this pile of loose, large lava blocks of point 7572. From it you see most of Lake Tahoe. Here, about 3.4 miles from our trailhead, we also see, to the north-northeast, broad, flat-topped Mt. Watson. The TRT traverses across its lower slopes, and although that stretch of trail is about 2 air miles away, it is about 6 trail miles away. Unseen Watson Lake, behind the mountain is about 3 air miles away, but is about 9 trail miles away. Between the mountain and our point lies the broad, fairly flat floored, Burton Creek drainage basin. In winter and early spring the drainage can lie under several feet of snow, but by midsummer even Burton Creek can dry up, due to the porosity of the underlying volcanic rocks.

From the minor gap we have about a mile traverse, first west then southwest, mostly along the southern edge of a lava plateau. Midway along this traverse, just past an old logging road, we have views south to Twin Peaks, to the high peaks of Desolation Wilderness, to western Lake Tahoe, and to the Freel Peak massif above the lake's southeast shore. From the end of the traverse, where the trail turns from southwest to northwest by our first trailside tobacco brush, you can head about 100 yards southwest to the top of a low knoll composed of large blocks of lava, and from it attain similar views. The trail goes only briefly northwest to a jog northeast, and from that spot you can walk 25 yards west to a **Truckee River canyon viewpoint**. There, along the east rim of the canyon, you see most of the Sierra crest from about the Five Lakes saddle north past the Squaw Valley peaks to

rugged Castle Peak, above unseen Donner Pass. For many trail users, this will be a turn-around point, for ahead there are no views worth the effort of the ups, downs, and arounds that lie ahead.

The first descent begins after we traverse for about ¼ mile along the north edge of the lava plateau, and we curve northeast down to a viewless **saddle crossed by a one-lane road**. Over the next mile, we climb north shortly to a large lava outcrop and descend north to another viewless saddle. It then makes a brief traverse east to sloping lava flows—with a small natural bridge—before descending north on a slackening grade to a **road crossing in Burton Creek headwaters**. Previous maps have shown a creek here, but in actuality there is no sign of even a dry creek bed. Once the snow melts, the headwaters area is dry. Ahead, the TRT takes almost a mile to climb 420 feet up past occasional large, andesite-lava boulders to the bouldery east end of Painted Rock. There, you have a tree-filtered view of Lake Tahoe, and a more open one of part of the Sierra crest lying north of Donner Pass.

From this fair viewpoint the TRT winds westward to the **Painted Rock saddle**, from which you could head over to the west end of Painted Rock, topped by a knoll, but views from it are similar to those that lie just ahead. Therefore, make a minor descent northward for 0.4 mile to a switchback, obtaining your last Sierra crest views along the winding route to it. Now you make a viewless descent, first southeast then east, to an abandoned road, just beyond which the gradient abates to make a level crossing of **Forest Route 73** (a.k.a. Mt. Watson Road 16N73). This begins at nearby Brockway Summit and also traverses above Watson Lake. From our crossing, this road goes 2.3 miles to a junction on a very broad saddle, from where you could continue eastward on a road that goes 0.7 mile down to the south shore of Watson Lake.

The TRT route is 1.2 miles longer, starting a 3-mile-traverse east by first crossing a usually dry tributary of Burton Creek, then climbing easily to a switchback on an abandoned road. We turn left onto it and make a ½-mile ascent east to the **start of a traversing road**, also abandoned. Overall, this road descends slightly, although it does have minor ascents. White firs and Jeffrey pines dominate the vegetation, although brush is locally abundant, and in the more open areas we have fair views of Lake Tahoe. After 1.8 miles we reach the **end of the traversing road**, and here at a road fork we diagonal left and first climb 0.3 mile northeast to a road's end, from which trail tread climbs a similar distance to a switchback just beyond a descending ridge and just before a usually dry creek. Now we make a climb of similar length and elevation gain up the descending ridge, having a rewarding **bedrock ridge viewpoint** of most of Lake Tahoe and the rim that surrounds it. But being about 11½ miles from the trailhead, this view is not worth the effort.

Nevertheless, it does give reason to pause before we reach, about 280 yards later, a closed road. Here, 400 feet above the end of the traversing road, our climbing effort is essentially over, although, heading northeast 0.2 mile on the closed road, we do climb a few feet on a gentle gradient before descending likewise to the road's sharp curve right. The closed road descends southeast, only to soon climb northwest to another sharp curve. The TRT route, however, continues straight ahead down 170 yards of trail tread that connects the two sharp curves. On closed road again, the TRT route curves from northeast to north to northwest down ⅓ mile to an abandoned, north-descending road, then traverses 300 yards west to a one-lane road. On it you walk 270 yards west gently up to a fork, where you branch right, northwest, for a 120-yard stroll over to **Watson Lake**, the first and only source of reliable water since the start of your 12½-mile trek. See the last two paragraphs of the previous hike for a description of the lake and its surroundings.

Appendix
Scientific Names of the Wildflowers on Plates 1-17
(Sources: The Jepson Manual, University of California Press, 1993;
Sierra Nevada Flora, Wilderness Press, 1996)

Plate 1 (p. 46)
1 *Perideridia parishii*
2 *Ligusticum grayi*
3 *Angelica breweri*
4 *Heracleum lanatum*
5 *Sphenosciadium capitellatum*
6 *Cirsium scariosum*
7 *Antennaria rosea*
8 *Hieracium albiflorum*
9 *Chaenactis douglassii*

Plate 2 (p. 47)
1 *Eriogonum nudum*
2 *Polygonum bistortoides*
3 *Polygonum phytolaccifolium*
4 *Lewisia nevadensis*
5 *Phlox dissusa*
6 *Pyrola picta*
7 *Zigadenus venenosus*
8 *Veratrum californicum*
9 *Platanthera leucostachys*

Plate 3 (p. 48)
1 *Anaphalis margaritace*
2 *Achillea millefolium*
3 *Erigeron peregrinus*
4 *Thalictrum fendleri*
5 *Caltha leptosepala*
6 *Streptanthus tortuosus*
7 *Pedicularis semibarbata*
8 *Calochortus leichtlinii*
9 *Polygonum davisiae*

Plate 4 (p. 49)
1 *Arnica longifolia*
2 *Arnica mollis*
3 *Balsamorhiza sagittata*
4 *Aster breweri*
5 *Eriophyllum lanatum*
6 *Microseris nutans*
7 *Senecio integerrimus*
8 *Senecio triangularis*
9 *Wyethia mollis*

Plate 5 (p. 50)
1 *Sedum obtusatu*
2 *Triteleia ixioides*
3 *Potentilla glandulosa*
4 *Eriogonum umbellatum*
5 *Verbascum thapsus*
6 *Mimulus guttatusr*
7 *Viola bakeri*
8 *Viola purpurea*
9 *Erysimum capitatum ssp. perenne*

Plate 6 (p. 51)
1 *Epilobium canum*
2 *Castilleja applegatei*
3 *Penstemon newberryi*
4 *Lilium parvum*
5 *Aquilegia formosa*
6 *Ipomopsis aggregata*

7 *Cirsium andersonii*
8 *Pterospora andromedea*
9 *Sarcodes saguinea*

Plate 7 (p. 52)
1 *Allium validum*
2 *Allium campanulatum*
3 *Agastache urticifolia*
4 *Dodecatheon alpinum*
5 *Geranium richardsonii*
6 *Pedicularis attollens*
7 *Sidalcea glaucescens*
8 *Calyptridium umbellatum*
9 *Epilobium angustifolium*

Plate 8 (p. 53)
1 *Lupinus arbustus*
2 *Phacelia hydrophylloides*
3 *Monardella odoratissima*
4 *Delphinium nuttallianum*
5 *Delphinium glaucum*
6 *Aconitum columbianum*
7 *Hackelia velutina*
8 *Penstemon heterodoxus*
9 *Penstemon rydbergii*

Plate 9 (p. 74)
1 *Adenocaulon bicolor*
2 *Montia perfoliata*
3 *Heuchera micrantha*
4 *Calochortus albus*
5 *Chlorogalum pomeridianum*
6 *Calochortus monophyllus*
7 *Iris hartwegii*
8 *Sedum spathulifolium*
9 *Dudleya cymosa*

Plate 10 (p. 75)
1 *Silene californica*
2 *Corallorhiza maculata*
3 *Pedicularis densiflora*
4 *Mimulus bifidus*
5 *Penstemon heterophyllus*
6 *Mimulus kelloggii*
7 *Brodiaea elegans*
8 *Dicentra formosa*
9 *Asclepias cordifolia*

Plate 11 (p. 108)
1 *Arenaria nuttallii*
2 *Raillardella argentea*
3 *Helianthella californica*
4 *Erythronium purpurascens*
5 *Chaenactis nevadensis*
6 *Penstemon deustus*
7 *Valeriana californica*
8 *Primula suffrutescens*
9 *Polemonium pulcherrimum*

Plate 12 (p. 221)
1 *Viola macloskeyi*
2 *Apocynum pumilum*

3 *Phacelia heterophylla*
4 *Lotus oblongifolius*
5 *Madia gracilis*
6 *Solidago canadensisd*
7 *Collomia grandiflora*
8 *Sidalcea oregana*
9 *Castilleja miniatash*

Plate 13 (p. 269)
1 *Camassia quamash*
2 *Smilacina racemosa*
3 *Calochortus minimus*
4 *Gentiana newberryi*
5 *Oxyria digyna*
6 *Hackelia micrantha*
7 *Orthilia secunda*
8 *Lupinus polyphyllus*
9 *Astragalus bolanderi*

Plate 14 (p. 292)
1 *Lewisia triphylla*
2 *Claytonia lanceolata*
3 *Dicentra uniflora*
4 *Saxifraga aprica*
5 *Ranunculus alismifolius*
6 *Sedum roseum)*
7 *Hieracium horridum*
8 *Crepis acuminata*
9 *Silene douglasii*

Plate 15 (p. 334)
1 *Senecio canus*
2 *Polemonium californicum*
3 *Castilleja nana*
4 *Mimulus tilingii*
5 *Mimulus lewisii*
6 *Penstemon speciosus*
7 *Linum lewisii*
8 *Swertia radiata*
9 *Mertensia ciliata*

Plate 16 (p. 369)
1 *Phacelia hastata*
2 *Arabis rectissima*
3 *Arabis platysperma*
4 *Orthocarpus cuspidatus*
5 *Linanthus nuttallii*
6 *Leptodactylon pungens*
7 *Eriogonum incanum*
8 *Paeonia brownii*
9 *Lupinus breweri*

Plate 17 (p. 377)
1 *Cryptantha humilis*
2 *Ipomopsis congesta*
3 *Phlox condensata*
4 *Phacelia hastata ssp. compacta*
5 *Stenotus acaulis*
6 *Erigeron compositus*
7 *Senecio fremontii*
8 *Hulsea algida*
9 *Penstemon davidsonii*

Recommended Reading and Source Materials

General

Aadland, Dan. 1993. *Treading Lightly with Pack Animals*. Missoula, MT: Mountain Press Pub. Co., 140 p.

Back, Joe. 1987. *Horses, Hitches and Rocky Trails*. Boulder, CO: Johnson Books, 117 p.

Carville, Mike. 1991. *Climber's Guide to Tahoe Rock*. Evergreen, CO: Chockstone Press, 295 p.

Crippen, J. R., and B. R. Pavelka. 1970. *The Lake Tahoe Basin, California-Nevada*. U.S. Geological Survey Water-Supply Paper 1972, 56 p.

Darville, Fred T., Jr., M.D. 1992. *Mountaineering Medicine*. Berkeley: Wilderness Press, 110 p.

Harmon, David, and Amy S. Rubin. 1992. *Llamas on the Trail: A Packer's Guide*. Missoula, MT: Mountain Press Pub. Co., 170 p.

Schaffer, Jeffrey P., and others. 1995. *The Pacific Crest Trail, Volume 1: California*. Berkeley: Wilderness Press, 525 p.

Winnett, Thomas, with Melanie Findling. 1994. *Backpacking Basics*. Berkeley: Wilderness Press, 134 p.

History

Egenhoff, Elizabeth L. 1949. *The Elephant As They Saw It; A Collection of Contemporary Pictures and Statements on Gold Mining in California*. Sacramento: California Division of Mines and Geology, 128 p.

Farquhar, Francis P. 1965. *History of the Sierra Nevada*. Berkeley: University of California Press, 262 p.

Reid, Robert L., ed. 1983. *A Treasury of the Sierra Nevada*. Berkeley: Wilderness Press, 363 p.

Scott, Edward B. 1957. *The Saga of Lake Tahoe*. Crystal Bay (Lake Tahoe), NV: Sierra-Tahoe Publishing Company, 519 p.

Biology

Basey, Harold E. 1976. *Discovering Sierra Reptiles and Amphibians*. El Portal: Yosemite Association, 50 p.

Carville, Julie Stauffer. 1989. *Hiking Tahoe's Wildflower Trails (formerly Lingering in Tahoe's Wild Gardens)*. Edmonton, Alberta, Canada T6E 1X5: Lone Pine Publishing. 350 p.

Fauver, Toni. 1992. *Wildflower Walking in Lakes Basin of the Northern Sierra*. Self-published: Toni Fauver, Box 2322, Orinda, CA 94563.

Gaines, David. 1988. *Birds of Yosemite and the East Slope*. Lee Vining: Artemisia Press, 352 p.

Graf, Michael. 1999. *Plants of the Tahoe Basin*. Sacramento: California Native Plant Society Press, 308 p.

Grater, Russell K., and Tom A. Blaue. 1978. *Discovering Sierra Mammals*. El Portal: Yosemite Association, 174 p.

Grillos, Steve J. 1966. *Ferns and Fern Allies of California* (California Natural History Guide 16). Berkeley: University of California Press, 104 p.

Hickman, James C., ed. 1993. *The Jepson Manual: Vascular Plants of California*. Berkeley: University of California Press, 1400 p.

Keator, Glenn. 1978. *Pacific Coast Berry Finder*. Berkeley: Nature Study Guild, 62 p.

McGinnis, Samuel M. 1984. *Freshwater Fishes of California* (California Natural History Guide 49). Berkeley: University of California Press, 316 p.

Niehaus, Theodore F., and Charles L. Ripper. 1976. *A Field Guide to Pacific States Wildflowers*. Boston: Houghton Mifflin, 432 p.

Peterson, P. Victor, and P. Victor Peterson, Jr. 1975. *Native Trees of the Sierra Nevada* (California Natural History Guide 36). Berkeley: University of California Press, 147 p.

Peterson, Roger Tory. 1990. *A Field Guide to Western Birds*. Boston: Houghton Mifflin, 432 p.

Powell, Jerry A., and Charles L. Hogue. 1979. *California Insects* (California Natural History Guide 44). Berkeley: University of California Press, 388 p.

Sawyer, John O., and Todd Keeler-Wolf. *A Manual of California Vegetation*. Sacramento: California Native Plant Society, 471 p.

Smith, Gladys L. 1973. "A Flora of the Tahoe Basin and Neighboring Areas." *The Wasmann Journal of Biology*, v. 41, no. 1-2, p. 1-231.

_____. 1983. "Supplement to a Flora of the Tahoe Basin and Neighboring Areas." *The Wasmann Journal of Biology*, v. 41, no. 1-2, p. 1-46.

Thomas, John Hunter, and Dennis R. Parnell. 1974. *Native Shrubs of the Sierra Nevada* (California Natural History Guide 34). Berkeley: University of California Press, 127 p.

Watts, Tom. 1973. *Pacific Coast Tree Finder*. Berkeley: Nature Study Guild, 62 p.

Weeden, Norman F., 1996. *A Sierra Nevada Flora*. Berkeley: Wilderness Press, 259 p.

Whitney, Stephen. 1979. *A Sierra Club Naturalist's Guide to the Sierra Nevada*. San Francisco: Sierra Club, 526 p.

Willard, Dwight. 1994. *Giant Sequoia Groves of the Sierra Nevada: A Reference Guide*. Self-published and (unfortunately) out of print, 372 p.

Geology

Bateman, Paul C., and Clyde Wahrhaftig. 1966. "Geology of the Sierra Nevada." In *Geology of Northern California* (Edgar H. Bailey, ed.). California Division of Mines and Geology Bulletin 190, p. 107-169. (Best overview, but *extremely* dated.)

Burchfiel, B. C., P. W. Lipman, and M. L. Zoback, eds. 1992. *The Cordilleran Orogen: conterminous U.S.* (Geology of North America, v. G-3). Boulder: Geological Society of America, 724 p.

Curtis, Garniss H. 1954. "Mode of origin of pyroclastic debris in the Mehrten Formation of the Sierra Nevada." *University of California Publications in Geological Sciences*, v. 29, no. 9, p. 453-502.

Dodge, F.C.W., and P.V. Fillo. 1967. *Mineral Resources of the Desolation Primitive Area of the Sierra Nevada, California.* U.S. Geological Survey Bulletin 1261-A, 25 p.

Fisher, G. Reid. 1990. "Middle Jurassic syntectonic conglomerate in the Mt. Tallac roof pendant, northern Sierra Nevada, California." In *Paleozoic and Early Mesozoic Paleogeographic Relations; Sierra Nevada, Klamath Mountains; and Related Terranes* (David S. Harwood and M. Meghan Miller, eds.). Geological Society of America Special Paper 255, p. 339-350.

Girty, Gary H., and eight others. 1995. "Timing of emplacement of the Haypress Creek and Emigrant Gap plutons: Implications for the timing and controls of Jurassic orogenesis, northern Sierra Nevada, California." In *Jurassic Magmatism and Tectonics of the North American Cordillera* (David M. Miller and Cathy Busby, eds.). Geological Society of America Special Paper 299, p. 191-201.

Graymer, Russell W., and David L. Jones. 1994. "Tectonic implications of radiolarian cherts from the Placerville Belt, Sierra Nevada Foothills, California: Nevadan-age continental growth by accretion of multiple terranes." *Geological Society of America Bulletin*, v. 106, p. 531-540.

Harwood, David S. 1991. *Stratigraphy of Paleozoic and Lower Mesozoic Rocks in the Northern Sierra Terrane, California.* Washington: U.S. Geological Survey Bulletin 1957, 78 p.

Jenkins, Olaf P. 1948. *The Mother Lode Country; Geologic Guidebook along Highway 49—Sierran Gold Belt.* Sacramento: California Division of Mines and Geology, 164 p. (An update appears in five issues of CDMG's *California Geology:* Mar./Apr., May/June, Jul./Aug., Sept./Oct., Nov./Dec. 1997.)

John, David A., and four others. 1993. *Geology and Mineral Resources of the Reno 1° by 2° Quadrangle, Nevada and California.* Washington: U.S. Geological Survey Bulletin 1957, 65 p.

Kistler, Ronald W. 1993. "Mesozoic intrabatholithic faulting, Sierra Nevada, California." In *Mesozoic Paleogeography of the United States - II* (George C. Dunne and Kristin A. McDougall, eds.). Los Angeles: Society of Economic Paleontologists and Mineralogists, Pacific Section, p. 247-261.

Schaffer, Jeffrey P. 1997. *The Geomorphic Evolution of the Yosemite Valley and Sierra Nevada Landscapes: Solving the Riddles in the Rocks.* Berkeley: Wilderness Press, 388 p.

Slemmons, David B. 1966. "Cenozoic volcanism of the central Sierra Nevada, California." In *Geology of Northern California* (Edgar H. Bailey, ed.). California Division of Mines and Geology Bulletin 190, p. 199-208.

Wolf, Michael B., and Jason B. Saleeby. 1995. "Late Jurassic dike swarms in the southwestern Sierra Nevada Foothills terrane, California: Implications for the Nevadan orogeny and North American plate motion." In *Jurassic Magmatism and Tectonics of the North American Cordillera* (David M. Miller and Cathy Busby, eds.). Geological Society of America Special Paper 299, p. 203-228.

Wolfe, Jack A., and Howard E. Schorn, Chris E. Forest, and Peter Molnar. 1997. "Paleobotanical evidence for high altitudes in Nevada during the Miocene." *Science*, v. 276, p. 1672-1675.

Yeend, Warren E. 1974. *Gold-Bearing Gravel of the Ancestral Yuba River, Sierra Nevada, California.* U.S. Geological Survey Professional Paper 772, 44 p.

Geologic Maps

CDMG = California Division of Mines and Geology, Sacramento, California

USGS = U.S. Geological Survey, Denver, Colorado

Scale 1:250,000 (1° x 2°)

Chico. 1992. CDMG.

Reno. 1991+. USGS Map MF-2154

Sacramento. 1981. CDMG.

Walker Lake. 1982+. USGS Map MF-1382

Scale 1:62,500

Fallen Leaf Lake 15' quadrangle. 1983. 2 maps plus 24-page text. CDMG Map Sheet 32.

Freel and Dardanelles Further Planning Areas. USGS Map MF-1322-A.

Freel Peak 15' quadrangle. 1983. USGS Map I-1424.

Granite Chief Wilderness Study Area. 1981-82. USGS Map MF-1273.

Scale 1:24,000

Mt. Tallac roof pendant. 1989. USGS Map MF-1943.

Index

Numbers in *italics* indicate photographs.

READ THIS

Hiking in the backcountry entails unavoidable risk that every hiker assumes and must be aware of and respect. The fact that a trail is described in this book is not a representation that it will be safe for you. Trails vary greatly in difficulty and in the degree of conditioning and agility one needs to enjoy them safely. On some hikes, routes may have changed or conditions may have deteriorated since the descriptions were written. Also, trail conditions can change even from day to day, owing to weather and other factors. A trail that is safe on a dry day or for a highly conditioned, agile, properly equipped hiker may be completely unsafe for someone else or unsafe under adverse weather conditions.

You can minimize your risks on the trail by being knowledgeable, prepared and alert. There is not space in this book for a general treatise on safety in the mountains, but there are a number of good books and public courses on the subject and you should take advantage of them to increase your knowledge. Just as important, you should always be aware of your own limitations and of conditions existing when and where you are hiking. If conditions are dangerous, or if you are not prepared to deal with them safely, choose a different hike! It's better to have wasted a drive than to be the subject of a mountain rescue.

These warnings are not intended to scare you off the trails. Millions of people have safe and enjoyable hikes every year. However, one element of the beauty, freedom and excitement of the wilderness is the presence of risks that do not confront us at home. When you hike you assume those risks. They can be met safely, but only if you exercise your own independent judgment and common sense.

The Tahoe Sierra **2002 Update**

p. 21–26, Wilderness Permits: For the latest information on US Forest Service wilderness permits, regulations, etc., use the US Forest Service's Region 5 internet address: *www.r5.fs.fed.us* (click on the appropriate national forest name). You can reach the Lake Tahoe Basin Management Unit at: *www.r5.fs.fed.us/ltbmu*. For the Eldorado National Forest Information Center, go to *www.r5.fs.fed.us./eldorado*. Only Desolation Wilderness overnight visitors must pay for wilderness permits: $5 per person per day for the first two days (additional days are free).

p. 35, height of Tahoe Sierra: The emerging view is that the Sierra Nevada proper reached its current height by about 75–80 million years ago. There was no last pulse of uplift (p. 35, col. 2, p. 36, col. 1).

p. 37, glacier dams across Truckee River canyon: New research indicates that major submarine landslides have occurred within the lake, creating tsunamis. So the "inconceivably large walls of water down the Truckee River canyon" could have been from broken ice dams, tsunamis, or both. (See *Geological Society of America Bulletin*, May 2000.)

Tioga glaciers were gone by about 13,000 years ago. These are carbon-14 years; corrected to calendar years, glaciers disappeared about 15,500 years ago, or about 13,500 B.C.

p. 120, Map 8, Wades Lake alternate route: From the Wades Lake Trail junction, a walk 0.6 mile south up the Rock & Jamison Lakes Trail gets you to a junction with a newer trail to Wades Lake. This trail starts near the right edge of Map 8's Section 2, immediately before the main trail curves east, just ¼ mile before reaching Jamison Lake's outlet creek. The newer trail winds 0.7 mile westward, first climbing and then mostly traversing before ending on the east side of Wades Lake's outlet creek opposite a large camping area by the lake's north shore.

p. 142, Hike 30, 2nd column, 2nd paragraph: diorite: Actually, it's metamorphic bedrock that superficially resembles the area's diorite.

p. 166, Hike 37, Trailhead: Sentence 3, which begins "In ¾ mile this starts south," is misleading. It should read: This starts south to a nearby bridge over the Little Truckee River, then in 0.7 mile winds east to an intersection . . .

p. 207–211, Hike 51, Twin Peaks: A shorter route, now part of the Tahoe Rim Trail (TRT), provides a more direct route to the summits. To reach the trailhead, drive to the Stanford Rock trailhead, Road 15N35. On the main road, continue 0.4 mile west up to a junction with Road 15N60, on the right, which is a part of the TRT route that climbs first to Paige Meadows (see next entry). On the main road, continue 0.2 mile west to a junction with gated Road 15N62. Your hiking route is along this closed road, shown on Map 24.

Hike about 1.7 miles west to a seasonal creek, shown as permanent on the map, a spot at the south edge of Section 16. One could camp along the north edge of the creek. Beyond the creek the road continues about ¼ mile to a junction. On the map, your road continues south-southwest while a trail starts south. In reality, the road ahead from this junction is quite abandoned (almost invisible), and the trail south is an obvious old road that is being narrowed by encroaching vegetation. After you traverse south for about ¼ mile, the route, now a trail, switchbacks to descend briefly northeast to cross Ward Creek proper, about 2¼ miles into your hike. On the trail you climb south-southwest up the creek, somewhat as depicted on the map. Near the four corners of Sections 20, 21, 28 and 29 it leaves the creek at mile 3.2 for a climb southward, at first via short switchbacks. As it approaches a bowl, the trail turns northeast for a climb to a prominent switchback, then climbs south to a junction at a ridge saddle, as shown on the map. Here, after 5.2 miles, you join the described route.

That trail west has been somewhat redesigned, so it winds more than as shown on Map 24. After 1.0 mile up it, you reach a junction with a use trail, the dotted line on the map, climbing northwest to the eastern Twin Peak. The TRT continues west below the peaks. You can head cross-country directly up to the saddle dividing the two peaks. The TRT drops slightly more than shown on the map, and where it reaches the cross-country route (dotted line) toward the western peak, the trail angles northwest to momentarily drop to the Pacific Crest Trail.

p. 209 & 390, Maps 24 and 55: Tahoe Rim Trail between Ward Creek and Tahoe City. The TRT is labeled on Map 55, but this was a temporary route. The official route, 4.6 miles long, differs and is described here in two directions: first north to Paige Meadows (Map 24), then southwest to them (Map 55). The official TRT route starts up Road 15N60, which begins barely off the right edge of Map 24, by the label "see MAP 55." This rough road, open to SUVs etc., climbs moderately to steeply northwest for 0.4 mile to a bend with a view up-canyon, then northeast almost 300 yards to a junction. From it a well-used road branches east, bound for a subdivision about one mile distant. Over the next 250 yards, a popular bike path first branches northeast immediately past the road junction while the TRT, still on the rough road, climbs north, quickly crossing two seasonal creeklets. The road over this brief stretch differs from that on Map 24. Ahead, as on Map 24 the road traverses ¼ mile northwest to a curve, from which a path starts west, traversing across the southwesternmost Paige Meadow. A walk about 150 yards west along the path gets you to the only reliable perennial source of water, a creek originating high on the east slopes of Scott Peak. This meadow, like several others, is bordered by aspens, which turn a blazing yellow in early autumn. From the curve the TRT heads ¼ mile northeast to another meadow, this one at the end of the dashed route on Map 24. This last stretch starts as a road but becomes a trail before reaching the meadow.

Because Paige Meadows often are boggy (great for wildflowers, but also a haven for myriad mosquitoes), the trail through this particular meadow is a slightly raised tread, which keeps your feet dry. Your trail quickly reaches a junction, located immediately left of the letter "P" in "Paige," on Map 24, and 1.3 miles into your hike. Mountain bikers make a loop that includes part of the TRT ahead and the conspicuous trail branching southeast.

This trail heads across "Paige" then northeast through a meadow identified as "Meadows," where you enter Map 55. That map correctly shows the trail then curving

southeast to a seasonal lakelet and a junction just past it. From it an old, closed road, now a bike path, descends southwest as well as rambles east, somewhat as shown on Map 55 as the "Tahoe Rim Trail."

Back at the junction by the letter "P" on Map 24, the official TRT curves from north to northwest over 170 yards, mostly staying close to the meadow's east edge. Then at a spot just east of the seasonal lakelet shown on Map 24, the TRT angles north into the forest. Your trail meanders for 0.2 mile, ascending relatively gently to a junction with an east-west trail, about 1.6 miles into your hike. This trail is not the one shown on Map 24, which doesn't exist, but a newer one, and the junction is located due north of the lakelet, on the 6960' contour line. This trail is part of a popular bike route. On it the TRT heads east, leaving Map 24 in about 0.4 mile.

To reach the last-mentioned junction from the Tahoe City environs, you need to find the trailhead. From the major junction by Lake Tahoe's outlet at Tahoe City, drive ⅓ mile south on Highway 89 to a road, branching right (west), and signed for the Truckee River Recreation Trail. This paved road goes about 270 yards to a conspicuous parking loop, on your right. Park in it and then walk about 0.1 mile west on the paved road to a junction from which a riverside trail heads northeast to just north of the north end of the parking loop. The trail continues eastward, but for those making the entire TRT loop, they take a short trail north to a bridge across the Truckee River to find themselves at Highway 89. To regain the TRT, they walk 70 yards northeast on 89 to Fairway Drive, then head north 0.2 mile up it to the trailhead (Hike 112). This spot is 0.7 mile from the start of the Truckee River Recreation Trail, mentioned just below.

Those bound for Paige Meadows and beyond, should continue about 50 yards on the paved road to a gate, then 220 yards on a closed dirt road leading to a conspicuous, straight road that climbs south from the Truckee River, as shown on Map 55. From its west edge the obvious Truckee River Recreation Trail begins. I start the mileage at this point although you'll have already walked 0.3–0.4 mile from where you've parked in the trailhead parking loop.

On the Truckee River Recreation Trail you walk just 0.1 mile west, paralleling the river, then branch left on the new segment of the Tahoe Rim Trail for a switchbacking climb south, staying above the largely unseen homes and buildings along Granlibakken Road. After about 0.7 mile, your trail peaks at about 6540', then traverses about ¼ mile southwest to a junction. From here an abandoned road, now narrowed by brush to a path, descends about ¼ mile east to the upper end of the loop of the Granlibakken Road.

The TRT route climbs moderately to steeply west-southwest up the abandoned, brush-encroaching road, staying on north slopes of a conspicuous gully shown on Map 55. After a 0.6-mile climb, the trail levels as it reaches the border of Sections 11–12. There it meets another trail, part of a popular bike route, then heads south. It crosses the gully's seasonal creeklet in 50 yards, then climbs 60 yards to an old, closed, east-west road (the "Tahoe Rim Trail" on Map 55). Ahead, the official TRT is nearly level, meandering westward, sometimes on old road segments, sometimes on new trail segments, reaching the junction north of Paige Meadows (mile 1.6) in about 1.4 miles, this spot about 3.0 miles from my designated starting point.

p. 217, Hike 53, Emerald Point: The northern trail east to Emerald Point is long abandoned. However, the southern trail east to it is still quite heavily used.

p. 218–219, Hike 54, Eagle Falls: A new trail goes to it, starting from the Visitors Center, which is just beyond the Vikingsholm. Partway up, a trail leaves to bridge nearby Eagle Creek, then goes about 1.6 miles to the amphitheater at the switchback at Upper Eagle Point Campground, in Emerald Bay State Park. This trail is for campers only; there is no day-use parking.

p. 223–224, Hike 58 via Clark Trail: Due to construction of homes in the 1990s, the start of the Clark Trail now is off limits to non-residents. If you stay at Fallen Leaf Lake, you'll have to ascend the Fallen Leaf-Angora Trail, or, like the vast majority of visitors to the Angora Lakes, drive up to the lakes' trailhead. Parking can be overflowing on hot summer days, since the upper lake is a popular sunbathing and swimming destination.

p. 242, Hike 62, Trailhead, Wrights Lake Road: "The Wrights Lake Road was permanently closed in 1997." This is not so; it has reopened. Besides Hike 62, Hikes 63–71 also are reached from this road. To reach it from the Eldorado National Forest Center east of Placerville, drive 26 miles east up Highway 50 to Kyburz, then 5 more miles. (The Wrights Lake Road junction is about 13 miles west from Echo Summit, and is easily missed. It is about 4 miles west beyond Strawberry Lodge.) The Lyons Creek trailhead for Hike 71 is about 4 miles up the Wrights Lake Road, while the trailheads for Hikes 62–70 are in the Wrights Lake area, about 4 miles farther. The existing trailhead directions still are fine.

p. 255, Map 32, Emerald Point: The northern trail east to Emerald Point is long abandoned. However, the southern trail east to it is still quite heavily used.

p. 270, Hike 72, Distances and Trailhead: Due to relocation of the trailhead, all distances now are 0.1 mile longer. The old Twin Bridges trailhead has been replaced with the Pyramid Creek trailhead, located at the old site of Twin Bridges, about 200 yards before Highway 50's bridge over Pyramid Creek. There is parking for almost 4 dozen vehicles. Be aware that there now is a $3 per day parking fee.

p. 271, Hike 72, 1st column, 1st sentence: Replace with: From an obvious trailhead, the trail winds about 400 yards east to the west side of Pyramid Creek, joining it about 0.1 mile north of the Highway 50 bridge.

p. 283, Hike 77, Trailhead parking: This can be completely full by 10 a.m. on a summer weekday and earlier on weekends. There is now a $3 per-day parking fee.

p. 289, Hike 79, 1st column, 2nd paragraph: Forget-me-not is another name for "stickseed".

p. 298, Map 35: See note regarding Haypress Meadows below, p. 304.

p. 299, Hike 84, Tamarack Trail: This now is an unmaintained primitive trail. It is potentially dangerous (as it was even when maintained).

p. 304, Hike 86, Description (Map 35), Haypress Meadows: From this vicinity you can reach the summit of Keiths Dome by a 200-foot ascent cross-country northward. This easy ascent, about ½ mile long, provides you with surprisingly fine views. From it one could descend first southwest and then curve northwest to Lake Lucille, or, traverse east along the "dome's" crest, down to Lost Lake or Triangle Lake. Lost Lake is best reached by a short cross-country jaunt from Triangle Lake. Even though Lost Lake is off the beaten path you can still find campers there, even on weekdays.

p. 305, Hike 87, 2nd column, last 4 lines: Most of the dead lodgepole snags have fallen by now. Few remain.

p. 306, Hike 87, 1st column, 1st line: Generally, it is true that the lake is very shallow. However, before it was flooded under the Aloha's water, the floor of Desolation Valley contained some lakes and ponds. Consequently there still are bodies of water, some 10–20 feet deep, that remain when the lake is emptied after Labor Day. So, swimming remains, although in a land with a conspicuous bathtub ring.

p. 310, Hike 88, Trailhead, Distances, Description: This has moved back and forth over the last few decades. It's again up at Sierra at Tahoe Ski Resort (formerly Sierra Ski Ranch). From Camp Sacramento, drive 2.7 miles east up Highway 50 (or 3.1 miles west from Echo Summit) to Sierra at Tahoe Ski Resort. Drive 1.4 miles up its paved road to a junction with a graded road, branching right. Take this road 2.0 miles, traversing a ski area before reaching the trailhead at road's end. Because this trailhead is about ½ mile above the lower, older one (for locals), change the hike's three distances as follows: 4.8 to 4.3, 5.6 to 5.0, 10.2 to 11.3. Also, delete the Description's first paragraph of prose up to the higher trailhead.

p. 314, Hike 89, Pacific Crest Trail, Description, 2nd paragraph: The trail is more obvious now. In the future, a ⅓-mile stretch of trail may be built to go from the existing westbound PCT at the entrance to the Sno-Park southward along the west edge of the Sno-Park's road.

p. 319, Hike 92, Distances: These likely now are about 01.–0.2 mile longer since the steep, initial trail tread was being replaced with

well-graded switchbacks in 2002, lengthening the route.

p. 375, Map 51: See note below for p. 378–381.

p. 378–381, Hike 109, Tahoe Rim Trail, and Maps 51–53: This was the last incomplete section on the TRT, and was finished in time for the TRT's September 22, 2001, dedication ceremony. As with the Paige Meadows section, this one has been changed from the proposed route shown on the maps. Counterclockwise, the TRT (Hike 109) now coincides with Hike 108 for the first 2½ miles up to a gated service road at a saddle. It continues west up the road, leaving Map 51 to switchback up to a saddle just south of the "Radio Tower" summit in the northeast corner of Map 52.

Next, it makes a crest route south—the only part of the entire route above 10,000'—first up to 10,338' Relay Peak and then down to its southern satellite, Peak 10,140, which offers great Lake Tahoe views. The TRT then switchbacks southwestward down a descending ridge to another ridge, above the Slab Cliffs, and goes about a mile along it to just north of Mud Lake. It arrives at a saddle with the word "Pack." West, the TRT to the saddle just east of Martis Peak may have last-minute route changes, particularly the part in eastern Map 53.

p. 390, Map 55: See write-up for page 209, above.

p. 394 Additions to the Recommended Reading and Source Materials:

General

Hauserman, Tim. 2002. *The Tahoe Rim Trail: A Complete Guide for Hikers, Mountain Bikers, and Equestrians.* Berkeley: Wilderness Press, 264 p.

Biology

If you want to do serious botanizing in the Sierra Buttes-Lakes Basin area, get the following book: Fauver, Toni. 1992. *Wildflower Walking in Lakes Basin of the Northern Sierra.* Self-published: Toni Fauver, P.O. Box 2322, Orinda, CA 94563.

A new book recently appeared on the flora of our area, and I heartily recommend it, since it covers more than 600 species and has over 380 color photographs: Graf, Michael. 1999. *Plants of the Tahoe Basin.* Sacramento: California Native Plant Society Press, 308 p.